RECONSIDERING REDD+

In *Reconsidering REDD+: Authority, Power and Law in the Green Economy*, Julia Dehm provides a critical analysis of how the REDD+ scheme operates to reorganise social relations and to establish new forms of global authority over forests in the Global South in ways that benefit the interests of some actors while further marginalising others. In accessible prose that draws on interdisciplinary insights, Dehm demonstrates how, through the creation of new legal relations, including property rights and contractual obligations, new forms of transnational authority over forested areas in the Global South are being constituted. This important work should be read by anyone interested in a critical analysis of international climate law and policy that offers insights into questions of political economy, power and unequal authority.

Julia Dehm is a Senior Lecturer at the School of Law, La Trobe University, Australia. Her research addresses international climate change law and regulation, transnational carbon markets and the governance of natural resources, as well as the relationship between human rights and economic inequality. She is the Co-Editor in Chief of the *Journal of Human Rights and the Environment*. Previously she was a Postdoctoral Fellow at the Rapoport Center for Human Rights and Justice at the University of Texas at Austin and a Resident Fellow at the Institute for Global Law and Policy, Harvard Law School. Her work has been widely published in journals such as the *Leiden Journal of International Law*, *Humanity: An International Journal of Human Rights, Humanitarianism, and Development* and the *Journal of Human Rights and the Environment*.

CAMBRIDGE STUDIES ON ENVIRONMENT, ENERGY AND NATURAL RESOURCES GOVERNANCE

Cambridge Studies on Environment, Energy and Natural Resources Governance publishes foundational monographs of general interest to scholars and practitioners within the broadly defined fields of sustainable development policy, including studies on law, economics, politics, history, and policy. These fields currently attract unprecedented interest due both to the urgency of developing policies to address climate change, the energy transition, food security and water availability and, more generally, to the progressive realization of the impact of humans as a geological driver of the state of the Earth, now called the "Anthropocene."

The general editor of the series is Professor Jorge E. Viñuales, the Harold Samuel Chair of Law and Environmental Policy at the University of Cambridge and the Founder and First Director of the Cambridge Centre for Environment, Energy and Natural Resource Governance (C-EENRG).

Reconsidering REDD+

AUTHORITY, POWER AND LAW IN THE GREEN ECONOMY

JULIA DEHM
La Trobe University

CAMBRIDGE
UNIVERSITY PRESS

University Printing House, Cambridge CB2 8BS, United Kingdom

One Liberty Plaza, 20th Floor, New York, NY 10006, USA

477 Williamstown Road, Port Melbourne, VIC 3207, Australia

314–321, 3rd Floor, Plot 3, Splendor Forum, Jasola District Centre, New Delhi – 110025, India

79 Anson Road, #06-04/06, Singapore 079906

Cambridge University Press is part of the University of Cambridge.

It furthers the University's mission by disseminating knowledge in the pursuit of education, learning, and research at the highest international levels of excellence.

www.cambridge.org
Information on this title: www.cambridge.org/9781108423762
DOI: 10.1017/9781108529341

© Julia Dehm 2021

This publication is in copyright. Subject to statutory exception and to the provisions of relevant collective licensing agreements, no reproduction of any part may take place without the written permission of Cambridge University Press.

First published 2021

A catalogue record for this publication is available from the British Library.

ISBN 978-1-108-42376-2 Hardback

Cambridge University Press has no responsibility for the persistence or accuracy of URLs for external or third-party internet websites referred to in this publication and does not guarantee that any content on such websites is, or will remain, accurate or appropriate.

Contents

Acknowledgements	*page* xi
List of Abbreviations	xv
Introduction: Reconsidering REDD+	1
A Introduction	1
B Assembling REDD+	7
1 REDD+ As a Relation	7
2 REDD+: Between Vision and Actualisation	12
C Critiquing REDD+	18
D Understanding REDD+	29
1 Climate Justice	30
2 The Green Economy	39
3 Power	42
4 Authority	47
E Beyond REDD+	50
F Outline of the Book	56
1 Background to REDD+	59
A Introduction	59
B REDD+ As a Part of the UNFCCC Framework	60
1 Result-Based Actions	67
(a) Forest Emission Reference Levels and/or Forest Reference Levels	69
(b) Measuring, Reporting and Verification	71
(c) Safeguards and Non-carbon Benefits	71
2 Alternative Policy Approaches	74

vii

viii   *Contents*

C REDD+ As Experimental Practices, Preparatory and
   Market-Construction Activities   76
   1 Demonstration Activities   77
   2 REDD+-Readiness   80
      (a) Forest Carbon Partnership Facility   81
      (b) UN-REDD Programme   86
      (c) Other Multilateral and Bilateral Channels   87
D REDD+ As a Concept, Idea and Way of Seeing   90
   1 REDD+ As a Vision of Economic Valuation of Forests   91
   2 REDD+ As a Vision of an 'Offset' in Transnational
     Carbon Markets   94
E REDD+ As Co-articulating Various Forms of
   Anthropocentric Governance   97
   1 Conservation   100
   2 Sustainable Management of Forests   102
F REDD+ As a Social Project   106
   1 Debates in the UNFCCC and by NGOs   106
   2 Debates within the UN Permanent Forum on Indigenous Issues 112
   3 The Gradual Elaboration of Safeguards   116
G Conclusion   121

2 Asserting Global Authority over the Carbon Sequestration
Potential of Forests   122
A Introduction   122
B Common Concern   124
C Climate Change and Supranational Jurisdiction   130
   1 Climate Change As a 'Global' Problem   132
   2 Climate Change As a Current or Future Problem   134
   3 Climate Change As a Problem of Emissions, Not Structural Causes 135
   4 The Imperatives of 'Efficiency'   136
   5 Substitution, Standardisation and Equivalence   140
   6 The Differentiated Actualisation of This 'Common Concern' 142
D Forests, 'Common Concern' and Authority   144
   1 Contestation and Authority over Forests   144
   2 From Proprietorial Claims over Forests to 'Concern' for
     Their Function   153
   3 Carbon Sequestration As a Global Concern   156
   4 The Differentiated Actualisation of This 'Common Concern' 164
E Conclusion   166

3 Actualising Authority through Public and Private Law:
REDD+ through the Lens of Property and Contract   168
A Introduction   168

Contents

	B Disrupting the Public–Private Boundary	170
	C REDD+ through the Lens of Transnational Carbon Contracting	177
	1 Challenges in Drafting Transnational Carbon Contracts for REDD+	178
	2 Establishing Norms through Carbon Contracting	184
	D REDD+ through the Lens of Property	191
	1 The Peculiar Properties of Rights in Carbon	192
	2 Initial Distribution and Unequal Allocation of Emission Allowances	196
	3 Carbon Units in a More Decentralised Climate Regime	201
	4 Inclusion of REDD+ in Post-Paris Markets	209
	E Conclusion	211
4	**Responsibility and Capacity: Recasting North–South Difference**	212
	A Introduction	212
	B The Contested Basis and Purpose of Differentiation in the Climate Regime	215
	C CBDR-RD: History of the Principle and Its Adoption in the Climate Regime	218
	1 Differentiation in the UNFCCC	218
	2 Kyoto Protocol: The 'High-Water Mark' of Differentiation	221
	3 The Road to Paris: Re-articulating Differentiation	223
	4 Differentiation in the Post-Paris Regime	227
	D Carbon Markets, Interests and Responsibility	230
	1 The Clean Development Mechanism (CDM), Offsets and Trade-Offs	232
	2 Post-Kyoto Discussions on Market Mechanisms	237
	3 REDD+: 'first ripe fruit in the pledge-and-review architecture'	240
	E Redressing Differentiated Capacity: Capacity-Building As Governance Reform	243
	1 REDD+-Readiness, Capacity-Building and International Partnerships	244
	2 REDD+-Readiness, Rule of Law and 'Good Governance' Promotion	247
	F Conclusion	255
5	**Scale, Multilevel Governance and the Disaggregation of Property Rights in REDD+**	256
	A Introduction	256
	B Rights in Forest Carbon	259
	1 Carbon Rights	260
	2 Forest Tenure	266

x   *Contents*

C Common Property Regimes and Natural Resources	269
1 Common Property Resources As a Development Strategy	272
2 Property Rights Regimes and Natural Resources	277
3 Decentralisation and Natural Resource Governance	280
4 Polycentric Governance and Nested, Multilevel Institutional Arrangements	283
5 Legal Pluralism and Customary Tenure	287
D Conclusion	293

6   REDD+ at the 'Local' Level: Between Rights and Responsibilisation   294

A Introduction	294
B Managing Social Risks	296
C Disciplinary Inclusion in the Green Economy	301
D Indigenous Human Rights, Recognition and Cultural Difference	304
E Identifying 'Stakeholders': The Constitution of Environmental Subjects	307
1 Indigenous Peoples	308
2 'Local Communities'	315
3 Identifying the 'Subjects' of Safeguards in REDD+	318
F Strategies to Manage the 'Social': Between Rights and Responsibilisation	322
1 Benefit Sharing	322
2 Tenure Reform	329
3 Free, Prior and Informed Consent	336
G Conclusion	349

7   Conclusion: Possibilities for Climate Justice and Planetary Co-habitation   351

Bibliography	357
Index	411

Acknowledgements

The friend....precedes and enables thought itself.... That one never thinks alone [but] always in common is an ancient truth of thought.... With my friend... I may come to think anew and differently.[1]

Writing is predominantly a solitary process, but the process of thinking through and formulating new ideas is necessarily a collective process grounded in collegial exchange. This project would not have been possible without the rich scholarly interactions I have been so fortunate to enjoy alongside the solidarity and support of family and friends. Unavoidably, too, one always writes from somewhere and with a specific orientation. I acknowledge that most of this book was written on the unceded lands of the Wurundjeri people of the Kulin nations, and I pay respects to their elders, past and present.

My passion for this project arose out of work with Friends of the Earth International on climate justice. Special thanks are due to Rebecca Pearse, Ellen Roberts and Holly Creanaune, as well as Pius Ginting, Muliardi, Norhadie, Deddy Ratih, Arie Rompas, Teguh Surya, Dipti Bhatnagar, Jeff Conant, Lucia Ortiz, Claudia Ramos-Guillén and Isaac Rojas for critical conversations on these themes. Thank you also to Teishan Ahearne and Jessica Malka Richter for travelling with me to Central Kalimantan, and to Daniel McIntyre for many discussions over many years.

This book developed out of a doctoral thesis, and particular thanks are due to Margaret Young, Maureen Tehan, Lee Godden and Kirsty Gover for their guidance throughout that project and for the freedom they allowed me to explore my ideas. Special thanks are due to Sundhya Pahuja for her continued support of this project, her critical encouragement and probing questions that opened up new lines of

---

[1] C. Casarino and A. Negri, *In Praise of the Common: A Conversation on Philosphy and Politics* (The University of Minnesota Press, 2008) p. 38.

enquiry. At Melbourne Law School I was fortunate to be part of an engaged community of scholars, including Tsegaye Regassa Ararssa, Marie Aronsson, Olivia Barr, Anna Driedzic, Debolina Dutta, Luis Eslava, Kathyrn Greenman, Jake Goldenfein, Anne Kellis, Tim Lindgren, Liz MacPherson, Shaun McVeigh, Caitlin Murphy, Erin O'Donnell, Di Otto, Rose Parfitt, Connal Parsley, James Parker, Peter Rush, Oishik Sircar and Cait Storr. A Residential Fellowship at the Institute of Global Law and Policy (IGLP) at the Harvard Law School allowed me precious time to write, and I am grateful to David Kennedy for this opportunity and to my colleagues Lina Céspedes-Báez, Tomaso Ferrando and Maya Savevska.

The book started to take its current shape whilst I was a postdoctoral fellow at the Rapoport Center for Human Rights and Justice at the University of Texas at Austin; this process of reformulation was enriched by conversations with Karen Engle as well as with Daniel Brinks, William Forbath and many others. The manuscript was finalised after I found a new academic home in the School of Law at La Trobe University, where I was welcomed and supported by Lola Akin Ojelabi, Madeline Chiam, Maria Elander, Fiona Kelly, Anita Mackay, Hannah Robert, Emma Russell, Kerstin Steiner, Savitri Taylor, Marc Trabsky and many others. Throughout the long process of writing, my thinking has been influenced in different ways by many colleagues, and I'm particularly grateful to Ben Golder, Rajshree Chandra, Deval Desai, Michael Fakhri, Isabel Feichtner, Anna Grear, Stephen Humphreys, Karin Mickelson, Usha Natarajan, Jordy Silverstein and Peer Zumbansen.

I was fortunate to present earlier versions of parts of this book at numerous academic conferences and workshops, including Law and Society Association annual meetings, the Third World Approaches to International Law Conferences (Cairo 2015 and Singapore 2018), the Institute for Global Law and Policy Workshops (2014 and 2015) and Conference (2015), the Transnational Law Summer School (2015), the Melbourne Doctoral Forum on Legal Theory (2010 and 2012), Critical Legal Conference (2014) and more. I am grateful to all my interlocutors and commentators, whose probing questions, insightful comments and constructive critiques provided generative impetus for deeper thinking.

Parts of Chapters 1, 6 and 7 build on arguments previously published in 'Indigenous peoples and REDD+ safeguards: Rights as resistance or disciplinary inclusion in the green economy?' (2016) 6(2) *Journal of Human Rights and the Environment* 170–217. Similarly, parts of the analysis in chapters 2 and 3 draws on my chapter 'One tonne of carbon dioxide equivalent' in Jessie Hohmann and Daniel Joyce (eds), *International Law's Objects* (Oxford University Press, 2018) pp. 305–18; and 'Carbon colonialism or climate justice?: Interrogating the international climate regime from a TWAIL perspective' (2016) 33(3) *Windsor Yearbook of Access to Justice* 129–61. Finally, Chapter 4 further develops some themes initially discussed in 'Reflections on Paris: Thoughts towards a critical approach to climate law' (2018) *Quebec Journal of International Law* 61–91. Throughout this manuscript the 'I' in

Acknowledgements xiii

'Indigenous' has been capitalised as a measure of respect and to reflect the plurality of diverse, sovereign peoples the term refers to. However, the lowercase 'i' has been retained in direct quotes from other materials.[2]

I am enormously indebted to those who generously read and provided comments on parts of earlier drafts, including Tom Andrews, Kathleen Birrell, Matt Canfield, Madelaine Chiam, Sara Dehm, Maria Elander, Lee Godden, Adil Hasan Khan, Sarah Mason-Case, Hannah Robert, Emma Russell and Ntina Tzouvala. I am enormously grateful to Stephanie Falconer, Julia Farrell, Laura Griffin, Carol Peterson and David Venema for all their assistance in finalising the manuscript. I was fortunate to enjoy the companionship of Tom Andrews, Polly Bennett, Katie Buckley, Vicky Huang, Jason Murphy as well as everyone at La Trobe Researchers Shut Up and Write, #melbwriteup and the Tuesday MLS Writing Group during the process of writing. Deep thanks are also due to Matt Gallaway, Cameron Daddis, Franklin Mathews Jebaraj and Catherine Smith everyone at Cambridge University Press for their support and patience throughout this process. I'm particularly grateful to Kathy McKenzie for her thoughtful, careful and perceptive edits on this manuscript.

My deepest thanks to my family: to Sara, Ben and Leo for their support, which has sustained me, to Anna for her patience, and to my parents, Doris and Burkhard, for their encouragement, belief in me and unwavering love. Finally, completing this project would not have been possible without the joy of countless conversations with Adil Hasan Khan as we work towards cultivating a companionship of care.

Finally, I acknowledge my daughter, Aalia, who was only a dream while this book was being written, but during the final pre-publication stages she has blessed my days with immense joy, providing a constant reminder of the fierce love that animates our ongoing struggles for ecologically just futures.

---

[2] G. Younging, *Elements of Indigenous Style: A Guide for Writing By an About Indigenous Peoples* (Brush Education, 2018)

Abbreviations

AAU	assigned amount unit
ADP	Ad Hoc Working Group on the Durban Platform for Enhanced Action
AFOLU	agriculture, forestry and other land use
A/R	afforestation and reforestation
AWG-KP	Ad Hoc Working Group on the Kyoto Protocol
AWG-LCA	Ad Hoc Working Group on Long-term Cooperative Action
BAU	business-as-usual
CAFI	Central African Forest Initiative
CBDR	common but differentiated responsibilities
CBDR-RC	common but differentiated responsibilities and respective capabilities
CDM	Clean Development Mechanism
CERs	certified emission reductions
CIFOR	Center for International Forestry Research
CMA	Conference of the Parties Serving as Meeting of the Parties to the Paris Agreement
CMP	Conference of the Parties Serving as Meeting of the Parties to the Kyoto Protocol
CO_2	carbon dioxide
CO_2e	carbon dioxide equivalent
COP	Conference of the Parties
CORSIA	Carbon Offset and Reduction Scheme for International Aviation
CPF	Collaborative Partnership on Forests
CPR	common property regime
CPRNet	Common Property Resources Management Network
ER	emission reduction
ERPA	Emission Reduction Purchase Agreement

ER-PIN	Emission Reduction–Program Idea Note
ESF	Environmental and Social Framework
ESS7	Environmental and Social Standard 7
ETS	emissions trading scheme
EU	European Union
FAO	Food and Agricultural Organization of the United Nations
FCPF	Forest Carbon Partnership Facility
FERL/FRL	forest emission reference level/forest reference level
FoEI	Friends of the Earth International
FPIC	free, prior and informed consent
FPP	Forest Peoples Programme
GHG	greenhouse gas
ICAO	International Civil Aviation Organization
IEL	international environmental law
IETA	International Emissions Trading Association
IIED	International Institute for Environment and Development
IIPFCC	International Indigenous Peoples' Forum on Climate Change
IISD	International Institute for Sustainable Development
ILA	International Law Association
INDC	intended nationally determined contribution
ITMO	internationally transferred mitigation outcome
ITTA	International Tropical Timber Agreement
IUCN	International Union for the Conservation of Nature
JI	Joint Implementation
KFCP	Kalimantan Forest Carbon Partnership
LULUCF	land use, land-use change and forestry
MMRV/	monitoring, measuring report and verification/ measuring, reporting
MRV	and verification
NAMA	nationally appropriate mitigation actions
NDC	nationally determined contributions
NGO	non-governmental organisation
NIEO	New International Economic Order
NMM	new market mechanisms
ODA	overseas development assistance
ODI	Overseas Development Institute
OECD	Organization for Economic Co-operation and Development
OHCHR	Office of the High Commissioner for Human Rights
PES	payment for environmental services
ppm	parts per million
PSNR	permanent sovereignty over natural resources
QELRC	quantified emission limitation or reduction commitments
RED	Reducing Emissions from Deforestation

REDD+	Reducing Emissions from Deforestation and Degradation
REL/RL	reference emission levels/reference level
R-Package	Readiness Package
R-PIN	Readiness Plan Idea Note
R-PP	Readiness Preparation Proposal
RRI	Rights and Resources Initiative
SSAHUTLC	Sub-Saharan African Historically Underserved Traditional Local Communities
SBI	Subsidiary Body for Implementation
SBSTA	Subsidiary Body for Scientific and Technological Advice
SFM	sustainable forest management
tCO_2e	tonne carbon dioxide equivalent
TEEB	The Economics of Ecosystems and Biodiversity
TFAP	Tropical Forest Action Plan
TWAIL	Third World Approaches to International Law
UK	United Kingdom
UN	United Nations
UNCRITAL	United Nations Committee on International Trade Law
UNDP	United Nations Development Programme
UNDRIP	United Nations Declaration on the Rights of Indigenous Peoples
UNEP	United Nations Environment Programme
UNFCCC	United Nations Framework Convention on Climate Change
UNFF	United Nations Forum on Forests
UNPFII	United Nations Permanent Forum on Indigenous Peoples
UN-REDD	United Nations collaborative initiative on Reducing Emission from Deforestation and Forest Degradation (REDD) in developing countries
US	United States of America
USAID	United States Agency for International Development
VGGT	Voluntary Guidelines on the Responsible Governance of Tenure of Land, Fisheries and Forests in the Context of National Food Security
WRI	World Resources Institute
WWF	World Wide Fund for Nature

Introduction

Reconsidering REDD+

A INTRODUCTION

The question of how we respond to the climate crisis – or even how such a 'we' is configured – is perhaps the most critical legal, political and moral question of our time. The globalisation of a fossil fuel-dependent capitalism has taken the world to the brink of ecological disaster. The climate crisis makes transformation of the status quo both urgent and unavoidable. Yet, the *form* this transformation will take is not inevitable: different visions of the future remain heavily contested, and the processes of transition and their elements and speed remain the subject of high-stake debate and struggle.

The realisation that humans have so fundamentally changed our environment that we have become a 'geological force' raises uncomfortable questions about responsibility, culpability and what it means to live well in the 'Anthropocene'.[1] On a theoretical level, the contemporary epoch has sparked exciting investigations about how core assumptions of many disciplines, including the doctrines, principles and processes of international law, will need to be rethought, in a context where a once presumed environmental stability no longer exists.[2] Similarly, the ecological crisis has led to a revitalisation of scholarship critically interrogating how international law has contributed to the production of Anthropocene conditions by perpetuating an extractivist relationship to nature. Such scholarship seeks to excavate the problematic assumptions about nature that lie at the heart of international

---

[1] P. J. Crutzen, 'Geology of mankind' *Nature* (2002) 415 Nature 23; a number of other terms have been proposed, such as the 'Capitalocene' in J. W. Moore (ed.), *Anthropocene or Capitalocene?: Nature, History, and the Crisis of Capitalism* (PM Press, 2016); and the 'Chthulucene' in D. J. Haraway, *Staying with the Trouble: Making Kin in the Chthulucene* (Duke University Press, 2016).

[2] D. Vidas, J. Zalasiewicz, and M. Williams, 'What is the Anthropocene – and why is it relevant for international law?' (2014) 25 *Yearbook of International Environmental Law* 3–23 at 23.

Introduction

law, and to remake international law's relationship with the natural world.[3] There is a growing chorus of scholarly voices calling for a different 'conception of law which acknowledges, and in fact emerges from, the entangled nature of existence'.[4]

Because the Anthropocene has given rise to such rich 'new' ways of thinking, some have suggested it marks a 'rupture' with the past.[5] However, the prosaic, day-to-day developments in the field of international legal practice are arguably marked more by *continuities* than by dramatic breaks from the norm. It is these questions of how existing structural power relations and sedimented historical conditions continue to influence responses to the climate crisis that are addressed by this book. This book is concerned with how the dominant international legal responses to climate change, particularly the marketised vision of a 'green economy', replicate – and indeed further intensify – already existing legal relations of domination, exploitation and marginalisation. While climate change arguably should have been the ultimate challenge to development and growth logic, in many ways it appears to have fuelled, rather than interrupted the expansion of these rationalities.

This book directs its attention to examining a specific response to the climate crisis – the Reducing Emissions from Deforestation and Forest Degradation scheme, commonly known by its acronym, REDD+.[6] REDD+ represents a particular way of framing and responding to the urgent challenge of addressing climate change that is not neutral in its effects, but has potential wide-ranging implications for how forests are governed and valued, both for biodiversity and for the estimated 1.6 billion people who live in and around forests and depend upon them to some degree for their livelihoods.[7] At stake in debates over REDD+ are struggles over the shape and contours of the necessary transition towards a low-carbon future, and

---

[3] U. Natarajan and J. Dehm (eds.), *Locating Nature: Making and Unmaking International Law* (Cambridge University Press, forthcoming); U. Natarajan and K. Khody, 'Locating nature: Making and unmaking international law' (2014) 27 *Leiden Journal of International Law* 573–93.

[4] M. Davies, *Asking the Law Question*, Fourth edition (Thomson Reuters, 2017) p. 497.

[5] See C. Hamilton, 'The Anthropocene as rupture' (2016) 3(3) *Anthropocene Review* 93–106.

[6] I use the term 'REDD+' throughout this book (unless directly quoting someone using a different term). When first proposed in 2005, this scheme was initially referred to as 'RED' (Reducing Emissions from Deforestation). It was subsequently known as 'REDD' (Reducing Emissions from Deforestation in Developing Countries or Reducing Emissions from Deforestation and Forest Degradation). The '+' on the end of the 'REDD+' refers to the additional components, beyond reducing emissions from deforestation and reducing emissions from forest degradation, namely conservation of forest carbon stocks, sustainable management of forests and enhancement of forest carbon stocks endorsed in the Cancun Agreements (Decision 1/CP16, 'The Cancun Agreements: Outcome of the Work of the Ad Hoc Working Group on Long-Term Cooperative Action under the Convention' FCCC/CP/2010/7/Add.1 (15 March 2011) para 70). Pursuant to this agreement these activities should receive as much emphasis as reducing emissions from deforestation and reducing emissions from forest degradation.

[7] J. Eliasch, *Climate Change: Financing Global Forests. The Eliasch Review* (Earthscan, 2008) p. 9. See discussion in Chapter 1 for more details.

A. Introduction

particularly with regards to how the burdens and benefits of any transition are distributed. REDD+ raises difficult questions about how global authority over resources, such as forests, located in the Global South should be distributed, as well as fraught questions about the present obligations arising from historical responsibility for greenhouse gas (GHG).[8] REDD+ therefore reflects broader debates about policy responses to climate change and underlying conflicts between the increased marketisation of climate policy and imperatives of global climate justice. Implicit in these debates are moral and justice arguments about whether questions of equity and (re)distribution should be central to climate change responses, or whether considerations of aggregate efficiency should be prioritised. Moreover, these contestations foreground how the present conjuncture is one that enlivens very different imaginaries of the future: an envisioned 'green capitalism' in which nature is scripted and valued in economic terms, commodified and financialised,[9] or alternative trajectories towards more decentralised decolonial frameworks of localised resource sovereignty.[10]

REDD+ is a scheme to address the contribution of GHG emissions from deforestation and forest degradation, which thereby brings together questions about the sustainable management of forests and climate mitigation. It therefore represents one part of a broader suite of 'nature-based' or 'natural' climate solutions that seek to preserve the integrity of ecosystems, improve sustainable management of ecosystems and restore degraded ecosystems.[11] The stated aim of REDD+ is to 'make forests more valuable standing than they would be cut down' by providing economic incentives to address tropical deforestation and forest degradation in the Global

---

[8] K. Mickelson, 'Seeing the forest, the trees and the people: Coming to terms with developing country perspectives on the proposed global forests convention' in Canadian Council of International Law (ed.), *Global Forests and International Environmental Law* (Kluwer Law, 1996) pp. 239–64; K. Mickelson, 'Beyond a politics of the possible? South–North relations and climate justice' (2009) 10(2) *Melbourne Journal of International Law* 411–23. I use the term 'Global North' and 'Global South' throughout this book, although this does not reflect the terminology in the climate regime. The 1992 United Nations Framework Convention on Climate Change established two lists: Annex I, which includes the 1992 members of the Organization of Economic Co-operation and Development (OECD) as well as some economies in transition, indicated by an asterisk; and Annex II, which includes only OECD countries. The 2015 Paris Agreement refers to 'developed country Parties' and 'developing country Parties', and also makes reference to 'least developed countries' and 'small island developing States'. Although my discussion necessarily has to adopt the language of the climate regime, where possible I choose to use the term 'Global North' and 'Global South' to avoid the implicit hierarchical ordering and developmental *telos* the concept of development implies.

[9] On this see *The Economics of Ecosystems and Biodiversity: Mainstreaming the Economics of Nature: A Synthesis of the Approach, Conclusions and Recommendations of the TEEB* (TEEB, 2010).

[10] On different trajectories arising out of the present conjuncture see also J. Wainwright and G. Mann, 'Climate leviathan' (2013) 45(1) *Antipode* 1–22; J. Wainwright and G. Mann, *Climate Leviathan: A Political Theory of Our Planetary Future* (Verso Books, 2018).

[11] See *Nature–Based Solutions to Address Climate Change* (International Union for the Conservation of Nature, 2016).

4   *Introduction*

South.[12] What has been particularly controversial is the proposal that REDD+ could operate as a carbon 'offset' scheme whereby countries in the Global North provide financial resources to promote the reduction of deforestation and forest degradation in the Global South, and in return can count the 'saved' carbon dioxide towards their own international mitigation commitments. Although at the time of writing no formal decision has been made about whether or how REDD+ would be included in international carbon markets under the United Nations Framework Convention on Climate Change (UNFCCC) or the Paris Agreement,[13] from its history and trajectory it is evident that REDD+ has been envisioned and planned as a market-orientated flexibility mechanism. Such proposals to incorporate deforestation and forest degradation into international carbon markets have been criticised as a 'false solution' by social movements and non-governmental organisations (NGOs) working towards climate justice, who question both the environmental integrity and social justice of carbon offsetting.[14]

This book argues that REDD+ needs to be analysed not just as a problematic 'false solution' to climate change but also as an ambitious project that is reorganising how forested land in the Global South becomes an object for international and transnational regulation. The analysis in this book is therefore not focused on the various limitations of REDD+, but rather draws attention to the productive effects of this type of international climate policy. It shows how REDD+ operates to reorganise social relations and to establish new forms of global authority over forests in the Global South in ways that benefit the interests of some actors while further marginalising others. It demonstrates how, through the creation of new legal relations, including new property rights and contractual obligations, new forms of transnational authority over forested areas in the Global South are being constituted. In doing so, it traces shifts in the location of authority to make decisions over forest resources; how this authority is actualised, enacted and materialised; and according

---

[12] UN-REDD Programme, *Frequently Asked Questions and Answers – REDD+ and the UN-REDD Programme* (June 2010).

[13] *United Nations Framework Convention on Climate Change*, opened for signature 4 June 1992, 1771 UNTS 107 (entered into force 21 March 1994) ('UNFCCC'); *Paris Agreement*, opened for signature on 22 April 2016, UNTS XXVII.7.d (entered into force 4 November 2016) ('Paris Agreement').

[14] See for example L. Lohmann, *Carbon Trading: A Critical Conversation on Climate Change, Privatisation and Power* (Dag Hammarskjöld Foundation, 2006); S. Böhm and S. Dabhi (eds.), *Upsetting the Offset: The Political Economy of Carbon Markets* (MayFly Books, 2009); S.-J. Clifton, *A Dangerous Obsession: The Evidence against Carbon Trading and for Real Solutions to Avoid a Climate Crunch* (Friends of the Earth England, Wales and Northern Ireland, 2009); R. Hall, *REDD Myths: A Critical Review of Proposed Mechanisms to Reduce Emissions from Deforestation and Degradation in Developing Countries* (Friends of the Earth International, 2008); R. Pearse and J. Dehm, in *REDD: Australia's Carbon Offset Project in Central Kalimantan* (Friends of the Earth International, 2011); A. Dawson, 'Climate justice: The emerging movement against green capitalism' (2010) 109(2) *South Atlantic Quarterly* 313–38; N. Klein, *This Changes Everything: Capitalism vs. the Climate* (Simon & Schuster, 2014).

A. Introduction

to what modalities of power it is deployed. In tracking these reconfigurations, this book focuses on how the legal arrangements constituting REDD+ not only operate to establish new forms of authority but also to rationalise and justify them.

Moreover, this book situates REDD+ as central to broader debates about the contours of and transition to a 'green economy'. REDD+ has been presented as a key part of a 'green economy transition',[15] with its proponents optimistic that it can contribute to a 'virtuous cycle' of investment that provides the catalyst for 'green development'.[16] More specifically, REDD+ proponents understand the scheme as central to post-2015 development objectives to ensure the socioeconomic benefits to be derived from forests are better 'valued',[17] while also holding 'transformative potential'[18] to facilitate a much wider valuation, commodification and financialisation of nature. REDD+ therefore should be seen as 'only a small and insignificant piece' of a broader trajectory of 'natural capital valuation' that frames conservation as a 'distinct "asset class" within conventional financial markets'.[19] Such expansive visions are reflected in comments made in 2011 by Christiana Figueres, the former Executive Secretary of the UNFCCC, when she described REDD+ as the 'spiritual core' of a 'global business plan for the planet'.[20] Similarly, the United Nations Environment Programme (UNEP) has 'placed REDD+ at the heart of its climate strategy' because of the opportunities REDD+ presents to 'catalyse further investments in other ecosystem services from forests, thus adding further "layers" of revenue streams from standing forests'.[21]

Contestations over REDD+ are therefore both important in their own right and also emblematic of broader struggles over differing modalities of environmental governance and how the relationship between the economy, society and the natural world should be configured. Grassroots Indigenous and climate justice activists have critiqued REDD+ as a 'land-grabbing false solution to climate change' that has 'privatized the air we breathe'; 'uses forests, agriculture, and water ecosystems in the Global South as sponges for industrialised countries' pollution'; and seeks to

---

[15] S. Sullivan, 'Banking nature?' (2013) 45(1) *Antipode* 198–217 at 200.

[16] P. Sukhdev, R. Prabhu, P. Kumar, A. Bassi, W. Patwa-Shah, T. Enters, G. Labbate, and J. Greenwalt, *REDD+ and the Green Economy: Opportunities for a Mutually Supportive Relationship* (UN-REDD Programme, 2012).

[17] 'State of the World's Forests: Enhancing the socioeconomic benefits from forests' (Food and Agricultural Organisation of the United Nations, 2014), www.fao.org/3/a-i3710e.pdf.

[18] I. Thiaw, 'Forward' in Xianli Zhu et al., *Pathways for implementing REDD+: Experiences from carbon markets and communities* (UNEP Riso Centre, 2010) p. 8.

[19] R. Fletcher, W. Dressler, B. Büscher, and Z. R. Anderson, 'Debating REDD+ and its implications: Reply to Angelsen et al.' (2017) 31(3) *Conservation Biology* 721–23 at 722.

[20] Transcribed by author from Center for International Forestry Research (CIFOR), 'Closing Remarks – Forest Day 5, 2011', blog.cifor.org/5782/countries-draft-%E2%80%9Cglobal-business-plan%E2%80%9D-for-planet-at-climate-summit-figueres-says/.

[21] I. Thiaw, 'Forward', p. 8.

'bring trees, soil, and nature into a commodity trading system'.[22] They have condemned REDD+ as a mechanism that 'steals your future, lets polluters off the hook and is a new form of colonialism'.[23] The Indigenous Environment Network has described REDD+ as a new form of neo-colonialism or 'CO$_2$lonialism'.[24] Indonesian villages affected by a REDD+ project have described it as the 'new face of capitalism in the shape of ecological imperialism' that is 'turning our homes into a carbon toilet'.[25] These groups and others have thus articulated their strong opposition to REDD+ and called for the 'defense of indigenous territories and forest dependent communities, their autonomy and control over their territories and the protection of Mother Earth'.[26] For some commentators, the REDD+ scheme represents a form of 'green grabbing', 'the appropriation of land and resources for environmental ends', which has been recognised as 'an emerging process of deep and growing significance'.[27]

Taking inspiration from these criticisms, this book provides a critical reading of the logics and effects of the REDD+ scheme. It engages with, and builds upon, numerous critiques of REDD+ that have highlighted its clear limitations as a climate mitigation strategy, but the primary contribution of the book is to examine the productive effects of this type of international climate policy and to interrogate the sort of world that REDD+ assumes and looks forward to. It understands REDD+ both as a vision of market-orientated environmental governance and as a series of practices and processes directed towards actualising and implementing this ideal. This book maps how REDD+ reconfigures global authority over forested land and forest resources in the Global South, paying attention to the processes of agreement-making under the UNFCCC and the development of legal and governance frameworks for REDD+ at the national level, but also to transnational practices of agreement-making and 'capacity building'. In doing so, this book intervenes in a number of key legal debates. First, it provides a critical account of the work of international climate law and some of the implications of the turn towards

---

[22] 'Media release: UN promoting potentially genocidal policy at World Climate Summit' (8 December 2015, Indigenous Environment Network), www.ienearth.org/un-promoting-potentially-genocidal-policy-at-world-climate-summit/

[23] Ibid.

[24] REDD: Reaping Profits from Evictions, Land Grabs, Deforestation and Destruction of Biodiversity (Indigenous Environment Network, 2009); No to CO$_2$lonialism! Indigenous Peoples' Guide: False Solutions to Climate Change (Indigenous Environment Network, 2009).

[25] Petak Danum Kalimantan Tengah, Our Land Is Not a Carbon Toilet for Dirty Industries of Developed Countries (2012), copy on file with author.

[26] Call to Action: To Reject REDD+ and Extractive Industries; to Confront Capitalism and Defend Life and Territories (December 2014), wrm.org.uy/wp-content/uploads/2014/11/Call-COP-Lima_NoREDD.pdf.

[27] See J. Fairhead, M. Leach, and I. Scoones, 'Green grabbing: A new appropriation of nature?' (2012) 39(2) The Journal of Peasant Studies 237–61 at 238.

market-orientated modes of governance.[28] In addition, it highlights the limitations of viewing international environmental law (IEL) as concerned with developing tools to bridge the North–South divide,[29] and shows instead how IEL is implicated in the reproduction of difference between the Global North and the Global South and the continuation of neo-colonial relations. It also reveals the ways in which international and transnational law is complicit in forms of appropriation of land and resources, thereby contributing to the literature about 'land grabbing'.[30] Further, the analysis speaks to the shifting ways in which global authority is articulated and actualised in the contemporary capitalist economy through the concurrent operations and mutual co-constitution of both public and private laws. It thus highlights the need for the standard public–private divide to be disrupted in the analysis of contemporary as well as historical relations of global domination and imperialism.[31] Finally, given that REDD+ implementation poses distinctive challenges for coordination between the global, national and local scales, this book interrogates how the operations of global governance distributes rights, power and obligations between scales, and illuminates processes by which authority is globalised while responsibility is localised.

B ASSEMBLING REDD+

1 REDD+ As a Relation

This section provides a background to REDD+ as an assemblage of international, national and transnational laws that make it possible to include forests in international markets and shows how this assemblage holds different practices and modes by which nature is governed in different parts of the world, in relation with each other. Throughout this book, REDD+ is understood simultaneously as a legal framework, a vision of market-orientated environmental governance and a project of materialising or actualising this vision through various programs and preparatory and experimental processes which is dependent upon a particular way of seeing forests and forest resources and particular forms of representation and legibility and modes of standardisation, comparison and calculation. This book develops a

---

[28] In doing so, it builds on my earlier analysis in J. Dehm, 'Carbon colonialism or climate justice: Interrogating the international climate regime from a TWAIL perspective' (2016) 33 *Windsor Yearbook of Access to Justice* 129–61; J. Dehm, 'Reflections on Paris: Thoughts towards a critical approach to climate law' (2018) *Revue Québécoise de Droit International* 61–91.

[29] S. Alam, S. Atapattu, C. G. Gonzalez, and J. Razzaque (eds.), *International Environmental Law and the Global South* (Cambridge University Press, 2015).

[30] For a discussion of the relationship between international law and land grabbing see 'Symposium on land grabbing' (2019) 32(2) *Leiden Journal of International Law*.

[31] M. Koskenniemi, 'Expanding histories of international law' (2016) 56(1) *American Journal of Legal History* 104–12; M. Koskenniemi, 'Empire and international law: The real Spanish contribution' (2011) 61 *University of Toronto Law Journal* 1–36.

8   *Introduction*

framework that brings these various conceptions together in order to understand REDD+ as a configuration of multiple legal frameworks; the vision they seek to actualise; the practices of implementation and materialisation pursuant to this objective; and the knowledge practices, forms of legibility and modes of calculation necessary for materializing REDD+. In doing so, it elucidates the complex nature of transnational norm creation at multiple sites and on multiple scales and identifies how REDD+ enables the actualisation of new forms of global authority as well as the reconfiguration of relations of power.

REDD+ and the capacity of forests to operate as 'carbon stocks' and to sequestrator carbon were affirmed as key parts of international climate mitigation efforts in the Paris Agreement.[32] The Paris Agreement sets ambitious objectives to hold the global average temperature increases below 2 °C and to 'pursue efforts' to limit temperature increases to 1.5 °C.[33] To achieve these goals countries aim to 'reach global peaking of emissions as soon as possible' and to undertake rapid emission reductions in order to 'achieve a balance between anthropocentric emissions by sources and removals by sinks',[34] affirming that international climate strategies are fundamentally concerned with both the reduction of GHG emissions and the intensification of carbon sequestration, through forests and other carbon sinks. The Paris Agreement specifically calls on Parties to 'take action to conserve and enhance ... sinks and reservoirs of greenhouse gases ... including forests'[35] and to implement and support the existing framework for REDD+. This 'potentially historic breakthrough'[36] has confirmed the centrality of REDD+ as a policy objective, a legal framework, a set of economic incentives and a series of practices aimed at protecting forests and promoting carbon sequestration as a climate change 'solution'.

One of the major – and still legally unresolved – controversies within the REDD+ negotiations relates to whether or not REDD+ will operate as an 'offset' scheme that allows parties to purchase carbon credits arising from sequestration activities in the Global South to meet their international mitigation commitments.[37] REDD+ is envisioned as a financial mechanism that relies upon valuing forests and the ecosystem services they provide, in economic terms, to provide incentives to address tropical deforestation by 'mak[ing] forests more valuable standing than they would

---

[32] *Paris Agreement*, Article 5.

[33] *Paris Agreement*, Article 2.1(a).

[34] *Paris Agreement*, Article 4.1.

[35] *Paris Agreement*, Article 5.1.

[36] 'Inclusion of REDD+ in Paris climate agreement heralded as a major step forward on deforestation' *Mongabay* 14 December 2015, news.mongabay.com/2015/12/inclusion-of-redd-in-paris-climate-agreement-heralded-as-major-step-forward-on-deforestation.

[37] For a discussion of country submissions and proposals see: UNFCCC Secretariat, *Financing Options for the Full Implementation of Results-Based Actions Relating to the Activities Referred to in Decision 1/CP.16, paragraph 70, Including Related Modalities and Procedures: Technical Paper*, FCCC/TP/2012/3 (26 July 2012).

B. Assembling REDD+

be cut down'.[38] However, whether REDD+ finance will come primarily from carbon markets or other public and private sources remains unclear. At the time of writing no formal decision has been made that 'result-based' actions arising from REDD+ can be sold as 'carbon credits' and counted towards the compliance obligations of the purchasing country; nor has it been decided[39] whether REDD+ will be part of the 'new era of international carbon trading'[40] enabled by the Paris Agreement framework that could facilitate a 'much deeper world of cooperation'[41] and the development of carbon markets, which together with carbon taxes could potentially be worth US$100 billion annually.[42]

REDD+ was initially conceived of as a market-based system,[43] and it was anticipated that the majority of funding would come from carbon markets.[44] However, other commentators have suggested that this 'historic vision' of REDD+ as a market-based instrument no longer reflects current realities,[45] and that REDD+ is now more akin to conditional or result-based aid programs than it is to a carbon market mechanism.[46] At present, almost all international REDD+ funding comes from bilateral and multilateral development aid budgets, rather than carbon

---

[38] UN-REDD Programme, *Frequently Asked Questions and Answers – The UN-REDD Programme and REDD+*, November 2010, www.unep.org/forests/Portals/142/docs/UN-REDD%20FAQs%20%5B11.10%5D.pdf.

[39] Note at COP24 in Katowice, Brazil opposed linking Article 6 of the *Paris Agreement* to REDD+ (see 'Summary of the Katowice Climate Change Conference: 2–15 December 2018' 12(747) *Earth Negotiations Bulletin* 18 December 2018, 17, although there are a number of suggestions of how such linkage could occur: P. Graham, *Cooperative Approaches for Supporting REDD+: Linking Articles 5 and 6 of the Paris Agreement* (Climate Advisors, 2017); C. Streck, A. Howard, and R. Rajão, *Options for Enhancing REDD+ Collaboration in the Context of Article 6 of the Paris Agreement* (Meridian Institute, 2017).

[40] Mike Szabo, 'Paris Agreement rings in new era of international carbon trading' *Carbon Pulse* 12 December 2015, carbon-pulse.com/13339/.

[41] 'After Paris, UN's new "light touch" role on markets to help spawn carbon clubs' *Carbon Pulse* 15 December 2015, carbon-pulse.com/13415/.

[42] *Carbon Pricing Watch 2016: An Advanced Brief from the State and Trends of Carbon Pricing 2016 Report, to be released in 2016* (The World Bank Group and ECOFYS, 2015) p. 3.

[43] C. Streck, 'In the market: Forest carbon rights: Shedding light on a muddy concept' (2015) 4 *Carbon & Climate Law Review* 342.

[44] M.-C. Cordonier Segger, M. Gehring, and A. Wardell, 'REDD+ instruments, international investment rules and sustainable landscapes' in C. Voigt (ed.), *Research Handbook on REDD-Plus and International Law* (Edward Elgar Publishing, 2016) p. 348.

[45] A. Angelsen, M. Brockhaus, A. E. Duchelle, A. M. Larson, C. Martius, W. D. Sunderlin, L. V. Verchot, G. Wong, and S. Wunder, 'Learning from REDD+: A Response to Fletcher et al.' (2017) 31(3) *Conservation Biology* 718–20.

[46] A. Angelsen, 'REDD+ as result-based aid: General lessons and bilateral agreements of Norway' (2017) 21(2) *Review of Development Economics* 237–64; result-based aid is part of the 'second generation' approach to conditionality in aid development policy that is increasingly promoted as a 'promising approach for implementing post-2050 development goals', that 'seeks to identify quantifiable and measurable results that can be attributed as directly as possible to the effects of development cooperation'; see S. Klingebiel and H. Janus, 'Results-based aid: Potential and limits of an innovative modality in development cooperation' (2014) 5(2) *International Development Policy\Revue Internationale de Politique de Développement*.

markets. However, the 'financial architecture' underpinning REDD+ has increasingly been understood as consisting of three phases, where the first two phases are funded by public and private domestic and international investments, and the third phase is based on public and private result-based payments.[47] Going forward, 'result-based' payments for REDD+ could flow through both fund-based and market-based models;[48] however, there is strong evidence that suggests the latter is the more likely trajectory. Currently, REDD+ frameworks allow for market-linking,[49] and the legal framework and accounting rules in place for REDD+ could enable REDD+ credits to be used as offsets by purchasing countries.[50] Considerable regulatory and technical work has gone into making it possible for forest carbon to become a 'fungible, compliance-grade asset' that could be treated as equivalent to other forms of carbon.[51] This market-based approach has been advocated for in key policy documents such as the 2008 *Eliasch Review*, which called for 'well-designed mechanisms for linking forest abatement to carbon markets' in order to access private and public finance.[52] Moreover, the explicit objective of key players working on REDD+ implementation, such as the World Bank's Forest Carbon Partnership Facility (FCPF), is to 'jump-start a forest carbon market', where provision of international finance for what has been called REDD+-readiness is a key enabling condition for the gradual construction of forest carbon markets.[53] Indeed, some analysts have suggested that REDD+ needs to be linked to carbon markets to be financially viable, given that a significant increase in overseas development aid would be necessary for non-market models of REDD+ to be financially viable.[54] Some analysis indicates that unless there is a strong demand for REDD+ credits such programmes 'may fail to be developed or not continue',[55] or even that it would not be possible to meet future emissions reduction commitments without tradeable REDD+ credits.[56]

---

[47] See for example, Green Climate Fund, *Green Climate Fund Support for the Early Phases of REDD+*, GCF/B.17/16 (2 July 2017) p. 2.

[48] J. Isenberg and C. Potvin, 'Financing REDD in developing countries: a supply and demand analysis' (2010) 10(2) *Climate Policy* 216–31.

[49] Streck, 'In the market: Forest carbon rights: Shedding light on a muddy concept', 342.

[50] K. Dooley and A. Gupta, 'Governing by expertise: The contested politics of (accounting for) land-based mitigation in a new climate agreement' (2017) 17(4) *International Environmental Agreements: Politics, Law and Economics* 483–500 at 488–9.

[51] W. Boyd, 'Ways of seeing in environmental law: How deforestation became an object of climate governance' (2010) 37 *Ecology Law Quarterly* 843–916 at 879.

[52] J. Eliasch, *Climate Change: Financing Global Forests. The Eliasch Review* (Earthscan, 2008) p. 165.

[53] 'Media Release: Forest Carbon Facility Takes Aim at Deforestation' (World Bank, 11 December 2007), web.worldbank.org/archive/website01290/WEB/0__-1493.HTM.

[54] *Emerging Compliance Markets for REDD+: An Assessment of Supply and Demand* (United States Agency for International Development, 2013).

[55] N. Linacre, R. O'Sullivan, D. Ross and L. Durschinger *REDD+ Supply and Demand 2015–2025: Forest Carbon, Markets and Communities Program* (United Stated Agency for International Development Forest Carbon, Markets and Communities Program, 2015) p. x.

[56] *Emerging Compliance Markets for REDD+: An Assessment of Supply and Demand.*

It is anticipated that a key source of demand for REDD+ credits will come from the Carbon Offset and Reduction Scheme for International Aviation (CORSIA) that was adopted by International Civil Aviation Organization (ICAO) in October 2016. CORSIA aims to implement ICAO's goal to have carbon neutral growth from 2020 and the scheme is projected to offset 2.5 billion tonnes of emissions from aviation over 15 years.[57]

REDD+'s potential confirmation as a carbon offset mechanism has been particularly controversial because of the impossibility of verifying that carbon 'saved' through sequestration is equivalent to carbon emissions released elsewhere, and because of how carbon markets operate to spatially displace the site of emission reductions from the Global North to the Global South. Indeed, 'offsets' have been decried by critics as a 'dangerous distraction' that legitimates the ongoing extraction of fossil fuels and avoids the deeper structural transformations necessary to move to a low-carbon society.[58] However, even if REDD+ is not eventually incorporated into international carbon markets as an 'offset' but rather uses other financial means to incentivise additional sequestration of carbon in forested lands, it is still indicative of a logic – reflected in the Paris Agreement – of seeking a 'balance' between 'emission sources' and 'removals by sinks' in order to meet aggregate global targets.[59] After 'long and intense' negotiations, the terminology of 'net-zero emissions', 'near zero' or carbon or climate neutrality was not included in the Paris Agreement due to fears that including it could provide political licence to offset industrial emissions with land-based sinks;[60] however, the final wording of 'balance' is generally seen as similar in effect and a 'concept akin to net zero GHG emissions'.[61] The language of the Paris Agreement thus leaves open the possibility of continued industrial and terrestrial emissions, provided they are (ostensibly) offset or 'balanced' by the 'enhancement of sinks'.[62] Given the urgency of both reducing

---

[57] D. Bodansky, J. Brunnée, and L. Rajamani, *International Climate Change Law* (Oxford University Press, 2017) pp. 270–3.

[58] S. Bullock, M. Childs, and T. Picken, *A Dangerous Distraction: Why Offsetting Is Failing the Climate and People: The Evidence* (Friends of the Earth England, Wales and Northern Ireland, 2009); for an overview of critiques of carbon trading see R. Pearse and S. Böhm, 'Ten reasons why carbon markets will not bring about radical emissions reduction' (2014) 5(4) *Carbon Management* 325–37.

[59] *Paris Agreement*, Article 4.1

[60] Dooley and Gupta, 'Governing by expertise: The contested politics of (accounting for) land-based mitigation in a new climate agreement', 494; for a critique of the term 'net zero' see T. Anderson and K. Stone, *Caught in the Net: How 'Net-Zero Emissions' Will Delay Real Climate Action and Drive Land Grabs* (ActionAid International, 2015).

[61] H. Winkler, 'Mitigation (Article 4)' in D. Klein, M. P. Carazo, M. Doelle, J. Bulmer, and A. Higham (eds.), *The Paris Agreement on Climate Change: Analysis and Commentary* (Oxford University Press, 2017) pp. 141–165, 144.

[62] Dooley and Gupta, 'Governing by expertise: The contested politics of (accounting for) land-based mitigation in a new climate agreement', 494; they also note that the authoritative modelling in the IPCC Fifth Assessment Report on long-term mitigation pathways that informs policy is based on assumptions about the availability of 'negative emissions', see P. Smith,

12 *Introduction*

GHG emissions *and* promoting enhanced carbon sequestration in forests, reducing emissions from fossil fuel sources and enhancing sequestration or 'draw down' should not be treated as substitutable and separate targets.[63]

Thus, although analysis of REDD+ is often focused on forested spaces and jurisdictions, this scheme needs to be understood within a broader frame that makes visible how it brings practices to reduce emissions from deforestation and forest degradation *into relation* with other practices producing emissions elsewhere. Offsets are often problematically conceptualised as a 'thing' when instead they should be conceived of as 'relational'.[64] Understanding offsets as instigating a relationship between carbon emitters in the North and carbon reducers in the South highlights their 'environmental-development' implications.[65] The logic of the 'offset', or of achieving a 'balance' between sinks and emission sources, is based on a *claim-of-equivalence* between GHG emissions produced from the combustion of fossil fuel in one place and emissions 'saved' in another. This claim of equivalence, although highly contested, is *performative* in that it has real effects, namely, it establishes a strategic relation between various activities in different parts of the world. The offset relation thus also holds together two very different modes of governing nature: one geared towards extractive ends and another geared towards enhancing and intensifying nature's capacity to sequester carbon. By establishing relations between different practices and different modes of governing nature, the offset relation establishes a new regime of global governance of nature and resources that is directed towards maximising the aggregate value to be derived from different types of resource use; however, where such value is defined in economically reductive ways.

2 REDD+: Between Vision and Actualisation

REDD+ has gained prominence in international climate debates because it promises a seductively simple response to the urgent, undeniable imperatives of addressing the crisis of deforestation and promoting climate mitigation and adaptation. Additionally, it also aims to address associated problems, including biodiversity protection, watershed quality and protection of the rights of forest communities. There is 'unequivocal' evidence of warming of the climate and its anthropocentric

'Chapter 11: Agriculture, forestry and other land use (AFOLU)' in O. Edenhofer (ed.), *Climate Change 2014: Mitigation of Climate Change* (Cambridge University Press, 2015).

[63] D. P. McLaren, D. P. Tyfield, R. Willis, B. Szerszynski, and N. O. Markusson, 'Beyond "Net-Zero": A case for separate targets for emissions reduction and negative emissions' (2019) 1 *Frontiers in Climate* 4.

[64] A. G. Bumpus and D. M. Liverman, 'Carbon colonialism? Offsets, greenhouse gas reductions, and sustainable development' in R. Peet, P. Robbins, and M. J. Watts (eds.), *Global Political Ecology* (Routledge, 2011) pp. 203–24, 212.

[65] Ibid.

B. Assembling REDD+

causes, with approximately 24 percent of global emission coming from agriculture, forestry and other land use (AFOLU).[66] From 2007 to 2016, between 2.6 and 7.8 $GtCO_2$ per year were produced from land-use change caused mostly by deforestation.[67] Reducing deforestation and forest degradation has an estimated technical mitigation potential of 0.4–5.8 $GtCO_2$ per year.[68] All of the pathways modelled to limit warming to 1.5 °C or well below 2 °C require land-based mitigation and land-use change involving different combinations of reforestation, afforestation, reduced deforestation and bioenergy.[69] In this context, 'natural climate solutions' such as conservation, restoration and improved land management of forests as well as wetlands, grassland and agricultural lands have been promoted as necessary to achieve the Paris objectives, together accounting for one of the most cost-effective forms of mitigation.[70] The 2015 *Global Forest Resources Assessment* by the UN Food and Agriculture Organization (FAO) found that, although rates of deforestation had declined in the previous decade, rates were still alarmingly high: between 2010 and 2015 there was an annual decrease in forest area of 3.3 million hectares per year.[71] Additionally, there is an urgent imperative to address high rates of deforestation, not just for climate reasons but also to protect biological diversity, water and other environmental objectives.

When REDD+ was first proposed, it was celebrated as a 'significant, cheap, quick and win-win way to reduce greenhouse gas',[72] widely seen as having the potential to deliver significant low-cost and quick emission reductions.[73] Since it was first suggested in 2005, REDD+ has been one of the most prominent ideas in international climate negotiations and has helped to give 'unprecedented visibility' to deforestation and global forest protection.[74] Yet, despite over a decade of discussion, debate and demonstration programmes, REDD+ has not had a major impact on

---

[66] 'IPCC, 2013: Summary for policymakers' in T.F. Stocker et al. (eds.), *Climate Change 2013: The Physical Science Basis: Contribution of Working Group I to the Fifth Assessment Report of the Intergovernmental Panel on Climate Change* (Cambrdige University Press, 2013) pp. 4–5.

[67] *IPCC Special Report on Climate Change, Desertification, Land Degradation, Sustainable Land Management, Food Security, and Greenhouse Gas Fluxes in Terrestrial Ecosystems: Summary for Policymakers (Approved Draft)* (2019) p. 7.

[68] Ibid., p. 24.

[69] Ibid., p. 26.

[70] B. W. Griscom, J. Adams, P. W. Ellis, R. A. Houghton, G. Lomax, D. A. Miteva, W. H. Schlesinger, D. Shoch, J. V. Siikamäki, and P. Smith, 'Natural climate solutions' (2017) 114(44) *Proceedings of the National Academy of Sciences* 11645–50.

[71] *Global Forest Resources Assessment 2015: How Are the World's Forests Changing?* 2nd edition (Food and Agricultural Organisation of the United Nations, 2016) p. 3.

[72] A. Angelsen and S. Atmadja, 'What is this book about?' in A. Angelsen (ed.), *Moving Ahead with REDD: Issues, Options and Implications* (CIFOR, 2008) pp. 1–9, 1.

[73] A. Angelsen (ed.), *Moving Ahead with REDD: Issues, Options and Implications* (CIFOR, 2008) p. viii.

[74] A. Angelsen, 'REDD+: What should come next?' in S. Barrett, C. Carraro and J. de Melo (eds.), *Towards a Workable and Effective Climate Regime* (CEPR Press, 2016) pp. 405–21, 406.

reducing forest loss.[75] The concept still has not been applied at scale, with proponents questioning whether it is ever likely to be realised on the scale at which it was envisioned.[76] The initial optimism that greeted REDD+ has now largely dissipated, and even key REDD+ proponents acknowledge that a 'thorough reality check is needed', given that the 'envisioned results in terms of reduced emissions have – by and large – not been delivered'.[77] Some commentators have therefore suggested that the hopes invested in REDD+ are unlikely to be satisfied,[78] and that REDD+ may simply be the latest conservation 'fad' that is 'embraced enthusiastically and then abandoned'.[79] While some suggest that 'REDD+ is dead; it's time to cut our losses and move on',[80] others maintain that REDD+, 'though troubled, is not dead'.[81]

Despite clear challenges in implementation, REDD+ remains a key part of international climate policy discussions. Almost 100 countries mentioned plans to reduce emissions from deforestation or to increase forest cover as part of their Paris Agreement commitments.[82] Over 70 countries have engaged in at least the early phases of REDD+ implementation, including through REDD+ initiatives such as the World Bank's Forest Carbon Partnership Facility and the UN-REDD Programme.[83] The Ecosystems Markets Map documents a total of 391 projects related to forest carbon, of which 43 are specifically REDD+ projects.[84] Between 2006 and 2014, more than US$8.7 billion was pledged for REDD+ from public and private sources (with the majority of funds coming from Norway, the United States [US], Germany, Japan and the United Kingdom [UK]) and directed to over 80 recipient countries, although 40 percent of funds went to Indonesia and Brazil.[85] The majority of these funds have gone to REDD+-readiness activities, and by mid-2017 only US$218 million of the US$2.9billion pledged to pay for actual REDD+ emission reductions had been disbursed.[86]

---

[75] Angelsen et al., 'Learning from REDD+: A response to Fletcher et al.', 718.

[76] Angelsen, 'REDD+: What should come next?', pp. 406–7.

[77] Ibid., p. 417.

[78] A. Wiersema, 'Climate change, forests and international law: REDD's decent into irrelevance' (2014) 47(1) *Vanderbilt Journal of Transnational Law* 1–66.

[79] K. H. Redford, C. Padoch, and T. Sunderland, 'Fads, funding, and forgetting in three decades of conservation' (2013) 27(3) *Conservation Biology* 437–8 at 437.

[80] R. Fletcher, W. Dressler, B. Büscher, and Z. R. Anderson, 'Questioning REDD+ and the future of market-based conservation' (2016) 30(3) *Conservation Biology* 673–5 at 673.

[81] A. Angelsen et al., 'Learning from REDD+: A response to Fletcher et al.', 718.

[82] K. Hamrick and M. Gallant, *Fertile Ground: State of Forest Carbon Finance 2017* (Ecosystem Marketplace, 2017) p. 1.

[83] Green Climate Fund, 'Green Climate Fund Support for the Early Phases of REDD+', 2.

[84] See 'Project list', www.forest-trends.org/project-list/#s (accessed on 15 February 2019). There is a wide geographical spread of projects, with 47 in Africa, 36 in Asia, 19 in Europe, 94 in Latin America, 47 in North America and 19 in Oceania.

[85] M. Norman and S. Nakhooda, *The State of REDD+ Finance* (Centre for Global Development Climate and Forest Paper Series, Working Paper 378, September 2014).

[86] K. Hamrick and M. Gallant, *Fertile Ground: State of Forest Carbon Finance 2017*, p. 38.

B. Assembling REDD+

Although the 'idea' of REDD+ still commands considerable support, the challenges of implementation and actualisation have raised important questions about the difficulties in realising this vision.[87] Many organisations and commentators remain heavily invested in the idea of REDD+, seeing it as the 'best' or even 'last' chance to save the world's forests,[88] and maintain that it remains a 'valid idea'[89] and continue to hope that 'momentum might eventually lead to results on the ground'.[90] Recurring difficulties in implementing REDD+ have led to calls to maintain faith in this vision, with proponents arguing that there is 'still time to right the ship' and 'still hope for REDD+ to be redeemed'.[91] However, there has also been a broader realisation regarding what an 'enormously ambitious and challenging endeavor'[92] REDD+ is and of the multiple complex challenges involved in operationalising the scheme.[93] These challenges have also promoted rethinking about the objectives of REDD+, which is increasingly viewed less as a unitary mechanism than as a 'broad set of policy instruments at different scales'.[94] This expansionary dynamic shows how the contours of REDD+ have been formed by a constant oscillation between an expanding ideal and the (as yet unrealised) materialisation of it in practice.

In this process REDD+ has been transformed from a project with one key objective – to minimise deforestation and forest degradation – into a project with multiple objectives,[95] including addressing livelihood reform, poverty reduction, biodiversity, adaptation and Indigenous rights and promoting good governance.[96] This book thus argues for the need to understand REDD+ as a continually expanding and proliferating project, whose scope and thus potential sphere of intervention has grown over time, often in response to criticisms directed against it. In response to criticisms that discrete REDD+ conservation projects would lead to 'leakage' or the displacement of deforestation to elsewhere, REDD+ is increasingly conceptualised at the national or sub-national scale. Responding to criticisms that REDD+ visualises forests reductively as 'carbon stocks', attempts have been made to

---

[87] Fletcher et al., 'Questioning REDD+ and the future of market-based conservation', 674.

[88] Former World Bank President Robert Zoellick cited in J. Conant, 'Do Trees Grow on Money?' (2011); see also W. Boyd, 'Climate change, fragmentation, and the challenges of global environmental law: Elements of a post-Copenhagen assemblage' (2010) 32 *University of Pennsylvania Journal of International Law* 457–550 at 471.

[89] A. Angelsen (ed.), *Transforming REDD+: Lessons and New Directions* (Center for International Forestry Research, 2018) p. xx.

[90] Angelsen, 'REDD+: What should come next?', p. 417.

[91] M. L. Brown, *Redeeming REDD+: Policies, Incentives, and Social Feasibility for Avoided Deforestation* (Routledge and Earthscan, 2013) pp. 274–5.

[92] Boyd, 'Climate change, fragmentation, and the challenges of global environmental law', 457–550 at 471.

[93] Angelsen and Atmadja, 'What is this book about?', p. 2.

[94] Angelsen, 'REDD+: What should come next?', p. 407.

[95] Ibid., pp. 407–8.

[96] Angelsen, 'REDD+ as result-based aid: General lessons and bilateral agreements of Norway', 238.

promote biodiversity protection as a co-benefit of REDD+. Most tellingly, in response to criticisms that REDD+ might have adverse social consequences and pose risks for peoples living in and around forested areas, increased focus has been placed on the rights of such peoples and on the realisation of co-benefits such as alleviating poverty, improving local livelihoods and tenure reform.[97] These have then authorised further interventions in local livelihoods, property rights and governance arrangements from international actors. Although such critiques have led to an expansion of REDD+'s objectives and sphere of intervention, in general they have not promoted a fundamental rethink of the current trajectory of the global conservation movement.[98] Thus understanding REDD+ as a proliferating project, constituted in part by critiques directed against it, draws attention to how REDD+ as a concept has managed to be quite malleable, while also 'retain[ing] enough immutable content to still be recognizable'.[99] This malleability has allowed REDD+ to remain 'plastic, open to interpretation by different actors and valuable to each for different reasons',[100] and explains the investments that different actors have in a specific idea of what REDD+ could be, and the commitment they have to helping realise that vision.

This understanding of REDD+ as a dynamic and expanding project also suggests the limitations of some of the rather diverse terminology used to describe REDD+, including: 'scheme', 'programme', 'policy approaches', 'mitigation actions', 'activities' and 'guidance'.[101] Increasingly, REDD+ is described as a 'regime', often in order to facilitate analysis of how it interacts with other legal regimes within an increasingly fragmented legal space.[102] However, unlike traditional definitions of regimes, REDD+ is not characterised by a coalescing of norms, decision-making procedures and organisations around a functional issue area,[103] because it does not establish overarching, unitary institutional arrangements. Instead it extends beyond a specific 'issue-area' to bring together and strategically link a number of different

---

[97] S. Howell, '"No RIGHTS–No REDD": Some implications of a turn towards co-benefits' (2014) 41(2) *Forum for Development Studies* 253–72.

[98] Fletcher et al., 'Debating REDD+ and its implications: Reply to Angelsen et al.', 722.

[99] C. L. McDermott, L. Coad, A. Helfgott, and H. Schroeder, 'Operationalizing social safeguards in REDD+: Actors, interests and ideas' (2012) 21 *Environmental Science and Policy* 63–72 at 64.

[100] Ibid.

[101] M. F. Tehan, L. C. Godden, M. A. Young, and K. A. Gover, *The Impact of Climate Change Mitigation on Indigenous and Forest Communities: International, National and Local Law Perspectives on REDD+* (Cambridge University Press, 2017) p. 13.

[102] Ibid., Chapter 2; see also M. A. Young, 'REDD+ and interacting legal regimes' in C. Voigt (ed.), *Research Handbook on REDD-Plus and International Law* (Edward Elgar Publishing, 2016) Chapter 4.

[103] Margaret Young defines 'regimes' as 'norms, decisionmaking procedures and organisations coalescing around functional issue-areas and dominated by particular modes of behaviour, assumptions and biases'. M. A. Young, 'Introduction: The productive friction between regimes' in M. A. Young (ed.), *Regime Interaction in International Law: Facing Fragmentation* (Cambridge University Press, 2012) pp. 1–19, 9.

B. Assembling REDD+

issues and associated legal regimes including climate,[104] forests,[105] biodiversity,[106] Indigenous rights,[107] poverty reduction and sustainable development.[108] The 'kaleidoscopic world' of REDD+ is made up of interaction between many varied international and national legal instruments.[109] REDD+ is thus better characterised as an 'emerging global assemblage' that holds together 'people, practices, organisations, law, technologies, and territories', and it is 'taking shape at multiple sites around the world'.[110] Understanding REDD+ as a 'transnational legal assemblage' productively directs attention to questions of 'materiality, distributed agency and heterogeneity' in the constitution, transmission and containment of norms.[111] Moreover, such a characterisation highlights both how REDD+ is more contingently assembled than legal formalist accounts might suggest, as well as showing the 'continuous work' that goes into 'pulling disparate elements together' in order to forge (provisional) alignment between the disparate (and at times contradictory) objectives of differentially situated actors.[112] REDD+ as an assemblage also highlights how the alignment between the differing (and expanding) objectives of REDD+ is not automatic, nor is the alignment between the interests and objectives of different actors on different scales, but rather it shows that any such alignment is both fraught and fragile. This account thus speaks to the difficulty and challenges of instantiating a global project on different scales and of effecting global objectives in the situated contingent settings of national and sub-national institutions or of finding

[104] For a detailed discussion of the UNFCCC Warsaw Framework for REDD+ and associated UNFCCC COP decisions, see Chapter 1.

[105] UNFF was established by the Economic and Social Council (Economic and Social Council Resolution 2000/35, *Report on the Fourth Session of the Intergovernmental Forum on Forests*, 46th plen mtg, E/RES/2000/35 (18 October 2000)). A key outcome of the UNFF process has been the *Non-legally Binding Instrument on All Types of Forests*, General Assembly Resolution 62/98, *Non-Legally Binding Instrument on All Types of Forests*, UN GAOR 62nd sess, 74th plen mtg, Agenda Item 54, A/RES/62/98 (31 January 2008).

[106] *Convention on Biological Diversity*, opened for signature 5 June 1992, 1760 UNTS 79 (entered into force 29 December 1993).

[107] International Labour Organisation (ILO), *Convention (No 169) Concerning Indigenous and Tribal Peoples in Independent Countries*, opened for signature 27 June 1989, 1650 UNTS 383 (entered into force 5 September 1991)('ILO 169') General Assembly Resolution 61/295, *United Nations Declaration on the Rights of Indigenous Peoples*, UN GAOR 61st sess, 107th plen mtg, Supp No 49, UN Doc A/61/67 (13 September 2007).

[108] General Assembly Resolution 66/288, *The Future We Want*, UN GAOR 66th sess, 123rd plen mtg, Agenda Item 19, Supp No 49, A/RES/66/288 (11 September 2012) General Assembly Resolution 70/1, *Transforming Our World: The 2030 Agenda for Sustainable Development*, UNGAOR 70th sess, 4th plen mtg, UN Doc A/RES/70/1 (21 October 2015).

[109] C. Voigt, 'Introduction: The kaleidoscopic world of REDD+' in C. Voigt (ed.), *Research Handbook on REDD-Plus and International Law* (Edward Elgar Publishing, 2016) p. 1.

[110] Boyd, 'Climate change, fragmentation, and the Challenges of global environmental law: Elements of a post-Copenhagen assemblage', 523.

[111] G. Sullivan, 'Transnational legal assemblages and global security law: Topologies and temporalities of the list' (2014) 5(1) *Transnational Legal Theory* 81–127 at 82.

[112] See T. M. Li, 'Practices of assemblage and community forest management' (2007) 36(2) *Economy and Society* 263–93 at 264–5.

18 *Introduction*

synergies between the imperatives 'from above' and demands 'from below'.[113] Finally, by highlighting how alignment between different objectives, practices and processes is not automatic, the analytical framework of assemblage speaks to how specific elements might need to be rearranged to enable coherence – for example, governance arrangements within nation-states might need to be 'reassembled' in specific ways in response to transnational processes in order for REDD+ to cohere.[114]

C CRITIQUING REDD+

What holds REDD+ together is the cultivation of a specific 'logic of problem amelioration' based upon a specific understanding of the 'problem' of carbon emissions from forest loss; a growing consensus around appropriate responses – namely, financial incentives; and a clear elaboration of the desired outcomes that has given rise to a 'shared community and norm generation'.[115] However, this 'logic of problem amelioration' depends on a framing the issues of deforestation and climate change mitigation in narrow and technical ways that risk obscuring many structural conditions that drive unsustainable deforestation and GHG emissions; and foreclosing more radical engagements that challenge unequal ecological exchange. As such, the 'solution' provided by REDD+ does not only fail to address these underlying global drivers; by focusing only on tropical deforestation sites in countries of the Global South, and not the global dynamics driving deforestation, it also operates to authorise further international interventions within these countries. REDD+ needs to be understood not just as a specific response to a particular way of articulating the problem of the climate crisis but also one that is itself productive of new configurations of authority and power over forested land and modes of governance of the peoples who live in and around forested areas and depend on them for their livelihoods. It is therefore insufficient for analyses of REDD+ to address whether and how it achieves its stated objectives; rather, it is necessary to interrogate the broader (potentially unintended) 'instrument-effects' it gives rise to.[116] Wendy Brown highlights that 'it is in the nature of every significant political project to ripple beyond the project's avowed target and action' and that '[n]o effective project

---

[113] Boyd, 'Climate change, fragmentation, and the Challenges of global environmental law: Elements of a post-Copenhagen assemblage', 468.

[114] Sullivan, 'Transnational legal assemblages and global security law', 92; see also S. Sassen, *Territory, Authority, Rights: From Medieval to Global Assemblages* (Princeton University Press, 2006).

[115] C. L. McDermott, K. Levin, and B. Cashore, 'Building the forest-climate bandwagon: REDD+ and the logic of problem amelioration' (2011) 11(3) *Global Environmental Politics* 85–103.

[116] M. Foucault, *Discipline and Punish: The Birth of the Prison* (Knopf Doubleday Publishing Group, 1977); cited in B. Rajagopal, *International Law from Below: Development, Social Movements and Third World Resistance* (Cambridge University Press, 2003) p. 76.

C. Critiquing REDD+

produces only the consequences it aims to produce'.[117] In this vein, this book departs from more pragmatically orientated scholarship focused on how to make REDD+ work – or how to 'redeem' its potential flaws – instead drawing attention to *the work that REDD+ does in the world*, how it operates to reorganise social relations and establish new forms of authority and new mechanisms of power.

While the literature on REDD+ is relatively new, it is already voluminous and substantial, consisting of both a diverse range of primary materials as well as extensive interdisciplinary secondary scholarships. The scholarship on REDD+ can be characterised as consisting of three main strands, each having different normative, scholarly and political orientations: the first directed towards making REDD+ work, or work better; the second focused on critiquing REDD+; and the third on understanding the conditions in and through which REDD+ becomes possible and its broader effects. The first strand, both functionalist and pragmatic, is primarily focused on analysing and explaining new developments in the legal frameworks of REDD+, being directed towards clarifying how REDD+ can be made to work and resolving potential legal and other challenges arising from its implementation. Specifically, legal scholars have examined the legal complexities involved in implementing REDD+ and proposed ways to better tailor and develop institutional and regulatory frameworks to promote a more effective and efficient realisation of REDD+ and a more equitable sharing of benefits.[118] Closely related to this work, are the scholarship or reports critically analysing aspects of REDD+ frameworks and implementation, in order to address specific failings in implementation and to propose responses that promote a better realisation of REDD+ goals and what has been termed the '3Es of REDD+'[119]: effectiveness, efficiency and equity. This body of scholarship includes mapping REDD+ development[120] and

---

[117] W. Brown, '"The most we can hope for. . .": Human rights and the politics of fatalism' (2004) 103(2/3) *The South Atlantic Quarterly* 451–63 at 452–53.

[118] See for example Tehan et al., *The Impact of Climate Change Mitigation on Indigenous and Forest Communities: International, National and Local Law Perspectives on REDD+*; see also C. Voigt, *Research Handbook on REDD-Plus and International Law* (Edward Elgar Publishing, 2016) focused on addressing the 'complexity of issues and interest to be taken into account' in achieving the goals of REDD+; S. Jodoin, *Forest Preservation in a Changing Climate: REDD+ and Indigenous and Community Rights in Indonesia and Tanzania* (Cambridge University Press, 2017).

[119] A. Angelsen (ed.), *Moving Ahead with REDD: Issues, Options and Implications* (CIFOR, 2008) p. viii.

[120] S. Engel and C. Palmer, '"Painting the forest REDD?" Prospects for mitigating climate change through reducing emissions from deforestation and degradation' (Institute for Environmental Decisions, 2008); Ian Fry, 'Reducing emissions from deforestation and forest degradation: Opportunities and pitfalls in developing a new legal regime' (2008) 17(2) *Review of European Community and International Environmental Law* 166; B. M. Campbell, 'Beyond Copenhagen: REDD+, agriculture, adaptation strategies and poverty' (2009) 19 *Global Environmental Change* 397; M. E. Recio, 'The Warsaw Framework and the future of REDD+' (2014) 24(1) *Yearbook of International Environmental Law* 37.

case study analysis of REDD+ projects.[121] There has also been considerable work on designing legal and governance frameworks for REDD+[122] that address the 'possibilities and limitations, promises and consequences' of the 'interplay and interaction between REDD+ and a wider spectrum of international legal instruments'.[123] A key focus in this work has been on identifying mechanisms to promote the environmental integrity of REDD+ and verifying that purported carbon 'savings' through REDD+ are 'real'. This includes the clarification of definitions of 'forests',[124] the construction of baselines, processes for preventing leakage, ensuring additionality[125] and promoting the permanence of carbon sequestration and associated processes for monitoring, reporting and verification.[126]

[121] See for example E. O. Sills (ed.), *REDD+ on the Ground: A Case Book of Subnational Initiatives across the Globe* (CIFOR, 2014); R. A. Clarke, 'Moving the REDD debate from theory to practice: Lessons learned from the Ulu Masen project' (2010) 6(1) *Law, Environment and Development Journal* 36; S. Wertz-Kanounnikoff and M. Kongphan-apirak, 'Emerging REDD+: A preliminary survey of demonstration and readiness activities' (CIFOR, 2009).

[122] J. Costenbader, *Legal Frameworks for REDD. Design and Implementation at the National Level* (International Union for the Conservation of Nature, 2009); R. Lyster, C. MacKenzie, and C. McDermott (eds.), *Law, Tropical Forests and Carbon: The Case of REDD+* (Cambridge University Press, 2013); S. Butt, R. Lyster, and T. Stephens, *Climate Change and Forest Governance: Lessons from Indonesia* (Routledge, 2015); R. Maguire, 'Deforestation, REDD and international law' in S. Alam, M. J. H. Bhuiyan, T. M. R. Chowdhury, and E. J. Techera (eds.), *Routledge Handbook of International Environmental Law* (Routledge, 2013) pp. 697–716.

[123] Voigt, 'Introduction: The kaleidoscopic world of REDD+', pp. 5 and 7; Young, 'REDD+ and interacting legal regimes', pp. 89–125; M. A. Young, 'Interacting regimes and experimentation' in *The Impact of Climate Change Mitigation on Indigenous and Forest Communities: International, National and Local Law Perspectives on REDD+* (Cambridge University Press, 2017) pp. 329–45.

[124] The current definition of 'forest' as a minimum land area of 0.05–1.0 hectare with tree cover of more than 10–30 per cent, with trees with the potential to reach a minimum height of 2–5 metres at maturity in situ is in the Annex of Decision 16/CMP.1 'Land use, land-use change and forestry'. FCCC/KP/2005/8/Add.3 (30 March 2006), for critiques see N. Sasaki and F. E. Putz, 'Critical need for a new definition of "forest" and "forest degradation" in a global climate change agreement' (2009) 20 *Conservation Letters* 1–20; A. Long, 'Taking adaptation value seriously: Designing REDD to protect biodiversity' (2009) 3 *Carbon & Climate Law Review* 314–23; for the need for forests to be understood as 'a socio-natural landscape shaped by past and present resource management practices' see B. A. Beymer-Farris and T. J. Bassett, 'The REDD menace: Resurgent protectionism in Tanzania's mangrove forests' (2012) 22(2) *Global Environmental Change* 332–41.

[125] C. F. Mason and A. J. Plantinga, 'The additionality problem with offsets: Optimal contracts for carbon sequestration in forests' (2013) 66(1) *Journal of Environmental Economics and Management* 1–14; on additionality, generally see M. Cames, R. O. Harthan, J. Füssler, M. Lazarus, C. M. Lee, P. Erickson, and R. Spalding-Fecher, 'How additional is the Clean Development Mechanism? Analysis of the application of current tools and proposed alternatives' (Institut für angewandte Ökologie, 2016); L. Schneider, 'Assessing the additionality of CDM projects: Practical experiences and lessons learned' (2009) 9(3) *Climate Policy* 242–54; M. Dutschke and A. Michaelowa, 'Development assistance and the CDM – How to interpret "financial additionality"' (2006) 11(2) *Environment and Development Economics* 235–46.

[126] See for example Angelsen, *Moving Ahead with REDD: Issues, Options and Implications*; A. Angelsen, *Realising REDD+: National Strategy and Policy Options* (CIFOR, 2009);

C. Critiquing REDD+

Another key focus has been on addressing risks and 'managing trade-offs' in order to protect the rights, interests and livelihoods of people living in and around forested areas;[127] and to address concerns that REDD+ might recentralise forest management[128] and that communities will be ill-informed about REDD+ and potentially dispossessed through conservation projects.[129] There has also been considerable attention given to the implementation of safeguards[130] and making REDD+ compatible with human rights norms,[131] as well as processes of clarifying and securing tenure rights[132] and

A. Angelsen, M. Brockhaus, W. D. Sunderlin, and L. V. Verchot (eds.), *Analysing REDD+: Challenges and Choices* (CIFOR, 2012); Angelsen, *Transforming REDD+: Lessons and New Directions*.

[127] F. Seymour, 'Forests, climate change and human rights: Managing risks and trade-offs' in S. Humphreys (ed.), *Climate Change and Human Rights* (Cambridge University Press, 2010) pp. 207–37.

[128] J. Phelps, E. L. Webb, and A. Agrawal, 'Does REDD+ threaten to recentralize forest governance?' (2010) 328(5976) *Science* 312–13.

[129] T. Griffiths, *Seeing 'REDD'? Forests, Climate Change Mitigation and the Rights of Indigenous Peoples*, updated version (Forest Peoples Programme, 2009).

[130] D. J. Kelly, 'The case for social safeguards in a post–2012 agreement on REDD' (2010) 6(1) *Law, Environment and Development Journal* 61–81; F. Daviet and G. Larsen, *Safeguarding Forests and People: A Framework for Designing a National System to Implement REDD+ Safeguards* (World Resources Institute, 2012); McDermott et al., 'Operationalizing social safeguards in REDD+: Actors, interests and ideas'; B. Dickson, M. Bertzky, T. Christophersen, C. Epple, V. Kapos, L. Miles, U. Narloch, and K. Trumper, *REDD+ Beyond Carbon: Supporting Decisions on Safeguards and Multiple Benefits* (UN-REDD Programme, Policy Brief: Issue No. 2, 2012); P. K. Sena, M. Cunningham, and B. Xavier, *Indigenous People's Rights and Safeguards in Projects Related to Reducing Emissions from Deforestation and Forest Degradation: Note by the Secretariat*, UN ESCOR, Permanent Forum on Indigenous Issues, 12th sess, Agenda Item 5, UN Doc E/C.19/2013/7 (5 February 2013); D. Ray, J. Roberts, S. Korwin, L. Rivera, and U. Ribet, *A Guide to Understanding and Implementing the UNFCCC REDD+ Safeguards* (Client Earth, 2013); B. Bodin, E. Vaananen, and H. van Asselt, 'Putting REDD+ environmental safeguards into practice: Recommendations for effective and country-specific implementation' (2015) *Carbon & Climate Law Review* 168.

[131] A. Savaresi, 'The human rights dimension of REDD' (2012) 21(2) *Review of European Community & International Environmental Law* 102–13; A. Savaresi, 'REDD+ and human rights: Addressing synergies between international regimes' (2013) 18(3) *Ecology and Society* 5–13.

[132] L. Cotula and J. Mayers, *Tenure in REDD – Start-Point or Afterthought?* (International Institute for Environment and Development, 2009); R. Lyster, 'REDD+, transparency, participation and resource rights: The role of law' (2011) 14 *Environmental Science and Policy* 118–26; R. Fisher and R. Lyster, 'Land and resource tenure: The rights of indigenous people and forest dwellers' in R. Lyster, C. MacKenzie, and C. McDermott (eds.), *Law, Tropical Forests and Carbon: The Case of REDD+* (Cambridge University Press, 2013) pp. 187–206; A. M. Larson, 'Forest tenure reform in the age of climate change: Lessons for REDD+' (2011) 21 *Global Environmental Change* 540–9; A. M. Larson, M. Brockhaus, W. D. Sunderlin, A. Duchelle, A. Babon, T. Dokken, T. T. Pham, I. A. P. Resosudarmo, G. Selaya, and A. A.-B. Huynh, 'Land tenure and REDD+: The good, the bad and the ugly' (2013) 23(3) *Global Environmental Change* 678–89; A. E. Duchelle, M. Cromberg, M. F. Gebara, R. Guerra, T. Melo, A. Larson, P. Cronkleton, J. Börner, E. Sills, and S. Wunder, 'Linking forest tenure reform, environmental compliance, and incentives: lessons from REDD+ initiatives in the Brazilian Amazon' (2014) 55 *World Development* 53–67.

Introduction

participation, consultation and consent processes,[133] with the aim of ensuring that benefits flow to local communities.[134]

Although this scholarship is diverse in its focus and methodologies, it exhibits a number of shared assumptions and a shared orientation. In these approaches, environmental law is generally invoked as a problem-solving or managerial tool.[135] In these accounts REDD+ research is presented as both neutral and progressive, and serving a clear pragmatic purpose; it is rare to see a more self-reflexive engagement with the role that knowledge production and specific forms of expertise play in developing, constituting and legitimising REDD+. Given that processes of knowledge production and expertise play a key role in shaping contemporary political economy and modes of governance,[136] greater interrogation of the effects of such scholarship is warranted, in terms of constituting a 'field of truth'[137] or establishing the 'sociotechnical imaginaries'[138] upon which REDD+ depends. Indeed, scholarship plays a significant role in the 'unconscious co-production of the global carbon imaginary',[139] allowing forest carbon to be treated as a standardised, fungible 'object' equivalent to other forms of carbon.[140] Moreover, the legitimacy of the claim that emissions emitted and emissions 'saved' through sequestration are equivalent ultimately relies on an 'implicit pact' with the public,[141] one dependent upon public trust in such expertise. This first strand of scholarship provides crucial insights into the novel problems that operationalising REDD+ presents, and it has proposed highly

---

[133] *Honest Engagement: Transparency and Civil Society Participation in REDD* (Global Witness, 2008); P. Anderson, *Free, Prior, and Informed Consent in REDD+: Principles and Approaches for Policy and Project Development* (RECOFTC [The Centre for People and Forests] and GIZ, 2011).

[134] D. Brown, F. Seymour, and L. Peskett, 'How do we achieve REDD co-benefits and avoid doing harm?' in A. Angelsen (ed.), *Moving Ahead with REDD: Issues, Options and Implications* (CIFOR, 2008) pp. 107–18; L. Godden, 'Benefit Sharing in REDD+: Linking Rights and Equitable Outcomes' in *The Impact of Climate Change Mitigation on Indigenous and Forest Communities: International, National and Local Law Perspectives on REDD+* (Cambridge University Press, 2017) pp. 172–200.

[135] See Andreas Philippopoulos-Mihalopoulos, 'Towards a critical environmental law' in A. Philippopoulos-Mihalopoulos (ed.), *Law and Ecology: New Environmental Foundations* (Routledge, 2011) for a critique of such managerial approaches.

[136] See in general D. Kennedy, *A world of Struggle: How Power, Law, and Expertise Shape Global Political Economy* (Princeton University Press, 2016).

[137] M. Foucault, *Security, Territory, Population: Lectures at the Collège de France 1977–1978* (Palgrave Macmillan, 2007) p. 118.

[138] S. Jasanoff, 'Future imperfect: Science, technology, and the imaginations of modernity' in S. Jasanoff and S.-H. Kim (eds.), *Dreamscapes of Modernity: Sociotechnical Imaginaries and the Fabrication of Power* (University of Chicago Press, 2015) pp. 1–33.

[139] I. P. Gray, *Climate finance, tropical forests and the state: Governing international climate risk in the Democratic Republic of Congo* (Master's thesis, Massachusetts Institute of Technology, 2012) p. 27.

[140] J. Dehm, 'One tonne of carbon dioxide equivalent (1tCO2e)' in J. Hohmann and D. Joyce (eds.), *International Law's Objects* (Oxford University Press, 2018) pp. 305–18.

[141] L. Lohmann, *Chronicle of a Disaster Foretold; REDD-with-Carbon-Trading* (The Corner House 2008).

C. Critiquing REDD+

innovative approaches to address these problems. However, the desirability of the overall REDD+ project is rarely called into question in this literature.

In contrast to this body of work focused on operationalising REDD+ and proposing reforms to address the concerns, failings or problems around implementation, a second strand of scholarship on REDD+ has engaged on a more critical register to highlight the ways REDD+ has not and cannot meet its stated objectives. Influenced by climate justice concerns and broader critiques of carbon markets and offsetting,[142] this more radical literature critiques the idea that terrestrial sequestration can offset fossil fuel emissions. In particular, such scholarship highlights the inherently problematic nature of the assumed equivalence of green carbon sequestered through REDD+ and brown carbon released from the burning of fossil fuels to the inherent indeterminacy of the regulatory and accounting concepts that purport to ensure 'additionality'.[143] In particular, there are concerns that as an offset scheme REDD+ cannot deliver permanent emission reductions, given the very distinct roles played in the carbon cycle by 'undisturbed fossil fuels ... locked away underground for millennia' and 'carbon being stored in trees, other plants and soils, for relatively short periods of time'.[144] Further, it voices concerns that even if REDD+ offset projects do not successfully reduce emissions, the offset relation can nonetheless be 'used to condone continued emissions elsewhere', therefore risking net increases.[145] Such analysis builds on broader arguments that carbon markets are flawed and unreformable, due to their empirical failings, their promotion of unjust development and 'green grabbing', their provision of loopholes for polluters, how they have operated as fossil fuel subsidies and the regressive nature of this form of taxation.[146] Rebecca Pearse and Steffen Böhm highlight how carbon is an 'unregulatable commodity',[147] and the problems with demonstrating 'additionality' and assuming commensurability, or 'like for like', referring to essentially different metabolic interactions. They also critique how carbon markets are political constructs

---

[142] Pearse and Böhm, 'Ten reasons why carbon markets will not bring about radical emissions reduction'; see also Lohmann, *Carbon Trading*; Böhm and Dabhi, *Upsetting the Offset: The Political Economy of Carbon Markets*; Clifton, *A Dangerous Obsession*.

[143] R. Hall, *REDD Myths: A Critical Review of Proposed Mechanisms to Reduce Emissions from Deforestation and Degradation in Developing Countries* (Friends of the Earth International, 2008); R. Hall, *REDD: The Realities in Black and White* (Friends of the Earth International, 2010); R. Hall, *The Great REDD Gamble. Time to Ditch Risky REDD for Community-Based Approaches that Are Effective, Ethical and Equitable* (Friends of the Earth International, 2014); Pearse and Dehm, *In the REDD: Australia's Carbon Offset Project in Central Kalimantan*.

[144] Hall, *The great REDD gamble. Time to ditch risky REDD for community-based approaches that are effective, ethical and equitable*, p. 8.

[145] Ibid., p. 8.

[146] Pearse and Böhm, 'Ten reasons why carbon markets will not bring about radical emissions reduction'.

[147] See also L. Lohmann, 'Regulation as corruption in the carbon offset markets' in Böhm and Dabhi (eds.), *Upsetting the Offset: The Political Economy of Carbon Markets*, pp. 175–91.

24 *Introduction*

that display a 'utopian faith in pricing', promote systems of technocratic rule managed by experts and are an obstacle to alternative policies promoting decarbonisation.[148] Thus critics in this camp see carbon markets – and especially the process of offsetting – as a 'dangerous distraction'[149] from the urgent and necessary structural changes in energy production use and distribution, an idea that risks facilitating 'carbon lock-in'.[150]

Further, critics of carbon markets have presented damning case study evidence of some of the economic, social and cultural consequences of offset projects and other payments for environmental services programmes for local communities upon whose lands they have been implemented.[151] In doing so, such critiques foreground broader justice and moral considerations about how the burdens of mitigating climate change have been displaced onto those who have done the least to cause the dangerous cumulation of GHG emissions in the atmosphere underlying the climate crisis.[152] These justice-based critiques have also been articulated in a series of statements released by grassroots social movements for climate justice that convey political opposition to market mechanisms such as REDD+ and promote alternatives. Such statements have been released by 'Climate Justice Now!' coalition at the UNFCCC Conference of the Parties (COP), in Bali (2007)[153] and Poznan (2008);[154] and also include 'System Change Not Climate Change – A People's Declaration from Klimaforum09' (2009);[155] 'Peoples Agreement', from the World People's Conference on Climate Change in Cochabamba (2010);[156] 'Scrap ETS: No

---

[148] Pearse and Böhm, 'Ten reasons why carbon markets will not bring about radical emissions reduction', 332–3.

[149] S. Bullock, M. Childs, and T. Picken, *A Dangerous Distraction: Why Offsetting Is Failing the Climate and People: The Evidence* (Friends of the Earth England, Wales and Northern Ireland, 2009).

[150] See for example G. C. Unruh, 'Understanding Carbon Lock-In' (2000) 28 *Energy Policy* 817–30.

[151] See for example Pearse and Dehm, *In the REDD: Australia's Carbon Offset Project in Central Kalimantan*; S. Lovera, 'REDD Realities' in U. Brand, E. Lander, N. Bullard, and T. Mueller (eds.), *Contours of Climate Justice: Ideas for Shaping New Climate and Energy Policies* (Dag Hammarskjöld Foundation, 2009) pp. 45–53; R. Hall, *REDD: The Realities in Black and White* (Friends of the Earth International, 2010); Böhm and Dabhi, *Upsetting the Offset: The Political Economy of Carbon Markets*.

[152] A. Dawson, 'Climate justice: The emerging movement against green capitalism'; N. Klein, *This Changes Everything: Capitalism vs. the Climate*.

[153] *Climate Justice Now! Statement*, www.carbontradewatch.org/take-action-archive/climate-justice-now-statement-4.html.

[154] *Radical New Agenda Needed to Achieve Climate Justice': Poznan Statement from the Climate Justice Now! Alliance*, www.carbontradewatch.org/archive/poznan-statement-from-the-climate-justice-now-alliance-2.html.

[155] *System Change Not Climate Change – A People's Declaration from Klimaforum09*, klimaforum.org.

[156] World People's Conference on Climate Change and the Rights of Mother Earth, *People's Agreement of Cochabamba* (2010), pwccc.wordpress.com/2010/04/24/peoples-agreement.

C. Critiquing REDD+

EU Emissions Trading Scheme' statement (2012)[157] and 'Margarita Declaration on Climate Change', from the Social PreCOP meeting (2014);[158] and the subsequent 'Call to Action to Reject REDD+ and Extractive Industries to Confront Capitalism and Defend Life and Territories', to which over 100 civil society groups are signatories.[159]

This book draws on these critiques of the marketisation of climate governance and particularly seeks to foreground the perspective of the often-marginalised communities who have been most impacted by these mechanisms and whose voices are amplified in such statements and reports. However, although there is a clear difference between critiques that are more narrowly focused on the problems with the implementation of REDD+ or other mechanisms and accounts that point to the inherent issues surrounding the marketisation of climate policy, both have tended to be taken up in ways that facilitate, rather than curtail, the expansion of carbon markets. The literature on REDD+ often displays an underlying imperative to 'redeem' REDD+ by proposing reforms, with the hope that actual implementation of REDD+ may better accord with the idealised vision of REDD+.[160] However, to date, highlighting the 'gap between vision and execution' or 'rhetoric and reality' has done little to deter proposals to 'scale up' markets.[161] Rather, criticisms of REDD+'s failures have often proven to be generative, leading to an expansion of the project in question.[162] Moreover, this gap between vision and realisation is 'seldom attributed to the fundamental nature of the market mechanisms themselves'[163] and instead the recognition of such failings takes the form of a 'simultaneous admission and denial' that promotes reform rather than an examination of any 'essential contradictions' in the performance of such mechanisms.[164] More generally, as Peter Newell and Matthew Paterson have observed, 'carbon markets are being shaped precisely by

---

[157] *Scrap the ETS* (2012), scrap-the-euets.makenoise.org/KV.

[158] Social PreCOP, *Margarita Declaration on Climate Change* (2014), https://redd-monitor.org/2014/08/08/the-margarita-declaration-on-climate-change-we-reject-the-implementation-of-false-solutions-to-climate-change-such-as-carbon-markets-and-other-forms-of-privatization-and-commodification-of-life/.

[159] *Call to Action to Reject REDD+ and Extractive Industries; To Confront Capitalism and Defend Life and Territories* (December 2014), wrm.org.uy/wp-content/uploads/2014/11/Call-COP-Lima_NoREDD.pdf.

[160] See for example M. L. Brown, *Redeeming REDD+: Policies, Incentives, and Social Feasibility for Avoided Deforestation* (Routledge and Earthscan, 2013).

[161] O. Reyes, 'Carbon markets after Durban' (2012) 12(1/2) *Ephemera: Theory and Politics in Organisation* 19–32.

[162] On the generative nature of failure and its conversion into institutions proliferation and expansion, see also (on prisons) Foucault, *Discipline and Punish: The Birth of the Prison*; and (on development) J. Ferguson, *The Anti-Politics Machine: 'Development,' Depolitization, and Bureaucratic Power in Lesotho* (Cambridge University Press, 1990).

[163] R. Fletcher, 'How I learned to stop worrying and love the market: virtualism, disavowal, and public secrecy in neoliberal environmental conservation' (2013) 31(5) *Environment and Planning D: Society and Space* 796–812.

[164] Ibid.

26	*Introduction*

the protests against them'.[165] The character of such markets, 'their operational rules, informal norms and changing dynamics', are thus a product of mediation between the proponents of markets and those who oppose carbon markets as a climate 'solution'.[166] As such, the way in which critiques have been taken up in generative ways suggests a danger that critiques of market mechanisms – both in the name of their (*not-yet* and *not-quite*) perfect ideal but also those based on a more structural analysis – can operate to (re)legitimate, (re)produce and (re)construct their object of concern.

A third strand of scholarship relevant to REDD+ has focused on understanding the techniques and processes that have enabled and facilitated the transformation of the human–nature relationship through economic valuation, commodification and marketisation, and on interrogating the broader effects of these techniques and processes. Drawing on science and technology studies, scholars have described the performative nature of the accountancy techniques that enable the construction of carbon markets[167] and the organisation and compression of 'space–time' they depend upon.[168] Scholars in the field of human geography have also demonstrated how such 'practices of calculation' that produce forest carbon offsets engage in the co-production of different forms of social ordering,[169] for example, by transforming understandings of space, territory and the practices of ordering that occur within them.[170] There has been considerable scholarship critically evaluating the effects of the marketisation of environmental services and the valuation of nature in increasingly economic terms,[171] often understanding these processes through the lens of

[165] P. Newell and M. Paterson, *Climate Capitalism: Global Warming and the Transformation of the Global Economy* (Cambridge University Press, 2010) p. 33.

[166] M. Paterson, 'Resistance makes carbon markets' in Böhm and Dabhi (eds.), *Upsetting the Offset Upsetting the Offset: The Political Economy of Carbon Markets*, pp. 244–55, 250.

[167] See for example H. Lovell and D. MacKenzie, 'Accounting for carbon: The role of accounting professional organisations in governing climate change' (2011) 43(3) *Antipode* 704–30; E. Lövbrand and J. Stripple, 'Making climate change governable: Accounting for carbon as sinks, credits and personal budgets' (2011) 5(2) *Critical Policy Studies* 187–200; M. Callon, 'Civilizing markets: Carbon trading between in vitro and in vivo experiments' (2009) 34(3–4) *Accounting, Organizations and Society* 535–48; on the performativity of economics see D. A. MacKenzie, F. Muniesa, and L. Siu, *Do Economists Make Markets?: On the Performativity of Economics* (Princeton University Press, 2007).

[168] J. Knox-Hayes, 'Constructing carbon market spacetime: Climate change and the onset of neo-modernity' (2010) 100(4) *Annals of the Association of American Geographers* 953–62; J. Knox-Hayes, 'The spatial and temporal dynamics of value in financialization: Analysis of the infrastructure of carbon markets' (2013) 50 *Geoforum* 117–28.

[169] On the concept of co-production, see S. Jasanoff, *States of Knowledge: The Co-production of Science and the Social Order* (Routledge, 2004).

[170] D. M. Lansing, 'Carbon's calculatory spaces: The emergence of carbon offsets in Costa Rica' (2010) 28(4) *Environment and Planning D: Society and Space* 710–25.

[171] For an overview of some of these debates, see for example B. Büscher, 'Nature on the move I: The value and circulation of liquid nature and the emergence of fictitious conservation' (2013) 6(1–2) *New Proposals: Journal of Marxism and Interdisciplinary Inquiry* 20–36; J. Igoe, 'Nature on the move II: Contemplation becomes speculation' (2013) 6(1–2) *New Proposals: Journal*

C. Critiquing REDD+

'neoliberalisation', 'commodification', 'marketisation', 'financialisation' and enclosure.[172] Drawing on Foucauldian frameworks of governmentality, some scholars have situated these developments as part of the configuration of a new 'power/knowledge' regime of green neoliberalism[173] or as part of a new 'eco-' or 'green governmentality'.[174] Finally, there has been considerable analysis of how these mechanisms reflect but also reproduce and (re)perpetuate unequal power relations. In this vein, carbon markets have been analysed as new forms of 'accumulation by decarbonisation' that extend supranational governance over the atmosphere.[175] Scholars have interrogated these mechanisms as a new form of 'privatisation of the atmosphere' that promotes unequal and inequitable appropriation of atmospheric space[176] and facilitates 'carbon colonialism'.[177] REDD+ specifically has been understood as part of a broader appropriation of land and resources for environmental ends – dubbed 'green grabbing' – linked to dynamics of accumulation and dispossession.[178] The questions such scholarship poses, pertaining to how such mechanisms are constituted and the effects they have in the world, are taken up this book. In this way, it departs from analysis of how REDD+ can be made to 'work', to instead interrogate the productive effects of REDD+, or what work REDD+ does in the world. However, while previous accounts have focused on the expansion of the economic sphere through processes of commodification, economisation and financialisation or the expansion of forms of power, appropriation and control, this book's focus is jurisprudential. Its primary focus is tracing the consolidation, reorganisation

of *Marxism and Interdisciplinary Inquiry* 37–49; S. Sullivan, 'Nature on the move III: (Re)countenancing an animate nature' (2013) 6(1–2) *New Proposals: Journal of Marxism and Interdisciplinary Inquiry* 50–71; N. Castree and G. Henderson, 'The capitalist mode of conservation, neoliberalism and the ecology of value' (2014) 7(1) *New Proposals: Journal of Marxism and Interdisciplinary Inquiry* 16–37.

[172] See for example N. Smith, 'Nature as accumulation strategy' (2007) 43 *Socialist Register* 16; Sullivan, 'Banking nature?', 198–217.

[173] M. Goldman, *Imperial Nature: The World Bank and Struggles for Social Justice in an Age of Globalization* (Yale University, 2006).

[174] S. Adelman, 'Tropical forests and climate change: A critique of green governmentality' (2015) 11(2) *International Journal of Law in Context* 195–212; S. Rutherford, 'Green governmentality: Insights and opportunities in the study of nature's rule' (2007) 31(3) *Progress in Human Geography* 291–307; K. Bäckstand and E. Lövbrand, 'Planting trees to mitigate climate change: Contested discourses of ecological modernisation, green governmentality and civic environmentalism' (2006) 6(1) *Global Environmental Politics* 50–75; see generally, A. Agrawal, *Environmentality: Technologies of Government and the Making of Subjects* (Duke University Press, 2005).

[175] A. Bumpus and D. Liverman, 'Accumulation by decarbonization and the governance of carbon offsets' (2008) 84(2) *Economic Geography* 127–55.

[176] P. Bond, *Politics of Climate Justice: Paralysis Above, Movement Below* (University of KwaZulu-Natal Press, 2012); M. Childs, 'Privatising the atmosphere: A solution or dangerous con?' (2012) 12(1/2) *Ephemera: Theory and Politics in Organisation* 12–18.

[177] H. Bachram, 'Climate fraud and carbon colonisation: The new trade in greenhouse gases' (2004) 15(4) *Capitalism, Nature, Socialism* 5–20.

[178] J. Fairhead, M. Leach, and I. Scoones, 'Green grabbing: A new appropriation of nature?' (2012) 39(2) *The Journal of Peasant Studies* 237–61.

28   *Introduction*

and rearticulation of new forms of global authority through REDD+. Considerations of authority, which arguably '[fall] somewhere between the reason and persuasion of equals and the forceful subordination of inferiors', connect questions regarding the force of law with questions about what it is that gives law legal force. That is, a focus on authority draws attention both to the fact of authority and how it is enacted and exercised, as well as to the modes by which authority is authorised, or the ways that authority is created, represented and justified.[179] Attention to questions of authority therefore allows for an examination of the effects of law, but it also brings into view that which conceptually precedes the articulation or enunciation of law, namely, the modes of authorisation that produce the authority or legitimacy to 'speak in the name of the law'.[180]

This focus on authority takes seriously how REDD+ exhibits the same dynamic of 'resistance and renewal', identified by scholars in international law more broadly, that tends to convert critiques of purported failures into 'institutional proliferation and practice'.[181] Therefore, as Balakrishnan Rajagopal has shown, it is important to pay attention to how critiques often produce their own 'instrument-effects', which, although unintended, have proven to be as important as intended effects.[182] This dynamic of 'resistance and renewal' has been particularly evident in discussions on the potential social risks from REDD+ projects to the 1.6 billion people who live in forests and depend on them to some degree for their livelihoods. These discussions have coalesced around the need to put certain safeguards in place, particularly those related to benefit sharing, tenure reform and processes for obtaining consent, in order to mitigate the risks to people who live in and around forest areas and allow them to realise the benefits arising from REDD+. The promotion of social safeguards has been underpinned by genuine concerns about protecting the rights of forest peoples, has mitigated potential abuses in REDD+ implementation and has provided important tools that can be deployed by communities to protect their interests *within* REDD+ projects. However, these mechanisms offer only limited possibilities for resisting REDD+ or the articulation of new forms of global authority produced through REDD+. Understanding these mechanisms not simply as potentially inadequate ameliorative measures, but as productive of new governance relations, allows for an examination of how they may, in fact, operate to create the forms of legibility, subjectivities and social relations that may further consolidate the reorganisation of authority that REDD+ represents.

---

[179] S. Dorsett and S. McVeigh, *Jurisdiction* (Routledge, 2012) pp. 32–4.

[180] P. Rush, 'An altered jurisdiction: Corporeal traces of law' (1997) 6 *Griffith Law Review* 144–68 at 150.

[181] Rajagopal, *International Law from Below*, p. 76; see also M. Sornarajah, *Resistance and Change in the International Law on Foreign Investment* (Cambridge University Press, 2015).

[182] Rajagopal, *International Law from Below*, p. 83.

D UNDERSTANDING REDD+

This book develops a unique conceptual apparatus to understand how REDD+ establishes and actualises new forms of authority over forested land and the peoples who live in and around forested areas. In particular, it presents a framework for understanding REDD+ that is attentive to the standpoint of those who are likely to be most affected by REDD+ – namely, the peoples living in and around forested areas – and is orientated towards the concerns and perspectives of the Global South. There is no unified or coherent 'Southern' perspective on either climate change or REDD+: the recognition by many states of the Global South – especially small island states – that climate change is an existential threat has also had to contend with the many forms of anti-colonial nationalism that have a commitment to and 'desire for energy-intensive, mostly fossil-fuel driven modernisation'.[183] Similarly, there is no unanimity within the countries of the Global South on carbon markets.[184] International endorsement of REDD+ was initiated and driven by countries of the Global South, particularly Papua New Guinea and Costa Rica and others in the Coalition for Rainforest Nations, and 'developing country repre- sentatives have been leaders in the movement to expand carbon markets to new jurisdictions',[185] even as these developments have been opposed by other countries, such as Bolivia.[186] Yet there are clear limitations to focusing exclusively on the positions of national governments, whose representatives tend to be part of a 'transnational ruling elite' who may act against the interests of their own peoples;[187] and thus legal scholarship orientated to the Global South must pay attention to the 'actualized experience of these peoples and not merely [to] that of the states which represent them'.[188]

This book therefore adopts a configuration of four concepts – organised as two pairs of two – through which to understand REDD+. The first pair of concepts – climate justice and the green economy – provides a means of situating and con- ceptualising REDD+. Below a formulation of the different registers of climate

---

[183] D. Chakrabarty, 'Planetary crises and the difficulty of being modern' (2018) 46(3) *Millennium: Journal of International Studies* 259–82 at 274–5.

[184] Pearse and Böhm, 'Ten reasons', 328.

[185] Ibid.

[186] See in particular the UNFCCC, *Submission by the Plurinational State of Bolivia to the Ad-Hoc Working Group on Long-Term Cooperative Action* (2010), unfccc.int/files/meetings/ad_hoc_ working_groups/lca/application/pdf/bolivia_awglca10.pdf.

[187] A. Anghie and B. S. Chimni, 'Third World approaches to international law and individual responsibility in internal conflicts' (2003) 2(1) *Chinese Journal of International Law* 77–103; Chimni, 'Third World approaches to international law: A manifesto' (2006) 8 *International Community Law Review* 3–27; see also S. Randeria, 'Cunning states and unaccountable international Institutions: Legal plurality, social movements and rights of local communities to common property resources' (2003) 44(1) *European Journal of Sociology* 27–60.

[188] Anghie and Chimni, 'Third world approaches to international law and individual responsibility in internal conflicts', 78.

30   *Introduction*

justice – procedural, distributive, corrective and structural – is provided, in order to set out a basis for analysing how REDD+ fails to meet climate justice demands, and instead actively forecloses distributive and corrective justice responses. The concept of the 'green economy' speaks to the wider transformations that REDD+ is inherently intertwined with, and therefore allows the analysis of REDD+ to be situated in this broader frame. The 'green economy' that is being co-produced alongside and through REDD+ is facilitating the re-legitimation of (green) growth and the greater economisation, marketisation and financialisation of nature. Together these two concepts – climate justice and the 'green economy' – therefore provide a conceptual apparatus to set out, understand, analyse and hold together both REDD+'s failures and productive effects.

The second pair of concepts – power and authority – speaks to the amalgamation and consolidation of global authority over forested areas, but also simultaneously the diffuse means by which authority is exercised in REDD+ through the devolution, decentralisation and pluralisation of governance. In order to understand the multiplicity of ways in which power manifests through REDD+, including by constituting objects and subjects, guiding their conduct and structuring the possible field of action, this book adopts Foucauldian-inspired concepts of 'environmentality' and 'green governmentality'. The language of authority directs attention both to the fact of authority, including how it is enacted and given institutional shape, and to the processes by which forms of legal authority are authorised, including through practices of representation. It thus provides a productive idiom for highlighting that what is at stake in REDD+ is the (as yet unrealised) aspiration to supplement a plurality of jurisdictions and ways of valuing forests with a singular frame for understanding, valuing, managing and governing forests, in accordance with internationally determined objectives. Yet, as an orientation or method, such a focus on authority also compels self-reflexivity to ensure that the way in which the consolidation of global authority is described in scholarly work does not also operate to further make invisible still existing rival forms of authority.

1 *Climate Justice*

Rather than understanding climate change within a primarily scientific frame, or an economic frame, the discourse of 'climate justice' names the profound questions of injustice that climate change raises. There is already an extensive literature on the concept of 'climate justice' that draws on political ecology and on frameworks of global justice and environmental justice.[189] It is widely recognised in scholarly,

---

[189] See for example, H. Shue, 'Subsistence emissions and luxury emissions' (1993) 15(1) *Law & Policy* 39–60; H. Shue, 'Global environment and international inequality' (1999) 75(3) *International affairs* 531–45; H. Shue, 'Historical Responsibility: Accountability for the Results of Actions Taken' (SBSTA Technical Briefing 2009); H. Shue, *Climate Justice: Vulnerability and Protection* (Oxford University Press, 2014); R. Kanbur and H. Shue,

D. Understanding REDD+

policy and activist contexts that climate change 'raises profoundly important questions about social justice, equity and human rights across countries and generations'.[190] The cruel reality of climate change is that, in general, an 'enormous global inequality' is evident when each country's contributions to global emissions are mapped against its vulnerability to the effects of climate change.[191] The impact and effect of climate change 'intensifies and exacerbates existing patterns of injustice',[192] and there is therefore a need for justice frameworks to inform climate mitigation and adaptation responses, in order to ensure equitable sharing of global resources and responsibilities for the global atmosphere among countries.[193] The term 'climate justice' speaks to multiple, different dimensions of justice: procedural, distributive, corrective and structural. The discussion below outlines these different conceptualisations of justice and identifies some of their potential limitations, in order to show why an expansive understanding of climate justice that encompasses all these registers is necessary.

Climate Justice: Integrating Economics and Philosophy (Oxford University Press, 2018); S. Caney, 'Cosmopolitan justice, responsibility, and global climate change' (2005) 18(4) *Leiden Journal of International Law* 747–75; D. Miller, *Global Justice and Climate Change: How Should Responsibilities Be Distributed?* (The Tanner Lectures on Human Values, 2008); K. Mickelson, 'Beyond a politics of the possible? South–North relations and climate justice' (2009) 10(2) *Melbourne Journal of International Law* 411–23; J. Baskin, 'The impossible necessity of climate justice?' (2009) 10(2) *Melbourne Journal of International Law* 424–38, and other articles in that Special Issue; A. Grear, 'Towards "climate justice"? A critical reflection on legal subjectivity and climate injustice: Warning signals, patterned hierarchies, directions for future law and policy' (2014) 5 *Journal of Human Rights and the Environment* 103–33; S. Humphreys, 'Climate justice: The claim of the past' (2014) 5 *Journal of Human Rights and the Environment* 134–48, and other articles in that Special Issue; drawing political economy J. T. Roberts and B. C. Parks, 'Ecologically unequal exchange, ecological debt, and climate justice: The history and implications of three related ideas for a new social movement' (2009) 50(3–4) *International Journal of Comparative Sociology* 385–409; B. C. Parks and J. T. Roberts, 'Climate change, social theory and justice' (2010) 27(2–3) *Theory, Culture and Society* 134–66; informing policy approaches, B. Adams and G. Luchsinger, *Climate Justice for a Changing Planet: A Primer for Policy Makers and NGOs* (United Nations and UN Non-Governmental Liaison Service, 2009); S. Klinsky and H. Dowlatabadi, 'Conceptualisations of justice in climate policy' (2009) 9(1) *Climate Policy* 88–108; from a social movement perspective; Bond, *Politics of Climate Justice*; U. Brand, N. Bullard, E. Lander, and T. Mueller (eds.), *Contours of Climate Justice: Ideas for Shaping New Climate and Energy Policies* (Dag Hammarskjöld Foundation 2009); B. Russell and A. Pusey, 'Movements and moments for climate justice: From Copenhagen to Cancun via Cochabamba' (2011) 11(3) *ACME: An International E-Journal for Critical Geographies* 15–32; Dawson, 'Climate justice: The emerging movement against green capitalism'.

[190] *Human Development Report 2007/2008: Fighting Climate Change – Human Solidarity in a Divided World* (United Nations Development Programme, 2007).

[191] G. P. Peters, R. M. Andrew, S. Solomon, and P. Friedlingstein, 'Measuring a fair and ambitious climate agreement using cumulative emissions' (2015) 10 *Environmental Research Letters* 105004.

[192] Humphreys, 'Climate justice: The claim of the past', 138.

[193] J. Gupta, *The Climate Change Convention and Developing Countries: From Conflict to Consensus?* (Kluwer Academic Publishers, 1997) p. 84.

Introduction

The focus on procedural justice, including questions of participation, voice and representation, is closely aligned with a human rights approach to climate change that emphasises how climate change impacts on the right to a safe, clean and healthy environment and other human rights.[194] It is now widely recognised that climate change threatens and could undermine the enjoyment of almost all protected human rights, including rights to life, health, water, food, housing, development and self-determination.[195] The human rights frame has been taken up in legal advocacy,[196] and the close connection between climate change and human rights has been articulated in different Human Rights Council resolutions[197] and explored by the Office of the High Commissioner for Human Rights (OHCHR)[198] and different mandate holders,[199] and UN treaty bodies.[200] Arguably such responses primarily remain 'patently inadequate and premised on forms of incremental managerialism and proceduralism which are entirely disproportionate to the urgency and magnitude of the threat'.[201] Moreover, human rights approaches have tended to focus on adaptation to climate change and the specific impacts of climate change on particularly vulnerable groups, having had much less to say about mitigation or 'confronting the core causes of climate change itself'.[202] Rights arguments have been usefully deployed to argue that failures to address

---

[194] On the relationship between climate change and human rights, see S. Humphreys (ed.), *Human Rights and Climate Change* (Cambridge University Press, 2009); S. Atapattu, *Human Rights approaches to Climate Change: Challenges and Opportunities* (Routledge, 2015).

[195] Atapattu, *Human Rights approaches to Climate Change: Challenges and Opportunities* p. 6.

[196] D. Esrin, and H. Kennedy, *Achieving Justice and Human Rights in an Era of Climate Disruption* (International Bar Association, 2014) p. 2.

[197] HRC resolution 7/23 (2008); 10/4 (2009); 18/22 (2011); 26/27 (2014); 29/15 (2015); 32/33 (2016); 35/20 (2017); 38/4 (2018).

[198] See A/HRC/10/61 (2009); A/HCR/32/23 (2016); A/HCR/35/13 (2017); A/HRC/37/35 (2017); A/HRC/38/21 (2018); A/HRC/41/26 (2019).

[199] See R. Rolnik, *The Right to Adequate Housing*, A/64/255 (6 August 2009); W. Kälin, *Protection of and Assistance to Internally Displaced Persons*, A/65/282 (11 August 2010); C. Beyani, *Protection of and Assistance to Internally Displaced Persons*, A/66/285 (9 August 2011); F. Crépeau, *Human Rights of migrants*, A/67/299 (13 August 2012); H. Elver, *Interim Report of the Special Rapporteur on the Right to Food*, A/70/287 (5 August 2015); J. Knox, *Report of the Special Rapporteur on the Issue of Human Rights Obligations Relating to the Enjoyment of a Safe, Clean, Healthy and Sustainable Environment*, A/HRC/31/52 (1 February 2016); V. Tauli Corpuz, *Report of the Special Rapporteur on the Rights of Indigenous Peoples*, A/HRC/36/46 (1 November 2017); P. Alston, *Climate Change and Poverty – Report of the Special Rapporteur on Extreme Poverty and Human Rights*, A/HRC/41/39 (25 June 2019).

[200] See in particular, Committee on Economic, Social and Cultural Rights, *Statement on Climate Change and the Covenant* (2018) Human Rights Committee, *General Comment No. 36 – Article 6: Right to Life*, CCPR/C/GC/36 (3 September 2019): 'Environmental degradation, climate change and unsustainable development constitute some of the most pressing and serious threats to the ability of present and future generations to enjoy the right to life.'

[201] P. Alston, *Climate Change and Poverty: Report of the Special Rapporteur on Extreme Poverty and Human Rights*, A/HRC/41/39 (25 June 2019), para 87.

[202] Ibid., para 23.

D. Understanding REDD+

climate change violate rights;[203] however, these frameworks provide little scope for engagement with the disproportionate contribution of some countries and companies to the underlying causes of climate change, or how responsibility for such mitigation action should be distributed.[204] Thus, while the human rights frame has given important impetus to discussions on climate change, opening up new forums for debate and potential for litigation, there remain clear limitations in using human rights as a means of challenging environmental injustice, both within nations and between the Global North and South.[205]

A key concern within the human rights scholarship has been centred around ensuring that states and companies meet their obligations to respect and/or protect human rights when taking mitigation and adaptation action.[206] The preamble to the Paris Agreement affirmed that 'Parties should, when taking action on climate change, respect, promote and consider their respective obligations on human rights';[207] however, the 'rulebook' subsequently developed to implement the Paris Agreement does not include any reference to human rights.[208] Such concerns about the violation of both procedural and substantive rights have arisen particularly in relation to carbon offset projects, both under the Kyoto Protocol's Clean Development Mechanism (CDM) and in relation to REDD+.[209] While a human rights framework provides a powerful language with which to identify and call for accountability for such harm at the project level, there are a number of challenges in deploying human rights in the service of developing a structural critique of carbon markets, given the 'fundamentally dissimilar' nature of these regimes.[210] In particular, human rights frameworks can highlight some of the adverse impacts of

---

[203] See J. Peel and H. M. Osofsky, 'A rights turn in climate change litigation?' (2018) 7(1) *Transnational Environmental Law* 37–67.

[204] In Knox, *Report of the Special Rapporteur on the Issue of Human Rights Obligations Relating to the Enjoyment of a Safe, Clean, Healthy and Sustainable Environment*, the Special Rapporteur acknowledges the relevance differentiated obligations in relation to climate change (para 46), however, he implies that the basis for this differentiation is 'capacity' rather than 'responsibility' (para 48).

[205] C. G. Gonzalez, 'Environmental justice, human rights, and the Global South' (2015) 13 *Santa Clara Journal of International Law* 151–95.

[206] Knox, *Report of the Special Rapporteur on the Issue of Human Rights Obligations Relating to the Enjoyment of a Safe, Clean, Healthy and Sustainable Environment*, para 55.

[207] *Paris Agreement*, preambular recital, 11.

[208] 'Katowice COP24 outcome incompatible with Paris Agreement' 15 December 2018, www.ciel.org/news/katowice-cop24-outcome-incompatible-with-paris-agreement; S. Duyck, 'Delivering on the Paris promises? Review of the Paris Agreement's implementing guidelines from a human rights perspective' (2019) 9(3) *Climate Law* 202–23.

[209] *Human Rights Implications of Climate Change Mitigation Actions* (CIDSE, Nature Code and Carbon Market Watch, 2015).

[210] S. Humphreys, 'Conceiving justice: Articulating common causes in distinct regimes' in S. Humphreys (ed.), *Climate Change and Human Rights* (Cambridge University Press, 2010) pp. 299–319, 316.

the marketisation of climate policy, yet they are arguably less capable of critiquing this process of marketisation or its distributional effects more broadly.[211] As a general rule, rights frameworks are better adapted to protecting minimum standards than contesting the constitution or distributional impacts of neoliberal markets.[212] Moreover, in a context where rights paradigms have become increasingly 'trade-related, market-friendly'[213] there is a risk that human rights can be 'manipulated to further and legitimise neo-liberal goals'.[214] Therefore, some scholars have warned against human rights becoming the main or exclusive language of Third World resistance.[215] Thus, while a focus on procedural and substantive rights provides a critical means of naming harms and calling for accountability for the impacts of carbon offsets at the project level, it has a number of limitations for critiquing the constitution of carbon markets and their distributional effects.

Considerable attention has also been given to the distributive justice dimensions of climate change and highlighting inequalities in relation to the responsibility for climate change, the vulnerability to its effects and the distribution of mitigation and adaptation burdens. The stark reality is that, '[p]erversely, the richest, who have the greatest capacity to adapt and are responsible for and have benefitted from the vast majority of greenhouse gas emissions, will be the best placed to cope with climate change, while the poorest, who have contributed the least to emissions and have the least capacity to react, will be the most harmed.'[216] While analysis of distributive inequalities has predominantly focused on the inequalities between countries, the 'extreme carbon inequality' and differentiated responsibility for GHG emissions is even more acute when mapped at the level of individuals.[217] To redress these inequalities, various frameworks of mitigation action have been proposed, including that emission rights should be based on an equal per capita allocation.[218]

---

[211] Similar arguments have been made about human rights in the context of globalisation, structural adjustment policy and neoliberalism. A. Lang, *World Trade Law after Neoliberalism: Reimagining the Global Economic Order* (Oxford University Press, 2011); S. Marks, 'Human rights and root causes' (2011) 74(1) *The Modern Law Review* 57–78; S. Moyn, 'A powerless companion: Human rights in the age of neoliberalism' (2014) 77(4) *Law and Contemporary Problems* 147–69.

[212] S. Moyn, *Not Enough: Human Rights in an Unequal World* (Harvard University Press, 2018).

[213] U. Baxi, *The Future of Human Rights*, 2nd edition (Oxford University Press, 2002) p. 234.

[214] Chimni, 'Third world approaches to international law', 3.

[215] B. Rajagopal, *International Law from Below*.

[216] P. Alston, *Climate Change and Poverty: Report of the Special Rapporteur on Extreme Poverty and Human Rights*, A/HRC/41/39 (25 June 2019), para 14; see also G. Althor, J. E. Watson, and R. A. Fuller, 'Global mismatch between greenhouse gas emissions and the burden of climate change' (2016) 6 *Scientific Reports* 20281.

[217] T. Piketty and L. Chancel, *Carbon and inequality: From Kyoto to Paris: Trends in the Global Inequality of Carbon Emissions (1998–2013) and Prospects for an Equitable Adaptation Fund* (Paris School of Economics, 2015); *Extreme carbon inequality* (Oxfam Media Briefing, 2015).

[218] R. W. Salzman, 'Distributing emission rights in the global order: The case for equal per capita allocation' (2010) 13(1) *Yale Human Rights and Development Journal* 281–306.

D. Understanding REDD+

Relatedly, the 'greenhouse development rights' model proposes a calculation of national obligations based on a country's current capacity or wealth and contribution to climate change, while protecting the 'right to development' by excepting from consideration emissions or income under a certain 'development threshold'.[219] The main institutional response to such concerns over distribution and North–South inequalities has been the inclusion of the principle of 'common but differentiated responsibilities and respective capacities' (CBDR-RC) and differentiation between 'developed' and 'developing countries' within the UNFCCC regime.[220] However, the potential of this principle to promote 'redistributive multilateralism'[221] has been undermined by moves towards a more nuanced model of self-differentiation within the regime. Such moves have been driven in part by concerns held by countries of the Global North about the growing emissions and economic power of the so-called BRICS countries (Brazil, Russia, India, China and South Africa), even though there has been no significant structural change in the comparative position of most countries in the Global South.[222] More recently, various methods have been proposed to assess whether parties are contributing their own 'fair share', variously based on cumulative or current emissions and capacity to take action.[223] These frameworks have provided critically important tools to critique the inequitable impacts of climate change; the inadequate climate mitigation measures taken by many countries, especially those of the Global North;[224] as well as how carbon markets could operate to spatially displace responsibility for mitigation actions.

However, on a conceptual level these frameworks exhibit a number of limitations. First, there is a realistic fear, based on the trajectory of developments within UN institutions and global conventions, that efforts towards distributive justice could be

---

[219] P. Baer, G. Fieldman, T. Athanasiou, and S. Kartha, 'Greenhouse development rights: Towards an equitable framework for global climate policy' (2008) 21(4) *Cambridge Review of International Affairs* 649–69.

[220] UNFCCC, Article 3.1; for a discussion of CBDR-RC within the climate regime see Chapter 4. See also Dehm, 'Reflections on Paris'.

[221] J. McGee and J. Steffek, 'The Copenhagen turn in global climate governance and the contentious history of differentiation in international law' (2016) 28(1) *Journal of Environmental Law* 37–63.

[222] P. Cullet, 'Differential treatment in environmental law: Addressing critiques and conceptualizing the next steps' (2016) 5(2) *Transnational Environmental Law* 305–28.

[223] *Fair Shares: A Civil Society Equity Review of INDCS. Report* (CSO Equity Review Coalition, 2015); Peters et al., 'Measuring a fair and ambitious climate agreement using cumulative emissions'; J. D. McBee, 'Distributive justice in the Paris Climate Agreement: Response to Peters et al.' (2017) 9(1) *Contemporary Readings in Law and Social Justice* 120–31.

[224] The CSO Equity Review Coalition found that 'all major developed countries fell well short of their fair shares', with Japan only contributing one-tenth of its fair share, the United States approximately one-fifth and the European Union contributing just over one-fifth of its fair share, ibid.

co-opted and repurposed in order to serve neoliberal ends.[225] When neoliberal economic and political conceptions monopolise policy and practice within environmental regimes, distributive justice concerns risk being reduced to: '(1) the insurance of a state's right to its property, (2) the free ability to trade this property globally and (3) the continual deregulation of this market in order to ensure everyone's equal and competitive position within commerce'.[226] This is evident in how distributive justice frameworks have been used to promote better equality of opportunity within carbon markets, including more equitable participation within mechanisms such as the CDM,[227] without fundamentally challenging the existence or structure of such markets or measures. Second, underpinning the demands for differentiation, especially by countries of the Global South, has been a concern that the necessity of taking climate mitigation action could undermine a country's 'right to development',[228] to reach an imagined future of fossil-fuel–driven industrialisation. Such demands can cynically be dismissed as a 'strategy for bargaining, in effect, for a longer life for a developmental regime ... for nations like India and China';[229] but what is more problematic is how such calls are based upon a specific imaginary of development as the only horizon and how they remain trapped in an 'inability to imagine development alternatives'.[230] Third, although valuable, such frameworks of distributive climate justice rely on the precepts of liberal egalitarianism, which assume the capacity to rearrange a current unjust distribution of quantifiable matter to make it conform to a universally valid conception of a just distribution of entitlements. Such conceptions of global justice, as Andrew Robinson and Simon Tormey have shown, thus dictate both the 'universality of equivalence' and the existence of some global 'state-form' that does this distributing.[231] These conceptions therefore require the establishment of an 'equivalential signifier' – such as one tonne of carbon dioxide equivalent ($1tCO_2e$) – that risks consolidating rather than contesting the premise that emissions arising from diverse social actions can be made legible in

---

[225] J. Mousie, 'Global environmental justice and postcolonial critique' (2012) 9(2) *Environmental Philosophy* 21–46; C. Okereke, *Global Justice and Neoliberal Environmental Governance: Ethics, Sustainable Development and International Co-operation* (Routledge, 2007).

[226] Mousie, 'Global environmental justice and postcolonial critique', 43.

[227] T. A. Eni-Ibukun, *International Environmental Law and Distributive Justice* (Routledge, 2014).

[228] General Assembly Resolution 41/128, *Declaration on the Right to Development*, 97th plen mtg, A/RES/41/128 (4 December 1986); the preamble to the UNFCCC recalls this Declaration (preambular recital 10) and – with a carefully placed comma – ambiguously affirms that 'Parties have a right to, and should, promote sustainable development' (Article 3(4)); see S. Biniaz, 'Comma but differentiated responsibilities: Punctuation and 30 other ways negotiators have resolved issues in the international climate change regime' (2016) 6 *Michigan Journal of Environmental & Administrative Law* 37–63.

[229] Chakrabarty, 'Planetary crises and the difficulty of being modern', 267.

[230] U. Natarajan, 'Human rights – help or hindrance to combatting climate change?' *OpenDemocracy*, 9 January 2015, www.opendemocracy.net/en/openglobalrights-openpageblog/human-rights-help-or-hindrance-to-combatting-climate-change/It.

[231] A. Robinson and S. Tormey, 'Resisting "global justice": Disrupting the colonial "emancipatory" logic of the West' (2009) 30(8) *Third World Quarterly* 1395–409 at 1397.

D. Understanding REDD+

standardisable and comparable terms.[232] Finally, such frameworks of distributive justice generally remain presentist, involving limited engagement with how climate justice is also a claim about the past.[233] The limitations outlined above speak to why distributive frameworks of climate justice, although highly pertinent and necessary, need to be supplemented by compensative and structural conceptions of justice.

Climate justice compels a compensative or reparative dimension because 'historical injustice saturates the problem of climate change'.[234] As Stephen Humphreys writes, a 'carbon footprint haunts every step of the history of industrial and colonial expansion of the last centuries',[235] and it is this cumulation of impacts that now constrains present and future possibilities. Reparative politics calls for reckoning with such acts that '*remain unrepaired* in the present, whose wrongs continue to disfigure generations, and which, in consequence, *call out* now for a just response'.[236] While it is not possible for all historical wrongs to be repaired, such calls for reparation 'confront us with pasts that are not past but remain unresolved or unreconciled such that they weigh upon the psyche like a blighted and hobbled and afflicted revenant' and thus highlight the unfinished – and perhaps unfinishable – project of justice.[237] Persistent claims have been raised (and strongly resisted) that the countries and peoples of the Global North owe a 'climate debt' to the countries and peoples of the Global South, as 'acknowledgment that the privileged position of the developed countries represents the culmination, and in many cases the perpetuation, of a history of unequal access'.[238] Thus this dimension of compensative justice provides a necessary supplement to other registers of climate justice, by foregrounding the 'uneven and persistent patterns of eco-imperialism and "ecological debt" as a result of the historical legacies of uneven use of fossil fuels and exploitation of raw materials'.[239]

Finally, frameworks of reparative or compensative justice should be supplemented with a deeper focus not on historical injustices alone but on critically interrogating the processes through which such injustices have been produced.

---

[232] See Dehm, 'One tonne of carbon dioxide equivalent (1tCO2e)'.

[233] Humphreys, 'Climate justice: The claim of the past', 134.

[234] Ibid.

[235] Ibid., 147.

[236] D. Scott, 'Preface: Evil beyond repair' (2018) 22(1) *Small Axe: A Caribbean Journal of Criticism* vii–x at viii (emphasis in original).

[237] Ibid., viii.

[238] K. Mickelson, 'Leading towards a level playing field, repaying ecological debt, or making environmental space: Three Stories about international environmental cooperation' (2005) 43 *Osgoode Hall Law Journal* 137–70 at 154; on climate debt see also A. Simms, A. Meyer, and N. Robbins, *Who Owes Who : Climate Change, Debt, Equity and Survival* (Christian Aid, 1999); T. Jones and S. Edwards, *The Climate Debt Crisis: Why Paying Our Dues if Essential for Tackling Climate Change* (Jubilee Debt Campaign and World Development Movement, 2009); *Climate Debt: A Primer* (Third World Network, 2009).

[239] P. Chatterton, D. Featherstone, and P. Routledge, 'Articulating climate justice in Copenhagen: Antagonism, the commons, and solidarity' (2013) 45(3) *Antipode* 602–20 at 606.

Joshua Mousie suggests that accounts of environmental justice need to be attentive to how contemporary political relationships have been shaped by 'current and historical political-material relationships of domination, exploitation, and consumption'.[240] He argues that 'Eurocentric projects of modernity, development, and globalization rarely (if ever) produce environmental relationships that promote equality' and proposes that a reformulation of environmental justice calls for a more general questioning of these projects.[241] It is consequently unsurprising that social movements have promoted a conceptualisation of 'climate justice' that focuses on the 'interrelationships between, and addresses the root causes of, the social injustice, ecological destruction and economic domination perpetuated by the underlying logics of pro-growth capitalism'.[242] Social movement declarations have highlighted that '[c]olonialism continues to operate', that it structures the historical context in which climate change occurs, that the 'structural causes' of climate change are linked to the 'current capitalist hegemonic system' and that there is a need for 'structural changes' to mainstream production, distribution and consumption models.[243] This reality compels critical reflection of the extent to which these projects of colonialism and hegemonic capitalist development models have been the foundation for the development of international legal doctrines and principles, and how they continue to provide 'transcendent grounds' to international law[244] and operate to '[secure] the putative objectivity of the categories of international law'.[245] Finally, social movements orientated towards climate justice have critiqued, as an underlying source of the climate crisis, the 'political and economic systems commercialising and reifying nature and life'.[246] Again, taking up these concerns within legal scholarship calls for an interrogation of how 'harmful understandings of nature were central to shaping the discipline', and of how a reconstructive 'remaking' of

---

[240] Mousie, 'Global environmental justice and postcolonial critique', 40.

[241] Ibid., 40–1.

[242] Chatterton, Featherstone, and Routledge, 'Articulating climate justice in Copenhagen: Antagonism, the commons, and solidarity', 606.

[243] Social PreCOP, *Margarita Declaration on Climate Change* (2014), redd-monitor.org/2014/08/08/the-margarita-declaration-on-climate-change-we-reject-the-implementation-of-false-solutions-to-climate-change-such-as-carbon-markets-and-other-forms-of-privatization-and-commodification-of-life/.

[244] S. Pahuja, *Decolonising International Law: Development, Economic Growth and the Politics of Universality* (Cambridge University Press, 2011), pp. 37–40; see generally A. Anghie, *Imperialism, Sovereignty and the Making of International Law* (Cambridge University Press, 2007).

[245] S. Pahuja, 'Laws of encounter: A jurisdictional account of international law' (2013) 1(1) *London Review of International Law* 63–98 at 66.

[246] Social PreCOP, *Margarita Declaration on Climate Change* (2014), redd-monitor.org/2014/08/08/the-margarita-declaration-on-climate-change-we-reject-the-implementation-of-false-solutions-to-climate-change-such-as-carbon-markets-and-other-forms-of-privatization-and-commodification-of-life.

international law requires both deconstructing these understandings and a radical reconceptualisation of the relationship between law and the natural world.[247]

Climate justice movements have foregrounded the need for transformative change to build a fair, egalitarian development model, one 'based on the principles of living in harmony with nature, guided by absolute and ecological sustainability limits'.[248] Key to realising such a transformative vision of change is the sharing of 'experiences from all over the world to understand and construct true solutions'; 'expressing solidarity' to those in other parts of the world and understanding their context, struggle and identity; and 'intercultural thinking'.[249] Within these alternative visions of climate justice there is thus a scepticism towards any attempts to 'impose a single social ordering, or even a general transcendental morality', and the focus is instead on allowing for a 'multiplicity of perspectives' as well as 'a range of different ways of relating to land, labour, nature, [and] territories'.[250] The challenge of 'trying to imagine ways in which diverse perspectives and lifeworlds can coexist in non-dominatory ways'[251] thus entails both a shared 'no' to the exploitative relationship over peoples and nature and an embrace of the potentialities of working towards many different visions of just, ecological justice. In doing so, such visions radicalise frameworks of 'climate justice' by authorising plural conceptions of 'climate *justices*'.

2 *The Green Economy*

REDD+ is one aspect of a much broader reconfiguration of relationships between humans and the natural world that is reflected in the changing ways in which the non-human world is 'conceived, valued, managed and governed globally'.[252] Analysis of REDD+ therefore needs to be situated against this background, in order to appreciate how the law is central to these transformations, through which an 'entire philosophy of nature [is] co-produced with a new "green" economy'.[253] The concept of the 'green economy' has become a new discursive frame for environmental politics, which gained traction in the lead-up to the 2012 UN Conference on

---

[247] Natarajan and Khody, 'Locating nature, 573–93; U. Natarajan and J. Dehm, 'Where is the environment? Locating nature in international law' *Third World Approaches to International Law Review (TWAILR)*, 30 August 2019, twailr.com/where-is-the-environment-locating-nature-in-international-law; Natarajan and Dehm, *Locating Nature: Making and Unmaking International Law*.

[248] Social PreCOP, *Margarita Declaration on Climate Change* (2014), https://redd-monitor.org/2014/08/08/the-margarita-declaration-on-climate-change-we-reject-the-implementation-of-false-solutions-to-climate-change-such-as-carbon-markets-and-other-forms-of-privatization-and-commodification-of-life/.

[249] Ibid.

[250] Robinson and Tormey, 'Resisting "global justice"', 1406.

[251] Ibid., 1407.

[252] S. Sullivan, 'Green capitalism, and the cultural poverty of constructing nature as service-provider' (2009) 3 *Radical anthropology* 18–27 at 19.

[253] Fairhead, Leach, and Scoones, 'Green grabbing: A new appropriation of nature?', 245.

Sustainable Development (Rio +20), even though, due to civil society pressure,[254] the concept only received cautious endorsement in the summit outcome document.[255] UNEP has promoted the 'green economy' as a response to the intertwined global food, energy and financial crises, and to catalyse renewed policy attention and international cooperation around sustainable development;[256] while the World Bank has foregrounded the concept of 'green growth',[257] which has been taken up in the strategies of the Organisation for Economic Co-operation and Development (OECD).[258] This discursive frame implies the possibility of reconciling ecological limits with capitalist imperatives of economic growth, through the rapid material decoupling of GDP growth from material throughput and carbon emissions. Jason Hickel and Giorgos Kallis have empirically examined such claims and found that such decoupling, although 'technically possible', is 'unlikely to be achieved even under highly optimistic conditions'.[259]

The 'green growth' or 'green economy' frame seeks to sustain the legitimacy of continual economic growth,[260] and, thereby facilitates the further expansion of economic logics and markets into previously uncommodified domains of life through the commodification, marketisation and financialisation of nature.[261] In particular, the frame of the green economy has helped to reconceptualise the 'natural commons' as 'natural capital',[262] and facilitated efforts to value nature and ecosystem services in economic terms,[263] on the premise that the abstraction and pricing of nature, and its transformation into assets, goods and services, will mean 'environmental risk and degradation can be measured, exchanged, offset and generally minimized'.[264] In doing so, this idea promotes a highly reductionist way of making nature visible and legible in substitutable and fungible terms, one that

---

[254] See N. Bullard and T. Müller, 'Beyond the "Green Economy": System change, not climate change?' (2012) 55(1) *Development* 54–62; D. Brockington, 'A radically conservative vision? The challenge of UNEP's towards a green economy' (2012) 43(1) *Development and Change* 409–22.

[255] General Assembly resolution 66/288, *The Future We Want*, A/RES/66/288 (11 September 2011), para 56.

[256] *Towards a Green Economy: Pathways to Sustainable Development and Poverty Eradication* (United Nations Environment Programme, 2011).

[257] *Inclusive Green Growth: The Pathway to Sustainable Development* (World Bank, 2012).

[258] *Towards a Green Economy: Pathways to Sustainable Development and Poverty Eradication.*

[259] J. Hickel and G. Kallis, 'Is green growth possible?' (2020) 25(4) *New Political Economy* 469–86 at 483.

[260] W. Sachs, 'Sustainable development and the crisis of nature: On the political anatomy of an oxymoron' in M. Hajer and F. Fischer (eds.), *Living with Nature: Environmental Politics As Cultural Discourse* (Oxford University Press, 1999).

[261] Smith, 'Nature as accumulation strategy'.

[262] J. Boehnert, 'The green economy: Reconceptualising the natural commons as natural capital' (2015) 10(4) *Environmental Communication* 395–417.

[263] See in particular, *The Economics of Ecosystems and Biodiversity: Mainstreaming the Economics of Nature: A Synthesis of the Approach, Conclusions and Recommendations of the TEEB* (TEEB, 2010).

[264] Sullivan, 'Green capitalism, and the cultural poverty of constructing nature as service-provider', 18.

D. Understanding REDD+

ignores complex social and ecological entanglements and dismisses other logics of evaluation, instead 'rationalising human and nonhuman natures to conform to an economic system that privileges price over other values, and profit-oriented market exchanges over the distributive and sustainable logics of other economic systems'.[265]

The frame of 'green growth' or the 'green economy' rejects claims of inherent ecological limits,[266] and instead embodies a specifically capitalist relationship with limits, with 'contradictory tendencies … to both overtake and posit limits'.[267] For capital, every limit appears as a barrier to be overcome in a drive towards a constantly expanding sphere of production that simply displaces contradictions elsewhere.[268] However, there is a simultaneous drive to re-establish limits, as the 'internal condition of value's realization as private wealth', and in order to 'capture the "new" within the property form'.[269] As such, even as the positing of aggregate limits or a 'cap' enables the constitution of carbon markets and generates the value of a new immaterial carbon commodity, the expansion of forest carbon offsets requires the delineation of new property rights in order to clarify ownership and entitlements in the forest carbon economy.

REDD+ has been widely described as key to enabling a broader transition to a 'green economy': proponents have suggested that integrating REDD+ in a 'green economy' transition can 'maximise synergies' and help create a 'virtuous circle' of investment in natural capital.[270] However, a more critical analysis suggests what is at stake is a process of capital expansion that takes both an *extensive* and an *intensive* form,[271] consisting of both the reorganisation of forest 'hinterland' spaces to more deeply accord with market logics as well as the further subsumption of nature within capitalist markets and the subjection of nature's productivity to marketised modes of

---

[265] Sullivan, 'Banking nature?', 200.

[266] See for example D. H. Meadows, D. L. Meadows, W. W. Behrens III, and J. Randers, *The Limits to Growth* (Universe Books, 1972); T. Jackson, *Prosperity without Growth: Economics for a Finite Planet* (Earthscan, 2009).

[267] A. Mitropoulos, *Contract and Contagion: From Biopolitics to Oikonomia* (Minor Compositions, 2012) p. 156.

[268] K. Marx, *Grundrisse: Foundations of the Critique of Political Economy* (Penguin Books, 1939) pp. 334, 410.

[269] M. Cooper, *Family Values: Between Neoliberalism and the New Social Conservatism* (MIT Press, 2017) p. 16; M. E. Cooper, *Life As Surplus: Biotechnology and Capitalism in the Neoliberal Era* (University of Washington Press, 2008) p. 25.

[270] Sukhdev et al., *REDD+ and the Green Economy: Opportunities for a Mutually Supportive Relationship*; C. Watson, E. Brickell, W. McFarland and J. McNeely, *Integrating REDD+ into a Green Economy Transition* (Overseas Development Institute, 2013).

[271] For a discussion of the expansion of capital through processes of so-called 'primitive accumulation' see K. Marx, *Capital: A Critique of Political Economy* (Lawrence and Wishart, 1887) vol. i Chapters 26–8; see also D. Harvey, *The New Imperialism* (Oxford University Press, 2005); J. Read, *The Micro-Politics of Capital: Marx and the Prehistory of the Present* (SUNY Press, 2003); M. D. Angelis, *The Beginning of History: Value Struggles and Global Capital* (Pluto Press, 2007); O. U. Ince, 'Primitive accumulation, new enclosures, and global land grabs: A theoretical intervention' (2013) 79(1) *Rural Sociology* 104–31.

production.[272] In contrast to counter-hegemonic imaginaries of ecological futures that create openings for the 'transformation of the current production model' and challenge policies that 'prioritize the reproduction of capital over the reproduction of life',[273] in this paradigm of the 'green economy' the 'environmental crisis has itself become a major new frontier of value creation and capitalist accumulation'.[274]

3 Power

REDD+ engages a complex form of transnational multi-sited, multi-layered and multi-actor governance – often described as 'polycentric'[275] – that extends beyond the formal climate regimes, transgresses the public/private divide and allows states, markets, laws and other institutions to cohere within a nested organisation of local, national and global scales.[276] The forms of power enacted through REDD+ are diffuse, plural and productive, directed towards constituting and fabricating their objects of governance and acting on and systematically modifying the variables of the background regulatory environment.[277] This book deploys a Foucauldian understanding of power as a 'way of acting on an acting subject', consisting of 'guiding the possibility of conduct and putting in order the possible outcome'.[278] For Foucault, to govern is therefore to 'structure the possible field of actions of others':[279] a process

---

[272] Smith, 'Nature as accumulation strategy'; Sullivan, 'Banking nature?'; N. Castree and G. Henderson, 'The capitalist mode of conservation, neoliberalism and the ecology of value' (2014) 7(1) *New Proposals: Journal of Marxism and Interdisciplinary Inquiry* 16–37.

[273] *Call to Action to Reject REDD+ and Extractive Industries; To Confront Capitalism and Defend Life and Territories* (December 2014), wrm.org.uy/wp-content/uploads/2014/11/Call-COP-Lima_NoREDD.pdf.

[274] Sullivan, 'Green capitalism, and the cultural poverty of constructing nature as service-provider', 18.

[275] A. Jordan, D. Huitema, H. Van Asselt, and J. Forster (eds.), *Governing Climate Change: Polycentricity in Action?* (Cambridge University Press, 2018).

[276] Boyd, 'Climate change, fragmentation, and the challenges of global environmental law: Elements of a post-Copenhagen assemblage', 471; On transnational climate governance see generally J. Peel, L. Godden, and R. J. Keenan, 'Climate Change Law in an Era of Multi-Level Governance' (2012) 1(2) *Transnational Environmental Law* 245–80; C. Okereke, H. Bulkeley, and H. Schroeder, 'Conceptualising climate governance beyond the international regime' (2009) 9(1) *Global Environmental Politics* 58–78; P. Pattberg and J. Stripple, 'Beyond the public and private divide: Remapping transnational climate governance in the 21st century' (2008) 8 *International Environmental Agreements* 367–88; L. B. Andonova, M. M. Betsill, and H. Bulkeley, 'Transnational climate governance' (2009) 9(2) *Global Environmental Politics* 52–73; H. Bulkeley, L. B. Andonova, M. M. Betsill, D. Compagnon, T. Hale, M. J. Hoffman, P. Newell, M. Peterson, C. Roger, and S. D. Vandveer, *Transnational Climate Change Governance* (Cambridge University Press, 2014).

[277] In M. Foucault, *The Birth of Biopolitics: Lectures at the Collège de France 1978–1979* (2008), Foucault theorises a type of 'governmentality which will act on the environment and systematically modify its variables' (p. 271).

[278] M. Foucault, 'The subject and power' (1982) 8(4) *Critical Inquiry* 777–95.

[279] Ibid., 790.

D. Understanding REDD+

of 'conducting the conduct'[280] of individuals so as to optimise relations in a specific milieu.[281] Governing through conduct, as Tania Murray Li has theorised, is thus 'a matter of "getting the incentives right" so that some conduct is encouraged and enabled, while other conduct becomes more difficult'.[282] These theoretical frameworks therefore help make visible that behind REDD+'s stated objectives to provide economic incentives to address tropical deforestation lies the work of organising the background regulatory environment to enable such incentives to become legible. Moreover, these theoretical frameworks illuminate that a necessary concurrent project is constructing the types of subject that modify their behaviours in line with such incentives.

Environmental scholars have taken up and adapted the 'ugly word'[283] 'governmentality' coined by Foucault to describe the ensemble of institutions, procedures, analyses, reflections, calculations and tactics that allow for a specific and complex form of power that operates at the level of populations, relies on knowledge of political economy and seeks to secure a complex balance between the interests of the collective and those of the individual.[284] The frameworks of 'environmentality', 'eco-governmentality' and 'green governmentality' provide conceptual tools for analysing the interconnections between power/knowledge, institutions and the production of subjectivities in contemporary environmental politics.[285] Specifically, Sam Adelman has identified how REDD+ constitutes a 'neoliberal green governmentality regime' that through the 'deployment of rationalities, techniques and legal regimes' has made tropical forests subject to market forces, and 'enabled them to be surveilled, monitored and measured, and their inhabitants rendered vulnerable to the discipline of markets'.[286] Central to this form of governmentality is the

---

[280] Foucault, *Security, Territory, Population: Lectures at the Collège de France 1977–1978* (Palgrave Macmillan, 2007), p. 193; see also T. M. Li, 'Fixing non-market subjects: Governing land and population in the Global South' (2014) 18 *Foucault Studies* 34–48.

[281] For an elaboration of governance as an attempt to direct conduct see Li, 'Fixing non-market subjects: Governing land and population in the Global South'; T. M. Li, 'Practices of assemblage and community forest management'; T. M. Li, *The Will to Improve: Governmentality, Development, and the Practice of Politics* (Duke University Press, 2007).

[282] Li, 'Fixing non-market subjects: Governing land and population in the Global South', 37.

[283] Foucault, *Security, Territory, Population: Lectures at the Collège de France 1977–1978*, p. 115.

[284] Ibid., pp. 108–9.

[285] Agrawal, *Environmentality*; A. Agrawal, 'Environmentality: Community, intimate government, and the making of environmental subjects in Kumaon, India' (2005) 46(2) *Current Anthropology* 161–90; Rutherford, 'Green governmentality: Insights and opportunities in the study of nature's rule'; T. W. Luke, 'On environmentality: Geo-power and eco-knowledge in the discourses of contemporary environmentalism' (1995) 31 *Cultural Critique* 57–81; T. W. Luke, 'Environmentality as green governmentality' in E. Darier (ed.), *Discourse of the Environment* (Blackwell Publishers, 1999) pp. 121–51; Luke, 'Environmentality' in Dryzek et al. (eds.), *The Oxford Handbook of Climate Change and Society* pp. 96–109; R. Fletcher, 'Environmentality unbound: Multiple governmentalities in environmental politics' (2017) 85 *Geoforum* 311–15.

[286] Adelman, 'Tropical forests and climate change: A critique of green governmentality', 196.

44   *Introduction*

constituting of 'nature' and human–nature relations such that the 'mechanisms of competition' are given 'freer play as regulatory principles'.[287] Such dynamics of competition are shaped and underpinned by legal relations – especially those of property and contract – and structured by a whole juridical, institutional ensemble. The close co-constitution of law and markets makes REDD+ an ideal site for examining 'the interplay between the ways the state creates "the market" and the ways market power feeds back into the politics'[288] as well as the non-egalitarian, asymmetrical, disciplinary micro-powers that support and constitute 'the other, dark side' of a formally egalitarian juridical framework.[289]

This conceptual apparatus also enables a more politicised understanding of how power is enacted through forms of 'polycentric' climate governance. The concept of 'polycentricity' has been taken up in climate law literature in descriptive and explanatory ways to analyse climate governance and has also been proposed as a normative prescription of how to better govern responses to the climate crisis.[290] The term was arguably popularised in the field through the publication of a background paper that Elinor Ostrom wrote for the World Bank's 2010 World Development Report, *Development and Climate Change.*[291] The term refers to governance arrangements that are multi-level, multi-tiered, multi-perspectival, functional, overlapping and made up of competing jurisdictions or spheres of authority,[292] and it has been taken up within the literature as 'hold[ing] significant potential for addressing some of the major challenges outlined for REDD'.[293] Conducting a quick genealogy of the term shows how it was first coined by Michael Polanyi, and then adopted in the work of the Indiana Workshop in Political Theory (directed by Vincent and Elinor Ostrom) as a means of rethinking questions of public choice economics.[294] For Michael Polanyi, the concept of

---

[287] Foucault, *The Birth of Biopolitics: Lectures at the Collège de France 1978–1979*, p. 147; Luke, 'Environmentality', p. 99.

[288] D. S. Grewal, A. Kapczynski, and J. Purdy, 'Law and political economy: Toward a manifesto' *Law and Political Economy Blog*, November 2017 lpeblog.org/2017/11/06/law-and-political-economy-toward-a-manifesto.

[289] Foucault, *Discipline and Punish: The Birth of the Prison*, p. 222.

[290] Jordan et al. (eds.), *Governing Climate Change: Polycentricity in Action?*

[291] E. Ostrom, *A Polycentric Approach for Coping with Climate Change: Background Paper to the 2010 World Development Report* (2009); see also E. Ostrom, 'Polycentric systems for coping with collective action and global environmental change' (2010) 20(4) *Global Environmental Change* 550–7.

[292] G. Marks and L. Hooghe, 'Contrasting visions of multilateral governance' in I. Bache and M. V. Flinders (eds.), *Multi-level Governance* (Oxford University Press, 2004) p. 15.

[293] H. Nagendra and E. Ostrom, 'Polycentric governance of multifunctional forested landscapes' (2012) 6(2) *International Journal of the Commons* 104–33.

[294] V. Ostrom, 'Polycentricity (Part 1)' in M. D. McGinnis (ed.), *Polycentricity and Local Public Economics: Readings from the Workshop in Political Theory and Policy Analysis* (University of Michigan Press, 1999) pp. 52–74; B. E. Wright, M. D. McGinnis, and E. Ostrom, 'Reflections on Vincent Ostrom, public administration, and polycentricity' (2011) 71(1) *Public Administration Review* 15–25; P. D. Aligica and P. Boettke, 'The social philosophy of

D. Understanding REDD+

polycentricity initially provided a way of theorising the process of epistemic innovation within a tradition, but in later work he used the term to refer to ordering by and through a pricing mechanism as a form of 'spontaneous arbitration'.[295] His theorisation of polycentricity – and polycentric tasks and orders – was thus intimately connected with his conceptualisation of the market as a system of 'spontaneous order'.[296] The term 'spontaneous order' was later popularised by the writing of fellow Mont Pèlerin Society member, Friedrich Hayek,[297] and the related language of self-organisation – especially in Hayek's usage – is 'tethered to a deeply conservative opposition to politics'.[298] The concept of the 'spontaneous order' assumes that the self-interested actions of individuals will converge and thereby promote the collective good, without the need for human or governmental coordination.[299] The theory not only holds that governmental intervention is unnecessary but also that it is impossible, because there is no standpoint from which the totality of economic relations is visible, and this lack of a totalising vantage point and ability to comprehend the order as a whole disqualifies the sovereign from intervening to moderate market relations. However, although direct interventions are disqualified, Polanyi (and Hayek) stress the fundamental importance of the background legal norms that '[frame] the economy', such that 'if the economy is a game', then legal institutions represent the 'rules of the game'.[300] Specifically in his discussion of the spontaneous order, Michael Polanyi notes that '[n]o marketing system can function without a legal framework that guarantees adequate proprietary powers and enforces contracts'.[301] It is this element of polycentric governance that is often obscured in the literature: namely, that polycentric governance is a system of spontaneous private

---

Ostrom's institutionalism' (2010) 10–19 Working Paper, Mercatus Centre, George Mason University; P. D. Aligica and P. J. Boettke, *Challenging Institutional Analysis and Development: The Bloomington School* (Routledge, 2009); P. D. Aligica and V. Tarko, 'Polycentricity: From Polanyi to Ostrom, and beyond' (2012) 25 *Governance: An International Journal of Policy, Administration, and Institutions* 237–62; P. D. Aligica, *Institutional Diversity and Political Economy: The Ostroms and Beyond* (Oxford University Press, 2014).

[295] M. Polanyi, 'Profits and private enterprise' in R. T. Allen (ed.), *Society, Economics and Philosophy: Selected Papers Michael Polanyi* (Transaction Publishers, 1948) and the essay 'Collectivist planning' in that edited collection; see also the chapter 'The span of central direction" in M. Polanyi, *The Logic of Liberty: Reflections and Rejoinders* (University of Chicago Press, 1981) pp. 136–69.

[296] See especially M. Polanyi, 'The manageability of social tasks' in *The Logic of Liberty: Reflections and Rejoinders*.

[297] S. Jacobs, 'Tradition in a free society: The fideism of Michael Polanyi and the rationalism of Karl Popper' (2010) 36(2) *Tradition & Discovery: The Polanyi Society Periodical* 8–25; On the Mont Pèlerin Society see P. Mirowski and D. Plehwe (eds.), *The Road from Mont Pèlerin. The Making of the Neoliberal Thought Collective* (Harvard University Press, 2009).

[298] J. Whyte, 'The invisible hand of Friedrich Hayek: Submission and spontaneous order' (2019) 47(2) *Political Theory* 156–84 at 160.

[299] Ibid., 161.

[300] Foucault, *The Birth of Biopolitics: Lectures at the Collège de France 1978–1979*, p. 173.

[301] Polanyi, 'The manageability of social tasks', p. 185; this is cited in M. Foucault, *The Birth of Biopolitics: Lectures at the Collège de France 1978–1979* (2008) p. 183 (fn 34).

ordering and mutual adjustment that occurs *within* a context that is already bounded and constituted by a system of predefined rules.[302] The analysis in this book therefore highlights the need to consider the 'background' conditions that constitute ostensible 'spontaneous ordering', especially the ways in which the definition and allocation of proprietary rights and the specificities of contractual terms structure the terrain in ways that compel competitive market interactions that further generate inequalities.

Finally, this analysis adds important nuances to descriptions of polycentric governance as systems in which 'authority is dispersed'.[303] Although polycentric governance is constituted by a multiplicity of actors, levels, institutions, decision-making nodes and potentially even legal pluralism, attention to the 'background' conditions of polycentric governance suggests a more singular basis of authorisation. This conceptual apparatus instead highlights the *simultaneous* consolidation of forms of global authority *alongside* the devolution, decentralisation and pluralisation of governance, as the means by which such authority is exercised. Therefore, even as the authority to shape and determine REDD+ objectives is amalgamated 'upwards' to the 'global' level, responsibility for REDD+'s enactment and implementation is increasingly devolved 'downwards' to the 'local' level. Nonetheless, the global objectives of REDD+ are made manifest in how international norms and institutional activities 'shape people's everyday lives and their local geographies'[304] to construct local spaces and subjects that are 'attuned with global expectations',[305] and increasingly 'responsibilised' to be accountable for the realisation of global imperatives.[306] Devolution therefore represents not a dismantling of global authority but a reconfiguration of its forms of exercise and implementation, whereby the 'local' can be strategically deployed as the level through which global visions come into being.

---

[302] See Vincent Ostrom's definition of a 'polycentric system' as one 'where many elements are capable of making mutual adjustments for ordering their relationships with one another within a general system of rules where each element acts with independence of other elements' 'Polycentricity (Part 1)'; this is a slight variation from the definition he had previously proposed in V. Ostrom, C. M. Tiebout, and R. Warren, 'The organisation of government in metropolitan areas: A theoretical inquiry' (1961) 55(4) *The American Political Science Review* 831–42.

[303] See for example A. Jordan, D. Huitema, J. Schoenefeld, and J. Forster, 'Governing climate change polycentrically: Setting the scene' in Jordan et al. (eds.), *Governing Climate Change: Polycentricity in Action?* (Cambridge University Press, 2018) pp. 3–26, 11.

[304] L. Eslava, 'Istanbul vignettes: Observing the everyday operation of international law' (2014) 2(1) *London Review of International Law* 3–47 at 6.

[305] L. Eslava, *Local Space, Global Life: The Everyday Operation of International Law and Development* (Cambridge University Press, 2015) p. 10.

[306] For a discussion of 'responsibilisation' as a 'regime in which the singular human capacity for responsibility is deployed to constitute and govern subjects and through which their conduct is organised and measured, remaking and reorientating them for a neoliberal order', see W. Brown, *Undoing the Demos: Neoliberalism's Stealth Revolution* (Zone Books, 2015) pp. 131–4; this is discussed further in Chapter 5.

4 *Authority*

Implementing REDD+ involves not just a 'protracted process in which power is being reorganised', but also the rationalisation of these processes, and the way in which such an 'expansive set of governmental practices' are underpinned by 'a coherent theoretical account of international authority'.[307] While the above discussion of power focused on the means by which authority is exercised, the concept of authority directs attention to the processes by which forms of legal authority are established: that is, the modes of authorisation of law.[308] Thinking with authority brings into view both the fact of legal authority and the institutional means by which it is enacted; but it also shows, given that 'authority always has to be authorized', the means by which international legal authority is given shape, including through practices of creation and representation.[309] In this sense, questions of authority draw attention to that which precedes law, namely, the ability to 'speak in the name of the law'.[310] The idiom of authority thus enlivens possibilities for acknowledging plural forms and sources of authority, including both state and non-state forms of authority, and therefore also conflicts over 'the authority to have authority',[311] and how the instantiation of new forms of political and legal authority can operate to displace 'rival forms of authority'.[312] Moreover, while political theory is often concerned with justifying authority or considering what constitutes legitimate authority, this book's focus on the way in which new forms of global authority are authorised allows for greater agonism about the normative basis of authority, and directs its consideration primarily to questions of *how* new forms of global authority come to be instituted, whether through practices of representation or other technical means.[313]

While authority has tended to be associated with public law and questions of sovereignty, in the context of a globalised world increased attention needs to be paid to how private mechanisms of governance and private arrangements gain standing as (de facto) forms of public authority.[314] In a globalised world, the expansion of markets beyond state borders is organising its own forms of authority.[315] It is therefore critical to interrogate how forms of climate governance that are 'an amalgam of

---

[307] A. Orford, 'On international legal method' (2013) 1(1) *London Review of International Law* 166–97 at 183.

[308] Dorsett and McVeigh, *Jurisdiction*, pp. 32–3.

[309] Ibid., p. 34.

[310] Rush, 'An altered jurisdiction: Corporeal traces of law', 150.

[311] S. Pasternak, *Grounded Authority: The Algonquins of Barriere Lake against the State* (University of Minnesota Press, 2017) p. 2.

[312] Dorsett and McVeigh, *Jurisdiction*, p. 4.

[313] See also Pahuja, 'Laws of encounter: A jurisdictional account of international law', 70.

[314] E. Hartmann and P. F. Kjaer, 'The status of authority in the globalizing economy: Beyond the public/private distinction' (2018) 25(1) *Indiana Journal of Global Legal Studies* 3–11 at 4.

[315] H. M. Watt, 'Private international law's shadow contribution to the question of informal transnational authority' (2018) 25(1) *Indiana Journal of Global Legal Studies* 37–60.

48 *Introduction*

private and public initiatives at multiple scales', of which carbon markets are now globally the most dominant feature, give rise to new forms of global or transnational authority.[316] Scholars have shown how climate governance is increasingly conducted 'by, through, and for the market',[317] and that law and regulations play a key role in co-constituting the carbon economy.[318] Examining this interplay between law and markets, and the complex interactions between the public and private domains, is critical to excavating and understanding contemporary shifts in transnational authority.[319]

Central to these dynamics are the roles played by private legal relations of property and contract that operate to supplement, complement and reorganise forms of public authority. Thinking with authority thus allows for a more nuanced engagement with how appropriation takes place, not only through direct, coercive means but also through the reorganisation of authority over land and resources via the restructuring of property and other legal rules.[320] It also provides a means of interrogating how mechanisms and technologies for expanding forms of appropriation and control do not just operate through the straightforward acquisition of property but are manifested by 'turning things into property' and 'establishing the conditions for the enjoyment of private property and exchange'.[321] It thus offers a lens through which to see how the establishment of new 'fictitious commodities'[322] in carbon, and the transnational carbon markets in which they circulate, is a means of authorising greater international power and control over land and land-use practices in the Global South.

A focus on questions of authority and modes of authorisation thus directs attention to the dynamics that are often grounded in discussions on REDD+: how specific representations of forests and climate change underpin a claim that the problem of deforestation is a matter of global 'common concern', and thus that forests should

---

[316] S. Bernstein, M. Betsill, M. Hoffmann, and M. Paterson, 'A tale of two Copenhagens: Carbon markets and climate governance' (2010) 39(1) *Millennium: Journal of International Studies* 161–73 at 170; see also Bulkeley et al., *Transnational Climate Change Governance*.

[317] Newell and Peterson cited in I. Bailey, A. Gouldson, and P. Newell, 'Ecological modernisation and the governance of carbon: A critical analysis' (2011) 43(3) *Antipode* 682–703 at 697.

[318] See J. Dehm, 'Tricks of perception and perspective: The disappearance of law and politics in carbon markets; Reading Alexandre Kossoy and Phillippe Ambrosi, "State and trends of the carbon market 2010"' (2011) 7 *Macquarie Journal of International and Comparative Environmental Law* 1–18; E. Boyd, M. Boykoff, and P. Newell, 'The "new" carbon economy: What's new?' (2011) 43(3) *Antipode* 601–11; Bernstein et al., 'A tale of two Copenhagens: Carbon markets and climate governance'.

[319] See Watt, 'Private international law's shadow contribution to the question of informal transnational authority'.

[320] Fairhead et al., 'Green grabbing: A new appropriation of nature?'.

[321] M. Craven, 'Colonisation and domination' in B. Fassbender and A. Peters (eds.), *The Oxford Handbook of the History of International Law* (Oxford University Press, 2012) p. 888.

[322] I take this term from K. Polanyi, *The Great Transformation: The Political and Economic Origins of Our Time* (Beacon Press, 2001), although Polanyi used the term 'fictitious commodities' to describe land, labour and money. See also Chapter 3.

D. Understanding REDD+

be understood, valued, managed and governed in accordance with internationally determined objectives. By describing these processes, this analysis draws attention to what is at stake in the work REDD+ does in the world, namely, the consolidation of a 'unitary agglomeration' of authority over forested areas that previously had been, and in many ways still are, subject to a plurality of jurisdictions.[323] In many ways, forests remain critical 'frontiers of land control': they are sites of struggles involving a range of actors, where the 'authorities, sovereignties, and hegemonies of the recent past have been or are currently being challenged by new enclosures, territorializations, and property regimes'.[324] Yet these struggles are too often narrated as an inevitable transition whereby 'development' and 'progress' come to 'wilderness' or 'traditional lands and peoples'.[325] In such accounts the concept of development provides a frame that suppresses and makes invisible rival authorities and law and thus allows their displacement to appear as both necessary and inevitable.[326] Most accounts of REDD+ presuppose the disappearance of plural authorities and the consolidation of a singular global authority; they are predominantly concerned with how global authority over forests can be made 'real' or with ensuring that it is exercised in humanitarian or rights-compliant ways. However, to focus only on questions of REDD+ implementation and the means by which the rights and tenures of forest peoples should be recognised *already presupposes* the authority of the institutions that are called upon to recognise such rights, and by doing so, also actively engages in the actualisation of such authority. As Thomas Sikar and Christian Lund show, the process of recognising rights or property claims 'simultaneously works to imbue the institutions that provide such recognition with the recognition of its authority to do so': it 'works to authorize the authorizers' and in doing so it 'undermine[s] rival claims to the same resources'.[327]

Thinking with authority thus calls for considerable reflexivity in how we, as international legal scholars, describe the world, given that modes of description are not neutral but can have prescriptive future effects – especially descriptions that represent power structures and forms of authority as totalising, impermeable or stable – and obscure from view already marginalised alternatives.[328] It also suggests the need to take responsibility for how legal writing and scholarship may participate in the 'actualisation of one form of authority, and one idea of what is lawful,

---

[323] I take this phrase from P. Goodrich, *The laws of Love: A Brief Historical and Practical Manual* (Springer, 2006) p. 11.

[324] N. L. Peluso and C. Lund, 'New frontiers of land control: Introduction' (2011) 38(4) *The Journal of Peasant Studies* 667–81 at 668.

[325] Ibid.

[326] Pahuja, 'Laws of encounter: a jurisdictional account of international law', 66.

[327] T. Sikor and C. Lund, 'Access and property: A question of power and authority' in T. Sikor and C. Lund (eds.), *The Politics of Possession* (Wiley-Blackwell, 2010) pp. 1–22.

[328] J. Dehm, 'The misery of international law: Confrontations with injustice in the global economy' (2018) 19 *Melbourne Journal of International Law* 763–72 at 767; A. Orford, 'In praise of description' (2012) 25(3) *Leiden Journal of International Law* 609–25.

over another form of authority, and a different idea of what is lawful'.[329] Thus, throughout this book, the concept of authority is used as a means to describe the consolidation of forms of global authority over forests, the modes of representation by which these new forms of global authority are authorised, and the means by which it is actualised and enacted. However, an orientation towards questions of authority also demands methodological reflexivity in how these transformations are described, in order to hold on to other rival forms of authority and alternative ways in which authority could be authorised, actualised and enacted.

E BEYOND REDD+

The conceptual apparatus used to understand REDD+ in this book also provides tools that can enable a more critical interrogation of the field of international environmental law (IEL) to highlight the ways in which this field is both structured by unequal power relations and complicit in their reproduction. Despite the urgency of environmental concerns – in a context where the number of 'planetary boundaries' within which humanity can safely operate have been transgressed, risking potentially catastrophic, non-linear abrupt environmental change[330] – IEL and international environmental lawyers seem unable to produce viable solutions to increasing inequality and environmental destruction.[331] Climate change has been probably the most high-profile environmental issue of the past three decades, and immense work, political commitment and technical skill have gone into reaching political agreements, building institutional capacity and developing regulatory frameworks in response at the international level. Nonetheless, *half of all greenhouse gas emissions currently in the atmosphere were emitted during this period in which climate change has been a key concern of international law.*[332] The most frequent explanations provided for this failure to curb emissions pertain to the lack of political will as well as the challenges around bridging the North–South divide; however, as Usha Natarajan and Kishan Khody have shown, there is a need for structural explanations of why IEL has 'failed to deliver on its promise to stem ecological harm, often serving as a barrier to, rather than a driver of, change'.[333] This requires complicating accounts that treat IEL as a neutral technical problem-solving tool to be applied by experts in instrumental ways. Instead, a critical interrogation of why

[329] Pahuja, 'Laws of encounter: A jurisdictional account of international law', 67.
[330] J. Rockström, W. L. Steffen, K. Noone, Å. Persson, F. S. Chapin III, E. Lambin, T. M. Lenton, M. Scheffer, C. Folke, and H. J. Schellnhuber, 'Planetary boundaries: Exploring the safe operating space for humanity' (2009) 14(2) *Ecology and Society* 32; W. Steffen, K. Richardson, J. Rockström, S. E. Cornell, I. Fetzer, E. M. Bennett, R. Biggs, S. R. Carpenter, W. De Vries, and C. A. De Wit, 'Planetary boundaries: Guiding human development on a changing planet' (2015) 347(6223) *Science* 1259855.
[331] Natarajan and Dehm, 'Where is the environment? Locating nature in international law'.
[332] D. Wallace-Wells, *The Uninhabitable Earth: Life after Warming* (Tim Duggan Books, 2019).
[333] Natarajan and Khody, 'Locating nature', 575.

E. Beyond REDD+

IEL has been unable to deter the 'general thrust of international law ... towards economic expansion at the expense of ecological decline', is needed, as well as of how it operates to 'obfuscate [international law's] disciplinary correlation with environmental harm'.[334] Although IEL continues to be – and presents itself as – relatively powerless within the discipline of international law, such a posture of marginality risks giving international environmental lawyers a pass on their responsibility for the effects of IEL and the work it does in the world,[335] which is especially important at a time when sustainability has arguably become a 'universal ideology, an international standard of legitimacy for sovereign power, [and] a common vernacular for justice'.[336] Therefore, greater interrogation is needed of how IEL has internalised and reflects – as well as occasionally resists – assumptions and ideologies that may be detrimental to its stated objectives of environmental protection, including the hegemony of 'liberal environmentalism',[337] the imperatives of development and economic growth[338] and neoliberal precepts.[339] As IEL increasingly takes on more market-oriented forms, where the imperatives of environmental protection are deployed to justify the greater privatisation and propertisation of nature, it becomes ever more urgent to pose questions about whether and how IEL might indeed be 'part of the problem' – not just because of its failures and limitations, but also more broadly because of its effects in the world, which may perpetuate inequalities.[340]

In particular, this examination of REDD+ offers tools for strengthening scholarship on IEL that is orientated towards the Global South and is inspired by and aligned with the political commitments and sensibility of Third World Approaches to International Law (TWAIL).[341] TWAIL scholarship has developed an important

---

[334] Ibid., 592.

[335] I expand on this argument in Dehm, 'Reflections on Paris', 72.

[336] I take this quote from D. Kennedy, 'The international human rights regime: Still part of the problem?' in R. Dickinson, E. Katselli, C. Murray, and O. W. Pedersen (eds.), *Examining Critical Perspectives on Human Rights* (Cambridge University Press, 2012) pp. 19–34, although, of course, Kennedy was discussing human rights not sustainability.

[337] S. Bernstein, *The Compromise of Liberal Environmentalism* (Columbia University Press, 2001).

[338] For a discussion of how these concepts underpin and structure international law see Pahuja, *Decolonising International Law: Development, Economic Growth and the Politics of Universality*.

[339] D. Ciplet, J. T. Roberts, and M. R. Khan, *Power in a Warming World: The New Global Politics of Climate Change and the Remaking of Environmental Inequality* (MIT Press, 2015).

[340] I take this phrase from D. Kennedy, 'The international human rights movement: Part of the problem?' (2002) 15 *Harvard Human Rights Journal* 101–25.

[341] On TWAIL see M. Mutua, 'What is TWAIL?' (2000) *Proceedings of the Annual Meeting (American Society of International Law)* 31–8; A. Anghie and B. S. Chimni, 'Third World approaches to international law and individual responsibility in internal conflicts' (2003) 2(1) *Chinese Journal of International Law* 77–103; Chimni, 'Third World approaches to international law: A manifesto' 3–27; K. Mickelson, 'Taking stock of TWAIL histories' (2008) 10(4) *International Community Law Review* 355–62; J. T. Gathii, 'TWAIL: A Brief history of it origins, its decentralised network, and a tentative bibliography' (2011) 3(1) *Trade, Law and Development* 26–64; L. Eslava, 'TWAIL Coordinates' *Critical Legal Thinking* 2 April 2019, criticallegalthinking.com/2019/04/02/twail-coordinates.

conceptual apparatus to interrogate the way in which 'liberal' international law remains structured and organised by a colonial 'dynamic of difference' that persists, despite formal decolonisation, and is reinscribed even as the discipline of international law purports to renew itself.[342] While modern international law seeks to represent itself as having broken with and transcended its imperial origins, Antony Anghie has shown how the imperial origins of international law have 'create[d] a set of structures that continually repeat themselves at various stages in the history of international law'.[343] TWAIL interventions seek to 'unpack and deconstruct the colonial legacies of international law, and to engage in efforts to support the decolonisation of the lived realities of the peoples of the Global South and the rupture or radical transformation of the international order which governs their lives'.[344] Environmental problems, and proposed responses to them, are deeply enmeshed in relations of power. As Karin Mickelson writes, 'environmental degradation does not arise in a vacuum' but rather 'has certain benefits associated with it, and it obviously has certain costs' that are unequally distributed such that 'some derive the benefits while others bear the costs'.[345] The exploitation and the desire to control such exploitation of natural resources were central to the colonial encounter.[346] It was also in the context of colonial administration that environmental discourses and management practices emerged.[347] In the aftermath of formal decolonisation, and particularly within debates about a New International Economic Order (NIEO),[348] questions pertaining to natural resources became a key concern for Third World lawyers and scholars.[349] When IEL started consolidating as a field,

---

[342] A. Anghie, *Imperialism, Sovereignty and the Making of International Law.*

[343] Ibid., p. 3.

[344] 'Founding Statement' *Third World Approaches to International Law Reviews (TWAILR)* August 2019, twailr.com/about/founding-statement.

[345] K. Mickelson, 'South, North, international environmental law, international environmental lawyers' (2000) 11 *Yearbook of International Environmental Law* 52–81 at 59.

[346] Ibid., 56.

[347] See R. Grove, *Green Imperialism: Colonial Expansion, Tropical Island Edens and the Origins of Environmentalism, 1600–1860* (Cambridge University Press, 1996); S. Humphreys and Y. Otomo, 'Theorizing international environmental law' in A. Orford, F. Hoffmann, and M. Clark (eds.), *The Oxford Handbook of the Theory of International Law* (Oxford University Press, 2016) pp. 797–819.

[348] See General Assembly Resolution 3202(S-VI), *Programme of Action on the Establishment of a New International Economic Order*, A/RES/S-6/3203 (1 May 1974); General Assembly Resolution 3281(XXIX), *Charter of Economic Rights and Duties of States*, 29th session, Agenda item 48, A/RES/29/3281 (12 December 1974) and for a discussion M. Bedjaoui, *Towards a New International Economic Order* (United Nations Educational, Scientific and Cultural Organization, 1979); N. Gilman, 'The new international economic order: a reintroduction' (2015) 6(1) *Humanity: An International Journal of Human Rights, Humanitarianism, and Development* 1–16.

[349] See U. Natarajan, 'Third World Approaches to International Law (TWAIL) and the environment' in A. Philippopoulos-Mihalopoulos and V. Brookes (eds.), *Research Methods in Environmental Law: A Handbook* (Edward Elgar Publishing, 2017) p. 207; for an overview of

E. Beyond REDD+

there was fear among some countries of the Global South that 'the inequitable economic order [would] be replaced and/or complemented by an inequitable environmental order'.[350] However, with the notable exception of Karin Mickelson's ground-breaking work, which highlighted how North–South tensions and the different perspectives of the Global North and the Global South on environmental issues raise fundamental, conceptual problems for the discipline,[351] there has been limited engagement with environmental issues in TWAIL scholarship from the 1990s until relatively recently.[352] In part, this was arguably because the field of IEL was, since the 1972 UN Conference on the Human Environment, acutely aware of North–South tensions and had focused on adopting international environmental law principles to mediate these tensions.[353] This included the recognition within the field of IEL that development and environmental concerns are inherently intertwined, reflected in the principle of 'sustainable development'[354] as well as operationalising differentiated treatment, pursuant to the principle of 'common but differentiated responsibilities and respective capabilities' that reflects both the greater responsibility of countries of the Global North for environmental degradation and the greater barriers that the countries of the Global South face in implementing environmental measures.[355] Nonetheless, IEL has historically been, and continues to be, 'a site of intense contestation over environmental priorities, over the allocation of responsibility for current and historic environmental harms, and over the relationship between economic development and environmental degradation'.[356] Scholars attentive to the

---

debates on permanent sovereignty over natural resources see N. Schrijver, *Sovereignty over Natural Resources: Balancing Rights and Duties* (Cambridge University Press, 1997).

[350] Gupta, *The Climate Change Convention and Developing Countries: From Conflict to Consensus?* p. 84.

[351] In particular Mickelson, 'South, North, international environmental law, international environmental lawyers'; see also K. Mickelson, 'Seeing the forest, the trees and the people: Coming to terms with developing country perspectives on the proposed global forests convention' in Canadian Council of International Law (ed.), *Global Forests and International Environmental Law* (Kluwer Law, 1996) pp. 239–64; Mickelson, 'Leading towards a level playing field, repaying ecological debt, or making environmental space'; K. Mickelson, 'Beyond a politics of the possible? South–North relations and climate justice'.

[352] See Natarajan, 'Third World Approaches to International Law (TWAIL) and the environment'.

[353] K. Mickelson, 'The Stockholm Conference and the creation of the South–North divide in international environmental law and policy' in S. Alam, S. Atapattu, C. G. Gonzalez, and J. Razzaque (eds.), *International Environmental Law and the Global South* (Cambridge University Press, 2015) pp. 109–29.

[354] Brundtland Commission Report, *Our Common Future World Commission on Environment and Development* (Cambridge University Press, 1987); N. Schrijver, *The Evolution of Sustainable Development in International Law: Inception, Meaning and Status* (Martinus Nijhoff Publishers, 2008).

[355] L. Rajamani, *Differential Treatment in International Environmental Law* (Oxford University Press, 2006); P. Cullet, *Differential Treatment in International Environmental Law* (Ashgate, 2003).

[356] S. Atapattu and C. G. Gonzalez, 'The North–South Divide in international environmental law: Framing the issues' in S. Alam, S. Atapattu, C. G. Gonzalez, and J. Razzaque (eds.),

concerns of countries and peoples of the Global South have highlighted the ongoing need for IEL to bridge this persistent North–South divide and to 'address historical inequities and inadequacies in the international environmental law regime' in order to ensure the effectiveness of IEL.[357] However, even though IEL principles might have initially reflected an agenda of 'redistributive multilateralism', over the past decade in particular this has been strongly resisted by the US and other countries of the Global North, with the effect that IEL and the global climate regime in particular have become a 'new area of distributive conflict between developed and developing countries'.[358]

In this regard, there is a need to understand not only the ways in which (neo)-colonial relations are reflected in IEL but also how IEL might be reproducing patterns whereby 'international law continuously disempowers the non-European world, even while sanctioning intervention within in'.[359] The discussion of REDD+ presented in this book suggests three key interlinked ways through which IEL operates to reproduce (neo)colonial dynamics. First, echoing the many mechanisms that international law has developed to prevent claims for colonial reparations,[360] IEL and climate law has adopted a forward-looking posture that operates to suppress and exclude the articulation of claims relating to historical environmental harms. This dynamic has arguably been the most overt within the climate regime, where responsibility for historical or cumulative emissions has persistently been foreclosed even though 'historical injustice saturates the problem of climate change'.[361] Second, IEL tends to frame environmental problems as a global 'common concern'. This focus on 'commonality' ignores the way in which both the causes and the effects of environmental harms reflect and are entangled in deeply stratified differentials of power, wealth and access to resources, along North–South lines as well as those of class, race and gender. Moreover, this frame also operates to authorise new forms of international authority to act in the name of this 'common concern', which however, in practice, impacts on countries and peoples of the Global North and Global South differently. Finally, environmental concern is mobilised to justify the further privatisation, propertisation and financialisation of nature, thus making nature – no longer just reductively characterised as a 'resource' but now also configured as the provider of 'ecosystem services'[362] – further enmeshed within, and increasingly subject to, globalised capitalist markets.

International Environmental Law and the Global South (Cambridge University Press, 2015) pp. 1–20, 2.

[357] Ibid., pp. 2, 5.

[358] McGee and Steffek, 'The Copenhagen turn in global climate governance', 51.

[359] Anghie, *Imperialism, Sovereignty and the Making of International Law* p. 312.

[360] Ibid., p. 2; see also A. Anghie, '"The heart of my home": Colonialism, environmental damage, and the Nauru case' (1993) 34(2) *Harvard International Law Journal* 445–506.

[361] Humphreys, 'Climate justice: The claim of the past', 134.

[362] Sullivan, 'Green capitalism, and the cultural poverty of constructing nature as service-provider'; V. Shiva, 'Resources' in W. Sachs (ed.), *The Development Dictionary: A Guide to Knowledge as Power* (Zed Books, 2010) pp. 228–42.

E. Beyond REDD+

This book also gestures towards, but does not posit, a rival vision of lawful ecological interrelations that are premised on a commitment to plurality and the coexistence of plural worlds and laws. Responses to the climate crisis have tended to privilege the scale of the global, or the planetary, and the adoption of an external epistemic vantage point that is at once totalising and withdrawn.[363] However, a rich body of literature drawing on political ecology has criticised both the necessity and the desirability of such globalist thinking in relation to ecological problems; it has warned how an imaginary of 'one world' globalism risks inflicting violence when imposed upon a world that is deeply stratified in relation to power and access to resources, along lines of class, race and gender, and where the problem of climate change – including its causes and effects – is deeply entangled in these differentials.[364] Such scholars have highlighted the multiple worlds that we 'share, co-constitute, create, destroy and inhabit with countless other life forms and beings'[365] and proposed working towards a 'pluriverse' or a 'world of many worlds'.[366] Although it can be seductive to posit that global environmental challenges are a 'common concern', especially in a context where everyone, albeit differentially and unequally, will be affected by environmental change, such pronouncements evade important political questions about the types of commonality that are envisioned, the ways in which commonality is patterned, the modes of being in common that are enacted, what modes of conduct are authorised and what responsibilities are compelled by this.[367] Moreover, to posit as fact that such a 'common concern' exists repeats the danger of globalist thinking, that is of 'unifying too quickly what first needs to be composed'.[368] It is this difficult work of composition, the unstable and difficult labour of building commonalities through grounded material practices of solidarity, that now demands our attention. Questions about how to create such a 'common

---

[363] Chakrabarty, 'Planetary crises and the difficulty of being modern', 265.

[364] W. Sachs, 'One World' in W. Sachs (ed.), *The Development Dictionary: A Guide to Knowledge As Power* (Zed Books, 2010) pp. 111–26; W. Sachs (ed.), *Global Ecology: A New Arena of Political Conflict* (Zed Books Ltd., 1993); The Ecologist, *Whose Common Future? Reclaiming the Commons* (Earthscan, 1993); S. B. Banerjee, 'Who sustains whose development? Sustainable development and the reinvention of nature' (2003) 24(1) *Organisation Studies* 143–80; A. Escobar, 'Beyond the third world: Imperial globality, global coloniality and anti-globalisation social movements' (2004) 25(1) *Third World Quarterly* 207–30; V. Argyrou, *The Logic of Environmentalism: Anthropology, Ecology and Postcoloniality* (Berghahn Books, 2005).

[365] A. Burke, S. Fishel, A. Mitchell, S. Dalby, and D. J. Levine, 'Planet politics: A manifesto from the end of IR' (2016) 44(3) *Millennium: Journal of International Studies* 499–523 at 518.

[366] F. Demaria and A. Kothari, 'The post-development dictionary agenda: Paths to the pluriverse' (2017) 38(12) *Third World Quarterly* 2588–99; M. de la Cadena and M. Blaser, *A World of Many Worlds* (Duke University Press, 2018).

[367] I develop this argument further in Dehm, 'Carbon colonialism or climate justice: Interrogating the international climate regime from a TWAIL perspective'.

[368] B. Latour, 'Fourth lecture: The Anthropocene and the destruction of (the image of) the globe' in *Facing Gaia: Eight Lectures on the New Climatic Regime* (John Wiley & Sons, 2017) p. 138.

56 _Introduction_

F OUTLINE OF THE BOOK

The first substantive chapter, Chapter 1, entitled 'Background to REDD+', examines the background and history of REDD+ on several registers. The chapter explores REDD+ as a _legal agreement,_ providing an account of the gradual and progressive development of norms under the institutional umbrella of the UNFCCC; as a _concept or idea_ that forest protection can be 'incentivised' through the increased financial valuation of nature and through payment for environmental services (PES) schemes; as a _series of practices,_ both experimental and preparatory, designed to actualise REDD+ projects in material ways, including via 'demonstration projects' and REDD+-readiness programmes; and finally as a project of _social transformation_ of the lives of people living in and around forested areas. This chapter argues that REDD+ is both a _vision_ of market-orientated environmental governance and the _processes and practices_ involved in creating and materialising this vision in the world.

Chapter 2 takes up the question of authority and is concerned with how a claim to global authority over land and resources in the Global South has been invoked and the shape or form this authority has been given. It shows how the designation of both climate change and biodiversity loss as matters of 'common concern' has operated to authorise a form of global jurisdiction over activities and processes that contribute to these very problems within nation-states. The chapter examines how this claim to global authority is based on both a specific representation of the problems of climate change and global deforestation and how these practices of representation have given a distinctive shape to the forms of global authority they authorise. The chapter pays attention to how climate change has come to be understood as an 'object' or 'problem' for law, and the specificity of this framing and its effects. Turning to the problem of deforestation, it shows how a focus on the functions of forests, especially their function as a carbon sink, makes it possible for deforestation to be understood as a matter of global, rather than local or national, concern.

The question of how this claim to global authority is actualised and enlivened in practice is taken up by Chapter 3. It examines how the legal forms of property and contract are central to the actualisation of new forms of global authority through REDD+. This chapter examines REDD+ through a consideration of the forms of transnational contracting used to secure future-orientated promises to ensure additional carbon sequestration in forested land in the Global South, paying attention to the power dynamics involved in the drafting of such contracts and the construction of their terms. Subsequently, it examines REDD+ through the idiom of property, interrogating the carbon commodity as a strange quasi-property right in 'emission

F. Outline of the Book

reductions', defined in international and domestic laws. The discussion in this chapter analyses the complex interactions between public and private international law that give shape to REDD+: the public international environmental law framework that defines and regulates carbon rights and the private transnational contracting that regulates specific projects. In doing so, it also highlights the key bridging or mediating role played by the World Bank's carbon funds that straddle the domains of the 'public' and 'private' by developing template emission reduction purchase agreements and experimenting with establishing the private law arrangements that enable the marketisation of climate governance.

Chapter 4 provides a critical examination of a key effect of REDD+: namely, the resignification of how questions of responsibility in the international climate regime are understood, alongside the foregrounding of the 'differentiated capacity' of developing countries to take climate mitigation action. This chapter explores the history of the controversial principle CBDR-RC within the climate regime and the contested and ambiguous rationale for differentiation. It shows how the transnational legal process of REDD+ norm production and implementation has consolidated a divergent understanding and application of CBDR-RC, one that further precludes (already marginalised) claims arising from the historical responsibilities of developed countries for the causes of climate change; and it shows how there has been a pronounced shift away from a vision that emphasises the relationality and respective share of global emissions from the Global North and the Global South and the distributive justice questions this raises. Finally, the chapter reveals how the foregrounding of 'differentiated capacity' has authorised 'capacity-building' within countries of the Global South, which has enabled further regulatory interventions to promote the regulatory infrastructure on which carbon markets depend.

Chapter 5 considers the question of scale and interrogates the multi-layered system of governance that REDD+ envisions. This chapter is focused on the property law dimension of vertical coordination across scales, describing and analysing how the disaggregation of property rights also operates as a key legal technology for globalising authority over forested land and transferring authority to international actors and away from local communities. It describes the definition and clarification of carbon right rights, but situates these technical debates about carbon rights in REDD+ alongside broader trends regarding property rights in natural resource governance, common property regimes (CPRs) and community resource management, to critically interrogate power relations within the emerging frameworks for the allocation of layered or nested rights in the forest carbon economy.

The final substantive chapter, Chapter 6, turns to examine REDD+ implementation 'on the ground' and the governance of REDD+ at the local level. It interrogates three of the strategies that have been central to debates on social safeguards: benefit sharing; tenure reform; and rights to consultation and free, prior and informed consent (FPIC). It shows that all these strategies are caught between imperatives of rights realisation 'from below' and greater responsibilisation 'from above'. It thus suggests that the impacts of such measures might not necessarily be emancipatory for forest people, but rather that such strategies may operate to facilitate the greater disciplinary inclusion of forest peoples in the so-called 'green economy'.

The conclusion of the book, Chapter 7, entitled 'Climate Justice and Planetary Co-habitation', returns to the underlying concerns animating this book – namely, the responsibilities and obligations that are entailed within a just co-habitation of a shared planet. It reiterates the ways in which REDD+ forecloses possibilities for climate justice, both by abrogating questions of historical responsibility and by legitimating ongoing fossil fuel extraction. In concluding, it suggests that there are other ways that the problem of climate change and deforestation could be approached and draws on statements by people living in or around forested areas who are resisting REDD+ to demonstrate some of these possible alternatives.

1

Background to REDD+

A INTRODUCTION

This chapter provides a background to and analysis of REDD+, examining it from multiple angles and across several different registers. The first section traces the history of REDD+ as a *legal agreement* that provides a framework through which activities addressing deforestation and forest degradation can be measured, reported and verified as 'result-based actions' and made legible in the rubric of one tonne of carbon dioxide equivalent ($1tCO_2e$). It describes the gradual and progressive development of norms under the institutional umbrella of the United Nations Framework Convention on Climate Change (UNFCCC), through a series of successive Conferences of the Parties (COPs), subsidiary bodies and expert meetings. The second section examines REDD+ as constituted through experimental practices and preparatory and market-construction activities. It examines 'demonstration activities' that seek to materialise REDD+ 'on the ground' as part of a process of 'learning-by-doing'; and it looks at the multilateral and bilateral 'REDD+-readiness' processes directed towards establishing the necessary background regulatory conditions to operationalise REDD+ in host nation-states. The third section analyses REDD+ as a concept or idea, one that arises from the field of environmental economics, namely, that forest protection can be 'incentivised' through the financial valuation of nature and through payment for environmental services (PES) schemes, including potentially the inclusion of forests in international carbon markets. It provides a brief history and lineage of these ideas about the economic valuation of nature. The fourth section provides an overview of the activities that are promoted through REDD+ and situates both conservation and sustainable forest management (SFM) in the context of their colonial origins. Finally, the fifth section outlines how, in response to concerns that REDD+ might impact the lives of peoples living in and around forested areas, the scope of REDD+ programmes and projects has extended beyond the initial environmental focus, so that REDD+ has now also become a

60 *Background to REDD+*

social project concerned with 'co-benefits' such as poverty alleviation, tenure reform and rights for forest peoples. It critically evaluates those discourses pertaining to the social impacts of REDD+ and shows how, through safeguards and other mechanisms, the sphere of REDD+ intervention has expanded to encompass developmental agendas that actively reshape the lives and livelihoods of forest peoples.

B REDD+ AS A PART OF THE UNFCCC FRAMEWORK

This section provides a background to the UNFCCC negotiations relevant to REDD+, including its endorsement in the Bali Action Plan (2007), the initial elaboration of a framework in the Cancun Agreements (2011), the Warsaw Framework for REDD+ (2013) and the conclusion of REDD+ agenda items in 2015.[1] The reference to REDD+ in Article 5.2 of the 2015 Paris Agreement confirmed that REDD+ will continue to be a significant element of the post-2020 climate regime,[2] however the Paris Agreement also left key issues unresolved, especially the controversial questions regarding the financing for REDD+.[3] Although negotiators were able to agree on most elements of the 'Paris Rule Book' at COP24 (2018), no decision was reached on guidelines for Article 5 or Article 6, pertaining to international flexibility mechanisms.[4] While a number of different proposals exist about how REDD+ could be included within the Article 6 carbon trading mechanisms, (at the time of writing) no formal decision had yet been reached on these questions.[5]

The institutional narrative of REDD+ generally begins with the decision to exclude 'avoided deforestation' from the Kyoto Protocol's Clean Development Mechanism (CDM).[6] When specific rules for the CDM were developed as part

---

[1] For an overview, see UNFCCC, *Key Decisions Relevant for Reducing Emissions from Deforestation and Forest Degradation in Developing Countries (REDD+)*, June 2014, unfccc .int/files/land_use_and_climate_change/redd/application/pdf/compilation_redd_decision_ booklet_v1.1.pdf.

[2] *Paris Agreement*, opened for signature on 22 April 2016, UNTS XXVII.7.d (entered into force 4 November 2016), Article 5.

[3] See A. G. M. La Viña and A. de Leon, 'Conserving and enhancing sinks and reservoirs of greenhouse gases, including forests (Article 5)' in D. Klein, M. P. Carazo, M. Doelle, J. Bulmer, and A. Higham (eds.), *The Paris Agreement on Climate Change: Analysis and Commentary* (Oxford University Press, 2017) pp. 166–77.

[4] See Decision 8/CMA.1 'Matters relating to Article 6 of the Paris Agreement and paragraphs 36–40 of decision 1/CP.21', FCCC/PA/CMA/2018/3/Add.1 (19 March 2019); for a summary of the 'Paris Rule Book' see M. Yang, 'COP 24 Round-Up Part 1: The Paris Rulebook' *Inside Energy & Environment*, 18 December 2018, www.insideenergyandenvironment.com/2018/12/cop-24-round-up-partone-the-paris-rulebook/; S. Evans and J. Timperley, 'COP24: key outcomes agreed at the UN climate talks in Katowice' *Carbon Brief*, 16 December 2018, www.carbonbrief.org/cop24-key outcomesagreed-at-the-un-climate-talks-in-katowice; see also H. van Asselt, K. Kulovesi, and M. Mehling, 'Editorial · negotiating the Paris Rulebook: introduction to the special issue' (2018) 12(3) *Carbon & Climate Law Review* and the articles in the special issue it introduces.

[5] For a more detailed discussion see Chapter 3.

[6] Decision 17/CP.7 'Modalities and procedures for a Clean Development Mechanism, as defined in Article 12 of the Kyoto Protocol', FCCC/CP/2001/13/Add.2 (21 January 2002), para 7(a) in

B. REDD+ As a Part of the UNFCCC Framework

of the Marrakech Accords in 2001, offsets from land use, land-use change and forestry (LULUCF) were limited to afforestation and reforestation (A/R) projects – albeit after heated debate.[7] At the time, proposals to include 'avoided deforestation' as an offset scheme were defeated due to concerns about methodological complexity and environmental integrity.[8] These methodological challenges have remained a major concern as REDD+ has developed. They include how to ensure the *permanence* of 'saved' or 'additional' forest carbon sequestration;[9] how to ensure carbon savings are *additional* to what would have otherwise happened;[10] how to establish credible *baselines* or reference levels against which to measure such a change;[11] and how to avoid *leakage*, that is, how to pevent deforestation shifting to other locations.[12] As the framework for REDD+ developed, it built on – but also significantly departed from – earlier efforts to include afforestation and reforestation (A/R) projects under the CDM. Afforestation and reforestation projects in the CDM have remained relatively marginal, as A/R accounts for only approximately 0.8 per cent of CDM projects and approximately 1 per cent of certified emission reductions (CERs) credits issued;[13] but REDD+ is envisioned as operating at a much larger scale. In addition, REDD+ differs from A/R projects in several significant ways. Firstly, while A/R credits accrue from *positive* actions, i.e. planting trees, REDD+ credits can also accrue from *preventing* certain actions, i.e. preventing deforestation and forest degradation that would otherwise take place. Secondly, the temporary credits issued from A/R projects are not strictly fungible with other carbon credits; in

---

2001. This is then confirmed in Decision 16/CMP.1 'Land use, land-use change and forestry', FCCC/KP/CMP/2005/8/Add.3 (30 March 2006), Annex, para 13 in 2005. 'Afforestation' and 'reforestation' are defined in 16/CMP.1, Annex, para 1.

[7] See Decision 17/CP.7, para 7(a) in 2001. This is then confirmed in Decision 16/CMP.1, Annex, para 13.

[8] For an overview of these debates, see P. Fearnside, 'Environmentalists split over Kyoto and Amazon deforestation' (2001) 28(4) *Environmental Conservation* 295–9.

[9] M. Dutschke and A. Angelsen, 'How do we ensure permanence and assign liability?' in A. Angelsen (ed.), *Moving Ahead with REDD: Issues, Options and Implications* (Center for International Forestry Research, 2008).

[10] E. Corbera, M. Estrada, and K. Brown, 'Reducing greenhouse gas emissions from deforestation and forest degradation in developing countries: Revisiting the assumptions' (2010) 100 *Climatic Change* 355–88.

[11] A. Angelsen, D. Boucher, S. Brown, V. Merckx, C. Streck, and D. Zarin, *Guidelines for REDD + Reference Levels: Principles and Recommendations* (Meridian Institute, 2011).

[12] The issue of leakage has now been somewhat better addressed due to the universal nature of the Paris Agreement in which all countries have taken on (some form of) climate mitigation or adaptation commitments. In contrast under the Kyoto Protocol and the Clean Development Mechanism the issue of leakage arose much more acutely, as developing countries had no mitigation commitments.

[13] Statistics from 2012, 'CDM projects by type', www.cdmpipeline.org/cdm-projects-type.htm (accessed 12 August 2015). See also S. Thomas, P. Dargusch, S. Harrison, and J. Herbohn, 'Why are there so few afforestation and reforestation Clean Development Mechanism projects?' (2010) 27 *Land Use Policy* 880–7.

contrast, many envision there would be exchangeability between REDD+ and other credits.[14] Thirdly, A/R projects are confined to the perimeters of the project itself, while the scale of REDD+ activities is often at the national or sub-national level. That is, whereas CDM A/R projects are discrete interventions, REDD+ requires a much more complex set of enabling regulatory conditions to be in place within the host nation-state. Sectoral carbon-trading schemes such as REDD+ may therefore facilitate much greater international interventions in REDD+ host states' regulatory environments as part of the process of REDD+-readiness. The possibility that REDD+ may 'incentivise' broader governance reforms in the Global South has been celebrated by some REDD+ proponents and linked to anti-corruption and rule-of-law initiatives.[15] As such, REDD+ raises broader questions of sovereignty and regulatory autonomy more acutely than the more discrete A/R CDM projects. For these reasons, and others, the inclusion of 'avoided deforestation' and 'forest degradation' in the climate regime continues to be controversial.[16]

The discussion paper 'Deforestation and the Kyoto Protocol', by Santilli et al.,[17] released at COP9 (2003) and published in 2005, which proposed 'compensated reductions', is often considered the 'starting point for the REDD proposal'.[18] 'Avoided deforestation' as a climate mitigation strategy was again raised in 2005 by Costa Rica and Papua New Guinea at the Montreal COP. They sought to highlight the 'climatic importance of deforestation' and asked 'how the UNFCCC can be used to draw developing countries toward emission reductions by functioning as a

---

[14] Market players have asserted that this lack of fungibility has operated to 'discourage carbon investors from acquiring forest credits', thereby leading to lack of demand for such credits, low prices, negative effects on project viability and limited support from carbon finance for forestry projects. Decisions on whether credits will be generated from REDD+ 'result-based actions' or how they will be integrated into global markets are not final, but subject to pressure for greater fungibility than under Kyoto; see *The BioCarbon Fund Experience: Insights from Afforestation/ Reforestation Clean Development Mechanism Projects* (The World Bank, 2012) siteresources .worldbank.org/INTCARBONFINANCE/Resources/57853-A_BioCarbon_LOW-RES.pdf, 3.1–3.6. See also A. Karsenty, 'The architecture of proposed REDD schemes after Bali: Facing critical choices' (2008) 10(3) *International Forestry Review* 443.

[15] P. Venning, '"REDD" at the convergence of the environment and development debates – international incentives for national action on avoided deforestation' (2010) 6(1) *Law, Environment and Development Journal* 82–101.

[16] For example, see C. Parker, A. Mitchell, M. Trivedi, and N. Mardas, *The Little REDD+ Book: An Updated Guide to Governmental Proposals for Reducing Emissions from Deforestation and Degradation* (Global Canopy Programme, 2009) for a useful overview of country positions (from 2009). See also UNFCCC Secretariat, *Financing Options for the Full Implementation of Results-Based Actions Relating to the Activities Referred to in Decision 1/CP.16, paragraph 70, Including Related Modalities and Procedures: Technical Paper*, FCCC/TP/2012/3 (26 July 2012), for 2012 positions.

[17] M. Santilli, P. Moutinho, S. Schwartzman, D. Nepstad, L. Curran, and C. Nobre, 'Tropical deforestation and the Kyoto Protocol' (2005) 71(3) *Climatic Change* 267–76.

[18] A. Karsenty, A. Vogel, and F. Castell, '"Carbon rights", REDD+ and payments for environmental services' (2014) 35 *Environmental Science & Policy* 20–29 at 21.

B. REDD+ As a Part of the UNFCCC Framework

mechanism to finance environmental sustainability'.[19] Their submission was 'noted' by the COP, and Parties and accredited observers were invited to submit their views on Reducing Emission from Deforestation (RED, as it was then called).[20] A subsidiary body to the Convention – the Subsidiary Body for Scientific and Technological Advice (SBSTA)[21] – was asked to consider this issue and report on it by COP13 in Bali in 2007. Numerous submissions by individual Parties and non-governmental organisations) (NGOs) were received,[22] two expert meetings held[23] and further submissions sought.[24]

In 2007, the Bali Action Plan agreed to at COP13 called for consideration of '[p]olicy approaches and positive incentives on issues relating to reducing emissions from deforestation and forest degradation in developing countries; and the role of conservation, sustainable management of forests and enhancement of forest carbon stocks in developing countries' as part of 'enhanced national/international action on mitigation of climate change'.[25] By then the actions included within this initiative had expanded beyond just deforestation and forest degradation to also encompass the role of conservation, sustainable management of forests and enhancement of forest carbon sinks. At Bali, the SBSTA, along with the Ad Hoc Working Group on Long-Term Cooperative Action (AWG-LCA), were tasked with developing norms and methodologies for such approaches.

---

[19] Costa Rica and Papua New Guinea, *Reducing Emissions from Deforestation in Developing Countries: Approaches to Stimulate Action: Submission from Parties* FCCC/CP/2005/MISC.1 (11 November 2005).

[20] UNFCCC, *Reducing Emissions from Deforestation in Developing Countries: Approaches to Stimulate Action: Draft Conclusions Proposed by the President* FCCC/CP/2005/L.2 (6 December 2005).

[21] SBSTA is established by Article 9 of the UNFCCC to provide the COP and other subsidiary bodies, as appropriate 'timely information and advice on scientific and technological matters relating to the Convention'.

[22] UNFCCC, *Issues Relating to Reducing Emissions from Deforestation in Developing Countries and Recommendations on Any Further Process: Submissions from Parties* FCCC/SBSTA/2006/ MISC.5 (11 April 2006) and Add.2 (10 May 2006).

[23] A workshop was held by SBSTA in Rome, Italy, 30 August–1 September 2006, see UNFCCC, *Report on a Workshop on Reducing Emissions from Deforestation in Developing Counties: Note by the Secretariat* FCCC/SBSTA/2006/10 (11 October 2006). A second workshop was held in Cairns, Australia, from 7–9 March 2007, see UNFCCC, *Report on the Second Workshop on Reducing Emissions from Deforestation in Developing Countries: Note by the Secretariat* FCCC/SBSTA/2007/3 (17 April 2007).

[24] UNFCCC, *Views on the Range of Topics and Other Relevant Information Relating to Reducing Emissions from Deforestation in Developing Countries: Submissions from Parties*, FCCC/ SBSTA/2007/MISC.2 (2 March 2007) and Add.1 (3 April 2007), as well as submissions from intergovernmental organisations FCCC/SBSTA/2007/MISC.3 (2 March 2007) and accredited observer groups, unfccc.int/parties_observers/ngo/submissions/items/3689.php.

[25] Decision 1/CP.13 'Bali Action Plan', FCCC/CP/2007/6/Add.1 (14 March 2008) ('Bali Action Plan'), para 1(b)(iii), see also Decision 2/CP.13 'Reducing emissions from deforestation in developing countries: approaches to stimulate action', FCCC/CP/2007/6/Add.1 (14 March 2008).

Background to REDD+

At Copenhagen (COP15, 2009), REDD+ received high-level political endorsement. The highly controversial Copenhagen Accord 'noted' by COP15[26] recognised

> the crucial role of reducing emission from deforestation and forest degradation and the need to enhance removals of greenhouse gas emission by forests and agree[d] on the need to provide positive incentives to such actions through the immediate establishment of a mechanism including REDD-plus, to enable the mobilization of financial resources from developed countries.[27]

The Copenhagen Accord further noted that REDD+, as a form of mitigation action, would require 'scaled up, new and additional, predictable and adequate funding' from developed to developing countries,[28] including through the newly established Green Carbon Fund.[29] A separate decision from COP15 provided greater methodological guidance for REDD+.[30] It crucially recognised the 'need for full and effective engagement of indigenous peoples and local communities'[31] and encouraged the development of guidance for their effective engagement.[32]

REDD+ was gaining momentum. The Cancun Agreements (COP16, 2010) established an initial framework for REDD+, which subsequent COP decisions have expanded upon.[33] Specifically, the Cancun Agreements encourage developing country Parties to contribute to mitigation actions in the forest sector by undertaking the following activities:

(a) reducing emissions from deforestation;
(b) reducing emissions from forest degradation;
(c) conservation of forest carbon stocks;
(d) sustainable management of forests and
(e) enhancement of forest carbon sinks.[34]

---

[26] The Copenhagen Accord was a last-minute agreement reached by a small group of countries behind closed doors. It was opposed by several countries, and as consensus on the Accord could not be reached, it was simply 'noted' by the COP in Decision 2/CP.15 'Copenhagen Accord' FCCC/CP/2009/11/Add.1 (30 March 2010) ('Copenhagen Accord').

[27] Copenhagen Accord, para 6.

[28] Copenhagen Accord, para 8.

[29] The Copenhagen Accord, para 10, also decided that the 'Copenhagen Green Climate Fund shall be established as an operating entity of the financial mechanism of the Convention to support projects, programme, policies and other activities in developing countries related to mitigation including REDD-plus, adaptation, capacity-building, technology development and transfer.'

[30] Decision 4/CP.15 'Methodological guidance for activities relating to reducing emissions from deforestation and forest degradation and the role of conservation, sustainable management of forests and enhancement of forest carbon stocks in developing countries', FCCC/CP/2009/11/Add.1 (30 March 2010).

[31] Decision 4/CP.15, preamble.

[32] Decision 4/CP.15, para 3.

[33] Decision 1/CP.16 'The Cancun Agreements: Outcome of the work of the Ad Hoc Working Group on the Kyoto Protocol', FCCC/CP/2010/7/Add.1 (15 March 2011) ('Cancun Agreements'), para 68–79.

[34] Decision 1/CP.16, para 70(a)–(e).

B. REDD+ As a Part of the UNFCCC Framework 65

The Appendix to the Cancun Agreements stipulates that such activities should contribute to Party commitments and the overall objective of the Convention, be consistent with 'objectives of environmental integrity', promote the sustainable management of forests and recognise the 'multiple functions of forests and other eco-systems', and that implementation should be in 'the context of sustainable development' and poverty eradication.[35] It also affirms the need to 'respect sovereignty' and for REDD+ to be 'country-driven', specifying that REDD+ activities should be undertaken in accordance with host-country national objectives, circumstances, capabilities and development priorities.[36] The role of the international community as envisioned in the Cancun Agreements is to support these activities through the provision of 'adequate and predictable' financial and technological support and capacity building.[37]

The most controversial question in REDD+ negotiations has been how avoided deforestation activities would be financed. The debate has essentially revolved around two models: a fund-based model, whereby developed countries financially support REDD+ activities in the Global South (for example, through aid or overseas development assistance), and a market-based model, where finance comes from global carbon markets. A market model also implies that carbon credits produced from REDD+ activities can be used towards the compliance obligations of purchasing countries.[38] The inclusion of forests in global carbon markets has been strongly opposed by Bolivia,[39] as well as many environmental justice-focused NGOs and social movements.[40] These questions have (at the time of writing) still not been conclusively resolved.

The Cancun Agreements establish a three-phased approach towards 'result-based actions'[41] and call for international public and private funds to support this transition:[42]

- The first phrase is the 'the development of national strategies or action plans, polices and measures and capacity building'.[43]
- The second phrase involves the 'implementation of national policies and measures and national strategies or action plans' as well as 'further

---

[35] Decision 1/CP.16, Appendix, para 1(a)–(k).
[36] Decision 1/CP.16, Appendix, para 1(c), (e)–(h).
[37] Decision 1/CP.16, para 69 and Annex, para 1.
[38] See UNFCCC Secretariat, *Financing Options for the Full Implementation of Results-Based Actions Relating to the Activities Referred to in Decision 1/CP.16, paragraph 70, Including Related Modalities and Procedures: Technical Paper*, FCCC/TP/2012/3 (26 July 2012).
[39] UNFCCC, *Submission by the Plurinational State of Bolivia to the Ad Hoc Working Group on Long Term Co-operative Action* FCCC/AWGLCA/2010/MISC.2 (30 April 2010).
[40] See 'The Cochabamba Protocol: People's Agreement on Climate Change and the Rights of Mother Earth' (People's Agreement from the World People's Conference on Climate Change in Bolivia, 2010).
[41] Decision 1/CP.16, para 73.
[42] Decision 1/CP.16, para 76.
[43] Decision 1/CP.16, para 73.

66   *Background to REDD+*

capacity-building, technology development and transfer and result-based demonstration activities'.[44]

- The final phrase is the evolution 'into results-based actions that should be fully measured, reported and verified'.[45]

This three-phrase approach echoes *The Eliasch Review*, an influential report commissioned by the UK government that aimed to provide a comprehensive analysis of international financing to reduce forest loss and associated impacts on climate change, which was released in 2008.[46] *The Eliasch Review* also envisioned a staged transition, made up of short, medium and long-term goals, towards a global cap and trade system that includes forests. Although the Cancun Agreements are silent on how eventual 'result-based actions' will be financed, *The Eliasch Review* was explicit that the long-term goal is 'the full inclusion [of forests] in a global carbon market'.[47] Both *The Eliasch Review* and the Cancun Agreements stress the need for public interventions and public funds to enable such a transition and to promote the sort of 'smooth transition path [that] is also important for building confidence in the system'.[48] This understanding of REDD+ as a staged or transitional program that encompasses not just 'result-based actions' but a three-phased 'progression' towards 'result-based actions', where each stage requires 'adequate and predictable' support from developed country Parties, was later confirmed in the 2013 Warsaw Framework.[49] The Warsaw Framework urges developed countries to support these stages of implementation 'through bilateral and multilateral channels' and to ensure the co-ordination of such readiness activities.[50] It further 'encourages' those entities financing such activities, including the Green Climate Fund, to 'collectively channel' resources in a 'fair and balanced manner' with the objective of increasing the number of countries that will be in a position to receive payment for result-based actions.[51]

Thus, even among those who envision of REDD+ as an eventual market-based scheme, there has been a strong focus on the need for initial *public* finance to establish the conditions and regulatory infrastructure for such markets. As such, REDD+ represents not simply a *vision* of the commodification, marketisation and financialisaton of forest mitigation actions, but also the *process* of constituting these markets and constructing the necessary regulatory apparatus through REDD+-readiness. Such an understanding of REDD+ unsettles the simple dichotomies that at times inform

---

[44] Decision 1/CP.16, para 73.
[45] Decision 1/CP.16, para 73.
[46] J. Eliasch, *Climate Change: Financing Global Forests: The Eliasch Review* (Earthscan, 2008).
[47] Ibid., pp. 126–7.
[48] Ibid., pp. 121–2.
[49] Decision 9/CP.19, 'Work programme on result-based finance to progress the full implementation of the activities referred to in Decision 1/CP.16, paragraph 70', FCCC/CP/2013/10/Add.1 (31 January 2014), para 2.
[50] Decision 1/CP.16, para 76 and 78.
[51] Decision 9/CP.19, para 5.

B. REDD+ As a Part of the UNFCCC Framework

debates on financing between public and private funding. It highlights the critical role played by public financing, from bilateral and multilateral sources, including overseas development assistance (ODA), in establishing the enabling conditions of a privatised market regime through the process of REDD+-readiness. As will be discussed in greater detail below, at stake in these processes of REDD+-readiness is not so much the retreat of the state in favour of the market, but rather a re-orientation of the host-state's function and purposes in market-constituting terms, a reorientation that is enabled, incentivised and disciplined by international public funds.

In 2011, Bolivia, due to concerns about the inclusion of forests in carbon markets, put forward a proposal that led to the introduction of non–market-based approaches as a separate agenda item for REDD+ discussions.[52] From then onwards, REDD+ discussions included agenda items on both 'alternative policy approaches' and 'result-based actions', and the wording of COP decisions left open the possibility of both market-based and non-market financing. The Warsaw decision on financing notes the possibility of the COP developing both market-based and non-market approaches,[53] and confirms that 'new additional and predictable' result-based finance could come from 'a wide variety of sources, public and private, bilateral and multilateral'.[54] Article 5.2 of the Paris Agreement is 'framed as a call to Parties to continue – and hopefully scale up' work already done on REDD+.[55] It encourages all Parties to 'take action to implement and support ... result-based payments' and the existing framework for REDD+; but it also encourages all Parties to 'take action to implement and support' 'alternative policy approaches, such as joint mitigation and adaptation approaches' and notes the 'non-carbon benefits' associated with such approaches.[56] However, all indicators suggest it is the former that will be the most dominant approach. The discussion below documents the development of frameworks for both 'result-based actions' and 'alternative policy approaches' in relation to REDD+.

1 Result-Based Actions

The primary effect of the 'Warsaw Framework for REDD+'[57] is to establish an accounting framework for the monitoring, reporting and verifying (MRV) 'result-based

---

[52] Submission by the Plurinational State of Bolivia, *Joint mitigation and adaptation mechanism: "Sustainable Forest Life"* (December 2011) unfccc.int/files/meetings/ad_hoc_working_groups/lca/application/pdf/submission_bolivia_redd.pdf.

[53] Decision 2/CP.17 'Outcome of the work of the Ad Hoc Working Group on Long-term Cooperative Action under the Convention', FCCC/CP/2011/9/Add.1 (15 March 2012), para 66 and 67.

[54] Decision 2/CP.17, para 65, and Decision 9/CP.19, para 1.

[55] La Viña and de Leon, 'Conserving and enhancing sinks and reservoirs of greenhouse gases', p. 172.

[56] *Paris Agreement*, Article 5.2.

[57] Constituted by Decisions 9/CP.19; Decision 10/CP.19, 'Coordination of support for the implementation of activities in relation to mitigation actions in the forest sector by developing countries, including institutional arrangements'; Decision 11/CP.19, 'Modalities for national forest monitoring systems'; Decision 12/CP.19, 'The timing and frequency of presentation of the summary of information on how all the safeguards referred to in Decision 1/CP.16, appendix I,

68   *Background to REDD+*

actions', one that allows the additional carbon sequestered due to policy approaches to reduce deforestation and forest degradation to become legible in terms of $1tCO_2e$. To be eligible to receive international ('results-based') finance, host nation-states are required to establish strategies, plans, reference levels and systems for monitoring, reporting and verifying the effects of forest mitigation activities. That is, countries are required to show results of, not merely steps towards, forest protection, and these results need to be measured in terms of saved emissions (as opposed to hectares of forests protected, for example). The Warsaw Framework is therefore primarily orientated towards establishing an internationally verifiable regime of accounting for carbon 'saved' from avoided deforestation, which renders divergent activities in different places legible as and accounted for as fully certified emission reductions measured in terms of carbon dioxide equivalent (CO_2e), that could be fungible, transferable and exchangeable within carbon compliance markets.[58] Such legibility is the essential precondition for the inclusion of forests in international carbon markets, and thus the current accounting rules create the regulatory conditions that could enable REDD+ credits to be used as offsets by purchasing countries or entities in the future.[59]

The Warsaw Framework did not set up an institutional arrangement for REDD+, but it calls for the 'effective and transparent coordination of support' for forest sector mitigation activities[60] and the transnational sharing of information and 'best practices'.[61] Institutional arrangements were the subject of 'much debate and disagreement during the negotiations';[62] however, no real decision was reached: rather, international co-ordination is to be organised through an 'information hub' on the UNFCCC Web Platform.[63] Countries are 'invited' to designate a 'national entity

---

are being addressed and respected'; Decision 13/CP.19, 'Guidelines and procedures for the technical assessment of submissions from Parties on proposed forest reference emissions levels and/or forest reference levels'; Decision 14/CP.19, 'Modalities for measuring, reporting and verifying'; Decision 15/CP.19, 'Addressing the drivers of deforestation and forest degradation', FCCC/CP/2013/10/Add.1 (31 January 2014).

[58] In addition, there is a decision on addressing the drivers of deforestation; however, it is not prescriptive: Decision 15/CP.19, para 1.

[59] K. Dooley and A. Gupta, 'Governing by expertise: The contested politics of (accounting for) land-based mitigation in a new climate agreement' (2017) 17(4) *International Environmental Agreements: Politics, Law and Economics* 483–500 at 448–9.

[60] Decision 10/CP.19, preamble.

[61] Decision 10/CP.19, para 3(a)–(g).

[62] *Briefing note: Unpacking the Warsaw Framework for REDD+: The requirements for implementing REDD+ under the United Nations Framework Convention on Climate Change* (Climate Law and Policy, 2014), 10. At Doha the COP recognised the need to 'improve the coordination of support' for the implementation of REDD+ activities and the need to 'provide adequate and predictable support, including financial resources and technical and technological' for developing countries: Decision 1/CP.18, 'Agreed outcome pursuant to the Bali Action Plan', FCCC/CP/2012/8/Add.1 (28 February 2013), para 34. SBSTA and SBI were requested to initiate a process to 'consider existing institutional arrangements or potential governance alternatives including a body, a board or a committee': Decision 1/CP.18, para 35.

[63] Decision 9/CP.19, paras 9–13.

B. REDD+ As a Part of the UNFCCC Framework

or focal point' to liaise with the Secretariat and other Convention bodies,[64] and 'encouraged' to meet with other Parties, financing entities and civil society representatives and other stakeholders annually on a voluntary basis.[65]

The Warsaw Framework establishes a decentralised model where responsibility for developing key aspects of the regulatory infrastructure for REDD+ is devolved to host nation-states but is subject to international review and verification. The elements of the framework were initially articulated in the Cancun Agreements that called on developing country Parties to develop:

- a national strategy or action plan;[66]
- a national forest emission reference level and/or forest reference level;[67]
- a 'robust and transparent' national forest monitoring system for monitoring and reporting;[68] and
- a system on providing information on how safeguards are being 'addressed and respected'.[69]

Host nation-states therefore formally establish their regulatory frameworks 'in accordance with national circumstances and respective capabilities', but must in practice do so with reference to internationally determined expectations and requirements. These processes therefore become 'internationalised': subsequent COP agreements have confirmed that many of these elements are subject to international technical verification. Whilst these processes are therefore formally decentralised, verification ensures some standardisation, not necessarily of content, but of in the methodologies, practices and modes of expertise relied upon. In the following section, I will briefly outline these aspects of the REDD+ regulatory framework in greater detail.

(a) Forest Emission Reference Levels and/or Forest Reference Levels

One key component of the carbon-accounting framework is the establishment of a benchmark or forest emission reference level and/or forest reference level (FERL/FRL) (expressed in tonnes of carbon dioxide equivalent per year) against which changes in carbon sequestration from REDD+ activities can be measured.[70]

---

[64] Decision 10/CP.19, para 1.

[65] Decision 10/CP.19, para 4–8. It calls on the Secretariat to facilitate the organisation of this meeting (para 6).

[66] Decision 1/CP.16, para 71(a).

[67] Decision 1/CP.16, para 71(b). The agreements also allow for sub-national rather than nationally based forest reference emission levels or forest reference level to be developed dependent upon national circumstances.

[68] Decision 1/CP.16, para 71(c).

[69] Decision 1/CP.16, para 71(d).

[70] Decision 12/CP.17 'Guidance on systems for providing information on how safeguards are addressed and respected and modalities relating to forest reference emission levels and forest reference levels as referred to in Decision 1/CP.16', FCCC/CP/2011/9/Add.2 (15 March 2012),

The question of how to define or determine a 'reference level' or 'baseline' has been justifiably controversial, because if baselines are over-inflated, credits could be produced from activities that do not result in 'real' emission reductions. Various approaches have been proposed, including: historical ('based solely on past emissions from each country'), 'stock/average' ('based on current carbon stock or forest area in each country and possibly an international deforestation rate average'), 'projected/modelled' ('based on past deforestation and estimates of future deforestation drivers and key social, economic, political and technological variables') and 'combined' ('based on a formula that combines a measure of individual country performance against their own historic emissions baseline, and performance against a global emission baseline').[71] The Copenhagen decision on methodological guidance states that reference levels should be developed transparently, 'taking into account historic data, and adjust(ed) for national circumstances'.[72] Subsequent COP decisions do not specify how baselines should be calculated, but have focused on procedural requirements. COP decisions have confirmed baselines should be established at the national level (although sub-national reference levels have been allowed as a possible interim measure),[73] and have endorsed an adaptive 'step-by-step' approach in which the sophistication and scale of reference levels will increase over time with improved information, financial resources and technical capacity.[74] The Durban decision invited Parties to submit 'information and rationale' to the COP about the development of their reference levels to allow for technical assessment.[75] The Warsaw Framework provides guidelines for the technical assessments of reference levels by two UNFCCC-approved LULUCF experts.[76] However, any counterfactual reference level – a projection of what would have otherwise

---

para 7. For the remaining discussions I will refer to both forest emission reference levels and forest reference levels as 'reference levels'. Generally, 'forest reference emission level' is used when LULUCF activities are a net source of GHG emissions, that is, in cases of deforestation and forest degradation. 'Forest reference level' is used where LULUCF activities are a net sink of GHG emissions, that is, the 'plus' activities that are part of REDD+. For my purposes, however 'reference level' captures the fact that what is being constructed, justified and assessed is the creation of a hypothetical baseline against which any additional carbon emissions of carbon sequestration can be compared.

[71] For a more detailed discussion of baselines see: A. Angelsen, 'How do we set the reference levels for REDD payments?' in A. Angelsen (ed.), *Moving Ahead with REDD: Issues, Options and Implications* (Center for International Forestry Research, 2008) pp. 53–63; Angelsen et al., *Guidelines for REDD+ Reference Levels*. See also UNFCCC, *Report on the Expert Meeting on Forest Reference Emission Levels and Forest Reference Levels for Implementation of REDD-plus Activities*, 14–15 November 2011, FCCC/SBSTA/2011/INF.18 (27 November 2011).

[72] Decision 4/CP.15, para 7.

[73] Decision 1/CP.16, para 71(b).

[74] Decision 12/CP.17, para 10–11.

[75] Decision 12/CP.17, para 9; see also 'Annex: Guidelines for submission of information on reference levels'.

[76] Decision 13/CP.19, 'Annex: Guidelines and procedures for the technical assessment of submissions from parties on proposed forest reference emission levels and/or forest reference levels'.

B. REDD+ As a Part of the UNFCCC Framework

happened but for the REDD+ activities – remains inherently indeterminate, and thus a danger remains that over-inflated baselines could generate credits that are not 'real'.

(b) Measuring, Reporting and Verification

The Warsaw Framework confirms that 'anthropogenic forest-related emissions by sources and removals by sinks, forest carbon stocks, and forest carbon stock and forest-area changes' resulting from the implementation of REDD+ activities need to be measured, reported and verified (MRV) in terms of tCO_2/year.[77] The MRV processes require host countries to develop 'robust and transparent' (sub)-national forest monitoring systems[78] using a combination of remote sensing and ground-based carbon inventory approaches[79] that take into account COP and IPCC guidelines.[80] Implementing MRV frameworks requires specialised knowledge and equipment, and it is recognised that MRV capacities will need to be developed and continuously improved over time.[81] Host states must provide biannual updates of MRV data and a technical annex to the COP[82] in a form consistent with its methodological guidance[83] and analysed by a technical team of UNFCCC-registered experts, in order to receive 'result-based payments'.[84] These MRV practices are to be consistent with previous methodological guidance on REDD+,[85] and other related or future COP decisions.[86]

(c) Safeguards and Non-carbon Benefits

One of the most fraught areas of REDD+ policy has been the development and verification of safeguards to ensure the environmental integrity of REDD+ and prevent negative social impacts. The Cancun Agreement affirmed social and environmental safeguards that should be 'promoted and supported' in REDD+ implementation:[87]

---

[77] Decision 14/CP.19, para 1.
[78] Decision 4/CP.15, para 3(d), see also Decision 1/CP.16, para 71(c).
[79] Decision 4/CP.15, para 3(d)(i)–(iii).
[80] Decision 11/CP.19, para 2.
[81] Decision 14/CP.19, para 2 and 5.
[82] Decision 14/CP.19, para 7; additional flexibility is given to the least developed countries and small island states Decision 14/CP.19, para 6.
[83] See Decision 4/CP.15 and 12/CP.17 as well as the guidelines in the Annex to Decision 14/CP.19.
[84] Decision 14/CP.19, para 10.
[85] The previous methodological guidance was set out in Decision 4/CP.15.
[86] Decision 14/CP.19, para 1.
[87] Decision 1/CP.16, para 69. The language of 'promoted and supported' in relation to the safeguards is criticised by environmental and social justice groups as 'too weak' to ensure safeguards are enforced. Note that in the draft Copenhagen text the words 'promoted and supported' in relation to the safeguards were still bracketed text as they were highly contentious

(a) That actions complement or are consistent with the objectives of national forest programmes and relevant international conventions and agreements;

(b) Transparent and effective national forest governance structures, taking into account national legislation and sovereignty;

(c) Respect for the knowledge and rights of indigenous peoples and members of local communities, by taking into account relevant international obligations, national circumstances and laws, and noting that the United Nations General Assembly has adopted the United Nations Declaration on the Rights of Indigenous Peoples;

(d) The full and effective participation of relevant stakeholders, in particular indigenous peoples and local communities,

(e) That actions are consistent with the conservation of natural forests and biological diversity, ensuring that the actions ... are not used for the conversion of natural forests, but are instead used to incentive the protection and conservation of natural forests and their ecosystem services, and to enhance other social and environmental benefits;

(f) Actions to address the risks of reversals; [and]

(g) Actions to reduce displacement of emissions.[88]

At Durban it was agreed that REDD+ host countries should provide to the COP a summary of information on how such safeguards are being 'addressed and respected'.[89] The Warsaw Framework invites Parties to provide such summaries to the UNFCCC REDD+ web platform specifically.[90] The Warsaw decision on results-based finance also provides that 'developing countries seeking to obtain and receive results-based payments ... should provide the most recent summary of information on how all the safeguards ... have been addressed and respected'.[91] However, unlike the carbon accounting aspects of the framework this information is *not* subject to international technical review. The European Union (EU) proposed a scheme of indicators for the achievement of safeguards; however, this was ultimately

---

(pre-Copenhagen draft used the strong language of 'shall implement'); these brackets have been removed in the Cancun text. Article 71(d) simply requests that countries develop a 'system for providing information on how the safeguards referred to in annex 1 are being addressed and respected'. The pre-Cancun draft text called for 'a system for *monitoring* and informing the Convention on how the safeguards referred to in Annex II ... [a]re being addressed and respected ...'. An entry on REDD-Monitor alleges it was PNG who proposed the weakened wording on safeguard monitoring. C. Lang, 'How Kevin Conrad dismissed NGO requests not to weaken safeguards in the REDD text in Cancun', *REDD-Monitor*, 5 January 2011.

[88] Decision 1/CP.16, Annex, para 2.

[89] Decision 12/CP.17, para 3.

[90] Decision 12/CP.19, para 3.

[91] Decision 9/CP.19, para 4.

B. REDD+ As a Part of the UNFCCC Framework

rejected due to concerns about costs and sovereignty.[92] Nonetheless, UN-REDD has issued guidance on how countries can achieve 'transparency, consistency, comprehensiveness and effectiveness' in their information summaries on safeguards.[93] A decision from the Paris COP on safeguards 'strongly encourages' (but does not strictly require) host countries to provide specific information to ensure transparency, consistency, comprehensiveness and effectiveness in reporting on REDD+ safeguards.[94] It also 'strongly encourages' developing country Parties, when providing safeguard information, to include relevant information on national circumstances, a description of each safeguard in accordance with national circumstances, a description of existing systems and processes relevant to addressing and respecting these safeguards, as well as information on how 'each of the safeguards has been addressed and respected, in accordance with national circumstances'.[95] Thus the COP guidance on safeguards was concluded with a decision which encouraged ways to ensure transparency, consistency and comprehensiveness and effectiveness of reporting on information system and processes, but did not mandate such reporting or make it subject to international review.[96]

A further COP decision at Paris also reaffirmed the 'importance of incentivising non-carbon benefits for the long-term sustainability of the implementation' of REDD+ activities and recognised the potential contribution of non-carbon benefits from reducing deforestation and forest degradation.[97] Stressing that such non-carbon benefits are 'unique to countries' national circumstances', the decision allows countries to provide information on 'the nature, scale and importance of the non-carbon benefits' and communicate this to financing entities.[98] However, the decision clarifies that non-carbon benefits 'do not constitute a requirement' in order to receive support for REDD+ activities or for 'result-based payments'; it imposes no obligations on financing entities to support such non-carbon benefits.[99] Thus overall, the framework for 'results-based actions' established the regulatory

---

[92] M. E. Recio, 'The Warsaw Framework and the future of REDD+' (2014) 24(1) *Yearbook of International Environmental Law* 37–69.

[93] UN-REDD Programme, *Info Brief 5: Summaries of Information: How to Demonstrate REDD+ Safeguards Are Being Addressed and Respected'* (2016), unredd.net/documents/global-pro gramme-191/safeguards-multiple-benefits-297/15299-info-brief-summaries-of-information-1-en .html.

[94] Decision 17/CP.21, 'Further guidance on ensuring transparency, consistency, comprehensiveness and effectiveness when informing on how all the safeguards referred to in decision 1/CP.16, appendix I, are being address and respected', FCCC/SBSTA/2015/L.5/Add.3 (29 January 2016).

[95] Decision 17/CP.21, para 5.

[96] Decision 17/CP.21, para 8.

[97] Decision 18/CP.21, 'Methodological issues related to non-carbon benefits resulting from the implementation of the activities referred to in Decision 1/CP.16, para 70', FCCC/2015/10/Add.3 (29 January 2016), preambular recitals 2 and 3.

[98] Decision 18/CP.21, para 1–4.

[99] Decision 18/CP.21, para 5.

74 *Background to REDD+*

framework for accounting for carbon 'saved' from avoided deforestation, based on establishing an internationally verifiable regime for establishing forest emission baselines and MRV processes, accompanied by a much more voluntarist, nationally based framework for social and environmental protections.

2 *Alternative Policy Approaches*

Since Bolivia proposed a further REDD+ agenda item on 'alternative policy approaches' in 2011, such non-result-based approaches have also been endorsed by COP decisions, but no real mechanisms have been established to support or incentivise such alternative approaches. The 2011 Durban decision on REDD+ noted that 'joint mitigation and adaptation approaches for the integral and sustainable management of forests as a non-market alternative'[100] and the 2012 Doha decision requested further methodological guidance on how 'non-market-based approaches, such as joint mitigation and adaptation approaches for the sustainable management of forests ... could be developed to support the implementation' of REDD activities.[101] The 2013 Warsaw framework for REDD+ likewise encouraged financing entities 'to continue to provide financial resources to alternative policy approaches, such as joint mitigation and adaptation approaches for the integral and sustainable management of forests'.[102] A 2015 COP decision at Paris explicitly concluded the consideration of alternative policy approaches including joint mitigation and adaptation approaches for the integral and sustainable management of forests.[103] It identified such 'alternative policy approaches' as 'one of the alternatives to result-based payments', noting that such policy approaches may 'contribute to the long-term sustainability of the implementation of [REDD+] activities'.[104] It also clarified that such approaches were subject to the previous methodological guidance and to the guidance on systems and safeguards.[105] This decision encouraged developing country Parties interested in such approaches to prepare national strategies or action plans, to identify their support needs, develop proposals about the potential contribution of such approaches and consider outcomes and areas of improvement.[106] The decision also noted that financing entities are encouraged to provide financial resources for alternative policy approaches.[107] Nevertheless, although the decision encouraged financial support for such activities it did not

---

[100] Decision 2/CP.17.
[101] Decision 1/CP.18, para 39 and 40.
[102] Decision 9/CP.19, para 8.
[103] Decision 16/CP.21, 'Alterative policy approaches, such as joint mitigation and adaptation approaches for the integral and sustainable management of forests' FCCC/CP/2015/10/Add.3 (29 January 2016) para 8.
[104] Decision 16/CP.21, para 4.
[105] Decision 16/CP.21, para 3.
[106] Decision 16/CP.21, para 5.
[107] Decision 16/CP.21, para 6.

B. REDD+ As a Part of the UNFCCC Framework

establish any mechanisms to incentivise such approaches to provide international support for their enactment.

The UNFCCC negotiations on REDD+ have therefore developed a regulatory framework that makes it possible for activities to avoid deforestation be made legible as 'result-based actions' measured in terms of one $1tCO_2e$, through an internationally verified process. This framework could therefore enable forest carbon to be incorporated in international carbon markets. Although there was also a separate agenda on 'alternative policy' approaches, the conclusions of this workstream are simply permissive and do not put in place measures to facilitative or mandate that such activities be undertaken or that support for them be provided. Despite extensive debate and deliberation, a number of key issues relating to environmental integrity remain unaddressed by the REDD+ framework. The problem of ensuring *permanence* of carbon sequestration and preventing reversals of carbon sequestration savings has not been properly resolved. As stated in a recent UNFCCC report, it is 'widely accepted that there are risks of reversals associated with … mitigation actions relating to forests'[108] that are inadequately addressed by current safeguards.[109] Although various risk-mitigation techniques to protect against such reversals have been proposed – including REDD+ unit reserves (or buffers) or the creation of an insurance system that requires compensation (financial or of credits) for reversals[110] – these are not required as a part of the Warsaw Framework. The problem of *additionality* – that is, ensuring that any carbon 'savings' attributed to REDD+ are 'additional' to what would otherwise have happened without the REDD+ project – also has not been satisfactorily resolved. Although reference levels are subject to international verification, the establishment of any counterfactual projection remains inherently indeterminate. There are also no real mechanisms in place to prevent *leakage* – the displacement of deforestation from the REDD+ jurisdiction to other jurisdictions sub-nationally or internationally. Although a safeguard calls for 'actions to reduce displacement of emissions',[111] the lack of universal participation as well as the mix of national and sub-national baselines means that leakage remains a real risk. Finally, although the Warsaw Framework talks about the need to address 'drivers of deforestation', REDD+ remains a mechanism that addresses 'supply-side' factors rather than any 'demand' leading to deforestation. REDD+'s narrow focus that locates the problem of deforestation in developing countries means that more structural drivers and internationalised demands for agricultural expansion, pulp,

---

[108] UNFCCC Secretariat, *Financing Options for the Full Implementation of Results-Based Actions Relating to the Activities Referred to in Decision 1/CP.16, Paragraph 70, including Related Modalities and Procedures: Technical Paper* FCCC/TP/2012/3 (26 July 2012) para 113.

[109] Decision 1/CP.16, Appendix, para 2(f).

[110] See UNFCCC Secretariat, *Financing Options for the Full Implementation of Results-Based Actions Relating to the Activities Referred to in Decision 1/CP.16, paragraph 70, including Related Modalities and Procedures: Technical Paper* FCCC/TP/2012/3 (26 July 2012) for a discussion of these proposals.

[111] Decision 1/CP.16, Appendix, para 2(g).

timber and palm oil remain unaddressed.[112] Therefore, despite the development of a complex accounting system, the inherent uncertainties in any attempt to posit what would have otherwise have happened in the future, to measure 'saved' emissions against that baseline, and then ensure that such 'savings' are permanent, means forest carbon remains an inherently indeterminate commodity.

C REDD+ AS EXPERIMENTAL PRACTICES, PREPARATORY AND MARKET-CONSTRUCTION ACTIVITIES

The preceding discussion outlined the REDD+ legal framework for producing, measuring and verifying REDD+ 'result-based actions', agreed through the UNFCCC process. However, activities carried out under the REDD+ banner are much broader than that framework might suggest. This section discusses the role of experimental practices, preparatory and market-construction activities that are directed towards materialising REDD+ in the world and establishing the broader national and transnational regulatory frameworks that REDD+ depends upon. The discussion shows that such exploratory and preparatory practices are not only directed towards the implementation of REDD+ but that they also play a significant role in the production of norms that complement but also exceed those of the formal UNFCCC framework. This section firstly discusses the role of 'demonstration activities' as critical experimental practices that test key methodologies for REDD+ as well as contributing to building the legitimacy of such projects. It then turns to discuss the various multilateral and bilateral programs – including the World Bank's Forest Carbon Partnership Facility (FCPF), the UN-REDD Programme and the Green Climate Fund (GCF) – and their role in promoting REDD+-readiness activities, and in the case of the FCPF establishing enabling conditions for a privatised market-based regime. Although it is beyond the scope of this book to examine the role of the voluntary markets and the various certification schemes that have been developed to verify forest carbon credits in that space, these voluntary markets – where approximately 42.8 million tonnes of CO_2e of forest carbon was traded in 2018[113] – clearly also constitute critical spaces of experimentation with REDD+ and the development of norms, methodologies and modes of implementation.[114]

---

[112] See M. A. Young, 'Interacting regimes and experimentation' in M. Tehan et al. (eds.), *The Impact of Climate Change Mitigation on Indigenous and Forest Communities: International, National and Local Law Perspectives on REDD+* (Cambridge University Press, 2017) pp. 329–45.

[113] K. Hamrick and M. Gallant, *Voluntary Carbon Market Insights: 2018 Outlook and First-Quarter Trends* (Ecosystem Marketplace 2018).

[114] See P. Newell and M. Paterson, *Climate Capitalism: Global Warming and the Transformation of the Global Economy* (Cambridge University Press, 2010).

1 Demonstration Activities

Demonstration activities represent a space of international/local REDD+ experimental 'learning-by-doing' that operate to generate specific knowledges, technologies and practices for REDD+ as well as producing new norms from on-the-ground facts. The REDD+ literature envisions that demonstration activities play a central role in 'build[ing] confidence and ensur[ing] that mechanisms and institutions are fit for purpose',[115] as well as testing approaches to MRV, benefit-sharing and credit transfer amongst others. By September 2016, the International Database on REDD+ Projects identified 454 projects, 344 of which were active, 67 completed prior to 2016 and 43 pending, located across 56 different countries.[116]

At the 2007 Bali COP, a methodological decision invited Parties to 'further strengthen and support ongoing efforts to reduce emissions from deforestation and forest degradation on a voluntary basis',[117] thereby encouraging action to prepare for the actualisation and implementation of REDD+ in parallel with the ongoing negotiations. The decision encouraged developed country Parties to support capacity-building and provide technical assistance and technology transfer (especially relating to data collection, estimating emissions and monitoring and reporting) and to address the institutional needs of developing countries to support the implementation of REDD+.[118] It also encouraged Parties to 'explore a range of actions, identify options and undertake efforts, including demonstration activities'.[119] Such 'demonstration projects' have become sites of experimental 'learning-by-doing', which not only seek to actualise the legal norms but actively influence their development. For example, the objectives of the Kalimantan Forest Carbon Partnership, an Australian-sponsored 'demonstration project' located in Central Kalimantan, Indonesia, included trialling an 'innovative market-orientated approach to financing and implementing measures for REDD+' in order to provide 'useful and practical lessons to support international efforts to establish a REDD+ mechanism' and 'inform a future climate change agreement'.[120] These practices and processes that are endorsed and encouraged, but are formally outside the official UNFCCC framework, therefore need to be understood as sites of norm construction. These are sites that produce and determine methodologies, processes and visions through

---

[115] Eliasch, *Climate Change: Financing Global Forest*, p. 121.
[116] These figures are from September 2016, see International Database on REDD+ Projects, ifri .snre.umich.edu/redd/index.html (accessed 15 November 2016).
[117] Decision 2/CP.13, para 1.
[118] Decision 2/CP.13, para 2.
[119] Decision 2/CP.13, para 3.
[120] UNFCCC, *Joint Submission under the Cancun Agreements: Reducing Emissions from Deforestation and Forest Degradation in Developing Countries*, submission by Australia and Indonesia to SBSTA, FCCC/SBSTA/2011/MISC.7/Add.3 (9 December 2011).

Background to REDD+

which REDD+ is actualised, *even as* these methodologies may be subject to intense contestation and controversy within the deliberative and consensus-driven formal negotiating spaces.

Critically, however, this process of learning-by-doing is not merely preparatory for REDD+ but is a key aspect of how REDD+ is envisioned. In this way REDD+ reflects several principles of 'experimentalist governance' frameworks, especially the concept of continuing iterative development and the need for continuous feedback, flexibility and adaptability.[121] In a different vein, scholars of science and technology studies have described carbon markets as 'on-going collective experiments'.[122] These scholars understand economics as performative, in that it is not simply 'a form of knowledge that depicts an already existing state of affairs but … a set of instruments and practices that contribute to the construction of economic settings, actors, and institutions'.[123] Timothy Mitchell has analysed the ways economic theory, as a method for testing its arguments, is required to conduct experiments in the world constituted as a laboratory.[124] He draws on Michel Callon's insight that economics is best understood 'not as a form of knowledge that pictures the world' but an activity that 'participates in the pre-formation of the worlds to which it belongs, by helping set up socio-technical agencies/arrangements' that are themselves part of a wider process of continuous experimentation.[125] Callon has described the process of establishing carbon markets as itself an economic experiment, writing that 'what is designed, tested and evaluated is a socio-technical *agencement* that combines material, textual and procedural elements'.[126]

When the construction of carbon markets is understood as a 'governance experiment' that operates not as a 'rational device to identify the best solution, but a social process in which a new reality is constructed', a much more complicated relation between vision and implementation in REDD+ becomes evident.[127] Rather than a straightforward relation between constructing a problem and proposing a solution, economic experiments are more ambitious attempts to 'reconfigure the world so that problem and solution works in it'.[128] Voß and Schroth define 'experimentation' as

---

[121] Young, 'Interacting regimes and experimentation'.

[122] See M. Callon, 'Civilizing markets: Carbon trading between in vitro and in vivo experiments' (2009) 34(3–4) *Accounting, Organizations and Society* 535–48.

[123] M. Callon cited in D. MacKenzie, F. Muniesa, and L. Siu (eds.), *Do Economists Make Markets?: On the Performativity of Economics* (Princeton University Press, 2005) p. 4; see also T. Mitchell, 'The work of economics: How a discipline makes its world' (2005) 46(2) *European Journal of Sociology* 297–320.

[124] Mitchell, 'The work of economics: How a discipline makes its world'.

[125] Cited in ibid.

[126] M. Callon, 'Civilizing markets: Carbon trading between in vitro and in vivo experiments', 535–48 at 527.

[127] F. Schroth, *The politics of governance experiments: Constructing the Clean Development Mechanism* (Unpublished PhD thesis, Technischen Universität Berlin, 2016) p. 69.

[128] Ibid., p. 69.

C. Experimental Practices, Preparatory & Market-Construction Activities   79

the 'deliberate production of experiences for finding out what works'.[129] They note how, in some understandings, experiments are not simply a process of *'adapting to reality'* but rather a process of *'making reality'*.[130] They thus highlight how experimentation is a 'way of deliberately changing the world' that 'enables learning, not about a pre-existing reality, but about the possibilities of knowing and doing reality differently'.[131] This means that experimentation is never a neutral process,[132] especially given that it is always 'deeply embedded in institutional, cultural and material settings and asymmetric power relations'.[133] Given how power shapes experimental practices 'leaving institutional development up to decentralized trials ... may not produce the best solutions, but in fact help already powerful actors to assert their vision of collective order against other[s]'.[134]

Demonstration projects, as sites of experimentation within the broader carbon market experiment, can therefore be understood not just as directed towards the *demonstration* of specific outcomes but an investment in the process of creating the conditions necessary for the realisation of carbon markets. 'Demonstration projects' should thus be understood as a 'laboratory' existing in a space of 'non-legality'[135] in that they are promoted by the UNFCCC framework, yet not subject to it. The constant reiteration that such projects are 'experimental' in nature moreover limits the perchance of critiques about their failures or problems, given that all failings can be rationalised as part of a process of 'learning-by-doing'. However, the practices promoted within this space nonetheless create specific realities: they enable the formation of particular expectations in and of different actors and stakeholders; they encourage particular forms of behaviours and interactions; and they require the establishment of particular organisational and institutional structures. These 'produced facts' are then taken as given within the spaces where institutionalised regulatory decisions are being made, where they retrospectively become 'inscribed into a law already prepared to accept it as a practice'.[136]

---

[129] J.-P. Voß and F. Schroth, 'The politics of innovation and learning in polycentric governance' in A. Jordan, D. Huitema, H. van Asselt, J. Forster (eds.), *Governing Climate Change: Polycentricity in Action?* (Cambridge University Press, 2018) pp. 99–116, 100.

[130] Ibid., p. 102 (emphasis in original).

[131] Ibid.

[132] Ibid.

[133] Ibid., p. 99.

[134] Ibid., pp. 99–100.

[135] See F. Johns, *Non-Legality in International Law: Unruly Law* (Cambridge University Press, 2013).

[136] S. Krasmann, 'Targeted killing and its law: On a mutually constitutive relationship' (2012) 25(3) *Leiden Journal of International Law* 665–82 at 667.

2 REDD+-Readiness

The process of 'REDD+-readiness' refers to '[a]ctions aimed at developing technical and institutional capacity in developing countries'.[137] It is broadly recognised that 'the legal framework will be the vehicle through which many of the international requirements for REDD+ will be translated by forest countries into tangible and specific national requirements, according to their unique circumstances'.[138] The Cancun Agreements followed *The Eliasch Review* recommendations in adopting a three-staged approach to REDD+ implementation. While *The Eliasch Review*'s explicit long-term goal is 'the full inclusion [of forests] in a global carbon market', it stresses the need for public interventions and public funds to enable and facilitate such a transition, given that a 'smooth transition path is also important for building confidence in the system'.[139] After reviewing three transition options *The Eliasch Review* recommends a hybrid model in which REDD+ countries would be 'accessing finance under incentive-based schemes from a combination of carbon markets (regional and national emissions trading schemes) and other sources while carbon markets grow smoothly over time'. This hybrid approach was specifically recommended over the alternative possibilities of either immediately moving to a market-based cap-and-trade system or remaining solely with funding from non-market sources.[140]

The process of REDD+-readiness involves preparing the following at the national level:

- REDD+ strategies and action plans;
- national or subnational reference levels;
- a robust and transparent system to measure, report and verify forest change;
- a system to provide information on how safeguards are being addressed and respected;
- a system for the receipt, management and disbursal of REDD+ finance.[141]

The process of REDD+-readiness therefore sits between easy delimitations of the global and the local. It is, as William Boyd describes, the process by which

> local and provincial level structures of forest governance are (re)combining with national and transnational capabilities to create technical, legal and institutional

---

[137] P. A. Minang, M. Van Noordwijk, L. A. Duguma, D. Alemagi, T. H. Do, F. Bernard, P. Agung, V. Robiglio, D. Catacutan, and S. Suyanto, 'REDD+ readiness progress across countries: Time for reconsideration' (2014) 14(6) *Climate Policy* 685–708 at 686.

[138] Denier et al., *The Little Book of Legal Frameworks for REDD+*, p. 16.

[139] Eliasch, *Climate Change: Financing Global Forests*, pp. 121–2.

[140] Ibid., p. 122.

[141] Denier et al., *The Little Book of Legal Frameworks for REDD+*, p. 22.

C. Experimental Practices, Preparatory & Market-Construction Activities   81

frameworks for generating compliance grade assets and moving them into GHG compliance systems and other pay-for-performance schemes.[142]

Similarly, the process of REDD+-readiness, unsettles distinctions between the public and private. It relies on public financing, but especially in the work of the FCPF, is arguably directed towards establishing the institutional conditions that can enable the expansion of private markets. Therefore, this discussion suggests REDD+-readiness should be understood as part of a process of 'market construction', where public funds are deployed to support the development of regulatory conditions that can enable private contracting and accumulation.

A number of multilateral processes have been established to support REDD+-readiness, including prominently the World Bank's Forest Carbon Partnership Facility (FCPF), the UN-REDD Programme (a collaboration between the FAO, UNDP and UNEP) and the Forest Investment Programme, which is part of the World Bank's Climate Investment Funds. In addition, the Green Climate Fund – the financial mechanism under both the UNFCCC and the Paris Agreement – is providing support and funding for REDD+-readiness. These initiatives are discussed below.

(a) Forest Carbon Partnership Facility

The World Bank's Forest Carbon Partnership Facility (FCPF) has played a key role in developing processes and norms for REDD+-readiness to promote its eventual objective: the inclusion of forest carbon in international markets. The FCPF was approved by the World Bank's Executive Board on 25 September 2007, launched at COP13 in Bali and became operational in June 2008.[143] Initially capitalized at $160 million, and valued at approximately $1.3 billion a decade later,[144] it has over 60 involved countries, including donors and 47 participant countries, as well as NGOs and the private sector.[145] The FCPF is one of 15 carbon initiatives of which the World Bank is trustee, through its Carbon Finance Unit capitalised at US$2.3 billion.[146] The FCPF describes its 'dual objectives' as 'building capacity for REDD in developing countries in tropical and subtropical regions' and 'testing a program of performance-based incentive payments in some pilot countries, on a relatively small

---

[142] W. Boyd, 'Climate change, fragmentation, and the challenges of global environmental law: Elements of a post-Copenhagen assemblage' (2010) 32 *University of Pennsylvania Journal of International Law* 457–550 at 544.

[143] The World Bank, 'Forest carbon partnership facility launched at Bali Climate Meeting' (Media release, 11 December 2007).

[144] *Forest Carbon Partnership Facility: 2018 Annual Report* (2018) p. 4.

[145] E. Baroudy, 'Why we should be more optimistic about forests and climate change' (2017) *The World Bank* https://blogs.worldbank.org/climatechange/why-we-should-be-more-optimistic-about-forests-and-climate-change, 18 December 2017.

[146] The World Bank, 'The World Bank Carbon Funds and Facilities', www.worldbank.org/en/topic/climatechange/brief/world-bank-carbon-funds-facilities.

82 *Background to REDD+*

scale, in order to set the stage for a much larger system of positive incentives and financing flows in the future'.[147] At its launch, it was explicit that the FCPF's 'ultimate goal' was to 'jump-start a forest carbon market'.[148] The FCPF Charter sets out a number of objectives: to 'pilot a performance-based payment system for Emission Reductions generated from REDD activities, with a view to ensuring equitable benefit-sharing and promoting future large scale positive incentives for REDD'; to provide eligible REDD countries with 'financial and technical assistance in building their capacity to benefit from possible future systems of positive incentives for REDD'; 'to test ways to sustain or enhance livelihoods of local communities and to conserve biodiversity'; and to disseminate broadly the knowledge gained through the Facility's work.[149] The FCPF Charter also specifically requires it to '[s]eek to ensure consistency with the UNFCCC Guidance on REDD',[150] and to '[m]aximize synergies with other bilateral and multilateral programs on REDD'.[151] It is also required to follow a 'learning-by-doing' approach, experimenting with how these international legal frameworks can be actualized in practice.[152] The FCPF has since established itself as a key norm-developer and driver in the field. A 2011 review by civil society organisations found that 'through the FCPF, the World Bank is now setting the post-Cancun agenda in terms of how forests are integrated into a global carbon regime, how the REDD will be implemented and how finance will be sourced'.[153]

The FCPF contains two separate funds: the Readiness Fund, which provides funds for the development of necessary policies and strategies in REDD+ host countries, and the Carbon Fund, which provides payments for verified emission reductions from REDD+ programs.[154] The FCPF has three different categories of participant: REDD+ country participants (to date, 47 developing countries have been selected to join the FCPF, including 18 from Africa, 18 from Latin America and 11 from the Asia–Pacific region),[155] Donor participants (14 developed countries and the European Commission),[156] and Carbon Fund participants (including

---

[147] The World Bank, 'Forest Carbon Partnership Facility', www.forestcarbonpartnership.org/fcp/node/12 (accessed 18 February 2010).

[148] The World Bank, 'Forest carbon partnership facility takes aim at deforestation,' (Press release, 11 December 2007).

[149] International Bank for Reconstruction and Development, *Charter Establishing the Forest Carbon Partnership Facility* (November 23, 2015), Article 2.1.

[150] Ibid., Article 3.1(c).

[151] Ibid., Article 3.1(f).

[152] Ibid., Article 3.1(b).

[153] K. Dooley, T. Griffiths, F. Martone, and S. Ozinga, *Smoke and Mirrors: A Critical Assessment of the Forest Carbon Partnership Facility* (FERN and Forest Peoples' Programme, 2011).

[154] *Charter Establishing the Forest Carbon Partnership Facility*, Article 2.2, see also 'About us: FPIC', www.forestcarbonpartnership.org/fcpf (accessed 21 October 2013).

[155] 'REDD+ countries', www.forestcarbonpartnership.org/redd-countries-1 (accessed 2 March 2019).

[156] 'Donor participants', www.forestcarbonpartnership.org/donor-participants#overlay-context=donor-participants-0 (access 2 March 2019). These are: European Commission, governments

C. Experimental Practices, Preparatory & Market-Construction Activities   83

governments and private sector entitles who contribute to the Carbon Fund).[157] The Participants Assembly, which meets annually, is made up of all countries and organizations involved in the FCPF, and it elects the Participants Committee, which meets twice a year and is made up of 14 forest countries and 14 donor countries.[158]

The Readiness Fund focuses on assisting countries to prepare for REDD+ implementation by adopting national REDD+ strategies and management arrangements, establishing reference emission levels, and designing measuring, reporting and verification systems and safeguard processes.[159] There are several stages of FCPF involvement in countries' national REDD+-readiness programs: participant countries are first required to submit a formal Readiness Plan Idea Note (R-PIN) to the FCPF. If this is accepted, participant countries can receive Readiness Preparation Grants to provide support for the preparation of a Readiness Preparation Proposal (R-PP), a plan for how the country will approach REDD+-readiness, which is assessed by the FCPF's governing body. At the end of the readiness phase the participant country is required to have completed a Readiness Package (R-Package), which should include a national REDD+ strategy, an implementation framework, a MRV system, a reference level scenario and a monitoring and evaluation framework for safeguards. As of June 2019, the Readiness Fund has US$400 million in funding, of which $314 million has been allocated and $200 million dispersed.[160] Between its 47 participants, 46 Readiness Proposals had been prepared, 44 Readiness Preparation Grant Agreements have been signed and 24 R-Packages have been endorsed.[161]

The Carbon Fund is 'set up to pilot incentive payments for REDD+ efforts in developing countries'.[162] It is focused on providing 'performance-based payments' to participant countries, by 'remunerat[ing] the selected countries in accordance with negotiated contracts for verifiable emission reductions'.[163] Countries '[making] progress towards REDD+ readiness' can apply to the Carbon Fund by submitting an Emission Reduction Program Idea Note (ER PIN). After the ER PIN is reviewed by a Technical Advisory Panel, a legal binding letter of intent between the World

---

of Australia, Canada, Denmark, Finland, France, Germany, Italy, Japan, Netherland, Norway, Spain, Switzerland, United Kingdom and the United States of America.

[157] 'Carbon Fund participants', www.forestcarbonpartnership.org/carbon-fund-participants (accessed 2 March 2019). These include: European Commission, governments of Australia, Canada, France, Germany, Norway, Switzerland, United Kingdom and the United States of America as well as BP Technology Venture Inc. and The Nature Conservancy.

[158] 'Participants page', www.forestcarbonpartnership.org/participants-page (accessed 2 March 2019).

[159] 'The Readiness Fund', www.forestcarbonpartnership.org/readiness-fund-0 (accessed 2 March 2019).

[160] *Forest Carbon Partnership Facility: 2019 Annual Report* (FCPF, 2019) 14.

[161] Ibid.

[162] 'The Carbon Fund', www.forestcarbonpartnership.org/carbon-fund (accessed 26 November 2019).

[163] 'The Carbon Fund', www.forestcarbonpartnership.org/carbon-fund-0 (accessed 26 November 2019).

Bank and the participating country is signed. The ER PIN is then translated into an Emission Reduction Program Document, which after undergoing a due diligence assessment is then developed into a legally binding Emission Reduction Payment Agreement (ERPA) between the host country and the World Bank (as trustee of the Carbon Fund). REDD+ activities are then implemented in the host country in accordance with the ERPA, and host countries receive payment for verified emission reductions (ERs) generated and these ERs transferred to Carbon Fund participants.[164] The first ERPAs were signed in February 2019 with Mozambique and the Democratic Republic of the Congo.[165] By June 2019, the Carbon Fund had US$900 million and included 19 participants, of whom all had signed letters of intent; 13 were in the process of developing ER Program Documents, and three Emission Reduction Payment Agreements had been signed.[166]

The FCPF has been an influential trend-setter in the REDD+-readiness space. A 2012 review by the World Bank's Independent Evaluation Group described the Fund's key activity as 'knowledge creation and knowledge transfer by defining and developing the modalities for REDD+' through expert meetings, capacity-building initiatives and dissemination of REDD+ lessons globally.[167] Its other major activity is 'capacity building through the Readiness Preparation Proposal (R-PP) process' at the country level.[168] The Review lauded the FCPF as an 'innovative' program 'willing to take risks and pioneer new ways of doing business', whose possibilities were, however, constrained due to uncertainties in the broader legal environment.[169] It also recommended greater alignment between 'country-generated REDD+ strategies' and other World Bank programs such as Country Assistance Strategies and Poverty Reduction Strategy Papers, and the prioritisation of 'no regrets' REDD+ interventions 'such as legal and policy support for land tenure and forest governance reforms that dovetail with the World Bank's wider objectives in the forest sector'.[170]

Civil society assessments, however, present a much more critical picture. A 2008 briefing prepared by the Forest Peoples Programme (FPP) presented a number of concerns of Indigenous peoples and forest-related organisations about the FCPF launch. These included concerns that the FCPF failed to take the United Nations

---

[164] This summary is primarily based on material in *The FCPF Carbon Fund: Piloting REDD+ Programs at Scale* (Forest Carbon Partnership Fund, June 2013), www.forestcarbonpartnership.org/sites/fcp/files/2013/june2013/CF%20Origination-web_0.pdf.

[165] 'Mozambique and Democratic Republic of Congo sign landmark deals with World Bank to cut emissions and reduce deforestation' (Press release, 19 February 2019), www.worldbank.org/en/news/press-release/2019/02/12/mozambique-and-democratic-republic-of-congo-sign-landmark-deals-with-world-bank-to-cut-carbon-emissions-and-reduce-deforestation.

[166] *Forest Carbon Partnership Facility: 2019 Annual Report* (FCPF, 2019), 15.

[167] *The Forest Carbon Partnership Facility* (Independent Evaluation Group, 2012); see also C. Lang, 'Independent Evaluation Group review of the FCPF: "World Bank needs a high-level strategic discussion on its overall approach to REDD"' REDD-Monitor, 22 November 2012.

[168] Independent Evaluation Group, *The Forest Carbon Partnership Facility*, p. xi.

[169] Ibid., p. xix.

[170] Ibid., p. xxi.

C. Experimental Practices, Preparatory & Market-Construction Activities 85

Declaration on the Rights of Indigenous Peoples (UNDRIP) into account, that REDD+ activities are contested and often opposed by forest-dwellers, and that the FCPF governance structure privileges the interests of governments and business over those of Indigenous peoples.[171] A 2008 joint report by FERN and the FPP also found that the Fund had been cutting corners, had failed to consult properly and had failed to apply its own internal safeguard policies.[172] Their 2011 updated review found:

> [T]he FCPF is still failing to fulfil its social and environmental commitments, whilst national REDD+ Readiness preparation Proposals (R-PPs) lack sufficient plans for policy and legal reforms that would uphold forest peoples' rights, improve forest governance and reduce deforestation.[173]

In a further 2014 assessment they warned that:

> Unless major changes are made in FCPF planning, design and validation of emissions reduction programmes to ensure alignment with the FCPF Charter and international human rights standards, the FCPF Carbon Fund risks enabling seriously flawed REDD pilots that could generate negative impacts on indigenous peoples and local communities as the FCPF moves towards implementation of activities on the ground.[174]

As it celebrated its tenth birthday, in 2017 the FCPF was described by a lead climate finance specialist at the World Bank as developing 'groundbreaking programs with tremendous potential for mitigating climate change and improving livelihoods.'[175] To mark this anniversary, over a dozen NGOs signed a letter calling for the suspension of the FCPF. They alleged that 'this approach to forest protection simply has not worked' and that the 'FCPF cannot point to a single gram of carbon that it has saved nor any emission reductions payments that have yet been made'.[176] Yet despite the FCPF's limited concrete achievements, it has had considerable influence on shaping how REDD+-readiness is understood and the processes by which it is implemented.

---

[171] *Briefing: Some views of Indigenous peoples and forest-related organisations on the World Bank's "Forest Carbon Partnership Facility" and proposals for a "Global Forest Partnership"* (Forest Peoples Programme, 2008).

[172] K. Dooley, T. Griffiths, H. Leake, and S. Ozinga, *Cutting Corners: World Bank's Forest and Carbon Fund Fails Forests and People* (FERN and Forest Peoples Programme, 2008).

[173] Dooley et al., *Smoke and Mirrors*, p. 7.

[174] *Implement in Haste, Repent at Leisure: A Call for Rethinking the World Bank's Carbon Fund, Based on an Analysis of the Democratic Republic of Congo Emissions Reduction: Project Idea Note (ER-PIN)* (FERN and Forest Peoples Programme, 2014) p. 5.

[175] Baroudy, 'Why we should be more optimistic about forests and climate change'.

[176] C. Lang, 'NGOs call for suspension of World Bank's REDD programme: "The approach to forest protection simply has not worked"', *REDD-Monitor*, 17 December 2017.

(b) UN-REDD Programme

The UN-REDD Programme, launched in 2008, seeks to build on the 'convening role' and 'technical expertise' of its member organisations – the UNDP, UNEP and the FAO – and to work in close partnership with other REDD+ initiatives, especially those operated by the World Bank. In its 2011–2015 Strategy the UN-REDD Programme articulated its mission thus:

> To support countries' efforts to reduce emissions from deforestation and forest degradation through national REDD+ strategies that transform their forest sectors so as to contribute to human well-being and meet climate change mitigation and adaptation aspirations.[177]

The 2016–20 strategy document includes an updated mission, namely 'to reduce forest emissions and enhance carbon stocks in forests while contributing to national sustainable development'.[178] The 2016–20 strategy also identifies a number of cross-cutting themes as relevant to the achievement of its intended outcomes and outputs, especially stakeholder engagement, improved forest governance, tenure security and gender equality.

Since its restructure in 2016 the UN-REDD Programme governance structure consists of an executive board, an assembly, national steering committees and a multi-party trust fund office.[179] The Programme provides support through: (i) 'direct support to the design and implementation of National REDD+ Programmes'; (ii) 'complementary tailored support to national REDD+ actions' and (iii) 'technical capacity building through the sharing of expertise'.[180] By early 2019 the UN-REDD Programme was supporting 65 partner countries located in Africa, Asia–Pacific, Latin America and the Caribbean.[181]

A 2014 external review of the UN-REDD Programme raised a number of issues.[182] In particular, it found the likelihood of impact was 'moderately unlikely' given that that while the Programme is 'helping to create enabling conditions for collective action at the country level' it was 'too early to tell what effects the Programme will have in terms of reduced deforestation, sustainable forest resource use, and

---

[177] UN-REDD Programme, *The UN-REDD Programme Strategy 2011–2015* (February 2011) 6.

[178] UN-REDD Programme, *UN-REDD Programme Strategic Framework 2016–20* (7 May 2015) iv.

[179] Young, 'Interacting regimes and experimentation', pp. 13–47 at p. 34.

[180] UN-REDD Programme, 'How we work', www.un-redd.org/how-we-work (accessed 20 April 2019).

[181] UN-REDD Programme, 'Partner countries', www.un-redd.org/partner-countries (accessed 4 March 2019).

[182] A. Frechette, M. de Bresser, and R. Hofstede, *External Evaluation of the United Nations Collaborative Programme on Reducing Emissions from Deforestation and Forest Degradation in Developing Countries (the UN-REDD Programme)* (2014).

C. Experimental Practices, Preparatory & Market-Construction Activities 87

improved socio-economic conditions."[183] It also found that while the UN-REDD Programme helped raise awareness at both national and international levels about the importance of safeguards, it remained 'a challenge to put such principles into practice, notably due to the high number of safeguards and the lack of clear guidance on how to implement, monitor and enforce these."[184] Whilst the UN-REDD Programme positions itself as giving greater focus to 'rights-based' approaches in contrast to the more economic orientation of the World Bank's FCPF, in practice the two initiatives are 'actively coordinating their efforts', have agreed early on to 'coordinate their global analytical work in a manner that builds on and leverages their comparative advantages' and to 'develop harmonised thinking on what constitutes REDD readiness'.[185]

(c) Other Multilateral and Bilateral Channels

There are a number of other multilateral and bilateral funds that are providing support for REDD+ and REDD+-readiness activities. The Forest Investment Programme, which become operational in 2009 and is valued at $8 billion, is a part of the World Bank's Climate Investment Fund. It 'represents one of the first global efforts to invest in a dedicated climate finance vehicle"[186] and supports REDD+ efforts by 'providing scaled-up financing to developing countries for readiness reforms and public and private investments, identified through national REDD readiness or equivalent strategies'.[187]

The World Bank's BioCarbon Funds Initiative for Sustainable Forest Landscape is another multilateral fund that promotes REDD+ as well as sustainable agriculture and 'smarter' land-use policies and practices.[188] It became operational in November 2013 and is currently capitalized at US$350 million, thanks to contributions from Germany, Norway, the United Kingdom (UK) and the United States of America. It focuses on an entire jurisdiction (whether national or sub-national) and adopts a 'landscape' approach, to consider the 'trade-offs and synergies between different sectors that may compete in a jurisdiction for land use – such as forests, agriculture,

---

[183] Ibid., p. v.

[184] Ibid., p. vi.

[185] UN-REDD Programme, *The UN-REDD Programme and the World Bank's Forest Carbon Partnership Facility: Working Together for Better National and International Coordination* (2009). See also UN-REDD Programme, *Harmonization of Readiness Components: Note by the Secretariat* (October 2009), UN-REDD/PB3/7.

[186] CIF, 'History of the CIF', www.climateinvestmentfunds.org/timeline-cif (accessed 28 March 2019).

[187] Carbon Funds Update, Forest Investment Programme, climatefundsupdate.org/the-funds/forest-investment-program (accessed 28 March 2019).

[188] BioCarbon Fund, Initiative for Sustainable Forest Landscapes, www.biocarbonfund-isfl.org/about-us (accessed 28 March 2019).

88   *Background to REDD+*

energy, mining, and infrastructure' in order to identify 'solutions that serve multiple objectives and influence a variety of sectors'.[189]

The Central African Forest Initiative (CAFI) is a collaborative partnership between Central African countries with high rainforest coverage (Cameroon, Central African Republic, Democratic Republic of the Congo, Equatorial Guinea and Gabon), a coalition of donors (the EU, France, Germany, the Netherlands, Norway, South Korea and the UK) and Brazil.[190] With an initial capitalisation of US$500 million for the 2015–25 period, its objective is to 'recognise and preserve the value of the forests in the region to mitigating climate change, reducing poverty, and contributing to sustainable development'.[191] The CAFI Declaration signed in September 2015 commits to financing one national investment framework per eligible country, following which a Letter of Intent is signed between the forest country and donors: disbursements may then flow, subject to a performance-based approach and agreed targets.[192]

The Green Climate Fund (GCF) 'represents a new kind of funding institution in the emerging field of climate finance governance', as it is directly created by COP decisions, has a mandate to engage directly with the private sector and pursue both mitigation and adaptation, and has a board with equal North–South representation.[193] It was established at COP16 in Cancun as an operating entity of the Convention's financial mechanism,[194] and the Paris Agreement confirmed it would serve as the financial mechanism for the Agreement.[195] Further, the Warsaw Framework on REDD+ recognised the 'key role the Green Climate Fund will play in channelling financial resources to developing countries and catalysing climate finance'.[196] The Warsaw Framework also specifically referred to the 'key role of the GCF, as well as other financing entities, to 'collectively channel adequate and predictable result-based finance in a fair and balanced manner … while working with a view to increasing the number of countries that are in a position to obtain and receive payments for result-based actions'.[197] In doing this, the GCF was requested to apply the methodological guidance from various COP decisions.[198]

---

[189] BioCarbon Fund, 'Approach', www.biocarbonfund-isfl.org/approach (accessed 28 March 2019).

[190] Central African Forest Initiative, 'Our Work', www.cafi.org/content/cafi/en/home/our-work .html (accessed 28 March 2019).

[191] Central African Forest Initiative, *The CAFI Declaration* (29 September 2015), www.cafi.org/ content/cafi/en/home/our-work/governance/the-cafi-declaration.html (accessed 28 March 2019).

[192] Central African Forest Initiative, *The CAFI Declaration* (29 September 2015), www.cafi.org/ content/cafi/en/home/our-work/governance/the-cafi-declaration.html (accessed 28 March 2019).

[193] M. Bowman and S. Minas, 'Resilience through interlinkage: The green climate fund and climate finance governance' (2019) 19(3) *Climate Policy* 342–53 at 1.

[194] Decision 1/CP.16, para 102, see also UNFCCC Article 11.

[195] *Paris Agreement*, Article 9.8.

[196] Decision 9/CP.19, preambular recital 5.

[197] Decision 9/CP.19, para 5.

[198] Decision 9/CP.19, para 7.

C. Experimental Practices, Preparatory & Market-Construction Activities 89

The GCF provides support for all three phases of REDD+, including considering forests as part of a broader landscape and addressing livelihood issues.[199] The GCF describes itself as providing

> support to maintain and amplify efforts to implement the early phases of REDD-plus in recognition that REDD-plus offers a cross-cutting approach to contribute to global efforts to reduce emissions and contribute to low-emission and climate resilient development pathways in developing countries, while simultaneously generating local benefits, which in some cases could assist with adaptation to climate change.[200]

Through the GCF's Readiness and Preparatory Support Programme countries can access support to establish and strengthen national entities such as National Designation Authorities and Direct Access Entities.[201] The GCF also has a Project Preparation Facility that provides support to accredited entities for project and programme preparation.[202] In 2014 the GCF started developing and subsequently approved a 'logic model and performance measurement framework for ex-post REDD+ result-based payments'.[203] The Fund's support for REDD+ is guided by a number of principles, namely: the degree to which the proposed activity can catalyse a paradigm shift, particularly considering forests as part of a broader 'landscape' than merely the 'forest sector'; the potential of a project/programme to deliver results; serving broader benefits to sustainable development; as well as the needs of the recipient, country-ownership and efficiency and effectiveness.[204] In 2017 the GCF's Board asked the Secretariat to develop 'a request for proposals ... for REDD+ results-based payments ... including guidance consistent with the Warsaw Framework for REDD+ and other REDD+ decisions under the United Nations Framework Convention on Climate Change (UNFCCC).'[205] In October 2017 the Board approved a pilot programme for REDD+ result-based payments.

[199] Green Climate Fund, 'REDD+ in GCF', www.greenclimate.fund/how-we-work/redd (accessed 28 March 2019); see also *GCF in Brief: REDD+* (Global Climate Fund), www.greenclimate.fund/documents/20182/194568/GCF_in_Brief_REDD_.pdf/16e4f020-da42-42a2-ad52-d18314822710.

[200] Green Climate Fund, *Green Climate Fund Support for the Early Phases of REDD+*, GCF/B.17/16 (2 July 2017), p. 2.

[201] Green Climate Fund, 'Readiness Support', www.greenclimate.fund/gcf101/empowering-countries/readiness-support (accessed 28 March 2019).

[202] Green Climate Fund, 'Project preparation', www.greenclimate.fund/gcf101/funding-projects/project-preparation (access 20 April 2019).

[203] Green Climate Fund, 'Decision B.08/08', *Decisions of the Board – Eighth Meeting of the Board 14–17 October 2014*, GCF/B.08/45 (3 December 2014); see also Green Climate Fund, *Initial Social Model and Performance Measurement Framework for REDD+ Result-based Payments*, GCF/B.08/08/Rev.01 (17 October 2014).

[204] GCF, *Green Climate Fund Support for the Early Phrases of REDD-Plus.*

[205] Green Climate Fund, 'Decision B.14/03', *Decisions of the Board – Fourteenth Meeting of the Board 12–14 October 2016*, GCF/B.14/17 (2 November 2016); Green Climate Fund, *Support for REDD-plus*, GCF/B.14/03 (10 October 2016).

Background to REDD+

Alongside these multilateral REDD+ funding mechanisms, REDD+ has also been the subject of bilateral agreements. The most significant agreements have been entered with Indonesia and Guyana by Norway's International Climate and Forest Initiative.[206] A central component of these has been moratoriums on licencing forest exploitation and the establishment of forest monitoring systems, including through GPS/GIS satellite land representational systems. The German Federal Ministry for Economic Cooperation and Development launched its REDD+ Early Movers program at Rio+20 in 2012.[207] The fund provides REDD+ with bridging finance, and the KfW Development Bank makes payments for independently verified REDD+ emission reductions achieved by Early Movers. Australia's International Forest Carbon Initiative also supported global REDD+ efforts, including through a bilateral agreement with Indonesia and through demonstration activities such as the Kalimantan Forest Carbon Partnership.[208]

To sum up, the preparatory processes discussed, including demonstration activities and support for REDD+-readiness practices, show the diffuse nature of REDD+ implementation as well as the dispersed processes of REDD+ norm production. Identifying how norms have been developed through these diverse experimental demonstration projects and REDD+-readiness processes highlights how powerful actors have been able to significantly influence REDD+ norm development, outside and beyond the formal UNFCCC decision-making processes.

D REDD+ AS A CONCEPT, IDEA AND WAY OF SEEING

REDD+ also needs to be understood as a deceptively simple *concept* or *idea* emerging from the field of environmental economics, namely that the economic value produced from leaving forests standing should be greater than that produced by their destruction. Understood as a vision or idea, REDD+ exemplifies the broader dominance of the field of environmental economics[209] in producing a neoliberal model of environmentalism, or 'market environmentalism', which has had a significant impact on law and policy-making.[210] Arild Angelsen has noted that REDD+ 'follows textbook recommendations' from the field of environmental economics to

---

[206] See Norway's International Climate and Forest Initiative, norad.no/en/front/thematic-areas/climate-change-and-environment/norways-international-climate-and-forest-initiative-nicfi (accessed 20 April 2019); on the agreement with Indonesia see F. Seymour, N. Birdsall, and W. Savedoff, *The Indonesia–Norway REDD+ Agreement: A Glass Half-Full* (Center for Global Development, 2015).

[207] 'REDD early movers – Tools and instruments', www.giz.de/en/worldwide/33356.html (accessed 20 April 2019).

[208] See R. Pearse and J. Dehm, *In the REDD: Australia's Carbon Offset Project in Central Kalimantan* (Friends of the Earth International, 2011).

[209] See D. Pearce, 'An intellectual history of environmental economics' (2002) 27 *Annual Review of Energy and Environment* 57–81.

[210] S. Bernstein, *The Compromise of Liberal Environmentalism* (Colombia University Press, 2001).

D. REDD+ As a Concept, Idea and Way of Seeing

'create a multilevel ... system of payments for ecosystem environmental services'.[211] Esteve Corbera likewise suggests that REDD+ is 'the world's largest [payment for ecosystem services] experiment'.[212] Fletcher et al. describe the vision of REDD+ thusly: [It is] conceptualized as a quintessential [market-based instrument] in its aim to incentivize forest conservation by correcting so-called market failure in sustainable forest management through ascribing monetary values to standing forest that would cover the opportunity costs of alternative land use and so make conservation more profitable than destruction.[213] This vision of REDD+ includes, at a minimum, making the 'value' of the carbon sequestration potential of forests legible in economic terms. However, for many key proponents and players in the REDD+ space the vision of REDD+ also includes incorporation of REDD+ as an offset within international carbon markets.

1 REDD+ As a Vision of Economic Valuation of Forests

The premise of REDD+ as a concept or idea is this: that making legible in economic terms the 'value' of forests' carbon sequestration potential will provide economic incentives for forest protection by enabling the 'value' of standing forests to be better factored into decision-making; this will thereby shift decision-making practices in ways that lead to better forest protection outcomes. The UN-REDD Programme describes how 'REDD+ ... creates a financial value for the carbon stored in forests by offering incentives for developing countries to reduce emissions from forested lands and invest in low-carbon paths to sustainable development'.[214] This idea that nature should be valued in economic terms underpins influential policy prescriptions to include forests in global carbon markets such as are found in the English *Stern Review*[215] and *The Eliasch Review*.[216] Eliasch writes that 'as long as forest carbon or other ecosystem services are not reflected in the price of commodities produced from converted forest land, forests will – in financial terms – generally be worth more to landowners cut rather than standing'.[217] He therefore argues that the costs of ecosystem services, including carbon storage and sequestration, need to be valued differently in order to change the current conditions in which it is 'more lucrative to deforest and sell the resulting timber and agricultural produce than to

---

[211] A. Angelsen, 'The 3 REDD "I's" (2010) 16 *Journal of Forest Economics* 253–6 at 253.

[212] E. Corbera, 'Problematizing REDD+ as an experiment in payments for ecosystem services' (2012) 4(6) *Current Opinion in Environmental Sustainability* 612–19 at 612.

[213] R. Fletcher, W. Dressler, B. Buscher, and Z. R. Anderson, 'Questioning REDD+ and the future of market-based conservation' (2016) 30(3) *Conservation Biology* 673–5 at 673.

[214] UN-REDD Programme, 'About REDD+', www.un-redd.org/aboutredd/tabid/102614/default .aspx (accessed 19 July 2014).

[215] N. H. Stern, *The Economics of Climate Change: The Stern Review* (Cambridge University Press, 2007).

[216] Eliasch, *Climate Change: Financing Global Forests*.

[217] Ibid., p. 41.

leave forests standing ... because the costs of the deforestation are not reflected in the price of the timber or agricultural produce'.[218] In this sense, *The Eliasch Review* conceptualises the costs of deforestation as 'externalities' whose exclusion from the market creates a market failure whereby the 'market will supply more timber and agricultural produce from deforested land than is efficient'.[219] The underlying rationale of this policy prescription is that 'if the costs of deforestation were factored into the price of products, their production would tend to shift to other land where they could be grown without deforestation'.[220] This conceptualisation, however, leaves unaddressed the concrete and material ways in which the demand for forest products drives processes of deforestation. Moreover, it is based on the assumption that there is a supply of available 'other' land, which ignores how such land may already be used for alternative purposes such as subsistence agriculture, which are critically important even if they bring low market returns. The rationality underpinning pricing mechanisms is that decisions about alternative land uses should be determined by relations of supply and demand rather than other – perhaps more deliberative – processes.

This focus on promoting the valuation of nature, including forests, in economic terms, has a longer history. In 1989, the *Blueprint for Green Economy* report commissioned by the UK government argued for the need to economically 'value' the environment and sought to outline mechanisms for that purpose.[221] The development of improved valuation, pricing and incentive mechanisms has been a principle of ecological sustainable development since the early 1990s, based on the assumption that the real costs of polluting activities – and the real value of natural resources – are reflected in the prices paid by industry and consumers.[222] This focus was adopted by the World Bank as the theme of their First Annual International Conference on Environmentally Sustainable Development in 1993.[223] Within the field of forest policy, a key message of the 1999 *Our Forests, Our Future* report produced by the World Commission on Forests and Sustainable Development was the need to value the 'natural capital' of forests.[224] These ideas were transferred into the forest regime through close collaborations between the epistemic community of environmental economic practitioners and those working

---

[218] Ibid., p. 63.

[219] Ibid.

[220] Ibid.

[221] D. Pearce, A. Markandya, and E. B. Barbier, *Blueprint for a Green Economy* (Earthscan, 1989).

[222] G. Bates, *Environmental Law in Australia*, 9th ed. (LexisNexis, 2016) pp. 321–2.

[223] I. Serageldin and A. Steer (eds.), *Valuing the Environment: Proceedings of the First Annual International Conference on Environmentally Sustainable Development, Held at the World Bank, Washington, D.C., September 30–October 1, 1993* (The World Bank, 1993).

[224] *Our Forests, Our Future: Summary Report of the World Commission on Forests and Sustainable Development* (World Commission on Forests and Sustainable Development, 1999); for a discussion see D. Humphreys, *Forest Politics: The Evolution of International Cooperation* (Earthscan, 1996) Chapter 3.

D. REDD+ As a Concept, Idea and Way of Seeing

on forest policy development. As documented by David Humphreys, some materials prepared for the Intergovernmental Panel on Forests (1995–97) for its work on 'methodologies for the proper valuation of the multiple benefits of forests' were in effect directly plagiarised from a report prepared by the International Institute for Environment and Development (IIED) for the UK Overseas Development Administration.[225] Subsequently the World Bank was made the lead agency for the Intergovernmental Forum on Forests (1997–2000) work program on the 'valuation of forest goods and services'.[226] In this role the Bank prepared background papers suggesting five areas where new markets could be established in forest goods and services to provide conservation incentives (including carbon sequestration, biodiversity and hydrological services as well as non-timber products and ecotourism).[227] Again Humphreys notes that 'in several cases, language from the documents was used as a basis for negotiating Intergovernmental Forum on Forests proposals for action ... [where in fact] in many cases the wording proposed by the World Bank survived the negotiations intact'.[228] These incidents, Humphreys argues, 'reveal the limits of genuine intellectual debate on environmental valuation' and the strong influence of certain actors that are part of 'a knowledge-based network that shares agreement on the methodologies for environmental valuation in general, and forest valuation in particular".[229]

Approaches focused on economic valuation have remained hegemonic in environmental policy-making, although for many proponents, economic valuation of nature is seen as only the first step in a much broader agenda. The *Millennium Ecosystem Assessment* highlighted that '[t]he mere act of quantifying the value of ecosystem services cannot by itself change the incentives affecting their use or misuse' and that changes to current practices are required to 'take better account of these values'.[230] The UNEP-sponsored *The Economics of Ecosystems and Biodiversity* (TEEB) initiative is perhaps the most prominent expression of this project of valuing nature in order to better factor ecosystem services within policy and decision-making.[231] These practices of 'valuing nature' – and accounting for this value within decision-making and cost benefit analysis – has become a central theme of the 'green economy'.[232] A critical observer of this trend, geographer Sian

---

[225] D. Humphreys, *Logjam: Deforestation and the Crisis of Global Governance* (Earthscan, 2006) p. 38.

[226] Ibid., p. 67.

[227] Ibid., p. 80.

[228] Ibid., p. 81.

[229] Ibid.

[230] The Millennium Ecosystem Assessment Board, *Ecosystems and Human Well-being: Current State and Trends, Vol 1* (2005) 34.

[231] *The Economics of Ecosystems and Biodiversity: Mainstreaming the Economics of Nature: A Synthesis of the Approach, Conclusions and Recommendations of the TEEB* (TEEB, 2010).

[232] C. Allen and S. Clouth, *A Guidebook to the Green Economy – Issue 1: Green Economy, Green Growth and Low-Carbon Development – History, Definitions and a Guide to Recent Publications* (UN-DESA, 2012); for a critique of this paradigm see D. Brockington, 'A radically

94 *Background to REDD+*

Sullivan, describes the development of a growing industry of 'accounting of socio-environmental relations'.[233] She highlights the reductive and repressive effects of an illusion of fixing the 'value of nature' in tradable and substitutable economic terms. Sullivan argues that when the 'messy materiality of life' is rendered 'legible as discrete entities, individualised and abstracted from complex social and ecological entanglements'[234] and standardised, it has the effect of dismissing other logics of evaluation.[235] She further expresses concern 'that diversities are lost in the world-making mission to fashion and fabricate the entire planet as an abstracted plane of (ac)countable, monetizable and potentially substitutable natural capital'.[236]

Thus, in understanding REDD+ as a vision of the economic valuation of forests it is critical to recognise that the underlying economic assumptions, theories and models are not simply a description of how forest conservation *does* work but a prescription of how forest conservation *should* work. Moreover, these models have embedded in them numerous presuppositions about human nature and human motivations. Actualising these prescriptions, or making them real, thus necessarily also entails a micro-politics addressed to altering human behaviour, responses, drives and motivations.

2 *REDD+ As a Vision of an 'Offset' in Transnational Carbon Markets*

For many proponents REDD+ is imagined, not just as a mechanism to 'value' forest carbon, but as a mechanism to incorporate forest carbon as an 'offset' into international carbon markets. The *Stern Review* noted that carbon markets could 'play an important role' in providing incentives for curbing deforestation.[237] Further, *The Eliasch Review* assumes that in order to tackle forest emissions it is necessary to have a 'well-designed mechanism for linking forest abatement to carbon markets', in order to access public and private finance.[238] Charlotte Streck writes that REDD+ was 'originally ... conceived of as a market-based system'[239] and others confirm it was

---

conservative vision? The challenge of UNEP's "Towards a Green Economy"' 43(1) *Development and Change* 409–22; N. Bullard and T. Müller, 'Beyond the "Green Economy": System change, not climate change?' (2012) 55(1) *Development* 54–62.

[233] S. Sullivan, 'The environmentality of "Earth Incorporated": On contemporary primitive accumulation and the financialisation of environmental conservation' (2010), Paper presented at the conference An Environmental History of Neoliberalism, Lund University, 6–8 May 2010; S. Sullivan, 'Banking nature? The Spectacular financialisation of environmental conservation' (2013) 45(1) *Antipode* 198–217.

[234] Prudham cited in Sullivan, 'The environmentality of 'Earth Incorporated'', p. 17.

[235] See also A. Robinson and S. Tormey, 'Resisting "Global Justice": Disrupting the colonial "emancipatory" logic of the West' (2009) 30(8) *Third World Quarterly* 1395–409 at 1399.

[236] S. Sullivan, 'On "natural capital", "fairy tales" and ideology' (2017) 48(2) *Development and Change* 397–423 at 398.

[237] Stern, *The Economics of Climate Change: The Stern Review*, p. xxvi.

[238] Eliasch, *Climate Change: Financing Global Forests*, p. 165.

[239] C. Streck, 'In the market: Forest carbon rights: Shedding light on a muddy concept' (2015) 4 *Carbon & Climate Law Review* 342–47.

D. REDD+ As a Concept, Idea and Way of Seeing

'originally conceived as a PES [payment for environmental services] system' where it 'was anticipated that the majority of funding would come from carbon markets'.[240]

If REDD+ were to be confirmed as an offset mechanism – whereby purchased 'emission reductions' from countries of the Global South were able to contribute towards the compliance obligations of countries of the Global North – such a mechanism would be structured around the assumption that 'emission reductions' through reducing deforestation and forest degradation are *equivalent to* GHGs emitted elsewhere. Scholars have critically described and elaborated the work – representational, accounting and regulatory – that goes into enabling diverse actions to be presented as equivalent and substitutable,[241] while simultaneously questioning these purported equivalences, especially the claimed equivalence between forest carbon and fossil carbon.[242] However, the present analysis is not primarily concerned with whether such purported equivalences are real or an illusion but is focused on interrogating the productive effects of such *claims to equivalence*: that is, the *effects* of designating the outcomes of these very different practices and processes as equivalent.

This claim of equivalence between carbon emitted in the Global North and additional carbon sequestered in forests in the Global South establishes a *strategic relation* between the practices of resource extraction on one hand and the practices of conservation, preservation, sustainable engagement of forests and management of carbon stocks that make up REDD+ on the other. As such, the offset relation holds together two different ways of governing nature – one directed towards the appropriation of nature and the other towards stewardship of nature – that have historically been viewed as being in *tension* with one another: that is, the offset relation holds together an 'extractive' power over nature alongside a 'productive' power over nature. Resource extraction operates through the form and modality of anthropocentric power over the natural world, in which an absolute human mastery and domination of nature is justified by a divine biblical right.[243] Thus, as a modality of

---

[240] M.-C. Cordonier Segger, M. Gehring, and A. Wardell, 'REDD+ instruments, international investment rules and sustainable landscapes' in C. Voigt (ed.), *Research Handbook on REDD-Plus and International Law* (Edward Elgar Publishing, 2016) p. 348.

[241] D. MacKenzie, 'Making things the same: Gases, emission rights and the politics of carbon markets' (2009) 34(3) *Accounting, Organizations and Society* 440–55; E. Lövbrand and J. Stripple, 'Making climate change governable: Accounting for carbon as sinks, credits and personal budgets' (2011) 5(2) *Critical Policy Studies* 187–200; L. Lohmann, 'Performative equations and neoliberal commodification: The case of climate' in B. Büscher, W. Dressler and R. Fletcher (eds.) *Nature^{TM} Inc.: Environmental Conservation in the Neoliberal Age* (The University of Arizona Press, 2014) 158–80.

[242] See for example L. Lohmann, 'The endless algebra of climate markets' (2011) 22(4) *Capitalism, Nature, Socialism* 93–116; J. Dehm, 'One tonne of carbon dioxide equivalent (1tCO2e)' in J. Hohmann and D. Joyce (eds.), *International Law's Objects* (Oxford University Press, 2018) pp. 305–18.

[243] King James Bible, Genesis 1:28 cited in S. Humphreys and Y. Otomo, 'Theorizing international environmental law' in A. Orford, F. Hoffmann, M. Clark (eds.), *The Oxford Handbook of the Theory of International Law* (Oxford University Press, 2016) pp. 797–819, 802.

power it exhibits a parallel with a sovereign 'power of life and death' or to '*take* life or *let* live', in which power is exercised primarily through deduction or subtraction and through a claim to a right of appropriation and seizure.[244] This biblical injunction to subdue the earth was, as Yoriko Otomo and Stephen Humphreys note, 'relied upon by the Dominicans in the pre-Reformation era and, most pointedly, the Puritans afterwards',[245] and it is a key organising principle of many legal theories.

Practices of conservation, preservation and scientific management display a different modality of anthropocentric power over the natural world to that of resource exploitation – namely stewardship or a form of pastoral power, whose motif is the shepherd rather than the king. In contrast to a despotic power based on its own absolute claim to sovereignty, stewardship manages its domain 'on the basis of its claim to be operating under the auspices of a higher ethical power that, properly understood, guides the rulers' concern for the well-being of those ruled'.[246] This is a 'beneficent power' whose purpose of doing 'good' manifests itself through a 'power of care'[247] or a 'duty' to undertake its tasks of keeping watch in order to achieve its objective of collective salvation, or salvation as subsistence.[248] Such a 'proper' management of individuals, goods and wealth derives from conceptions of the art of governing a family and the paternal control exercised by a (male) household head over his wife, children and servants. The Greek word *oïkos*, meaning 'home' or household, is the etymological root of both economy and ecology.[249] The strategic relation that REDD+ instigates between these two different modalities of power therefore requires us not to bracket or downplay either one, but to think of them together, and 'to account for and critically engage the integral co-implication and coevalness of "repressive" and "productive" formations' by which life is governed.[250] Moreover, through the offset relation these practices are *co-articulated* and jointly encompassed in a broader framework directed towards maximising the aggregate productivity of nature. The strategic relation produced by the offset generates a rationality of aggregate global resource maximisation that is made concrete through the concept of 'value'. The danger of such an approach, focused on maximising the aggregate 'value' of nature, is that an economic understanding of 'value' increasingly operates as a substitute for, or it displaces, the contestation over competing values.

---

[244] M. Foucault, *The Will to Knowledge: The History of Sexuality: Volume I* (Penguin, 1998) p. 136.

[245] Humphreys and Otomo, 'Theorizing international environmental law', p. 802.

[246] M. Smith, *Against Ecological Sovereignty: Ethics, Biopolitics, and Saving the Natural World* (University of Minnesota Press, 2011) p. 22.

[247] M. Foucault, *Security, Territory, Population: Lectures at the Collège de France 1977–1978* (Palgrave Macmillan, 2007) p. 127.

[248] Ibid., p. 126.

[249] Angela Mitropoulos notes that the term 'ecology' was coined by zoologist Ernst Haeckel in attempting to 'articulate a nascent behaviourism (that psychology is a branch of physiology) and biopolitics (his infamous phrase: 'politics is applied biology'); see A. Mitropoulos, 'Oikopolitics, and storms' (2009) 3(1) *The Global South* 66–82 at 68.

[250] This quote is taken from J. Butler and A. Athanasiou, *Dispossession: The Performative in the Political* (Polity, 2013) p. 30, where coevalness is discussed in relation to a different context.

E REDD+ AS CO-ARTICULATING VARIOUS FORMS OF ANTHROPOCENTRIC GOVERNANCE

What is thereby lost are the 'irreducible contestations over the values underlying and informing ecological science and environmental law'.[251]

As well as understanding REDD+ as a legal or regulatory framework, as series of practices and processes and as a concept, vision or idea, REDD+ can also be understood as being made up of mechanisms to promote specific activities to avoid deforestation and forest degradation. This section provides an overview of such activities, their origins, history and exclusionary dynamics, focusing primarily on practices of conservation and sustainable forest management (SFM). When REDD+ (or RED, as it then was) was first proposed, the focus was primarily on activities to reduce deforestation and avoid forest degradation; however, this scope expanded over time.[252] The Bali Action Plan extended this initial focus when it called for positive incentives and policy approaches relating to 'reducing emissions from deforestation and forest degradation in developing countries; and the role of conservation, sustainable management of forests and enhancement of forest carbon stocks in developing countries and forest degradation'.[253] However, at that stage a strategically placed semi-colon suggested that the latter activities would not be subject to the same policy approaches and positive incentives as reducing deforestation and forest degradation.[254] The following year at COP14, however, actors who wanted to make conservation and sustainable forest management more prominent in these discussions pushed to change the semi-colon to a comma.[255] At Copenhagen (COP15), the punctuation separating 'activities relating to reducing emissions from deforestation and forest degradation and the role of conservation, sustainable management of forests and enhancement of forest carbon stocks in developing countries' was removed[256] – and the term 'REDD+ was officially born'.[257] The Cancun Agreements clarified that the same polices and incentives were applicable to all of the following activities: reducing emissions from

---

[251] V. De Lucia, 'Competing narratives and complex genealogies: The ecosystem approach in international environmental law' (2015) 27(1) *Journal of Environmental Law* 91–117 at 99.

[252] A. Wiersema, 'Climate change, forests and international law: REDD's descent into irrelevance' (2014) 47(1) *Vanderbilt Journal of Transnational Law* 1–66 at 25–6.

[253] Decision 1/CP.13, para 1(b)(iii).

[254] I. Fry, 'Reducing emissions from deforestation and forest degradation: Opportunities and pitfalls in developing a new legal regime' (2008) 17(2) *Review of European Community and International Environmental Law* 166–82 at 167.

[255] Wiersema, 'Climate change, forests and international law: REDD's descent into irrelevance', 33–4.

[256] Decision 4/CP.15.

[257] Wiersema, 'Climate change, forests and international law: REDD's descent into irrelevance', 35.

Background to REDD+

deforestation; reducing emissions from forest degradation; conservation of forest carbon stocks; sustainable management of forests; and enhancement of forest carbon sinks.[258]

Due to the contested histories of such activities, the language adopted to describe them was at times controversial. The use of the phrase 'conservation of forest carbon stocks', which departed from the phrase used in earlier decisions 'the role of conservation', raised concerns that this shift in language suggested forests would be viewed simply in terms of their carbon conservation value, rather than in terms of a broader conception of conservation, which also encompasses biodiversity protection. The semantic distinction between 'sustainable forest management' (SFM) – which has been used in other international forest agreements – and 'sustainable management of forests' – which was adopted in the Cancun Agreements – was also the subject of heated debate. The Bali Action Plan referred to 'sustainable management of forests', but Decision 2/CP.13 on approaches to stimulate action on REDD+ included the term SFM, alongside references to the provisions of the United Nations Forum on Forests, the UN Convention to Combat Desertification and the Convention on Biological Diversity.[259] Both phrases, 'sustainable management of forests' and 'sustainable forest management', were included in parentheses in the pre-Copenhagen texts.[260] Several environmental groups strongly contested the inclusion of the term SFM, concerned it would allow strong vested interests in logging and agribusiness to benefit from REDD+ under the guise of SFM.[261] According to the FAO, the key faultline in the debate was between those who supported the inclusion of the term SFM, who sought 'a comprehensive scope for REDD+ in order to maximise potential greenhouse gas reductions and removals from forests', and those who opposed the inclusion of the term, who were advocating a more 'restrictive' scope 'that [would exempt] forests managed for commercial timber production, due to the concern that REDD+ might subsidise industrial-scale timber extraction at the expense of small-scale local enterprise or non-timber forest values, such as biodiversity'.[262] The fact that the term SFM was not included in the Cancun Agreements was thus celebrated by environmental NGOs.[263] Margaret Young reads this failure to fully endorse the SFM approach from the forest regime in REDD+ as

---

[258] Decision 1/CP.16, para 70.
[259] Decision 2/CP.13, Annex, para 8.
[260] See K. Dooley and N. Reisch, 'Bonn II: REDD discussions at the June 2009 UNFCCC Climate Meeting', *EU Forest Watch* July 2009, www.redd-monitor.org/wp-content/uploads/2009/07/document_4448_4450.pdf.
[261] *Vested Interests: Industrial Logging and Carbon in Tropical Forests* (Global Witness, 2009) p. 6.
[262] *Sustainable management of forests and REDD+: Negotiations need clear terminology: Information Note* (Food and Agricultural Organization, 2009) p. 1; see also *Trick or Treat? REDD, Development and Sustainable Forest Management* (Global Witness, 2009).
[263] See for example (writing about Copenhagen) Patrick Alley, 'As the dust settles, some cause for optimism' *Global Witness* (blog), 2009, www.globalwitness.org/archive/dust-settles-some-cause-optimism.

E. REDD+ As Co-articulating Various Forms of Anthropocentric Governance   99

potentially constraining '[the way in which] REDD+ would be influenced by, and influence, other regimes', such as the international forest governance regime.[264] While the rejection of the formation of 'sustainable forest management' may reduce the influence of some established practices, the boundaries are probably not so neat: for example, the Global Environmental Facility in its 2010–14 strategy refers to REDD+ and SFM interchangeably.[265]

A brief history of what will probably be the two most common REDD+ activities, conservation and sustainable forest management, is provided below. By making these very different activities subject to the same policy approaches and incentives, REDD+ brings together activities that have arisen from very different imperatives and have very different rationalities. Stephen Humphreys and Yoriko Otomo have demonstrated how international environmental law is constituted by the animating tension between two 'non-negotiable' imperatives, which can be traced to the practices of the scientific management of nature and the ideology of romanticism, respectively.[266] The practices of SFM arise from the former whilst conservation is a key enactment of the latter. Humphreys and Otomo have highlighted the key tension between these practices, given that 'the promise to respect an inherent bound within "nature itself" is destabilised by the necessity of exploiting, developing, applying the non-human as a resource'.[267] They have therefore stressed the 'extraordinary difficulty in achieving any such mediation' because of the inherent irreconcilability of the two: 'what one holds sacred, the other profanes'.[268] The effect of the way REDD+ holds these different activities together and makes them subject to the same policy approaches and incentives therefore deserves further investigation. Thinking about REDD+ as an assemblage that somehow holds together these 'constituent conceptual elements that generate [international environmental law's] specific energy and propel its contradictions'[269] explains some of the contradictions internal to REDD+ and helps make evident the work needed to allow REDD+ (however uneasily) to cohere. However, on a deeper level, despite the inherent tensions and contradictions between these activities and their underlying imperatives, one can also observe a shared coloniality underpinning both these activities, as well as a shared anthropocentric assumption of 'ecological sovereignty'.[270]

---

[264] M. A. Young, 'REDD+ and interacting legal regimes' in C. Voigt (ed.), *Research Handbook on REDD-plus and International Law* (Edward Elgar Publishing, 2016), pp. 89 and 108.

[265] 'GEF 5 Focal Areas Strategies' (Global Environmental Facility, 2009), www.thegef.org/gef/sites/thegef.org/files/publication/English%20-%20Strategies-may2012-optimized.pdf, 90–98.

[266] Humphreys and Otomo, 'Theorizing international environmental law'.

[267] Ibid., pp. 818–19.

[268] Ibid., p. 819.

[269] Ibid., p. 799.

[270] M. Smith, *Against Ecological Sovereignty: Ethics, Biopolitics, and Saving the Natural World* (University of Minnesota Press, 2011).

100   *Background to REDD+*

1 *Conservation*

Practices of forest conservation or preservation have historically been counterpoised to processes of extraction, appropriation and translation of nature into a 'resource'. Nonetheless, like practices of extraction, practices of conservation and the romanticised wilderness ideology that underpins them are structured by colonialist assumptions, that historically operated to make invisible the practices and histories of peoples living in places imagined as 'wild'.[271] National Parks or 'wilderness areas', whilst not autonomous jurisdictions,[272] nonetheless remain a troubling figure of exclusion/inclusion in the law.[273] The 'nature resource', as Mick Smith argues, exists in a paradoxical legal position whereby it 'is exempted from being a resource, freed from human domination, only by being already and always included within the remit of human domination'.[274] These practices were underpinned by the concept of 'wilderness' as a central theme of Romantic political and artistic movements. This concept, Humphreys and Otomo argue, has 'implanted lasting notions of the beauty of "unspoilt" wilderness, imbued with a profound moral significance, that have endured to the present and provide the ideational backdrop specific to this body of international law'.[275] This fantasy of wilderness as a primitive Eden arose in a specific context, namely that of the nineteenth century colonising and industrialising bourgeoisie;[276] it did so to enable the Romantic bourgeois dreams of 'authentic' self-realisation; and it had dangerous effects, because this idea as 'ideal' sustains itself only through the erasure of people, law and livelihoods from these spaces.[277] As Robert Fletcher shows, the illusion that a wilderness free of human manipulation could engage with Indigenous peoples in only one of two ways: either through their deliberate erasure and making invisible the record of inhabitation and transversion of these spaces by, interventions in and transformation of 'wilderness' spaces by humans for millennia; or by recognising their presence, but 'pronouncing indigenous people sub-human, and therefore incapable of diluting wilderness in the same manner as 'civilized man'.[278]

---

[271] R. Fletcher, 'Against wilderness' (2009) 5(1) *Green Theory & Praxis: The Journal of Ecopedagogy* 169–79; for a critique of the idea of 'wilderness' see W. Cronon, 'The trouble with wilderness; or, getting back to the wrong nature' in W. Cronon (ed.), *Uncommon Ground: Rethinking the Human Place in Nature* (W. W. Norton & Company, 1995) pp. 69–90; and for an historical overview see R. Guha, *Environmentalism: A Global History* (Oxford University Press, 1999) Chapter 4.

[272] S. Dorsett and S. McVeigh, *Jurisdiction* (Routledge, 2012) p. 46.

[273] For a discussion of nature as 'other' see also L. Godden, 'Preserving natural heritage: Nature as other' (1998) 22(3) *Melbourne University Law Review* 719–42.

[274] Smith, *Against Ecological Sovereignty: Ethics, Biopolitics, and Saving the Natural World*, p. xiii.

[275] Humphreys and Otomo, 'Theorizing international environmental law', p. 799.

[276] Cronon, 'The trouble with wilderness; or, getting back to the wrong nature'.

[277] See Godden, 'Preserving natural heritage: Nature as other'.

[278] See Fletcher, 'Against wilderness', 175.

The establishment of 'protected areas' has been the main vehicle for in-situ conservation for 'the protection of ecosystems, natural habitats and the maintenance of viable populations of species in natural surroundings',[279] and it is 'deeply embedded in the forest regime and other areas of global environmental governance'.[280] In the contemporary era, the conflicts between nature conservation and local livelihoods remain acute. Anthropologist Nancy Peluso has shown that a Romantic gaze continues to underpin 'coercive conservation' practices,[281] and Mark Dowie has documented how such practices have produced 'conservation refugees'.[282] In the last two decades there has been a strong focus on 'rights-based conservation',[283] since the Durban Accord passed at the fifth International Union for the Conservation of Nature (IUCN) World Parks Congress announced a 'new paradigm' for protected areas that foregrounded the rights of Indigenous peoples and local communities.[284] To facilitate 'rights-based approaches' to conservation various 'soft law' mechanisms have been developed and adopted such as codes of practice, principles and internal policies; nonetheless, the challenges of implementing such 'rights-based approaches' in practice have been considerable.[285] Since 2010 the issue of 'green grabbing', where large conservation projects have led to forced evictions, resettlement or decreased livelihood or subsistence access for local communities, has again come into sharp focus.[286] The UN Special Rapporteur on the rights of indigenous peoples, Victoria Tauli-Corpuz, highlighted in 2016, how the 'impact that conservation initiatives have on indigenous peoples has been a

---

[279] *Convention on Biological Diversity*, opened for signature 5 June 1992, 1760 UNTS 79 (entered into force 29 December 1993), article 8(d).

[280] Humphreys, *Logjam: Deforestation and the Crisis of Global Governance*, p. 194.

[281] N. L. Peluso, 'Coercing conservation? The politics of state resource control' (1993) *Global Environmental Change* 199–217.

[282] M. Dowie, *Conservation Refugees: The Hundred-Year Conflict between Global Conservation and Native Peoples* (MIT Press, 2009).

[283] For a discussion see L. Siegele, D. Roe, A. Giuliani, and N. Winer, 'Conservation and human rights : Who says what? A review of international law and policy' in J. Campese, T. Sunderland, T. Greiber, and G. Oviedo (eds.), *Rights-Based Approaches: Exploring Issues and Opportunities for Conservation* (Center for International Forestry Research and International Union for Conservation of Nature, 2009); T. Greiber, M. Janki, M. Orellana, A. Savaresi, and D. Shelton, *Conservation with Justice: A Rights-Based Approach* (Center for International Forestry Research and International Union for Conservation of Nature, 2009).

[284] IUCN, *The Durban Action Plan*, Revised version, March 2004, cmsdata.iucn.org/downloads/durbanactionen.pdf.

[285] V. Tauli-Corpuz, *Report of the Special Rapporteur of the Human Rights Council on the rights of indigenous peoples, Victoria Tauli-Corpuz*, General Assembly, A/71/229 (29 July 2016), para 39–50.

[286] See J. Fairhead, M. Leach, and I. Scoones, 'Green grabbing: A new appropriation of nature?' (2012) 39 *Journal of Peasant Studies* 237–61 and the article in the special issue it introduces; for some case studies see F. Pearce, *The Land Grabbers: The New Fight Over Who Owns the Earth* (Random House, 2012).

constant and recurring theme'.[287] She noted that conservation measures have resulted in a number of human rights violations, including the expropriation of land, forced displacement, denial of self-governance, lack of access to livelihoods and loss of culture and spiritual sites, non-recognition of Indigenous peoples' own authority over land and resources, and denial of access to justice and reparation, including restitution and compensation.[288] She has noted specific concerns that '[w]hile the conservation community is in the process of adopting conservation measures that respect the human rights of indigenous peoples, considerable implementation gaps remain and new threats to human rights-based conservation are emerging'.[289] It is therefore unsurprising that the provision of further incentives for such activities through the carbon economy has raised concerns about the potential impact on peoples living in and around forested areas, something which will be discussed in greater detail in the next section.

2 Sustainable Management of Forests

The concept of 'sustainable forest management' (SFM) has been notoriously difficult to define. The 'deliberately vague' term was included in the 1992 Non-legally Binding Authoritative Statement of Principles for a Global Consensus on the Management, Conservation and Sustainable Development of All Types of Forests (the 'Forest Principles'), which was agreed to at the Rio Earth Summit in 1992.[290] Several regional processes have since attempted to define this term and develop indicators and criteria.[291] As David Humphreys argues, the formulation of the concept of 'sustainable development' had a strong impact on the emergence of 'sustainable forest management' as a legal idea.[292] This concept is central to the International Tropical Timber Agreement (1983, 1994 and 2006),[293] the first

---

[287] V. Tauli-Corpuz, *Report of the Special Rapporteur of the Human Rights Council on the Rights of Indigenous Peoples* (2016) para 8.

[288] Ibid., para 9.

[289] Ibid., para 11.

[290] *Non-Legally Binding Authoritative Statement of Principles for a Global Consensus on the Management, Conservation and Sustainable Development of All Types of Forests*, Report of the United Nations Conference on Environment and Development, Rio de Janeiro, A/CONF.151/26 (Vol. III) (14 August 1992) paragraph 8(d) states that 'Sustainable forest management and use should be carried out in accordance with national development priorities and on the basis of environmentally sound national guidelines. In the formation of such guidelines, account should be taken, as appropriate and if applicable, of relevant internationally agreed methodologies and criteria.' For a discussion of these processes see Humphreys, *Logjam: Deforestation and the Crisis of Global Governance* , Chapter 6.

[291] See for example the Montreal Process, the Helsinki Process, the Tarapoto Proposal, and the Lepaterique Process for Central America.

[292] D. Humphreys, *Forest Politics: The Evolution of International Cooperation* (Earthscan, 1996) p. 21.

[293] *International Tropical Timber Agreement, 1983*, opened for signature 18 November 1983, 1393 UNTS 119 (entered into force 1 April 1985); *International Tropical Timber Agreement, 1994*, opened for signature 1 April 1994, 1955 UNTS 81 (entered into force 1 January 1997);

commodity agreement to also include conservation provisions. Subsequent to the articulation of the Forest Principles, the 1995 protocol to the Lomé IV Convention was the first international legal agreement between governments from the North and South on SFM.[294] The concept of SFM is central to the four global objectives that organise the 2007 Non-Legally Binding Instrument on All Types of Forests, especially the first objective – to 'reverse the loss of forest cover worldwide through sustainable forest management, including protection, restoration, afforestation and reforestation, and increase efforts to prevent forest degradation'.[295] This instrument also recognises that SFM, as a 'dynamic and evolving concept, aims to maintain and enhance the economic, social and environmental values of all types of forests, for the benefit of present and future generations'.[296]

However, the concept of SFM has been critiqued for its environmental and social limitations. Global Witness writes that 'SFM is a poorly defined term that in practice has included highly destructive activities such as industrial-scale logging in intact natural (primary) forests'.[297] Similar to how 'sustainable development' has been critiqued as a paradigm that facilitates the sustaining of capitalism rather than promotion of ecological values, SFM has been described as a 'nasty little euphemism', that in practice allows the continuation of destructive logging practices.[298] As Global Witness alleges:

> The lack of clear performance thresholds has allowed high-impact industrial logging companies to call their practices "SFM" without changing those practices at all. These companies were quick to co-opt the term and use it in their communications strategies. As a result, SFM has become strongly associated with industrial forestry, without requiring any changes to status quo logging practices.[299]

The development of forestry science can be traced to seventeenth century European attempts to understand the detrimental consequences of over-utilisation of resources alongside the need to safeguard them for future generations. Eighteenth century German scientific forestry formulated the concept of 'Nachhaltigkeitsprinzip' (sustainability principle) and developed quantitative methods to estimate growing stock and develop a yield-based system directed towards the maximisation of 'sustained yield'.[300]

International Tropical Timber Agreement, 2006, opened for signature 3 April 2006, 2797 UNTS 75 (entered into force 7 December 2011).

[294] Humphreys, *Forest Politics: The Evolution of International Cooperation*, p. 153.

[295] General Assembly Resolution 62/98, *Non-Legally Binding Instrument on All Types of Forests*, UN GAOR 62nd sess, 74th plen mtg, Agenda Item 54, A/RES/62/98 (31 January 2008), para 5.

[296] Ibid.

[297] *Trick or Treat? REDD, Development and Sustainable Forest Management*, p. 1.

[298] C. Lang, 'REDD+ myth: Sustainable forest management' (2014) 207 *World Rainforest Movement Bulletin*; see also *Pandering to the Loggers: Why WWF's Global Forest and Trade Network Isn't Working* (Global Witness, 2011).

[299] *Trick or Treat? REDD, Development and Sustainable Forest Management*, p. 4.

[300] See K. F. Wiersum, '200 years of sustainability in forestry: Lessons from history' (1995) 19 *Environmental Management* 321–9.

104   *Background to REDD+*

In these practices, nature is still fundamentally legible as a resource, extractable for human use, but where the impetus of resource utilisation needs to be tempered with the capacity of the resource to reproduce and regenerate. This ideology of scientific conservation was given impetus through colonial exploitation.[301] When the practices were deployed in the colonies, their 'actual experience' and 'professed aims' often conflicted.[302] .

Governance of forests has tended to assume a highly centralised form, one that depends on development of standardised measures and 'ways of seeing'. These practices have had the effect of strengthening the centralisation of political authority and strengthening state control over forested lands.[303] In anthropologist James Scott's influential account, practices of scientific forest management are emblematic of a specific modernist governance paradigm. He documents the emergence of a specific way of seeing the world that has sought to make phenomena legible in quantifiable terms from a top-down perspective.[304] This model of colonial forestry produced conflict given the reality that areas now delineated as 'forest reserves' were owned, inhabited, managed and used by peoples in those areas: 'curtailing the rights of these peoples inevitably sparked resistance, which either had to be suppressed through forced removals, fines, exactions or worse punishments or accommodated by permitting certain forest-based activities to continue as "privileges" subject to strict controls.'[305] Practices of forest management continue to generate social conflict, as well as excluding and impoverishing local communities. For example, a 2000 World Bank evaluation report describing the impact of 'large-scale commercial interests' in Indonesia found as follows:

> Not only has the use of forest resources been unsustainable, the distribution of the benefits has been highly inequitable. Since the inception of the New Order Regime in 1967, the Indonesian forest policy has subordinated the traditional rights of indigenous forest dwellers and communities dependent on forests for their livelihoods. The denial of access to forest resources has resulted in conflict and created one of the most serious social problems facing Indonesia at present.[306]

---

[301] R. Grove, *Green Imperialism: Colonial Expansion, Tropical Island Edens and the Origins of Environmentalism, 1600–1860* (Cambridge University Press, 1996) p. 3.

[302] Guha, *Environmentalism: A Global History* (Oxford University Press, 1999) Chapter 3.

[303] See N. L. Peluso and P. Vandergeest, 'Genealogies of the political forest and customary rights in Indonesia, Malaysia, and Thailand' (2001) 60(3) *The Journal of Asian Studies* 761.

[304] J. C. Scott, *Seeing Like a State: How Certain Schemes to Improve the Human Condition Have Failed* (Yale University Press, 1998) Chapter 1.

[305] M. Colchester, T. Apte, M. Laforge, A. Mandondo, and N. Pathak, *Learning Lessons from International Community Forestry Networks: Synthesis Report* (Center for International Forestry Research, 2003) p. 8; see also N. L. Peluso, *Rich Forests, Poor People: Resource Control and Resistance in Java* (University of California Press, 1992).

[306] *Indonesia: The Challenges of World Bank Involvement in Forests* (World Bank Operations Evaluation Department, 2000) xvi.

E. REDD+ As Co-articulating Various Forms of Anthropocentric Governance

In the mid twentieth century, the concept of 'sustained yield' was progressively broadened from a singular focus on timber, to encompass the multiple uses of forests, and consider social, as well as economic factors. The Collaborative Partnership on Forests, founded in 2000 and made up of 14 intergovernmental organisations[307] in 2008, promoted SFM as 'an effective framework for forest-based climate change mitigation and adaptation'.[308] In recent years there has been increasing attention to the 'multiple benefits' or 'multiple functions' of forests.[309] For example, a report of the United Nation Forum on Forests (UNFF) meeting states:

> Forests provide multiple goods and services that are essential for people worldwide and crucial for sustainable development. Forests make significant contributions to addressing the complex and interconnected global challenges relating to economic and social development, poverty eradication, environmental sustainability, energy, water and mitigation of and adaptation to climate change. Forests are also vital for the livelihoods of local and indigenous peoples, providing a repository for a large portion of the world's terrestrial biodiversity.[310]

This focus on multiple uses suggests that 'the different forest interests were reconcilable and that no intrinsic value conflicts existed between different ideas of future use', and therefore such 'win-win' rhetoric can be 'efficient as a way of holding different agendas together'.[311] However, in practice, this conception of the multiple uses of forests and the optimal yield of a range of different benefits is often quickly narrowed to a focus on the most economically productive uses. In the case of REDD+ such a rhetoric of 'multiple benefits' is arguably in tension with the focus in REDD+ on 'the conservation of forest carbon stocks' and the 'enhancement of forest carbon stocks'.[312] Thus, in many ways, although its focus is carbon rather than timber, REDD+ arguably replicates many of problematic dynamics of SFM. Finally, the recognition that the activities of conservation and sustainable forest management each have conflicted histories highlights the need to be attentive to the social impact of REDD+ programs and how they risk perpetuating dangerous dynamics that consolidate power and inequalities. It is therefore unsurprising that

---

[307] The Collaborative Partnership on Forests was established in April 2001, based on a recommendation by the UN Economic and Social Council. Its purpose is to support the work of the UNFF and increase cooperation and collaboration on forest governance.

[308] Collaborative Partnership on Forests, *Strategic Framework for Forests and Climate Change*, 2008, www.fao.org/forestry/16639-1-0.pdf.

[309] See United Nations Forum on Forests, *Report of the Tenth Session (4 February 2011 and 8 and 9 April 2013)*, E/2013/42, E/CN.18/2013/18, 42, 'Significance of forests'.

[310] Ibid.

[311] See J. Andersson and E. Westholm, 'Closing the future: Environmental research and the management of conflicting future value orders' (2019) 44(2) *Science, Technology and Human Values* 237–62, 250.

[312] Decision 1/CP.16, para 70(c) and (e).

106   *Background to REDD+*

the potential social impacts of REDD+ have been a key concern, as the next section discusses.

F REDD+ AS A SOCIAL PROJECT

While REDD+ was initially understood primarily as an environmental project, it quickly became evident that it had clear social implications for peoples living in and around forested areas. This section considers how the scope of REDD+ has expanded to additionally become a 'social' project, concerned also with the livelihood and governance of people living in and around forested areas. As Signe Howell notes, 'What was listed in the original REDD documents as one of several co-benefits to the conservation of tropical forests, namely "governance and rights", is rapidly turning into a major preoccupation.'[313] In discussions on REDD+ implementation there is now a broad concern about protecting the rights of people living in and area forested areas,[314] as well as a recognition of the 'rights dimension' of REDD+ and the need to create synergies between human rights instruments and REDD+.[315] This section analyses how social concerns have been discussed in debates on REDD+, tracing the shift from the initial marginalisation of social considerations to the growing consensus that REDD+ must minimise social risks ('do no harm') and promote social benefits ('do good') in order to be both equitable and effective.[316] In particular, the implementation of safeguards, as well as mechanisms of benefit sharing, tenure reform and free, prior and informed consent, have all been seen as key ways to minimise risks and promote benefits to forest peoples. The discussion shows how the manner in which REDD+ debates have taken up social concerns marginalised more radical voices opposed to REDD+, and the question of *whether* REDD+ should proceed has been increasingly obscured by a focus on *how* REDD+ should be implemented.

1 *Debates in the UNFCCC and by NGOs*

It is important to recognise the background conditions under which the push for REDD+ safeguards has gained particular traction, namely the intensification of processes that restructure land relations and promote human dispossession in the

---

[313] S. Howell, '"No RIGHTS–No REDD": Some implications of a turn towards co-benefits' (2014) 41(2) *Forum for Development Studies* 253–72 at 254.

[314] Ibid., 257.

[315] See A. Savaresi, 'The human rights dimension of REDD' (2012) 21(2) *Review of European Community & International Environmental Law* 102–13; A. Savaresi, 'REDD+ and human rights: Addressing synergies between international regimes' (2013) 18(3) *Ecology and Society*.

[316] E. O. Sills (ed.), *REDD+ on the Ground: A Case Book of Subnational Initiatives across the Globe* (Center for International Forestry Research, 2014) p. 430; see also the discussion in Chapter 6.

F. REDD+ As a Social Project

Global South. A key characteristic of the present era is the 'explosion' of (trans) national commercial land transactions and speculation ('land grabbing') driven by large-scale, export-orientated agricultural production (including biofuels), as well as extractive industries and conservation practices.[317] The LandMatrix database documented over 1000 large-scale land concluded deals (over 200 hectares) affecting almost 40 million hectares of land, an area over 4,300 times the size of Manhattan, between 2000 and 2015.[318] These new forms of 'accumulation by dispossession'[319] have produced, as Saskia Sassen documents, a new global logic of expulsion.[320] The expulsion of life deemed 'superfluous'[321] or 'disposable',[322] she argues, is not accidental. Rather, such expulsions are produced by a 'systemic logic at work' in 'predatory formations' that are part of 'larger assemblage of elements, conditions and mutually reinforcing dynamics'.[323] This global context has made concerns that REDD+ could represent a form of 'green grabbing' particularly acute.[324]

The first major report to address the potential social impacts of REDD+ was *Seeing 'RED'? Forests, Climate Change Mitigation and the Rights of Indigenous Peoples'*, written by Tom Griffiths for the Forest Peoples' Program and launched to coincide with COP13 (Bali, 2007).[325] It highlighted that implementing such projects

---

[317] For a discussion of 'land grabbing', see N. L. Peluso and C. Lund, 'New frontiers of land control: Introduction' (2011) 38(4) *The Journal of Peasant Studies* 667–81 and the Special Edition of which it is an introduction; for a discussion of the methods of land grabbing see I. Scoones, R. Hall, S. M. Borras, Jr., B. White, and W. Wolford, 'The politics of evidence: Methodologies for understanding the global land rush' (2013) 40(3) *The Journal of Peasant Studies* 469–83 and the remainder of the Special Edition; for a discussion of biofuels see S. M. Borras, Jr., P. McMichael, and I. Scoones, 'The politics of biofuels, land and agrarian change: Editors' introduction' (2010) 37(4) *The Journal of Peasant Studies* 575–92 and the remainder of the Special Issue; for a discussion of 'green grabbing' see Fairhead et al., 'Green grabbing: A new appropriation of nature?' and the remainder of the Special Issue.

[318] 'Land Matrix' website, www.landmatrix.org/en (accessed 6 February 2015).

[319] D. Harvey, *The New Imperialism* (Oxford University Press, 2005).

[320] S. Sassen, *Expulsions: Brutality and Complexity in the Global Economy* (Harvard University Press, 2014); see also S. Sassen, 'A savage sorting of winners and losers: Contemporary versions of primitive accumulation' (2010) 7(1) *Globalisations* 23–50.

[321] J. Biehl and T. Eskerod, *Vita: Life in a Zone of Social Abandonment* (University of California Press, 2013).

[322] See M. Duffield, *Development, Security and Unending War: Governing the World of Peoples* (Polity, 2007).

[323] Sassen, *Expulsions: Brutality and Complexity in the Global Economy*, pp. 77–8.

[324] Fairhead et al., 'Green grabbing: A new appropriation of nature?'.

[325] T. Griffiths, *Seeing 'RED'?: Avoided Deforestation' and the Rights of Indigenous Peoples and Local Communities* (Forest Peoples Programme, 2007). Revised and updated versions of this report were released in December 2008, see T. Griffiths, *Seeing 'REDD'?: Forests, Climate Change Mitigation and the Rights of Indigenous Peoples and Local Communities – Update for Poznań* (UNFCCC COP14) (Forest Peoples Programme, 2008); and in May 2009, see T. Griffiths, *Seeing 'REDD'?: Forest, Climate Change Mitigation and the Rights of Indigenous Peoples and Local Communities – Updated Version* (Forest Peoples Programme, 2009).

Background to REDD+

without proper regard for rights and social and livelihood issues could give rise to the following risks:

- renewed and even increased state and 'expert' control over forests;
- overzealous government support for anti-people and exclusionary models of forest conservation (evictions, expropriation) to protect lucrative forest carbon 'reservoirs';
- unjust targeting of indigenous and marginal peoples as the 'drivers' of deforestation;
- violations of customary land and territorial rights;
- state and NGO zoning of forest lands without the informed participation of forest dwellers;
- unequal imposition of the costs of forest protection on indigenous peoples and local communities;
- unequal and abusive community contracts;
- land speculation, land grabbing and land conflicts (competing claims on [avoided deforestation] compensation);
- corruption and embezzlement of international funds by national elites;
- increasing inequality and potential conflict between recipients and non-recipients of [avoided deforestation] funds;
- potential conflict among indigenous communities (over acceptance or rejection of [avoided deforestation] schemes)[.][326]

The report argued that any effective policy 'on forests and climate change mitigation must be based on the recognition of rights, respect for the principle of free, prior and informed consent (FPIC) and requirements for progressive forests sector tenure and governance reforms', otherwise it would perpetuate injustices.[327] These concerns were quickly taken up by human rights advocates and civil society actors. At the launch of the World Bank's Forest Carbon Partnership Facility at the Bali COP in 2007 the (then) Chair of the United Nations Permanent Forum on Indigenous Peoples (UNPFII), Victoria Tauli-Corpuz, strongly condemned the World Bank's failure to consult properly with Indigenous peoples prior to the Facility's launch.[328]

By 2008, questions concerning the social impacts of REDD+ had permeated into UNFCCC processes. The report from a June 2008 SBSTA workshop on methodo-logical issues associated with REDD+ noted:

---

[326] Griffiths, *Seeing 'RED'? Avoided Deforestation' and the Rights of Indigenous Peoples and Local Communities*, p. 1.

[327] Ibid.

[328] V. Tauli-Corpuz, 'Statement on the Announcement of the World Bank Forest Carbon Partnership Facility' 11 December 2007, www.un.org/esa/socdev/unpfii/documents/statement_vtc_toWB11dec.2007.doc.

F. REDD+ As a Social Project

Some participants stressed the importance of involving local communities in the sustainable management of forests. It has been shown that training these communities enables them to manage their forest resources on a more sustainable basis.

It was noted that social implications, particularly for indigenous people and local communities, associated with any system for reducing emissions from deforestation and forest degradation in developing countries should be taken into consideration.[329]

Simultaneously, social mobilisation around the potential social implications of REDD+ continued. The 'Accra Briefing' (August 2008) by NGOs stressed the need for the 'recognition and enforcement of customary and territorial land rights' and reference to the United Nations Declaration on the Rights of Indigenous Peoples (UNDRIP) in any REDD+ policy.[330] More critically, Director of the Global Forest Coalition Simone Lovera described REDD+ as 'another disaster in the making' and a 'fairy-tale about a simple solution to climate change'.[331] In November 2008 the Friends of the Earth International (FoEI) report *REDD Myths* concluded that if REDD+ were to significantly increase the value of forests 'it is likely [would have] extremely detrimental impacts on some of the poorest people in the world'.[332] It argued that REDD+ implementation could potentially displace millions, and that there were no guarantees that Indigenous peoples would benefit from its implementation unless secure land rights were ensured.[333] The report also cited additional risks of REDD+ such as 'conflict between and within communities (especially where land rights are unclear), changes to local power structures and shifts in social and traditional values and behaviours'.[334] Survival International's *The Most Inconvenient Truth of All: Climate Change and Indigenous Peoples* (2009) likewise suggested REDD+ could make recognition of land rights more difficult and undermine existing recognition as well as potentially restrict traditional land use activities.[335]

Alongside this focus on the risks REDD+ could present to forest peoples, a distinct but related discourse emerged that emphasised potential benefits REDD+ could provide to peoples living in and around forest areas. A 2008 report by Overseas Development Initiative (ODI) canvassed design and policy options for how REDD+

---

[329] UNFCCC Secretariat, *Report on the Workshop on Methodological Issues Relating to Reducing Emissions from Deforestation and Forest Degradation in Developing Countries: A Note from the Secretariat*, FCCC/SBSTA/2008/11 (8 September 2008) paras 71–72.

[330] C. Lang, 'FoEI: Forests are more than carbon' *REDD-Monitor* 29 October 2008.

[331] See C. Lang, 'Global Forest Coalition attacks REDD' *REDD-Monitor* 6 October 2008.

[332] R. Hall, *REDD Myths: A Critical Review of Proposed Mechanisms to Reduce Emissions from Deforestation and Degradation in Developing Countries* (Friends of the Earth International, 2008) p. 16.

[333] Ibid.

[334] Ibid., p. 16.

[335] *The Most Inconvenient Truth of All: Climate Change and Indigenous People* (Survival International, 2009).

110 *Background to REDD+*

could be made to 'work for the poor'.[336] It identified that there were pragmatic as well as moral reasons for a 'pro-poor' approach to REDD+, including improved long-term project sustainability, reduced risks for investors and buyers, the potential for increased returns or 'niche' market opportunities as well as donor contractual and legal obligations.[337] These discussions highlighted REDD+ as a potential opportunity to promote co-benefits and stressed that the viability of REDD+ depended upon it being perceived as not causing harm and in fact as having positive impacts. A report by the Center for International Forestry Research (CIFOR) highlighted that REDD+ 'deriv(es) much of its legitimacy and potential effectiveness from its ability to improve the welfare of the forest-dependent poor and foster development in some of the poorest regions of the world'.[338] Similar conclusions were reached by the influential *Eliasch Review* that recognised the potential risks REDD+ could pose to those living in and around forest areas. For Eliasch, participation was key to mitigating these risks: 'the full participation of forest communities will make reforms more likely to succeed and benefit the poor.'[339]

This emphasis on 'rights-based' or 'pro-poor' REDD+ has become central to the mandate of the UN-REDD Programme, whose *Framework Document* articulates the Programme's guiding principles as a 'human-rights-based approach', 'gender equity', 'environmental sustainability', 'results-based management' and 'capacity development'.[340] At the Programme's launch in September 2008, participation and benefit-sharing were emphasised, with UN Under-Secretary-General and UNEP Executive Director Achim Steiner stating, 'REDD must benefit local communities and indigenous peoples as much as it benefits national economies and the global environment. If that is done the prospects are exciting and potentially far reaching.'[341]

The importance of participation was reiterated in Global Witness' report *Honest Engagement: Transparency and Civil Society Participation in REDD* (February 2009) that stressed 'enhancing transparency and understanding of the process, and ensuring broad engagement of civil society organizations and indigenous groups, must move to the top of the agenda if REDD is to avoid failure.'[342] Other civil society reports, such as FERN's *An Overview of Selected REDD+ Proposals*

---

[336] L. Peskett, D. Huberman, E. B. Jones, G. Edwards, and J. Brown, *Making REDD Work for the Poor* (Poverty Environmental Partnership, 2008).

[337] Ibid.

[338] D. Brown, F. Seymour, and L. Peskett, 'How do we achieve REDD co-benefits and avoid doing harm?' in A. Angelsen (ed.), *Moving Ahead with REDD: Issues, Options and Implications*, (Center for International Forestry Research, 2008) pp. 107–18, 109.

[339] Eliasch, *Climate Change: Financing Global Forests*, p. xiii.

[340] UN-REDD Programme, *Framework Document* (2008) p. 7.

[341] United Nations, '"REDD"-letter day for forests: United Nations, Norway unite to combat climate change from deforestation, spearheading new programme' (Press release, 24 September 2008), www.un.org/press/en/2008/envdev1005.doc.htm.

[342] *Honest Engagement: Transparency and Civil Society Participation in REDD* (Global Witness, 2008) p. 1.

F. REDD+ As a Social Project

(November 2008), similarly focused on the centrality of rights as 'crucial to forest conservation' and the imperatives of tenure reform, warning that without clearly defined property rights REDD+ would fail.[343] Released in May 2009, the International Institute for Environment and Development (IIED) report *Tenure in REDD: Start-point or Afterthought?* foregrounded the issues of tenure and forest governance, and emphasised that questions of land and resource tenure needed to be given greater attention in REDD+ implementation to ensure both the equity and effectiveness of REDD+.[344] A subsequent consensus quickly developed that tenure clarification was a precondition for, and potentially co-benefit arising from, REDD+ activities.

A 2009 report by CIFOR and IUCN lists potential benefits that REDD+ for people living in and around forest areas, including:

- encouraging government action to secure and formalize land tenure for forest dwellers;
- generating revenue that governments could direct to social services in rural areas (health care centres, schools, water systems, etc.);
- creating new income streams for forest-dwellers;
- maintaining forests' regulating ecosystem services ... which may enhance adaptive capacity in a changing climate; and
- maintaining forests' provisioning ecosystem services ... which may also help buffer communities from the shocks of [climate related] reduced agricultural yields.[345]

A further IUCN briefing document noted that REDD+ projects may improve livelihoods and provide opportunities to strengthen capacity of Indigenous peoples' organisations and communities, whilst an increased awareness of Indigenous peoples' role in forest management may contribute to further recognition to Indigenous peoples' traditional knowledge systems.[346] It concluded that *if* rights are recognised REDD+ is more likely to achieve mitigation and sustainable development objectives.[347]

The discussions on the social impacts of REDD+ increasingly came to be structured in accordance with two dominant frames: firstly, one focused on the *risks*

---

[343] K. Dooley, *An Overview of Selected REDD Proposals* (FERN and Forest Peoples Programme, 2008) p. 10.

[344] L. Cotula and J. Mayers, *Tenure in REDD – Start-Point or Afterthought?* (International Institute for Environment and Development, 2009).

[345] K. Lawlor and D. Huberman, 'Reduced emissions from deforestation and forest degradation (REDD) and human rights' in J. Campese et al. (eds.), *Rights-Based Approaches: Exploring Issues and Opportunities for Conservation,* (Bogor, Indonesia: CIFOR and IUCN, 2009), pp. 269–85, 269 and 272.

[346] *Briefing Document: Indigenous Peoples and Climate Change/REDD: An Overview of Current Discussions and Main Issues* (IUCN, 2010).

[347] Ibid., p. 9.

REDD+ projects might present to people living in and around forested areas that emphasises the need to *manage* these risks; and secondly, one focused on *benefits* REDD+ projects might present to people living in and around forested areas that emphasised the need to put in place measures to ensure that such benefits were *realised*. Both these discourses, around risks and around benefits, focused on *how* REDD+ could be carried out, rather than *whether* it should be. That is, the two dominant positions taken in debates over social impacts both seemed to accept the existence or rolling out of REDD+ as a given, and primarily focused on ways in which REDD+ could be implemented in order to either minimise risks or materialise potential benefits for forest people. Thus, the dominant framing of social debates increasingly foreclosed critiques of REDD+ *as a project* and instead directed attention to its *mode of implementation*.[348]

2 Debates within the UN Permanent Forum on Indigenous Issues

This section turns to consider how a similar grammar of argumentation, as that analysed in civil society debates above, was adopted in discussions about REDD+ at the UNPFII between 2008 and 2013. It shows how within the UNPFII debates, individuals and organisations that were critical of the idea of REDD+ were increasingly sidelined, and the institutional focus shifted to addressing how REDD+ should be implemented in order to best manage risks and realise potential benefits for people living in forested areas.

'We want to speak' was the collective call from a caucus in the back of the room on 2 May 2008, the concluding day of the Seventh Session of the UNPFII. Initially, the Chair of the session, Victoria Tauli-Corpuz, attempted to continue through the agenda, but she was prevented from doing so as the clapping and chanting from the back of the room intensified in speed and volume. Delegates in the two back rows were on their feet calling out: 'We want to make a statement!', 'You have to listen to us — we want that you hear us.', 'Indigenous peoples want to make a statement!' 'Madame Chair — we want to speak.' The Chair offered to give the interjectors the floor once 'business' had been finished, but the protests continued and security personnel were called into the session. It was only when the situation risked spiralling out of control, after Indigenous delegates were almost forcefully evicted from the United Nations space that claimed to represent and facilitate their voices, that the Chair requested security staff to leave and reorganised proceedings to allow time to listen to a statement prepared by the Caucus Indigenas de Abya Yala.[349]

---

[348] This argument is made in the context of debates on land grabbing here: S. Borras and J. Franco, 'From threat to opportunity? Problems with the idea of a "code of conduct" for land-grabbing' (2010) 13 *Yale Human Rights and Development Law Journal* 507–23.

[349] See 'PROTEST: Indigenous peoples "2nd MAY REVOLT" at the UNPFII', *Carbon Trade Watch*, 12 May 2008, www.carbontradewatch.org/video/protest-indigenous-peoples-2nd-may-revolt-at-the-unpfii-4.html.

F. REDD+ As a Social Project

The commotion was sparked by recommendations that had been presented to the UNPFII on carbon market 'offset' mechanisms under the CDM and REDD+.[350] One of the recommendations described the CDM as a 'good example of the kind of partnership that will become increasingly important',[351] and called for greater engagement with Indigenous peoples in the process of designing and implementing such programs. Another recommendation called on World Bank carbon funds to centrally involve Indigenous peoples in their project design, implementation and evaluation.[352] These recommendations calling for more Indigenous *participation and voice in* REDD+ projects ran counter to the *opposition to* REDD+ articulated by some Indigenous groups and their representatives in the UNPFII, who saw the commodification of nature as fundamentally incompatible with their worldview and cosmology. Tom Goldtooth, executive director of the Indigenous Environment Network, recalls that throughout the Seventh Session 'intervention after intervention of our Indigenous brothers and sisters from the Global South said, "This is wrong, we do not support REDD, we do not support these offset initiatives."'[353] He recounts that 'despite this overwhelming opposition [to carbon trading] we got [a report] from the permanent forum members promoting ... these World Bank initiatives'.[354]

After the commotion subsided, a petition addressed to the UNPFII expressing opposition to REDD+ was read out, which asserted that '[t]he vast majority of indigenous peoples feel that the REDD will not benefit Indigenous Peoples, but in fact will result in [further] violations of Indigenous Peoples' rights'.[355] In response, some amendments were made to the recommendations, and the Permanent Forum recommended that REDD+ and the 'renewed political focus on forests' should be *'used towards securing the rights* of indigenous peoples living in forests'.[356] The Permanent Forum also noted that

> [The] current framework for REDD is not supported by most indigenous peoples [and that all] new proposals for avoided deforestation or reduced emissions from

[350] V. Tauli-Corpuz and A. Lynge, *Impact of Climate Change Mitigation Measures on Indigenous Peoples and Their Territories and Lands*, UNPFII, Seventh Session, E/C.19/2008/10 (20 March 2008).

[351] Draft recommendations E/C.19/2008/L.3, para 5, reflected in Economic and Social Council, *Permanent Forum on Indigenous Issues: Report on the Seventh Session (21 April–2 May 2008) E/2008/43*, E/C.19/2008/13 (14 May 2008) para 8.

[352] Ibid., para 88. Note, the recommendation also stated: 'Those who opt not to participate in reduction of emissions from deforestation in developing countries or in the Forest Carbon Partnership Facility-supported projects should be respected.'

[353] Transcribed by author from 'PROTEST: Indigenous peoples "2nd MAY REVOLT" at the UNPFII'.

[354] Ibid.

[355] Ibid.

[356] Economic and Social Council, Permanent Forum on Indigenous Issues: Report on the Seventh Session (21 April–2 May 2008) E/2008/43, E/C.19/2008/13 (14 May 2008) para 44 (emphasis added).

114   *Background to REDD+*

deforestation must address the need for global and national policy reforms and be guided by the United Nations Declaration on the Rights of Indigenous Peoples, respecting rights to land, territories and resources; and the rights of self-determination and the free, prior and informed consent of the indigenous peoples concerned.[357]

Since this incident several reports by Special Rapporteurs appointed by the UNPFII have addressed the impacts of carbon-offset mechanisms on Indigenous peoples.[358] The 2013 report, by Paul Kanyinke Sena, Myrna Cunningham and Bertie Xavier, briefly reviews the experiences and positions of Indigenous organisations and communities around the world in relation to REDD+. It acknowledges the

numerous reported cases of REDD-plus projects involving indigenous communities that appear to have signed highly disadvantageous agreements as a consequence of a lack of understanding of the implications, a lack of access to advice or information, bad faith on the part of the REDD-plus developer and in some cases, a breakdown in community governance arrangements or corruption on the part of local officials. Terms of such purported contracts have included, for example, "agreements" that the community will cease to use its forests for any production purposes, including subsistence, hunting and gathering activities. Notwithstanding the fact that the community (or certain members of the community claiming to act on its behalf) may have signed an agreement, clearly the free, prior informed consent of the community has not been given, nor are the terms mutually agreed by any reasonable definition of the terms. In some cases, the document has been prepared in the language of the developer with no faithfully translated version provided to the community. Such cases have been observed in many regions, including the Amazon and the Congo Basin countries and in the Asia–Pacific region.[359]

---

[357] Ibid., para 45.

[358] These include the report by Tauli-Corpuz and Lynge, *Impact of Climate Change Mitigation Measures on Indigenous Peoples and Their Territories and Lands*, UNPFII, Seventh Session, E/C.19/2008/10 (20 March 2008); V. Tauli-Corpuz and L.-A. Baer, *Results of the Copenhagen meeting of the Conference of the Parties to the United Nations Framework Convention on Climate Change; Implications for Indigenous Peoples' Local Adaptation and Mitigation Measures*, Permanent Forum on Indigenous Issues, 9th session, E/C.19/2010/18 (2 March 2010); H. Id Balkassm and P. Hasteh, *Study on the Extent to which Climate Change Policies and Project Adhere to the Standards Set Forth in the United Nations Declaration on the Rights of Indigenous Peoples: Note by the Secretariat*, UNPFII, Ninth Session, E/C.19/2010/7 (2 February 2010) and the background concept note, *The Extent to which Climate Change Policies and Projects Adhere to the Standards Set Forth in the United Nations Declaration on the Rights of Indigenous Peoples: Concept Note Submitted by the Permanent Forum Special Rapporteurs*, UNPFII, Eighth Session, E/C.19/2009/5 (25 March 2009); and P. Kanyinke Sena, M. Cunningham, and B. Xavier, *Indigenous People's Rights and Safeguards in Projects Related to Reducing Emissions from Deforestation and Forest Degradation: Note by the Secretariat*, UN ESCOR, Permanent Forum on Indigenous Issues, 12th sess, Agenda Item 5, UN Doc E/C.19/2013/7 (5 February 2013).

[359] Kanyinke Sena et al., *Indigenous People's Rights and Safeguards in Projects Related to Reducing Emissions from Deforestation and Forest Degradation*, para 26.

F. REDD+ As a Social Project

This passage speaks to critical 'on the ground' realities about how REDD+ is being implemented and the abuses of power evident in some REDD+ schemes – echoing similar documentation of abuses in REDD+ implementation that have been confirmed in other NGO reports.[360] However, the UNPFII report positions these examples as at one end of a 'wide spectrum', and also highlights opposite cases, 'where the initiative for a project springs from a community decision, perhaps as a way of funding its own previously determined territorial management and community development aspirations.'[361] The report thereby implies that the problems associated with REDD+ are not inherent to the scheme but are instead produced by a lack of good governance, information or understanding, or are the product of corruption or bad faith. The report further positions properly implemented REDD+ schemes as an opportunity for Indigenous peoples to consolidate their rights.[362] It therefore reflects the growing convergence between rights discourses and REDD+ imperatives evident both at a rhetorical level but also in a proliferation of reports on rights in REDD+ and 'best practice' guidelines.

The report acknowledged that there are at least two divergent positions adopted by Indigenous groups in relation to REDD+, but it failed to acknowledge the deeper ontological and normative reasons why some groups might have rejected REDD+. It described 'two different scenarios', namely:

(a) Organizations radically oppose REDD-plus owing mainly to insecurity as to the rights of indigenous peoples, the weakness of existing national legal frameworks to protect those rights and the uncertainties of the Framework Convention negotiations on REDD-plus. Those organizations are strongly opposed to the carbon market.

(b) Organizations consider the REDD-plus model as [offering] opportunities for indigenous peoples. Although they share reservations about the risks that this model offers if indigenous peoples' rights are not fully recognized and strong safeguards are not in place, some organizations are open to the voluntary carbon market.[363]

Despite acknowledging many reports of communities signing 'highly disadvantageous agreements',[364] the report engages only minimally with the former position,

---

[360] See for example J. Kill, *REDD: A Gallery of Conflicts, Contradictions and Lies* (World Rainforest Movement, 2014); cf. the more optimistic accounts provided in E. O. Sills (ed.), *REDD+ on the Ground: A Case Book of Subnational Initiatives across the Globe* (Center for International Forestry Research, 2014).

[361] P. K. Sena, M. Cunningham and B. Xavier, *Indigenous People's Rights and Safeguards in Projects Related to Reducing Emissions from Deforestation and Forest Degradation: Note by the Secretariat*, UN ESCOR, Permanent Forum on Indigenous Issues, 12th sess, Agenda Item 5, UN Doc E/C.19/2013/7 (5 February 2013), para 25.

[362] Ibid., para 59.

[363] Ibid., para 58.

[364] Ibid., para 24.

Background to REDD+

and concludes that 'REDD-plus offers opportunities for indigenous peoples to consolidate their rights, including tenure of their territories and the implementation of community-led livelihood strategies.'[365] It thus focuses on 'the nature of potential benefits to indigenous peoples and how those benefits could be secured through the various safeguard mechanisms being developed'.[366] As in the discussions of safeguards described above, this focus eludes the normative question of whether REDD+ *should* be implemented. Instead, the attention is directed to questions of REDD+'s implementation: how to manage the potential risks of REDD+ and how to promote benefits through REDD+.

3 The Gradual Elaboration of Safeguards

As discussions about the social impacts on REDD+ progressed, a consensus developed that the implementation of social safeguards is a key means to minimise risks and promote benefits to forest peoples. The road towards the elaboration of safeguards in the UNFCCC was, however, far from smooth. At Poznań (COP14, 2008), Parties and observers were invited 'to submit . . . their views on issues relating to indigenous people and local communities for the development and application of methodologies'.[367] This wording was the subject of intense dispute: initial draft wording had also included 'noting the rights and importance of engaging indigenous peoples and other local communities'. However, this reference to 'rights' was removed after lobbying by the US, Canada, New Zealand and Australia,[368] sparking civil society protests[369] that demanded 'an unequivocal reference to rights and the UN Declaration on the Rights of Indigenous peoples be reinserted into the draft COP14 Decision text on REDD.'[370] The language used by SBSTA also ignored the earlier address to the session by UNPFII Chair Victoria Tauli-Corpuz, who had called for the UNDRIP to 'be used as an overarching framework for the design, methodologies, implementation and monitoring and evolution of REDD+' and had stated that no projects should occur on Indigenous lands without free, prior and

---

[365] Ibid., para 59.

[366] Ibid., summary.

[367] UNFCCC, *Report of the Subsidiary Body for Scientific and Technological Advice on Its Twenty-Ninth Session, Held in Poznań from 1 to 10 December 2008*, FCCC/SBSTA/2008/13 (17 February 2009), para 45.

[368] Australia, New Zealand, Canada and the United States all voted against the United Nations Declaration on the Rights of Indigenous People when it was adopted by the General Assembly on 13 September 2007. However, all four of these settler-colonial states have since endorsed the Declaration: Australia on 3 April 2009, New Zealand on 19 April 2010, Canada on 12 November 2010 and the United States on 16 December 2010.

[369] Third World Network, 'Indigenous Peoples outraged at removal of rights in REDD outcome, Poznań news update 12' (December 2008).

[370] C. Lang, 'Rights struck from draft text on REDD', *REDD-Monitor* 9 December 2008.

F. REDD+ As a Social Project

informed consent.[371] At the final SBSTA session, a representative from the International Indigenous Peoples' Forum on Climate Change sought to speak to express profound disappointment over the removal of 'rights' language and the use of the singular rather than the collective term 'indigenous peoples'.[372] The Chair prevented her from speaking by saying:

> I'm sorry, I'm going to have to stop you there because you [civil society groups] have exceeded the two minutes allocated to you for the statement and in the interests of time we are going to have to move on and close the meeting.[373]

Although the UNFCCC COP process allows for more civil society participation and inclusion of Indigenous voices than many other international legal institutions,[374] this incident highlights how there are still broader institutional failings to provide space and meaningful participation for diverse and oppositional voices. Moreover, this incident reveals the limitations of calls for participation and the broader issue of to what extent these institutional spaces are able to hear and take on board such voices, even if they are allowed to speak.

Subsequent to the Poznań COP14 multiple submissions from Parties and observer groups were received by SBSTA.[375] Many submissions stressed the need to fully involve local communities in monitoring and implementation and the necessity for safeguards and tenure clarification; many submissions also stressed the necessity of a rights-based approach, including provisions for consultation towards free, prior and informed consent and other rights articulated in the UNDRIP. At Copenhagen a methodological decision on REDD+ recognised the 'need for full and effective engagement of indigenous peoples and local communities in, and the potential contribution of their knowledge to, monitoring and reporting of activities',[376] although a separate draft text on safeguards could not be agreed upon.[377]

As discussed previously, the 2010 Cancun Agreements listed seven safeguards that should be 'promoted and supported', and also requested that countries, 'when

---

[371] C. Lang, 'UN Permanent Forum on Indigenous Issues intervenes on REDD in Poznań' *REDD-Monitor* 2 December 2008.

[372] C. Lang, 'Indigenous Peoples censored at Poznań' *REDD-Monitor* 15 December 2008.

[373] *REDD: Indigenous Peoples Not Allowed to Speak at UNFCCC* (2008), www.youtube.com/watch?v=brsqUgbBHuo.

[374] C. Betzold and A. Flesken, 'Indigenous peoples in international environmental negotiations: Evidence from biodiversity and climate change' in T. Kaime (ed.), *International Climate Change Law and Policy: Cultural Legitimacy in Adaptation and Mitigation* (Routledge, 2014), pp. 63–83.

[375] UNFCCC, *Issues Relating to Indigenous Peoples and Local Communities for the Development and Application of Methodologies: Submissions from Parties*, FCCC/SBSTA/2009/MISC.1 (10 March 2009), Add.1 (17 April 2009) and Add.2 (27 June 2009).

[376] Decision 4/CP.15, preamble.

[377] Draft Decision -/CP.15 Policy, 'Approaches and positive incentives on issues relating to reducing emissions from deforestation and forest degradation in developing countries; and the role of conservation, sustainable management of forests and enhancement of forest carbon sinks in developing countries' FCCC/AWGLCA/2009/L.7/Add.6 (15 December 2009).

preparing national REDD+ strategies or plans ... ensur[e] the full and effective participation of relevant stakeholders, inter alia indigenous peoples and local communities'.[378] Debates about the processes by which the implementation of safeguards is verified in order to ensure environmental integrity and to prevent negative social impacts has been one of the most fraught areas of REDD+ policy and there has been significant criticism of the fact that the extent to which safeguards are realised is not subject to international review.[379] While the safeguards, as expressed in UNFCCC agreements on REDD+, lack clear legal enforcement, they nonetheless have had a significant a normative impact. Several guides have been prepared on how to actualise safeguards within national REDD+ projects,[380] and it is assumed 'host' governments of REDD+ projects should develop capacity to implement and enforce safeguards as part of REDD+-readiness programs.[381] Further, the language, style and approach of the UNFCCC safeguards is reflected in social and environmental safeguard provisions that have been adopted by other agencies involved in REDD+-readiness or the regulation of carbon markets in more tangible ways. As Margaret Young argues, there is an entire 'plethora of informal or soft-law processes which have developed outside of the UNFCCC negotiations but which influence and draw upon these negotiations', predominately arising out of bilateral and multilateral processes engaged in supporting REDD+-readiness activities.[382] Safeguards have also been promoted through an emerging transnational governance network that includes the internal guidelines and procedures governing donors' activities (such as international development agencies of countries, including Australia, Norway and Germany, and multilateral development banks) and policies or voluntary Codes of Conduct of implementing agencies (transnational conservation or aid bodies such as The Nature Conservancy, Flora and Fauna International, World Wide Fund for Nature (WWF), Wetlands International or CARE) alongside market-based certification schemes.[383]

UN-REDD and the FCPF have developed harmonised *Guidelines on Stakeholder Engagement in REDD+ Readiness with a Focus on the Participation of Indigenous Peoples and Other Forest-Dependent Communities*, defining stakeholders broadly as 'those groups that have a stake/interest/right in the forest and those that will be affected either negatively or positively by REDD+ activities', but

---

[378] Cancun Agreements, para 72.

[379] See for example C. Lang, 'REDD safeguards: What are they?', *REDD-Monitor*, 20 March 2015.

[380] D. Rey and S. Swan, *A Country-Led Safeguards Approach: Guidelines for National REDD+ Programmes* (SNV–The Netherlands Development Organisation, REDD+ Programme, 2014); F. Daviet and G. Larsen, *Safeguarding Forests and People: A Framework for Designing a National System to Implement REDD+ Safeguards* (World Resources Initiative, 2012).

[381] See for example, Pillar Five of Indonesia REDD+ Strategy, 'REDD+ National Stategy' (Indonesian REDD+ Task Force, 2012), www.satgasreddplus.orgon the inclusion of stakeholders.

[382] Young, 'REDD+ and interacting legal regimes', p. 93.

[383] See for example *REDD+ Social & Environmental Standards, Version 2* (10 September 2012).

F. REDD+ As a Social Project

focusing primarily on 'indigenous peoples and other forest-dependent communities'.[384] It refers to further applicable standards, which for the FCPF includes the FCPF Charter and the World Bank Operational Policies, and for the UN-REDD Programme includes international instruments on human rights and Indigenous peoples' rights. The UN-REDD Programme has additionally prepared its own *UN-REDD Programme Guidelines on Free, Prior and Informed Consent* (January 2013) and its complementing legal companion.[385] In August 2016, the World Bank adopted a new Environmental and Social Framework (ESF)[386] made up of ten standards, including Environmental and Social Standard 7 (ESS7) on Indigenous Peoples/Sub-Saharan African Historically Underserved Traditional Local Communities (IP/SSAHUTLCs).[387] The adoption of these standards was preceded by a major consultation with civil society and contentious debates,[388] given that these standards are 'likely to give rise to new norms and/or trigger reinterpretation of existing rules in international law more generally'.[389] Although the ESF 'symbolically' invokes international human rights norms in its vision, as María Victoria Cabrera Ormaza and Franz Christian Ebert have shown, the World Bank's operationalisation of it entails 'a form of discourse-content-decoupling'.[390] That is, although the World Bank 'symbolically' refers to human rights concepts in order to suggest coherence and build legitimacy, its discourse on human rights does not 'fully correspond to the actual content of the ESF".[391] Although ESS7 aims to 'foster full respect for the human rights' of Indigenous Peoples and Sub-Saharan African Historically Underserved Traditional Local Communities, it does not refer to the UNDRIP or ILO 169, the major international instruments concerned with such rights.[392] Further, although ESS7

---

[384] UN-REDD Programme and FCPF, *Guidelines on Stakeholder Engagement in REDD+ Readiness with a Focus on the Participation of Indigenous Peoples and Other Forest-Dependent Communities* (20 April 2012).

[385] UN-REDD Programme, *Legal Companion to the UN-REDD Programme Guidelines on Free, Prior and Informed Consent (FPIC): International Law and Jurisprudence Affirming the Requirement of FPIC* (January 2013).

[386] The World Bank, *Environmental and Social Framework* (2017), pubdocs.worldbank.org/en/837721522762050108/Environmental-and-Social-Framework.pdf.

[387] The World Bank, *ESS7: Indigenous Peoples/Sub-Sahara African Historically Underserved Traditional Local Communities*; see also G. Jokubauskaite, 'The World Bank Environmental and Social Framework in a wider realm of public international law' (2019) 32(3) *Leiden Journal of International Law* 457–63.

[388] R. Houghton, 'Looking at the World Bank's safeguard reform through the lens of deliberative democracy' (2019) 32(3) *Leiden Journal of International Law* 465–82.

[389] Jokubauskaite, 'The World Bank Environmental and Social Framework in a wider realm of public international law', 458.

[390] M. V. C. Ormaza and F. C. Ebert, 'The World Bank, human rights, and organizational legitimacy strategies: The case of the 2016 Environmental and Social Framework' (2019) 32(3) *Leiden Journal of International Law* 483–500 at 488.

[391] Ibid.

[392] Ibid., 491–2.

requires 'meaningful consultation' in ways that are 'culturally appropriate',[393] it also 'appears to distance itself from relevant human rights standards in different ways'.[394] However, a positive development is that it departs from the World Bank's earlier Operational Directive 4.20 (1991) and Operational Policy 4.10 (2005), which only provided for free, prior and informed *consultation*. ESS7 now requires *consent* in three situations: where a project will 'have adverse impacts on land and natural resources subject to traditional ownership or under customary use or occupation'; where a project will cause 'relocation'; and where a project will have 'significant impacts' on 'cultural heritage that is material to their identity and/or cultural, ceremonial, or spiritual aspects'.[395] Although this inclusion was widely welcomed, a detailed analysis of how the World Bank has defined and articulated FPIC suggests that '[t]he scope of application of FPIC under the ESF appears to be narrower than under the UNDRIP'.[396] Ormaza and Ebert therefore warn that consultation and FPIC might 'turn out to be legitimation tools to validate Bank-sponsored projects and not primarily consensus-building devices and safeguards for indigenous peoples'.[397]

When evaluating safeguards it is critical to examine not just their limitations but also their productive effects. Safeguard mechanisms are key sites through which REDD+ implementation interacts with and engages other legal regimes as well as broader development objectives.[398] As Feja Lesniewska argues, 'Since Cancun, safeguards have been seen as the opportunity through which the interactions between these different law making processes could be more formally co-ordinated.'[399] Safeguards thereby operate as a 'missing link' that connects REDD+ with other fields of law; they 'provide formal justification [for] the increasing cross-fertilization and collaboration between forest law and governance processes beyond the UNFCCC'.[400] In this way they facilitate the integration of REDD+ with broader development objectives, including those relating to improved forest governance, tenure reform and livelihood interventions. Such agendas are not politically neutral in either their conceptualisation or implementation and have long and often contentious histories.[401] The promotion of social safeguards has therefore also

---

[393] ESS7, para 23.

[394] Ormaza and Ebert, 'The World Bank, human rights, and organizational legitimacy strategies, 492.

[395] ESS, para 24.

[396] Ormaza and Ebert, 'The World Bank, human rights, and organizational legitimacy strategies', 493.

[397] Ibid., 495.

[398] Young, 'REDD+ and interacting legal regimes', pp. 89–125.

[399] F. Lesniewska, 'UNFCCC REDD+ COP Decisions: The cumulative effect on forest related law processes' (2013) 15 *International Community Law Review* 103–21 at 121.

[400] Ibid., 119–20.

[401] In relation to tenure reform see A. Manji, *The Politics of Land Reform in Africa: From Communal Tenure to Free Markets* (Zed Books, 2006).

operated to expand the sphere of authorised intervention by international financial institutions and other bilateral and multilateral bodies into the lives of peoples living in and around forested areas as part of REDD+-readiness and REDD+ implementation processes. The effects of key mechanisms promoted to address social concerns – especially tenure reform and benefit sharing – go beyond merely minimising risks or promoting benefits to people living in and around forested areas: they represent an active transformation of lives and livelihoods.[402]

G CONCLUSION

This chapter has analysed REDD+ from a number of different standpoints. It has provided a critical overview of REDD+ as a legal framework under the UNFCCC directed towards measuring, monitoring and verifying 'savings' from sequestered carbon as 'result-based actions' expressed in terms of $1tCO_2e$. REDD+ was also analysed as a series of practices and programmes to implement REDD+ on the ground, including 'demonstration activities' and REDD+-readiness programs, and to reduce deforestation and forest degradation. On a different register, this chapter scrutinised REDD+ as a concept or idea promoting the economic valuation of nature. It also provided an analysis and history of the key activities that are likely to be promoted through REDD+, namely, conservation and sustainable management of forests. Finally, this chapter analysed REDD+ as a social project concerned with safeguards, rights, participation and governance at the local level. Understanding REDD+ as both a vision or idea and a project to actualise this vision requires engaging with REDD+ on all these registers. It is, as the subsequent chapters of this book illustrate, only by examining all these different aspects of REDD+ as part of an integrated analysis that more complex understandings of its operations and effects can emerge.

---

[402] See Chapter 6 for a more detailed discussion.

2

Asserting Global Authority over the Carbon Sequestration Potential of Forests

A INTRODUCTION

This chapter is concerned with how a claim to global authority over land and resources in the Global South has been invoked and the shape or form it has been given. It shows how the designation of both climate change and tropical deforestation as matters of 'common concerns' has operated to authorise global authority over activities within national states that contribute to these processes. This chapter unpacks the specific representational practices through which climate change and tropical deforestation have become understood as an 'object' or 'problem' for law, and how this has given the international regimes a distinctive – and contingent – shape and inaugurated specific types of legal relations. It analyses how specific representational practices and the ways in which the problems of climate change and deforestation have been framed have led to the actualisation of forms of global authority that are actually highly differentiated in their operations and effects. The analysis suggests that this has created a dynamic whereby international actors are empowered to exercise greater authority over land use decisions in the Global South, even as many polluting actors in the Global North are not subject to the same degree of intervention and scrutiny. Problematically, this means that the process of 'acting' to address climate change has been configured to demand more of those who have done the least to cause the problem of climate change. Therefore, this chapter shows that a key effect of the REDD+ scheme has been to internationalise authority over land and resources in the Global South while simultaneously localising responsibility for addressing the dual and related crisis of climate change and deforestation.

This chapter departs from more technical accounts about REDD+ implementation, by foregrounding the often obscured, background representational and framing practices that authorise international authority over forested areas in the Global South that REDD+ depends upon. The first section introduces and outlines the

A. Introduction

principle of 'common concern', exploring how this principle authorises a specific claim to global authority or jurisdiction over a matter of concern, although this jurisdiction must be balanced with national domestic jurisdiction over the same matter. It thus treats the invocation of a 'common concern' as a jurisdictional technology that gives rise to global authority over a specific problem. A global jurisdiction organised around a so-called common concern in relation to dangerous processes of environmental degradation could take a number of different forms. Indeed, there are many ways a global 'commonality' might be patterned or enacted, and similarly a diversity of different legal relations to which the invocation of a 'global common' might give rise. An invocation of 'common concern' could manifest an 'ethic of the commons as community',[1] and aspire to enact worlds that might be that are very different from the very unequal and divided world that is.[2] There is an inherent indeterminacy in any such invocation of 'commonality': while such a claim can be deployed to mask or disguise differentials in power, wealth and responsibility, it can also serve as a beacon or motivator to construct the conditions of a more genuine commonality. Thus, framing the climate crisis as a 'common concern' of the international community could open space for political and ethical contestation over how to respond collectively to the differentiated responsibilities that climate change reflects and the differentiated vulnerabilities and capacities it exposes. Similarly, framing tropical deforestation as a 'common concern' of the international community could give rise to a critical interrogation of the global dynamics and processes driving deforestation and a disruption of the global political economy of land clearing. The focus of this chapter, however, is not on imagining the different possible ways in which an invocation of 'common concern' might be manifested. Instead, it traces how such an invocation has been given a specific shape *in practice*, and the forms of global authority it has authorised in the world and their effects.[3] In order to do so, it shows how specific representations or framing of the 'problem' of climate change and the 'problem' of tropical deforestation have given a distinctive shape to this claim to international authority.

The second section interrogates how climate change has come to be understood in specific ways as an 'object' or 'problem' for law, and how this has given a distinctive shape to the climate regime. This section shows how representations of climate change as a 'common' future problem as well as a focus on greenhouse gas (GHG) emissions and their effects, rather than their structural causes, has foregrounded a specific understanding of the 'problem' of climate change – one that privileges certain responses to the crisis while marginalising others. Moreover,

---

[1] S. Pahuja, 'Conserving the world's resources?' in J. Crawford and M. Koskenniemi (eds.), *The Cambridge Companion to International Law* (Cambridge University Press, 2012) pp. 398–420, 416.

[2] R. M. Cover, 'Foreword: Nomos and narrative' (1983) 97 *Harvard Law Review* 4–68.

[3] For a more detailed discussion see J. Dehm, 'Carbon colonialism or climate justice?: Interrogating the international climate regime from a TWAIL perspective' (2016) 33 *Windsor Yearbook of Access to Justice* 129–61.

124 *Asserting Global Authority over the Carbon Sequestration Potential of Forests*

it shows how an underlying imperative of development underpins demands of efficiency within the regime, giving rise to a number of 'flexibility mechanisms' directed towards enabling and incentivising the least-cost mitigation options. These in turn depend upon an ability to think about different actions contributing to climate change as if they were 'equivalent', and thus comparable, substitutable and exchangeable. These abstractions allow emission reductions to be disembedded and decontextualised from the broader social and economic conditions that produce them and their underlying political economy, in ways that risk disabling the political and economic transformations necessary to address the crisis. Instead, of addressing structural drivers of climate change this innovation of 'common concern' has thus authorised increased mechanisms for the measuring, monitoring, reporting and verifying (MMRV) of emission reductions, particularly in the Global South. These mechanisms thereby enable the exercise of international authority, power and control over sites and spaces of particular concern, such as tropical forests located in the Global South.

The third section addresses how reducing tropical deforestation and increasing carbon sequestration in forests came to be understood as a matter of global 'common concern'. It highlights how forests have historically been subject to competing claims of ownership and contestation over whether they should be understood as an international, national or local resource. It shows how it became possible to sidestep these controversial questions about who owns or has a legitimate stake in the world's forests, by focusing not on proprietorial questions but instead on the global functions that forests provide. Such a focus on the capacity of forests to sequester carbon and their function as carbon sinks allowed the issue of deforestation, and thus also forest management, to be understood as a matter of global concern, rather than simply matters of local or national concern. Finally, this section shows how international authority over forests pursuant to this 'common concern' has also been differentially actualised, due to a particular framing that locates the problem of deforestation in countries of the Global South and thereby renders invisible the global political economy and the global drivers of tropical deforestation.

B COMMON CONCERN

The principle of 'common concern' is central to the two key conventions arising out of the 1992 UN Conference on Environment and Development (UNCED) in Rio de Janeiro: the UNFCCC declares that the 'the change in the Earth's climate and its adverse effects are a matter of common concern',[4] while the Convention on Biological Diversity (CBD) declares that the 'conservation of biological diversity is

---

[4] *United Nations Framework Convention on Climate Change*, opened for signature 4 June 1992, 1771 UNTS 107 (entered into force 21 March 1994) preambular recital 1.

B. Common Concern

a common concern of humankind'.[5] This section explores the history of this concept and distinguishes it from other potentially applicable principles relevant to international environmental law and resource governance, including transboundary harm, 'common interests' and 'common heritage of mankind'. It describes how designating processes of atmospheric change and conservation as matters of 'common concern' can be understood as a 'jurisdictional technology ... capable of authorising, changing or altering lawful relations'.[6]

Although the principle of 'common concern' draws on earlier international environmental law principles, it was first articulated just prior to the Rio Earth Summit. General Assembly Resolution 43/53 (1988) affirmed that 'climate change is a common concern of mankind (sic)'.[7] Further, conceptual foundations of the principles of 'common concern' and 'common but differentiated responsibility' were articulated in the 1990 General Assembly Declaration on International Economic Co-operation.[8] That Declaration acknowledges the current threat to the environment as 'the common concern of all' and that '[a]ll countries should take effective actions for the protection and enhancement of the environment in accordance with their respective capabilities and responsibilities and taking into account the specific needs of developing countries'.[9] However, the principle of 'common concern' arguably has a longer conceptual history – one that can be traced, as Dinah Shelton has done, to frameworks of 'humanitarian' law or the 'laws of humanity and the dictates of public conscience' focused on protecting humans because of their status as human, not due to their citizenship of a specific state.[10] Doctrinally, the principle of 'common concern' is generally seen not as creating either specific rules or specific obligations but as 'establish[ing] the general basis for the community concerned to act'.[11]

The principle thus differs in important ways from other international environmental law principles directed towards either the prevention of transboundary

---

[5] *Convention on Biological Diversity*, opened for signature 5 June 1992, 1760 UNTS 79 (entered into force 29 December 1993) preambular recital 3.

[6] S. Dorsett and S. McVeigh, *Jurisdiction* (Routledge, 2012) p. 14.

[7] General Assembly, *Provisional Record of the Thirty-Fifth Meeting*, 43rd session, A/43/PV.35 (25 October 1988) para 17.

[8] General Assembly Resolution S-18/3, *Declaration on International Economic Co-operation, in Particular the Revitalization of Economic Growth and Development of the Developing Countries*, 11th plen mtng, A/RES/S-18/3 (1 May 1990) para 29; N. Schrijver, *The Evolution of Sustainable Development in International Law: Inception, Meaning and Status* (Martinus Nijhoff Publishers, 2008) pp. 65–6.

[9] *Declaration on International Economic Co-operation*, para 29. For a discussion of the Declaration and its context see J. Dehm, 'Rupture and continuity: North/South struggles over debt and economic co-operation at the end of the Cold War' in M. Craven, S. Pahuja, and G. Simpson (eds.), *International Law and the Cold War* (Cambridge University Press, 2020) pp. 287–314.

[10] D. Shelton, 'Common concern of humanity' (2009) 39 *Environmental Policy and Law* 83–6.

[11] A. Kiss, 'The common concern of mankind' 27 *Environmental Policy and Law*, cited in International Law Commission, *Second report on the protection of the atmosphere, by Shinya Murase, Special Rapporteur*, 67th session, A/CN.4/681 (2 March 2015).

126 Asserting Global Authority over the Carbon Sequestration Potential of Forests

pollution or the governance of shared resources. Principles regarding transboundary pollution have had to balance the right of states to pursue domestic policies based on territorial sovereignty with the right of other states not to be harmed.[12] These principles, developed in bilateral disputes, have clear limitations for regulating pollution in a multilateral or global context.[13] Arguably too, such an approach might more clearly foreground questions of historical and ongoing responsibility for pollution – and potentially enliven the polluter pays principle – more so than framing emissions as a 'common' concern.[14] The 'commons' framing instead suggests a 'global' problem, and the attribution of collective responsibility, in ways that may blur discussions of responsibility or liability.[15]

The concept of 'common concern' also differs from the principle of 'common heritage' used in the governance of the deep sea bed and outer space, which are beyond the limits of national jurisdictions.[16] This principle was first proposed in 1967 by Malta's ambassador, Arvid Pardo,[17] and in 1988 Malta's representative argued that the principle of 'common heritage of mankind' could also be productively applied to the atmosphere.[18] Malta argued that the concept of common heritage was relevant to the problems raised by climate change, as it would 'recognize one of climate's fundamental characteristics: climate is one of the few truly natural conditions which determine life on earth and is, therefore, an integral part of man's natural heritage'.[19] Malta proposed that the principle of 'common heritage', which 'entails major proprietary and economic considerations'[20] to ensure the equitable sharing of the benefit of exploitation, could be applied to climate change. Although Malta accepted that the principle would require appropriate modification if it were extended to the climate context, ultimately, the principle was deemed inappropriate for the climate regime – perhaps because it has principles of equity and benefit-sharing at its core.[21] Although the General Assembly 'welcomed' Malta's proposal,

---

[12] M. Koskenniemi, 'International Pollution in the System of International Law' (1984) 17 Oikeustiede Jurisprudentia 91–181.

[13] On this principle see, *Trail Smelter Arbitration* (USA v Canada, 1938/1941) UN.RIAA, Vol III.

[14] J. Gupta, 'International law and climate change: The challenges facing developing countries' (2006) 16(1) *Yearbook of International Environmental Law* 119 at 130.

[15] Ibid., 129.

[16] F. Biermann, '"Common concern of humankind": The emergence of a new concept of international environmental law' (1996) 34(4) *Archiv des Völkerrechts* 426–81; see also S. Mason-Case, 'Inaugurating a new kind of "commons"' (draft manuscript on file with the author).

[17] M. W. Lodge, 'The common heritage of mankind' in D. Freestone (ed.), *The 1982 Law of the Sea Convention at 30: Successes, Challenges and New Agendas* (Martinus Nijhoff Publishers, 2013) pp. 59–68.

[18] General Assembly, *Provisional Record of the Thirty-Fifth Meeting*, 43rd session, A/43/PV.35 (25 October 1988) pp. 14–15.

[19] Ibid., p. 16.

[20] Ibid., p. 17.

[21] See S. Mason-Case, 'Inaugurating a new kind of "commons"' (draft manuscript on file with the author)

B. Common Concern

the subsequent resolution instead described climate change as 'a common concern of mankind, since climate is an essential condition which sustains life on earth'.[22]

The concept of 'common concern' is most similar to the earlier concept of 'common interest' in international environmental law, which was directed towards established international jurisdiction over shared resources or areas beyond the jurisdiction of any nation states.[23] In the lead up to the United Nations Conference on Environment and Development the concept of 'common interest' was welcomed as a 'frame of reference for an international law meeting the challenges of the future', but it was also recognised that the principle would need to be significantly rethought in a context where international law was seen as being 'at a turning point from a system of balancing conflicting sovereign interests to one of constructive interaction for the common good'.[24] In 1989, Jutta Brunnée argued that while the 'coinciding interests' of states provides the 'foundation' for the principle of 'common interest', this principle also 'could not function relying exclusively on the reciprocity mechanism underlying much of the contemporary international law'. Instead, she argued that 'where the emerging, shared or coinciding interests are of such intensity that their realization commands actions on the international level', the notion of 'common interest' could 'assume another quality', such that 'it permits – factually and legally – only one mode of conduct'.[25] In this analysis, the concept of 'common interest' is transformed; it no longer operates as an expression of shared concern that *brings into being* an international community; instead it treats this imagined 'international community' as a *pre-existing entity* that compels specific action. This subtle difference in jurisdictional terms could be described as reflecting two rival accounts of the international domain: 'one giving shape to the international domain in terms of the free meeting of sovereign territorial nation states, the other shaping the international domain around forms of cosmopolitan order that treat [it] as having an independent existence'.[26] The latter account, which treats the 'international community' as a pre-given entity, presumes that the international community is already structured in specific ways, and thereby implicitly constrains the type and nature of action that is authorised in its name.

While there are clear resonances between the concept of 'common concern' and 'common interest', the concept of 'common concern' differs from that of 'common

---

[22] General Assembly Resolution 43/53, *Protection of global climate for present and future generations of mankind*, 70th plen mtng, A/RES/43/53 (6 December 1988) para 1.

[23] Shelton, 'Common concern of humanity', pp. 84–5.

[24] J. Brunnée, '"Common interest" echoes from an empty shell?: Some thoughts on common interest and international environmental law' (1989) 49 *Zeitschrift für ausländisches öffentliches Recht und Völkerrecht* 791–808 at 792.

[25] Ibid at 794.

[26] Dorsett and McVeigh, *Jurisdiction*, p. 118; on 'rival jurisdictions' see also S. McVeigh and S. Pahuja, 'Rival jurisdictions: The promise and loss of sovereignty' in C. Barbour and G. Pavlich (eds.), *After Sovereignty: On the Question of Political Beginnings* (Routledge, 2009) pp. 97–114.

interest' in key ways. Firstly, Frank Biermann has suggested that the language of 'concern' 'may indicate a certain higher status' compared to the weaker term 'interest', previously applied to Antarctica, whaling and the protection of the seabed from military installations.[27] As such, he suggests that this could 'imply that international governance regarding those "concerns" is not only necessary or desired but rather essential for the survival of humankind'.[28] Brunnée elaborates:

> Although the concept of common concern does not imply a specific rule for the conduct of states, it does signal that their freedom of action may be subject to limits even where other states' sovereign rights are not affected in the direct transboundary sense envisaged by the harm principle. Such limits flow precisely from the fact that the concept identifies certain types of environmental degradation as of concern to all, which would imply that obligations are owed *erga omnes*.[29]

Secondly, the two principles have different spatial or geographical scopes. While the principle of 'common interest' generally applies to resources and areas beyond the jurisdiction of any nation-state, the principle of 'common concern' pertains to matters *spatially within* nation-states. Therefore, while the principle of 'common interest' calls for international co-operation on matters outside of national jurisdiction, the designation of something as a matter of 'common concern' operates to remove the topic of concern from a state's *exclusive* jurisdiction and makes it a 'legitimate matter for international regulation'.[30] Such a designation of 'common concern' does not entirely remove a state's sovereignty in relation to the topic in question, rather it establishes a complicated *balancing* between international and domestic jurisdictional authority over the domain of common concern, whereby the right of the international community to act is balanced against national sovereignty, and the exercise of national jurisdiction is made subject to international obligations.[31]

This complicated balancing between international and domestic jurisdictions means that the extent to which the global authority authorised through an innovation of 'common concern' is actualised in practice remains highly uneven. When discussing the principle of 'common concern', international environmental law

---

[27] Biermann, '"Common concern of humankind": The emergence of a new concept of international environmental law', 426–81 at 431.

[28] Ibid.

[29] J. Brunnée, 'A conceptual framework for an international forests convention: Customary law and emerging principles' in Canadian Council of International Law (ed.) *Global Forests and International Environmental Law* (Kluwer Law, 1996) pp. 41–77; in 1989 she wrote that 'common interest' can become so compelling that 'it alone formulates the rule and coincides with the rule's content' or so vital that 'it permits – factually and legally – only one mode of conduct'; J. Brunnée, '"Common interest" echoes from an empty shell?: Some thoughts on common interest and international environmental law' at 791–808 at 794.

[30] A. C. Kiss and D. Shelton, *Guide to International Environmental Law* (Martinus Nijhoff Publishers, 2007).

[31] Ibid.

B. Common Concern

scholarship is generally caught between a pessimistic realist apology that such principles are neither 'precise enough' nor 'forceful enough to impose' themselves,[32] and utopian arguments about the imperatives of realising the normative, cosmopolitan vision this principle proclaims.[33] In such international environmental law scholarship there is often a sense of despair that despite invocations of 'common concern' the '[l]ack of cooperation among states, lack of appropriate international institutions, a host of collective action problems, and free-riding, all render concerted efforts difficult, if not impossible'. [34] But in the literature, there is also a frequently expressed hope of possibilities for realising the more '"communitarian" strain' in international law.[35] Oscillating between a pessimistic assessment of practice and an optimistic view of principle, international legal responses have generally sought in a top-down fashion to reassert the *necessity* of 'mutual interdependence' of all states within a 'world order in which every sovereign State depends on the same global environment',[36] or to seek in a more bottom-up way 'any evidence in international law of . . . the idea that there exists not just a community of necessity, but also of values'.[37] Regardless of whether such writing either adopts an optimistic valance that such a community will yet emerge or a more pessimistic tone that it has not yet, it generally holds on to a vision of what a cosmopolitan global law based around a 'common concern' could look like, and either seeks to explain why this vision has not yet been realised or continues to call for its realisation.

Rather than focusing on the persistent gap between such a vision and its actualisation, the analysis in this chapter focuses on the effects such an invocation of 'common concern' has had in practice. It pays attention to the uneven and differentiated kind of global authority that is gradually being actualised in the name of a 'common concern' as a matter of fact and examines how the international authority authorised by the claim of a 'common concern' is, in concrete and material ways, actualised differently in the Global North and Global South. It shows that despite

---

[32] J. Brunnée, 'International environmental law: Rising to the challenge of common concern?' (2006) 100 *Proceedings of the Annual Meeting (American Society of International Law)* 307–10 at 308.

[33] On this dynamic in international law generally see, M. Koskenniemi, *From Apology to Utopia: The Structure of International Legal Argument* (Cambridge University Press, 2005).

[34] T. Cottier et al., 'The principle of common concern and climate change' (2014) 53(3) *Archiv des Völkerrechts* 293–324 at 294.

[35] See S. Pahuja, 'Conserving the world's resources?' p. 416.

[36] See how these sentiments were expressed in by Justice Christopher Weeramantry in *Legality of the Threat of Use of Nuclear Weapons*, Advisory Opinion (8 July 1996), *ICJ Reports 1996*, p. 505; see also Justice Weeramantry's separate opinion in the *Gabčicovko–Nagymaros Project (Hungary/Slovakia)*, Judgement (15 September 1997), *ICJ Reports 1997*, p. 118, where he wrote: '[W]e have entered an era of international law in which international law serves not only the interests of individual States, but looks beyond them and their parochial concerns to the greater interests of humanity and planetary welfare.'

[37] J. Brunnée, 'Common areas, common heritage, and common concern' in D. Bodansky, J. Brunnée, and E. Hey (eds.), *The Oxford Handbook of International Environmental Law* (Oxford University Press, 2008).

the purported universality of the claim to 'common concern' and the fact that its domain is necessarily *formally* global in scope, in practice the form and shape of the international authority it authorises can be enacted very differently in different parts of the world. This assessment echoes key insights of Third World Approaches to International Law (TWAIL) scholarship, which has importantly demonstrated the much more 'porous' nature of Third World sovereignty in relation to international intervention; it reveals how for some countries sovereignty acts as a strong 'bulwark' against international obligations while for others sovereignty provides only a very limited 'shield' against imposed international forms of action.[38]

There are two key implications arising from this analysis that the invocation of a 'common concern' in the context of climate change and forest protection has given rise to forms of international authority that are actualised differently in the Global North and the Global South. Firstly, it points to how countries in the Global South can be differently compelled to act pursuant to a 'common concern', including through mechanisms of conditionality and finance. Secondly, it highlights to a responsibility gap, where those countries responsible for the greatest proportion of current and historical GHG emissions are also least subject to an international jurisdiction pursuant to a 'common concern' seeking to address these urgent environmental imperatives. Recognising these differences therefore brings to light the politics and political economy that have crafted the way in which this invocation of a global 'common concern' has in practice been actualised in ways that are highly differentiated and that parallel pre-existing relations of power.

C CLIMATE CHANGE AND SUPRANATIONAL JURISDICTION

This section describes how the problem of climate change has come to be understood and represented in a specific way and how this representation has authorised new forms of international authority, which are however actualised in highly differentiated ways. There is ample evidence and scientific consensus that anthropocentric GHG emissions are impacting the climate in ways that have serious consequences for the ability of the planet to sustain the possibilities of life.[39] In a context where there has been a deliberately orchestrated and targeted attack on the credibility of climate science by vested interests promoting 'sceptic' and 'denier' positions,[40] paying attention to how we have come to know things the way we have

---

[38] A. Anghie, *Imperialism, Sovereignty and the Making of International Law* (Cambridge University Press, 2007).

[39] *Global Warming of 1.5° C: An IPCC Special Report on the Impacts of Global Warming of 1.5° C Above Pre-industrial Levels and Related Global Greenhouse Gas Emission Pathways, in the Context of Strengthening the Global Response to the Threat of Climate Change, Sustainable Development, and Efforts to Eradicate Poverty* (Intergovernmental Panel on Climate Change, 2018).

[40] B. Latour, 'Why has critique run out of steam? From matters of fact to matters of concern' (2004) 30(2) *Critical Inquiry* 225–48.

C. Climate Change and Supranational Jurisdiction

can be a fraught endeavour.[41] Yet it remains critical to recall that '[s]cience is not the only, nor even the primary, medium through which people experience climate change',[42] and that 'climate change' as a scientific phenomenon is a very different epistemological beast than is the knowledge that the climate is changing.[43] The question of how knowledge is produced and validated, and thus how specific 'truths' are constructed, is inherently tied to questions of power.[44] Thus, the way in which the 'problem' of climate change is framed is not neutral; it is already the effect of specific assemblages of material and discursive power, which create a 'field of intelligibility' with the effect of enabling certain forms of actions and actors while marginalising others.[45] It is, therefore, both possible and necessary to simultaneously affirm human-induced climatic change as an ecological reality while simultaneously interrogating the ways in which these process coalesce into specific representations and how they are understood as a 'scientific phenomenon', as an 'object' of governance and as a 'problem' for international law.[46] Questioning how particular problems are framed is critically important, because, as Sara Dehm has highlighted, at stake in the framing of issues are 'questions of authority, jurisdiction and institutional responsibility' given that 'particular frames set the conditions for apprehension, recognition and regulation' even as frames are always 'open to redescription, contestation and reconfiguration'.[47] Martti Koskenniemi has likewise observed how 'political conflict is waged on the description and re-description of aspects of the world so as to make them fall under the jurisdiction of particular institutions'.[48]

This section therefore draws attention to how the jurisdiction of the UNFCCC is authorised and given a specific shape through a specific representation of climate change as: (i) a global, common or aggregate problem; (ii) a current or future problem and (iii) primarily a problem of excessive GHG concentrations rather than of the political and social conditions that enabled them. It subsequently examines how the imperatives of efficiency and economic growth have underpinned how the targets and methods of climate mitigation has been conceptualised. Finally, it describes how climate action becomes understood in standardised and substitutable terms through market-based responses. The analysis shows that this specific framing of climate change is not inevitable and that the problem of climate

---

[41] Ibid.; see also S. Jasanoff and H. R. Simmet, 'No funeral bells: Public reason in a "post-truth"age' (2017) 47(5) *Social Studies of Science* 751–70.

[42] S. Jasanoff, 'A new climate for society' (2010) 27(2–3) *Theory, Culture and Society* 233–53 at 235.

[43] Ibid, 237.

[44] See generally M. Foucault, *Power/Knowledge: Selected Interviews and Other Writings, 1972–1977* (Pantheon, 1980).

[45] B. T. Russell, *Interrogating the Post-Political: The Case of Radical Climate and Climate Justice Movements* (PhD Thesis, University of Leeds, 2012) p. 15.

[46] F. Johns, *Non-Legality in International Law: Unruly Law* (Cambridge University Press, 2013) Chapter 5.

[47] S. Dehm, 'Framing international migration' (2015) 3(1) *London Review of International Law* 133–68 at 137.

[48] M. Koskenniemi, *The Politics of International Law* (Hart Pub, 2011) pp. 336–8.

change could be (perhaps more politically) conceptualised otherwise, possibly giving rise to different ways of conceptualising legal frameworks and legal obligations to respond to this crisis.

1 Climate Change As a 'Global' Problem

The UNFCCC preamble acknowledges that 'change in the earth's climate and its adverse effects are a common concern of humankind' and the main object of this concern is 'global emissions' and specifically the stabilisation of aggregate, global levels of GHG emissions.[49] The preamble also acknowledges the 'global nature of climate change',[50] and in doing so, affirms the inadequacy of using territorially organised sovereignty to address harms and ecological processes that persistently transverse borders and stresses the need for 'the widest possible cooperation by all countries'.[51] Underpinning this claim is an imaginary of the Earth as a distinct, bounded, blue-green sphere – a collective 'life-boat' suspended in a vast universe, which demands collective responsibility and threatens collective vulnerability or annihilation.[52] Such a framing of climate as a 'common' problem has been critiqued, because it too easily 'creates the image of a tragedy' and implies it is a problem of 'widespread harm with no clear culprit'.[53] It is therefore risks obscuring how climate change is 'inextricably linked to economic inequality': it is 'a crisis that is driven by the greenhouse gas emissions of the "haves" that hits the "haves-nots" the hardest'.[54] The language of 'one world' globalism in scientific and political representation of 'climate change' thus risks inflicting violence when imposed upon a globe that has historically been deeply stratified in relation to power and access to resources, along lines of class, race and gender, and where the problem of climate change – its causes and effects – is deeply entangled with these differentials.[55] Jason Moore warns against a simplified positioning of a collective humanity or 'anthropos' as the causal agent responsible for climate change. He writes:

[49] UNFCCC, preambular recital 1.
[50] UNFCCC, preambular recital 3.
[51] UNFCCC, preambular recital 6.
[52] For a discussion of 'one world' globalism see W. Sachs, 'One world' in W. Sachs (ed.), *The Development Dictionary: A Guide to Knowledge as Power* (Zed Books, 2010) pp. 111–26; see also A. Escobar, 'Beyond the Third World: imperial globality, global coloniality and antiglobalisation social movements' (2004) 25(1) *Third World Quarterly* 207–30.
[53] Gupta, 'International law and climate change', 128.
[54] T. Gore, *Extreme carbon inequality: Why the Paris climate deal must put the poorest, lowest emitting and most vulnerable people first* (Oxfam International, 2015) p. 1.
[55] V. Tauli-Corpuz and L.-A. Baer, *Results of the Copenhagen Meeting of the Conference of the Parties to the United Nations Framework Convention on Climate Change; Implications for Indigenous Peoples' Local Adaptation and Mitigation Measures*, Permanent Forum on Indigenous Issues, 9th session, E/C.19/2010/18 (2 March 2010) para 10. See also N. Smith, 'There's no such thing as a natural disaster', *Understanding Katrina: Persepctives from the Social Sciences* 11 June 2006, understandingkatrina.ssrc.org/Smith.

C. Climate Change and Supranational Jurisdiction

The Anthropocene makes for an easy story. Easy, because it does not challenge the naturalized inequalities, alienation, and violence inscribed in modernity's strategic relations of power, production, and nature. It is an easy story to tell because it does not ask us to think about these relations *at all*.[56]

It is therefore valuable to recall that it is neither innate nor inherent to understand climate change as a predominately 'global' issue, and that understandings of climate change and questions of scale and space have been linked to political imperatives.[57] Considerable work was required to consolidate a specific idea of climate as a 'global' problem. In particular, the Intergovernmental Panel on Climate Change (IPCC) presented a specific scientific framing of climate change that 'explicitly challenged the prior, local framing of climate change and mobilized the backing of the international community behind a global framing' to 'boost the credibility of the claim that the Earth's climatic system should be treated in international law as an ontologically unitary system that spans the entire globe'.[58] Clark Miller has shown how from the first IPCC reports onwards, the notion of a global 'climate system' was adopted as 'the totality of the atmosphere, hydrosphere, biosphere, and geosphere and their interactions'.[59] Moreover, Miller shows that in order to 'reinforce its authority', the IPCC 'articulated a new model of science and politics' by offering a vision of global governance that did not foreground states but rather in which 'experts and expert knowledge, as politically neutral agents, were accorded significant power to define problems of global policy'.[60]

Framing climate change as a global problem and articulating the objectives of international climate policy in aggregate global terms has real effects. Such a globalist frame does not inevitably lead to treating emission reductions from different actions and places as exchangeable; however, it is a necessary precondition for the later abstractions that international carbon trading as a mitigation strategy would introduce. Such a focus on the global as the relevant scale for climate action is the necessary (although not sufficient, or inevitable) precondition for the standardisation and exchangeability of different mitigation actions in different places globally.

---

[56] J. W. Moore, 'Anthropocene or capitalocene?' *Verso*, 1 December 2015 www.versobooks.com/blogs/2360-jason-w-moore-anthropocene-or-capitalocene; see also the various contributions in J. W. Moore (ed.), *Anthropocene or Capitalocene?: Nature, History, and the Crisis of Capitalism* (PM Press, 2016); as well as A. Grear, 'Deconstructing anthropos: A critical legal reflection on "anthropocentric" law and Anthropocene "humanity"' (2015) 26(3) *Law and Critique* 225–49.

[57] See D. R. Coen, *Climate in Motion: Science, Empire, and the Problem of Scale* (University of Chicago Press, 2018).

[58] C. A. Miller, 'Democratization, international knowledge institutions, and global governance' (2007) 20(2) *Governance: An International Journal of Policy, Administration, and Institutions* 325–57 at 341; see also Johns, *Non-Legality in International Law: Unruly Law*, Chapter 5.

[59] Cited in C. A. Miller, 'Climate science and the making of a global political order' in S. Jasanoff (ed.), *States of Knowledge: The Co-production of Science and the Social Order* (Routledge, 2004) p. 57.

[60] Miller, 'Climate science and the making of a global political order', 47.

2 Climate Change As a Current or Future Problem

The different temporalising narratives that are used to structure accounts of climate change, and their modes of employment, enliven different possibilities of thinking about actions, responsibility and agency in the present.[61] The preamble to the UNFCCC acknowledges in the (conditional) future tense that substantial increases in anthropogenic GHG emissions 'will result . . . in an additional warming' and 'may adversely affect natural ecosystems and humankind'.[62] In response to these threats, which are projected into the future, the Convention seeks to achieve, 'within a timeframe sufficient to allow' for adaptation and development, the 'stabilization of greenhouse gas concentrations in the atmosphere at a level that would prevent dangerous anthropogenic interference with the climate system'.[63] The temporal account of the climate crisis provided by the Convention is of climate change as a future threat, and mitigation and adaptation as future-orientated obligations. It thus presents climate change as a future – not present – crisis and configures obligations that arise as obligations to the future ('for the benefit of present and future generations'),[64] rather than recognising that climate change is also a 'claim of the past', given that 'a carbon footprint haunts every step of the history of industrial and colonial expansion of the last centuries'.[65] The historical cumulation of emissions – predominantly from a small number of individuals and entities located primarily in the Global North[66] – now over-determines planetary futures. Such a recognition of the past's hold on the present underpins calls for the acknowledgment of climate debts.[67] However, instead of engaging with how the past has constituted the present and constrains future possibilities – and thus the legal obligations arising from historical causes for future effects – the temporal orientation of the UNFCCC inscribes a break with the past in the name of instigating a new future-orientated regime.

---

[61] For a longer discussion see J. Dehm, 'International law, temporalities and narratives of the climate crisis' (2016) 4(1) *London Review of International Law* 167–93.

[62] UNFCCC, preambular recital 2.

[63] UNFCCC, Article 2.

[64] UNFCCC, Article 3.1.

[65] S. Humphreys, 'Climate justice: The claim of the past' (2014) 5 *Journal of Human Rights and the Environment* 134–48 at 147.

[66] R. Heede, 'Tracing anthropogenic carbon dioxide and methane emissions to fossil fuel and cement producers, 1854–2010' (2014) 122(1–2) *Climatic Change* 229–41.

[67] T. Jones and S. Edwards, *The Climate Debt Crisis: Why Paying Our Dues Is Essential for Tackling Climate Change* (Jubilee Debt Campaign and World Development Movement, 2009); K. Mickelson, 'Leading towards a level playing field, repaying ecological debt, or making environmental space: Three stories about international environmental cooperation' (2005) 43 *Osgoode Hall Law Journal* 137–70; R. Warlenius, G. Pierce, V. Ramasar, E. Quistorp, J. Martínez-Alier, L. Rijnhout, and I. Yanez, 'Ecological debt: History, meaning and relevance for environmental justice' (2015) 18 *EJOLT Report*.

C. Climate Change and Supranational Jurisdiction

3 Climate Change As a Problem of Emissions, Not Structural Causes

The 'ultimate objective' of the UNFCCC is the 'stabilisation of greenhouse gas concentrations in the atmosphere at a level that would prevent dangerous anthropocentric interference with the climate system'.[68] This framing is primarily concerned with the direct *effects* that produce climate change – GHG emissions – rather than their *causes*, namely the type of 'human activities [that] have been substantially increasing the atmospheric concentration of greenhouse gases'.[69] As such, the objectives of the agreement are translated from a *political* goal of transforming the underlying political economy and 'overcoming fossil fuel dependence by entrenching a new historical pathway' to a more *technical* goal of 'placing progressive numerical limits on emissions' and achieving 'measurable, divisible greenhouse-gas "emission reductions"'.[70]

Narrowly focusing on reducing CO_2 emissions rather than envisioning the necessary pathways to a low-carbon society has several consequences. Social theorist Erik Swyngedouw has criticised the 'fetishist invocation of CO_2 as the "thing" around which our environmental dreams, aspirations, contestations as well as policies crystallize', which he suggests, leads to a reductionist approach to addressing climate change, focused on stabilizing the CO_2 content in the atmosphere'.[71] He further argues that this hegemonic vision of mitigation obscures both the 'multiple and complex relations through which environmental change unfolds',[72] as well as the complex processes and social relations through which this 'hybrid socio-natural quasi-object came into its problematic being'.[73] Moreover, this focus on abstract goals related to temperature targets and concentrations of GHG emissions in the atmosphere, rather than concrete trajectories to a low-carbon society, makes it possible to avoid fraught questions of what is involved in a social, political and economic transition to a low-carbon future and away from fossil fuel dependence, including questions of 'carbon lock-in'[74] as well as critical normative questions about justice and the distributional impact of such a transition.[75] A narrow focus on reducing GHG emissions also brackets ethical or moral considerations that might seek to distinguish between the 'survival emissions' of the poor and

---

[68] UNFCCC, Article 2.

[69] UNFCCC, preambular recital 2.

[70] L. Lohmann, 'Uncertainty markets and carbon markets: Variations on Polanyian themes' (2010) 15(2) *New Political Economy* 225–54 at 237–8.

[71] E. Swyngedouw, 'Apocalypse forever?: Post-political populism and the spectre of climate change' (2010) 27(2–3) *Theory, Culture and Society* 213–32 at 219 and 217.

[72] Ibid., 220.

[73] Ibid., 220.

[74] On 'carbon lock-in' see G. C. Unruh, 'Understanding carbon lock-in' (2000) 28 *Energy Policy* 817–30.

[75] J. Dehm, 'Post Paris reflections: Fossil fuels, human rights and the need to excavate new ideas for climate justice' (2017) 8(2) *Journal of Human Rights and the Environment* 280–300 at 291–2.

136 *Asserting Global Authority over the Carbon Sequestration Potential of Forests*

'luxury emissions' of the rich.[76] Moreover, such an approach, which does not draw qualitative distinctions between different activities that produce GHG emissions or subject them to different policy approaches, may create incentives to 'pick the lowest hanging fruit' rather than promote what might be initially more costly, but longer-term more strategic interventions. This framing therefore encourages a more reductionist and calculative approach to climate policy, one that is less attentive to how the production of GHG emissions are embedded in social and economic configurations.

4 *The Imperatives of 'Efficiency'*

The UNFCCC also articulates further imperatives that direct how the objective of 'stabilization of greenhouse gas concentrations in the atmosphere at a level that would prevent dangerous anthropocentric interference with the climate system' should be achieved.[77] In particular, Article 2 also provides that 'such a level should be achieved ... [in a manner] to enable economic development to proceed in a sustainable manner'.[78] In doing so, it reflects the 'compromises of liberal environmentalism' and the discourse of 'sustainable development' that have sought to reconcile environmental protection with the imperatives of growth.[79] The articulation of the objectives in this way not only demonstrates the quasi-transcendental position of economic growth in relationship to international law[80] but also constrains a deeper questioning of the ways in which the continual pursuit of economic growth and ecological limits are irreconcilable.[81] Additionally, the endorsement of these economic imperatives gives weight to assumptions about the need for *efficient* and *cost-effective* mitigation strategies and impacts the quantification of emission reduction targets and the means by which they might be achieved.

There still has not been any agreement on a precise level for the 'stabilization of greenhouse gas emissions' that 'would prevent dangerous anthropocentric

---

[76] A. Agarwal and S. Narain, *Global Warming in an Unequal World: A Case for Environmental Colonialism* (Centre of Science and the Environment, 1990); see also H. Shue, 'Subsistence emissions and luxury emissions' (1993) 15(1) *Law & Policy* 39–60.

[77] UNFCCC, Article 2.

[78] UNFCCC, Article 2.

[79] D. Ciplet and J. T. Roberts, 'Climate change and the transition to neoliberal environmental governance' (2017) 46 *Global Environmental Change* 148–56; see also S. Bernstein, *The Compromise of Liberal Environmentalism* (Colombia University Press, 2001).

[80] See S. Pahuja, *Decolonising International Law: Development, Economic Growth and the Politics of Universality* (Cambridge University Press, 2011).

[81] In contrast, see current discussion on the ecological need to adopt 'degrowth' perspectives: see for example G. D'Alisa, F. Demaria, and G. Kallis, *Degrowth: A Vocabulary for a New Era* (Routledge, 2014); and for a critique of growth paradigms see P. Ferguson, *Post-Growth Politics: A Critical Theoretical and Policy Framework for Decarbonisation* (Springer International Publishing, 2018).

C. Climate Change and Supranational Jurisdiction

interference with the climate system'.[82] The targets adopted in the 1997 Kyoto Protocol – a 5 percent reduction of developed states' GHG emissions from their 1990 levels – were primarily a result of political negotiation. The Paris Agreement articulated its objectives not in terms of aggregate GHG levels but in terms of 'holding the increase in the global average temperature to well below 2 °C above pre-industrial levels and pursuing efforts to limit the temperature increase to 1.5 °C above pre-industrial levels'.[83] This temperature goal reflects a political compromise, and the inclusion of the 1.5 °C aspirational target was seen by many as a key victory for small island states.[84] Discussions on temperature limitations have been strongly influenced by the scientific evidence on climate change. For example, the Copenhagen Accord recognised 'the scientific view that the increase in global temperatures should be below 2 degrees Celsius'.[85] However, as Benoit Mayer writes, 'Science alone cannot determine what *should* be' nor can it 'tell us what increase in global temperature is acceptable; such a determination is only possible based on particular values and interests.'[86]

In practice, considerations of economic efficiency have strongly influenced the quantification of emission reduction targets. Within the field of environmental economics there has been considerable discussion about 'efficient strategies to reduce the costs of climate change'[87] and the 'economics of stabilisation' based upon calculations 'comparing the marginal costs of abatement with the social costs of carbon'.[88] For example, the *Stern Review* suggested stabilisation within the range of 450–550 ppm, arguing that any high ambition would 'impose very high adjustment costs in the near term for relatively small gains and might not even be feasible'.[89] Internal to debates within environmental economics about the appropriate level of stabilisation have been many controversial questions of how future benefits from climate action should be weighed against the present-day costs of such action, especially the discount rate that should be applied or the weight that

---

[82] UNFCCC, Article 2.

[83] *Paris Agreement*, Article 2.1(a).

[84] M. Burkett, 'Small island states and the Paris Agreement' *Wilson Center*, 21 December 2015, www.wilsoncenter.org/article/small-island-states-and-the-paris-agreement; I. de Águeda Corneloup and A. P. Mol, 'Small island developing states and international climate change negotiations: The power of moral "leadership"' (2014) 14(1) *International Environmental Agreements: Politics, Law and Economics* 281–97.

[85] Decision 2/CP.15 'Copenhagen Accord', FCCC/CP/2009/11/Add.1 (30 March 2010) Annex, para 2.

[86] B. Mayer, *The international Law on Climate Change* (Cambridge University Press, 2018) p. 20 (emphasis in original).

[87] See for example W. D. Nordhaus, 'To slow or not to slow: The economics of the greenhouse effect' (1991) 101(407) *The Economic Journal* 920–37; W. Nordhaus, *A Question of Balance: Weighing the Options on Global Warming Policies* (Yale University Press, 2008).

[88] N. H. Stern, *The Economics of Climate Change: The Stern Review* (Cambridge University Press, 2007) p. 284.

[89] Ibid.

138   *Asserting Global Authority over the Carbon Sequestration Potential of Forests*

should be given to the interests of future peoples.[90] Following Fleur Johns, the influence of environmental economics can be understood as a form of 'supra-legal' phenomenon that can be 'understood to enliven, elicit or constrain international legal doings from a plane above or beyond the terrain of international legal work'.[91]

Similar to the way considerations of efficiency have influenced how the optimal balance between present costs of mitigation and future costs of climate change is quantified, an imperative of aggregate economic efficiency has also underpinned assumptions about the types and form of mitigation action that should be taken in the present. Underpinning market-based approaches to climate governance is the notion that 'using price-driven instruments (through tax or trading) will allow flexibility concerning how, where and when emission reductions are made, providing opportunities and incentives to keep down the cost of pollution'.[92] The idea of regulating social costs through the use of private property rights and compliance markets emerged, unsurprisingly, from economics. Through such mechanisms, tradable private rights have become a key way that policy makers seek to 'balance' collective public interest in a 'safe' climate against private freedoms to pursue accumulative growth and development and displace the inevitable tensions between them.[93] Historically, the Pigouvian tradition of welfare economics calculated the social costs of activities by subtracting the additional private benefit of an activity from its uncompensated cost in production elsewhere.[94] However, this approach was directly attacked, and turned on its head, by Ronald Coase's highly influential analysis.[95] Coase agnostically treated pollution as neither good nor bad, calling instead for an analysis about whether the 'gain from preventing harm is greater than the loss suffered elsewhere as a result of stopping the action which produces the harm'.[96] This reframing of the problem of social costs influenced J. H. Dales, who in his book *Pollution, Property and Prices: An Essay in Policy-Making and Economics*, first proposed permit trading as a mechanism for addressing pollution.[97]

---

[90] This is a key point of disagreement between Stern, *The Economics of Climate Change: The Stern Review*, and Nordhaus, *A Question of Balance: Weighing the Options on Global Warming Policies*; W. D. Nordhaus, *The Climate Casino: Risk, Uncertainty, and Economics for a Warming World* (Yale University Press, 2013).

[91] F. Johns, *Non-Legality in International Law: Unruly Law* (Cambridge University Press, 2013) p. 154.

[92] Stern, *The Economics of Climate Change: The Stern Review*, p. 309.

[93] For a discussion of liberal governmental reason as a 'game' between individual freedom and the protection of collective interests against individual interests that is subject to a continuous 'principle of calculation' to calibrate the appropriate balance, see M. Foucault, *The Birth of Biopolitics: Lectures at the Collège de France 1978–1979* (Palgrave, 2008) p. 65.

[94] A. C. Pigou, *The Economics of Welfare* (Macmillan and Co., Ltd., 1932).

[95] R. H. Coase, 'The problem of social cost' (1960) 3 *The Journal of Law and Economics* 1–44; see also Coase interview in T. W. Hazlett, 'Looking for results', *Reason* January 1997, reason.com/archives/1997/01/01/looking-for-results.

[96] Coase, 'The problem of social cost', 27.

[97] J. H. Dales, *Pollution, Property and Prices: An Essay in Policy-Making and Economics* (University of Toronto Press, 1968).

C. Climate Change and Supranational Jurisdiction

He argued that the role of policy is to maintain a 'proper balance' between pollution prevention costs, public and private expenditure to avoid pollution damage and the welfare damage of pollution; he thus proposed taking public goods such as air and water out of the 'category of unrestricted common property' and creating private property rights in the right to use them, which could be traded in markets.

From the 1970s onwards, a range of actors – including banks and business – took on key roles in the establishment of global environmental governance and contributed towards the development and promotion of key ideas.[98] Within the United States, emissions trading schemes (ETSs) were established for sulphur dioxide and later nitrogen oxide under the *Clean Air Act* (1963, USA).[99] Although economists 'offered the initial intellectual foundation and justification for pursuing the development of emission trading', there was a subsequent handover to different professional groups, notably policy analysts.[100] The concept of 'flexibility' was pushed by the US in the negotiations for the Kyoto Protocol as a 'cornerstone of its position in the negotiations' and a precondition to considering binding targets.[101] Although this concept was at the time very unpopular outside the 'Umbrella Group',[102] it has, as Peter Newell and Matthew Paterson have shown, come to dominate the policy response to climate change, especially since the EU (an initial opponent to carbon trading) launched the first ETS.[103]

The 1997 Kyoto Protocol provided a legally binding framework for signatories to achieve an aggregate 5 percent reduction (from 1990 levels)[104] for the first

---

[98] G. Sluga, 'Capitalists and climate', *Humanity Journal* (Blog) 6 November 2017.

[99] See for example F. Green and R. Denniss, 'Cutting with both arms of the scissors: The economic and political case for restrictive supply-side climate policies' (2018) 150(1) *Climatic Change* 73–87; F. Ackerman, B. Biewald, D. White, T. Woolf, and W. Moomaw, 'Grandfathering and coal plant emissions: The cost of cleaning up the Clean Air Act' (1999) 27(15) *Energy Policy* 929–40.

[100] M. Paterson, M. Hoffmann, M. Betsill, and S. Bernstein, 'Professions and policy dynamics in the transnational carbon emissions trading network' in *Professional Networks in Transnational Governance* (Cambridge University Press, 2017) pp. 182–202.

[101] D. Stowell, *Climate Trading: The Development of Greenhouse Markets* (Palgrave Macmillan, 2005).

[102] 'The Umbrella Group is a loose coalition of non-EU developed countries which formed following the adoption of the Kyoto Protocol. Although there is no formal list, the Group is usually made up of Australia, Canada, Japan, New Zealand, Kazakhstan, Norway, the Russian Federation, Ukraine and the US.' UNFCCC, *Party Groupings*, unfccc.int/parties_and_obser vers/parties/negotiating_groups/items/2714.php.

[103] P. Newell and M. Paterson, *Climate Capitalism: Global Warming and the Transformation of the Global Economy* (Cambridge University Press, 2010); C. Haywood, 'The European Union's emissions trading scheme: International emissions trading lessons for the Copenhagen Protocol and implications for Australia?' (2009) 26 *Environmental and Planning Law Journal* 310.

[104] *Kyoto Protocol to the United Nations Framework Convention on Climate Change*, opened for signature 16 March 1998, 2303 UNTS 148 (entered into force on 16 February 2005) Article 3.1 and Annex B; for a discussion see C. Breidenich, D. Magrow, A. Rowley, and J. W. Rubin, 'The Kyoto Protocol to the United Nations Framework Convention on Climate Change' (1998) 92(2) *American Journal of International Law* 315–31.

140   *Asserting Global Authority over the Carbon Sequestration Potential of Forests*

commitment period (2008–12).[105] Pursuant to the principles of 'common but differentiated responsibilities', only Annex I, or 'developed' countries, were expected to take on 'quantified emission limitation and reduction commitments' as listed in Annex B of the Protocol.[106] The most controversial aspects of the Protocol were the last minute addition of three 'flexibility mechanisms': carbon trading between states and two offset mechanisms, the Joint Implementation and the Clean Development Mechanism.[107] Article 17 of the Protocol authorises Annex B parties to 'participate in emissions trading for the purposes of fulfilling their commitments', provided such trading is 'supplemental' to domestic action.[108] These three 'flexibility mechanisms' are based on the premise that mitigation *should* take place where it is cheapest to do so, reflecting the assumptions explicit in the *Stern Review*, namely that '[e]conomic efficiency points to the advantages of a common global carbon price: emission reductions will then take place wherever they are cheapest'.[109]

5 *Substitution, Standardisation and Equivalence*

Market-based flexibility mechanisms rely on understanding climate action in standardised and substitutable terms: they depend on the ability to think of different actions contributing to climate change as 'equivalent' in some way and therefore easily exchangeable. The imaginary of one tonne of carbon dioxide equivalent ($1tCO_2e$) as a standardised 'object' makes it possible to render very different actions commensurable: the rubric of $1tCO_2e$ operates as a 'general equivalent' that makes it possible to compare, standardise and substitute different actions in different parts of the world.[110] There is nothing 'natural' or 'inherent' in thinking about carbon as standardised, commensurable, substitutable and exchangeable. Rather, this specific imaginary of carbon as a fungible 'object' is a mode of legibility structured by international law.

The 'object' of $1tCO_2e$ is therefore the product of various techniques that make it possible to abstract climate mitigation actions from their 'place, technology, history and greenhouse gas type' and other contextual factors.[111] The international climate

---

[105] Annex I countries are those countries listed in Annex I of the UNFCCC.

[106] Note the following countries have alternative baseline years: Bulgaria (1988), Hungary (the average of the years 1985–87), Poland (1988), Romania (1989) and Slovenia (1986).

[107] C. Hepburn, 'Carbon trading: A review of the Kyoto mechanisms' (2007) 32(1) *Annual Review of Environment and Resources* 375–93.

[108] *Kyoto Protocol*, Article 17.

[109] Stern, *The Economics of Climate Change: The Stern Review* p. xviii.

[110] For a more detailed discussion see J. Dehm, 'One tonne of carbon dioxide equivalent (1tCO2e)' in Jessie Hohmann, and D. Joyce (eds.), *International Law's Objects* (Oxford University Press, 2018) pp. 305–18.

[111] Lohmann, 'Uncertainty markets and carbon markets: Variations on Polanyian themes', 237; see also L. Lohmann, 'Neoliberalism and the calculable world: The rise of carbon trading' in K. Birch and V. Mykhnenko (eds.), *The Rise and Fall of Neoliberalism: The Collapse of an Economic Order?* (Zed Books, 2010) pp. 77–93.

regime has facilitated numerous substitutions that render commensurable different types of mitigation actions. One such substitution involves enabling emissions of different GHGs – each with their own properties, characteristics and lifetimes or period of potency – to be expressed and measured in terms of their carbon dioxide equivalence.[112] A further substitution that creates the 'object' of $1tCO_2e$ involves making it possible to compare and exchange 'green' carbon emissions 'saved' by sequestration in 'sinks', such as forests and grasslands, with emission from 'grey' carbon stored in fossil fuels (coal, oil and gas deposits in the lithosphere). Arguably the most controversial substitutions have been those relating to so-called offset credits, or reductions in GHGs in one location that seek to compensate for GHGs emitted elsewhere. The purported equivalence that 'CO_2e reduction under a cap = "avoided" CO_2e emission outside of the cap' enables offset projects to 'license the emissions of still more greenhouse gases elsewhere – as long as they emit less than "would have been released" in the absence of carbon finance'.[113] With REDD+ a further substitution takes place, between actual emissions and those that will be saved through future sequestration against counterfactual baselines of what *would have otherwise have happened* 'but for' the project.

All these substitutions – the 'endless algebra of carbon markets'[114] – are fraught and presents many challenges of how to ensure the commensurability performed by these purported equivalences and require complex technical arrangements to construct and stabilise.[115] Our ability to think of $1tCO_2e$ as substitutable, exchangeable and fungible depends on numerous 'performative equations'[116] that are themselves the outcomes of various contested political and legal decisions, an elaborate regulatory and accounting architecture, as well as a regime of truth that creates and stabilises these equivalences. The Marrakech Accords played a key role in legally defining various different carbon trading units, issued pursuant to specific rules, including the 'emission reduction unit', the 'certified emission reduction', the 'assigned amount unit', and the 'removal unit', specifying that each was 'equal to one metric tonne of carbon dioxide equivalent'.[117] It was therefore through the Marrakech Accords, and the carbon accounting rules they laid out, that $1tCO_2e$

---

[112] See Dehm, 'One tonne of carbon dioxide equivalent ($1tCO2e$)'.

[113] L. Lohmann, 'The endless algebra of climate markets' (2011) 22(4) *Capitalism, Nature, Socialism* 93–116.

[114] Lohmann, 'The endless algebra of climate markets'.

[115] D. MacKenzie, 'Making things the same: Gases, emission rights and the politics of carbon markets' (2009) 34(3) *Accounting, Organizations and Society* 440–55.

[116] L. Lohmann, 'Performative Equations and Neoliberal Commodification: The Case of Climate' (The Corner House, 2012).

[117] See Decision 15/CP.7, 'Principles, nature and scope of the mechanisms pursuant to Articles 6, 12 and 17 of the Kyoto Protocol'; Decision 16/CP.7, 'Guidelines for the implementation of Article 6 of the Kyoto Protocol'; Decision 17/CP.7, 'Modalities and procedures for a Clean Development Mechanism, as defined in Article 12 of the Kyoto Protocol' Decision 18/CP.7, 'Modalities, rules and guidelines for emissions trading under Article 17 of the Kyoto Protocol', FCCC/CP/2001/13/Add.2 (21 January 2002).

142 *Asserting Global Authority over the Carbon Sequestration Potential of Forests*

was 'invented as a functional unit, an Archimedean point of reference that enabled commensurability and exchangeability with other units'.[118] The Warsaw Framework for REDD+, as Chapter 1 showed, similarly made it possible for activities that reduce deforestation and forest degradation to become legible in terms of $1tCO_2e$, which could enable REDD+ 'result-based actions' to be understood as commensurable and exchangeable with other carbon units.

6 *The Differentiated Actualisation of This 'Common Concern'*

This section has shown how addressing climate change has come to be understood in a narrow, abstracted and socially disembedded way, which assumes that a set of activities aimed at reducing the amount of one type of GHG emitted in one part of the world is essentially the same as or equivalent to a different set of activities reducing the amount of emissions (from perhaps another GHG) in another part of the world. There are numerous critiques of how this framing of climate change presents political, ethical and practical dangers and enables carbon trading to coalesce as a potential 'solution'. For example, thinking about climate mitigation in terms of this 'object' can distract attention from the social and economic conditions that produce emissions and might therefore be disabling of the more transformative social change towards a low-carbon society. Further, scholars have questioned the environmental integrity of these purported equivalences and so-claimed emission reductions, especially whether offset emissions are actually 'additional'.[119] There have also been concerns that such markets operate as a 'spatial fix', one that shifts the geographical site of mitigation activities,[120] thereby enabling continued 'lock-in' of carbon intensive growth in the Global North,[121] sustained by export-oriented production of immaterial carbon commodity in the Global South, with its potential local, social and environmental consequences.[122] However, the

---

[118] E. Lövbrand and J. Stripple, 'Making climate change governable: Accounting for carbon as sinks, credits and personal budgets' (2011) 5(2) *Critical Policy Studies* 187–200 at 194.

[119] L. Schneider, 'Assessing the additionality of CDM projects: Practical experiences and lessons learned' (2009) 9(3) *Climate Policy* 242–54; L. R. Schneider, 'Perverse incentives under the CDM: An evaluation of HFC-23 destruction projects' (2011) 11(2) *Climate Policy* 851–64; see also L. Schneider and A. Kollmuss, 'Perverse effects of carbon markets on HFC-23 and SF6 abatement projects in Russia' (2015) 5 *Nature Climate Change* 1061–3.

[120] A. G. Bumpus and D. M. Liverman, 'Accumulation by decarbonization and the governance of carbon offsets' (2008) 84(2) *Economic Geography* 127–55.

[121] S.-J. Clifton, *A Dangerous Obsession: The Evidence Against Carbon Trading and for Real Solutions to Avoid a Climate Crunch* (Friends of the Earth England, Wales and Northern Ireland, 2009); S. Bullock, M. Childs, and T. Picken, *A Dangerous Distraction: Why Offsetting Is Failing the Climate and People: The Evidence* (Friends of the Earth England, Wales and Northern Ireland, 2009).

[122] See in particular the case studies documented in L. Lohmann, *Carbon Trading: A Critical Conversation on Climate Change, Privatization and Power* (2006); and S. Böhm and S. Dabhi (eds.), *Upsetting the Offset: The Political Economy of Carbon Markets* (MayFly Books, 2009).

C. Climate Change and Supranational Jurisdiction

analysis in this chapter highlights how this particular framing of climate change, one that focuses on emission reductions and treats these as substitutable, especially when it is underpinned by a utilitarian focus on promoting greatest aggregate efficiency, then makes it seem self-evident that achieving 'low cost' emission reductions anywhere in the world is a matter of global 'common concern'. This then grounds a claim of global authority to promote action in countries of the Global South in order to enable, support and encourage such 'low cost' emission reductions.

This framing of the problem of climate change as a 'common concern' enlivens an expansion of supranational law rather than promoting a more critical engagement with the complex ways in which (international) law is already intertwined with the climate crisis. Such a framing excludes an examination of the way in which, as Shirley Scott writes, international law is *already* 'complicit in creating the climate crisis' through its 'facilitating of an oil-based, capitalist economy'.[123] Moreover, it avoids addressing also the many ways in which international and transnational laws are intertwined with and facilitate the extraction, circulation and combustion of fossil fuels.[124] It is a framing that predominantly authorises 'demand-side' measures, focused on restricting demand for GHG emissions, rather than 'supply-side' measures,[125] and 'instruments that aim to *restrict the supply* of commodities or products [such as fossil fuels] whose downstream consumption causes greenhouse gas emissions'.[126] In a context where the world is on track to produce more coal, oil and gas than is consistent with the Paris Agreement objectives,[127] approaches are urgently needed that focus not on disembodied 'emission reductions' but which critically interrogate the global political economy and modes of production that drive and underpin deadly levels of GHG emissions. However, dominant framing of climate action not only forecloses more critical interrogations of the broader global political economy that enables and promotes excessive GHG emissions, it also has productive effects in that it simultaneously directs international attention to what are seen as 'low-cost' emission reduction options. By doing so it helps authorise

---

[123] S. V. Scott, 'Is the crisis of climate change a crisis for international law: Is international law too democratic, too capitalist and too fearful to cope with the crisis of climate change?' (2007) 14 *Australian International Law Journal* 31–43.

[124] Dehm, 'Post Paris reflections', 294–96; for example, the need to tackle fossil fuel subsidies has been largely ignored in the UNFCCC; H. van Asselt, *The Politics of Fossil Fuel Subsidies and Their Reform* (Cambridge University Press, 2018); H. van Asselt and K. Kulovesi, 'Seizing the opportunity: Tackling fossil fuel subsidies under the UNFCCC' (2017) 17(3) *International Environmental Agreements: Politics, Law and Economics* 357–70.

[125] M. Lazarus, P. Erickson, and K. Tempest, *Supply-Side Climate Policy: The Road Less Taken* (SEI Working Paper No. 2015–13, 2015); M. Lazarus and H. van Asselt, 'Fossil fuel supply and climate policy: Exploring the road less taken' (2018) 150 *Climatic Change* 1–13.

[126] Green and Denniss, 'Cutting with both arms of the scissors', 74 (emphasis in original).

[127] *The Production Gap Report* (Stockholm Environment Institute, International Institute for Sustainable Development; Overseas Development Institute; Climate Analytics; Center for International Climate research and UN Environment Programme, 2019).

and legitimate claims that international authority should be asserted over land use and forestry in the Global South in the interests realising the global 'common concern' of climate change mitigation.

D FORESTS, 'COMMON CONCERN' AND AUTHORITY

Historically, any articulation of a claim to global authority over tropical forests in the Global South has been very contentious. This section provides a background of the struggles to assert international, national and 'local' ownership and control over tropical forests and of the competing claims of ownership of – or sovereignty over – forests. It suggests that over the past two decades these tensions were able to be productively sidestepped, by avoiding the conflictual 'proprietorial' question and instead focusing on the functions – both global and local – that forests serve. It shows how, through the growing recognition of forests' capacity to sequester carbon and thus function as global carbon sinks, a gradual consensus coalesced that forests should be subject to global forms of governance. This section shows that although this understanding (i.e., that forests play a critical role in the global carbon system) now seems obvious and self-evident, it 'rests on a distinctive way of seeing that took years, even decades, to cultivate and one that has profound implications for climate governance'.[128] Finally, this section highlights how this frame, by locating the problem of deforestation predominantly within nation-states, thus obscuring global drivers of deforestation, gives rise to international authority over the problem of deforestation that is shaped, applied and exercised in uneven and differentiated ways.

1 Contestation and Authority over Forests

Areas designated as 'forests' have been – and continue to be – subject to competing claims to authority by numerous actors, including international institutions (both environmental and economic), the domestic nation-state, foreign states, transnational organisations (conservation NGOs and corporate interests) and local populations. These claims are based on diverse assertions of rights over such spaces and are directed toward divergent purposes, including resource exploitation for maximum profit, preservation and conservation, or the maintenance of livelihoods and reproduction of lifeworlds. Due to their often remote and difficult-to-access terrain, forested landscapes are typically spaces where formal assertions of authority do not necessarily coincide with the manifestation of effective control. The term 'forest' has

---

[128] W. Boyd, 'Ways of seeing in environmental law: How deforestation became an object of climate governance' (2010) 37 *Ecology Law Quarterly* 843–916 at 884.

D. Forests, 'Common Concern' and Authority 145

historically been an administrative category, and the designation of land as 'forest' has often been linked to specific forms of political control, which have often been resisted.[129] The concept of a category of land called 'forest' and the assertion of state territorial sovereignty over such land emerged in tandem, creating, as Nancy Peluso and Peter Vandergeest argued, 'new, almost inescapable means of imagining land, resources and people' as well as revolutionising livelihoods.[130] The discourse and concept of 'political forest' operated as 'a critical part of colonial-era state-making, both in terms of the territorialisation and legal framing of forests and the institutionalisation of forest management as a technology of state power'.[131] Colonial forest practices consisted of various legal strategies for asserting control and techniques of power and discipline including 'territorial zoning and mapping, the enactment of land and forest laws delimiting legal and illegal forest uses, the constitution of state forestry institutions to implement these laws according to specialised procedures, the constitution of forest police, and the creation of legal exceptions that became Customary Rights'.[132]

The political designation of land as 'forest' has been inherently intertwined with the assertion of territorial sovereignty and national jurisdiction over such areas; however, this has been contested by 'global' as well as 'local' claims to authority over forests. This 'proprietorial dimension' and these competing claims about how forests should be understood, who should 'own' them, and who has a 'legitimate stake' in how they should be governed has presented considerable barriers to developing an international regime for the management of forests. David Humphreys elaborates:

> First, many actors concerned about the global environmental ramifications of forest destruction have inclined towards, though often stopped short of, asserting that forests are a global commons. This has been resisted by governments of the South who have asserted a counter claim, namely that forests are a national resource to be used in line with national policy. Third, many local peoples, especially indigenous peoples, acting with the help of international NGO networks such as the World Rainforest Movement, have asserted that forests are a commons belonging to local peoples.[133]

The claim made by governments of the Global South – that forests are a national resource to be exploited in the interests of their people – is grounded in the international legal principle of permanent sovereignty over natural resources

---

[129] See for example P. Linebaugh, *The Magna Carta Manifesto: Liberties and the Commons for All* (University of California Press, 2008).

[130] N. L. Peluso and P. Vandergeest, 'Genealogies of the political forest and customary rights in Indonesia, Malaysia, and Thailand' (2001) 60(3) *The Journal of Asian Studies* 761–812 at 762.

[131] Ibid.

[132] Ibid., 764–5.

[133] D. Humphreys, *Forest Politics: The Evolution of International Cooperation* (Earthscan, 1996) p. 24.

146 *Asserting Global Authority over the Carbon Sequestration Potential of Forests*

(PSNR) as a 'right of peoples and nations' to be 'exercised in the interest of their national development and of the well-being of the peoples of the State'.[134] For countries of the Global South the concept of PSNR was a central component of asserting a new, post-colonial international law while contesting the persistence of colonial relations of dependency and unequal terms of trade, and promoting both political and economic self-determination, and subsequently a New International Economic Order (NIEO).[135] As Karin Mickelson writes:

> The concept evolved as a direct response to the inequities which marked the colonial period, during which resources were exploited mainly for the benefit of colonial powers and their nationals, and in particular to the types of concession agreements that allowed the beneficiaries virtual free reign over large tracts of land and resources of critical importance to the national economy.[136]

Based on this model of the state as the public trustee of resources, many national, post-colonial Constitutions then authorised the state to control natural resources within a territory and to exploit them for the benefit of the country's people. For example, the Indonesian Constitution declares that the 'land and the waters as well as the natural riches therein are to be controlled by the state to be exploited to the greatest benefit of the people'.[137] To dismiss such a claim to sovereignty as simply a 'legal fiction' whose assertion 'serv[es] to insulate the state from the international environmental effects of its policies'[138] fails to properly recognise how claims to sovereignty over resources and claims of political and economic self-determination were very fundamentally intertwined for post-colonial states and central to efforts to achieve 'sovereign equality'. Nonetheless, over time, as Nico Schrijver documents, the principle of PSNR has been reshaped so that it is increasingly interpreted and applied as 'a source of duties as well as rights', especially in relation to the protection of foreign investment as well as the imperatives of sustainable development.[139] Therefore, domestic sovereignty over resources has increasingly become subject to both international responsibilities and local rights claims, entailing a delicate balancing of rights and responsibilities.[140]

---

[134] General Assembly Resolution 1803 (XVII), *Permanent Sovereignty over Natural Resources*, UNGAOR 17th sess, 1194th plen mtg, Agenda Item 39, UN Doc. A/5217 (14 December 1962).

[135] C. R. Dietrich, *Oil Revolution* (Cambridge University Press, 2017); on the NIEO see N. Gilman, 'The new international economic order: A reintroduction' (2015) 6(1) *Humanity: An International Journal of Human Rights, Humanitarianism, and Development* 1–16.

[136] K. Mickelson, 'Seeing the forest, the trees and the people: Coming to terms with developing country perspectives on the proposed global forests convention' in Canadian Commission on International Law (ed.) *Global Forests and International Environmental Law* (Kluwer Law, 1996) pp. 239–64, 243.

[137] *Constitution of the Republic of Indonesia 1945* (Indonesia) Article 33.3.

[138] Humphreys, *Forest Politics: The Evolution of International Cooperation*, p. 171.

[139] N. Schrijver, *Sovereignty over Natural Resources: Balancing Rights and Duties* (Cambridge University Press, 1997) p. 171.

[140] Ibid., Chapters 4 and 6.

D. Forests, 'Common Concern' and Authority

A different, or 'rival', claim to authority over forested areas is made by those living in and around forested areas, based on customary possession and traditional law, often against a '[colonialist] logic based on exclusion and dispossession'.[141] Although such forest communities are often designated by the state as 'squatters', many assert ownership over forested lands based on 'traditional' or 'customary' laws.[142] This reality of legal pluralism underlies many forest conflicts. Scholarship on natural resource governance, and particularly forest governance, has highlighted the need to recognise that on 'the ground' there is commonly 'a mixture of several normative orders, which are based on long tradition': these include customary law as well as new forms of self-regulation, elements of old and new state laws and donor laws.[143] Such claims also find endorsement in international law, including in arguments that the right of PSNR understood as a right of 'peoples' could also protect the claims of Indigenous communities asserting ownership or usage rights over resources within a state.[144] The United Nations Declaration of the Rights of Indigenous Peoples (UNDRIP) asserts that 'Indigenous peoples have the right to the lands, territories and resources which they have traditionally owned, occupied or otherwise used or acquired'.[145] In their 2018 report, Rights and Resources Initiative found that Indigenous peoples and local communities have been legally recognised as owning at least 447 million hectares (12.2 percent) of forest land within the 58 countries analysed.[146] While this represented a slight increase on 2013 figures, the pace of recognition has generally slowed since 2008.[147] However, it remains the case that 'despite the substantial forest area held, claimed, and managed by Indigenous Peoples, local communities, and rural women, the vast majority of the world's forests formally remain under government administration as national or provincial forests, protected areas, or forests allocated to third parties under concessions'.[148]

The development of global environmental consciousness and the rise of international environmental protection obligations have together produced a 'fundamental impact on the understanding of sovereignty in general, and sovereignty over

---

[141] *Protecting Carbon to Destroy Forests: Land, Enclosure and REDD+* (Carbon Trade Watch, 2013) p. 9.

[142] A. Mutolib and H. Ismono, 'Forest ownership conflict between a local community and the state: A case study in Dharmasraya, Indonesia' (2017) *Journal of Tropical Forest Science* 163–71.

[143] R. S. Meinzen-Dick and R. Pradhan, 'Implications of legal pluralism for natural resource management' (2001) 32(4) *IDS Bulletin* 10–17.

[144] R. Pereira and O. Gough, 'Permanent sovereignty over natural resources in the 21st century: Natural resource governance and the right to self-determination of indigenous peoples under international law' (2013) 14(2) *Melbourne Journal of International Law* 451–95.

[145] General Assembly Resolution 61/295, *United Nations Declaration on the Rights of Indigenous Peoples*, UN GAOR 61st sess, 107th plen mtg, Supp No 49, UN Doc A/61/67 (13 September 2007) Article 26.1.

[146] C. Ginsburg and S. Keene, *At a Crossroads: Consequential Trends in Recognition of Community-Based Forest Tenure From 2002–2017* (Rights and Resources Initiative, 2018) p. 9.

[147] Ibid., p. 13.

[148] Ibid., p. 7.

148 *Asserting Global Authority over the Carbon Sequestration Potential of Forests*

resources in particular'.[149] Following the rise of global environmental consciousness in the 1960s, tropical forest deforestation became a matter of international concern, with temperate and boreal forests only later gaining similar prominence on the international agenda.[150] Attempts to 'internationalise' forest protection and their underlying implication that 'people in the North were entitled to some of the values inherent in forests of the South' were unsurprisingly controversial.[151] This means that negotiations at the international level concerning the protection of and questions of rights and responsibilities in relation to tropical forests located in the Global South have always been 'politically charged', with forested nations 'unwilling to negotiate binding commitments limiting their sovereign use of natural resources when the natural resource in question contributes to the state's economy and the livelihoods of local people'.[152]

The United Nations Conference on the Human Environment held in Stockholm, in 1972, affirmed that 'man (sic) has a special responsibility to safeguard and wisely manage the heritage of wildlife and its habitat, which are now gravely imperilled by a combination of adverse factors'.[153] It also articulated a delicate balance between the imperatives of global environmental protection and national sovereign rights to exploit resources: Principle 21 of the Stockholm Declaration affirmed that

> [s]tates have, in accordance with the Charter of the United Nations and the principles of international law, the sovereign right to exploit their own resources pursuant to their own environmental policies, and the responsibility to ensure that activities within their jurisdiction or control do not cause damage to the environment of other States or areas beyond the limits of national jurisdiction.[154]

Subsequent to Stockholm, there were some attempts to 'internationalise' forest issues by positing that forests should be preserved for the 'common good' or that forests were the 'common heritage of mankind (sic)'.[155] Proponents of this claim – that products of the biosphere are humankind's common heritage – saw the assertion of sovereignty over forests by countries of the Global South as 'virulently nationalistic and definitely opposed to the larger view of the biosphere as a single system'.[156] Yet it is important to

---

[149] Mickelson, 'Seeing the forest, the trees and the people', p. 246.

[150] Humphreys, *Forest Politics: The Evolution of International Cooperation*, p. 1.

[151] D. S. Davenport, 'An alternative for the failure of the UNCED forest negotiations' (2005) 5(1) *Global Environmental Politics* 105–30 at 107.

[152] R. Maguire, 'Deforestation, REDD and international law' in S. Alam, M. J. H. Bhuiyan, T. M. R. Chowdhury, and Re. J. Techera (eds.), *Routledge Handbook of International Environmental Law* (Routledge, 2013) pp. 697–716, 699.

[153] *Declaration of the United Nations Conference on the Human Environment* (Report of the United Nations Conference on the Human Environment, Stockholm, 5–16 June 1972) A/CONF.48/14/Rev.1.

[154] *Declaration of the United Nations Conference on the Human Environment*, principle 21.

[155] G. Porter and J. W. Brown, *Global Environmental Politics* (Westview Press, 1991).

[156] L. H. Miller, *Global Order, Values and Power in International Politics*, 3rd edition (Westview Press, 1994) 247–8, cited in Mickelson, 'Seeing the forest, the trees and the people', p. 247.

D. Forests, 'Common Concern' and Authority

recognise how for many countries of the South, such invocations of common heritage 'raise[d] the spectre of the past' and provoked fears of 'environmental colonialism' and concerns that while 'the North used to exploit resources directly, it now does so indirectly by asserting a quasi-proprietary interest in their preservation'.[157] Moreover, as comments by prominent Third World lawyer Mohammed Bedjaoui make clear, the Southern position was not necessarily inherently opposed to understanding forest basins as part of 'mankind's common heritage'. Rather, he highlights how the application of such principles could operate to impose additional burdens on countries of the Global South. Responding in 1979 to arguments that the basins of the Congo and the Amazon were part of 'mankind's common heritage', Bedjaoui wrote:

> Such an idea is in itself in no way outrageous, but it must nevertheless be part of a joint pooling of all the riches and resources of the planet, a pooling free of any national self-seeking. In the manifest or implicit behaviour of nations, it nonetheless seems to be assumed that only the Third World is to shoulder the obligations resulting from the application of the concept of mankind's common heritage, while only the industrialized States would have the benefit of the corresponding rights and advantages. A sort of international division of labour, which would perpetuate and even aggravate domination patterns[,] would, for example, compel Brazil and the Congo to conserve the oxygen so that the industrialized powers could burn it at will. Thus, nothing is said about the rich countries being obliged to take care not to destroy the earth's thin atmosphere layer by immoderate use of the internal combustion engine in any of its time-honoured and disorderly applications.[158]

Bedjaoui supported a universal approach to ecological challenges and supported the concept of 'common heritage' as fundamental to the development of a new international economic order and a *future* law of solidarity for the international community. What he opposed, however, was its selective application and the 'co-option of the concept' to serve the interests of dominant powers.[159]

By the 1980s deforestation was considered by scientists and world leaders alike to be one of 'the earth's most serious environmental problems'.[160] There was increased awareness of the consequences of 'alarming' rates of deforestation, including impacts on local weather and rainfall, as well as impacts on the global climate as threatening biological diversity, thereby 'depleting the "world's genetic pool"'.[161] In particular, the 1985 report *Tropical Forests: A Call for Action*, by the World Resources Institute (WRI), the World Bank and the International Union for the Conservation of Nature (IUCN), enhanced earlier efforts to broaden discussions on

---

[157] Mickelson, 'Seeing the forest, the trees and the people', p. 247.
[158] M. Bedjaoui, *Towards a New International Economic Order* (United Nations Educational, Scientific and Cultural Organization, 1979) p. 235.
[159] Ibid., p. 239.
[160] L. Tangley, 'Saving tropical forests' (1986) 36 *BioScience* 4–8 at 4.
[161] T. B. Hamlin, 'Debt-for-nature swaps: A new strategy for protecting environmental interests in developing nations' (1989) 16 *Ecology Law Quarterly* 1065 at 1065–88.

150 *Asserting Global Authority over the Carbon Sequestration Potential of Forests*

deforestation to an audience that extended beyond foresters and to bring questions of deforestation, resource management, conservation and development into the conversation.[162]

Over this period a number of different initiatives sought to foster co-operative arrangements for the management of forests and timber resources, and to provide international incentives for domestic conservation activities. From the late 1970s the negotiations of the International Tropical Timber Agreements (ITTAs) went beyond standard commodity agreements by also incorporating sustainability considerations. The first ITTA, concluded in 1983, established a framework for international co-operation that sought to mediate conflicting interests to promote 'proper and effective conservation and development of tropical timber forests with a view to ensuring their optimum utilization while maintaining the ecological balance of the regions concerned and of the biosphere'.[163] In 1986 the International Tropical Timber Organization was established to monitor the agreement, and in the process started to serve as an inter-state forum outside of the UN system.[164] The year 1985 saw the launch of the Tropical Forestry Action Plan (TFAP), sponsored by the World Bank, UNDP, the FAO and the World Resources Institute. It was presented as a 'global forest conservation and development program' with objectives to 'increase the financial aid to forests, to act against deforestation and to promote the sustainable use of tropical forests';[165] it also supported tropical forest countries to develop their own national forestry action plan, based on guidelines articulated in the TFAP. However, the Plan was strongly criticised by environmental NGOs, who saw it as a 'loggers charter' and suggested it may have led to increased deforestation in some areas, given that it prioritised the interests of forestry and failed to address the root causes of deforestation or protect rights and livelihoods.[166]

In the lead up to the 1992 United Nations Conference on Environment and Development (UNCED) in Rio de Janeiro, growing awareness of the 'importance of the world's forests, especially in the context of climate change' afforded forest protection a 'high priority on the international agenda'.[167] The 1990 G7 Summit affirmed they were 'ready to begin negotiations' for a global forest convention 'to curb deforestation, protect biodiversity, stimulate positive forestry action and address threats to the world's forests'.[168] However, as Karin Mickelson noted:

---

[162] See B. Johnson, 'The forestry crisis: What must be done' (1984) 13(1) *Ambio* 48–9.

[163] *International Tropical Timber Agreement, 1983*, opened for signature 18 November 1983, 1393 UNTS 119 (entered into force 1 April 1985) preamble.

[164] V. de Campos Mello, *North–South Conflicts and Power Distribution in UNCED Negotiations: The Case of Forestry* (International Institute for Applied Systems Analysis, 1993) p. 17.

[165] Ibid., p. 16.

[166] See R. Winterbottom, *Taking Stock: The Tropical Forestry Action Plan after Five Years* (World Resources Institute, 1990); Boyd, 'Ways of seeing in environmental law, 863.

[167] J. Cameron, 'Forests' (1991) 1 *Yearbook of International Environmental Law* 201.

[168] Cited in de Campos Mello, *North–South Conflicts and Power Distribution in UNCED Negotiations*, p. 18.

D. Forests, 'Common Concern' and Authority

An essential difficulty that arises in the context of developing a forest convention is that of avoiding the perception that such an agreement constitutes an infringement of sovereignty. In fact, if an instrument on forests is qualitatively different from previous international instruments in the environmental area it is precisely because its potential impact on sovereignty over resources appears to be much more direct.[169]

Ultimately, there was a failure to negotiate a global forest convention at Rio. Although accounts differ on how significant the question of sovereignty was, according to many observers it was the critical reason why a legally binding instrument was not negotiated.[170] In the first UNCED preparatory committee meeting the FAO proposed developing a Convention on forest protection, but this suggestion was strongly opposed by timber-exporting, developing countries, especially Brazil, Malaysia and Indonesia, who feared and resisted any suggestions that forests were a 'global commons' rather than a 'national resource'.[171] The claim advanced in these negotiations – that forests were part of the 'global commons' or the 'common heritage of mankind' – was strongly rejected by G77. Tensions persisted at the second preparatory meeting, especially as the G77 refused to allow further discussion of a legally binding agreement on forests.[172] Eventually a decision was made not to negotiate a Convention or legal instrument at UNCED, but instead to produce a non-legally binding statement of principles on all types of forests, addressing both tropical and boreal and temperate forests. The statement made by Malaysian Prime Minister Mahathir Mohamad during UNCED encapsulates the resistance to a Convention:

> The North wants to have a direct say in the management of forests in the poor South at next to no cost to themselves. The pittance they offer is much less than the loss of earnings by the poor countries and yet it is made out as generous compensation ...
>
> The poor are not asking for charity. When the rich chopped down their own forests, built their own poison-belching factories and scoured the world for cheap resources, the poor said nothing. Indeed, they paid for the development of the rich. Now the rich regulate the development of poor countries. And yet any suggestion that the rich compensate the poor adequately is regarded as outrageous. As colonies we were exploited. Now as independent nations we are to be equally exploited.[173]

---

[169] Mickelson, 'Seeing the forest, the trees and the people, p. 248.

[170] Humphreys, *Forest Politics: The Evolution of International Cooperation*, Chapter 4; Davenport, 'An alternative for the failure of the UNCED forest negotiations'.

[171] de Campos Mello, *North–South Conflicts and Power Distribution in UNCED Negotiations*, p. 18.

[172] Ibid., p. 19.

[173] Cited in Mickelson, 'Seeing the forest, the trees and the people', p. 240.

152 Asserting Global Authority over the Carbon Sequestration Potential of Forests

Thus, after 'extensive and often acrimonious negotiations' the UNCED did not produce a forest convention.[174] All that could be agreed upon were some 'elements for a global consensus', to which the 'curious warning label [of] "non-legally binding"' was affixed.[175] The *Non-Legally Binding Authoritative Statement of Principles for a Global Consensus on the Management, Conservation and Sustainable Development of All Types of Forests* [176] ('Forest Principles') was 'itself the subject of fierce debates'.[177] In its first principle, it rearticulated the balance between rights of sovereignty and international environmental obligations,[178] adopting the same formula as Principle 2 of the Rio Declaration.[179] The second principle affirmed:

> States have the sovereign and inalienable right to utilize, manage and develop their forests in accordance with their development needs and level of socio-economic development and on the basis of national policies consistent with sustainable development and legislation, including the conversion of such areas for other uses within the overall socio-economic development plan and based on rational land-use policies.[180]

As Rowena Maguire notes, this strong statement 'actually provides for and allows for further deforestation', and even 'suggests that states are not able to delegate or transfer power to regulate forest use and management outside the state – so, standards and rules concerning forest use and management prescribed by international institutions would be inconsistent with this statement'.[181] However, the Forest Principles also included a shared agreement that 'sound management and conservation is of concern to the Governments of the countries to which they belong and are of value to local communities and to the environment as a whole'[182] and that '[f]orest resources and forest lands should be sustainably managed to meet the social, economic, ecological, cultural and spiritual needs of present and future generations'.[183] The Forest Principles also agreed that the 'full incremental costs of achieving benefits associated with forest conservation and sustainable development'

---

[174] P. H. Sand, 'International environmental law after Rio' (1993) 4(3) *European Journal of International Law* 377–89 at 383.

[175] Ibid.

[176] *Non-Legally Binding Authoritative Statement of Principles for a Global Consensus on the Management, Conservation and Sustainable Development of All Types of Forests*, Report of the United Nations Conference on Environment and Development, Rio de Janeiro, A/CONF.151/26 (Vol. III) (14 August 1992) ('Forest Principles').

[177] Mickelson, 'Seeing the forest, the trees and the people', p. 240.

[178] Forest Principles, principle 1(a).

[179] *Rio Declaration on Environment and Development* UN Doc. A/CONF.151/26 (vol. I); 31 ILM 874 (1992) principle 2 (which reiterated with slight modification Stockholm Principle 21).

[180] Forest Principles, principle 2(a).

[181] R. Maguire, *Global Forest Governance: Legal Concepts and Policy Trends* (Edward Elgar Publishing, 2013) p. 47.

[182] Forest Principles, preambular recital (f).

[183] Forest Principles, principle 2(b).

D. Forests, 'Common Concern' and Authority

both required both international co-operation and must be equitably shared by the international community.[184] Concurrently, the Convention on Biological Diversity prompted a significant expansion of conversation activities and protected areas,[185] which also indirectly facilitated the protection of forest areas. However, as Boyd notes, this approach 'has been unable to alter the basic incentives driving deforestation and [it has been] incapable of supporting governance solutions sufficient to address the problem at scale'.[186] The promotion of global agenda for forest protection still required the articulation of a rationale for global governance of forest areas that was able to avoid the fraught questions of sovereignty and claims about national ownership over forests.

2 From Proprietorial Claims over Forests to 'Concern' for Their Function

In the post-Rio context it was clear that any attempts to assert international property or control over forests in the Global South would be strenuously resisted. Those arguing for the need internationalise forest management were therefore careful to avoid environmental claims being perceived as an infringement of state sovereignty. In this period, there was a subtle but important shift in terminology, to foreground the global functions that forests provide rather than consideration of questions pertaining to ownership of or sovereignty over forests. In 1996, Jutta Brunnée proposed a conceptual framework for an international forest convention that sought to 'overcome the *apparent* contradiction between the sovereignty of states over their natural resources and the interests of the international community in the preservation of these resources'.[187] She suggested that 'despite polarization and conflicting interests, there is room for terms that could help make the competing positions sufficiently compatible for a common interest in a binding agreement to develop', within a paradigm of equity that pays due regard to conservation interests, the right to development and the human rights of forest peoples.[188] The emerging principle that she suggested had the potential to bridge these tensions was that of 'common concern'.[189]

Brunnée argued that the principle of 'common concern' was better suited for this context than the principle of 'common heritage' because unlike the 'common heritage' principle, the 'common concern' principle 'does not purport to circumscribe the *"ownership"* dimension of state sovereignty of natural resources, but

---

[184] Forest Principles, principle 1(b).
[185] Boyd, 'Ways of seeing in environmental law', 864.
[186] Ibid.
[187] Brunnée, 'A conceptual framework for an international forests convention' pp. 41–77, 41 (emphasis added).
[188] Ibid., p. 42.
[189] Ibid., p. 55.

merely its *"use"* dimension'.[190] Further, she stressed that the 'concern' should pertain not to forests themselves as a resource, but to their *functions* or uses, and thus better able to reflect the 'global ramifications of [forest] depletion'[191] and other matters such as 'climate change'.[192] The principle of 'common concern', she argued, does not attempt to 'internationalise' forest resources, but the 'normative effect' is to suggest a shared obligation to contribute to a solution that would 'limit state sovereignty in the interest of the international community'.[193] Additionally, Brunnée argued that the notion of 'common concern' goes 'hand in hand' with the concept of 'common but differentiated responsibility' and therefore implies the need for financial and technical assistance from the North to the South to address deforestation.[194]

This formulation made it possible to shift the framing of forest debates away from questions of who 'owns' or 'controls' forests to instead focus on the global responsibilities 'owners' have, arising from global functions performed by forests. In this way, the national ownership of forests is affirmed but simultaneously made subject to an overarching functional imperative about how the control arising from ownership should be exercised. This understanding of forests as nationally owned but serving global functions dovetails well with the emerging focus on 'global public goods' – products that tend toward 'universality in the sense that they benefit all countries, population groups and generations'.[195] The language of 'global public goods' provides a language whereby forests might be owned nationally, yet their preservation contributes to the 'global public good', especially through biodiversity preservation as well as climate stabilisation – and thus preserving them provides global benefits outcomes, for which 'humanity' as a whole is the beneficiary.[196]

This rationalisation resonated with and reinforced what was already happening in practice. For example, when the World Bank hosted its First Annual International Conference on Environmentally Friendly Development post-Rio, Ismail Serageldin, then Vice-President for Environmentally and Socially Sustainable Development at the Bank, highlighted the need to 'recognise that *national activities do have global payoffs* and that this is an area in which much can be done to promote the global agenda from a national sovereignty decision-making framework'.[197] Around this time the World Bank elaborated its own specific

---

[190] Ibid., p. 59 (emphasis added).
[191] Ibid., p. 59.
[192] Ibid., p. 60.
[193] Ibid., p. 56.
[194] Ibid., p. 60.
[195] I. Kaul, I. Grunberg, and M. A. Stern (eds.), *Global Public Goods: International Cooperation in the 21st Century* (Oxford University Press, 1999) p. 16.
[196] D. Humphreys, 'Forests as public goods' in *Logjam: Deforestation and the Crisis of Global Governance* (Earthscan, 2006) Chapter 1.
[197] I. Serageldin and A. Steer (eds.), *Valuing the Environment: Proceedings of the First Annual International Conference on Environmentally Sustainable Development, Held at the World Bank, Washington, DC, September 30–1 October 1, 1993* (The World Bank, 1993) p. 15 (emphasis in original).

D. Forests, 'Common Concern' and Authority

discourse on the environment and the promotion of regulatory incentives for the preservation of environmental resources in the global interest, consolidated its role in environmental aid and finance, and incorporated environment conditionality in its operations.[198] The World Bank's forest strategy, articulated in the 1991 World Bank policy paper *The Forest Sector* sought to better 'promote the conservation of natural forests and the sustainable development of managed forestry resources',[199] and it introduced forest sector conditionality and linked forest issues to broader governance and anti-corruption agendas.[200] Thus, although the ownership, control and management of forests were affirmed as a national matter, there were increasing international incentives and pressures for nation-states to manage their forests in internationally directed ways.

The focus on the global functions forest serve also provided a rationalisation for ongoing bilateral and private forest protection initiatives. In the 1980s the concept of 'debt-for-nature' swaps was suggested and developed as a 'practical tool' to address the Third World debt crisis and tropical deforestation simultaneously.[201] Such debt-equity swaps offered to cancel or restructure a developing country's national debt in return for environmental protection action.[202] Initially, 'first generation' swaps were primarily funded privately by private actors, but subsequent 'second generation' swaps were increasingly funded publicly and involved public actors.[203] However, such projects 'generated only a very small amount of debt forgiveness, with minimal acreage protected, while provoking significant concerns about sovereignty and indigenous rights in tropical forest countries'.[204] These internationalised arrangements were orientated towards formally affirming national sovereignty over forest resources while increasingly transforming how decision-making power over forests is exercised, even while seeking to ensure 'national ownership of reforms'. They therefore foreshadowed the way in which international arrangements would seek to incentivise specific forms of national forest governance with REDD+.

Additionally, as the forest regime has developed post-Rio it has emphasised globally shared objectives on forest management that should be implemented nationally with international coordination, in order to promote multiple forest functions and balance the interests of various stakeholders. Discussions continued

---

[198] P. Gibbon, 'The World Bank and the new politics of aid' (1993) 5(1) *The European Journal of Development Research* 35–62 at 50–51; J. W. Head, 'Environmental conditionality in the operations of international development finance institutions' (1991) 1 *The Kansas Journal of Law & Public Policy* 15–26; see also M. Goldman, *Imperial Nature: The World Bank and Struggles for Social Justice in an Age of Globalization* (Yale University, 2006).

[199] *The Forest Sector* (The World Bank, 1991) p. 5.

[200] U. Lele, N. Kumar, S. A. Husain, A. Zazueta, and L. Kelly, *The World Bank Forest Strategy: Striking the Right Balance* (World Bank Operations Evaluations Department, 2000).

[201] J. E. Knicley, 'Debt, nature, and indigenous rights: Twenty-five years of debt-for-nature evolution' (2012) 36 *Harvard Environmental Law Review* 79–122 at 81.

[202] Ibid., 83.

[203] Ibid.

[204] Boyd, 'Ways of seeing in environmental law', 863.

156 *Asserting Global Authority over the Carbon Sequestration Potential of Forests*

through the Intergovernmental Panel on Forests (1995–97), whose work was taken up by the Intergovernmental Forum on Forests (1997–2000), then replaced by the UN Forum on Forests (UNFF) in 2000.[205] The 2002 UNFF Ministerial Declaration reiterated national sovereignty over forests, but also 'underscore[d] ... that the economic, social and environmental well-being of the planet and humanity is closely tied with sustainable forest management'.[206] The purpose of the 2007 Non-Legally Binding Instrument on All Kinds of Forests is to 'strengthen political commitment and action at all levels to implement effectively sustainable management of all types of forests and to achieve the shared global objectives on forests'.[207] The 2007 instrument reiterates again the principle of sovereignty in its preamble, although the reaffirmation of sovereignty is not included in the articles of the agreement. Maguire suggests this might be explained by the 'voluntary and non-legally binding nature of the agreement, and perhaps a small shift in states' willingness to accept some small limitation upon domestic forest use and management'.[208] There was, therefore a growing acceptance that forests served local, national and international functions and thus that their protection required international co-operation and support; however, as the next section will show, it was the growing understanding of the role of forests as global carbon sinks that consolidated a claim to global authority over forested lands.

3 *Carbon Sequestration As a Global Concern*

It was through the growing recognition of the global importance of forests' carbon sequestration functions that the problem of deforestation came to be seen as unavoidably a 'global' problem and a matter of international 'common concern'. Alexander Zahar, Jacqueline Peel and Lee Godden pose the question of whether deforestation could be characterised as a truly global problem, and reflect:

> If we approach this question [of deforestation] from the perspective of biodiversity protection or ecosystem services (clean water, prevention of erosion, human amenity and so forth), forest destruction may seem to be a local, national, or at most a transnational (cross-border) environmental problem. But if forests are conceptualised as carbon storage systems, which also actively remove carbon dioxide from the atmosphere, then their preservation and enhancement become strategies in the mitigation of climate change, and deforestation turns into a global issue.[209]

---

[205] Economic and Social Council Resolution 2000/35, *Report on the Fourth Session of the Intergovernmental Forum on Forests*, 46th plen mtg, E/RES/2000/35 (18 October 2000).

[206] *Ministerial Declaration and Message from the United Nations Forum on Forests to the World Summit on Sustainable Development*, A/CONF.199/PC/8 (19 March 2002).

[207] General Assembly Resolution 62/98, *Non-Legally Binding Instrument on All Types of Forests*, UN GAOR 62nd sess, 74th plen mtg, Agenda Item 54, A/RES/62/98 (31 January 2008) para 1(a).

[208] Maguire, *Global Forest Governance*, p. 47.

[209] A. Zahar, J. Peel, and L. Godden, *Australian Climate Law in Global Context* (Cambridge University Press, 2013) p. 237.

D. Forests, 'Common Concern' and Authority

Key to enabling deforestation to be seen as a global 'common concern' was the foregrounding of a specific 'frame' or 'way of seeing' the problem of global deforestation – one which focuses on the role that forests play in the global carbon cycle. The emergence of carbon cycle research and the application of remote sensing techniques were key to enabling deforestation to be understood as a climate – and thus also an international – problem.[210] William Boyd shows how carbon cycle research 'provided the basis for viewing tropical forests as an important component of the global carbon budget and, consequently, served to highlight the role that tropical deforestation (and land-use change more generally) played in global anthropogenic carbon emissions'.[211] However, because 'deforestation is not a unitary phenomenon amenable to easy generalization'[212] this framing also 'necessarily resulted in a radical simplification of diverse tropical forest ecosystems to their functional, aggregated role in carbon cycling'.[213] Thereby 'efforts to simplify, reduce, and translate tropical forests into compliance carbon [put] significant pressure on previous ways of conceiving and governing forests'.[214]

Prior to the 1970s most research on the carbon cycle focused on ocean-atmosphere exchange; however, from the 1970s onwards, increased attention was directed to the role of land use and forests in the carbon cycle.[215] In the 1980s, ecologists proposed that emissions from deforestation and land use be included in models of the global carbon budget, a suggestion initially resisted by geologists.[216] By 1990 there was scientific awareness that '[d]eforestation in the tropics has contributed to the rise in atmospheric concentrations of carbon dioxide'.[217] There was some acknowledgement of the limitations of forests' role, given that emission from fossil fuels is two to three times the amount derived from deforestation and sequestration of carbon in forests is not permanent. Nonetheless, halting deforestation was seen as a 'permanent solution to stabilizing the concentration of CO_2 in the atmosphere'.[218] The first IPCC assessment, released in 1990, 'recognized the importance of tropical deforestation as a source of global anthropogenic GHG emissions' and suggested a World Forest Conservation Protocol to a framework climate convention as a potential response.[219] In 1991 a special issue of the journal *Climatic Change*, which focused on 'Tropical Forests and Climate' (subsequently published as a book)[220]

---

[210] Boyd, 'Ways of seeing in environmental law', 878.
[211] Ibid., 878–9.
[212] Ibid., 866.
[213] Ibid., 884.
[214] Ibid., 880.
[215] Ibid.
[216] Ibid., 881.
[217] R. A. Houghton, 'The future role of tropical forests in affecting the carbon dioxide concentration of the atmosphere' (1990) 19(4) *Ambio* 204–9 at 204.
[218] Ibid., 209.
[219] Boyd, 'Ways of seeing in environmental law', 882.
[220] N. Myers (ed.), *Tropical Forests and Climate* (Springer, 1992).

158 *Asserting Global Authority over the Carbon Sequestration Potential of Forests*

responded to considerable 'discussion in recent years about whether tropical forests affect climate, and hence whether the removal of the forests will change [the] climate'; the authors sought further clarity on the key question of 'how far, if at all, does tropical deforestation lead to climatic change?'[221] Researchers identified that 'forests globally are much more important in determining the composition of the atmosphere on a year-to-year basis than climatologists, oceanographers, and others involved in anticipating climatic changes have recognized'.[222] George Woodwell argued that '[r]ecognition of the importance of forests in affecting, possibly controlling, the composition of the atmosphere, therefore the temperature of the earth and global climate, moves forests and forested land into a new realm of public interest'.[223] He argued forests were 'a part of the common property'[224] and part of the 'global commons ... essential to the welfare of all, now and for the future',[225] and this recognition necessitated 'a transition in management of forests'.[226] Because '[a]ny amelioration of the warming of the earth will require a cessation of deforestation globally', he posited that it seemed evident that 'common interests of the nations globally will force innovations in governments that would not come otherwise'.[227] Hence, Woodwell declared, 'The time when forests in their entirety can be considered local, regional, or even national resources to be managed for personal or local interests has passed.'[228]

The IPCC *Climate Change 1992* report, which supplemented its 1990 scientific assessment in order to inform discussions at Rio, documented that emissions due to fossil fuel combustion contributed roughly 70–90 percent of the total anthropogenic emissions of CO_2 into the atmosphere, with the remaining 10–30 percent coming from anthropogenic use of terrestrial ecosystems. It noted that '[a] major decrease of the rate of deforestation as well as an increase in afforestation would contribute significantly to slowing the rate of CO_2 concentrations increase in the atmosphere, but it would be well below that required to stop it'; it therefore stressed that 'other measures to limit or reduce greenhouse emissions should not be neglected'.[229] The *Conservation and Development of Forests* preparatory report released by the UNCED Secretariat prior to Rio argued that the 'role of forests as carbon sinks to reduce the effects of CO_2 in the atmosphere, and thereby helping to contain

---

[221] N. Myers, 'Tropical deforestation and climatic change: The conceptual background – guest editorial' in N. Myers (ed.), *Tropical Forests and Climate* (Springer, 1992) pp. 1–2, 1.

[222] G. M. Woodwell, 'Forests in a warming world: A time for new policies' *Tropical Forests and Climate* (Springer, 1992) pp. 245–51, 245.

[223] Ibid.

[224] Ibid.

[225] Ibid., p. 249.

[226] Ibid., p. 246.

[227] Ibid.

[228] Ibid., p. 248.

[229] 'Overview' 1992 *IPCC Supplement*, p. 57, www.ipcc.ch/site/assets/uploads/2018/05/ipcc_90_92_assessments_far_overview.pdf.

D. Forests, 'Common Concern' and Authority

warming of the atmosphere, has extended the services rendered by the forests to a global level.'[230] This understanding of forests as playing a 'global' role and providing 'global' services had important political implications. As a 1993 working paper reflected:

> It means that forests are now considered "strategic" resources which act as stabilizers in the crisis caused by climate change. They can reabsorb and store the emissions of gases linked to the burning of fossil fuels. The existence of an important forested area in the world could thus mean that the effort to "clean" industrial activities responsible for greenhouse gas emissions – and the heavy investments it would require – could be postponed or even avoided. In a simplistic manner, one could say that this means that tropical forests of the South could clean the atmosphere polluted by the North free of charge.
>
> The North is then interested in obtaining a recognition of this "global role" of forests, and in curving down the deforestation rate in order to guarantee the continuity of this "free cleaning of the atmosphere". This interest is magnified by the fact that the convention of climate change in UNCED turned out to be extremely vague and weak in terms of obligations with no binding timetable for the phasing out of emissions. For the North, focusing on forests could be a way of having some results in the area of climate change without having to bear the burden of the costs of developing more efficient energy options, and of reassuring public opinion that something is being done.[231]

Over the 1990s, more studies 'reveal[ed] that rainforests play a far more vital role in keeping our planet liveable than was previously realized'.[232] Not only were forests seen to provide critical ecosystem services, stabilise rivers and watersheds and soils and have vital impacts on regional climate, but it was noted particularly that the 'effects of deforestation are being manifested globally [given that the] rapid burning, logging, and fragmentation of tropical forests is a major source of greenhouse gases like carbon dioxide and methane'.[233] During this period, scientists issued dire warnings that 'as the area of cleared and degraded forest increases, the positive effects of rainforests will diminish accordingly [and that] areas that had formerly been carbon sinks will instead become sources of greenhouse gases'.[234]

In 2000 the IPCC released its special report on *Land Use, Land-Use Change and Forestry*, providing more guidance on how to account for 'afforestation, reforestation, and deforestation and other agreed land use, land-use change, and

---

[230] Cited in de Campos Mello, *North–South Conflicts and Power Distribution in UNCED Negotiations*, p. 25.

[231] de Campos Mello, *North–South Conflicts and Power Distribution in UNCED Negotiations*, pp. 25–6.

[232] W. F. Laurance, 'Reflections on the tropical deforestation crisis' (1999) 91(2–3) *Biological Conservation* 109–17.

[233] Ibid., 110.

[234] Ibid.

160   *Asserting Global Authority over the Carbon Sequestration Potential of Forests*

forestry'.[235] It provided key definitions and addressed methodological issues, such as accounting rules for 'carbon stock changes and for emissions and removals of greenhouse gases from LULUCF activities'.[236] Even as the Marrakech Accords confirmed that 'the eligibility of land use, land-use change and forestry project activities under the clean development mechanism is limited to afforestation and reforestation',[237] scientific discussions continued to consider the role of terrestrial sinks of carbon, and how '[e]nhanced carbon storage on land can play a small but important role in this endeavor' – that is, in avoiding excessive climate change.[238]

At COP9 in 2003, further modalities and procedures on afforestation and reforestation (A/R) under the Clean Development Mechanism (CDM) were adopted, confirming that only temporary certified emission reductions (tCERs) credits would be granted.[239] At this COP a proposal by Santilli et al. on avoided deforestation (discussed in Chapter 1) was presented at a side event, and scientific and policy debate continued. For some it was welcomed as 'show[ing] refreshing new thought' with its idea that tropical forest degradation and conservation 'should be an integral part of the efforts to reduce global GHG emissions'.[240] Whereas A/R in the CDM was seen as 'an effort to "fix the damage after it has occurred" in an "end-of-pipe" manner', in contrast, 'avoidance of deforestation prevents the damage in the first place'.[241] Commentators also stressed the further benefit that avoiding deforestation could provide in terms of biodiversity, watersheds, livelihoods and ecosystems, and how this could address problems of 'leakage' associated with A/R efforts. The 2006 *Stern Review* stressed that '[c]urbing deforestation is a highly cost-effective way to reduce emissions' with 'the potential to offer significant reductions fairly quickly' and provide key environmental co-benefits.[242] The subsequent 2008 *Eliasch Review* likewise emphasised the 'central role' forests would need to play in any global climate stabilisation strategy.[243] It presented as self-evident not just that '[u]rgent action to tackle the loss of global forests needs to be a central part of any future

---

[235] R. T. Watson, I. R. Noble, B. Bolin, N. H. Ravindranath, D. J. Verardo, and D. J. Dokken, *Land Use, Land-Use Change and Forestry: A Special Report of the Intergovernmental Panel on Climate Change* (Cambridge University Press, 2000).

[236] Ibid.

[237] Decision 17/CP.7, para 7.

[238] R. J. Scholes and I. R. Noble, 'Storing carbon on land' (2001) 294(5544) *Science* 1012–13 at 1013.

[239] Decision 19/CP.9, 'Modalities and procedures for afforestation and reforestation project activities under the Clean Development Mechanism in the first commitment period of the Kyoto Protocol' FCCC/CP/2003/6/Add.2 (30 March 2004).

[240] B. Schlamadinger, L. Ciccarese, M. Dutschke, P. M. Fearnside, S. Brown, and D. Murdiyarso, 'Should we include avoidance of deforestation in the international response to climate change?' in D. Murdiyarso and H. Herawati (eds.), *Carbon Forestry: Who Will Benefit?: Proceedings of Workshop on Carbon Sequestration and Sustainable Livelihoods held in Bogor on 16–17 February 2005* (Center for International Forestry Research, 2005), pp. 26–41, 29.

[241] Ibid., 55.

[242] Stern, *The Economics of Climate Change: The Stern Review*, p. 537.

[243] J. Eliasch, *Climate Change: Financing Global Forests: The Eliasch Review* (Earthscan, 2008) p. xv.

D. Forests, 'Common Concern' and Authority 161

international deal on climate change', but that a 'central element in making this shift work will be the inclusion of the forest sector in global carbon markets'.[244]

A further key factor in the process of understanding forests as global carbon sinks was the development of tools for seeing changes in forest cover remotely from the air, and the growing sense that viewing forests from the outside was the proper epistemic standpoint. Remote sensing, Boyd reflects, 'allowed for the first truly synoptic view of changes in forest cover ... establishing the basis for visualizing forests as terrestrial carbon stocks and as components of the earth's carbon budget'.[245] Seeing forests as repositories of 'saved carbon' requires not just a new body of knowledge but also new ways of seeing the forest, as well as the consolidation of a specific epistemological vantage point or position.[246] It depends upon developing a whole series of technologies for satellite remote sensing of forested areas, including those developed by Google, the Group on Earth Observations, a partnership between the Clinton Foundation and the Environmental Systems Research Institute (ESRI) amongst others.[247] Launched in 2014, the Global Forest Map, building on almost two decades of work by the World Resources Institute's (WRI's) Forest Watch programme, seeks to make 'the best available data about forests available online for free, creating unprecedented transparency about what is happening in forests worldwide'.[248] This online platform, used by thousands of people daily, provides data and tools for monitoring forests by allowing users to access real-time information about changes in forest cover. They write: '[b]etter information supports smarter decisions about how to manage and protect forests for current and future generations, and greater transparency helps the public hold governments and companies accountable for how their decisions impact forests'.[249]

---

[244] Ibid., pp. xi–xii.

[245] Boyd, 'Ways of seeing in environmental law', 879.

[246] Ibid.; see also C. Fogel, 'The local, the global, and the Kyoto Protocol' in M. L. Martello and S. Jasanoff (eds.), *Earthly Politics: Local and Global in Environmental Governance* (MIT Press, 2004).

[247] For a discussion of REDD+ and satellite mapping see 'Google tool to help watch over world's forests', *AFP* 10 December 2009 2009, www.google.com/hostednews/afp/article/ ALeqM5j4dCO6c-YK2xBy36xtnIX7B6RR5A; A. Doyle, 'Space agencies, Google seek ways to save forests', *Reuters, AlertNet* 20 October 2009, www.alertnet.org/thenews/newsdesk/LK385966 .htm; GEO, 'Comprehensive new global monitoring system to track deforestation and forest carbon' (Media release, 19 October 2009), www.earthobservations.org/documents/pressreleases/ pr_09_10_forest_carbon_monitoring.pdf; Department of Climate Change and Energy Efficiency (Australia) *Global Carbon Monitoring System*, www.climatechange.gov.au/en/gov ernment/initiatives/global-carbon-monitoring.aspx (accessed 26 March 2010); GEO, *About GEO*, www.earthobservations.org/about_geo.shtml (accessed 26 March 2010); Clinton Foundation, *Measuring the Carbon Content of Forests*, clintonfoundation.org/what-we-do/ clinton-climate-initiative/our-approach/forests/measuring-carbon (accessed 26 March 2010).

[248] Global Forest Watch, 'About', www.globalforestwatch.org/about (accessed 10 January 2019).

[249] Ibid.; see also P. Potapov, A. Yaroshenko, S. Turubanova, M. Dubinin, L. Laestadius, C. Thies, D. Aksenov, A. Egorov, Y. Yesipova, and I. Glushkov, 'Mapping the world's intact forest landscapes by remote sensing' (2008) 13(2) *Ecology and Society* 51.

162 *Asserting Global Authority over the Carbon Sequestration Potential of Forests*

Implicit in these technologies is also an epistemological claim, namely that a globalist view – a view from outside and above – is the more accurate, if not 'better', way to see forests. This is evidenced in the statement by Jose Achache, director of the Group on Earth Observations, who explained that 'the only way to measure forests efficiently is from space'.[250] Such epistemological standpoints and ways of seeing are not neutral or objective but are themselves productive of a political regime of visibility. Timothy Mitchell has observed that 'accuracy is always a question of where one stands',[251] and that therefore the key effect of representation practices is not to increase the accuracy or quantity of knowledge but to 'redistribute forms of knowledge, increasing it in some places and decreasing it in others'.[252] What has been fostered through these remote sensing technologies and framing of forests as a 'global' concern, is a perspective orientated to Earth System Science that presents a view of the 'globe' as a planet from the outside. From such a vantage point the planet appears as a 'single system' within an imagination that also has 'other planets in view' and thereby 'lays out a perspective on humans and other forms of life where humans cannot be at the centre of the story'.[253] As Dipesh Chakrabarty has highlighted, this view of the 'globe' in Earth Systems Science is very different from the view of the 'globe' in discussions of 'globalisation', which places humans and human connection at its centre, and how histories of imperial expansion led to the 'creation of a world-market' that remains 'crisscrossed by issues of identity and difference'.[254]

This background work, including 'knowledge practices and supporting infrastructures' through which deforestation was increasingly understood as both a 'global' concern and a problem for climate governance,[255] was necessary to 'create the conceptual space' to enable REDD+ to cohere as a 'climate solution'. This understanding of deforestation as a global problem is reflected in COP decisions on REDD+ that foreground the 'contribution of emissions from deforestation to global anthropocentric greenhouse gas emissions',[256] and the 'potential role of further actions to reduce emissions from deforestation and forest degradation in developing countries in helping to meet the ultimate objective of the Convention', the stabilisation of GHG emissions.[257] COP decisions on REDD+ are careful to affirm that the collective aim to 'slow, halt and reverse forest cover and carbon loss … consistent with the ultimate objective of the Convention' must nonetheless be 'in accordance

---

[250] Doyle, 'Space agencies, Google seek way to save forests'.

[251] T. Mitchell, *Rule of Experts: Egypt, Techno-Politics, Modernity* (University of California Press, 2002) p. 92.

[252] Ibid.

[253] D. Chakrabarty, 'Planetary crises and the difficulty of being modern' (2018) 46(3) *Millennium: Journal of International Studies* 259–82 at 265.

[254] Ibid., 261.

[255] Boyd, 'Ways of seeing in environmental law', 878.

[256] Decision 2/CP.13, 'Reducing emissions from deforestation in developing countries: approaches to stimulate action', FCCC/CP/2007/6/Add.1 (14 March 2008) preambular recital 2.

[257] Decision 2/CP.13, preambular recital 6.

D. Forests, 'Common Concern' and Authority

with national circumstances',[258] and that REDD+ activities should be 'country-driven'.[259] Although participation in REDD+ remains formally voluntary and host-country driven, as David Takacs reflects, '[As once] intact forests are deemed essential to mitigating GHG buildup, they inch closer to an international resource that states no longer control.'[260] Articulating carbon sequestration in forests as a matter of global 'common concern' provides a rationale for international support to incentivise, encourage and enable such activities, including through capacity-building initiatives.[261] In addition, the rules around measuring, monitoring, reporting and verification (MMRV) have become a key site of struggle over the degree of national control and international oversight to which forest preservation activities are subjected. In practice, although REDD+ remains formally country driven, it goes much further than any previous mechanisms in making national actions to address deforestation subject to international verification and oversight through extensive MMRV processes. Takacs reflects:

> Once forests are internationalized as part of efforts to mitigate global GHG build-ups, the concomitant MMRV regime further threatens the PSNR: The resource is no longer under the exclusive control of the nation that ensconces it, and efforts to conserve that resource include explicit intrusions into a nation's traditional sovereign prerogatives.'[262]

He suggests that 'mutual insistence on reciprocal, quid pro quo MMRV for REDD+ provides a paradigmatic example of how "sovereignty" is being reconstructed to forge contractual co-operation among nations and between nations and emerging powerful actors'.[263] Through these technical processes, REDD+ is thereby further 'reshaping traditional understandings of territory – in part by opening up possibilities for new value forms and new claims on the environmental and resource practices taking place within the boundaries of the nation state'.[264] As William Boyd reflects,

---

[258] Decision 1/CP.16 'The Cancun Agreements: Outcome of the work of the Ad Hoc Working Group on Long-term Cooperative Action under the Convention' FCCC/CP/2010/7/Add.1 (15 March 2011) part C, preambular recital 1; see also Decision 2/CP.17 'Outcome of the work of the Ad Hoc Working Group on Long-term Cooperative Action under the Convention' FCCC/CP/2011/9/Add.1 (15 March 2012) part C, preambular recital 4.

[259] Decision 1/CP.16, Appendix 1, para 1(c).

[260] D. Takacs, 'Forest carbon (REDD+), repairing international trust, and reciprocal contractual sovereignty' (2012) 37 *Vermont Law Review* 653–736 at 704–5.

[261] See Decision 2/CP.13, para 2; Decision 4/CP.15 'Methodological guidance for activities relating to reducing emissions from deforestation and forest degradation and the role of conservation, sustainable management of forests and enhancement of forest carbon stocks in developing countries', FCCC/CP/2009/11/Add.1 (30 March 2010) para 4; Decision 1/CP.16, para 76.

[262] Takacs, 'Forest carbon (REDD+), repairing international trust, and reciprocal contractual sovereignty', 704–5.

[263] Ibid., 696.

[264] W. Boyd, 'Climate change, fragmentation, and the challenges of global environmental law: Elements of a post-Copenhagen assemblage' (2010) 32 *University of Pennsylvania Journal of International Law* 457–550 at 513.

164 *Asserting Global Authority over the Carbon Sequestration Potential of Forests*

in effect 'the integration of forests into emerging GHG compliance regimes represents a potentially fundamental transformation of the law governing forests at multiple levels with significant implications for traditional understandings of national territory and sovereign control of forest resources'.[265] Thus, although formally national sovereignty over forests is affirmed, the consolidation of a specific understanding that forests' carbon sequestration functions are a matter of global 'common concern' – coupled with the development of extensive international regulatory process to incentivise, direct, monitor and verify national management of forests – has in effect actualised global authority over forested areas.

4 *The Differentiated Actualisation of This 'Common Concern'*

The previous sections have shown how international authority has come to be actualised over forests in the Global South through conceptualising the global carbon sequestration functions of forests as a matter of global 'common concern'. Such a conceptualisation of deforestation as a matter of international 'common concern' could enliven genuinely global strategies to address the root causes of deforestation based on a framework of equitable burden sharing; however, in practice international authority has been directed primarily to interventions at the sites of deforestation in the Global South rather than towards disentangling the broader mesh of global commodity relations that drive tropical deforestation. In their 2010 report, *Getting to the Roots*, the Global Forest Coalition documents some of the underlying causes of deforestation and forest degradation.[266] They identify the 'persistently high demand for wood' as a key driver of deforestation – arising from both international demand 'primarily generated by over-consuming industrialized countries' alongside high levels of domestic demand – as well as 'spiralling' demand for land for industrial tree plantations, monocultural palm oil plantations, intensive agriculture and cattle ranching.[267] In addition, ongoing uncertainty surrounding land tenure is a further factor underlying deforestation and conflict, processes of industrialisation, urbanisation and the spread of infrastructures, as well as regulatory issues including lack of good governance and central planning, illegal logging and corruption.[268] More recent reports have highlighted how the underlying or indirect drivers of deforestation act on multiple scales, including 'international (markets, commodity prices), national (population growth, domestic markets, national policies, governance) and local circumstances (subsistence poverty)', and

---

[265] Boyd, 'Ways of seeing in environmental law', 880.

[266] *Getting to the Root: Underlying Causes of Deforestation and Forest Degradation, and Drivers of Forest Restoration* (Global Forest Coalition, 2010).

[267] Ibid., pp. 7–8; see also J. Costenbader, *Legal Frameworks for REDD. Design and Implementation at the National Level* (IUCN, 2009) p. 7.

[268] *Getting to the Root*, pp. 11, 12, 14, 16.

that '[p]ressures from many international drivers to clear forests are expected to increase'.[269] Therefore, taking deforestation seriously as a matter of global 'common concern' should involve addressing the many international drivers of deforestation, which include the global financing that enables it; the production of commodities such as timber, agricultural goods and palm oil that contribute to deforestation; the global supply chains through which these commodities circulate; and the global consumers of these products.

However, rather than acknowledge these 'entanglements' and reconstituting these international pressures, REDD+ as a policy approach has explicitly resisted any engagement with the manner in which tropical deforestation is embedded in a broader global economic and political economy. REDD+ has predominantly located the problem of deforestation *within* the host nation state, instead of adopting a perspective that *internationalises* the problem of deforestation, that recognises the ways in which the drivers of deforestation are already situated within transnational commodity chains and a complex matrix of international consumer demand and international financing, export trade and currency flows. REDD+ thereby presents the international community as intervening to assist the countries of the Global South to reduce their unsustainable rates of deforestation, rather than recognising how the international community is already implicated in driving deforestation.[270] COP decisions on REDD+ have 'reaffirm[ed] the importance of addressing drivers of deforestation and forest degradation [and] encourag[ed] all Parties ... to continue their work to address drivers of deforestation and forest degradation'.[271] However, although these decisions acknowledge that 'drivers of deforestation and forest degradation have many causes', they presume that action to address these drivers should be taken in the Global South, 'in the context of the development and implementation of national strategies and action plans by developing country Parties'.[272] Reviews of REDD+ implementation have found that '[c]ountries largely define strategies and interventions to deal with national and local scale drivers, but face problems addressing international drivers and acknowledge that international pressure will increase'.[273] This represents a real problem for REDD+ implementation given that the 'long-term viability of REDD+ depends on altering business-as-usual activities in

---

[269] G. Kissinger, M. Herold, and V. De Sy, *Drivers of Deforestation and Forest Degradation: A Synthesis Report for REDD+ Policy Makers* (Lexeme Consulting, 2012) p. 5. This report identifies agriculture as a proximate driver of 80 percent of global deforestation globally, and timber extraction as responsible for 70 percent of degradation in Latin America and (sub) tropical Asia.

[270] See also M. C. Thompson, M. Baruah, and E. R. Carr, 'Seeing REDD+ as a project of environmental governance' (2011) 14 *Environmental Science and Policy* 100–10.

[271] Decision 15/CP.19, 'Addressing the drivers of deforestation and forest degradation', FCCC/CP/2013/10/Add.1 (31 January 2014) paras 1 and 4.

[272] Decision 15/CP.19, paras 1 and 2.

[273] Kissinger et al., *Drivers of Deforestation and Forest Degradation: A Synthesis Report for REDD+ Policy Makers*, p. 5.

166 *Asserting Global Authority over the Carbon Sequestration Potential of Forests*

sectors currently driving greenhouse gas (GHG) emissions from forests'.[274] A number of important, initiatives have sought to address international drivers of tropical deforestation, including the EU Voluntary Partnership Agreements, voluntary procurement and sourcing commitments and import controls; however, these are generally seen as outside of the scope of REDD+.[275] Therefore, even as greater global authority over tropical forests is asserted through REDD+, there is a simultaneous denial of responsibility for the transnational processes that incentivise and drive tropical deforestation and the international processes that have compelled the adoption of export-orientated capitalist economic development in the Global South.

E CONCLUSION

This chapter has shown how international authority over the carbon sequestered in tropical forests has been authorised by the representation of global climate change and deforestation as matters of global 'common concern'. In particular, it has demonstrated that the way both climate change and tropical deforestation have come to be framed has given a distinctive shape to this claim to global authority, with the effect that it is unevenly and differently actualised in the Global South and Global North. As a result, greater international intervention within countries of the Global South is authorised, even as the underlying global drivers of deforestation and the historical responsibilities of countries of the Global North for cumulative GHG emissions escape the purview of international intervention. This chapter showed how climate change has come to be understood as a 'global' and 'future-orientated' problem, and how a more narrow focus on GHG emissions rather than the social and economic processes that produce them has led to a focus on 'measurable, divisible greenhouse-gas emission reductions' – instead of more situated, embedded approaches focused on a vision of transition to a more sustainable society. This understanding of climate change, together with imperatives of efficiency, grounds the substitutions of global carbon markets and the move to make all actions that increase or reduce emissions understandable in substitutional and ultimately exchangeable terms. Yet this is a highly specific framing, one that renders invisible the way international law is *already* implicated in promoting a fossil-fuel intensive economy and in the transnational legal processes that facilitate the extraction, circulation and combustion of fossil fuels. This chapter also showed how forests have historically been – and continue to be – spaces of contested authority. The growing recognition of the important global functions that forests play through their carbon sequestration potential has made it possible to sidestep fraught questions about the 'ownership' of forests, and gradually consolidate a regime where the national management of forested lands is increasingly done with reference to

[274] Ibid., p. 4.
[275] Ibid., p. 6.

E. Conclusion

international objectives. Framing forests' carbon sequestration capacities as a matter of 'common concern' thus authorises greater international control over land and resources in the Global South, but it has done so in ways that simultaneously ignore how the complex drivers of deforestation are already international.

By situating REDD+ within a longer history of international forest governance, this chapter highlighted how the forms of global authority being authorised over forested areas in the Global South through REDD+ are the continuation and expansion of pre-existing trends and developments. Moreover, it is critical to recall that the forms of global authority being authorised through claims that environmental issues are a matter of global 'common concern' are not the only way in which the exercise of international authority impacts upon the processes driving either climate change or deforestation: international authority is also exercised through trade, investment and development regimes that arguably facilitate and enable these processes.[276] Therefore, the new forms of international authority established through REDD+ should not be understood as a *transition away from* existing forms of international authority asserted over countries in the Global South but as more of a *layering over*. It is this complex layering of different claims to authority – each with its own rationales, objectives and purposes – which gives shape to the complex and arguably contradictory assemblage of the 'green economy'. The next chapter turns to consider the technical means by which this claim to global authority articulated over forests in the Global South is actualised and made real, namely through the creation of new forms of property rights in sequestered carbon as well as new forms of transnational carbon contracting.

---

[276] As Sundhya Pahuja has argued, 'Just as the "sovereigntist" claims of the 'Third World' were met on one side by those who favoured the 'common interest' of the world understood in terms of the earth, so were those claims met on the other side by those who favoured the common interest of the world understood in terms of the "world economy."' 'Conserving the world's resources?', pp. 398 and 405.

3

Actualising Authority through Public and Private Law

REDD+ through the Lens of Property and Contract

A INTRODUCTION

The previous chapter showed how international authority over the carbon sequestered in forests, and thus over forests in the Global South, was asserted by understanding both climate change and tropical deforestation as matters of 'common concern'. This specific way the problems of climate change and tropical deforestation came to be represented provided a rationale and justification for these new forms of global authority – an authority that was not, however, actualised in material and concrete ways. This chapter turns to consider how this claim to authority is materialised or made real, doing so through an examination of the mechanisms of private law that structure the REDD+ mechanism, namely the creation of new quasi-property rights in carbon and the establishment of new contractual relations.

Legally, REDD+ takes a strange hybrid form, as it is constituted by the interaction between contractual arrangements and property rights. REDD+ is based on forms of transnational contracting and represents promises of future-orientated action to ensure additional carbon sequestration at a specific location. If REDD+ is adopted as a market-based mechanism, these contracts would also produce credits that can become disembedded from the specificities of place and made exchangeable and fungible, in order to be traded (and financialised) in international and transnational carbon markets. Therefore, if REDD+ takes the form of a market-based offset it would be legally structured through both quasi-property rights and contractual obligations. This chapter therefore examines REDD+ through the lens of both contract and property in order to make visible the different areas of law that are engaged and involved in its constitution and regulation. REDD+ carbon commodities are established and defined under the international climate regime and through various UNFCCC decisions; however, the transnational conservation or carbon

A. *Introduction*

contract between investors and host countries or entities that also structure REDD+ are enforced through private international law and/or investment law. REDD+ thereby sits at the intersection of two bodies of law and is regulated by a 'dual cycle system', given that the 'whole contractual procedure is a process that occurs in parallel to the formal procedures required by the climate regime'.[1] Although separate and distinct, these two processes necessarily need to refer to one another: the content of REDD+ carbon contracts needs to reflect and reference the international climate law framework in relation to REDD+; however, these private arrangements arguably also play a norm-setting role where the international climate law framework is ambiguous or does not cover a specific issue. Scholarship on REDD+ rarely bridges this public–private divide to consider both the public and private law aspects of REDD+ together, as each of these facets of REDD+ engages different epistemic communities and is underpinned by different forms of professional expertise, divergent forms of knowledges and modes of practice as well as different objectives and background norms.[2] This chapter shows how understanding REDD+ as a hybrid creature of public international environmental law that is also structured and enforced by private international law can provide a more complex account of the ways in which new forms of power and authority over land in the Global South are actualised and made real through both public and private law.

This chapter shows how forms of global authority in REDD+ are manifested in and through private law arrangements and the legal forms of property and contract that structure the strange 'object' that is the REDD+ carbon offset. In doing so, it builds on the insights of legal realistic scholars, who almost a century ago identified in the domestic context the ways in which supposedly private relations of property and contract established public forms of authority, power and coercion akin to 'economic sovereignty'.[3] This chapter also draws on scholarship that has examined how modern forms of social power are structured by delineating the political and economic as distinct institutional spheres, the constructed nature of this boundary, and the interactions between these domains.[4] In international legal scholarship, increasing attention is being paid to the need for scholarship to breach the

---

[1] A.-M. Klijn, J. Gupta, and A. Nijboer, 'Privatizing environmental resources: The need for supervision of Clean Development Mechanism contracts?' (2009) 18(2) *Review of European Community & International Environmental Law* 172–84 at 176.

[2] H. Lovell and N. S. Ghaleigh, 'Climate change and the professions: The unexpected places and spaces of carbon markets' (2013) 38(3) *Transactions of the Institute of British Geographers* 512–16.

[3] See particularly M. R. Cohen, 'Property and sovereignty' (1927) 13 *Cornell Law Quarterly* 8; and R. L. Hale, 'Coercion and distribution in a supposedly non-coercive state' (1923) 38(3) *Political Science Quarterly* 470–94.

[4] J. Rosenberg, *The Empire of Civil Society: A Critique of the Realist Theory in International Relations* (Verso, 1994); S. Pahuja, *Decolonising International Law: Development, Economic Growth and the Politics of Universality* (Cambridge University Press, 2011).

'intransgressible boundaries' between public and private law and sovereignty and property in order to tell compelling histories of power and authority in international society.[5]

This chapter unfolds in three main parts. The first section draws attention to the limitations of analyses that address only either the 'public' or the 'private' aspects of climate and carbon governance and demonstrates why it is necessary to disrupt this constructed public–private dichotomy in order to develop a more comprehensive analyses of REDD+. It provides a brief overview literature that has shown how private law mechanisms can actually operate as forms of quasi-public power, and thus how authority can be actualised through private law arrangements. The second section examines REDD+ through the lens of contract and situates the transnational private contracts that underpin REDD+ within a broader history of transnational conservation contracts, while also highlighting the novel challenges that arise in translating REDD+ provisions into contractual terms. It also highlights the key norm-production role played by actors involved in developing template or standard form forest carbon contracts, especially the role of the World Bank carbon funds, which have played a leading role in experimenting with and developing novel forms of carbon contracting. The final section examines REDD+ through the lens of property as a potential carbon credit and strange quasi-property right. Although the technical legal question of whether carbon credits constitute property is complex, this chapter draws on the idiom of property as a lens for thinking about how the processes of creating, defining and allocating new rights that concern scarce and valuable resources reflects existing power relations and highlights the distributional effects of such choices.

B DISRUPTING THE PUBLIC–PRIVATE BOUNDARY

This section explores how new perspectives on the actualisation and operation of authority and power in REDD+ can emerge if we pay attention to both the public and the private aspects of REDD+'s ordering. The legal arrangements of property and contract that structure REDD+ are distinct but also inherently intertwined: private forms of transnational carbon contracting give rise to novel carbon commodities that are defined in public law frameworks; therefore, inversely, these private forms of contractual ordering have as their *necessary precondition* an international and national public law regulatory framework. The REDD+ carbon contract is a future-orientated transnational conservation agreement to ensure permanent, additional carbon sequestration; however, it is distinguishable from other

---

[5] M. Koskenniemi, 'Expanding histories of international law' (2016) 56(1) *American Journal of Legal History* 104–12; M. Koskenniemi, 'Empire and international law: The real Spanish contribution' (2011) 61 *University of Toronto Law Journal* 1–36.

B. Disrupting the Public–Private Boundary

transnational conservation contracts, because this contractual promise potentially gives rise to a 'new abstraction' – namely a novel property right in sequestered forest carbon.[6] Such a property right in sequestered carbon – or the 'carbon *actually retained by the soil or vegetation*' – is not a right in or an attribute of the land per se, but rather the right to a 'potential "product" or value of the land'.[7] If this 'right' is recognised as a 'compliance grade asset' that can be decoupled from its referent – the immobile and often difficult to access forested land – it becomes 'free' to circulate within transnational carbon markets as a 'separate, alienable property right'[8] that is fungible, substitutable and exchangeable with other carbon credits.[9] Additionally, as Natasha Affolder notes, forest carbon contracts also 'pose a new way of thinking about environmental regulation', because '[e]ven though the forest carbon contracts are closely linked with "public" values, and contentious "public" processes such as REDD, they are legally constructed as transnational commercial contracts', thereby raising important questions about legitimacy, accountability and fairness in this complex emerging architecture.[10] This section therefore explores these two aspects of REDD+'s ordering in order to show the conceptual and methodological implications of understanding these as public and private aspects as concurrent and mutually co-constitutive.

Viewing REDD+ only through the lens of the public international legal framework that gives it shape risks obscuring from analysis many of the legal relations structuring REDD+, including the 'key actors, the dense networks of contracts, the applicable law, even the venues of dispute resolution'.[11] As Affolder has identified, '[A] byproduct of contract law's transposition of the "public" good of carbon sequestration into the private law sphere of contracts' is that the role played by private law in these arrangements is 'shield[ed] from view'.[12] Paying attention to the often invisibilised role that private law plays in structuring contractual relations helps to make 'otherwise hidden dynamics of this form of governance become apparent'.[13]

---

[6] The complexities of understanding carbon credits as 'property' are discussed in greater detail in section D.

[7] S. Kennett, A. J. Kwasniak, and A. R. Lucas, 'Property rights and the legal framework for carbon sequestration on agricultural land' (2005) 37 *Ottawa Law Review* 171–213 at 178 (emphasis in original).

[8] A. Savaresi and E. Morgera, 'Ownership of land, forest and carbon' in J. Costenbader (ed.), *Legal Frameworks for REDD: Design and Implementation at the National Level* (IUCN, 2009) pp. 15–34, 27.

[9] Ibid.

[10] N. Affolder, 'Transnational carbon contracting: Why law's invisibility matters' in C. Cutler and T. Dietz (eds.), *The Politics of Private Transnational Governance by Contract* (Routledge, 2017) pp. 215–36, 221; see also N. Affolder, 'Transnational conservation contracts' (2012) 25(2) *Leiden Journal of International Law* 443–60.

[11] Affolder, 'Transnational carbon contracting', pp. 215–16.

[12] See C. Cutler and T. Dietz, 'The politics of private transnational governance by contract: Introduction and analytical framework' in Cutler and Dietz (eds.), *The Politics of Private Transnational Governance by Contract* (Routledge, 2017) pp. 1–36.

[13] Affolder, 'Transnational carbon contracting', p. 216.

172   *Actualising Authority through Public and Private Law*

Bringing these private legal arrangements into view is particularly important in a context where this invisibility has played a key role in 'allow[ing] the unknown dimensions of this market to remain unidentified' and 'hid[ing] the ideological underpinnings of the transfers of legal forms and technologies that shape this market'.[14]

Understanding REDD+ as constituted by both property and contract also brings into view how REDD+ arrangements depend upon and are regulated by two different bodies of international law. The contours of what constitutes 'result-based actions' and thus the parameters of a potential REDD+ commodity have been defined by public international environmental law under the umbrella of the UNFCCC; however, as a transnational conservation contract, REDD+ is also regulated by international private law. What emerges is a hybrid public–private regime for the production, regulation and enforcement of environmental action *qua* commodity, which has paradoxical effects and implications from an environmental perspective and for North–South justice, because the public and private regimes have different objectives, norms and actors. Some of the potential tensions arising in this 'duel system' are identified by Anne-Marie Klijn, Joyeeta Gupta and Anita Nijboer, who note that information about the public and private aspects are kept distinct, the private law aspect gets little attention, private contracts are often confidential, posing challenges for transparency, and different issues are raised in both spaces requiring different expertise, amongst others.[15] These consequences are elaborated in greater detail below.

Firstly, different objectives, purposes and rationales structure these different legal regimes. The public environmental law framework is underpinned by the objective of climate mitigation as well as considerations about North–South equity, but international contractual enforcement is predominantly orientated towards ensuring compliance and managing risks. As a result, issues arising in REDD+ are discussed and framed in very different ways in these two distinct fields and very different mechanisms are proposed to address them. For example, issues that raise deeply political and regulatory questions within the public law framework tend to be discussed in the contracting literature as 'risks' that need to be managed through technical means, such as financial risks (risk that the project will not be fully funded), technology and implementation risks (such as unproven technology and an inexperienced program entity), social and environmental risks, methodological monitoring and verification risks, host country regulatory risks and host country political risks.[16]

---

[14] Ibid.

[15] Klijn et al., 'Privatizing environmental resources', 177–8.

[16] 'Forest Carbon Partnership Facility, Carbon Fund: Introduction to managing risk delivery (PowerPoint slides of talk at FCPF Carbon Fund, 3rd Meeting, 2012) slide 5; *Legal Issues Guidebook to the Clean Development Mechanism* (UNEP Riso Centre on Energy, Climate and Sustainable Development, 2004) p. 89 also provides a legal discussion of risks associated with offset projects including international regulatory risks, monitoring risks, risks associated

B. Disrupting the Public–Private Boundary

The technical language of delivery risks in contractual frames – which include the risk of reversal (non-permanence), displacement or leakage (domestic and international), social risk (social disruption or conflict that affects delivery), political risks (in the host country) and regulatory risks (such as verification and issuance) – downplays how critically important these factors are to ensuring the environmental integrity of REDD+. The contractual literature recommends various strategies for buyers to protect themselves from these risks, including prudent risk assessment by investors prior to entering into contracts, careful drafting of contract clauses (clarity in *force majeure* clauses, inclusion of scheduled performance criteria, minimum performance criteria or regular independent assessment or rights to inspect),[17] as well as aggregate risk management strategies such as risk buffers, carbon pooling vehicles or re-insurance approaches.[18] This technical language of 'risk management' masks the distributional implications of these different approaches for the various contracting and state parties affected as well as for people living in and around forested areas.[19] For example, as Phillipe Cullet has identified, contractual clauses may indirectly shift responsibility from 'investor' to 'host' states, against the principles of 'common but differentiated responsibilities and respective capabilities' (CBDR-RC) in the UNFCCC and that therefore it is 'fundamental that responsibility be allocated not only according to normal contract principles but also according to the principles of the Convention'.[20] However, any suggestion that the principle of CBDR-RC or considerations of equity should influence terms in carbon contracting has generally been resisted.[21] Making these questions a matter of private rather than public law

---

with legal title to the CERs; financial risks associated with rising and falling market prices; and risks related to the social legitimacy of the project.

[17] *Legal Issues Guidebook to the Clean Development Mechanism*, pp. 87–8.

[18] R. Bayon, A. Hawn, and K. Hamilton, *Voluntary Carbon Markets: An International Business Guide to What They Are and How They Work* (Earthscan, 2007).

[19] In general see, L. Peskett and Z. Harkin, *Risk and Responsibility in Reduced Emissions from Deforestation and Degradation* (Forest Policy and Environment Programme and Overseas Development Institute, 2007).

[20] Cullet continues: 'Among the two (private) entities signing the contract for the implementation of the project, contract rules should apply if the host, for instance, fails to deliver the carbon benefits specified in the contract. However, the host entity implementing the project cannot be held responsible if the investor country is in breach of its own international commitments under the Convention. Similar principles should apply in case of non-completion of a project due, for instance, to force majeure. If, say, a forest under flexible management is destroyed by a natural cause, such as a volcanic eruption, contractual principles should apply between the two private entities at stake, but the investor country should remain responsible for meeting its commitments. In other words, flexibility mechanisms should not become a vehicle for the transfer of responsibility for fulfilling international obligations from a country to a private entity in another country.' *Differential Treatment in International Environmental Law* (Ashgate, 2003) p. 124.

[21] C. Palmer, M. Ohndorf, and I. A. MacKenzie, *Life's a Breach! Ensuring 'Permanence' in Forest Carbon Sinks under Incomplete Contract Enforcement* (CER-ETH – Center of Economic Research at ETH Zurich, 2009).

174   *Actualising Authority through Public and Private Law*

renders these equitable and distributional implications less transparent and thus less subject to contestation.

Secondly, different types of actors operate in both systems. While states predominate in public international environmental negotiations, in contrast private, often commercial, entities dominate within contracting spaces. In addition, these processes engage quite different epistemic communities with different expertise. Scholars and practitioners engaged with the UNFCCC process generally have expertise in international law; however, scholars and practitioners engaged with the contracting dimensions generally have expertise in commercial law. As a result the growing body of literature focused on the development of transnational carbon contracts remains, for the most part, hermetically sealed from the literature on carbon markets orientated towards understanding the public law framework.[22] Consisting primarily of 'legal manuals' regarding the international carbon markets, carbon contracts literature is primarily orientated towards lawyers working in private practice, and to those who will play a key role in drafting, interpreting and enforcing these transnational forest carbon contracts. These manuals discuss the legal aspects of carbon markets from a contractual perspective and describe how the legal relationship between the seller and the buyer of carbon offsets is structured through a specialised contract called an Emission Reduction Purchase Agreement (ERPA).

Thirdly, the enforcement mechanisms available in the public and private legal regimes differ considerably. The mechanism established to promote compliance of the Paris Agreement is facilitative, non-adversarial and non-punitive.[23] In contrast, domestic courts and international arbitration provide binding mechanisms to enforce compliance of transnational contractual arrangements, as provided by the applicable choice of law clause. For example, the template contract developed by the Forest Carbon Partnership Facility (FCPF) Carbon Fund provides that the governing law of the contract is English law, that dispute conciliation is in accordance with United Nations Commission on International Trade Law (UNCITRAL) Conciliation Rules, and that arbitration is in accordance with the UNCITRAL Arbitration Rules.[24] The sample ERPA produced by the International Emissions Trading Association (IETA) recommends the law of England and Wales as the

---

[22] An important exception is S. Mason-Case, 'On being companions and strangers: Lawyers and the production of international climate law' (2019) 32(4) *Leiden Journal of International Law* 625–51.

[23] *Paris Agreement*, opened for signature on 22 April 2016, UNTS XXVII.7.d (entered into force 4 November 2016), Article 15.

[24] International Bank for Reconstruction and Development, *General Conditions Applicable to Emission Reductions Payment Agreements for the Forest Carbon Partnership Facility Emission Reductions Programs* (1 November 2014), sections 18.02 and 18.03. In 2001 the PCA adopted *Optional Rules for the Arbitration Relating to Natural Resources and/or the Environment* and in 2002 adopted *Optional Rules for Conciliation of Disputes Relating to the Environment and/or Natural Resources*, see C. Q. Wu, 'A Unified Forum? The New Arbitration Rules for Environmental Disputes under the Permanent Court of Arbitration' (2002) 3(1) *Chicago Journal of International Law* 263–70; D. P. Ratliff, 'The PCA optional rules for arbitration of

B. Disrupting the Public–Private Boundary

governing law of the contract, while another sample Forest Carbon Agreement proposes the law of State of New York.[25] In addition, a whole system of international arbitration as well as of bilateral and multilateral investment agreements and dispute resolution has developed to protect investor expectations.[26] Alongside these coercive forms of contractual enforcement, other strands of World Bank literature on REDD+ have emphasised the relational aspects of contracting, focusing on internalised morality and perceived trust as key means by which to guarantee performance.[27] The literature makes evident how contracts compel compliance not just through external enforcement mechanisms but also through promoting interiorised self-governance and self-discipline by the contracting subject and a form of morality premised on the contract. Therefore, when the operations of private law are foregrounded, a much more complex understanding of how REDD+ obligations are enforced emerges, compared to the more limited frame of reference when 'international lawyers focus almost exclusively on states to explain treaty compliance'.[28] Finally, while public international environmental law encourages transparency and public debate, international commercial rules often promote confidentiality, secrecy and non-discrimination.[29]

In examining the ways in which new forms of authority are articulated over land in the green economy, it is imperative one pay attention to how private law mechanisms such as property and contract operate alongside public law framework as key technologies through which authority is actualised. Martti Koskenniemi has stressed the need for international legal analysis not just to focus on the 'legal trajectories of the foreign policy of states' but also to pay increased attention 'to the private law relations that undergird and support state action'.[30] He has emphasised the need to not side-line analysis of the 'relations of property and contract that support state policy' and to unsettle the 'prejudice that public law has to do with matters that by their nature are "political", while private law deals with non-political

---

disputes relating to natural resources and/or the environment' (2001) 14(4) *Leiden Journal of International Law* 887–96.

[25] International Emissions Trading Association, Emission Reduction Purchase Agreement, Version 3.0 (2006), www.ieta.org/resources/Resources/Trading%20Documents/cdmerpav.3 .ofinal.doc; S. Hawkins et al., *Contracting for Forest Carbon: Elements of a Model Forest Carbon Purchase Agreement* (Duke Law, Forest Trends and The Katoomba Group, 2010).

[26] See M. Sornarajah, *Resistance and Change in the International Law on Foreign Investment* (Cambridge University Press, 2015); see also K. Miles, *The Origins of International Investment Law: Empire, Environment and the Safeguarding of Capital* (Cambridge University Press, 2013).

[27] On relational contracting see E. J. Lieb, 'Contracts and friendships' (2009) 59 *Emory Law Journal* 649–726; and R. W. Gordon, 'Macneil, Macaulay, and the discovery of power and solidarity in contract law' (1985) *Wisconsin Law Review* 565–79.

[28] Affolder, 'Transnational conservation contracts', 510.

[29] Klijn et al., 'Privatizing environmental resources', 180.

[30] Koskenniemi, 'Expanding histories of international law', 109.

and "only technical" matters'.[31] In particular, his work highlights the need for international legal scholars to be alert to the ways in which private law rules concerning property and contract establish and sustain imperial forms of authority and jurisdiction. He writes:

> While it is understandable that public international lawyers and historians have traditionally focused on the public activities of sovereigns and on the formal imperial relationships that may be embodied in international law rules and institutions, these are only a small part of imperial relations, one arguably less important than the relations that operate through the universal functioning of such private-law rules as those concerning property and contract.[32]

These insights build on the work of historians of empire who showed how the establishment and maintenance of imperial relations has taken both 'formal' and 'informal' forms and demonstrated the 'inter-relation' of the political and economic arms of empire.[33]

The intimate relationship between the recognition of property rights and constitution of forms of public authority has also been extensively explored in the domestic context. Early twentieth century US legal realists theorised how private authority granted through property and contract (when protected by the state) accords forms of quasi-public power. While there is, as Peer Zumbansen has warned, clear methodological dangers in directly translating these insights to a different time period and from domestic to international spheres, legal realist insights nonetheless provide a useful reference point for any analysis of the exercise of international authority through private law mechanisms such as property and contract.[34] Robert Hale has shown that those with the *power* to acquire all the rights of ownership in the products produced from a site are thereby (provided property rights are enforced by the state) delegated by the law 'a discretionary power over the rights and duties of others.'[35] In his essay 'Property and Sovereignty', Morris Cohen argued that when property law protects future revenue from property, alongside an economic power to command the services of those who are economically dependent, 'we have the essence of what had historically constituted political sovereignty'.[36] Elsewhere, Cohen analysed contract law in terms of public law principles, writing that

---

[31] Ibid., 110.

[32] Koskenniemi, 'Empire and international law: The real Spanish Contribution', 2.

[33] J. Gallagher and R. Robinson, 'The imperialism of free trade' (1953) 6(1) *The Economic History Review: New Series* 1–15; see also Rosenberg, *The Empire of Civil Society: A Critique of the Realist Theory in International Relations*.

[34] For a discussion of the challenges of transposing these insights from the domestic to the international/transnational space see P. Zumbansen, 'The law of society: Governance through contract' (2007) 14(2) *Indiana Journal of Global Legal Studies* 191–233.

[35] R. L. Hale, 'Rate making and the revision of the property concept' (1922) 22(3) *Columbia Law Review* 209–16 at 214.

[36] Cohen, 'Property and sovereignty', 8.

C. REDD+ through the Lens of Transnational Carbon Contracting

'enforcement, in fact, puts the machinery of the law in the service of one party against the other', vesting state power, or sovereignty, in a private party.[37] Karl Llewellyn was concerned with inquiring into the 'social and political effects of contract, and especially contract as an instrument of unofficial government'.[38] In this assessment the 'bottom-up creation of contractual rules' has '"constitution-making" dimensions' in that it lays the basis of a 'constitutional order on which parties can fall back'.[39] These analyses provide tools for thinking critically about the 'work of property' in the international domain as *concealing* a sovereign in an order that claims to have no sovereign'.[40] Moreover, such analysis helps make visible how the establishment of new rights in sequestered carbon and the development of new forms of transnational contracting are therefore not simply technical matters but key technologies through which a global claim to authority over the land is actualised or made real.

C REDD+ THROUGH THE LENS OF TRANSNATIONAL CARBON CONTRACTING

This section discusses how REDD+ is underpinned by forms of transnational carbon contracting, as the production of forest carbon rests on contracts about how land will be used.[41] The rise in forest carbon contracting should be understood against the background of a broader, and still understudied, trend towards contracts becoming a key mechanism of transnational environmental law.[42] Forest carbon contracts represent a form of 'transnational conservation contract', defined by Affolder as 'agreements to conserve discrete areas of land or water, including valued,

---

[37] M. R. Cohen, 'The basis of contract' (1933) 46(4) *Harvard Law Review* 553–92.

[38] K. N. Llewellyn, 'What price contract? – An essay in perspective' (1931) 40(5) *The Yale Law Journal* 704–51.

[39] Zumbansen, 'The law of society', 191–233 at 195.

[40] S. McVeigh and S. Pahuja, 'Rival jurisdictions: The promise and loss of sovereignty' in C. Barbour and G. Pavlich (eds.), *After Sovereignty: On the Question of Political Beginnings* (Routledge, 2009) pp. 97–114, 106.

[41] M. Wilder and L. Fitz-Gerald, 'Carbon contracting' in D. Freestone and C. Streck (eds.), *Legal Aspects of Implementing the Kyoto Protocol Mechanisms: Making Kyoto Work* (Oxford University Press, 2005) pp. 295–309; S. Mahanty, W. Dressler, S. Milne, and C. Filer, 'Unravelling property relations around forest carbon' (2013) 34(2) *Singapore Journal of Tropical Geography* 188–205 at 189.

[42] N. Affolder, 'Transnational conservation contracts'; on transnational environmental law see also N. A. Affolder, 'The Private Life of Environmental Treaties' (2009) 103(3) *American Journal of International Law* 510–25; N. Affolder, 'A market for treaties' (2010) 11(1) *Chicago Journal of International Law* 159–96; and on transnational climate law see H. Bulkeley, L. B. Andonova, M. M. Betsill, D. Compagnon, T. Hale, M. J. Hoffman, P. Newell, M. Peterson, C. Roger, and S. D. Vandveer, *Transnational Climate Change Governance* (Cambridge University Press, 2014); L. B. Andonova, M. M. Betsill, and H. Bulkeley, 'Transnational climate governance' (2009) 9(2) *Global Environmental Politics* 52–73.

endangered, or critical habitat, between actors in more than one country',[43] which include debt-for-nature swaps, private protected areas, company reserve agreements, conservational performance payment agreements and conservation concessions agreements as well as forest carbon agreements. However, transnational carbon contracts underpinning REDD+ differ from other transnational conservation contracts, because in many cases REDD+ carbon contracts purport to transfer title to the emission reductions arising from such projects. Forest carbon contracts can be structured as either a 'service contract' or a 'purchasing agreement': in the former the 'paying entity pays for a service provided and reserves the right that the benefits of this service not be sold twice';[44] in the latter, the purchaser actually acquires title to the verified emission reductions, which can then be used to meet voluntary or compliance commitments.[45] In order for REDD+ to operate as a market-based scheme, the latter option – where there is a shift in title of verified emission reductions produced through the transnational contract – would need to be adopted. This approach is reflected in the contractual terms prepared by the FCPF Carbon Fund (discussed further below); however, some other bilateral funds have adopted a different approach where no such transfer of title to emission reductions is required.[46] This section discusses first some of the challenges involved in drafting forest carbon contracts and legally translating contentious 'public' concerns into private contractual arrangements. It then turns to consider the key norm-setting role played by the World Bank carbon funds including by its work on developing template carbon contracts.

1 Challenges in Drafting Transnational Carbon Contracts for REDD+

In general, the legal relationship between a seller and a buyer of carbon credits is structured through an aforementioned specialised contract called an Emission Reduction Purchase Agreements (ERPA). An ERPA is 'an agreement between a seller and buyer for the sale and purchase of an agreed amount of emission reductions (ERs) generated by an ER Program during a certain time'.[47] These contractual arrangements legally delineate responsibilities and rights relating to project management, allocate project risks and outline commercial terms including price, volume and delivery schedule of emission reductions.[48] A direct carbon

---

[43] Affolder, 'Transnational conservation contracts', 444.

[44] C. Streck, 'In the market: Forest carbon rights: Shedding light on a muddy concept' (2015) 4 *Carbon & Climate Law Review* 342–7 at 346.

[45] Ibid.

[46] Ibid.

[47] Forest Carbon Partnership Facility, 'ERPA Elements & Roadmap to ERPA General Condition' (Powerpoint slides of talk at FCPF Participants Committee, 11th Meeting, 2012) slide 5.

[48] *What Is an Emission Reduction Purchase Agreement (ERPA)?* (Overseas Development Institute) p. 1. It lists the key elements of ERPAs as: quantity and price of ERs; delivery and

C. REDD+ through the Lens of Transnational Carbon Contracting 179

supply chain might consist of a single contract between supplier and purchaser, where the seller could be a government agency, a private company specialised as a provider of offsets (or potentially an NGO) or even a certifying agency.[49] However, more commonly a range of intermediaries is involved. Further, while purchasers could directly contract with land users on the ground, the more likely scenario is that an ERPA will be finalised between the buyers and an intermediary, who will then enter into other (potentially less legally binding) agreements with community groups or individuals within the proposed project area.[50] The way such contracts are structured, and their specific terms, 'can create substantial risks and liabilities for governments while threatening the access that local communities have to land and other resources'.[51] Asymmetries of information and knowledge of carbon markets,[52] unequal power or negotiating capacity[53] and different levels of commercial law expertise can all mean that the wording of specific clauses 'can easily turn an ERPA from an asset into a liability'.[54]

Carbon contracts may provide for either a fixed price for the credits produced or a floating (linked to market fluctuations) market price or some moderation of this that imposes a floor or ceiling on a market-indexed price.[55] Like many commodities, the price of carbon has been volatile, adding further difficulties in terms of planning and in pricing.[56] Contracts can also be structured as spot agreements, future delivery agreements or options. Future delivery agreements are most common types of ERPA, as the agreement is made while a project is being delivered and thus the emission reduction may not be issued for some period of time.[57] Substantial risks are thus involved, and contractual terms can allocate this risk to either the buyer or the seller; if a buyer provides upfront payment for future delivery and the project then fails, the investment could be lost;[58] however, it is also generally recognised that an

payment schedule of ERs; consequences of non-delivery; consequences of default; general obligations of the Seller; general obligations of the Buyer; and project risks, responsibilities and management strategies.

[49] G. C. van Kooten, 'Forest carbon offsets and carbon emissions trading: Problems of contracting' (2017) 75 *Forest Policy and Economics* 83–6 at 86.

[50] Ibid., 84.

[51] K. Tienhaara, 'The potential perils of forest carbon contracts for developing countries: cases from Africa' (2012) 39(2) *The Journal of Peasant Studies* 551–72 at 553.

[52] On asymmetric information and how buyers know more about carbon markets than sellers and are more familiar with legal/technical language, see Peskett and Harkin, *Risk and Responsibility in Reduced Emissions from Deforestation and Degradation*.

[53] S. Hawkins, *Contracting for Forest Carbon: Elements of a Model Forest Carbon Purchase Agreement* (Forest Trends and the Katoomba Group, 2010).

[54] Klijn et al., 'Privatizing environmental resources', 177.

[55] Wilder and Fitz-Gerald, 'Carbon contracting', p. 303.

[56] 'EU carbon price volatility in January a sign of things to come', S&P Global Platts Insight, 10 January 2019, 56–9, blogs.platts.com/2019/01/10/eu-carbon-price-volatility-sign-of-things-to-come/.

[57] *What Is an Emission Reduction Purchase Agreement (ERPA)?*

[58] Ibid.

upfront payment will usually be required to cover project establishment costs.[59] Other analyses have shown that pricing provisions and whether price is fixed or floating can increase or decrease certainties for parties in ways that advantage one over the other.[60] Similarly, the way payment and delivery terms are structured – whether as spot agreements (simultaneous payment and delivery), future delivery agreements (payment prior to delivery) or options where the purchaser/seller has the right but no obligation to buy/sell – determines the allocations of risks between parties.[61]

Forest carbon contracts seek to establish legally enforceable, contractually organised forms of future control over land and land-use activity at referred sites for the time-period of the project. Sample forest carbon purchase agreements produced to assist parties in the development of such conservation contracts recommend the following terms:

> Participating Landholders shall manage their land and forest in order to decrease greenhouse gas emissions from deforestation and degradation and increase carbon sequestration ("Project Activities") in accordance with the project plan in annex 1 (the "Project Plan").[62]

What is promised, and sought to be guaranteed, in a REDD+ conservation contract is that the carbon sequestration from avoided deforestation or forest degradation be *additional* to what would otherwise have occurred; that the carbon sequestration be *permanent*; and that *leakage* (the shifting of deforestation from one site to another, see Chapter 1) be prevented. These requirements pose major challenges for the drafting of forest carbon contracts, because while their form must comply with the 'demands of commercial contractual practices', as Affolder notes, their 'subject matter implicates legal issues that commercial contracts cannot resolve'.[63]

The need to ensure *additionality* means that contractual terms must require parties to take on obligations to undertake activities that would not have otherwise gone ahead in the absence of the project, and also to establish counterfactual 'business-as-usual' baselines or reference levels against which additional emission reductions can be measured. The need to ensure *permanence* means that contracts need to ensure emissions are 'saved' over the time period of the contract and to protect against risks that may impact contractual performance as well as reversals in the future. Various different types of risks are identified that may impact on the permanence of carbon storage: natural/ecological risks (where natural events such as

---

[59] van Kooten, 'Forest carbon offsets and carbon emissions trading', 87.
[60] *What Is an Emission Reduction Purchase Agreement (ERPA)?*, p. 2.
[61] Ibid., pp. 2–3.
[62] Hawkins, *Contracting for Forest Carbon: Elements of a Model Forest Carbon Purchase Agreement*, p. 5.
[63] Affolder, 'Transnational carbon contracting', p. 221.

C. REDD+ through the Lens of Transnational Carbon Contracting 181

storm, drought, pests or fire affect carbon stocks); climate-change-related risks (where climate change leads to systemic carbon losses in some areas); demand-side risks (where increased prices for agricultural commodities might shift opportunity costs, making forest conversion more profitable); failure of project partners (caused by ineffective project management, insecure tenure rights leading to encroachment, or bankruptcy); and political risks (change of government or reversal of policy).[64] Thus, as well as regular contractual enforcement mechanisms, discussions on ensuring permanence have asserted the need for two 'layers' of risk management: a general strategy layer to manage the risks of re-emissions by projects or countries, and a layer that puts a system of commercial liability in place where the credits are produced for use in either compliance or voluntary markets. While the former is underpinned by concerns about environmental integrity, the latter is a matter of 'commercial necessity', where the resulting credits are traded.[65] For example, Michael Dutschke and Arild Angelsen have argued that 'if REDD credits from subnational activities are to be made fungible with other mitigation credits of allowances units, the resulting commercial risks need to be securitised'; they argue that 'assigning liability is a precondition for credit fungibility'.[66] The literature also discusses a number of different risk management techniques to protect against reversals including risk pooling, REDD+ unit reserves (or buffers) or the creation of insurance systems.[67]

The need to avoid *leakage* raises complex questions of contractual privity, or who has rights and obligations under a contract, because a proponent of a particular project generally cannot guarantee that emissions saved there have not simply been emitted elsewhere; nor can they promise they will prevent deforestation and forest degradation activities from being displaced to elsewhere. Concerns about leakage have led to the promotion of 'jurisdictional' approaches to REDD+, focused on reducing emissions for deforestation across an entire national or sub-national area rather than just in a single project site. Such a jurisdictional approach 'highlights the critical role of government and the need for wall-to-wall, holistic approaches to forest and land-use governance across a defined territory as key components of any realistic effort to protect forests and reduce land-use emissions at scale'.[68] Something

---

[64] M. Dutschke and A. Angelsen, 'How do we ensure permanence and assign liability?' in A. Angelsen (ed.), *Moving Ahead with REDD: Issues, Options and Implications* (Center for International Forestry Research, 2008) pp. 77–85, 79.

[65] Ibid., pp. 78–9.

[66] Ibid., pp. 80 and 83.

[67] Ibid.; C. Palmer, 'Property rights and liability for deforestation under REDD+: Implications for "permanence" in policy design' (2011) 70(4) *Ecological Economics* 571–6. See also UNFCCC Secretariat, *Financing Options for the Full Implementation of Results-Based Actions Relating to the Activities Referred to in Decision 1/CP.16, paragraph 70, Including Related Modalities and Procedures: Technical Paper*, FCCC/TP/2012/3 (26 July 2012).

[68] W. Boyd, C. Stickler, A. E. Duchelle, F. Seymour, D. Nepstad, N. H. A. Bahar, and D. Rodriguez-Ward, *Ending Tropical Deforestation: A Stocktake of Progress and Challenges. Jurisdictional Approaches to REDD+ and Low Emissions Development: Progress and Prospects*

else underpinning any jurisdictional approach is the recognition that individual projects are unlikely to scale to a level needed for significant emission reductions and that 'government policies and programs at multiple levels must be a foundational component of any successful approach to protecting forests and climate'.[69] As such, the performance of contractual obligations is also dependent upon policy, environmental and other developments within the jurisdiction in which the project is situated. At a minimum, a jurisdictional approach will require governmental buy-in as well as forms of cooperation and communication between different private sector actors within a jurisdiction.[70] To date, there has been limited private sector demand for participation in jurisdictional approaches or direct financial or technical investment in them, although this interest is growing.[71] Therefore, a number of key questions still need to be resolved about how to reconcile 'result-based payment' or the transfer of verified emission reduction credits to purchases within a jurisdictional approach.[72]

Finally, one of the most controversial questions in relation to forest carbon contracts is determining who the appropriate contracting party is, in a context where the owner of the forested land is often not the person or people on the ground who will ultimately determine how the forested land is used in practice. The supply chain for carbon can be relatively simple in cases where there is a 'clear "owner" of the rights to the carbon stored in the trees, who develops an offset project and then either sells carbon "credits" directly to individuals, governments and firms or instead sells them to an intermediary that will resell them at a profit'.[73] However, commonly the supply chain in relation to forest carbon is more complex than this direct buyer/seller relationship, and it involves a number of intermediaries, whose relationships are generally also structured through contracts. Kyla Tienhaara identifies that a situation may arise where 'the owner of the land/ trees/carbon may lease his/her rights to another party that wishes to develop a project'.[74] Alternately, the contract may take the form of an investment contract ('state contracts' or 'investor-state contracts') such as a concession agreement or a joint venture where the owner of the land is the state entity and the purchaser is a foreign investor.[75]

(World Resources Institute and Laboratory for Energy and Environmental Policy Innovation, 2018) p. 1. The development of such jurisdictional approaches is being trialled by Acre and Mato Grosso in Brazil, Central Kalimantan in Indonesia, Sabah in Malaysia, San Martin in Peru, and Yucatan State in Mexico.

[69] *A REDD+ Jurisdictional Approach to Achieve Green Development in Indonesia* (Bandan Pengelola REDD+, 2014) p. 2.

[70] A. Fishman, E. Oliveira, and L. Gamble, *Tackling Deforestation through a Jurisdictional Approach: Lessons from the Field* (WWF, 2017) p. ii.

[71] Ibid., p. iv.

[72] Ibid., p. 10.

[73] Tienhaara, 'The potential perils of forest carbon contracts for developing countries', 554.

[74] Ibid.

[75] Ibid.

C. REDD+ through the Lens of Transnational Carbon Contracting

Two distinct but interrelated issues arise when forest contracts do not include or engage with the people living in and around forested land. The first, arising from a perspective focused on contractual enforcement, is what the literature has called the 'principal–agent' problem: namely that the 'agent has information that is unavailable to the principal and the agent often acts in ways hidden from and contrary to the desires of the principal'.[76] For example, Gerrit van Kooten discusses the potential contractual challenges caused by an 'on-the-ground agent who is ultimately responsible for how the land is used' but who is often not the actual landowner. Van Kooten is concerned that such a land user, who might not be in a formal rental arrangement with the owner and 'may not even be aware that there is a contract to use the land to generate environmental services or create carbon offsets', may violate terms of the contract inadvertently or even deliberately if a 'better opportunity' presented itself.[77] He suggests one way to approach this problem is to have a series, or a chain, of different contracts with different actors.[78] Such an approach therefore requires identifying who the appropriate people 'on the ground' are to enter into a contract, ensuring they are adequately informed about contractual conditions and that there are mechanisms to enforce their compliance. The second issue, arising from a perspective concerned with the rights of people living in and around forested lands, relates to how exclusion from such contracts and the process of negotiating them could impact on the rights and interests of forest communities. For example, in a contract between an investor and the state, forest-communities are unlikely to have a formal role as parties, and even though they 'may be referred to in the contract . . . it is unlikely that they will have any role in the negotiation process.'[79] In response, there have been calls by advocates for improvement by 'increasing transparency and opportunities for the participation of local communities and forest-dwelling peoples'.[80] These divergent concerns of contractual enforcement and forest peoples' rights have therefore tended to converge on a shared agreement that it is necessary to transform forest peoples from 'unrecognised counterparties' into contractual partners.[81] That is, those concerned that communities can only be legally bound by contractual obligations to the extent they are recognised as relevant parties *and* those concerned that communities might be disadvantaged if they are excluded from contracts or their negotiations have both posited greater inclusion as a necessary response in order to ensure social feasibility of the scheme and to promote rights. In this way the contractual frame facilitates convergence between

---

[76] van Kooten, 'Forest carbon offsets and carbon emissions trading', 85–6.

[77] Ibid., 86.

[78] Ibid., 83.

[79] Tienhaara, 'The potential perils of forest carbon contracts for developing countries', 558.

[80] Ibid., 568.

[81] This terminology is taken from A. Alforte, J. Angan, J. Dentith, K. Domondon, L. Munden, S. Murday, and L. Pradela, *Communities As Counterparties: Preliminary Review of Concessions and Conflict in Emerging and Frontier Market Concessions* (Rights and Resources Initiative, 2014).

184 Actualising Authority through Public and Private Law

demands for rights and participation 'from below' with demands for further mechanisms of responsibilisation 'from above'. Yet, in doing so, it fosters a highly disciplinary inclusion of forest peoples into the legal arrangements that structure and underpin the green economy.

2 Establishing Norms through Carbon Contracting

The legal form of the contract provides considerable flexibility for parties to determine their own terms and arrangements for carbon contracting; however, standardisation of key terms has also been promoted through the development of template or 'boilerplate' contracts by key players such as the World Bank and the International Emissions Trading Association (IETA). Through such standard form contracts, specific norms can be developed and disseminated across a sector, outside of the formal, transparent deliberative UNFCCC processes. There is, as Affolder writes, a distinct power 'that accompanies first-mover advantage in establishing methodologies that become the "defaults" for later regulatory regimes'.[82] Scholars have highlighted the need to attend to the role played by such standard form contracts in transnational private ordering, given that their proliferation raises 'pressing questions about legitimacy, democracy and the accountability of the trade associations who are the authors of these standard terms'.[83]

The World Bank has, over the past two decades, been a central actor in initiatives to build carbon markets, especially through its various carbon funds that aim to encourage the development of a global carbon market.[84] These funds have played a key role bridging the UNFCCC regime and private carbon contracting. The World Bank's promotion of environmental initiatives, Michael Goldman has argued, should not be dismissed as an exercise in mere 'greenwash', but rather understood as part of a broader strategy of promoting the power/knowledge regime of green neo-liberalism, 'the Bank's latest and most profound discursive framework'.[85] Goldman argues that green neo-liberalism has reactively allowed the Bank to respond to – but more crucially, incorporate within its activities – many of its environmental critics. It has also productively enabled the World Bank to 'expand into more places and insinuate its worldview into more lifeworlds than [it did] before',[86] and to further its goal of 'restructuring and capitalisation of nature–society relations that exist as

---

[82] Affolder, 'Transnational carbon contracting', p. 230.

[83] J. P. Braithwaite, 'Standard form contracts as transnational law: Evidence from the derivatives markets' (2012) 75(5) *The Modern Law Review* 779–805 at 780.

[84] 'Carbon finance: The role of the World Bank in carbon trading markets', *Bretton Woods Project*, 26 September 2018, www.brettonwoodsproject.org/2018/09/carbon-finance-role-world-bank-carbon-trading-markets/ (accessed 27 April 2019).

[85] M. Goldman, *Imperial Nature: The World Bank and Struggles for Social Justice in an Age of Globalization* (Yale University, 2006) p. 5.

[86] Ibid., p. 6.

C. REDD+ through the Lens of Transnational Carbon Contracting

uncommodified or underutilised by capital markets'.[87] Similarly, the World Bank's engagement in the space of climate finance is best understood as actively promoting a specific, market-driven response to the climate crisis and facilitating the development of carbon markets by enabling the creation of the requisite background regulatory conditions.

The World Bank is now the trustee of fifteen different climate funds capitalised at over \$6 billion that have supported activities in at least seventy-eight countries.[88] Subsequent to the launch of the Prototype Carbon Fund in 2000, the World Bank established ten so-called Kyoto funds and since 2007 the World Bank has developed a number of so-called next generation carbon instruments.[89] The key objectives of the World Bank's carbon finance work, as articulated in a 2005 position paper, are:

1. to ensure carbon finance contributes substantially to sustainable development;
2. to assist in building, sustaining and expanding the international market for carbon emission reductions and its institutional and administrative structure; and
3. to further strengthen the capacity of developing countries to benefit from the emerging market for ER credits.[90]

Through its work developing new financial instruments and building 'supportive' policy and regulatory environments to promote 'market-readiness', the World Bank has consistently engaged in activities that '[pre-empt] a political decision within international climate negotiations'.[91] Therefore, despite attempts by the World Bank to depict its work as merely a 'technical exercise', its effects are deeply political, enabling it to exert a powerful normative effect on the development of international carbon markets.

In April 2000, the World Bank launched its first climate fund, the Prototype Carbon Fund (PCF). It was called a prototype, because as David Freestone (the PCF's legal advisor and former Deputy General Counsel at the Bank) has explained, 'its primary intent was that it would be able to act as a "trail blazer" for other similar funds that might be launched by the other international financial institutions or the

---

[87] Ibid., p. 7.
[88] The World Bank, 'Climate finance and initiatives', www.worldbank.org/en/topic/climate change/brief/world-bank-carbon-funds-facilities (accessed 29 November 2019).
[89] These include the Carbon Partnership Facility, the Forest Carbon Partnership Facility, the Partnership for Market Readiness, the Carbon Initiative for Development, the BioCarbon Fund Tranche 3: Initiative for Sustainable Forest Landscapes and Pilot Auction Facility.
[90] 'The role of the World Bank in carbon finance: An approach for further engagement' (approved by the Bank's Board of Directors on 6 December 2005) cited in World Bank, *Forest Carbon Partnership Facility: Information Memorandum* (13 June 2008), 10.
[91] O. Reyes, *More Is Less: A Case Against Sectoral Carbon Markets* (Carbon Trade Watch, 2011) p. 6.

private sector'.[92] Freestone describes the Bank's objectives as 'to "lead from behind" in climate finance to try and help ease the path for the private sector'.[93] Given the many uncertainties regarding the modalities for carbon trading, the PCF was 'deliberately seeking to use risk capital from the public sector and other early movers to address the most difficult early challenges'.[94] Key to its achievements was the development of the first ERPA, which was then adopted as a standard form contract for such transactions for a number of years.[95] The PCF is widely seen as 'the pioneer of the global carbon market, piloting transactions several years before the Kyoto Protocol to the UNFCCC entered into effect and acting as a "role model" for other similar funds'.[96] Indeed, the World Bank's development of the technical modalities of carbon trading preceded many parts of the UNFCCC processes, where key decisions about carbon accounting were not made until the Marrakech Accords were instituted in 2001. By the time the first Kyoto Protocol was operational in 2005 and its first commitment period (2008–12) commenced, these World Bank-sponsored carbon funds had already been launched and projects developed, thereby materialising and actualising the market on the ground.

In 2003 the World Bank established the BioCarbon Fund (BCF) – the same year that COP9 in Milan reached agreement on rules for afforestation and reforestation (A/R) projects under the CDM. The BCF has two explicit purposes: first, to finance forest sequestration projects with the aim that they should generate ERs that can be verified as meeting Kyoto Protocol requirements, and second, a more exploratory aim to finance sustainable agriculture projects and other sequestration projects – which at the time were not eligible under the Kyoto Protocol rules – in order to demonstrate 'how practical solutions can be found to many of the problems surrounding the generation of emission reductions by such [A/R] activities'.[97] In 2006 the World Bank started consulting with stakeholders on an initiative to scale up the BCF 'by supporting capacity building and providing performance-based payments'.[98] Shortly after this, at COP13 in Bali in 2007 the World Bank launched its Forest Carbon Partnership Facility (FCPF).[99] Since 2007 the World Bank has launched a number of 'next generation carbon instruments', including Partnership for Market Readiness, designed to assist major emerging and middle-income economies to expand carbon markets to sectoral trading mechanisms.[100] In doing so, the

---

[92] D. Freestone, *The World Bank and Sustainable Development: Legal Essays* (Martinus Nijhoff Publishers, 2013) p. 174.

[93] 'Interview with David Freestone' (2017) 3 *Carbon & Climate Law Review* 196–7 at 196.

[94] Ibid.

[95] Ibid.

[96] C. Carr and F. Rosembuj, 'World Bank experiences in contracting for emission reductions' (2007) 2 *Environmental Liability* 114–19 at 114.

[97] Freestone, *The World Bank and Sustainable Development: Legal Essays*, p. 177.

[98] World Bank, *Forest Carbon Partnership Facility: Information Memorandum* (13 June 2008), 11.

[99] See Chapter 1.

[100] See the Partnership for Market Readiness Fund website, www.thepmr.org.

C. REDD+ *through the Lens of Transnational Carbon Contracting*

World Bank sought to take on a 'leadership role in shaping the next generation of carbon instruments for the post-2012 period by developing new approaches to performance-based payments'. In November 2013, at the Warsaw COP, the World Bank announced a major new initiative managed by the BCF, namely the 'Initiatives for Sustainable Forest Landscapes'.[101] It seeks to 'scale up land-management practices across large landscapes, including improved livestock management, climate-smart agriculture, and sustainable forest management, with a focus on protecting forests and greening and securing supply chains', and as such to build connections between REDD+, climate-smart agriculture and land-use planning.[102] In particular, it seeks trial approaches to public–private partnerships within a 'landscape' approach to REDD+.[103]

The World Bank has also played an influential role through its work disseminating knowledge and developing contractual models. David Freestone together with Charlotte Streck (from the World Bank's senior counsel) edited two 'bibles' of climate law.[104] In addition, the World Bank's climate finance section has 'created business models and examples that have been followed by government and the private sector' and 'spurred the development of ERPAs'.[105] The World Bank's first contracts to buy and sell carbon subsequently formed the basis of templates produced and distributed by IETA.[106] The structure of these contracts has altered over time: in line with the initial objective to '[catalyse] the carbon market before the Kyoto Protocol entered into force', early ERPAs were individually tailored to projects and provided more upfront cash without strict remedies for under-delivery,[107] but they were subsequently refined to a 'payment on delivery approach'.[108] Other actors have also produced and shared sample or template ERPAs, including UNEP and Baker McKenzie,[109] the Norwegian Ministry of Finance and

---

[101] 'BioCarbon Fund launches $280 million initiative for sustainable forest landscapes' *The World Bank*, 20 November 2013, www.worldbank.org/en/news/feature/2013/11/20/biocarbon-fund-initiative-promote-sustainable-forest-landscapes.

[102] Ibid.

[103] *Engaging the Private Sector in Results-Based Landscape Programs: Early Lessons from the World Bank's Forests and Landscapes Climate Finance Funds* (Forest Carbon Partnership Facility and BioCarbon Fund Initiative for Sustainable Forest Landscapes, 2017).

[104] D. Freestone and C. Streck (eds.), *Legal Aspects of Implementing the Kyoto Protocol Mechanisms: Making Kyoto Work* (Oxford University Press, 2005); D. Freestone and C. Streck (eds.), *Legal Aspects of Carbon Trading: Kyoto, Copenhagen, and Beyond* (Oxford University Press, 2009).

[105] Carr and Rosembuj, 'World Bank experiences in contracting for emission reductions', 115.

[106] R. O'Sullivan, 'CERSPA: A new template agreement for the sale and purchase of certified emission reductions (CERs)' (2007) 2 *Environmental Liability* 120–4 at 120–1.

[107] Ibid.

[108] Carr and Rosembuj, 'World Bank experiences in contracting for emission reductions', 116.

[109] UNEP, *Legal Issues Guidebook to the Clean Development Mechanism*.

International Emissions Trading Association[110] as well as specialised Forest Carbon Purchase Agreements.[111]

World Bank climate funds have also developed general contractual conditions for REDD+ contracts. In November 2014 the Carbon Fund of the World Bank's FCPF approved the adoption of general conditions applicable to forest ERPAs.[112] These General Conditions will be incorporated into any ERPA concluded between the FCPF and a REDD+ country. However, in the same way that the terms and conditions of the ERPAs produced by the initial Prototype Carbon Fund were taken up more generally by carbon trading industry players, it is likely the terms articulated in these General Conditions will be taken up more broadly by other actors. This presumption is supported by the FCPF's stated objective to 'pilot a performance-based payment system for ERs generated from REDD activities' and to 'disseminate broadly the knowledge gained'.[113] These 'General Conditions' set out the general legal rules that should be followed during the Emission Reduction Program design, preparation and implementation and build on the earlier Methodological Framework developed by the FCPF. In addition, each negotiated ERPA contains negotiable commercial terms covering the contract ER volume, their unit price, advance payments, conditions of sale and purchase, options and cost recovery discount. The General Conditions include clauses relating to:

- transfer and payment of ERs (including which rights/titles/interests are attached to such ERs);
- title to ERs (seller demonstrates ability to transfer title to ERs);
- ER program Operation and Management (including validation, monitoring, reporting and verification);
- benefits (including non-carbon benefits) and benefit-sharing (obligation of seller to share its revenue with other stakeholders affected by the project);

---

[110] For sample ERPSs see J. Cameron, M. Guli, A. Hobley and D. Reid-Thomas, 'Carbon contracts cornerstones: Drafting contracts for the sale of project based emission reductions' (Discussion Paper No 02-01, Version 1.2, International Emissions Trading Association and Baker & McKenzie, 2002). For sample ERPAs see those collated at Forest Carbon Asia, *Sample Emission Reduction Purchase Agreements (ERPAs)* www.forestcarbonasia.org/other-resources/sample-emission-reduction-purchase-agreements-erpas/.

[111] Hawkins, *Contracting for Forest Carbon: Elements of a Model Forest Carbon Purchase Agreement.*

[112] International Bank for Reconstruction and Development, *General Conditions Applicable to Emission Reductions Payment Agreements for the Forest Carbon Partnership Facility Emission Reductions Programs* (1 November 2014), www.forestcarbonpartnership.org/requirements-and-templates ('General Conditions'); FCPF Participants Committee, Resolution PC/18/2014/2 'Adoption of FCPF General Conditions Applicable to Emissions Reductions Payment Agreement', 18th Meeting (PC18), Arusha, Tanzania 31 October–4 November 2014, www .forestcarbonpartnership.org/sites/fcp/files/2014/october/FCPF%20ERPA_General% 20Conditions_November%201%202014.pdf.

[113] International Bank for and Reconstruction and Development, *Charter Establishing the Forest Carbon Partnership Facility* (2013), section 2.1 (b) and (d).

C. REDD+ *through the Lens of Transnational Carbon Contracting*

- ER Program Buffer;
- events of default and remedies; and
- dispute resolution and governing law.

Further, each ERPA must contain several 'additional elements' including:

- Safeguard Plans (which include Environmental Management Plan, Resettlement Plan, Indigenous Peoples Plan and any other environmental or social related plan or document required under the World Bank operational policies);
- Benefits Sharing Plan, regarding how monetary and non-monetary benefits will be shared with beneficiaries;
- ER Program Document and ER Monitoring Plan;
- Action Plan (documenting further steps and timelines in order for the seller to demonstrate ability to transfer title of ERs);
- Letter of Approval (from department in host country responsible for approving REDD+ projects).

The General Conditions require that as part of periodic ER monitoring reports, 'evidence satisfactory to the Trustee [the World Bank]' is to be provided, that all the measures are all implemented in accordance with the Safeguard Plan(s) and Benefits Sharing Plan.[114] They also require that the program entity 'shall share a significant part of the Monetary and non-Monetary Benefits achieved' with beneficiaries and develop a Benefits Sharing Plan to affect this.[115] The Methodological Framework requires that such benefit-sharing arrangements be 'designed in a consultative, transparent, and participatory manner appropriate to the country context ... [and] reflect] inputs by relevant stakeholders, including broad community support by affected Indigenous peoples', and be in a 'form, manner and language understandable to the affected keyholders'.[116]

A number of concerns about these contractual conditions have been raised by NGOs, including how the language presumes that all documents relating to the ERPA will be confidential if requested by one of the parties, rather than subject to public disclosure.[117] NGOs have also expressed concern that although the Methodological Framework calls for consultation with the affected community during the early stages of ER

---

[114] International Bank for Reconstruction and Development, *General Conditions Applicable to Emission Reductions Purchase Agreements for Forest Carbon Partnership Facility Emission Reductions Programs* (1 November 2014), section 5.01(b)(i).

[115] Ibid., section 6.03.

[116] Forest Carbon Partnership Facility, *Carbon Fund: Methodological Framework* (Revised final, 22 June 2016), Criterion 31 and Indicator 31.3.

[117] Letter from Bank Information Center, Environmental Investigation Agency and Rainforest Foundation Norway to Members of the FCPF Participants Committee, 29 October 2014, https://d5i6isoeze552.cloudfront.net/documents/Politiske-utspill/2014/FCPF-EIA-BIC-RFN-Letter-to-PC-on-ERPA-GC-CT-ID-17490.docx?mtime=20150630145459.

190 *Actualising Authority through Public and Private Law*

program design, the commercial terms of the contract allow that the preparation of safeguards and benefits sharing plans can be delayed until the time of sale of ER credits. Concerned NGOs wrote:

> Delaying the final version of these plans until ERPA signature, or worse[,] after the ERPA is signed and the project is already being implemented or making them conditions of effectiveness will be highly detrimental to indigenous peoples and forest dependent communities unless the indigenous people and forest dependent people and other stakeholders affected by the ER Program have been actively consulted about these plans prior to the signing of the ERPA and during the negotiations and drafting of these plans.[118]

Significantly, the General Conditions structure the arrangement as a 'purchasing agreement' rather than a 'service contract' and provide that title to ERs be transferred: they require the seller to transfer 'title to ERs [emission reductions]' – that is, 'the full legal and beneficial title and exclusive right' – to the purchaser.[119] Additionally, before an ERPA is signed the seller is required to demonstrate to the buyer their ability to transfer title to such ERs.[120] The development of domestic legal frameworks to clarify rights to such emission reductions is considered a matter for national governments; however, NGOs have raised concerns that the General Conditions risk 'incentivizing a rush to nationalize or otherwise assign carbon rights when there may be insufficient development of a national legal framework to clarify these rights or where awareness and good faith negotiations between the ER Program Proponent and affected stakeholders on these issues has not occurred'.[121] Although, the FCPF has been careful to clarify that only the title to the verified ERs is transferred, and that such transfer does not affect the beneficial, legal or customary interests or rights in the land and territories of the project area,[122] NGOs have warned that 'title to carbon rights, and the transfer of those rights to the Carbon Fund, impacts the fundamental rights of people to their lands and forests'.[123] Civil society groups have therefore stressed the need for this 'to be approached with greater caution and with greater remedies for potentially affected peoples and other stakeholders'.[124] However, despite clear concerns that contractual terms developed

---

[118] Ibid.

[119] International Bank for Reconstruction and Development, *General Conditions Applicable to Emission Reductions Purchase Agreements for Forest Carbon Partnership Facility Emission Reductions Programs* (1 November 2014), sections 5.02, 5.03 and 15.01, the definition of 'Title to ERs' is provided in section 2.01.

[120] See Forest Carbon Partnership Facility, 'ERPA General Conditions', www.forestcarbonpartnership .org/erpa-general-conditions (accessed 27 April 2019).

[121] Letter from Bank Information Center, Environmental Investigation Agency and Rainforest Foundation Norway to Members of the FCPF Participants Committee, 29 October 2014.

[122] For a discussion of 'carbon rights' see Chapter 5.

[123] Letter from Bank Information Center, Environmental Investigation Agency and Rainforest Foundation Norway to Members of the FCPF Participants Committee, 29 October 2014.

[124] Ibid.

D. REDD+ *through the Lens of Property*

by the FCPF could have adverse consequences for forest peoples, it is likely that the General Conditions developed by the FCPF will exert a strong influence on how the legal arrangements for forest carbon are consolidated. Therefore, the key role played by actors such as the World Bank, including through the development of contractual conditions, highlights the need for analysis to 'pay attention to peripheral legal and political orders as well as central ones',[125] and to be attentive to how public environmental and social concerns are manifested through private contractual terms, and how power relations shape their translation.

D REDD+ THROUGH THE LENS OF PROPERTY[126]

This section examines REDD+ through the lens of property in order to interrogate the strange characteristics of carbon credits and the distributive effects of creating and allocating new rights in carbon. Before embarking on this analysis, two preliminary objections – namely, that it has not been confirmed that REDD+ activities will create tradable credits, and that such credits do not constitute 'property' – will be addressed in brief. Carbon markets, like all environmental markets, require for their operation rights that are defined, enforced and transferable.[127] Indeed, the creation of transferable rights is a key difference between emissions trading schemes and either traditional 'command and control' regulatory policy or environmental taxes.[128] Within emission trading schemes (ETSs) two different types of rights can circulate: 'emission allowances', which 'represent the authorization or entitlement to emit a certain amount of GHGs',[129] and 'emission credits', which are generated privately and 'represent a reduction of GHG emissions resulting from a defined project activity, calculated on the basis of a comparison between the level of verified action emissions and a counterfactual scenario (defined as the baseline scenario)'.[130] At the time of writing, no formal decision has been made to allow ERs resulting from REDD+ activities to be traded in international carbon markets, although the accounting rules set out in the Warsaw Framework for REDD+ potentially enables such ERs to be treated as equivalent, fungible and tradable with other carbon credits. Moreover, the discussion above showed that private contractual arrangements already provide for transfer of ERs from REDD+ activities. It is therefore

---

[125] Affolder, 'Transnational carbon contracting', p. 230.

[126] REDD+ raises a number of complex legal issues pertaining to property. This section examines the 'emission reductions' arising from REDD+ projects through the lens of property. Associated questions about how rights in emission reductions are related to rights to management the carbon sequestration potential of lands, rights to benefit from carbon sequestration and rights in the underlying land are discussed in Chapter 5.

[127] M. Wemaere, C. Streck, and T. Chagas, 'Legal ownership and nature of Kyoto Units and EU Allowances' in Freestone and Streck (eds.), *Legal Aspects of Carbon Trading* pp. 35–58, 44.

[128] Ibid., p. 37.

[129] Ibid., p. 43.

[130] Ibid.

appropriate to consider REDD+ credits as legally taking the form of quasi-property rights for two reasons: firstly, this accords with how REDD+ has been imagined and visualised as a market-based instrument; and secondly, current trajectories suggest key institutional players will continue to work towards implementing a market-based REDD+ scheme.

There is also a technical legal debate (discussed in greater detail below) about whether carbon credits constitute 'property'. Such discussions are complicated by the fact that '[property is] a dangerously slippery word' with arguably 'chameleonic qualities',[131] which itself is difficult to define with precision, and also that legal rules regarding property, and whether carbon credits constitute property, differ between jurisdictions. Nonetheless, carbon allowances and credits, defined as equivalent to $1tCO_2e$, are enforceable and transferable and are widely understood as type of 'hybrid, regulatory created property right'.[132] The discussion in this section is, however, less concerned with technical legal questions surrounding property or 'what allowances or emission rights are' but rather with 'what they entitle the holder to do',[133] and in particular, the forms of power and authority these rights actualise. In particular, the analysis in this section is concerned with how the international climate framework creates an unequal initial allocation of carbon allowances and how this unequal initial allocation influences the subsequent shape of the climate regime and the carbon markets it authorises. It thus adopts property as a lens or rubric for thinking about how rights in scarce and valued resources – namely carbon or rights to emit GHGs into the atmosphere – are defined and allocated. This section considers first the peculiar nature of the carbon commodity, before considering the how the Kyoto Protocol authorised an unequal distribution of emission allowances, the subsequent development of a more decentralised climate regime and the effect of the Paris Agreement; finally, it discusses how REDD+ credits could be incorporated into post-Paris carbon markets.

1 The Peculiar Properties of Rights in Carbon

There have been 'prolonged difficulties' in resolving the technical 'classification of carbon as a legal entity' and whether carbon credits or emissions allowances constitute property or quasi-property rights.[134] The technical legal questions about whether such credits or allowances constitute a commodity, a financial instrument,

---

[131] K. F. Low and J. Lin, 'Carbon credits as EU like it: Property, immunity, tragiCO$_2$medy?' (2015) 27(3) *Journal of Environmental Law* 377–404 at 387 and 388.

[132] C. M. Rose, 'The several futures of property: Of cyberspace and folk tales, emission trades and ecosystems' (1998) 83 *Minnesota Law Review* 129–82 at 144; see also Wemaere et al., 'Legal ownership and nature of Kyoto units and EU allowances', p. 44.

[133] Wemaere et al., 'Legal ownership and nature of Kyoto units and EU allowances', p. 44.

[134] Lovell and Ghaleigh, 'Climate change and the professions', 514.

D. REDD+ through the Lens of Property

an asset, private property or a personal right are complex.[135] In addition, because carbon units are 'legally defined units', the legal rights that they give rise to '[depend] on the legal system that brought them into existence',[136] and under different legal systems they might be understood as an authorisation or permit to emit, an administrative or public right, a private property right, a security, a financial instrument, a good or a commodity.[137] As Charlotte Streck clarifies, it is therefore the legal system that brought a particular carbon credit into existence which also determines the 'extent to which a carbon right represents a property right (with its accompanying guarantees), and if so, what type of property right (i.e. a "real" or "personal" right)'.[138] Where carbon credits or emission allowances are traded internationally, additional complications might arise if different governing laws apply once this intangible right is traded across borders.[139] As issues arise, courts in different jurisdictions may be called on to determine the legal nature of these statutory entitlements to resolve disputes, and they may adopt different analyses.[140] In the UK, for example, courts have pronounced the carbon credits from the EU emission trading schemes as 'property rights of some sort', without clarifying exactly what private law rights this property conferred.[141] How these legal questions are resolved, and whether they are resolved in uniform ways across different jurisdictions, will have important legal implications in a range of areas including security rights, insolvency law, accounting and taxation.

This analysis however foregrounds the strange and peculiar characteristics of the 'hybrid, regulatory created property right' in carbon, and thus also its complex relationship to law and regulation. Carbon markets require as an essential precondition for their operation a capacity to think about and imagine $1tCO_2e$ as a 'thing' or 'object'. Yet, this is a very strange 'object' in that it does not exist as an object prior to processes of reification (in the German *Verdinglichung*), that is, 'thingification' or 'objectification' through which social processes come to be expressed and understood as an objects.[142] The carbon commodity is thus not so much an 'object' but rather, as Jerome Whitington has argued, 'an assemblage of agreements, conventional practices, durable artefacts and rules held by people who operate in different

---

[135] Ibid.

[136] Streck, 'In the market: Forest carbon rights', 343–4.

[137] Wemaere et al., 'Legal ownership and nature of Kyoto units and EU allowances', p. 43.

[138] Streck, 'In the market: Forest carbon rights', 344.

[139] Low and Lin, 'Carbon credits as EU like it', 402.

[140] H. Johnson, P. O'Connor, W. D. Duncan, and S. A. Christensen, 'Statutory entitlements as property: Implications of property analysis methods for emissions trading' (2018) 43 *Monash University Law Review* 421–62.

[141] *Armstrong v Winnington* [2012] EWHC 10 (Ch), [2013] Ch 156 discussed in Lin and Low, 'Carbon credits as EU like it '.

[142] J. Dehm, 'One tonne of carbon dioxide equivalent (1tCO2e)' in J. Hohmann and D. Joyce (eds.), *International Law's Objects* (Oxford University Press, 2018) pp. 305–18, 317–18.

contexts around the world'.[143] Understanding the carbon commodity as an object is therefore a *productive fiction* that depends upon a social acceptance and agreement: as Larry Lohmann has argued, the establishment of carbon markets and of property rights in carbon is dependent upon a 'contract with the public' about the legitimacy of all these transactions and substitutions, as well as public faith in the regulation, monitoring and verification of these markets.[144] It is perhaps best understood as a 'fictitious commodity' in a Polanyian sense – as something not inherently or obviously a commodity (defined as something made to be bought and sold in markets) but something subject to a social decision that it should be treated *as if* it was a commodity.[145]

Therefore, as a commodity, carbon is caught within a performative double bind: its commodification is legitimated through claims that such propertisation serves a social purpose, purportedly enabling cost-effective climate mitigation. Because of this explicit social purpose, Peter Newell and Matthew Peterson argue that carbon markets are – or *should* be – different from other markets: they should not be treated as '*ends* in themselves' but can only legitimately exist as 'a means to achieve a specific social purpose'.[146] Yet, within the literature on carbon markets, carbon is imagined *as if* it were a commodity like any other,[147] and this creates an ongoing tension between whether the carbon commodity is treated as a means or an end and whether the nature of the commodity is understood in purely formal terms or with reference to the social function is it envisioned to perform. There is also an inherent tension between the 'particular' and 'universal' aspects of the carbon commodity: a 'credit' refers to specific emission reductions that are the product of a 'production process embedded in a material context', but in order to facilitate exchange it is treated as a disembodied 'product unrestricted in spatial or temporal mobility' that can be treated as substitutable with any other carbon commodity.[148] Matthew Paterson and Johannes Stripple refer to this as the difference between 'boutique carbon', where there might be an explicit relationship between buyer and seller or a focus on 'virtue of particular reductions' and associated co-benefits, as compared to 'Walmart carbon', wherein the units become financialised and are traded as an

---

[143] J. Whitington, 'The prey of uncertainty: Climate change as opportunity' (2012) 12(1/2) *Ephemera: Theory and Politics in Organisation* 113–37 at 118–19.

[144] L. Lohmann, 'Carbon trading, climate justice and the production of ignorance: Ten examples' (2008) 51 *Development* 359–65.

[145] K. Polanyi, *The Great Transformation: The Political and Economic Origins of Our Time* (Beacon Press, 2001).

[146] P. Newell and M. Paterson, *Climate Capitalism: Global Warming and the Transformation of the Global Economy* (Cambridge University Press, 2010) p. 142.

[147] See for example A. Kossoy and P. Ambrosi, *State and Trends of the Carbon Market 2010* (World Bank, 2010) and my analysis; J. Dehm, 'Tricks of perception and perspective: The disappearance of law and politics in carbon markets; Reading Alexandre Kossoy and Phillippe Ambrosi, "State and trends of the carbon market 2010"' (2011) 7(2) *Macquarie Journal of International and Comparative Environmental Law* 1–18.

[148] J. Knox-Hayes, 'The spatial and temporal dynamics of value in financialization: Analysis of the infrastructure of carbon markets' (2013) 50 *Geoforum* 117–28 at 123.

D. REDD+ through the Lens of Property

'"empty" unit, detached from climate mitigation as ethical duty', including, in even more abstracted ways, as derivatives (including options, swaps and bond) or arbitrage.[149] This tension resurfaces therefore in alternative imperatives underpinning how carbon markets should be governed: whether there should be increased regulatory measures to guarantee the authenticity of specific credits or whether governance mechanisms should assume greater commensurability between credits in order to facilitate faster transactions.

Finally, the carbon commodity is an 'object' that is entirely constituted and produced by law: its existence and its value depend upon political agreements and legal regulations, as well as public faith in those regulatory arrangements. As Charlotte Streck and Jolene Lin write:

> [C]ompared to traditional commodities markets, the success of a market in carbon rights is more dependent on investor confidence in the robustness of the market and the regulatory framework, simply because the creation, authenticity and consequent value of the commodity in question are entirely dependent upon the regulatory framework.[150]

In addition, to public regulatory frameworks that constitute this novel commodity, a whole network of private certification schemes has developed in order to 'provide stakeholders with an independent guarantee of environmental sustainability and credibility'.[151] Due to the intangible nature of the carbon commodity, a rights holder is not in possession of something physical but rather a certificate that 'is a representation by the issuer of the certificate that an emission reduction in the terms described in the certificate has occurred'.[152] Law and regulation thus play a particularly crucial role in generating confidence that the certificate actually represents that which it purports to represent, that is, 'good title to a commodity of substance, namely genuine carbon credits'; they guarantee that carbon credits have both a 'value' and a 'proper foundation'.[153]

---

[149] M. Paterson and J. Stripple, 'Virtuous carbon' (2012) 21(4) *Environmental Politics* 563–82 at 570.

[150] C. Streck and J. Lin, 'Making markets work: A review of CDM performance and the need for reform' (2008) 19(2) *The European Journal of International Law* 409–42 at 420–1.

[151] Abyd Karmail, of Merrill Lynch, cited in Newell and Paterson, *Climate Capitalism: Global Warming and the Transformation of the Global Economy*, p. 123. Such certification schemes include the Gold Standard, The Voluntary Carbon Standard, Green e-Climate, the Climate, Community & Biodiversity Standard, the Chicago Climate Exchange, Plan Vivo, Greenhouse Friendly VER+, ISO14064, Voluntary Offset Standard, Social Carbon and more.

[152] I take this phrasing from *Shift2Neutral Pty Limited v Fairfax Media Publications Pty Limited* [2014] NSWSC 86 (18 February 2014), para 21; see also *Shift2Neutral Pty Ltd v Fairfax Media Publications Pty Ltd* [2015] NSWCA 274 (10 September 2015). This was a defamation case regarding claims in newspaper articles that carbon credits sold by Shift2Neutral were worthless, and thus the court had to consider whether the carbon offset certificates actually represented 'real' emission reductions.

[153] I take this phrasing from *Shift2Neutral Pty Limited v Fairfax Media Publications Pty Limited* [2014] NSWSC 86, para 44 and 48. This problem of the 'genuineness' of carbon credits, or more abstractly of the authenticity of their foundation, is increasingly recognised as a problem for law enforcement more generally, with carbon fraud emerging as a potential form of white collar crime; see *Carbon Credit Fraud: The White Collar Crime of the Future* (Deloitte, 2009).

2 Initial Distribution and Unequal Allocation of Emission Allowances

The international climate regime enabled an unequal initial allocation and distribution of emission allowances, which has ongoing implications for the international political economy of carbon markets. The analysis below builds on critiques of how carbon trading represents the 'privatization of the atmosphere',[154] but focuses how the process of initially allocating of emission allowances favoured the Global North over the Global South, because of the way the regime was established and how the allocation of emission allowances favoured historical polluters. In classical international law approaches, air (along with the high seas) was conceived as being *res communis* (that is, a common thing) on account of its being limitless and therefore available for the use of all.[155] Climate science has, however, conclusively demonstrated clear limits to the atmosphere's capacity to absorb GHGs and/or waste gases, and the key struggles around the drafting of the Kyoto Protocol concerned how to distribute the total 'carbon budget' between countries.[156] The Kyoto Protocol thus provided that developed countries should take the lead and that:

> The Parties included in Annex I shall, individually or jointly, ensure that their aggregate anthropogenic carbon dioxide equivalent emissions of the greenhouse gases listed in Annex A do not exceed their assigned amounts, calculated pursuant to their quantified emission limitation and reduction commitments inscribed in Annex B and in accordance with the provisions of this Article, with a view to reducing their overall emissions of such gases by at least 5 per cent below 1990 levels in the commitment period 2008 to 2012.[157]

Further, the Protocol provided that Parties included in Annex B may 'participate in emissions trading for the purposes of fulfilling their commitments under Article 3' by transferring 'parts of assigned amounts' to one another, provided that such trading is 'supplemental' to domestic action.[158]

The articulation of quantified emission limitation and reduction commitments (QELRCs) within a regime where emissions units have become tradable rights, does not just impose restrictions but operates to simultaneously establish the *entitlement* of Parties included in Annex B to emit their assigned amount (which is a certain percentage of their base year, generally 1990 emissions). Although the Marrakech Accords state that the rules have 'not created or bestowed any right, title or entitlement

---

[154] See for example G. Torres, 'Who owns the sky' (2001) 19 *Pace Environmental Law Review* 515.

[155] H. Grotius, *Mare Liberum: Free Sea or a Dissertation on the Right which the Dutch Have to Carry on Indian Trade* (Brill, 1609) p. 28.

[156] See R. Felli, 'On climate rent' (2014) 22(2–3) *Historical Materialism* 251–80 at 261.

[157] *Kyoto Protocol to the United Nations Framework Convention on Climate Change*, opened for signature 16 March 1998, 2303 UNTS 148 (entered into force on 16 February 2005), Article 3.1.

[158] *Kyoto Protocol*, Article 17.

D. REDD+ through the Lens of Property 197

to emissions of any kind on Parties included in Annex I',[159] they cannot through such an utterance performatively prevent property rights being created by this regulatory regime.[160] This clause, as Matthieu Wemaere, Charlotte Streck and Thiago Chagas write, 'needs to be understood in the political context of the Kyoto Protocol' – specifically the need to affirm politically that the Kyoto Protocol does not formally create 'rights to emission or the atmosphere' but only 'the right to a defined pollution in a defined timeframe' and that allocation of units does not therefore formally 'grandfather any future authorizations to emit a certain quantity of pollutants'.[161] Despite the clear political imperative to avoid any suggestion that countries of the Global North were granted property rights or entitlements to emit by taking on QERLCs, experts agree that resulting 'assigned amount units' (AAUs) can be 'regarded as a mixture of a sovereign right (to be used to fulfil an international obligation) and a public property right of an Annex B government (to make use of the value of its assigned units, for instance, by selling them to another Annex B party'.[162] Therefore, although Parties' QERLCs should become more ambitious in subsequent commitment periods, for the duration of the first commitment period at least, the regime established not only limits on emissions but also – simultaneously – established the 'constitution of public entitlements to emit greenhouse gases'.[163]

At COP 18 in 2012, Parties to the Kyoto Protocol adopted an amendment to the Protocol to allow for a second commitment period from 2013 to 2020.[164] The amendment allowed Annex I countries to revisit their QELRCs for the second commitment period.[165] In order to ensure that QERLCs for the second commitment period represented an increase of ambition compared to the QERLCs for the first commitment periods, the relevant COP decision stated that Parties 'shall either adjust the calculation of its assigned amount or cancel, upon the establishment of its assigned amount, a number of AAUs equivalent to the decrease in its quantified emission limitation and reduction commitment'.[166] However, this decision also allows for the carryover of any surplus credits from the first commitment period

---

[159] Decision 15/CP.7 'Principles, nature and scope of the mechanisms pursuant to Articles 6, 12 and 17 of the Kyoto Protocol', FCCC/CP/2001/13/Add.2 (21 January 2002), preambular recital 5; this language is reiterated in the preamble of Decision 2/CMP.1 'Principles, nature and scope of the mechanisms pursuant to Article 6, 12 and 17 of the Kyoto Protocol', FCCC/KP/CMP/2005/8/Add.1 (30 March 2006).

[160] B. Yandle, 'Grasping for the heavens: 3-D property rights and the global commons' (1999) 10(1) *Duke Environmental Law and Policy Forum* 14–44.

[161] Wemaere et al., 'Legal ownership and nature of Kyoto units and EU allowances', p. 45.

[162] Ibid., p. 43.

[163] Felli, 'On climate rent', 254.

[164] *Doha Amendment to the Kyoto Protocol*, adopted 8 December 2012, UNTS XXVII.7.c (entered into force 31 December 2020); Decision 1/CMP.8, 'Amendment to the Kyoto Protocol pursuant to its Article 3, paragraph 9 (the Doha Amendment)', FCCC/KP/CMP/2012/13/Add.1 (28 February 2013).

[165] Decision 1/CMP.8, para 7.

[166] Decision 1/CMP.8, para 8.

into the second commitment period.[167] This is significant given that almost all Annex I countries ended the first commitment period with surplus credits; indeed, this oversupply of credits raised serious concerns about the environmental integrity of the system.[168] This ability to carry over credits from the first commitment period therefore means that the initial allocations in the regime created rights to pollute over an extended timeframe.[169]

In practice the initial allocation of rights and obligations had the effect of creating an 'unequal distribution of these entitlements amongst states',[170] a situation that advantaged states with high levels of GHG emissions in their base year (generally 1990).[171] Farhana Yamin notes that '[b]y requiring only modest cuts from current emissions levels (and in some cases allowing increases), the Kyoto targets appear to sanction grandfathering as a formula for allocating emissions' – an approach that gives developed countries 'considerable advantages because it sanctions their high levels of current emissions' and works to the disadvantage of developing countries.[172] This process of so-called grandfathering, Romain Felli argues, 'ensured that the distribution of entitlements amongst countries favoured the wealthiest and most "polluting" countries: those with the highest amount of emissions received the largest amount of entitlements to emit'.[173] Similarly, Diana Liverman notes that '[b]ecause the baseline for reductions was based on emissions in 1990 the atmosphere was effectively "enclosed" according to pollution levels in 1990': this affirmed and endorsed 'prior appropriation' such that 'those who first polluted the atmosphere then [would] acquire a right to pollute under international law'.[174] This approach, based on 'grandfathering', differs sharply from other principles that could be used to

---

[167] Decision 1/CMP.8, para 24.

[168] *Carry-Over of AAUs from the CP1 to CP2 – Future Implications for the Climate Regime* (Point Carbon, 2012).

[169] At the time of writing no formal decision had been reached on whether such carry-over of credits could be used towards commitments under the Paris Agreement. Although such use had been rejected by many countries, Australia was controversially seeking to use Kyoto 'carry over credits' towards its Paris Agreement commitments, although has subsequently committed not to; see Graham Readfearn and Adam Morton, 'Australia is the only country using carryover climate credits, officials admit' *The Guardian*, 22 October 2019, www.theguardian.com/environ ment/2019/oct/22/australia-is-the-only-country-using-carryover-climate-credits-officials-admit.

[170] Felli, 'On Climate rent', 254.

[171] *Kyoto Protocol*, Article 3.5, provided that countries included in Annex I that were undergoing the process of transition to a market economy could use base years as established in Decision 9/CP.2, or where they had not yet submitted their first national communication to the Convention, such countries could notify the COP that it intended to use an historical base year or period other than 1990 for the implementation of its commitments.

[172] F. Yamin, 'Equity, entitlements and property rights under the Kyoto Protocol: The shape of "things" to come', (1999) 8(3) *Review of European, Comparative & International Environmental Law* 265–74 at 267.

[173] Felli, 'On Climate rent', 262.

[174] D. M. Liverman, 'Conventions of climate change: Constructions of danger and the dispossession of the atmosphere' (2009) 35(2) *Journal of Historical Geography* 279–96 at 294.

D. REDD+ *through the Lens of Property*

determine allocations, such as claims of equal per capita rights to emit GHGs,[175] or frameworks such as greenhouse development rights, in which the allocation of obligations is based on considerations of both responsibility (contribution to the problem) and capacity (ability to pay), as well as a 'right to development'[176] or the application of the 'polluter pays' principle in relation to historical emissions.[177] In contrast to these latter approaches, which are based on consideration of equality or equity, 'grandfathering' favours those countries who have historically been the main polluters. Farhana Yamin suggests the grandfathering approach reflects 'two traditional legal principles regulating the appropriation of things and territory historically favoured by [countries of the Global North]': firstly that 'whoever possesses as territory and exercises actual control over it acquires a legal title'; and secondly, where something is consider *terra nullius* 'the "first come-first served" principles establishes title, provided there is an actual display of sovereignty and authority'.[178] Therefore, although many commentators argued that the key problem with the Kyoto Protocol was that it allowed 'the underdeveloped world ... to continue to emit with impunity',[179] because non-Annex I countries, pursuant to the principle of common but differentiated responsibilities (CBDR) were not required to commit to emission reductions, arguably a more problematic effect of the Kyoto Protocol was that it constitutionalised an unequal and inequitable allocation of rights to emit that favoured the historical polluters of the Global North. Although, countries of the Global South were excluded from immediate ER obligations, as Felli notes, 'they agreed to a principle of GHG emission rights distribution ('grandfathering') that would be disadvantageous to them, should they be subjected to it in the future'.[180]

The hybrid system established by the Kyoto Protocol does not simply permit the trading of allowances but also provides for the production of allowances or credits from activities considered to represent 'saved' or 'prevented' emissions. These two mechanisms are the 'Joint Implementation' authorised by Article 6,[181] and the 'Clean Development Mechanism' authorised by Article 12.[182] Article 12 authorises

---

[175] D. Miller, *Global Justice and Climate Change: How Should Responsibilities Be Distributed?* (2008) p. 138; see also R. W. Salzman, 'Distributing emission rights in the global order: The case for equal per capita allocation' (2010) 13 *Yale Human Rights and Development Journal* 281–306.

[176] P. Baer, G. Fieldman, T. Athanasiou, and S. Kartha, 'Greenhouse development rights: Towards an equitable framework for global climate policy' (2008) 21(4) *Cambridge Review of International Affairs* 649–69.

[177] F. Yamin, 'Equity, entitlements and property rights under the Kyoto Protocol: The shape of "things" to come', 270.

[178] Ibid.

[179] Yandle, 'Grasping for the heavens', 39; see also D. Campbell, M. Klaes, and C. Bignell, 'After Copenhagen: The impossibility of carbon trading' (2010) 22 *LSE Law, Society and Economy Working Papers*.

[180] Felli, 'On Climate rent', 263.

[181] *Kyoto Protocol*, Article 6, see also Articles 3.10 and 3.11.

[182] *Kyoto Protocol*, Article 12, see also Article 3.12.

the creation of certified emission reductions (CERs) from projects located in non-Annex I countries, provided the ERs resulting from each project represent 'real, measurable and long-term benefits related to the mitigation of climate change'[183] and that such reductions are 'additional to any that would occur in the absence of the certified project activity'.[184] The objectives of the CDM are to deliver globally aggregate and symbiotic benefits; to assist in 'achieving sustainable development' in non-Annex I countries, while also assisting Annex I parties to achieve compliance in the most cost-effective manner by allowing 'certified emission reductions accruing from such projects to contribute to compliance'.[185] The voluntary participation[186] of both 'producing' and 'purchasing' countries should '[contribute] to the ultimate objective of the Convention'.[187] The CDM depends upon a complex regulatory infrastructure, including a supervisory Executive Board[188] as well as validation and verification by private 'Operational Entities'.[189] Such emission credits are of private 'origin', and generated by private actors, but come into existence through the issuance of the Executive Board, based on the independent verification report.[190] Article 6 allows an Annex I party to 'transfer to, or acquire from' emission reduction units (ERUs) that result from 'projects aimed at reducing anthropogenic emissions by sources' or 'enhancing anthropocentric removals by sinks of greenhouse gases' located in another Annex I country, provided that such projects have the approval of all Parties involved and provide a 'reduction in emissions by sources, or an enhancement of removals by sinks, that is additional to any that would otherwise occur'.[191] Such Joint Implementation ERUs represent 'a hybrid between an allowance and an emission credit'.[192]

Detailed rules and modality for all these mechanisms were set out in the Marrakech Accords agreed to at COP7 in 2001.[193] The Marrakech Accords also legally defined and codified various different carbon trading units, issued pursuant to specific rules, including the 'emission reduction unit' (ERU), the 'certified emission reduction' (CER), the 'assigned amount unit' (AAU) and the 'removal unit' (RMU), specifying that each was 'equal to one metric tonne of carbon dioxide

---

[183] *Kyoto Protocol*, Article 12.5(b).

[184] *Kyoto Protocol*, Article 12.5(c).

[185] *Kyoto Protocol*, Articles 12.2 and 12.3(b).

[186] *Kyoto Protocol*, Article 12.5(a).

[187] *Kyoto Protocol*, Article 12.2.

[188] Subject of course to the 'authority and guidance of the Conference of the Parties serving as the Meeting of the Parties to this Protocol' Article 12.4.

[189] *Kyoto Protocol*, Article 12.5.

[190] Wemaere et al., 'Legal ownership and nature of Kyoto units and EU allowances', pp. 43–4.

[191] *Kyoto Protocol*, Article 6.1(b).

[192] Wemaere et al., 'Legal ownership and nature of Kyoto units and EU allowances', p. 44.

[193] Decisions 1–39/CP.7, FCCC/CP/2001/13/Add.1–4 (21 January 2002), these decisions were later confirmed at the first Conference of the Parties serving as the meeting of the Parties to the Kyoto Protocol (CMP) in 2005.

D. REDD+ *through the Lens of Property*

equivalent'.[194] Subsequent decisions confirmed that afforestation and deforestation activities under the CDM were only able to generate temporary credits – either temporary Certified Emission Reductions (tCERs) or long-term Certified Emission Reductions (lCERs) – which were therefore not strictly fungible with other credits.[195] Overall, the Kyoto Protocol established an initial allocation that benefits countries of the Global North whilst also positioning countries of the Global South as producers of carbon credits to satisfy demand from the Global North. This framework had ongoing implications for the political economy of carbon markets, even as the international climate regime gradually transformed away from the 'top down' architecture of the Kyoto Protocol towards the more decentralised 'bottom up' approach of the Paris Agreement.

3 Carbon Units in a More Decentralised Climate Regime

There has been a progressive transformation of the UNFCCC regime away from a 'top-down' legal architecture consisting of aggregate, legally binding ER targets informed by climate science, allocated according to principles of distributive justice. What has emerged in its place is a decentralised 'bottom-up' pledge and review framework, where countries put forward their 'nationally determined contributions' (NDCs) on the basis of their own 'national interests'. This more 'bottom-up' approach, organised around more flexible nationally determined targets, is complemented by international norms to promote transparency and accountability and encourage increased ambition. Even as the overall architecture of the international climate regime has transformed from Kyoto to Paris, the 'carbon commodity' continues to play a key role as it allows for interlinkages between actions in different Parties through the possibility of trading standardised carbon units.[196]

The beginning of a shift away from the 'top down' Kyoto approach of internationally negotiated emission reductions towards a more 'bottom up' approach where countries put forward their own nationally determined contributions (NDCs) is observed in the Bali Action Plan (COP13, 2007).[197] This shift also represented a transformation from a contractual or prescriptive function for the regime towards a new facilitative function that 'starts from what countries are doing

---

[194] Decision 17/CP.7, 'Modalities and procedures for a Clean Development Mechanism, as defined in Article 12 of the Kyoto Protocol', FCCC/CP/2001/13/Add.2 (21 January 2002), Annex.

[195] Decision 19/CP.9, 'Modalities and procedures for afforestation and reforestation project activities under the Clean Development Mechanism in the first commitment period of the Kyoto Protocol', FCCC/CP/2003/6/Add.2 (30 March 2004) and Decision 5/CMP.1.

[196] J. D Macinante, 'Operationalizing cooperative approaches under the Paris Agreement by valuing mitigation outcomes' (2018) 12(3) *Carbon & Climate Law Review* 258–71.

[197] Decision 1/CP.13, 'Bali Action Plan', FCCC/CP/2007/6/Add.1 (14 March 2008) ('Bali Action Plan').

on their own, and seeks to find ways to reinforce and encourage these',[198] or a move away from a focus on 'compliance' towards 'incentiv[ising] action'.[199] The Bali Action Plan launched a 'comprehensive process to enable the full, effective and sustained implementation of the Convention through long-term cooperative action'.[200] This was tasked to the Ad Hoc Working Group on Long-term Cooperative Action (AWG-LCA), and the outcomes of this work stream, alongside that of the Ad Hoc Working Group on Further Commitments for Annex I Parties under the Kyoto Protocol (AWG-KP),[201] were intended to help form the basis of a post-Kyoto agreement at Copenhagen (COP15, 2009). The Bali Action Plan committed Parties to agreeing to 'a shared vision for long-term co-operative action' in accordance with and in order to achieve the Convention objections that also addressed 'enhanced' action on mitigation, adaptation, technology development, transfer and provision of financial resources and investment to support action on mitigation and adaptation.[202] It was under the heading of 'enhanced national/ international action on mitigation of climate change' that REDD+ clearly became part of the official UNFCCC agenda.[203]

In 2009 the highly controversial Copenhagen Accord (that was 'noted' by, but not approved by, the COP)[204] set a political goal of limiting warming to 2 degrees Celsius, but it also introduced a more 'bottom up' architecture.[205] The Accord is structured around a 'pledge and review' system through which Annex I countries 'commit to implement individually or jointly the quantified economy-wide emissions targets for 2020' and non-Annex I countries 'will implement mitigation actions' as well.[206] This 'pledge and review' structure was formally adopted the

---

[198] D. Bodansky, *The Durban Platform Negotiations: Goals and Options* (Harvard Project on Climate Agreements, 2012).

[199] See for example D. Bodansky, 'A tale of two architectures: The once and future UN climate change regime' (2011) 43 *Arizona State Law Journal* 697–712.

[200] Bali Action Plan, para 1.

[201] The AWG-KP was mandated to 'initiate a process to consider further commitments' at Montreal (2005), Decision 1/CMP.1 'Consideration of commitments for subsequent periods for Parties included in Annex I to the Convention under Article 3, paragraph 9, of the Kyoto Protocol', FCCC/KP/CMP/2005/8/Add.1 (30 March 2006).

[202] Bali Action Plan, para 1(b)–(e).

[203] Bali Action Plan, para 1(b)(iii). The other forms of mitigation actions the Bali Action Plan agreed to consider were: (i) quantified emission limitation and reduction objective for developed country parties; (ii) nationally appropriate mitigation actions (NAMAs) by developing country Parties; (iv) cooperative sectoral approaches and sector-specific actions; (v) various approaches, including opportunities for using markets, to enhance the cost-effectiveness of, and to promote, mitigation actions; (vi) economic and social consequences of response measures; and (vii) ways to strengthen the catalytic role of the Convention. See Chapter 1 for a more detailed discussion.

[204] Decision 2/CP.15, 'Copenhagen Accord', FCCC/CP/2009/11/Add.1 (30 March 2010) ('Copenhagen Accord').

[205] Copenhagen Accord, para 2.

[206] Copenhagen Accord, paras 4 and 5.

D. REDD+ through the Lens of Property

following year in the Cancun Agreements, which 'note' the 'quantified economy-wide emission reduction targets' that were communicated by Annex I countries and urged them to increase their ambition.[207] The Cancun Agreements also decided to enhance reporting requirements, guidelines and information review processes and international assessment processes.[208]

This transformation in the architectural framework of the international climate regime was contentious. For example, the 2011 inter-sessional meeting prior to COP17 in Durban was described as 'tumultuous', after a 'stark challenge' was posed from developing to developed countries about the future of the Kyoto Protocol.[209] The Philippines negotiator colourfully noted that the Kyoto Protocol was in 'intensive care' and, 'instead of oxygen, is being fed a supply of carbon dioxide'.[210] The surprise, 36-hour-delayed outcome of the COP17 (2011), the Durban Platform for Enhanced Action, was an artfully worded agreement to launch 'a process to develop a protocol, another legal instrument or an agreed outcome with legal force under the Convention applicable to all Parties' to come into effect and be implemented by 2020.[211] This work, which was to be concluded before COP21 in 2015, was tasked to the Ad Hoc Working Group on the Durban Platform of Enhanced Action (ADP).[212] The ADP agenda comprised two work-programs: (1) development a post-2020 agreement[213] and (2) addressing pre-2020 levels of ambition, given growing concern about the 'significant gap' between aggregate mitigation pledges and pathways consistent with holding the increase in global temperature to 1.5 or 2 degrees Celsius.[214]

At Doha (COP18, 2012), alongside an agreement to amend the Kyoto Protocol to enable a second commitment period, the 'determination' to adopt a post-2020 agreement was reiterated and a decision was made that the ADP would 'consider

---

[207] Decision 1/CP.16 'The Cancun Agreements: Outcome of the work of the Ad Hoc Working Group on Long-term Cooperative Action under the Convention', FCCC/CP/2010/7/Add.1 (15 March 2011), paras 36 and 37 ('Cancun Agreements').

[208] Cancun Agreements, paras 40–4. In Durban biannual reporting guidelines for developed country parties were developed (Decision 2/CP.17 'Outcome of the work of the Ad Hoc Working Group on Long-term Cooperative Action under the Convention' FCCC/CP/2011/9/Add.1 (15 March 2012), paras 12-22 and Annex I) and modalities for international assessment and review adopted (Decision 2/CP.17, paras 23–32 and Annex II).

[209] Third World Network, 'Bangkok Climate News Updates' (April 2011), www.twnside.org.sg/title2/climate/news/bangkok03/bkk3_news_up04.pdf.

[210] Ibid.

[211] Decision 1/CP.17, 'Establishment of an Ad Hoc Working Group on the Durban Platform for Enhanced Action', FCCC/CP/2011/8/Add.2 (15 March 2011), para 2. For a discussion of the politics, compromises and legal implications of the wording of the Durban Platform see L. Rajamani, 'The Durban Platform for Enhanced Action and the future of the climate regime' (2012) 61(2) *International & Comparative Law Quarterly* 501–18.

[212] Decision 1/CP.17, paras 2–4.

[213] Decision 1/CP.17, paras 2–6 for mandate.

[214] Decision 1/CP.17, paras 5–8; see also preambular recital 2.

elements of a draft negotiating text' no later than COP20 in Lima (2014).[215] At Warsaw (COP19, 2013) it was confirmed that draft text of the post-2020 agreement should include elements on mitigation, adaptation, finance, technology development and transfer, capacity-building and transparency of action and support.[216] Parties were invited to 'initiate or intensify domestic preparation for their intended nationally determined contribution' (INDC), without prejudgement as to their legal nature, towards a post-2020 agreement by the first quarter of 2015.[217] The Lima Call for Climate Action and the 'Elements for a Draft Negotiating Text' included in its Annex reiterated the invitation to Parties to communicate their INDC and confirmed that such nationally determined contributions (NDCs) would be key to the architecture and arrangements of the post-2020 agreement.[218] It was also agreed that each Parties' INDC should 'represent a progression beyond the current undertaking of that Party',[219] that INDCs could include both mitigation and adaptation components,[220] and that they should be communicated in a manner that facilitates 'clarity, transparency and understanding'.[221] Most of the academic commendatory that analysed this shift to a framework where countries put forward their own nationally determined commitments was generally optimistic that this facilitative 'bottom-up' regime offered possibilities for incentivising ambitious action.[222] However, many civil society groups were scathing about the Lima Outcome, dubbing it a 'Roadmap to Global Burning', because they feared, based on projections, it could lead to the catastrophic outcome of 4 degrees of temperature increase.[223]

The Paris Agreement, agreed to in 2015, adopts a hybrid architecture with 'bottom up' nationally determined commitments (NDCs) put forward by all countries, which are, however, 'complemented by international norms to ensure transparency and accountability and to prod states to progressively ratchet up their efforts'.[224] The Agreement also adopts a hybrid legal form: although it is a legally binding instrument, it also includes many non-binding elements.[225] Each country is legally

---

[215] Decision 2/CP.18, 'Advancing the Durban Platform', FCCC/CP/2012/8/Add.1 (28 February 2013), paras 4 and 9.
[216] Decision 1/CP.19, 'Further advancing the Durban Platform', FCCC/CP/2013/10/Add.1 (31 January 2014), para 2(a).
[217] Decision 1/CP.19, para 2(b).
[218] Decision 1/CP.20, 'Lima call for climate action', FCCC/CP/2014/10/Add.1 (2 February 2015) and Annex, 'Elements of a draft negotiating text'.
[219] Decision 1/CP.20, para 10.
[220] Decision 1/CP.20, para 12.
[221] Decision 1/CP.20, paras 13 and 14.
[222] D. Bodansky, *Durban Platform: Issues and Options for a 2015 Agreement* (Centre for Climate and Energy Solutions, 2012); Bodansky, *The Durban Platform Negotiations: Goals and Options*; Bodansky, 'A tale of two architectures'.
[223] See C. Lang, 'More reactions to COP20 and Lima's "Roadmap to global burning"', *REDD-Monitor*, 2 January 2015.
[224] D. Bodansky, 'The Paris Climate Change Agreement: A new hope?' (2016) 110(2) *American Journal of International Law* 288–319 at 289.
[225] Ibid., 290.

D. REDD+ through the Lens of Property

required to 'prepare, communicate and maintain successive nationally determined contributions that it intends to achieve', although none is legally required to achieve these stated targets.[226] There are two main consequences of this more decentralised approach to mitigation commitments.[227] Firstly, the aggregate effect of all the Parties' NDCs is insufficient to meet the stated objectives of the Agreement, namely to 'hold the increase in global average temperature to well below 2 °C' and 'pursu[e] efforts to limit the temperature increase to 1.5 °C'.[228] Indeed, the commitments put forward by Parties, even if implemented fully, would lead to a warming of 2.7–3.4 degrees Celsius.[229] Although, successive NDCs should represent a 'progression beyond' earlier targets and reflect the 'highest possible ambition'[230] and periodic stock-take to assess collective progress towards achieving the objectives of the Agreement provide a means for assessing 'the collective progress toward achieving the purposes of this Agreement',[231] these gaps are highly concerning, especially in a context where the 'emission gap' is large, and achieving the 1.5-degree Celsius objective is quickly slipping out of reach.[232] Secondly, this more decentralised approach means there is no framework for determining whether countries' contributions reflect their 'fair share' of mitigation effort, and a number of studies have found that many, if not all, developed countries are contributing less than what would be equitable considering their contribution to cumulative emissions and their capacity to take action.[233]

The Paris Agreement has been welcomed by Carbon Pulse as 'ring[ing] in a new era of international carbon trading'.[234] The Director of the IETA likewise described it as 'set[ting] up the framework for a much deeper world of cooperation'[235] on carbon markets. In its response to the Paris Agreement, the World Bank promised to 'explor[e] ways to create incentives for large scale cuts in emissions by widening and

---

[226] *Paris Agreement*, Article 4.2.

[227] See also J. Dehm, 'Reflections on Paris: Thoughts towards a critical approach to climate law' (2018) *Revue québécoise de droit international* 61–91.

[228] *Paris Agreement*, Article 2.1(a).

[229] UNFCCC, *Synthesis Report on the Aggregate Effects of the Intended Nationally Determined Contributions: Note by the Secretariat*, FCCC/CP/2015/7 (30 October 2015).

[230] *Paris Agreement*, Article 4.3.

[231] *Paris Agreement*, Article 14.1.

[232] *Emissions Gap Report 2019* (United Nations Environment Programme, 2019).

[233] *Fair Shares: A Civil Society Equity Review of INDCS. Report* (CSO Equity Review Coalition, 2015); G. P. Peters, R. M. Andrew, S. Solomon, and P. Friedlingstein, 'Measuring a fair and ambitious climate agreement using cumulative emissions' (2015) 10 *Environmental Research Letters* 105004; J. D. McBee, 'Distributive justice in the Paris Climate Agreement: Response to Peters et al.' (2017) 9(1) *Contemporary Readings in Law and Social Justice* 120–31. These concerns are discussed in greater detail in Chapter 4.

[234] M. Szabo, 'Paris Agreement rings in new era of international carbon trading', *Carbon Pulse*, 12 December 2015, carbon-pulse.com/13339/.

[235] M. Szabo, 'After Paris, UN's new "light touch" role on markets to help spawn carbon clubs', *Carbon Pulse*, 15 December 2015, carbon-pulse.com/13415/.

deepening carbon markets'.[236] Over half the NDCs put forward by Parties state that they intend to use or will consider using carbon trading mechanisms,[237] suggesting that carbon trading will continue to be utilised as key tool for achieving climate mitigation.[238] The words 'carbon trading' or 'carbon markets' are not explicitly mentioned in the Paris Agreement; however, Article 6 provides for 'voluntary cooperation in the implementation' of NDCs in order to 'allow for higher ambition in their mitigation and adaptation actions' and also 'promote sustainable development and environmental integrity'.[239] Article 6 sets out three different approaches that reflect more 'decentralized' as well as 'centralised' ways of organising carbon trading alongside non-market approaches. Firstly, Article 6.2 provides that countries are allowed to trade 'internationally transferred mitigation outcomes' (ITMOs), provided this also promotes sustainable development, environmental integrity and transparency.[240] Such trades are subject to 'robust accounting' to avoid double counting, which at the time of writing had not yet been finalised. This language of 'cooperative approaches' suggests a more decentralised model of bilateral and multilateral linking between so-called carbon clubs in order to trade units of carbon, or ITMOs.[241] Article 6.2 has a strong 'bottom up flavour' and 'displays the overriding logic of the Paris Agreement – a bottom up process whereby those countries – or entities – wishing to participate in internationally transferred mitigation outcomes can do so'.[242] While there is still at the time of writing no clear agreed definition of ITMOs, the negotiating text calls for the expression of those units in terms of $1tCO_2e$ (as well as some additional options),[243] and the IETA favours adopting $1tCO_2e$ as the 'universal metric to measure ITMOs'.[244]

---

[236] '"Historic" Paris Agreement paves way for World Bank to help countries deliver on climate commitments', *World Bank*, 12 December 2015, www.worldbank.org/en/news/feature/2015/12/12/paris-agreement-paves-way-for-world-bank-group-helping-countries-deliver-on-climate-commitments.

[237] G. Bryant, 'Climate Change: Back to the Market or … ?', *Progress in Political Economy*, 24 November 2014, ppesydney.net/climate-change-back-to-the-market-or/.

[238] S. Böhm, 'How emissions trading at Paris climate talks has set us up for failure', *The Conversation*, 15 December 2015, theconversation.com/how-emissions-trading-at-paris-climate-talks-has-set-us-up-for-failure-52319.

[239] *Paris Agreement*, Article 6.1.

[240] *Paris Agreement*, Article 6.2.

[241] *Paris Agreement*, Articles 6.2 and 6.3.

[242] R. R. Bhandary, 'Trying to eat an elephant (again)': Opportunities and challenges in international cooperative approaches of the Paris Agreement' (2018) 12(3) *Carbon & Climate Law Review* at 240.

[243] Ibid., 241; see also S. Evans and J. Gabbatiss, 'COP25: Key outcomes agreed at the UN climate talks in Madrid' *Carbon Brief*, 15 December 2019, www.carbonbrief.org/cop25-key-outcomes-agreed-at-the-un-climate-talks-in-madrid

[244] International Emission Trading Association, *Key Design Options for Article 6: IETA Priorities* (April 2018), www.ieta.org/resources/International_WG/2018/Key%20design%20priorities%20for%20Article%206.pdf.

D. REDD+ through the Lens of Property

Secondly, Article 6.4 establishes a new 'mechanism to contribute to the mitigation of greenhouse gas emissions and contribute to sustainable development' that is established under the authority, guidance and supervision of the Conference of the Parties serving as the meeting of the Parties to the Paris Agreement (CMA).[245] This 'Sustainable Development Mechanism' is flagged to replace the 'Clean Development Mechanism' (CDM).[246] It shall aim to contribute to emission reductions in host Parties whilst allowing another Party to use any resulting emission reductions towards the fulfilment of its own NDCs while also 'deliver[ing] an overall mitigation in global emissions' and to 'incentivise and facilitate' participation in mitigation activities by public and private entities.[247] The purpose of this mechanisms is not just to offset emissions but to 'obtain an actual deviation in global emissions': in the provisions at least, cost-effectiveness and ambition are 'intrinsically linked'.[248] The scope of this mechanism also is much broader than the CDM, as it does not assume the same North–South bifurcation: instead, any country can either host abatement activities or use outcomes towards compliance.[249] Additionally, it is likely to move beyond the project-based offsets of the CDM to also include 'sectoral' offsets. IETA has stressed that Article 6.4 of the Paris Agreement should generate mitigation units from a number of different activities, including the 'quantification of emissions projected within a sector or sectors covered by the NDC'.[250] In 2010 the World Bank launched a new carbon development fund, the Partnership for Market Readiness, to help major emerging and middle-income economies expand their carbon markets towards sectoral trading.[251] Since then, there have also been sustained critiques of the 'inadequacy of existing mechanisms [namely, CDM and Joint Implementation (JI)] to drive the level of mitigation needed to meet the global climate challenge' and to mobilise the levels of private sector and market support necessary. There have been proposals to create 'new mechanisms operating on a considerably broader level of aggregation than projects or even programs of activities, these operating across entire policy areas, subsectors, sectors or even entire countries'.[252] Such a shift from 'project' to 'sectoral' trading was also one of the recommendations of the High-Level Policy Dialogue, *Climate Change, Carbon Markets and the CDM: A Call for Action*, released in late 2012.[253] Finally, Article 6.8

---

[245] *Paris Agreement*, Article 6.4

[246] S. Zwick, 'The road from Paris: Green lights, speed bumps, and the future of carbon markets' (Ecosystem Marketplace, 2016).

[247] *Paris Agreement*, Article 6.4.

[248] Bhandary, 'Trying to eat an elephant (again)', 241.

[249] Ibid., 240–1.

[250] International Emission Trading Association, *Key Design Options for Article 6*, p. 4.

[251] See also the discussion on sectoral trading in Chapter 4.

[252] UNFCCC, *Synthesis Report on Information on Various Approaches in Enhancing the Cost-Effectiveness of, and Promoting, Mitigation Actions. Note by the Secretariat* FCCC/AWGLCA/2011/4 (30 March 2011), para 19.

[253] *Climate Change, Carbon Markets and the CDM: A Call to Action. Report of the High-Level Panel on the CDM Policy Dialogue* (2012).

also provides for a framework for non-market approaches to sustainable development that are 'integrated, holistic and balanced', an assist in implementing NDCs, promotes ambition, enhances public and private participation and 'enable[s] opportunities for coordination across instruments and relevant institutional arrangements'.[254] At COP24 in Katowice, negotiations agreed on an incomplete 'rulebook' for the implementation of the Paris Agreement.[255] However, consensus could not be reached on draft texts relating to Article 6 and so this was deferred for later consideration.[256] Commentators observed that the Katowice outcome left carbon markets 'intact but incomplete', and noted that although 'carbon clubs' or regional platforms could develop their own guidance, the lack of 'clear global guidance' risked slowing efforts.[257] However, as civil society groups have highlighted, there are real risks that the Article 6.2 markets could repeat earlier failures and trade 'hot air'; for example, if countries' NDCs are too weak, any 'transferred credits will have no value for the climate'.[258] Similarly, the Article 6.4 mechanism risks double counting emissions and creating perverse incentives that hamper ambition and would undermine its stated objective to deliver overall mitigation in global emissions. Additionally, many have highlighted the need to incorporate safeguards and human rights provisions to avoid harmful local impacts arising from such projects.[259]

Overall the trajectory from a top-down to a bottom-up architecture means that even as the *political* organisation of the regime has become more decentralised and the understanding of the 'international' as a space for setting collective goals contesting how mitigation burdens should be distributed based on principles of equity has been gradually dismantled, the *economic* organisation of the regime continues to be organised around ideas of aggregate efficiency, embodied in the carbon commodity. Whilst in the Kyoto Protocol the flexibility mechanisms were

---

[254] *Paris Agreement*, Article 6.8.

[255] For a good summary of the outcomes see S. Evans and J. Timperley, 'COP24: Key outcomes agreed at the UN climate talks in Katowice', *Carbon Brief* 16 December 2018, www.carbonbrief.org/cop24-key-outcomes-agreed-at-the-un-climate-talks-in-katowice; see also IISD Reporting Service, *Katowice Climate Change Conference – December 2018 – Summary & Analysis* (2018); see also H. van Asselt, K. Kulovesi, and M. Mehling, 'Editorial: Negotiating the Paris rulebook: Introduction to the special issue' (2018) 12 *Carbon & Climate Law Review* and the other articles in the special issue.

[256] Decision 8/CMA.1 'Matters relating to Article 6 of the Paris Agreement and paragraphs 36–40 of Decision 1/CP.21', FCCC/PA/CMA/2018/3/Add.1 (19 March 2019).

[257] S. Zwick, 'Katowice climate deal leaves carbon markets intact but incomplete', *Ecosystem Marketplace*, 15 December 2018, www.ecosystemmarketplace.com/articles/carbon-markets-look-set-to-emerge-from-katowice-intact-but-incomplete/.

[258] *Carbon Markets 101: The Ultimate Guide to Carbon Offsetting Mechanisms* (Carbon Market Watch, 2019) p. 6.

[259] R. Webb and J. Wentz, *Human Rights and Article 6 of the Paris Agreement: Ensuring Adequate Protection of Human Rights in the SDM and ITMO Frameworks* (Sabin Center for Climate Change Law, Columbia Law School, 2018); S. Duyck, 'Delivering on the Paris promises? Review of the Paris Agreement's implementing guidelines from a human rights perspective' (2019) 9 *Climate Law* 202–23.

D. REDD+ *through the Lens of Property*

primarily understood as a means to achieve pre-determined QERCLs, in the current framework, considerations about the availability of carbon markets – the possibility of buying or selling credits – are arguably taken into account by many countries when determining their NDCs. Although this relationship is not straightforward, it is often posited that the availability of carbon trading mechanisms can 'lower political resistance to more ambitious targets' and incentivise more ambitious targets,[260] even though it is 'very difficult to establish a clear relationship between the ability to buy cheap carbon credits and a country's willingness to commit to more climate action'.[261] Nonetheless, there is now a much more dynamic relationship between the level of ambition articulated in NDCs and the availability and structure of carbon markets. It is therefore more descriptively accurate to see the regime as an amalgam between formally decentralised 'bottom-up' political commitments and the aggregate, overarching context in which they are made, namely a transnational carbon market that embodies a rationality of aggregate global efficiency. In this way, the 'work of property' – through the carbon commodity – continues to play a key role stabilising and pre-supposing questions of power and authority within that regime.[262]

4 *Inclusion of REDD+ in Post-Paris Markets*

The question of how REDD+ fits within the current carbon trading provisions being developed as part of the Paris Agreement's 'rulebook' remains contentious.[263] Whilst some Parties maintain an opposition to the inclusion of REDD+ in carbon markets (see for example the position taken by Brazil at COP24 in Katowice), commentators have suggested that REDD+ could be included through both the Article 6.2 modalities and the Article 6.4 mechanism. Indeed, some commentators have suggested that no further decisions would be necessary to include REDD+ within the Article 6.2 modalities. In a 2017 paper, 'Issue for Discussion to Operationalise Article 6 of the Paris Agreement' for the International Centre for Trade and Sustainable Development, Andrei Marcu suggests that cooperative approaches such as REDD+ are already within the scope of Articles 6.2 and 6.3.[264] This is the position adopted by the Coalition for Rainforest Nations, who maintain that the existing REDD+ Framework 'extensively addresses environmental and social integrity regarding the implementation of REDD+ activities', and thus '[o]nce REDD+

---

[260] See 'The power of markets to increase ambition: New evidence supports efforts to realize the promise of Paris' (Environmental Defense Fund, 2018).

[261] *Carbon Markets 101: The Ultimate Guide to Carbon Offsetting Mechanisms*, p. 4.

[262] S. McVeigh and S. Pahuja, 'Rival jurisdictions: The promise and loss of sovereignty' in C. Barbour and G. Pavlich (eds.), *After Sovereignty: On the Question of Political Beginnings* (Routledge, 2009) pp. 97–114, 106.

[263] Bhandary, 'Trying to eat an elephant (again)', 246.

[264] A. Marcu, *Issues for Discussion to Operationalise Article 6 of the Paris Agreement* (International Centre for Trade and Sustainable Development, 2017).

results successfully complete the agreed process under the REDD+ Framework and are posted on the UNFCCC's REDD+ Information Hub, those outcomes are fully eligible for international transfer as referred to in Article 6, paragraph 2 and paragraph 3 of the Paris Agreement subject to the avoidance of double counting'.[265] Similarly, in their submission the Republic of Rwanda on behalf of the Member States of the Central African Forestry Commission states the following: 'The rules and procedures and modalities for REDD+ activities are already defined by the Warsaw [F]ramework for REDD+. As such, no new or additional rules, modalities and procedures for REDD+ are needed.'[266] In a subsequent analysis on linking REDD+ with Article 6 provisions, Peter Graham, in a report 'Cooperate Approaches for Supporting REDD+: Linking Article 5 and 6 of the Paris Agreement', also suggests that '[s]o long as Parties to agreements on the international transfer of mitigation outcomes (ITMOs) of REDD+ take the necessary steps to avoid double-counting emission reductions and follow the rules and guidance of the Warsaw Framework, no other international approval for such agreements is necessary'.[267] Although this report's analysis found that no additional agreements are necessary to include REDD+ in Article 6, it proposed that in order to secure broad support for REDD+ and redress concerns that ITMOs may reduce overall ambition, further 'clarity and consistency of information of REDD+ results' will need to be provided.[268] In addition, it has been argued that the Article 6.4 mechanism could incorporate REDD+ or the agriculture forestry and other land-use sector (AFOLU). In their submission, the Versified Carbon Standard (VSC) argues that 'it will be critical for the success of Article 6.4 [of the Paris Agreement] to embrace reductions in the AFOLU [agriculture, forestry and other land use] sector, especially REDD+ given its potential for reducing global emissions and drawing down atmospheric carbon'.[269] Although at the time of writing the question of how that REDD+ will be incorporated in either or both the Article 6.2 modalities and Article 6.4 mechanism and how these arrangements would operate had not yet been finalised, it appears very likely that REDD+ will become a key part of the carbon markets supported by this more decentralised regime.

---

[265] UNFCCC, *Submission of Views by the Democratic Republic of Congo on Behalf of the Coalition for Rainforest Nations on Article 6, Paragraph 2 of the Paris Agreement. Views on Guidance on Cooperative Approaches* (2017).

[266] UNFCCC, *Submission of Views by the Republic of Rwanda on Behalf of the Member States of the Central African Forestry Commission (COMIFAC) on APA Agenda Item 3* (2017).

[267] P. Graham, *Cooperative Approaches for Supporting REDD+: Linking Articles 5 and 6 of the Paris Agreement* (Climate Advisors, 2017) p. 2.

[268] Ibid.

[269] VCS Submission: Operationalizing Article 6 of the Paris Agreement (29 September 2017), www .ieta.org/resources/International_WG/Article6/Portal/VCS%20Submission%20on%20Operationalizing%20Article%206,%2029%20SEP%202017.pdf.

E CONCLUSION

This chapter has shown how the international claim to authority over forested areas in the Global South has been actualised in practice, by focusing on the private law mechanisms – namely property and contract – that structure REDD+. In doing so, this chapter has highlighted the need to examine the co-constitutive operations of both international public law and international private law and how the two work together to establish new forms of authority in the so-called green economy. REDD+ arrangements are underpinned by transnational carbon contracting; however, the viability of these forms of private contractual ordering depends upon the emission reductions transferred by such contracts being defined and recognised as a form of quasi-property in international and national laws. Conversely however, the establishment of compliance operations in international environmental law and the authorisation of carbon markets is a necessary background condition to incentivise entering into transnational forest carbon contracts as well as to make the other 'politically challenging, complex long-term reforms needed to make REDD+' succeed.[270] There are, however, a number of reasons to be wary about the key role played by private arrangements in establishing norms and constitutionalising this hybrid regime, in particular, because of the lack of transparency, the clear power that specific actors have to influence norm-development in this space; how questions of environmental integrity have been translated into 'risks' to be managed; and sidelining of North–South equity considerations. The next chapter raises further questions about how questions of North–South differentiation have been recast within the REDD+ regime, in ways that arguably place less emphasis on the responsibilities that countries of the Global North have due to their contribution to climate change, and which instead foreground a purported 'lack' of capacity in the Global South.

---

[270] P. Cowling, *REDD+ Market: Sending Out an SOS* (Conservation International, 2013) p. 1.

4

Responsibility and Capacity

Recasting North–South Difference

A INTRODUCTION

This chapter explores a key effect of REDD+, namely that it recasts how the North–South differentiation in the climate regime is understood and how questions of responsibility and capacity for climate mitigation are conceptualised. This reconfiguration has the effect of enabling the countries of the Global North – who bear the greater responsibility for GHG production – to avoid taking the types of actions necessary to ameliorate the climate crisis; at the same time, an increased focus on the purported lack of capacity of Global South countries to take climate mitigation measures has provided a justification or authorisation for greater international intervention in the name of assisting them to act on climate change.

REDD+ is an experiment with approaches that allow developing countries to make voluntary, sectoral level emission reductions (ERs) while receiving international support for capacity-building and finance, and thereby considered a 'trail-blazer' for the more decentralised, pledge-and-review climate architecture that was confirmed in the Paris Agreement. The ways in which questions of responsibility and capacity are reconfigured through REDD+ therefore foreshadow broader trends with implications for the climate regime as a whole. This resignification precludes proper accounting of the differentiated responsibilities countries have arising from their contributions to the causes of climate change and how this impacts the types of obligations and mitigation ambition they should take on; instead REDD+ makes central the imperatives of capacity-building within countries of the Global South, in ways directed towards the development of the regulatory infrastructure on which carbon markets depend. This chapter situates these developments within broader debates about differentiated responsibilities and capacities within the climate regime and the divergent underlying visions of justice that underpin different approaches.

A. Introduction

Global inequalities are reflected in both the causes and consequences of climate change among countries, namely: their differentiated responsibilities as contributors to climate change, their vulnerabilities to the impacts of climate change and their capacities for taking mitigation and adaptation action. The issue of how to respond to and address these inequalities has been a key point of international contestation within climate negotiations. The key legal and institutional means to mediate these tensions has been the recognition that developed countries should take the lead in mitigation, and the principle of 'common but differentiated responsibilities and respective capacities' (CBDR-RC). The principle of CBDR-RC is however the product of 'constructive ambiguity',[1] and thus, since the drafting of the UNFCCC there have been divergent interpretations by countries of the Global North and Global South about whether developed country leadership is or should be grounded in those countries bearing heightened responsibility for the GHG emissions causing climate change or whether the focus should be on the purported lack of capacity of developing countries to take climate action. As this chapter shows, REDD+ supports the consolidation of a broader recasting of North–South differentiation that emphasises the purported lack of capacity of Southern countries, rather than the greater responsibility of Northern countries, as the key ground or rationale for differentiated treatment.

In conceptualising REDD+ as a scheme for compensated reductions, where developed countries would provide financial, technical and capacity-building support to developing countries that willingly take on voluntary commitments, the international community reaffirmed, but also reinterpreted, the principle of CBDR-RC .[2] As Sébastien Jodoin and Sarah Mason-Case have compellingly shown, '[A]ctors have used the principle of CBDR in a new way to support the emergence and effectiveness of the transnational legal process for REDD'.[3] They identify that while the principle of CBDR-RC was interpreted and applied to require ERs to occur exclusively or primarily in developed countries, the emergence of REDD+ was co-constitutive with 'an innovative conception of differentiation which broke with previous efforts'.[4] In this way, the transnational legal process of REDD+ norm production and implementation has solidified a novel interpretation and application of CBDR-RC, one in which 'developing country governments may take on voluntary commitments to reduce their carbon emissions, with the multilateral, bilateral, and private sources of financial support and technical assistance provided by

---

[1] S. Biniaz, 'Comma but differentiated responsibilities: Punctuation and 30 other ways negotiators have resolved issues in the international climate change regime' (2016) 6 *Michigan Journal of Environmental & Administrative Law* 37–63 at 39–40.

[2] S. Jodoin and S. Mason-Case, 'What difference does CBDR make? A socio-legal analysis of the role of differentiation in the transnational legal process for REDD+' (2016) 5(2) *Transnational Environmental Law* 255–84 at 282.

[3] Ibid., 259.

[4] Ibid., 282.

developed countries, international organizations, NGOs and corporations'.[5] Jodoin and Mason-Case identify a number of benefits arising from this dynamic recasting of CBDR-RC, including that the principle no longer hindered countries taking greater action on deforestation and that it provided a 'normative frame by which actors could legitimate a new division of responsibilities among parties to the UNFCCC' that was a 'prerequisite to achieving consensus on an international agreement for the post-2012 period'.[6]

This chapter affirms the analysis provided by Jodoin and Mason-Case but raises additional normative concerns about implications of how CBDR-RC has been recast in REDD+ and the ways this subsequently was reflected in the Paris Agreement. This chapter identifies some of the consequences of this recasting, including that it further precludes (already marginalised) claims of compensative justice for historical responsibility for climate change within the regime. Moreover, this recasting represents a pronounced shift away from an underpinning redistributive justice frame and a focus on the *relationality* or the *respective shares* of emissions produced in the Global North and the Global South. Instead, the approach to North–South differentiation consolidated through REDD+ is underpinned by a utilitarian, welfarist notion of justice – committed to minimising the aggregate cost of emission reductions – that accepts as a pragmatic constraint a model of 'international Paretianism',[7] a concept that seeks to ensure no one is worse off from changes that benefit some. This much thinner conception of fairness, even though it contains a commitment to a minimal protective floor, is unable to contest persistent inequalities between countries or prevent their increase.

The recasting of CBDR-RC to focus on purported differentiated levels of capacity in the Global North and the Global South also operates to authorise expanded interventions in countries of the Global South in the name of remedying this purported lack of capacity. Such international interventions within countries of the Global South operate not so much to remedy this purported lack, but rather to facilitate, actively produce and shape a specific political economy in states of the Global South in the name of 'sustainable development' or the 'green economy'. This chapter shows how the focus on a 'lack' of capacity in the Global South authorises expanded international interventions in REDD+ host countries in the name of promoting the so-called green economy, in particular the establishment of the regulatory infrastructure necessary to enable expanded carbon markets. Through these processes the expansion of carbon markets is presented as a neutral, inevitable

---

[5] Ibid., 259.

[6] Ibid., 282–3.

[7] This is advocated for in E. A. Posner and D. Weisbach, *Climate Change Justice* (Princeton University Press, 2010); see also E. A. Posner and D. Weisbach, 'International Paretianism: A defense' (2012) 13 *Chinese Journal of International Law* 347–58; for a critique of this approach see M. Prost and A. T. Camprubí, 'Against fairness? International environmental law, disciplinary bias, and Pareto justice' (2012) 25(2) *Leiden Journal of International Law* 379–96.

B. The Contested Basis and Purpose of Differentiation in the Climate Regime 215

and necessary development, while the question of who benefits most from the market mechanisms is avoided.

The chapter unfolds as follows. The first section explores the different interpretations of the purposes and basis of the principle CBDR-RC. The following section provides a history of how the principle of CBDR-RC has been formally included in the climate regime. The third section examines how the adoption of flexibility mechanisms within the regime have shaped the way differentiation is operationalised in practice. The final section then turns to critically interrogate how the process of REDD+-readiness uses the language of 'capacity-building' to authorise interventions that actively reshape the internal political economy and regulatory frameworks.

B THE CONTESTED BASIS AND PURPOSE OF DIFFERENTIATION IN THE CLIMATE REGIME

The principle of CBDR-RC recognises that 'states whose societies impose a disproportionate pressure on the global environment, and which command high levels of technological and financial resources, bear a proportionally higher degree of responsibility in the international pursuit of sustainable development'.[8] This principle has been translated into practice through differentiated standards, compliance timelines and commitments for differently situated countries.[9] However, underlying the principle of CBDR-RC is a key constructive ambiguity, namely, is the principle anchored in an historic, moral and legal *'responsibility* to pay'[10] or does it simply reflect a 'pragmatic problem solving formula' based on *'ability* to pay'.[11] Central to this debate is the question of whether the purpose of the principle is to promote compensative and redistributive justice and thereby 'recompense to some states for the excessive use of ecological space by others', or is it meant to incentivise universal action by recognising the 'difference in the abilities of nations to participate in the global effort to protect the environment'.[12] As a result, there has been ongoing North–South debate about how the principle should be interpreted and actualised,

---

[8] United Nations Commission on Sustainable Development, *Report of the Expert Group Meeting on Identification of Principles of International Law for Sustainable Development*, Geneva, 26–28 September 1995, para 89.

[9] Ibid., para 90.

[10] See for example contribution to historical emissions cited in T. Deleuil, 'The common but differentiated responsibilities principle: Changes in continuity after the Durban Conference of the Parties' (2012) 21(3) *Review of European Community & International Environmental Law* 271–81 at 273.

[11] J. Brunnée and C. Streck, 'The UNFCCC as a negotiation forum: Towards common but more differentiated responsibilities' (2013) 13(5) *Climate Policy* 589–607 at 592; K. Mickelson, 'South, North, international environmental law, international environmental lawyers' (2000) 11 *Yearbook of International Environmental Law* 52–81 at 70.

[12] L. Rajamani, *Differential Treatment in International Environmental Law* (Oxford University Press, 2006) p. 9.

and parties have 'continued to simultaneously evoke contrasting iterations of CBDR in deeply contentious debates over the future of climate action'.[13]

The critical political question this debate raises is this: Should the basis of differentiation in the climate regime be understood as grounded in historical or current *responsibility*; or should it be centred on *capacity* to act? A focus on *responsibility* brings to the front questions of historical and ongoing inequalities in causing the problem of climate change, and therefore reflects calls for restorative and compensative justice. In contrast, a focus on *capacity* foregrounds differences in resources, technology and finances and is therefore focused on present realities and the possibilities for future action. Likewise, whereas the focus on responsibility highlights the need for countries of the Global North to acknowledge their climate debt and take additional action as a matter of justice, the focus on capacity points to a lack in the Global South that needs international action and additional support to remedy. Already in 1992 Oliver Tickell and Nicolas Hildyard identified that although such demands for additional support have often come from Southern governments, it is 'demand that has fitted well with the agendas of many Northern interests', as such calls 'effectively [frames] environmental problems in terms of "solutions" which only the North can provide'.[14] They continued:

> Underpinning the call for new funds is the view that environmental and social problems are primarily the result of insufficient *capital* (solution: increase Northern investment in the South); *outdated technology* (solution: open up the South to Northern technologies); *a lack of expertise* (solution: bring in Northern educated mangers and experts) and *faltering economic growth* (solution: push for an economic recovery in the North).[15]

The key concern of Tickell and Hildyard is that 'casting environmental problems in the language of development diverts attention from the policies, values, and knowledge system that have led to the crisis – and the interest groups that have promoted them'.[16]

Foregrounding current capacity rather than historical responsibility as the basis differentiation is problematic because it displaces questions of unequal appropriation of atmospheric space and the relations of colonialism and neo-colonialism which led to some countries appropriating more natural resources and accumulating more wealth. Additionally, focusing on capacity rather than responsibility as the basis of differentiation is also productive as the identification of a 'lack' within countries of the Global South operates to authorise further intervention within those countries. That is, the language of 'differentiated capacity', in ascribing a *lack*

---

[13] Jodoin and Mason-Case, 'What difference does CBDR make?', 283.

[14] Cited in J. Gupta, *The Climate Change Convention and Developing Countries: From Conflict to Consensus?* (Springer, 1997) p. 110.

[15] Ibid. (emphasis in original).

[16] Ibid.

B. The Contested Basis and Purpose of Differentiation in the Climate Regime   217

to the Global South – whether this is configured as a lack of resources, lack of knowledge or expertise or lack of appropriate regulatory frameworks – characterises the South as necessarily requiring additional intervention to remedy this purported 'lack'.

Understanding a specific attribute or characteristic as universal, but differentially realised, has historically (and in ongoing ways) enabled the operation of a 'dynamic of difference' in international law. Antony Anghie has described this 'dynamic of difference' as 'the endless process of creating a gap between two cultures, demarcating one as "universal" and civilized and the other as "particular" and uncivilized, and seeking to bridge the gap by developing techniques to normalize the aberrant society'.[17] The development project has always relied on defining the Global South as characterised by 'lack' vis-à-vis the Global North and offering (conditional) finance, technical skills and forms of knowledge and expertise to supposedly close what is in fact an ever-growing 'gap'. As Sundhya Pahuja reminds us, 'International law's effect in the world hinges largely on its capacity to *authorise*, including the practices it authorises under the rubric of development'.[18] While a focus on differentiation on the basis of capacity may facilitate some additional assistance and resources for states of the Global South, it does not disrupt the distribution of power and authority in the global economy, and arguably operates instead to re-authorise the authority of these international bodies and actors who can position themselves as addressing this purported lack.

In REDD+ discussions, the assistance provided by countries in the Global North to countries in the Global South for REDD+-readiness is presented as a 'reflection' and enactment of the principles of CBDR-RC.[19] Critically, this focus on capacity also closes down discussion on what 'acting on climate change' should look like or involve. Within this frame, support from countries of the Global North to countries of the Global South in relation to technology, finance and capacity-building appears as necessary assistance and an ameliorative response to global inequalities in skills and resources. However, the 'assistance' offered is not apolitical, and is often directed towards putting in place a specific way of responding to and addressing climate change. The 'capacity-building' that is central to REDD+-readiness programs is orientated towards putting in place the accounting, regulatory and legal infrastructure for the measurement, monitoring, reporting and verification of 'result-based actions'. However, arguably the scope of REDD+-readiness activities extends beyond this, to

---

[17] A. Anghie, *Imperialism, Sovereignty and the Making of International Law* (Cambridge University Press, 2007) p. 4.

[18] S. Pahuja, 'Global poverty and the politics of good intentions' in R. Buchanan and P. Zumbansen (eds.), *Law in Transition: Human Rights, Development and Restorative Justice* (Hart Publishing, 2016), pp. 31–48, 32.

[19] P. Venning, '"REDD" at the convergence of the environment and development debates – international incentives for national action on avoided deforestation' (2010) 6(1) *Law, Environment and Development Journal* 82–101.

218   *Responsibility and Capacity: Recasting North–South Difference*

promote and support regulatory interventions for the construction of the infrastructure necessary to enable and secure international carbon markets. In this way 'capacity-building' activities work to promote a specific approach to mitigating and adapting to climate change that is heavily reliant on the expansion of carbon markets.

C CBDR-RD: HISTORY OF THE PRINCIPLE AND ITS ADOPTION IN THE CLIMATE REGIME

1 *Differentiation in the UNFCCC*

The principle of CBDR has since the late 1980s played a 'pivotal'[20] role as a key concept of international environmental law.[21] The principle of differentiation is widely understood as an attempt to 'bridge the gap between the formal equality of states under international law and the deep inequalities in wealth, power and responsibility that divide them',[22] and thereby 'to promote substantive equality between developed and developing States . . . rather than mere formal equality'.[23] Commentators have highlighted how differential treatment is based on notions of 'solidarity and partnership',[24] 'builds on ideas of global distributive justice'[25] and seeks to 'foster equity' and possibly even enact in practice a form of 'redistributive multilateralism'[26] that draws on struggles to remake the international order in a more equitable way.[27] General Assembly resolution Resolution 44/228 (1989) highlighted that because most pollution originates in developed countries, those countries should therefore take on 'primary responsibility' for addressing it.[28] The resolution affirmed that 'responsibility for containing, reducing and eliminating

[20] C. Voigt and F. Ferreira, 'Differentiation in the Paris Agreement' (2016) 6(1–2) *Climate Law* 58–74.
[21] P. Cullet, 'Principle 7–Common but differentiated responsibilities' in J. Viñuales (ed.), *The Rio Declaration on Environment and Development: A Commentary* (Oxford University Press, 2015) pp. 229–44, 229.
[22] Voigt and Ferreira, 'Differentiation in the Paris Agreement', 286.
[23] M.-C. C. Segger, A. Khalfan, M. Gehring, and M. Toering, 'Prospects for principles of international sustainable development law after the WSSD: Common but differentiated responsibilities, precaution and participation' (2003) 12(1) *Review of European Community & International Environmental Law* 54–68 at 57.
[24] P. Cullet, 'Differential treatment in international law: Towards a new paradigm of inter-state relations' (1999) 10(3) *European Journal of International Law* 549–82 at 551.
[25] P. Cullet, 'Differential treatment in environmental Law: Addressing critiques and conceptualizing the Next Steps' (2016) 5(2) *Transnational Environmental Law* 305–28 at 306.
[26] J. McGee and J. Steffek, 'The Copenhagen turn in global climate governance and the contentious history of differentiation in international law' (2016) 28(1) *Journal of Environmental Law* 37–63.
[27] N. Gilman, 'The new international economic order: A reintroduction' (2015) 6(1) *Humanity: An International Journal of Human Rights, Humanitarianism, and Development* 1–16.
[28] General Assembly Resolution 44/228, *United Nations Conference on Environment and Development*, 85th plenary meeting, A/RES/44/228 (22 December 1989).

global environmental damage must be borne by the countries causing such damage ... in accordance with their respective capabilities and responsibilities'.[29] However, including this principle in the declarations and treaties arising out of the United Nations Conference on Environment and Development (1992) in Rio de Janeiro was contentious. At Rio, the US immediately advanced an interpretation of CBDR-RC that rejected any 'acceptance of any international obligation' by countries of the Global North or 'diminution in the responsibilities of developing countries'.[30] Instead the US highlighted 'the special leadership role of developed countries, based on our industrial development, our experience with environmental protection policies and actions, and our wealth, technical expertise and capabilities'.[31] While Principle 7 of the Rio Declaration on Environment and Development states that 'developed countries acknowledge the responsibility that they bear in the international pursuit of sustainable development', it offers a duel basis for this acknowledgement namely both differentiated responsibility for environmental harm ('the pressures their societies place on the global environment') and differentiated capacity to take action, due to the 'technologies and financial resources they command'.[32]

Although the North–South differentiation was evident in some earlier treaties, such as the Montreal Protocol[33] and the Basel Convention,[34] the UNFCCC represents the first explicit and 'unambiguous adoption' of the principle of differentiation in a multilateral environmental treaty,[35] and it is here that the principle is, arguably, 'best reflected'.[36] The principle of CBDR-RC in Article 3.1 of the UNFCCC has become an 'anchor provision' of the global climate regime.[37] This provision states that 'developed country Parties should take the lead in combating climate change and the adverse effects thereof',[38] but it does not specify the underpinning normative reasons for developed country leadership, nor does it 'specify on what basis differentiation is to be made between countries – capability and/or culpability'.[39] Article 4 makes a distinction between on the one hand the commitments that all Parties,

---

[29] General Assembly Resolution 44/228, preambular para 15.

[30] U. Beyerlin and T. Marauhn, *International Environmental Law* (Hart Publishing, 2011) p. 65.

[31] Ibid.

[32] *Rio Declaration on Environment and Development*, UN Doc. A/CONF.151/26 (vol. I); 31 ILM 874 (1992), principle 7; Cullet, 'Principle 7–Common but differentiated responsibilities'.

[33] See Cullet, 'Principle 7–Common but differentiated responsibilities', pp. 230–1.

[34] L. Rajamani, 'The changing fortunes of differential treatment in the evolution of international environmental law' (2012) 88(3) *International Affairs* 605–23 at 608.

[35] C. D. Stone, 'Common but differentiated responsibilities in international law' (2004) 98(2) *American Journal of International Law* 276–301 at 279.

[36] Rajamani, *Differential Treatment in International Environmental Law*, p. 10.

[37] Brunnée and Streck, 'The UNFCCC as a negotiation forum', 590.

[38] *United Nations Framework Convention on Climate Change*, opened for signature 4 June 1992, 1771 UNTS 107 (entered into force 21 March 1994), Article 3.1.

[39] Rajamani, *Differential Treatment in International Environmental Law*, p. 195; see also Deleuil, 'The common but differentiated responsibilities principle', 272.

'taking into account their common but differentiated responsibilities and their specific national and regional development priorities', shall undertake, and on the other hand the specific, additional commitments for Annex I countries.[40] Significantly, it also provides that developed country Parties shall provide new and additional financial resources to assist other countries in complying with their reporting obligations as well as providing financial resources, including for the transfer of technology, to assist developing countries to take action.[41]

Due to resistance from countries of the Global North, the 'main responsibility principle' from General Assembly resolution 44/128 was not incorporated in the UNFCCC, and the additional phrase 'respective capacities' was added to the principle of 'common but differentiated responsibilities'. As the US has always strongly contested any suggestion that the principle of CBDR-RC might give rise to international responsibility for historic emissions,[42] it was important for them 'to put responsibilities and capacities on an equal footing'.[43] This 'constructive ambiguity'[44] in the wording has sparked ongoing interpretive debates: the principle of CBDR-RC has been interpreted as suggesting two distinct reasons why developed countries should take the lead – namely their greater contribution to causing the problem of climate change but also their greater capacity to take action[45] – as well as two notions of equity.[46] However, scholars orientated to the Global South have read this provision in light of the preambular recital which states:

> [That the] largest share of historical and current global emissions of greenhouse gases has originated in developed countries, that per capital emissions in developing countries are still relatively low and that the share of global emissions originating in developing countries will grow to meet social and development needs.[47]

Therefore, Lavanya Rajamani has interpreted the principle of CBDR-RC in the UNFCCC as supporting a 'contract and convergence' vision that seeks an equitable per capital allocation of GHG entitlements within a framework of climate limits.[48]

---

[40] UNFCCC, Article 4.1 and 4.2.

[41] UNFCCC, Article 4.3.

[42] McGee and Steffek, 'The Copenhagen turn in global climate governance', 52.

[43] Deleuil, 'The common but differentiated responsibilities principle', 272.

[44] Biniaz, 'Comma but differentiated responsibilities', 40.

[45] McGee and Steffek, 'The Copenhagen turn in global climate governance', 52.

[46] L. Rajamani, 'The principle of common but differentiated responsibility' (2000) 9(2) *Review of European Community & International Environmental Law* 120–31 at 123.

[47] UNFCCC, preambular recital 3.

[48] Rajamani, *Differential Treatment in International Environmental Law*; on the 'contract and convergence' or 'greenhouse development rights' model see P. Baer, G. Fieldman, T. Athanasiou, and S. Kartha, 'Greenhouse development rights: Towards an equitable framework for global climate policy' (2008) 21(4) *Cambridge Review of International Affairs* 649–69; on per capita allocations see R. W. Salzman, 'Distributing emission rights in the global order: The case for equal per capita allocation' (2010) 13(1) *Yale Human Rights and Development Journal* 281–306.

C. CBDR-RD: History of Principle & Its Adoption in Climate Regime   221

Similarly, Joyeeta Gupta has read it as 'implicitly referring to the notion of "ecospace"', and endorsed the claim that '[t]he convergence principle on the basis of an agreed per capita global equitable and sustainable GHG emissions threshold is fundamental to FCCC'.[49] However, Jutta Brunnée and Charlotte Streck have stressed that the Convention 'carefully avoids a direct linkage' between the CBDR-RC principle in the operative text and the preambular provisions regarding developed countries' historical emissions and developing countries' low per capita emissions.[50] Overall, it is clear that a deliberate 'constructive ambiguity' from the drafting has thus allowed parties to hold different interpretations about the basis for the leadership role of developed countries.

2 Kyoto Protocol: The 'High-Water Mark' of Differentiation[51]

The decade between the 1992 Rio Earth Summit and the 2002 World Summit on Sustainable Development is widely seen as a period for the 'consolidation and expansion' of international environmental law alongside the 'flowering of differential treatment in favour of developing countries'.[52] The 1994 Berlin Mandate provided that a future agreement be guided by '[t]he fact that the largest share of historical and current global emissions of greenhouse gas emissions has originated in developed countries, that per capita emissions in developing countries are still relatively low and that the share of global emissions originating in developing countries will grow to meet their social and developmental needs'.[53] The 1997 Kyoto Protocol, which represents 'the high-water mark of differentiation treatment',[54] is widely considered the 'clearest attempt to transform CDR [sic] from a legal concept to a policy instrument'.[55] The Kyoto Protocol provided for differentiation between developed and developing countries with respect to core obligations, as well as in relation to provisions on implementation, compliance and assistance.[56] Pursuant to the principles of 'common but differentiated responsibilities'

---

[49] Gupta, *The Climate Change Convention and Developing Countries*.
[50] Brunnée and Streck, 'The UNFCCC as a negotiation forum, 589–607.
[51] Rajamani, 'The changing fortunes of differential treatment in the evolution of international environmental law', 606.
[52] Ibid.
[53] Decision 1/CP.1, 'The Berlin Mandate: Review of the adequacy of article 4, paragraph 2(a) and (b), of the Convention, including proposals related to a protocol and decisions on follow up' FCCC/CP/1995/7/Add.1 (6 June 1995), para 1(d); see also the affirmation of the principle of CBDR in para 1(e).
[54] Rajamani, 'The changing fortunes of differential treatment in the evolution of international environmental law', 606.
[55] C. C. Joyner, 'Common but differentiated responsibility' (2002) 96 *Proceedings of the Annual Meeting (American Society of International Law)* 358–9; cited in Rajamani, *Differential Treatment in International Environmental Law*, p. 176.
[56] Rajamani, 'The changing fortunes of differential treatment in the evolution of international environmental law', 611.

only Annex I or 'developed' countries were expected to take on 'quantified emission limitation and reduction commitments' as listed in Annex B of the Protocol.[57] In addition, the Kyoto Protocol's Article 4.7 provided a 'linking clause'[58] between developing country commitments and developed country support, acknowledging as follows:

> The extent to which developing country Parties will effectively implement their commitments under the Convention will depend on the effective implementation by developed country Parties of their commitments under the Convention related to financial resources and transfer of technology and will take fully into account that economic and social developments and poverty eradication are the first and overriding priority of the developing country Parties.[59]

The Protocol thus provided for developed country leadership both in relation to mitigation commitments and in relation to the provision of finance and assistance to developing countries for mitigation and adaptation.

However, the approach the Kyoto Protocol took to differentiation, and the fact that it did not require developing countries to adopt binding emission reduction commitments, has been highly contentious. The US in particular has taken the position that both developed and developing countries should make 'meaningful' contributions to global mitigation efforts, and moreover has characterised this position not as a rejection of the principle of CBDR-RC but as representing a different interpretation of it.[60] After the negotiations on operationalising the Kyoto Protocol concluded and questions again arose about the 'next step in the evolutionary process' of differentiation,[61] the US interpretation became increasingly influential. US climate negotiator Susan Biniaz attacked the principle of CBDR-RC as 'not necessary' and 'not helpful'.[62] Other commentators argued that not imposing limits on developing countries was causing 'irrevocable damage to the environment', and that 'absolute and universal norms of compliance were necessary',[63] suggesting

---

[57] *Kyoto Protocol to the United Nations Framework Convention on Climate Change*, opened for signature 16 March 1998, 2303 UNTS 148 (entered into force on 16 February 2005), Annex B. Annex B lists the quantified emission limitation or reduction commitments of each of the countries listed in Annex I of the UNFCCC, as a percentage of base year or period.

[58] Rajamani, 'The changing fortunes of differential treatment in the evolution of international environmental law', 612.

[59] *Kyoto Protocol*, Article 4.7.

[60] P. G. Harris, 'Common but differentiated responsibility: The Kyoto Protocol and United States policy' (1999) 7 *NYU Environmental Law Journal* 27–48 at 28. See also the Resolution 98 (SR-98), the Byrd-Hagel Resolution, adopted by the US Senate in July 1997.

[61] Rajamani, 'The principle of common but differentiated responsibility', 130.

[62] S. Biniaz, 'Common but differentiated responsibility: Remarks by Susan Biniaz' (2002) 96 *Proceedings of the Annual Meeting (American Society of International Law)*, pp. 359–63, 361.

[63] M. Weisslitz, 'Rethinking the equitable principle of common but differentiated responsibility: Differential versus absolute norms of compliance and contribution in the global climate change context' (2002) 13 *Colorado Journal of Environmental Law and Policy* 473–509 at 477–8.

C. CBDR-RD: History of Principle & Its Adoption in Climate Regime 223

disputes over the scope of CBDR-RC was a primary cause for 'stalemate' in the climate negotiations.[64] Even those who were supportive of the principle acknowledged the need to address 'salient questions' about its operationalisation, especially in light of the US' refusal to participate in Kyoto unless developing countries took on binding emission commitments.[65] The growth in emissions from emerging economies also sparked concerns that the Kyoto Protocol 'contained no automatic evolution of the differentiation',[66] and that the principle of differentiation must be 'designed to evolve' in order to address ongoing tensions in an equitable manner and promote universal participation and timely action.[67]

3 The Road to Paris: Re-articulating Differentiation

As negotiations increasingly focused on the shape of the post-2012 regime, 'questions concerning the legal nature and scope of the CBDR principle ... re-emerged'.[68] In 2001 there was a clear gap between the position of the US, who insisted that 'the notions of "responsibilities" and "capabilities" [must] evolve as the circumstances of countries evolve in the global economy', and that countries of the Global South such as India, who maintained that emissions should be based on equal per capita rights to the atmosphere and aim towards a gradual convergence of developed and developing country per capita emissions.[69] However, since around 2007 there has been a shift in how the principle of CBDR-RC is discussed, as 'progressively more nuanced notions of differentiation' have been articulated.[70] Significantly, the Bali Action Plan used the terms 'developed' and 'developing' countries (rather than the UNFCCC formulation of 'Annex I' and 'non-Annex I'), arguably to provide an opening for these categories to 'be negotiated anew' and enable a 'more flexible and evolving categorisation of Parties'.[71] As Rajamani described, this change in wording gave parties 'the option of destabilizing the conceptual apparatus of the existing climate regime, and making a fundamental departure from the premises on which Kyoto is built'.[72]

Alongside this shift, the US and some other countries of the Global North have pushed 'to reinterpret ... CBDR in a manner that accommodates self-selected, nationally determined emission reduction targets' as part of a 'move away from

---

[64] Stone, 'Common but differentiated responsibilities in international law', 280.
[65] Joyner, 'Common but differentiated responsibility', 358.
[66] Biniaz, 'Common but differentiated responsibility: Remarks by Susan Biniaz', p. 361.
[67] Rajamani, 'The principle of common but differentiated responsibility', 120.
[68] Deleuil, 'The common but differentiated responsibilities principle', 272.
[69] L. Rajamani, 'From Berlin to Bali and beyond: Killing Kyoto softly?' (2008) 57(4) *International & Comparative Law Quarterly* 909–39 at 919–20.
[70] Brunnée and Streck, 'The UNFCCC as a negotiation forum', 594.
[71] Rajamani, 'From Berlin to Bali and beyond', 924.
[72] Ibid., 917.

top-down, prescriptive, differentiation between developed and developing countries based on equity and responsibility concerns'.[73] In Copenhagen, US chief negotiator Todd Stern 'categorically' rejected responsibility for a 'sense of guilt or culpability or reparations' by the US, despite recognition of their 'historic role in putting emissions in the atmosphere ... that are there now'.[74] The failure to reach agreement at Copenhagen can be partially attributed to 'deep disquiet over the nature and extent of differentiation' in the regime, especially 'differentiation in central obligations'.[75] Even as the Copenhagen Accord did not resolve 'fundamental cleavages' and left 'most substantive disagreements unresolved', including 'the nature and extent of differential treatment',[76] it also marked a clear turning point from a more 'top-down' to a 'bottom-up' regime architecture.[77] In the aftermath of Copenhagen, critics continued to argue that CBDR was 'politically and practically flawed',[78] and call for its application to be reassessed, stating that a 'more nuanced categorization model is necessary',[79] especially in light of the increased emissions and wealth of emerging economies such as China. However, although many developing countries were politically and economically 'far better placed' than in 1992, it remained the case – as Dubash and Rajamani highlighted – that there were 'vast disparities between developing countries' and 'heavy burdens of underdevelopment within many developing countries.'[80] Therefore, the arguments against differentiation need to be understood as part of a highly political agenda that was resistant to the 'redistributive multilateralism' this principle represented.[81]

As negotiations progressed, a subtle shift in language, alongside a broader transformation of the climate regime from a 'top-down' to a 'bottom-up' architecture, transformed understandings of differentiation. While the Kyoto Protocol referred to CBDR alone, the Bali Action Plan and the Copenhagen Accord articulated the principle as 'common but differentiated responsibilities and *respective capabilities*',[82]

---

[73] McGee and Steffek, 'The Copenhagen turn in global climate governance', 62.

[74] J. M. Broder, 'U.S. climate envoy's good cop, bad cop roles' *New York Times*, 10 December 2009, www.nytimes.com/2009/12/11/science/earth/11stern.html

[75] Rajamani, 'The changing fortunes of differential treatment in the evolution of international environmental law', 615.

[76] L. Rajamani, 'The making and unmaking of the Copenhagen Accord' (2010) 59(3) *International & Comparative Law Quarterly* 824–43 at 840.

[77] See Chapter 3.

[78] See for example M. J. Bortscheller, 'Equitable but ineffective: How the principle of common but differentiated responsibilities hobbles the global fight against climate change' (2009) 10 *Sustainable Development Law & Policy* 49–69 at 49.

[79] Ibid., 53.

[80] N. K. Dubash and L. Rajamani, Beyond Copenhagen: Next steps (2010) 10(6) *Climate Policy* 593–9 at 598.

[81] McGee and Steffek, 'The Copenhagen turn in global climate governance', 54.

[82] Decision 1/CP.13 'Bali action plan' FCCC/CP/2007/6/Add.1 (14 March 2008), para 1(a); Decision 2/CP.15 'Copenhagen Accord' FCCC/CP/2009/11/Add.1 (30 March 2010) ('Copenhagen Accord'), para 1 (emphasis added).

C. CBDR-RD: History of Principle & Its Adoption in Climate Regime   225

and the Cancun Agreements further '[added] on the basis of equity'.[83] Drawing attention to this subtle shift in language and the return to the phrase used in the UNFCCC, Thomas Deleuil argued that the phrase 'CBDR-RC' rather than 'CBDR' should be used going forward, citing as a rationale 'developed countries' resistance to the mentioning of historical responsibilities'.[84] More generally, the Cancun Agreements formally confirmed 'a gradual erosion of the form of differentiation'[85] given both its 'less prescriptive tone' in relation to mitigation, as well as the greater 'parallelism' in how developed and developing country obligations were described and the 'near-identical framing language' adopted.[86] At Durban (COP17, 2011) an impasse arose when countries of the Global North insisted that the future regime must be 'applicable to all' and that references to CBDR-RC should be interpreted in light of 'contemporary economic realities'.[87] To circumvent this standoff, the text of the Durban Platform on Enhanced Action did not include any explicit reference to CBDR-RC;[88] however, the wording of the decision to 'develop a protocol, another legal instrument or an agreed outcome with legal force under the Convention applicable to all Parties' nodded to it.[89] Analysing the wording of these texts, including their more frequent references to 'equity', 'national circumstances' and 'specific needs', Thomas Deleuil argued there had been 'a shift in the conception of States' responsibilities under CBDR'.[90] The practice and conception of CBDR-RC was changing, he argued, as well as its legal nature, scope and consequences.[91] Although the parties continued to have a wide range of different and divergent approaches to and interpretations of differentiation,[92] it was undeniable that a 'new, more pragmatic, regime based on flexibility for all, rather than North–South transfers ... [was] in the process of taking hold', raising concerns that space for 'meaningful conversations on issues of equity between nations' was shrinking.[93] Even as many developing countries continued to stress issues of

---

[83] Decision 1/CP.16 'The Cancun agreements: Outcome of the work of the Ad Hoc Working Group on Long-Term Cooperative Action under the Convention', FCCC/CP/2010/7/Add.1 (15 March 2011), para 1.

[84] Deleuil, 'The common but differentiated responsibilities principle', 274.

[85] L. Rajamani, 'The Cancun Climate Agreements: Reading the text, subtext and tea leaves' (2011) 60(2) *International & Comparative Law Quarterly* 499–519 at 512.

[86] Ibid., 502–3.

[87] Rajamani, 'The changing fortunes of differential treatment in the evolution of international environmental law', 618.

[88] Decision 1/CP.17, 'Establishment of an Ad Hoc Working Group on the Durban Platform for Enhanced Action', FCCC/CP/2011/9/Add.1 (15 March 2012).

[89] Decision 1/CP.17, para 2.

[90] Deleuil, 'The common but differentiated responsibilities principle', 277.

[91] Ibid. 274.

[92] R. Maguire, 'The role of common but differentiated responsibility in the 2020 climate regime' (2013) 4 *Carbon & Climate Law Review* 260–9.

[93] Rajamani, 'The changing fortunes of differential treatment in the evolution of international environmental law', 222–3.

historical responsibility and the need for developed country leadership in mitigation,[94] commentators suggested there was growing support for a 'dynamic interpretation of the principle'.[95]

The lack of any explicit reference to CBDR-RC in the Durban Platform for Enhanced Action arguably 'opened a window for a recasting of the principle'.[96] In early 2013 the US negotiators called on parties to 'move beyond old ways of thinking about differentiation', proposing that differentiation should be 'thought of along a spectrum' and based on 'real, material circumstances, not on ideology'.[97] Given there was consensus that the principle of CBDR-RC was 'essential to the legitimacy and hence viability of a long-term, global regime',[98] the US' objective was not so much to 'eliminate differentiation and put every country on the same footing' but rather to radically reinterpret the principle.[99] A number of other developed countries and commentators also advocated for the abolition of the Kyoto Protocol 'firewall' in favour of a more 'nuanced, multifaceted understanding' to replace the 'binary' approach to CBDR-RC.[100] Although scholars orientated to the Global South accepted the need to 'instil dynamism', they highlighted that real differences in responsibility and capacity persisted and that therefore while '[a]ll must do more ... some must do still more than others'.[101] In contrast, other commentators suggested that '[t]he only feasible approach ... may therefore be for each party to decide for themselves which aspects of their national circumstances are relevant'.[102] Such a move – towards a more 'bottom-up' architecture and 'a self-differentiated approach for the 2015 agreement' – was confirmed at Warsaw (COP19, 2013) when countries were invited to prepare their own intended nationally determined contributions (INDCs).[103] Nonetheless, many countries from the Global South remained

---

[94] See UNFCCC, *Views on a workplan for the Ad Hoc Working Group on the Durban Platform for Enhanced Action: Submissions from Parties*, FCCC/ADP/2012/MISC.3 (30 April 2012)

[95] Brunnée and Streck, 'The UNFCCC as a negotiation forum', 597.

[96] Ibid., 599.

[97] 'The new climate negotiations: Ambition, differentiation and flexibility', speech by Todd Stern, Special Envoy for Climate Change at World Futures Energy Summit, Abu Dhabi, 15 January 2013 <https://2009-2017.state.gov/e/oes/rls/remarks/2013/202824.htm>.

[98] Brunnée and Streck, 'The UNFCCC as a negotiation forum: Towards common but more differentiated responsibilities', 602.

[99] 'The new climate negotiations: Ambition, differentiation and flexibility', speech by Todd Stern (2013).

[100] Brunnée and Streck, 'The UNFCCC as a negotiation forum: towards common but more differentiated responsibilities', 602.

[101] H. Winkler and L. Rajamani, 'CBDR&RC in a regime applicable to all' (2014) 14(1) *Climate Policy* 102–21 at 118.

[102] Brunnée and Streck, 'The UNFCCC as a negotiation forum: Towards common but more differentiated responsibilities', 591.

[103] Decision 1/CP.19, 'Further advancing the Durban platform' FCCC/CP/2013/10/Add.1 (31 January 2014), para 2(b); L. Rajamani and E. Guérin, 'Central concepts in the Paris Agreement and how they evolved' in D. Klein, M. P. Carazo, M. Doelle, J. Bulmer, and A. Higham (eds.), *The Paris Agreement on climate change: Analysis and commentary* (Oxford University Press, 2017), pp. 74–90, 83.

C. CBDR-RD: History of Principle & Its Adoption in Climate Regime 227

concerned that this approach 'failed to address the matter of equitable effort sharing' and that differentiation was necessary as a 'vital corrective concept to ensure that distributional fairness remained part of the international climate agenda'.[104] Differentiation therefore remained a critical point of contention in the lead-up to Lima (COP20, 2014).[105] The Lima Call for Climate Action once again explicitly included the principle of CBDR-RC but added the proviso 'in light of national circumstances',[106] drawing on the language of the November 2014 US–China Agreement.[107] It is this formulation of the principle that appears in the Paris Agreement.[108]

4 Differentiation in the Post-Paris Regime

The principle of CBDR-RC 'in light of national circumstances' is explicitly articulated in several parts of the Paris Agreement,[109] and differentiation is also present in other parts of the Agreement through reference to equity,[110] 'different capacities'[111] or 'respective national capacities and circumstances of Parties'.[112] Given the contentious negotiations about the role of CBDR-RC, 'every instance of its articulation in the Paris Agreement is a product of careful negotiation'.[113] Overall, the Paris Agreement 'endorses a markedly different notion of differentiation under the CBDRs principle from that of previous understandings'.[114] It adopts a more 'nuanced' approach to differentiation and includes 'different forms of differentiation in different areas' tailored to the pillars of mitigation, adaptation, finance, technology, capacity-building and transparency.[115] In addition, concepts of CBDR-RC and equity 'also take on a new meaning'[116] and the principle of differentiation is substantially reinterpreted in the context of the more 'bottom-up' architecture of

---

[104] Voigt and Ferreira, 'Differentiation in the Paris Agreement', 292.

[105] Ibid.

[106] Decision 1/CP.20, 'Lima call for climate action' FCCC/CP/2014/10/Add.1 (2 February 2015).

[107] S. Maljean-Dubois, 'The Paris Agreement: A new step in the gradual evolution of differential treatment in the climate regime?' (2016) 25(2) *Review of European, Comparative & International Environmental Law* 151–60 at 153.

[108] Rajamani and Guérin, 'Central concepts in the Paris Agreement and how they evolved', p. 84.

[109] *Paris Agreement*, preambular recital 3, Article 2.2, Article 4.3 and Article 4.19.

[110] *Paris Agreement*, Articles 4, 14.

[111] *Paris Agreement*, Article 13.

[112] *Paris Agreement*, Article 15. This analysis draws on Maljean-Dubois, 'The Paris Agreement: A new step in the gradual evolution of differential treatment in the climate regime?'.

[113] L. Rajamani, 'Ambition and differentiation in the 2015 Paris Agreement: Interpretative possibilities and underlying politics' (2016) 65(2) *International & Comparative Law Quarterly* 493–514 at 507.

[114] J. Peel, 'Re-evaluating the principle of common but differentiated responsibilities in transnational climate change law' (2016) 5(2) *Transnational Environmental Law* 245 at 248.

[115] Rajamani, 'Ambition and differentiation in the 2015 Paris Agreement: Interpretative possibilities and underlying politics', 509.

[116] Maljean-Dubois, 'The Paris Agreement', 153.

Responsibility and Capacity: Recasting North–South Difference

the agreement. In relation to mitigation commitments, given that countries put forward their own nationally determined contributions (NDCs), a model of 'self-differentiation'[117] or 'individual differentiation' is promoted.[118] There is therefore a 'diminished role' for CBDR-RC in relation to mitigation commitments, notwithstanding that the principle still plays a key role in 'shap[ing] procedurally orientated implementation and support mechanisms'.[119]

Numerous commentators have welcomed the Paris Agreement's approach as a 'subtle, creative and more dynamic' way of addressing differentiation,[120] especially in conjunction with the new principles of *highest possible ambition* and *progression* introduced in the Agreement.[121] Other have argued that it represents a more 'nuanced' and 'dynamic' approach to differentiation than the strict 'binary' differentiation of the Kyoto Protocol,[122] and that this more diversified approach allows for 'the creation of an evolutionary "policy space" under the Convention'.[123] However, the 'self-differentiation' approach adapted in the Paris Agreement has also been critiqued. For example, even though Lavanya Rajamani and Emmanuel Guérin see self-differentiation as a 'pragmatic choice for mitigation because it provides flexibility, privileges sovereign autonomy, and encourages broader participation', they regret that this approach 'leaves little room for collectively tailoring commitments to differentiated responsibilities for environmental harm'.[124] Civil society groups have also been critical of the fact that 'self-differentiation' means that no real process exists to ensure each country is contributing its 'fair share' to global mitigation efforts.[125] A civil society report released before Paris, *Fair Shares: A Civil Society Equity Review of INDCs*, found that 'all major developed countries fell well short of their fair shares',[126] and that the 'majority of developing countries have made

---

[117] L. Rajamani, 'The devilish details: key legal issues in the 2015 climate negotiations' (2015) 78(5) *The Modern Law Review* 826–53 at 852.

[118] Cullet, 'Differential treatment in environmental law: Addressing critiques and conceptualizing the next steps', 318.

[119] A. Huggins and M. S. Karim, 'Shifting traction: Differential treatment and substantive and procedural regard in the international climate change regime' (2016) 5(1) *Transnational Environmental Law* 427–48 at 428.

[120] Maljean-Dubois, 'The Paris Agreement', 152.

[121] Voigt and Ferreira, 'Differentiation in the Paris Agreement', 295.

[122] See particularly Rajamani, 'Ambition and differentiation in the 2015 Paris Agreement'; Maljean-Dubois, 'The Paris Agreement'; Voigt and Ferreira, 'Differentiation in the Paris Agreement'.

[123] Voigt and Ferreira, 'Differentiation in the Paris Agreement', 294.

[124] Rajamani and Guérin, 'Central concepts in the Paris Agreement and how they evolved', p. 85.

[125] See also G. P. Peters, R. M. Andrew, S. Solomon, and P. Friedlingstein, 'Measuring a fair and ambitious climate agreement using cumulative emissions' (2015) 10 *Environmental Research Letters* 105004; H. Winkler, N. Höhne, G. Cunliffe, T. Kuramochi, A. April, and M. J. de Villafranca Casas, 'Countries start to explain how their climate contributions are fair: More rigour needed' (2018) 18(1) *International Environmental Agreements: Politics, Law and Economics* 99–115.

[126] *Fair Shares: A Civil Society Equity Review of INDCs. Report* (CSO Equity Review Coalition, 2015).

C. CBDR-RD: History of Principle & Its Adoption in Climate Regime   229

mitigation pledges that exceed or broadly meet their fair share'.[127] While the report stressed that all countries should aim to do as much as possible, contributing one's 'fair share' – based on historical responsibility and current capacity – was seen as representing an ethical minimum.[128] As such, the self-differentiated approach to mitigation within a more 'bottom-up' architecture risks allowing countries to avoid the level of commitment, they should morally – if not legally – take on to address climate change.[129]

Moreover, while it is necessary for approaches to differentiation to evolve in response to changing geopolitical and economic circumstances, as Philippe Cullet has highlighted, the calls for more 'dynamic interpretation' of CBDR-RC seem to '[presuppose] a context in which structural inequalities are showing signs of significantly decreasing', whereas in fact, despite absolute gains, most countries in the Global South remain as comparatively disadvantaged as they were in the early 1990s.[130] Global inequalities, both of wealth and of carbon emissions, remain stark.[131] There is a common critique that a bifurcated approach to differentiation disallows distinctions within the broad North–South categories and thus does not properly account for the growing power of emerging economies (such as the 'BRICS'[132] countries). However, this critique should not 'become a wedge [i.e. justification] to abolish differentiation altogether'.[133] Instead, the limitations of the bifurcated approached in shifting international context should have promoted 'new thinking about criteria which could become the basis for differentiation and ... avoid the pitfalls of the current approach'.[134] However, rather than of developing such criteria, the Paris Agreement problematically enshrines a 'move away from internationally negotiated differentiation in the context of the environmental issue most easily identified as being global'.[135] The Paris Agreement's focus on national

---

[127] Ibid.

[128] Ibid.

[129] See also J. Dehm, 'Reflections on Paris: Thoughts towards a critical approach to climate law' (2018) *Revue québécoise de droit international* 61–91.

[130] Cullet, 'Differential treatment in environmental law: Addressing critiques and conceptualizing the next steps', 315–16.

[131] On carbon inequality see T. Piketty and L. Chancel, 'Carbon and inequality: From Kyoto to Paris' (2015) *Trends in the Global Inequality of Carbon Emissions (1998–2013) and Prospects for An Equitable Adaptation Fund. Paris: Paris School of Economics*; T. Gore, 'Extreme carbon inequality: Why the Paris climate deal must put the poorest, lowest emitting and most vulnerable people first' (2015); on inequality generally, see J. Hickel, *The Divide: A Brief Guide to Global Inequality and Its Solutions* (Random House, 2017); B. Milanovic, *Global Inequality: A New Approach for the Age of Globalization* (Harvard University Press, 2016); T. Piketty, *Capital in the Twenty-First Century* (Harvard University Press, 2015).

[132] i.e. Brazil, Russia, India, China, South Africa.

[133] Cullet, 'Differential treatment in environmental law: Addressing critiques and conceptualizing the next steps', 319.

[134] Ibid., 318; see also K. Mickelson, 'Beyond a politics of the possible? South–north relations and climate justice' (2009) 10(2) *Melbourne Journal of International Law* 411–23.

[135] Cullet, 'Differential treatment in environmental law', 323.

230 Responsibility and Capacity: Recasting North–South Difference

interest does not 'point the way towards new forms of international cooperation' to comprehensively and effectively address climate change.[136] Instead it moves away from an approach of 'redistributive multilateralism'[137] and promotes an understanding of self-differentiation that has no aspiration of gradual convergence or equalisation of emissions. The Paris Agreement thus promotes an approach to differentiation that masks inequitable burden-shifting and thereby further accentuates the deadly inequalities of the climate crisis.[138]

D CARBON MARKETS, INTERESTS AND RESPONSIBILITY

Building on the previous section, which discussed how the principle of CBDR-RC was formally included in the climate regime, this section turns to consider how the adoption of flexibility mechanisms within the regime have shaped the way differentiation is operationalised in practice. The objective of flexibility mechanisms is to facilitate aggregate emission reductions at the cheapest costs, and in the case of market mechanisms to provide finance for mitigation action in developing countries and for the resulting emission reductions to be counted towards developing country commitments. These mechanisms reconfigure understandings of differentiation in (at least) two ways, as the discussion below explains.Firstly, the flexibility mechanisms promote a trade-off between two different aspects of the differentiated obligations that countries of the Global North have under the Convention: namely to provide leadership on mitigation action *and* to provide financial support for climate action in developing countries. Flexibility mechanisms allow countries of the Global North to provide financial support for emission reduction activities located elsewhere and to count the resulting emission reductions towards the achievement of their international commitments. In practice, this means the provision of financial support makes possible the spatial displacement of mitigation actions from countries of the Global North to those of the Global South. The provision of finance through flexibility mechanisms can lead to an 'induced convergence of different interests', whereby countries of the Global North who are 'anxious for cost-effective reduction opportunities' provide financial assistance to countries of the Global South who are 'enthusiastic to be at the receiving end'.[139] Unsurprisingly, such opportunities to receive financial compensation from offset programs was appealing to many governments from the Global South, who then considered it more pragmatic to engage with these mechanisms than to insist on Global North

---

[136] Ibid.

[137] McGee and Steffek, 'The Copenhagen turn in global climate governance and the contentious history of differentiation in international law'.

[138] For more see Dehm, 'Reflections on Paris'.

[139] Gupta, *The Climate Change Convention and Developing Countries*, p. 186.

D. Carbon Markets, Interests and Responsibility

leadership on mitigation.[140] The possibility of receiving such international finance through trading mechanisms therefore can operate to divide developing country coalitions, thereby weakening demands that countries of the Global North just take more ambitious mitigation action domestically.[141] In addition, commentators associated with the World Bank have sought to argue that the provision of finance through such market mechanisms might *in itself* fulfil the principle of CBDR-RC. David Freestone, former Deputy General Counsel at the World Bank, suggested that the Global Environmental Facility might represent an operationalisation of the principle of CBDR.[142] Likewise, in 2002 Charles DiLeva, Lead Counsel from the Office of the General Council at the World Bank, suggested that '[o]ne concrete example that several developing countries might contend fulfils [common but differentiated responsibility] is the creation within the World Bank of a Prototype Carbon Fund' to help implement (and pre-empt the norms of) the Kyoto Protocol's flexibility mechanisms.[143] These practices, and the discourses promoting them, therefore operate to reconfigure understandings of what sort of developed country leadership is required pursuant to the principle of CBDR-RC.

Secondly, and perhaps more importantly, the promotion of flexibility mechanisms undermines an understanding of CBDR-RC that emphasises the *relationality* of emissions from the Global North and the Global South and the need to consider what *share* of global emissions were produced where, one that is underpinned by a commitment to distributive justice and a normative vision that there should be a convergence between emission levels of different countries. In contrast, flexibility mechanisms are underpinned by a focus on aggregate efficiency and a utilitarian conception of justice, namely, that they should help increase aggregate ambition at the lowest cost. Already during the drafting of the UNFCCC, observers noted a potential conflict or tension between the principles of developed country leadership and cost-effectiveness, especially in a context where 'cost effectiveness concerns have tended to dominate debates about implementation.'[144] The provision of financial support from countries of the Global North to countries of the Global South was one way such tensions were moderated and addressed.

---

[140] L. Lohmann, *Beyond Patzers and Clients: Strategic Reflections on Climate Change and the 'Green Economy'* (The Corner House, 2012) p. 9.

[141] Gupta, *The Climate Change Convention and Developing Countries*, pp. 125–30.

[142] D. Freestone, 'The establishment, role and evolution of the global environment facility: Operationalising common but differentiated responsibility?' in T. M. Ndiaye and R. Wolfrum (eds.), *Law of the Sea, Environmental Law and Settlement of Disputes: Liber Amicorum Judge Thomas A. Mensah* (Brill Nijhoff, 2007) pp. 1077–1107.

[143] C. DiLeva, 'Common but differentiated responsibility: Remarks by Charles E. DiLeva' 96 *Proceedings of the Annual Meeting (American Society of International Law)* 363–6 at 364. For a further discussion of World Bank climate funds see Chapter 2.

[144] D. M. Driesen, 'Free lunch or cheap fix: The emissions trading idea and the climate change convention' (1998) 26 *Boston College Environmental Affairs Law Review* 1 at 17.

Responsibility and Capacity: Recasting North–South Difference

In the post-Kyoto context, commentators and policy makers suggested structuring flexibility and market mechanisms so they had embedded within them assumptions about the inevitability of economic growth in developing countries in order to incentivise developing country participation and make such mechanisms more attractive to developing country governments. Proposals for sectoral markets assumed 'growth' or 'business as usual' baselines that would allow developing countries to sell credits, even if their overall emissions increased, provided that emissions did not increase as much as they otherwise would have in the absence of the mitigation projects. These embedded assumptions about the inevitability of economic growth in business as usual trajectories, resonated with the affirmation in the UNFCCC of the 'legitimate priority' of sustained economic growth and the eradication of poverty for developing countries,[145] as well as how many countries of the Global South understand climate change in both environmental and development terms, but often place 'a decided emphasis on development'.[146] However, from an environmental perspective the purported equivalence that this approach presumes between actual emissions and future emissions 'saved' (because projected emissions are less than would have otherwise have been the case in a counterfactual baseline) is highly problematic, given that any such calculations necessarily involve speculative assumptions about potential alternative futures.

The following discussion examines how these embedded assumptions of growth and dynamics of 'induced acceptance'[147] make it possible for participation in market mechanisms to come to be understood as the 'interests' of countries of the Global South. It shows how this legibility also depends upon reconceptualising understandings of fairness, both by adopting a 'future-orientated' frame (rather than one attentive to historical inequalities) and by sidelining notions of redistributive justice, adopting instead a much narrower focus of ensuring that no party be worse off. Finally, the discussion highlights how through these developments the tensions between environmental imperatives and assumptions of the inevitability of economic growth again resurface. Below, I discuss first the CDM, then the policy debates around sectoral market and 'growth' baselines before examining how these dynamics play out in REDD+.

1 The Clean Development Mechanism (CDM), Offsets and Trade-Offs

The CDM – described by one observer as the 'biggest trade-off of the negotiations' – allows for the *voluntary* participation of non-Annex I countries in mitigation

---

[145] UNFCCC, preambular recital 21.

[146] R. Gordon, 'Climate change and the poorest nations: Further reflections on global inequality' (2007) 78 *University of Colorado Law Review* 1559–624 at 1601.

[147] Gupta, *The Climate Change Convention and Developing Countries*, pp. 127–9.

D. Carbon Markets, Interests and Responsibility

measures.[148] It had it forerunners in the contested 1995 Activities Implemented Jointly pilot phrase of the UNFCCC, which was only agreed upon on the basis that it was voluntary and did not produce any credits.[149] What was to become the CDM was initially proposed by Brazil as a Clean Development Fund to finance sustainable development in the South, financed by compliance penalties imposed on Annex I countries.[150] Instead, the CDM became a means of facilitating emission reduction projects in developing countries financed by developed countries, but by which the certified emission reductions (CERs) produced could be counted towards developed country commitments. This idea arguably gained 'unstoppable momentum as the US recognized it as a politically correct avenue for getting some key developing countries on board', paradoxically creating a situation whereby the developing countries that 'helped craft the CDM, eventually accept[ed] the flexibility and differentiation approach to QELROs [quantified emission limitation reduction objectives] that they had earlier resisted'.[151] Although the 'offset' nature of the mechanism was objected to by some developing countries, most of these objections were overcome through the inclusion of a clause that provided a 'share of the proceeds from certified project activities [be] used ... to assist developing country Parties that are particularly vulnerable to the adverse effects of climate change meet the costs of adaptation'.[152] Although the G77 and China had previously opposed market mechanisms, which they argued unfairly shifted the burden of ERs under the pretext of 'cost effectiveness', they nonetheless agreed to the CDM because it allowed them to demonstrate their participation in a global endeavour to reduce emissions without having to sacrifice developmental desires,[153] while also providing a means to access the technology and finances to promote sustainable development.[154] Most of these discussions took place within informal contact groups in last days of COP3 (1997) by only handful of delegates, and '[t]he speed of these negotiations and the lack of transparency meant that many issues were left to be clarified during the CDM's operationalization'.[155]

---

[148] 'Report of the Third Conference of the Parties to the United Nations Framework Convention on Climate Change: 1–11 December 1997' (1997) 12(76) *Earth Negotiations Bulletin* 15.

[149] For an overview see Gupta, *The Climate Change Convention and Developing Countries*, Chapter 6.

[150] A. E. Prouty, 'The clean development mechanism and its implications for climate justice' (2009) 34 *Columbia Journal of Environmental Law* 513–40 at 520.

[151] 'Report of the Third Conference of the Parties to the United Nations Framework Convention on Climate Change: 1–11 December 1997', p. 15.

[152] *Kyoto Protocol*, Article 12.8; J. Gupta, *The History of Global Climate Governance* (Cambridge University Press, 2014) pp. 83–4.

[153] Rajamani, 'The principle of common but differentiated responsibility', 130.

[154] A. Krajnc, 'Survival emissions: A perspective from the south on global climate change negotiations' (2003) 3(4) *Global Environmental Politics* 98–108 at 102, discussing M. J. Mwandosya, *Survival Emissions: A Perspective from the South on Global Climate Change Negotiations* (Dar es Salaam: Centre for Energy, Environment, Science and Technology, 2000).

[155] N. H. Ravindranath and J. A. Sathaye, *Climate Change and Developing Countries* (Kluwer Academic Publishers, 2002) p. 198.

234   *Responsibility and Capacity: Recasting North–South Difference*

The overarching objective of the CDM was to create a market-based system that both promoted sustainable development in the Global South and provided low-cost compliance to incentivise further action for the Global North.[156] Both Lavanya Rajamani and Philippe Cullet therefore argued it was 'a direct emanation of the principle of common but differentiated responsibility', given that it represented a North–South partnership in solving a global problem, on the basis of different commitments.[157] In their accounts the CDM is presented as a 'win-win' scenario where 'developed countries benefit from project activities in their countries, [and] industrial countries benefit from the certified emission reduction units accruing from such projects'.[158] Similarly, it is presented as a mechanism through which both developing and developed countries 'fulfil their share of "common responsibility"' – the former by participating in the CDM and the latter by 'accepting and reaching their emission reduction or limitation targets'.[159] Putting to one side broader potential objections to these arguments that the idea of the CDM reflects the principle of CBDR, in order to analyse whether and how this mechanism operationalises the principle it is critical one consider the rules and modalities agreed to subsequently at COP7 (2001) in the Marrakech Accords, as well as how the mechanism operates in practice. This requires an analysis of: whether the mechanism does indeed lead to additional mitigation outcomes; if it has let developed countries avoid domestic emission reductions; and whether it has in fact provided 'additional' finance to developing countries and promoted sustainable development.[160]

Since the CDM became operational in 2006 there have been numerous critiques of its operations, with commentators suggesting 'several reasons that the CDM may be wholly inadequate' to achieve its objectives.[161] Firstly, there are real questions about whether the Kyoto Protocol requirement that all ERs resulting from projects be 'additional to any that would occur in the absence of the certified project activity'[162] has been met. The conception of additionality[163] is 'difficult to define, implement, and secure',[164] and although tools have been developed to determine baselines and additionality by the CDM methodologies panels, it remains inherently

---

[156] Prouty, 'The clean development mechanism and its implications for climate justice', 520.

[157] Rajamani, 'The principle of common but differentiated responsibility', 130; Cullet, 'Differential treatment in international law', 571.

[158] Rajamani, 'The principle of common but differentiated responsibility', 130.

[159] Ibid.

[160] Y. Matsui, 'Some aspects of the principle of "common but differentiated responsibilities"' (2002) 2(2) *International Environmental Agreements* 151–70 at 162.

[161] Prouty, 'The clean development mechanism and its implications for climate justice', 520.

[162] *Kyoto Protocol*, Article 12.5(c).

[163] Decision 17/CP.7 'Modalities and procedures for a clean development mechanism as defined in Article 12 of the Kyoto Protocol', Annex, para 43; Decision 3/CMP.1 'Modalities and procedures for a clean development mechanism as defined in Article 12 of the Kyoto Protocol', para 43.

[164] D. Bodansky, J. Brunnée, and L. Rajamani, *International Climate Change Law* (Oxford University Press, 2017) p. 183.

D. Carbon Markets, Interests and Responsibility

uncertain.[165] Studies by Lambert Schneider have demonstrated key problems with the tools for demonstrating additionality and have concluded that '[a]dditionality seems unlikely or questionable for a significant number of projects that were registered' in the early years of the CDM's operations.[166] Although reforms have been made, a more recent analysis found that the 'the CDM still has fundamental flaws in terms of overall environmental integrity' given that it is 'likely that the large majority of the projects registered and CERs issued under the CDM are not providing real, measurable and additional emission reductions'.[167]

Secondly, although the Kyoto Protocol specified that flexibility mechanisms were to be 'supplementary' to domestic action, and therefore indicates that 'domestic actions should be the main means of meeting emission limitation and reduction commitments',[168] this particular term was never clearly defined.[169] In subsequent debates the Umbrella Group (made up of Australia, Belarus, Canada, Iceland, Israel, Japan, New Zealand, Kazakhstan, Norway, the Russian Federation, Ukraine and the United States) maintained there was no requirement that domestic action be the 'primary means' and took the position that it was not necessary to define 'supplementarity'; this position was opposed by other Parties, especially the EU, who wanted to formulate for a 'concrete ceiling' on the use of flexible mechanisms.[170] Although there was contentious discussion over a number of different definitions of 'supplementarity' at COP6,[171] only a very 'vague and open'[172] definition – namely that 'domestic actions ... thus constitute a *significant element* of the effort made by each Party included in Annex I to meet its quantified emission limitation and reduction commitments under Article 3, paragraph 1'[173] – was subsequently

---

[165] L. Schneider, 'Assessing the additionality of CDM projects: Practical experiences and lessons learned' (2009) 9(3) *Climate Policy* 242–54; L. R. Schneider, 'Perverse incentives under the CDM: An evaluation of HFC-23 destruction projects' (2011) 11(2) *Climate Policy* 851–64.

[166] Schneider, 'Assessing the additionality of CDM projects: Practical experiences and lessons learned', 253.

[167] M. Cames, R. O.Harthan, J. Füssler, M. Lazarus, C. M. Lee, P. Erickson, and R. Spalding-Fecher, *How Additional Is the Clean Development Mechanism? Analysis of the Application of Current Tools and Proposed Alternatives* (DG CLIMA, 2016) p. 11.

[168] F. M. Platjouw, 'Reducing greenhouse gas emissions at home or abroad? The implications of Kyoto's supplementarity requirement for the present and future climate change regime' (2009) 18(3) *Review of European Community & International Environmental Law* 244–56 at 224.

[169] *Kyoto Protocol*, Article 6.1(d), Article 17 and Article 12.3(b). Article 6.1(d) provides that the acquisition of ERUs from Joint Implementation and Article 17 provides that participation in international emission trading 'shall be supplemental to domestic action', and Article 12.3(b) states that use of CDM CERs can be used only for compliance with 'part of' QELRCs.

[170] Platjouw, 'Reducing greenhouse gas emissions at home or abroad?', 245; L. Rajamani, 'Re-negotiating Kyoto: A review of the Sixth Conference of Parties to the Framework Convention on Climate Change Air and Atmosphere' (2001) 12 *Colorado Journal of International Environmental Law and Policy* 201–38 at 215–18.

[171] From Platjouw, 'Reducing greenhouse gas emissions at home or abroad?', 246.

[172] Ibid.

[173] Decision 5/CP.6, 'The Bonn Agreement on the implementation of the Buenos Aires Plan of Action' FCCC/CP/2001/5 (29 October 2001).

included in the Marrakech Accords.[174] Given that this principle of supplementarity was never quantified or clearly defined, it has left 'wide scope for discretion, with some countries being more responsible than others when it comes to using, or abusing, carbon credits'.[175]

Thirdly, there are serious questions about whether the CDM has in fact contributed to assisting non-Annex I countries in 'achieving sustainable development'.[176] The term 'sustainable development' is nowhere defined in either the UNFCCC or the Kyoto Protocol,[177] and the Marrakech Accords affirmed that 'it is the host Party's prerogative to confirm whether a clean development mechanism project activity assists it in achieving sustainable development'.[178] Thus, whether a CDM project contributes to sustainable development in the host country is not subject to international oversight but rather affirmed by a Designated National Authority in the host country.[179] Although there are difficulties in assessing the extent to which CDM projects have contributed to sustainable development, evidence suggests 'benefits have been limited',[180] and a 2009 study concluded that '[t]he CDM in its current form has not realized sustainable development benefits envisioned in its creation'.[181] There have been many concerns about 'equity in the geographical distribution of CDM projects' and that CDM investment is being directed only to a small number of countries and excluding those countries 'without the financial and technical capacity to unilaterally develop and implement projects'.[182] Finally, there are questions about whether payments transferred through the CDM represent 'financial additionality', that is whether money flowing to host countries for CDM projects is additional to existing overseas development assistance, including commitments to support climate mitigation and sustainable development in developing countries. During the negotiations on operationalising these provisions the G77 called for CDM funds to be 'additional' to overseas development aid, but it was the

---

[174] Decision 15/CP.7 'Principles, nature and scope of the mechanisms pursuant to Article 6, 12 and 17 of the Kyoto Protocol' FCCC/CP/2001/13/Add.2 (21 January 2002), preambular recital 7.

[175] F. Sindico, 'Paris, climate change, and sustainable development' (2016) 6(1–2) *Climate Law* 130–41 at 134.

[176] *Kyoto Protocol*, Article 12.2.

[177] Bodansky et al., *International Climate Change Law*, p. 185.

[178] Decision 17/CP.7, preambular recital 4.

[179] Decision 17/CP.7, Annex, para 40(a).

[180] Bodansky et al., *International Climate Change Law*, p. 185; see also C. Streck and J. Lin, 'Making markets work: A review of CDM performance and the need for reform' (2008) 19(2) *The European Journal of International Law* 409–42 at 419.

[181] E. Boyd, N. Hultman, J. T. Roberts, E. Corbera, J. Cole, A. Bozmoski, J. Ebeling, R. Tippman, P. Mann, K. Brown, and D. M. Liverman, 'Reforming the CDM for sustainable development: Lessons learned and policy futures' (2009) 12 *Environmental Science and Policy* 820–31 at 829.

[182] T. A. Eni-Ibukun, *International Environmental Law and Distributive Justice* (Routledge, 2014) pp. 3–4; see also A. Cosbey, J.-E. Parry, J. Browne, Y. D. Babu, P. Bhandari, J. Drexhage, and D. Murphy, *Realizing the development dividend: Making the CDM work for developing countries* (International Institute for Sustainable Development, 2005).

D. Carbon Markets, Interests and Responsibility

formulation proposed by both the Umbrella Group and the EU – which avoided the term 'additional' and developed a new term 'diversion' – that prevailed.[183]

This analysis shows that although the CDM was promoted as a 'win-win' solution that would deliver benefits to countries of the Global North and Global South as well as overall mitigation outcomes, the process of drafting rules and modalities weakened key provisions that would be necessary to ensure host country benefits and the environmental integrity of the scheme. Moreover, in the operationalisation of the CDM, such 'win-win' outcomes have not been achieved. Of the three stated objectives of the CDM – assisting in the achievement of sustainable development, contributing towards overall environmental goals and assisting Northern countries in complying with their emissions reduction requirements – the first two have arguably been 'abyssal failures' and only the latter goal a 'resounding' but 'paradoxical' success.[184] Rather, what the flexibility mechanisms have done is 'allow[ed] countries to make less domestic reductions than the national quantitative limits seem to require, if they purchase something deemed equivalent from elsewhere',[185] while providing a 'spatial fix' by 'organizing costly emission reductions through a geographic expansion of markets that provides cheaper alternatives in the developing world as well as creative opportunities for some investors'.[186] Given these realities, it is arguably the case that the CDM in its actual operations is undermining rather than promoting the principle of CBDR-RC.

2 Post-Kyoto Discussions on Market Mechanisms

After the Kyoto Protocol negotiations concluded, a number of Northern policy makers and commentators sought to find ways to incentivise greater developing country participation in the regime. At Kyoto, the US position had been that developing countries should take on voluntary commitments, and it specifically proposed including emission growth targets to 'abate the increase' in emissions, which it argued would not inhibit economic growth in these countries.[187] Although

---

[183] M. Dutschke and A. Michaelowa, 'Development assistance and the CDM – How to interpret "financial additionality"' (2006) 11(2) *Environment and Development Economics* 235–46 at 236; it provides that 'public funding for clean development mechanisms projects from Parties in Annex I is not to result in the diversion of official development assistance and is to be separate from and not counted towards the financial obligations of Parties included in Annex I', Decision 17/CP.7, preambular recital 7.

[184] K. Smith, 'Offsets under Kyoto: A dirty deal for the South' in S. Böhm and S. Dabhi (eds.), *Upsetting the Offset* (MayFlyBooks, 2009) pp. 2–4, 2.

[185] Driesen, 'Free lunch or cheap fix', 30.

[186] A. G. Bumpus and D. M. Liverman, 'Accumulation by decarbonization and the governance of carbon offsets' (2008) 84(1) *Economic Geography* 127–55 at 134.

[187] Harris, 'Common but differentiated responsibility', 44–5. On the US favouring 'emissions growth targets' see 'Report of the Third Conference of the Parties to the United Nations Framework Convention on Climate Change: 1–11 December 1997' (1997) 12(76) *Earth Negotiations Bulletin* 3.

238 *Responsibility and Capacity: Recasting North–South Difference*

the US presented its proposal not as a rejection of CBDR but as a different interpretation of the principle,[188] this approach was strongly opposed at Kyoto. However, a decade later the Bali Action Plan endorsed voluntary 'nationally appropriate mitigation actions' (NAMAs) by developing countries, to be 'supported and enabled by technology, financing and capacity-building'.[189] It similarly called for consideration of 'cooperative sectoral approaches and sector-specific actions' to enhance the development, application, diffusion and transfer of technologies, practices and processes to reduce GHG emissions in relevant sectors.[190] These were promoted amid consideration of 'various approaches, including opportunities to use markets, to enhance the cost-effectiveness of, and to promote, mitigation actions'.[191] There are many different factors that contributed to these changes. Here, I focus solely on how the move away from the project-based offsets of the CDM to more comprehensive sectoral approaches[192] has been seen as a 'potential avenue to bridge the North–South divide in international climate politics'.[193]

As post-Kyoto discussion sought to envision the shape of the future climate regime, a number of commentators and policy makers proposed an expanded carbon trading regime based on 'growth baselines' and 'no-regrets' reductions to incentivise developing country participation.[194] In such a model developing country emissions would not be capped in 'absolute terms' but allowed to 'rise above current levels', provided 'emissions grew at a slower rate than their economies'.[195] Writing in 2000, Cédric Philibert argued that such models of voluntary participation and compensated reductions could help incentivise carbon market participation by developing countries, which otherwise feared that firm, legally binding targets would act as a potential restraint on their development. Instead of requiring reductions of actual emissions, he proposed that developing countries could be given an 'emissions trading budget' for a future period and then be permitted to sell allowances if their actual emissions for that period were less than the budget, without the threat of sanctions if the budget was exceeded.[196] Philibert argued that because such 'emissions budgets' could be based on growth projections, 'negotiating emission budgets [would] not provoke the same fears of possible constraints upon economic

---

[188] Harris, 'Common but differentiated responsibility', 45–8.

[189] Decision 1/CP.13, para 1(b)(ii).

[190] Decision 1/CP.13, para 1(b)(iv), see also UNFCCC, Article 4.1(c).

[191] Decision 1/CP.13, para 1(b)(v).

[192] See generally J. O. Meckling and G. Y. Chung, 'Sectoral approaches for a post-2012 climate regime: A taxonomy' (2009) 9(6) *Climate Policy* 652–68.

[193] Ibid., 653.

[194] C. Philibert, 'How could emissions trading benefit developing countries' (2000) 28 *Energy Policy* 947–56; see also C. Philibert, 'Lessons from the Kyoto Protocol: Implications for the future' (2004) 5(1) *International Review for Environmental Strategies* 311; K. Karousakis, B. Guay, and C. Philibert, *Differentiating Countries in Terms of Mitigation Commitments Actions and Support* (Organisation for Economic Co-operation and Development, 2008).

[195] Philibert, 'How could emissions trading benefit developing countries', 951.

[196] Ibid., 948.

D. Carbon Markets, Interests and Responsibility

growth as negotiating emission limits', and could thereby 'ease the negotiating process'.[197] In subsequent papers he proposed that the Kyoto Protocol could be transformed and greater developing country participation in the regime incentivised by including such non-binding, voluntary, dynamic targets that were based on business-as-usual projections.[198] In particular, he argued that it would be easier to encourage developing country participation in a global emissions trading regime based on this model, given that developing countries 'would have everything to gain and nothing to lose from accepting targets'.[199]

In sum, what was proposed was a model where emissions in the Global South could still grow in absolute terms, provided these emissions were less than they would have been under a business-as-usual trajectory. In this model climate finance is transferred from the North to the South *in return* for future emissions *opportunities* being transferred from the South to the North as purchasable emissions *credits/ rights*. This model therefore operates to transform potential future developing country emissions from a projected possibility to a quasi-entitlement, given that they can be transformed into a saleable credit if not realised. Moreover, the model assumes that 'actual' and 'future' emissions can be treated as equivalent, substitutable and exchangeable, even though any projection of counterfactual business-as-usual baselines is necessarily indeterminate, and inherently based on contestable assumptions and speculations. Such a projected 'growth baseline' also reflects the how economic growth is treated as a quasi-transcendental imperative in international law.[200] Therefore, even though such an equation of 'actual' emission reductions with reductions compared to business-as-usual scenarios allows sectoral mechanisms *to be seen as* being in the 'interests' of both host and purchaser countries, it is based on a problematic assumption of equivalence between 'actual' and 'future' emissions that threatens the environmental integrity of the whole exchange.

This vision of an expanded carbon market – in which developing countries take on 'no regrets' emission reductions in relation to a 'growth baseline' – reflects a very specific understanding of fairness or equity. Underlying this vision of an expanded carbon market is a vision of utilitarianism and welfarism committed to minimising the aggregate cost of ERs – that nonetheless accepts as a pragmatic constraint the need for actions to comply with 'international Paretianism',[201] that is, the requirement that any change must make at least one person better off without making

---

[197] Ibid., 952.
[198] Philibert, 'Lessons from the Kyoto Protocol', 318; See also C. Philibert and J. Pershing, 'Considering the options: Climate targets for all countries' (2001) 1(2) *Climate Policy* 211–27.
[199] Philibert, 'Lessons from the Kyoto Protocol', 318.
[200] S. Pahuja, *Decolonising International Law: Development, Economic Growth and the Politics of Universality* (Cambridge University Press, 2011).
[201] This is advocated for in Posner and Weisbach, *Climate Change Justice*; see also Posner and Weisbach, 'International Paretianism'; for a critique of this approach see Prost and Camprubí, 'Against fairness?.

anyone worse off.[202] Therefore, although models of compensated reductions offer limited North–South financial transfers, they also sideline a conceptualisation of CBDR-RC that is underpinned by concerns about the *share* of emissions and emission reductions originating in the Global North and the Global South, the need to see these in relation to one another, and an aspiration towards a future equalisation of emissions levels (within ecological limits). In contrast, the focus in models of compensated reductions are the 'interests' of specific parties, conceptualised only in a future-orientated manner (and not a historically orientated way) and in terms of immediate benefits; moreover this approach does not interrogate how the political economy of carbon markets unequally distributes relative benefits.

3 REDD+: 'first ripe fruit in the pledge-and-review architecture'[203]

REDD+ was one of the first concrete proposals to reflect these ideas of sectoral, voluntary compensated reduction and should therefore be understood as a trailblazer for such models. The REDD+ mechanism is an early experimentation with establishing approaches for 'enabling developing countries to reduce emissions on a voluntary basis, with developed countries providing them with the finance to do so, while appropriating carbon offsets'.[204] Hence Annalisa Savaresi describes REDD+ as 'the first ripe fruit in the pledge-and-review architecture for international climate governance', and highlights how lessons from REDD+ offer many insights for understanding the framework of the Paris Agreement.[205] Additionally, as Jodoin and Mason-Case have shown, the way the Paris Agreement 'requires developing countries to elaborate targets that are to be self-determined and bolstered by international transfers' clearly 'resembles the way in which CBDR was first applied to REDD+'.[206]

As discussed in Chapter 1, the initial proposal leading to REDD+ was presented at a COP9 side event. Central to the proposal was the notion of 'compensated reductions', a model the authors argued provided 'substantial incentives for developing countries to meaningfully participate in emission reductions in the near term, while respecting the UNFCCC's guiding principle of "common but differentiated responsibilities"'.[207] Santilli et al. wrote:

---

[202] Prost and Camprubí, 'Against fairness?, 389.

[203] A. Savaresi, 'A glimpse into the future of the climate regime: Lessons from the REDD+ architecture' (2016) 25(2) *Review of European, Comparative & International Environmental Law* 186–96 at 187.

[204] Ibid.

[205] Ibid.

[206] Jodoin and Mason-Case, 'What difference does CBDR make?', 283.

[207] M. Santilli, P. Moutinho, S. Schwartzman, D. Nepstad, L. Curran, and C. Nobre, 'Tropical deforestation and the Kyoto Protocol' (2005) 71 *Climatic Change* 267–76 at 269.

D. Carbon Markets, Interests and Responsibility

Compensated reductions is a voluntary mechanism that offers tropical countries access to substantial market incentives for reducing emissions, while respecting their sovereignty in selecting means and investing returns. It is in essence a strategy for an equitable global distribution of the costs and allocation of benefits for reducing deforestation. It may thus allow negotiators to move beyond ineffective good intentions on one hand and unacceptable mandatory targets for developing countries on the other.[208]

A number of commentators recognised that approaches to limit emissions from deforestation could operate as a 'first step in the direction of "meaningful participation" of developing countries in the climate regime'.[209] This proposal was endorsed by key developing countries, in particular Papua New Guinea and Costa Rica, who submitted that such a proposal presented opportunities for them and other developing countries to take up their own climate responsibilities, provided adequate international support was provided. In their submission they attested:

> As developing nations, we are prepared to stand accountable for our own contributions toward global climate stability, provided international frameworks are appropriately modified, namely through fair and equitable access to carbon emission markets. Lasting climate stability will depend upon the equitable expansion of the market systems ... that actively facilitate and integrate developing country participation.[210]

In a later submission on REDD+, Peru, Colombia, Costa Rica, Ecuador, Mexico, Nicaragua and Panama argued that REDD+ represented 'a unique opportunity to enhance the effective participation of developing countries in the climate regime on a "voluntary" basis, whilst also providing industrialized countries an opportunity to positively fulfil their historical commitments for additional financing to support forest conversation and reduced deforestation in developing countries'.[211]

In this way REDD+ came to provide a 'new cooperative solution to an important collective action problem', because it provided a means for incentivising those countries who could take action on deforestation to do so.[212] Moreover, it provided

---

[208] Santilli et al. 'Tropical deforestation and the Kyoto Protocol', 273.

[209] B. Schlamadinger, L. Ciccarese, M. Dutschke, P. M. Fearnside, S. Brown, and D. Murdiyarso, 'Should we include avoidance of deforestation in the international response to climate change' in D. Mudiyarso and H. Herawati (eds.), *Carbon Forestry: Who Will Benefit?: Proceedings of Workshop on Carbon Sequestration and Sustainable Livelihoods Held in Bogor on 16–17 February 2005* (Center for International Forestry Research, 2005) pp. 26–41, 30.

[210] UNFCCC, *Reducing Emission from Deforestation in Developing Countries: Approaches to Stimulate Action: Submissions from Parties*, FCCC/CP/2005/MISC.1 (11 November 2005), 7.

[211] UNFCCC, *Submission by Peru, on Behalf of Colombia, Costa Rica, Ecuador, Mexico, Nicaragua, Panama and Peru, in Subsidiary Body for Implementation (SBI), Issues Relating to Reducing Emissions from Deforestation in Developing Countries and Recommendations on Any Further Process* (FCCC/SBSTA/2006/MISC.5, 11 April 2006) p. 111 cited in Deleuil, 'The common but differentiated responsibilities principle', 275.

[212] Jodoin and Mason-Case, 'What difference does CBDR make?', 270.

242   *Responsibility and Capacity: Recasting North–South Difference*

a means by which countries in the Global South could be supported in taking mitigation action and thus also take up take up global responsibility for the reduction of emissions from deforestation within their jurisdiction. Through the development of REDD+ norms, as Jodoin and Mason-Case have described,

> [Actors] reached a shared understanding to the effect that voluntary commitments by developing countries to reduce emissions from forest-based sources and the related provision of financial compensation and technical assistance provided a legitimate way of differentiating between the roles and responsibilities of various countries in global climate governance.[213]

However, even as the concept of 'compensated reductions' facilitated this new shared understanding, conflict was displaced to a new terrain – namely the question of how to measure the 'emission reductions' to be compensated, and specifically how to quantify the baselines against which any reductions in emissions were calculated. The question of how baselines should be determined and their scale or scope in REDD+ has been the subject of significant policy debate because although quantification of credible 'emission reference levels' is necessary to make REDD+ viable,[214] any quantification of a 'but for' business-as-usual scenario is inherently indeterminate. The initial proposal by Santilli et al. suggested that baselines be based on historical rates of deforestation.[215] *The Eliasch Review* canvassed different options for baseline construction,[216] and two SBSTA expert meetings (in March 2009[217] and November 2011[218]) addressed the question of reference levels. A report prepared by the Meridian Institute for the Government of Norway, titled *Guidelines for REDD+ Reference Levels: Principles and Recommendations*,[219] made influential proposals for the establishment of reference levels, which it defines as 'business-as-usual (BAU) baselines developed by taking into account historical

---

[213] Ibid., 271.

[214] On baselines see R. Lyster, 'The new frontier of climate law: Reducing emissions from deforestation and degradation' (2009) 26 *Environmental and Planning Law Journal* 417–56; I. Fry, 'Reducing emissions from deforestation and forest degradation: Opportunities and pitfalls in developing a new legal regime' (2008) 17(2) *Review of European Community and International Environmental law* 166–82; A. Angelsen, D. Boucher, S. Brown, V. Merckx, C. Streck, and D. Zarin, *Guidelines for REDD+ Reference Levels: Principles and Recommendations. Prepared for the Government of Norway* (Meridian Institute, 2011); A. Angelsen, 'How do we set the reference levels for REDD payments?' in A. Angelsen (ed.), *Moving Ahead with REDD: Issues, Options and Implications* (Center for International Forestry Research, 2008).

[215] Santilli et al., 'Tropical deforestation and the Kyoto Protocol', 270.

[216] J. Eliasch, *Climate Change: Financing Global Forests: The Eliasch Review* (Earthscan, 2008) p. 133.

[217] UNFCCC Secretariat, *Report on the Expert Meeting on Methodological Issues Relating to Reference Emission Levels and Reference Levels. Note by the Secretariat.* (2009).

[218] See UNFCCC Secretariat, *Report on the Expert Meeting on Forest Reference Emission Levels and Forest Reference Levels for Implementation of REDD-Plus Activities* (2011).

[219] Angelsen et al., *Guidelines for REDD+ Reference Levels.*

GHG emissions and removals, adjusted for national circumstances where necessary to improve reliability'.[220] This report is alert to the clear dangers inherent in overestimations, warning that such overestimations risk undermining both the political credibility and the environmental integrity of REDD+, and suggesting that such adjustments only be allowed when justified by empirical evidence.[221] A further CIFOR report proposed developing increasingly sophisticated baselines over time, as technological monitoring and prediction capacities increase.[222]

The Warsaw Framework for REDD+ provides considerable scope for host countries to determine their own baselines and baseline methodologies, but it requires them to be subject to internationalised expert review.[223] However, this invocation of expertise as an objective and rational domain *in itself* cannot sufficiently depoliticise the inherently indeterminate task of establishing a projected counterfactual baseline. The quantification of any 'but for' baseline is inherently political; its determination has implications for the degree of revenue generated for the host state, the environmental integrity and credibility of the offset credits as well as questions of equity. Moreover, there are risks that these imperatives could operate in tension with one another' that is, incentivising participation may be facilitated by unduly pessimistic future projections of 'business-as-usual' resource exploitation, that will lead to the production of 'valueless' carbon offset credits that do not represent any 'genuine' emission reductions. The model of compensated reductions therefore operates to make participation in such schemes legible as in the 'interests' of countries of the Global South, but it only does so by displacing underlying tensions onto a seemingly technical – but inherently political – domain and embedding assumptions of development and economic growth within the model. Additionally, this relies upon the recasting of underlying notions equity, away from an understanding of CBDR-RC informed by aspirations of redistributive justice towards a much stronger focus on aggregate efficiency, moderated by a much thinner principle of 'international Paretianism'.

E REDRESSING DIFFERENTIATED CAPACITY: CAPACITY-BUILDING AS GOVERNANCE REFORM

The previous section traced how the operationalisation of flexibility mechanisms recast understandings of CBDR-RC in ways that enabled the evasion of the responsibility of countries of the Global North for their greater contribution to the causes of

---

[220] Ibid., p. 1.
[221] Ibid., p. 8.
[222] M. Herold, A. Angelsen, L. V. Verchot, A. Wijaya, and J. H. Ainembabazi, 'A stepwise framework for developing REDD+ reference levels' in A. Angelsen, M. Brockhaus, W. D. Sunderlin, and L. V. Verchot (eds.), *Analysing REDD+: Challenges and Choices* (Center for International Forestry Research, 2012) pp. 279–300.
[223] See Chapter 1 for further discussion.

244   *Responsibility and Capacity: Recasting North–South Difference*

climate change. This section shows how the corresponding foregrounding of the 'differentiated capacity' of countries to take climate action operates to authorise further interventions in countries of the Global South in the name of 'assisting' them to take climate action. It examines how the discourse of capacity-building within the climate regime is orientated to establishing a regulatory and legal infrastructure that can support neoliberal markets by interrogating the politics of the forms of support and capacity-building being offered by developed countries in REDD+-readiness programs.[224] Therefore, REDD+-readiness activities undertaken as part of such capacity-building should be understood not as neutral 'assistance' but as a way by which specific forms of international authority are actualised and enacted.

1 REDD+-Readiness, Capacity-Building and International Partnerships

The process of 'REDD+-readiness' refers to the establishment of the legal, regulatory as well as technical and accounting infrastructure to enable and to guarantee REDD+ at the national level.[225] As discussed in Chapter 1, multilateral and bilateral programs play a key role in supporting these processes of REDD+-readiness through technical assistance and capacity-building. The first objective of the Forest Carbon Partnership Facility (FCPF) is to assist countries in achieving ERs from the forest sector 'by providing them with financial and technical assistance in building their capacity to benefit from possible future systems of positive incentives for REDD+'.[226] Similarly, the UN-REDD Program's 2011–15 Strategy stressed the importance of capacity-building for REDD+-readiness and envisioned the role of the programme as 'supporting governments to prepare national REDD+ strategies, build monitoring systems, engage stakeholders and assess multiple benefits'.[227] In its 2015–20 Strategic Framework, UN-REDD describes '[d]eveloping and managing REDD+ knowledge and enhancing capacity development' as key parts of its work, alongside the development of guidance, tools and briefs to 'move the REDD+ discussion forward'.[228]

While there is a strong focus on ensuring these activities are nationally directed and that 'countries are in the driving seat', the process of capacity-building for REDD+-readiness nonetheless enables considerable international influence over national policy development. The UN-REDD Programme, for example, celebrates its member agencies' 'proven ability to influence policy and build capacity'.[229]

---

[224] For further discussion of REDD+-readiness processes see Chapter 1.

[225] Forest Carbon, 'What is REDD-Readiness' forest-carbon.org/faq/what-is-redd-readiness.

[226] International Bank for Reconstruction and Development, *Charter Establishing the Forest Carbon Partnership Facility* (November 23, 2015), Article 2.1(a) ('FCPF Charter').

[227] UN-REDD Programme, *UN-REDD Programme Strategy 2011–15*, 1.

[228] UN-REDD Programme, *UN-REDD Programme Strategic Framework 2016–20* (revised 7 May 2015), UNREDD/PB14/2015/III/3, vi.

[229] *UN-REDD Programme Strategic Framework 2016–20*, p. 5.

The FCPF Charter operating principles prescribe an uneasy balance between 'respect[ing] a REDD Participant Country's sovereign right and responsibility to manage its own natural resources' alongside 'encouraging effective monitoring and implementation of the Readiness Preparation Proposal and Emission Reductions Programs'.[230] Under both the FCPF and the UN-REDD Programme, host countries are required to prepare a Readiness Preparation Proposal (R-PP).[231] The R-PP requires the preparation of a REDD+ strategy (R-PP component 2b); an assessment of land use, forest law, policy and governance (R-PP component 2a); the preparation of reference emission levels and/or forest reference levels (R-PP component 3); the development of a monitoring system (R-PP component 4); and an assessment of social and environmental risks and potential impacts (R-PP component 2d). The R-PP is then subject to an assessment process,[232] which for the FCPF involves the FCPF Participants Committee and the independent Technical Advisory Panel experts. In preparing their R-PPs, host countries are encouraged to consider 'emerging good practices' that have been developed through this assessment process, which 'should be followed, to the extent feasible'.[233]

Couched in the language of 'partnerships', these REDD+-readiness programs reflect the turn to 'participatory development' thinking.[234] Critical commentators have highlighted how questions of power imbalances are often obscured within such partnerships, and how inclusion, voice, and participation often operate to legitimise foreign policy imperatives and obfuscate Western power.[235] The literature shows how such partnerships are a new 'practice of governance'[236] that evade political contestation by foregrounding technical and depoliticised ways of engaging.[237] As

---

[230] *FCPF Charter*, Article 3.1(a).

[231] See Forest Carbon Partnership Facility, *R-PP Template Version 6, for Country Use* (April 20, 2012).

[232] Forest Carbon Partnership Facility, *A Guide to the FCPF Readiness Assessment Framework* (June 2013).

[233] *R-PP Template Version 6, for Country Use* (April 20, 2012) 8.

[234] B. Bhatnagar and A. C. Williams, 'Introduction' in B. Bhatnagar and A. C. Williams (eds.), *Participatory Development and the World Bank: Potential Directions for Change* (World Bank, 1992) p. 2; *The World Bank Participation Sourcebook* (The World Bank, 1996).

[235] D. Chandler, *Empire in Denial: The Politics of State-Building* (Pluto Press, 2006) p. 76.

[236] Chatterjee writes that while 'participation' from the standpoint of the governed is a 'practice of democracy' it is a 'practice of governance' from the standpoint of those who govern, P. Chatterjee, *The Politics of the Governed; Reflections on Popular Politics in Most of the World* (Columbia University Press, 2004).

[237] See B. Cooke and U. Kothari (eds.), *Participation: The New Tyranny?* (Zed Books, 2001); other critiques have focused on participation as 'infinitely malleable', such that it has 'become mired in a morass of competing referents', A. Cornwall, 'Unpacking "participation": Models, meanings and practices' (2008) 43(3) *Community Development Journal* 269–83; as 'mere rhetoric' disguising what are pre-formulated plans or as a 'mere technical tool' to increase the efficiencies of projects and decrease costs, J. Gideon, '"Consultation" or co-option? A case study from the Chilean health sector' (2005) 5(3) *Progress in Development Studies* 169–81; as exclusionary, extending only to the 'most presentable, upper-middle class emissaries' while the 'uncivil' are excluded, K. Anderson, 'Global governance: The problematic legitimacy relationship between

Rita Abrahamsen argues, although capacity-building is commonly presented by donors as 'technical transfers of knowledge and procedures', these can in fact be highly political interventions.[238] Partnerships, capacity-building and indicators are all technologies that facilitate governance by self-management rather than by command, in which power operates not through direct domination but through the 'conduct of conduct'.[239] She shows that within such partnerships power does not operate through imposition, but instead as a form of training in the 'responsible' exercise of government freedom, 'simultaneously empowering and disciplinary, in that it both constitutes and regulates the identities, behaviours and choices of their target country'.[240]

Therefore, financial support from countries of the Global North for the process of REDD+-readiness in host countries cannot be understood simply as aid or assistance. Rather, it is important to critically engage with the broader political transformation which these bilateral and multilateral processes facilitate, enable and justify. The process of REDD+-readiness should be understood more broadly as a process of 'market construction' in which public funding is deployed to develop the institutional conditions for markets that will enable further private accumulation. Practices of REDD+-readiness are based on a recognition that a global carbon market cannot function without the tangible and intangible infrastructure established by the state, including law and regulations.[241] As such, they reflect a broader acknowledgement in what has been called the 'post-Washington Consensus'[242] about the imperative of 'building institutions that support the development of markets'.[243] Described as a retreat from the deregulatory focus of the so-called Washington Consensus, this revised understanding pays more attention to national institutions, including legal institutions, given that '[w]ell-functioning institutions and an effective legal system are now recognized as the necessary prerequisites for efficient markets'.[244] Within this approach to development, the state is not

---

global civil society and the United Nations' (2008) Working Paper No 2008-71, Washington College of Law.

[238] R. Abrahamsen, 'The power of partnerships in global governance' (2004) 25(8) *Third World Quarterly* 1453–67.

[239] S. E. Merry, 'Measuring the world: Indicators, human rights, and global governance' (2011) 53(3) *Current Anthropology* 83–95; see also K. E. Davis, B. Kingsbury, and S. E. Merry, 'Indicators as a technology of global governance' (2010) 46(1) *Law & Society Review* 71–104.

[240] Abrahamsen, 'The power of partnerships in global governance', 1453–67 at 1462.

[241] See R. Buchanan and S. Pahuja, 'Legal imperialism: Empire's invisible hand?' in P. A. Passavant and J. Dean (eds.), *Empire's New Clothes: Reading Hardt and Negri* (Routledge, 2004) pp. 73–93, 81.

[242] On the 'post Washington Consensus' see J. E. Stiglitz, *More Instruments and Broader Goals: Moving toward the Post-Washington Consensus* (Citeseer, 1998); Z. Öniş and F. Şenses, 'Rethinking the emerging post-Washington Consensus' (2005) 36(2) *Development and Change* 263–90.

[243] *World Development Report 2002: Building Institutions for Markets* (The World Bank, 2001) p. 4.

[244] Buchanan and Pahuja, 'Legal imperialism: Empire's invisible hand?', p. 81.

E. Redressing Differentiated Capacity

marginalised or displaced to enable a regime of globalised market governance, but rather it 'becomes the site of the legal instantiation and governance of the market'.[245] Since the turn of the century, a key focus of law and development interventions has been the regularisation of property rights in the Global South, on the (contested) assumption that the legal clarification of property rights operates to facilitate greater development.[246] In the context of REDD+, the establishment, formalisation and securitisation of the types of property rights that are necessary for the carbon economy to operate become central to what is considered to be 'acting on climate change'.

More recently there has been an even greater convergence between institutionalist and market agendas in the post-Washington Consensus as 'part of a new push towards constituting capitalist social relations, in a particular neo-liberal image, on a truly global scale'.[247] Development policy, while remaining orientated towards market construction, is drawing on a broader range of measures to work towards this end and to manage the contradictions inherent in this process.[248] This is based on an assumption that

> the incomplete constitution of capitalism in a particular image requires energetic 'remedial' attempts to push forms of 'knowledge' (via technical assistance), 'build' particular institutions and foster whole new spheres of private sector activity via mitigation and new instruments of financial support (often directly to the private sector).[249]

REDD+-readiness reflects this framework, in which public/state and private markets are understood not as dichotomised and subject to different intervention but as increasingly 'fused' within what Toby Carroll describes as a 'heavily institutionalised pro-market order'.[250]

2 REDD+-Readiness, Rule of Law and 'Good Governance' Promotion

Essential elements of REDD+-readiness include undertaking an assessment of current governance and institutional practices within the host nation state, especially within the forest sector, as well as undertaking reforms to promote 'good

---

[245] Ibid., p. 83.
[246] See D. Kennedy, 'The "Rule of Law", political choices, and development common sense' in D. M. Trubek and A. Santos (eds.), *The New Law and Economic Development: A Critical Appraisal* (Cambridge University Press, 2006) pp. 95–173.
[247] T. Carroll, 'Introduction: Neo-liberal development policy in Asia and beyond the post-Washington Consensus' (2012) 42(3) *Journal of Contemporary Asia* 350–8 at 350; see also U. Brand and N. Sekler, *Postneoliberalism – A beginning debate* (The Dag Hammarskjöld Foundation, 2009).
[248] Carroll, 'Introduction: Neo-liberal development policy in Asia and beyond the post-Washington Consensus', 351.
[249] Ibid.
[250] Ibid.

governance'. Commentators have argued that successful national implementation of REDD+ also depends on 'addressing the governance challenges which underlie deforestation through a number of broader, cross-cutting measures that are at the foundation of good governance'.[251] The Cancun Agreement identified 'forest governance issues' as key to developing and implementing national strategies or action plans for REDD+.[252] The UN-REDD Programme, as part of their strategic framework, therefore highlights the need to identify 'the governance deficits that lead to deforestation, forest degradation and unsustainable management as well as conversely, governance enablers that have or would facilitate successful policies and measures'.[253] While there are clearly many problematic gaps in the way forests have been governed within many tropical nations, the focus of this analysis is on how the promotion of 'good governance' is not a neutral agenda but rather one that carries its own politics and implicit assumptions.

To enable an identification of 'governance defects' the UN-REDD Programme calls for country-level assessments to address drivers of deforestation including 'weak governance of institutions in forest-related sectors, including capacity deficiencies, conflicting cross-sectoral legislation and policies and illegal activities (related to corruption and weak enforcement)'.[254] Hence the preparation of an R-PP requires an 'assessment of land use, forest law, policy and governance' (component 2a of the R-PP). Additionally, countries are required to address proposed institutional issues for implementing REDD+, especially associated with governance. As part of the assessment of forest governance, countries are encouraged to '[s]trongly consider using a forest or other governance assessment framework consisting of principles and criteria for good forest and/or other relevant sector governance', and to develop their own indicators to assess and monitor the proposed governance reform strategy.[255] The development of a national REDD+ strategy (component 2b of the R-PP) requires addressing the governance issues identified, as well as the provision of 'support for the emergence of a more transparent, participatory, and accountable governance system'.[256] Further, the purpose of the implementation framework (component 2c of the R-PP) is described as being to 'set out credible and transparent institutional, economic, legal and governance arrangements that may be necessary'.[257] Alongside reforms more specific to REDD+, the R-PP also calls on countries to consider if further institutional and governance reforms might be necessary, such as 'anti-corruption laws and measures, national best practices for fiscal

---

[251] L. Denier, S. Korwin, M. Leggett, and C. MacFarquhar, *The Little Book of Legal Frameworks for REDD+* (Global Canopy Programme, 2014) p. 35.

[252] Decision 1/CP.16, para 72.

[253] *UN-REDD Programme Strategic Framework 2016–20*, p. v.

[254] Ibid., 10.

[255] *R-PP Template Version 6, for Country Use* (April 20, 2012), 34.

[256] Ibid., 37.

[257] Ibid., 40.

E. Redressing Differentiated Capacity

transparency, clarifying roles and responsibilities within a decentralized forest management system, role and the capacity of governmental and non-governmental institutions, including the local and traditional institutions'.[258]

REDD+-readiness programs therefore operate as a key site for intervention in the legal and governance frameworks in host countries relating to the forest sector but also more broadly. This is especially the case because unlike project-based offsets such as the CDM, sector-based offsets, and particularly REDD+, require much greater integration with a country's national policies and planning.[259] It is widely acknowledged that REDD+ both depends upon not merely specific laws but also a legal framework that addresses broader governance challenges.[260] Well-designed legal frameworks are understood as not only critical to the 'effective development of REDD+ nationally', but also as having the potential to have 'wide-reaching impacts across sectors beyond forests, such as agriculture and water, while also requiring greater integration of policy planning and implementation among these sectors'.[261]

REDD+ thus has clear implications for national development planning – in the sense that REDD+ will incentivise not just action on reducing deforestation but more generally will 'incentivise governance improvements'.[262] Phillipa Venning writes that '[w]here national governments wish to attract private investment in REDD activities, competing with other countries for scarce capital could provide incentives for governments to improve governance and address regulatory and corruption impediments'.[263] She thus recommends that REDD+-readiness 'should focus not only on monitoring and accounting capacity, but also on broader development planning and social policies'.[264] Similarly, the possibility that REDD+ may incentivise broader governance reforms in the Global South, especially in relation to anti-corruption and rule of law initiatives, has been celebrated by some REDD+ proponents.[265]

The concept of 'good governance' and the promotion of the 'rule of law' has played an important role in international development discourses since the late 1980s,[266] alongside a more specialised focus on the need for 'forest governance'

---

[258] Ibid., 42.

[259] Venning, '"REDD" at the convergence of the environment and development debates', 97.

[260] Denier et al., *The Little Book of Legal Frameworks for REDD+*, p. 16.

[261] Ibid.

[262] Venning, '"REDD" at the convergence of the environment and development debates', 98.

[263] Ibid.

[264] Ibid.

[265] See for example L. Tacconi, F. Downs, and P. Larmour, 'Anti-corruption policies in the forest sector and REDD+' in A. Angelson (ed.), *Realising REDD+: National Strategy and Policy Options* (Center for Independent Forestry Research, 2009) pp. 163–74.

[266] For a critical examination of 'good governance' discourses see J. T. Gathii, 'Good governance as a counter-insurgency agenda to oppositional and transformative social projects in international law' (1995) 5 *Buffalo Human Rights Law Review* 107; J. T. Gathii, 'The limits of the new international rule of law on good governance' in E. K. Obiora and O. C. Quashigah (eds.),

reforms.[267] The 'law and development' agenda has for several decades now presented law as both a *means to* development and more recently as a *measure of* development.[268] The programs of REDD+-readiness can therefore be situated amid the broader programs of rule of law promotion as a development strategy that is a key plank of the post-1989 Washington Consensus. This vision of economic reform seeks to integrate new political economy and new institutional economy perspectives,[269] retreating from the extreme deregulation promoted through structural adjustment projects in the 1980s with a renewed focus on how 'institutions matter'[270] and the role of 'the state in a changing world'.[271]

In its second wave, around the time of the 1996 Asian Financial Crisis, rule of law (or lack thereof) came to be understood as 'an explicit site of development's failure' requiring transformative interventions, where questions of governance were articulated as both a cause and effect of development.[272] This framing enabled an expansion of the mandate of international financial institutions, like the World Bank, into previously excluded 'political' domains.[273] Moreover, as Antony Anghie has highlighted, the discourse of 'good governance' was 'developed in relation to, and principally applied to, Third World states'.[274] It therefore replicates what Stephen Humphreys has identified as a key distinction in rule of law promotion, namely that 'the presence of the rule of law at home is contrasted with, and privileged over, its absence abroad'.[275]

Nonetheless, what constitutes 'good governance' or the 'rule of law' is inherently indeterminant. Stephen Humphreys has identified how the term 'rule of law' is 'a

---

Legitimate Governance in Sub-Saharan Africa (Kluwer Publishers, 1999) pp. 207–31; J. T. Gathii, 'Neoliberalism, colonialism and international governance: Decentering the international law of governmental legitimacy' (2000) 98 *Michigan Law Review* 1996.

[267] See for example D. Brown, K. Schreckenberg, G. Shepherd, and A. Wells, *Forestry as an Entry Point for Governance Reform* (ODI Forestry Briefing, 2002); *Forests Sourcebook: Practical Guidance for Sustaining Forests in Development Cooperation* (The World Bank, 2008) especially Chapter 5 'Improving forest governance'.

[268] On law and development see D. M. Trubek and A. Santos, *The New Law and Economic Development: A Critical Appraisal* (Cambridge University Press, 2006).

[269] T. Tanner and J. Allouche, 'Towards a new political economy of climate change and development' (2011) 42(3) *IDS Bulletin* 1–14.

[270] S. J. Burki and G. E. Perry, *Beyond the Washington Consensus: Institutions Matter* (The World Bank, 1998).

[271] *World Development Report 1997: The State in a Changing World* (The World Bank, 1997) for a discussion see also ; U. Brand and N. Sekler, 'Postneoliberalism: Catch-all word or valuable analytical and political concept? – Aims of a beginning debate' in U. Brand and N. Sekler (eds.), *Postneoliberalism – A Beginning Debate* (Dag Hammarskjold Centre, 2009) pp. 5–15.

[272] Pahuja, *Decolonising International Law: Development, Economic Growth and the Politics of Universality*, p. 193.

[273] Ibid.

[274] A. Anghie, 'Civilisation and commerce: The concept of governance in historical perspective' (2000) 45 *Villanova Law Review* 887–912 at 893–4.

[275] S. Humphreys, *Theatre of the Rule of Law: Transnational Legal Intervention in Theory and Practice* (Cambridge University Press, 2010) p. 10.

E. Redressing Differentiated Capacity

locus of numerous, varied, and sometimes apparently incompatible claims'.[276] The rule of law can be understood narrowly as 'encompass[ing] the collective importance of property rights, respect for legal institution, and the judiciary',[277] or a more in more expansive terms as a means to 'consolidate democracy, promote human rights, reduce corruption, and, not least, secure economic growth'.[278] There has been significant contestation over the content of this indeterminate norm of 'good governance': that is, whether to adopt a thin definition whereby the 'purpose of law is reduced to the facilitation of utility maximizing exchange and optimal market allocation',[279] representing a dangerous neoliberal narrowing of the political and policy environment, in contrast to a more expansive conception of rights-based governance directed to empowerment.[280]

The way these terms are taken up by different actors is also highly political. For example, the World Bank defines 'good governance' in broad terms, as 'epitomized by predictable, open and enlightened policy making; a bureaucracy imbued with a professional ethos; an executive arm of government accountable for its actions; a strong civil society participating in public affairs; and all behaving under the rule of law'.[281] However, as Sundhya Pahuja and Ruth Buchanan note, 'this purportedly generalized conception of governance clearly refers to a specific set of principles and institutions',[282] which have arguably been 'instrumentalised' to support a broader neoliberal agenda.[283] As an example, a critical reading of an Indonesian government report on REDD+ shows that what is being promoted is an 'investor-friendly' version of 'good governance'.[284] This report discusses how the REDD+ offset is distinguished from other commodities, and that particularly because of its intangible nature, it is 'very important that the seller be able to *cultivate trust among potential buyers through consistent demonstration of good governance*'.[285] The nature of REDD+ as a 'performance-based commodity', the Report writes, necessitates 'credible governance and a strong regulatory framework to mediate transactions, reduce transaction costs and assure buyers of quality emission reductions balancing risks

---

[276] Ibid., p. 5.

[277] *World Development Report 2002: Building Institutions for Markets* (The World Bank, 2002) p. 7.

[278] T. Krever, 'The legal turn in late development theory: The rule of law and the World Bank's development model' (2011) 52 *Harvard International Law Journal* 287–319 at 313.

[279] Ibid.

[280] For an overview of different accounts of the rule of law see Humphreys, *Theatre of the Rule of Law*, Chapter 1; see also; Pahuja, *Decolonising International Law*, pp. 213–33.

[281] *Governance: The World Bank's Experience* (World Bank, 1994) cited in *World Development Report 2002: Building Institutions for Markets*, p. 203.

[282] Buchanan and Pahuja, 'Legal imperialism', p. 86.

[283] See T. Krever, 'The legal turn in late development theory'.

[284] *Consolidation Report: Reducing Emissions from Deforestation and Forest Degradation in Indonesia* (Ministry of Forestry of the Republic of Indonesia, 2008).

[285] Ibid., p. 63 (emphasis added).

252 *Responsibility and Capacity: Recasting North–South Difference*

and returns'.[286] It describes Indonesia's ability to 'be in a competitive position by establishing a REDD carbon credit production process *credible to international buyers*'.[287] The aspiration is the demonstration of 'good governance' as determined and assessed by international market players. Subsequently, this thin, market-orientated understanding of good governance has been supplemented – at least in rhetoric – in REDD+ discourses by a strong focus on participation of stakeholders and the recognition of rights. However, NGOs have criticised programs such as the FCPF for not taking their own rhetoric seriously,[288] and have highlighted that this more expansive version of what constitutes 'good governance' appears more like an optional add-on, subject to less international oversight than what is given to the neoliberal core.

In addition to a general focus on 'good governance', there has been a specific focus on forest governance reform within REDD+-readiness. Although REDD+ is not primarily about governance reform, observers highlight how REDD+ will 'affect and be affected by forest governance', given that it 'can improve forest governance or be undermined by its failures and, therefore, it depends on good forest governance if it is to be efficient, effective and equitable'.[289] Some have even described REDD+ as a potential 'tool' for (global) forest governance.[290] Others have asserted that 'an effective REDD+ regime can be built around national and sub-national policy settings for forest conservation and management', such that international attention to REDD+ can be directed towards 'building national, sub-national and local capacities to implement existing forest conservation and management requirements in ways that are consistent with the principles of good forest governance'.[291]

Forest governance is generally focused on principles of accountability, inclusion and transparency in decision-making processes, even though understanding of how such principles translate into better outcomes for forests remains limited.[292] Like 'good governance', definitions of what constitutes 'good' forest governance are necessarily contested. For example, Anne Larson and Elena Petkova claim that good forest governance 'means decisions are fair, transparent and just, rights are respected, laws and rules are enforced equitably, decision makers are accountable, and decisions are made based on the analysis of what is good for people and forests

---

[286] Ibid., p. 70.

[287] Ibid. (emphasis added).

[288] See discussion of FCPF in Chapter 1.

[289] A. M. Larson and E. Petkova, 'An introduction to forest governance, people and REDD+ in Latin America: Obstacles and opportunities' (2011) 2(1) *Forests* 86–111 at 87.

[290] See E. R. Neto, 'REDD+ as a tool of global forest governance' (2015) 50(1) *The International Spectator: Italian Journal of International Affairs* 60–73.

[291] P. J. Kanowski, C. L. McDermott, and B. W. Cashore, 'Implementing REDD+: Lessons from analysis of forest governance' (2011) 14(2) *Environmental Science & Policy* 111–17 at 114–15.

[292] Ibid., 113.

E. Redressing Differentiated Capacity

in general and not personal interest'.[293] Compare this to the World Bank's definition of good forest governance, which replicates almost exactly its definition of 'good governance' with its focus on 'predictable, open, and informed policy making based on transparent processes, a bureaucracy imbued with a professional ethos, an executive arm of government accountable for its actions, and a strong civil society participating in decisions related to sector management and in other public affairs – and all behaving under the rule of law'.[294]

Despite these indeterminacies, scholars have suggested that 'standardised comparisons' could help 'build international support for effective national forest governance'.[295] Indeed, the last decade has seen a proliferation of frameworks for assessing, monitoring and comparing forest governance. These include the Framework for Assessing and Monitoring Forest Governance (2011), developed by Program on Forests and FAO,[296] and the Governance of Forests Initiative Indicator Framework (2013), developed by World Resources Initiative.[297] This can be understood as part of a broader focus on metrics and indicators that have become increasingly central to modes of governance.[298] Through such metrics a specific ideal of what constitutes good forest governance is consolidated. The R-PP Template specifically refers to a range of forest governance guidelines toolkits or documents available as resources, including the Governance of Forest Toolkit by the World Resources Institute, the World Bank's Analytical Framework for Governance Reform, and the REDD+ Social and Environmental Standards by the Climate Community and Biodiversity Alliance and Care International.[299]

Through the process of enacting a specific notion of 'good governance', the nature of developmental state is itself reconfigured – away from being understood as having authority over its jurisdiction and towards being seen as playing an appropriate managerial role within its territory, mediating various national, local and international imperatives. The process of REDD+-readiness thus envisions sovereignty as *managerial*; the role of the state becomes that of *facilitating* and *securing* a promise of future-orientated carbon sequestration, such that the signification of this promise is

---

[293] Larson and Petkova, 'An introduction to forest governance, people and REDD+ in Latin America', 87.

[294] *Forests Sourcebook: Practical Guidance for Sustaining Forests in Development Cooperation*, p. 151.

[295] Kanowski et al., 'Implementing REDD+', 114.

[296] *Framework for Assessing and Monitoring Forest Governance* (The Program on Forests (PROFOR) and FAO, 2011).

[297] C. Davis, L. Williams, S. Lupberger, and F. Daviet, *Assessing Forest Governance: The Governance of Forests Initiative Indicator Framework* (World Resources Institute, 2013); N. Kishor and K. Rosenbaum, *Assessing and Monitoring Forest Governance: A User's Guide to a Diagnostic Tool* (PROFOR, 2012).

[298] Davis et al., 'Indicators as a technology of global governance'; Merry, 'Measuring the world'; A. Perry-Kessaris, 'The re-co-construction of legitimacy of/through the doing business indicators' (2017) 13(4) *International Journal of Law in Context* 498–511.

[299] *R-PP Template Version 6, for Country Use* (April 20, 2012) 24.

able to be decoupled from the physical forest which is its referent, and circulated as an 'asset-grade' commodity in international carbon markets. Underpinning REDD+-readiness interventions is a specific ideal sovereignty in which the state is envisioned as the facilitator and guarantor of the circulation of commodities within globalised capital markets. Yet this is also a highly differentiated account of sovereignty, in which it is only the sovereignty of countries of the Global South that are pathologised and made malleable, differentiable and 'tradable';[300] it is only the self-governance of Southern states that is essentially suspect. Moreover, this approach prescribes that global objectives of forest protection are best achieved by subjecting internal forest governance to internationally determined standards of 'good governance' and their indicators, even as it fastidiously avoids locating the drivers of deforestation in broader internationalised demand-side dynamics and globalised export-orientated trade, and the international legal frameworks facilitating these. In particular, the notion that the international financial institutions should help promote good forest governance in tropical forested countries invisibilises the role of these organisations in promoting and putting in place a legal framework that facilitated and enabled an export-orientated model of development in countries of the Global South, a model reliant on resource extraction. These tensions were articulated by Hadi Daryanto, former Indonesian Secretary-General of the Ministry of Forestry, when he discussed barriers to acting on climate change:

> There is $10bn coming in from palm oil, $4bn from pulp and paper, and the people who work in these concessions are many, so we cannot just stop it all or the [International Monetary Fund] will collapse us as an economy. ... We were told to democratise and this is the price of democracy. Climate change is the price of democracy. Indonesia is trying to be a good boy, but we can't paint the sky for you.[301]

In a perverse illustration of such international entanglements, investigations showed that illegal logging that took place in Central Kalimantan on the first day of the moratorium agreed to as part of a US$1 billion Norway–Indonesian REDD+ agreement, was being carried out by Kuala Lumpur Kepong – a company in which the Norwegian state pension fund had a $41.5 million shareholding (and would therefore directly profit from the breach).[302] This suggests that before intervening to

---

[300] David Takacs, drawing on the work of Tyler Welti, understands REDD+ as reflecting a 'market sovereignty' where '[s]overeignty is less an indivisible, inalienable entitlement, and more accurately a commodity that a nation can divide into quanta and put up portions for bid; provided a nation doesn't give up too many quanta of sovereignty, international efficiency and cooperation can improve through sovereignty commodity trading', see D. Takacs, 'Forest carbon (REDD+), repairing international trust, and reciprocal contractual sovereignty' (2012) 37 *Vermont Law Review* 653–736 at 731.

[301] T. McVeigh, 'Borneo's majestic rainforest is being killed by the timber mafia', *The Guardian* 24 October 2010.

[302] *Caught REDD Handed: How Indonesia's Logging Moratorium Was Criminally Compromised on Day One and Norway Will Profit* (Environmental Investigation Agency (EIA) and Telapak, 2011).

F. Conclusion

'assist' countries of the Global South address deforestation, there is an urgent need for international actors to recognise the ways they are, already, intervening in and implicated in processes of deforestation.

F CONCLUSION

This chapter has analysed shifts in how North–South differentiation has been conceptualised and enacted within the international climate regime. It has shown that a key consequence of these shifts has been to recast the principle of CBDR-RC so that it is orientated less towards promoting 'redistributive multilateralism' and the normative visions of convergence between the emissions of the North and South. Instead, this principle can operate to authorise increased interventions in countries of the Global South in the name of 'capacity-building'. This can be understood as a further marginalisation of an understanding of CBDR-RC as part of a 'justice paradigm' and its re-interpretation within a 'capacity paradigm'.[303] Within a 'justice paradigm', North–South difference is understood as being produced through modes of appropriation and expropriation central to historical colonialism as well as ongoing forms of neo-colonialism and persistent unequal terms of trade,[304] and poverty is understood as a product of processes of impoverishment[305] or 'planned misery'.[306] Thus, questions of responsibility, restitution and compensation are seen as central to addressing and responding to this difference. In contrast, a 'capacity paradigm' conceptualises North–South difference in terms of a 'lack', located in the Global South, where the focus is not on questions of historical and ongoing responsibility but on the need for the countries of the Global South to build their capacity in order to overcome this naturalised North–South gap. The implications of this shift from a 'justice' to 'capacity' paradigm become more acute when the broader political economy of the so-called green economy – and who benefits within it – are interrogated. In practice, the focus on lack of capacity operates to authorise further intervention in countries of the Global South, which are not neutral, but often entails deeply political regulatory and governance reform, in order to enable the expansion of privatised markets in new environmental commodities.

---

[303] For an elaboration of this argument in a different context see J. Dehm and A. Hasan Khan, 'North–South transboundary movement of hazardous wastes: The Basel ban and environmental justice' in P. Cullet and S. Koonan (eds.), *Research Handbook on Law, Environment and the Global South* (Edward Elgar Publishing, 2019) pp. 109–37.

[304] For scholarship attentive to the constitutive relationship between poverty and wealth see U. Baxi, *Law and Poverty: Critical Essays* (NM Tripathi, 1988); S. Marks, 'Human rights and the bottom billion' (2009) 1 *European Human Rights Law Review* 37–49; S. Marks, 'Human rights and root causes' (2011) 74(1) *The Modern Law Review* 57–78; M. E. Salomon, 'Why should it matter that others have more? - Poverty, inequality and the potential of international human rights law' (2011) 37(5) *Review of International Studies* 2137–55.

[305] Baxi, *Law and Poverty: Citical Essays*, p. vi.

[306] Marks, 'Human rights and the bottom billion'; Marks, 'Human rights and root causes'.

5

Scale, Multilevel Governance and the Disaggregation of Property Rights in REDD+

A INTRODUCTION

This chapter turns to consider questions of scale by interrogating the multilayered system of governance REDD+ envisions that is established through the allocation of forest resource rights to diverse social actors at the local, national and international levels. It addresses debates about carbon rights in REDD+ alongside broader trends relating to property rights in natural resource governance, common property regimes (CPRs) and community resource management. It thus aims to show how the emerging frameworks for the allocation of layered, or nested, rights in the forest carbon economy is another legal technology through which authority over land is transferred to international actors and away from peoples who live in and around forested areas. This chapter does not recommend models for the definition or allocation of carbon rights in REDD+, but rather analyses how the proposed models for carbon rights in REDD+ map onto broader trajectories in the fields of natural resource governance, common property rights and community-based resource management, and critically evaluates how such arrangements are operating to unequally distribute power between differently situated social actors.

In his discussion of the evolution of resource property rights, Anthony Scott reflects that '[n]ew natural resource uses almost always give rise to demand for changes in the powers and characteristics of the rights over of the resource, both among current holders and would-be users'.[1] Unsurprisingly, therefore, the sudden attribution of value to carbon sequestered in forests has led to intense legal and political debates over how carbon rights should be defined, allocated and governed. The issue of resource rights in the carbon economy raises a number of complex questions, including how the distribution of different entitlements, powers, privileges and duties should be allocated to various actors in the carbon economy.

---

[1] A. Scott, *The Evolution of Resource Property Rights* (Oxford University Press, 2008) p. 41.

A. Introduction

Moreover, the process of clarifying tenure rights to enable the forest carbon economy is highly political, and often both reflects existing inequalities whilst also giving rise to new inequalities. Much of the literature on REDD+ implementation has been concerned with how Indigenous peoples and local communities can establish their rights to the carbon sequestered in forested land so they can share the benefits arising from REDD+ projects and be protected from potential harms such as exclusion and dispossession.[2] However, in these discussions on how the rights of local communities can be recognised and protected through tenure reform, the political question about the actual content of these rights and what degree of relational social power they confer are often sidelined. Property theorists have stressed that property is not a 'thing' but rather a social relation that consists of 'individuals exercising control over external things and (therefore) over others':[3] it is thus fundamentally a relational concept that involves 'dynamic power relations between contending groups'[4] to establish forms of social power.[5] This chapter therefore focuses less on how to address the unresolved, and often jurisdiction-specific, technical legal questions relating to the definition and characteristics of carbon rights,[6] and instead poses critical questions about the 'set of *powers* conveyed by' carbon rights within the green economy.[7]

The chapter brings together the theoretical literature on natural resource governance with the technical legal literature, which is concerned with the definition and allocation of property rights in the forest carbon economy and the clarification of the various 'carbon rights' necessary for REDD+. It shows how understandings of property as a 'bundle of rights' have facilitated the disaggregation of the different rights in this 'bundle', the allocation of separate rights to different actors in the carbon economy and their governance at different scales – local, national and international. The result of this has been the establishment of a layered, multilevel system of rights where 'higher-order' rights to excise authority and control over resources are increasingly granted to international actors, while 'lower-order' rights to use and receive direct and indirect benefits arising from resources are granted to local communities, as form of compensation. The analysis therefore shows that even when local communities are recognised as having carbon rights, the nature of

---

[2] See, for example, R. Lyster, 'REDD+, transparency, participation and resource rights: The role of law' (2011) 14 *Environmental Science and Policy* 118–26 at 120.

[3] M. Davis, *Property: Meanings, Histories, Theories* (Routledge, 2007) p. 2.

[4] S. M. Borras, *Competing Views and Strategies on Agrarian Reform, Volume 1: International Perspective* (Ateneo de Manila University Press, 2008) p. 20.

[5] K. Gray, 'Property in thin air' (1991) 50(2) *The Cambridge Law Journal* 252–307 at 295–6.

[6] Resource rights generally have certain characteristics such as exclusivity, duration, flexibility, quality of title, transferability and divisibility; see Scott, *The Evolution of Resource Property Rights*, p. 6.

[7] In discussions of resource rights it is common to distinguish between the power to use and manage, powers to transfer or alienate it and powers to take the income or rent from its use; see Scott, *The Evolution of Resource Property Rights*, p. 5 (emphasis in original).

these rights and the social powers they convey are constrained. Moreover, it high-lights how the (often very technical) discussion on carbon rights has implications not only for the distribution of benefits in the carbon economy but also for the distribution of authority and power between international, national and local actors.

Finally, the chapter contextualises debates on carbon rights in REDD+ by situating them within the broader literature on natural resource governance, CPRs and community-based resource management. This chapter describes REDD+ as an experiment in how to effectively integrate two of the most commonly discussed 'solutions' to common action problems. At the global level, the governance solution most frequently proposed to address complex common action problems tend to be market-orientated and property-based approaches, as can be seen in the global climate regime where emissions trading has been the predominant international mitigation strategy.[8] At the local level, in contrast, the establishment of CPRs and community-based resource management have become key policy responses to common action problems. However, as Carol Rose identifies, at the turn of the millennium there was a growing realisation in global environmentalism that 'these two different management structures [could] to some degree be combined or at least mixed'.[9] Combining market-orientated regimes and CPRs might appear paradox-ical, as these 'organizational forms are mirror images'; yet, as Rose suggests, this contrast can mean that 'the strengths of one are apt to be the weaknesses of the other, and vice versa'.[10] Rose documents the emergence of new arrangements for environ-mental governance based around a 'combination of hybrid, governmentally created property rights and CPRs'.[11] REDD+ reflects such a hybrid approach: it combines elements of market-orientated regimes, given the potential inclusion of REDD+ credits in international carbon markets; but debates about REDD+ implementation at the local level and how to organise the governance structures for the underlying forested land have also been influenced by the CPR literature. Understanding REDD+ as reflecting this hybridity therefore requires moving beyond a dichotom-ous understanding of markets and 'commons',[12] to consider how these different institutional forms have been combined in multilevel arrangements. Specifically, the analysis in this chapter shows how this hybridity facilities the disciplinary inclusion of CPRs and community-based resource management – which are often perceived of as alternatives to, or even counterposed to, marketised approaches – within global markets. Through such processes of disciplinary inclusion, these

---

[8] C. M. Rose, 'Expanding the choices for the global commons: Comparing newfangled tradable allowance schemes to old-fashioned common property regimes' (1999) 10 *Duke Environmental Law & Policy Forum* 45–72 at 70.

[9] Ibid.

[10] Ibid., 68.

[11] Ibid., 70.

[12] E. Ostrom, 'Beyond markets and states: Polycentric governance of complex economic systems' (2010) 100(3) *American Economic Review* 1–33.

B. Rights in Forest Carbon

'commons' arrangements no longer appear as potentially disruptive alternatives to regimes of private property rights and globalised markets, but instead they are neutralised and transformed so they become a means to facilitate ever greater expansion of capitalist market relations.

B RIGHTS IN FOREST CARBON

Historically, rights in sequestered carbon were mostly not legally recognised, since in most jurisdictions these rights were not protected as 'excludable benefits'; rather, the sequestration of carbon in forests and other biomass created only collective (and non-excludable) benefits, namely a cleaner environment.[13] However, with REDD+, sequestered carbon now has become an 'excludable economic benefit', and this is therefore driving calls to more clearly define the nature of 'carbon rights' and clarify legal questions about who is entitled to them and the relationship between carbon rights and other property rights within the carbon economy. The term 'carbon rights' or 'forest carbon rights' is frequently found in national, international and donor documents pertaining to REDD+; however, there remains considerable legal ambiguity, even at a conceptual level, about the nature and content of such 'carbon rights' or 'forest-based carbon rights', and there is 'no generally accepted legal definition'.[14] David Takacs describes 'carbon rights' as 'the bundle of rights allowing an entity to explore and exploit the potential that natural sources have to store carbon',[15] which 'usually encompasses the bundle of property rights to control a resource (trees, land) that may contain and preserve carbon, and may connote the right to manage the land to maximize the potential carbon sequestration'.[16] A report by the United States Agency for International Development (USAID) defines 'carbon rights' as 'the right to benefit from sequestered carbon and/or reduced greenhouse gas emissions'.[17] A report by REDDnet and the World Bank describes them as 'intangible assets created by legislative and contractual arrangements that allow the recognition of separate benefits arising from the sequestration of carbon in the biomass'.[18] Lasse Loft defines carbon rights as relating to 'which parties have the right to sell, trade and purchase a carbon credit (i.e., a fixed quantity of carbon)

---

[13] A. Knox, D. Vhugen, S. Aguilar, L. Peskett, and J. Miner, *Forest Carbon Rights Guidebook: A Tool for Framing Legal Rights to Carbon Benefits Generated through REDD+ Programming* (United States Agency for International Development, 2012) p. 8.

[14] C. Streck, 'In the market: Forest carbon rights: Shedding light on a muddy concept' (2015) 4 *Carbon & Climate Law Review* 342, 243.

[15] D. Takacs, *Forest Carbon: Law and Property Rights* (Conservation International, 2009) p. 14.

[16] Ibid.

[17] Knox et al., *Forest Carbon Rights Guidebook*, p. 7.

[18] L. Peskett and G. Brodnig, *Carbon Rights in REDD+: Exploring the Implications for Poor and Vulnerable People* (The World Bank, 2011).

in the world's voluntary and compulsory markets, or through bilateral agreements'.[19] According to the International Institute for Environment and Development (IIED), carbon rights are a 'form of property right' that 'separate rights to carbon from broader rights to the forest and land' and also 'define management responsibilities and liabilities'.[20] The *Little Book of Legal Frameworks for REDD+* states that carbon rights 'create rights over an "intangible asset" and introduce carbon as a new form of property, separate from the trees/biomass in which it resides, and which may be transferred or purchased separately'.[21] This lack of clarity has significant implications for the legal nature of such rights, their status as property, the rules of allocation and transfer, as well as how 'land-bound carbon rights relate to regulated carbon units'.[22]

1 Carbon Rights

The discussions about carbon rights are complicated by the fact that different dimensions of rights can be attached to carbon taken up from the atmosphere and converted through photosynthesis into carbon stored in biomass.[23] One can think about rights in forest carbon as the whole 'bundle of rights and obligations to the resource or good itself: the carbon sequestered and stored in the biomass of the trees that make up a forest'.[24] The rights in this bundle include the right to carbon credits created through sequestration processes, the right to manage the land to promote carbon sequestration and right to be compensated or rewarded for the provision of carbon sequestration and storage services or to benefit from these processes.[25] The various forms such rights can take therefore adds complexity[26] and necessitates careful elaboration and differentiation between the different, but related, rights.[27]

In addition, complex questions arise about how such carbon rights are related to potentially separate rights either in the underlying land[28] or in 'emission reductions'

---

[19] Extracted in W. D. Sunderlin, A. M. Larson, and J. P. Sarmiento Barletti, 'Land and carbon tenure: Some – but insufficient – progress' in A. Angelsen, C. Martius, V. De Sy, A. E. Duchelle, A. M. Larson, and P. T. Thuy (eds.), *Transforming REDD+: Lessons and New Directions* (Center for International Forestry Research, 2018) pp. 93, 95.

[20] L. Cotula and J. Mayers, *Tenure in REDD – Start-Point or Afterthought?* (International Institute for Environment and Development, 2009) p. 9.

[21] L. Denier, S. Korwin, M. Leggett, and C. MacFarquhar, *The Little Book of Legal Frameworks for REDD+* (Global Canopy Programme, 2014) p. 137.

[22] Streck, 'In the market: Forest carbon rights', 342.

[23] L. Loft, A. Ravikumar, M. Gebara, T. Pham, I. Resosudarmo, S. Assembe, J. Tovar, E. Mwangi, and K. Andersson, 'Taking stock of carbon rights in REDD+ candidate countries: Concept meets reality' (2015) 6(4) *Forests* 1031–60 at 1035.

[24] Ibid.

[25] Ibid.

[26] Takacs, *Forest Carbon: Law and Property Rights*, p. 13.

[27] Streck, 'In the market: Forest carbon rights'.

[28] See K. L. Rosenbaum, D. Schoene, and A. Mekouar, *Climate Change and the Forest Sector: Possible National and Subnational Legislation* (Food and Agricultural Organisation of the United Nations, 2004); A. Savaresi and E. Morgera, 'Ownership of land, forest and carbon' in

B. Rights in Forest Carbon

or 'carbon credits' that could circulate in international carbon markets. In some jurisdictions (for example, Brazil) which recognise separate and distinct rights in trees and land, carbon rights might also need to be distinguished from rights in trees.[29] Although legal frameworks are still evolving, most of the proposed frameworks conceptually distinguish between:

(i) rights in sequestered carbon or carbon credits;
(ii) right to the carbon sinks or the 'reservoirs in which the carbon is stored', also described as the right to the carbon sequestration potential of the land, that is, 'the bundle of rights allowing an entity to explore and exploit the potential that land and forests have to store carbon'[30] and/or benefit from these activities and
(iii) the right or title to the land on which the trees or biomass are located.

'Carbon rights', or rights in the carbon sequestration potential of the land, (i.e., (ii) above), is a novel type of property right, referring to a right or property in the 'ability of soil and vegetation that can be grown on land to absorb and retain atmospheric carbon', which is an 'existing attribute or product of the land'.[31] Such carbon rights are thus inherently linked to – and arguably a bridge between – international legal frameworks regulating emission reductions and national laws pertaining to forests and forested land. As Mahanty et al. write, '[The] need to store carbon in forested land connects the intangible commodity of forest carbon to material natural resources.'[32] Although the rights in 'carbon credits' or 'emission reductions'[33] that arise from avoided deforestation could potentially circulate in international carbon markets and are defined by reference to UNFCCC guidance, 'the bundle of rights allowing an entity to explore and exploit the potential that land and forests have to store carbon'[34] and to benefit from the sequestration of carbon in land are – pursuant to the principle of permanent sovereignty over natural resources – governed by domestic law.[35]

Therefore, legal frameworks to establish these novel property rights and the rules for their transfer and enforceability will need to be developed at the national or subnational level in jurisdictions seeking to produce REDD+ carbon credits. It is widely accepted that clarification of the nature of 'carbon rights' is critical for REDD+ to

---

J. Costenbader (ed.), *Legal Frameworks for REDD: Design and Implementation at the National Level* (IUCN, 2009) pp. 15–34.

[29] Takacs, *Forest Carbon: Law and Property Rights*, p. 14.

[30] Peskett and Brodnig, *Carbon Rights in REDD+*, 4.

[31] S. Kennett, A. J. Kwasniak, and A. R. Lucas, 'Property rights and the legal framework for carbon sequestration on agricultural land' (2005) 37 *Ottawa Law Review* 171.

[32] S. Mahanty, W. Dressler, S. Milne, and C. Filer, 'Unravelling property relations around forest carbon' (2013) 34(2) *Singapore Journal of Tropical Geography* 188–205 at 189.

[33] For a discussion of these see Chapter 3.

[34] Peskett and Brodnig, *Carbon Rights in REDD+*, 4.

[35] Loft et al., 'Taking stock of carbon rights in REDD+ candidate countries, 1035.

work, especially for project or market-based approaches to REDD+.[36] Scholars have identified that clarity over tenure and resource rights will be 'critical to prevent disruptive conflicts between competing stakeholders' and to avoid uncertainties and complications for REDD+ sellers/providers and buyers/beneficiaries.[37] As Loft et al. write, '[I]t is critical for project partners to know who manages and controls the forest' and therefore to 'ensure that those who are responsible for activities that may lead to emission reductions have the long-term right to conduct such activities and ... can be rewarded in case of successful reductions or held responsible in case of failure'.[38] Furthermore, the clarification of carbon rights is needed to establish who has the right to benefit from performance-based mechanisms, and thus who should be included in benefit-sharing mechanisms. As the Rights and Resources Initiative (RRI) states, 'Clarifying who owns the carbon – and the land and forest containing the carbon – is essential to fulfilling the promise of result-based payments'.[39] The clarification of carbon rights is also a prerequisite for transnational carbon contracting. For example, the FCPF requires that any 'program entities' who have been authorised by the host country, to implement an emission reduction programme must demonstrate before they enter into the ERPA that they have the ability to transfer the title to emission reductions to the Carbon Fund.[40] However, the UNFCCC framework does not provide guidance on frameworks for carbon rights,[41] and leaves the question of defining and allocating 'carbon rights' to be resolved in accordance with national circumstance and existing property law regimes and regulatory objectives in host nations.[42]

Although the development of national-level frameworks of carbon rights has become a key element of REDD+-readiness programmes, only a few countries have legislated to define carbon rights, and in most jurisdictions there remain high levels of ambiguity about the nature of carbon rights, the rights they confer to different actors and how they should be regulated.[43] A review by the RRI of 24 countries that collectively contain over 50 percent of global tropical and subtropical forests found that, although most of these countries are involved in the carbon trade, they continue to struggle to define carbon rights, and only four countries (Brazil, Costa

---

[36] Peskett and Brodnig, *Carbon Rights in REDD+*, 1; A. Karsenty, A. Vogel, and F. Castell, '"Carbon rights", REDD+ and payments for environmental services' (2014) 35 *Environmental Science & Policy* 20–9 at 21.

[37] Loft et al., 'Taking stock of carbon rights in REDD+ candidate countries', 1033.

[38] Ibid., 1034.

[39] A. Corriveau-Bourque, F. Almeida, and A. Frechette, *Uncertainty and Opportunity: The Status of Forest Carbon Rights and Governance Frameworks in Over Half of the World's Tropical Forests* (Rights and Resources Initiative, 2018) p. 4.

[40] *FCPF Carbon Fund Methodological Framework*, June 22, 2016, Criterion 36, and related discussion on p. 27.

[41] Denier et al., *The Little Book of Legal Frameworks for REDD+*, p. 138.

[42] Kennett et al., 'Property rights and the legal framework for carbon sequestration on agricultural land'.

[43] Denier et al., *The Little Book of Legal Frameworks for REDD+*, p. 137.

B. Rights in Forest Carbon

Rica, Guatemala and Peru) have explicitly defined such rights in national law.[44] Moreover, only five of the countries examined (Brazil, Costa Rica, Ecuador, Peru and Vietnam) have introduced national legal frameworks establishing and regulating carbon rights, while the majority of forested countries have not done so.[45]

There has been considerable debate over how such a right in the carbon sequestration potential of land would be defined and structured, including in a number of reports[46] as well as scholarly work seeking to clarify these concepts[47] and to draw lessons from experiences in comparable jurisdictions.[48] A number of distinct legal questions are addressed in the literature about various aspects of 'carbon rights' including:

- whether carbon rights should be explicitly defined in legislation or simply addressed implicitly under existing laws;
- whether carbon rights will be recognised as a form of property or simply a 'benefit' or 'credit';
- how carbon rights are allocated and whether they exist as a separate proprietary interest, or are tied to resource rights or land (use) rights;
- who the carbon rightsholder is, namely the nation/state, a community or an individual;
- the nature of the liability associated with the carbon right.[49]

A key focus of such analysis has been identifying what legal form and structure is most suited to these novel carbon rights. One report by the FAO suggests that carbon rights could be defined as: (a) inseparable from the land; (b) inseparable from the land but the subject of a covenant binding land owners; (c) a transferable easement over land (which is however not a property right) or (d) a separate alienable property right.[50] Additionally, it states that such a right could be regarded as a 'public good'

---

[44] Corriveau-Bourque et al., *Uncertainty and Opportunity*, p. 5.

[45] Ibid.

[46] J. Costenbader, *Legal Frameworks for REDD. Design and Implementation at the National Level* (IUCN, 2009), especially the chapter 'Ownership of land, forest and carbon' by Savaresi and Morgera; *Background Analysis of REDD Regulatory Frameworks* (Baker & McKenzie, 2009); Takacs, *Forest Carbon: Law and Property Rights*; Peskett and Brodnig, *Carbon Rights in REDD+*; Knox et al., *Forest Carbon Rights Guidebook*; Denier et al., *The Little Book of Legal Frameworks for REDD+*.

[47] Streck, 'In the market: Forest carbon rights'; R. Fisher and R. Lyster, 'Land and resource tenure: The rights of indigenous peoples and forest dwellers' in R. Lyster, C. MacKenzie, and C. McDermott (eds.), *Law, Tropical Forests and Carbon: The Case of REDD+* (Cambridge University Press, 2013) pp. 187–206.

[48] See for example N. Durrant, 'Legal Issues in biosequestration: Carbon sinks, carbon rights and carbon trading' (2008) 31(3) *UNSW Law Journal* 906–18; S. Hepburn, 'Carbon rights as new property: The benefits of statutory verification' (2009) 31 *Sydney Law Review* 239–71; A. Zahar, J. Peel, and L. Godden, *Australian Climate Law in Global Context* (Cambridge University Press, 2013) Chapter 10.

[49] Loft et al., 'Taking stock of carbon rights in REDD+ candidate countries', 1034.

[50] Rosenbaum et al., *Climate Change and the Forest Sector*.

that is either not ownable by private entities or wholly owned by the state and unalienable.[51] Scholars have also canvassed multiple options for defining carbon rights, including that such rights could be structured as a personal usufruct right, whereby a person or entity may use and derive benefit from property that belongs to another entity, provided the property is not impaired;[52] or as a separate property right that is tied to the land. Further, there are several ways in which carbon rights could be established: through defining new rights in legislation, as well as through usufruct rights, including easements, leases or *profits a prendre*,[53] as well as a chose in action or as a *sui generis* separate interest in land.[54] In the Australian context, carbon rights legislation has confirmed that 'carbon rights' denote 'a land interest separate from the land upon which it is situated', rebutting the common law presumption that would see carbon stored in trees as part of the land.[55] However, a number of commentators have warned that potential 'dangers lurk for local tenure security where carbon rights are separated from land tenure'.[56]

These discussions operate primarily on a technical register, and although the authors are all undoubtedly aware of how such policy making is saturated with political significance, they nonetheless present their analysis in 'vocabularies of economic and legal expertise that obscure the political stakes of development policy making'.[57] Yet the recommendations and proposals presented by such scholars about how these novel property rights should be defined and allocated are highly political, given that different approaches will necessarily affect the distribution of resources among groups and individuals, and thereby also impact upon the distribution of power between these groups and individuals.[58] Questions about the nature and allocation of carbon rights are shaped by existing dynamics of knowledge, culture and power and are 'enacted, embedded, legitimated and/or resisted within changing political, economic and cultural contexts'[59] that are marked by the historical dispossession of forest peoples. Forest landscapes are often the product of colonial and postcolonial histories, where states have sought to control access to forest areas and have granted concessions to state-owned or private logging companies while ignoring the rights and interests of forest communities. Such landscapes are also often subject to 'persistent agricultural frontier expansion' and

---

[51] Ibid.
[52] Takacs, *Forest Carbon: Law and Property Rights*, p. 14.
[53] Ibid.; Karsenty et al., '"Carbon rights", REDD+ and payments for environmental services', 24.
[54] M. Parry, 'A property law perspective on the current Australian carbon sequestration laws, and the Green Paper model' (2010) 36 *Monash University Law Review* 321.
[55] Hepburn, 'Carbon rights as new property', 247.
[56] Cotula and Mayers, *Tenure in REDD – Start-point or afterthought?*, p. 25.
[57] D. Kennedy, 'The "rule of law", political choices, and development common sense' in D. M. Trubek, and A. Santos (eds.), *The New Law and Economic Development: A Critical Appraisal* (Cambridge University Press, 2006) pp. 95–173.
[58] Ibid.
[59] Mahanty et al., 'Unravelling property relations around forest carbon', 189.

B. Rights in Forest Carbon

resulting conflict between those holding customary tenure and those seeking to appropriate land and resources.[60] REDD+, and the need to clarify carbon rights, therefore introduces further contestation to landscapes already marked by a history of competing 'dynamic and overlapping claims to forested land'.[61]

Debates about carbon rights are particularly fraught in a context where questions pertaining to such rights effectively become 'a proxy for unresolved and contested land tenure, which often derives, in turn, from the historic marginalization of indigenous forest communities and their long struggle to assert land and resource rights'.[62] The majority of forest land remains owned by governments,[63] and despite persistent calls to transfer rights to forest peoples, according to the RRI, only approximately 12 percent of land in forested countries is owned by Indigenous peoples or local communities.[64] Its analysis of trends over 15 years (2002–17) shows that governments have been slow to recognise community rights and that 'the global slowdown in tenure recognition ... has reached a plateau, with recognition increasing only marginally'.[65] The degree to which the land and resource rights of forest dwellers have been recognised and/or formalised by nation-states is highly variable, and the lack of legal security afforded such rights can, in certain contexts, give rise of conflict.[66] The 'entry of forest carbon as a new "resource" could precipitate a renegotiation of property relations in land and forests'[67] in ways that might further disadvantage already marginalised communities. Concerns have been expressed that REDD+ could promote greater centralised control over forested lands and deincentivise current trends to recognise local rights. However, alongside these concerns others have suggested REDD+ also presents an opportunity to leverage more progressive tenure reform.[68] However, it is generally the case, as Lee Godden and Maureen Tehan warn, that '[t]he degree of recognition of indigenous and local

---

[60] E. Corbera, M. Estrada, P. May, G. Navarro, and P. Pacheco, 'Rights to land, forests and carbon in REDD+: Insights from Mexico, Brazil and Costa Rica' (2011) 2(1) *Forests* 301–42 at 305.

[61] Mahanty et al., 'Unravelling property relations around forest carbon', 199.

[62] Streck, 'In the market: Forest carbon rights', 346.

[63] The 2015 FAO Global Forest Resources Assessment found that in 2010, 76 percent of global forest area was publicly owned, 20 percent was private and 4 percent was of unknown ownership: *Global Forest Resources Assessment 2015: How Are the World's Forests Changing?* 2nd edition (FAO, 2016) p. 38.

[64] Rights and Resources Initiative analysed ownership trends in 58 forested countries and found that Indigenous peoples and local communities owned 12.2 percent (447 million hectares), individual and firms own 11.4 percent (419 million hectares), and governments claimed administrative responsibility for over two-thirds of all forest lands: C. Ginsburg and S. Keene, *At a Crossroads: Consequential Trends in Recognition of Community-Based Forest Tenure from 2002–2017* (Rights and Resources Initiative, 2018) p. 9.

[65] Ibid., p. 7.

[66] L. Godden, 'Benefit-sharing in REDD+: Linking rights and equitable outcomes' in *The Impact of Climate Change Mitigation on Indigenous and Forest Communities: International, National and Local Law Perspectives on REDD+* (Cambridge University Press, 2017) pp. 172–200, 196.

[67] Mahanty et al., 'Unravelling property relations around forest carbon', 190–1.

[68] See discussion in Chapter 1.

266 *Scale, Multilevel Governance & Disaggregation of Property Rights in REDD+*

community "rights" in relation to REDD+ often hinges on the extent to which the land and resource rights of the groups are accepted by the governing state'.[69] There are therefore serious concerns that if the 'existing configuration of property [is] referenced to legitimize forest carbon claims',[70] such processes would be biased in favour of the current possessors and users of land and would therefore disadvantage communities claiming rights based on prior possession.[71] The next section discusses how even if local communities are recognised as having such rights or are granted such rights, the nature of these rights and the relational power they confer is likely to be highly constrained.

2 *Forest Tenure*

Land tenure is a 'multivariate term',[72] but can be understood as 'the right, whether defined in customary or statutory terms, that determines who can hold and use land (including forests and other landscapes) and resources, for how long, and under what conditions'.[73] In practice, however, as Godden and Tehan write, 'The term "tenure" typically indicates a formalization of rights in a state-based system', and thus may exclude informal rights, even if they are strongly grounded in Indigenous or local community law.[74] More expansive understandings of tenure include 'property rights, understood as social relationships that contain enforceable claims to rights in something, and informal relations governing access to, use of and exclusion from resources, and involving potentially multiple authorities'.[75] By extension, forest tenure refers to who owns forest land, but also who uses, manages and makes decisions about forest resources. That is, it 'determines who is allowed to use which resources, in what way, for how long and under what conditions, as well as who is entitled to transfer rights to others and how'.[76]

Since the mid-1980s there have been important trends pertaining to forest tenure reform and recognition that have been shaped and driven by a number of different

---

[69] L. Godden and M. Tehan, 'REDD+: Climate justice and indigenous and local community rights in an era of climate disruption' (2016) 34(1) *Journal of Energy & Natural Resources Law* 95–108 at 105.

[70] Mahanty et al., 'Unravelling property relations around forest carbon', 190–1.

[71] K. Gover, 'REDD+, tenure and Indigenous property claims' in *The Impact of Climate Change Mitigation on Indigenous and Forest Communities: International, National and Local Law Perspectives on REDD+* (Cambridge University Press, 2017) pp. 130–71.

[72] Godden, 'Benefit-Sharing in REDD+', p. 195.

[73] Corbera et al., 'Rights to land, forests and carbon in REDD+', 303.

[74] Godden and Tehan, 'REDD+: Climate justice and indigenous and local community rights in an era of climate disruption', 105.

[75] Corbera et al., 'Rights to land, forests and carbon in REDD', 303.

[76] A. Larson, *Tenure Rights and Access to Forests: A Training Manual for Research – Part I. A Guide to Key Issues* (Center for International Forestry Research, 2012) p. 8.

B. Rights in Forest Carbon

forces, both 'from above' and 'from below'.[77] This has involved titling of territories, the granting of new formal statutory rights as part of an uneven process of recognising or formalising customary or de facto rights, and at times transferring, constraining or limiting rights.[78] However, often the process of forest tenure reform has been 'imposed from the top' in a way that has not properly taken into account 'peoples' own customs, institutions and forms of land ownership' or provided an appropriate enabling framework.[79]

Discussions on carbon rights need to be attentive to how forest tenure arrangements are distinct from arrangements governing agricultural land as well as the 'unique set of conditions that distinguish rights to collective or common property resources, like forests, that are particularly important in developing countries'.[80] Forest tenure arrangements depart from agrarian tenure arrangements in a number of ways. First, forest tenure generally involves 'groups of people with multiple and simultaneous rights and hence a shared interest in a common resource'.[81] Processes of forest tenure reform or formalisation therefore need to engage 'an entire array of rights holders bound by a complex web of interests', who all have different kinds of rights, including some rights or interests that may 'vary with the season, climate, price of forest goods or political factors'.[82] The dynamic and overlapping nature of rights claimed in forested land poses challenges for identifying both the various rights and the rights holders affected by REDD+.[83] Such affected rights might include access rights (to enter a specific area), withdrawal rights (to contain products of a resource), management rights (to establish rules and sanctions), exclusion rights (to determine who has access and withdrawal rights) and alienation rights (to transfer rights to another).[84] Second, processes of forest tenure reform are distinct from other processes of agrarian tenure reform because the former have been shaped by three global forces or dynamics – namely, demands for Indigenous rights, conservation and decentralisation. As Barry et al. identify, forest tenure reform processes have generally been driven by and aimed at the following three objectives simultaneously: ensuring greater rights for forest peoples and local communities in forest areas, improving their livelihoods and promoting conservation of forests and their

---

[77] A. M. Larson, D. Barry, and G. R. Dahal, 'Tenure change in the global south' in A. M. Larson, D. Barry, G. R. Dahal, and C. Colfer (eds.), *Forests for People: Community Rights and Forest Tenure Reform* (Earthscan, 2010) pp. 3–18, 3.

[78] Ibid.

[79] M. Colchester, *Beyond Tenure: Rights-Based Approaches to Peoples and Forests. Some Lessons from the Forest Peoples Programme* (Forest Peoples Programme, 2007) p. 3.

[80] D. Barry, A. M. Larson, and C. J. P. Colfer, 'Forest tenure reform: An orphan with only uncles' in Larson et al. (eds.), *Forests for People: Community Rights and Forest Tenure Reform* (Earthscan, 2010) pp. 19–40, 20.

[81] Ibid.

[82] Ibid., p. 22.

[83] Streck, 'In the market: Forest carbon rights', 346.

[84] Ibid.

biodiversity.[85] These different – and occasionally in tension – drivers and objectives have given a distinctive shape to the nature and process of forest tenure reform.

As a result, the nature of the rights granted through processes of forest tenure reform often differs from the rights granted through other processes of agrarian tenure reform. In contrast to agrarian land reform, which may involve the granting of individual private property rights, forest tenure reform has generally involved 'granting collective rights but maintaining the state as a principal rights holder'.[86] Moreover, alienation rights have generally not been granted to communities through processes of forest tenure reform, but rather these rights have remained with the state, which also maintains a key role in forest management and often imposes expectations that the forest should remain intact.[87] Therefore, even when land is formally 'community owned' the associated rights often remain 'highly circumscribed'[88] and as Barry et al. discuss, communities whose tenure rights are recognised are 'bound in relationships that could be considered co-ownership or co-management of forests with the state'.[89] Finally, given that the division and sale of forested land is generally prohibited, forests are not considered 'property' or 'commodities' as forested land 'does not enter into formal land markets'.[90] In sum, forest tenure reforms, even when they recognise pre-existing community rights or transfer rights to communities, 'rarely transfer the full bundle of rights' related to forested land, consisting of right to access, sell or otherwise alienate, manage, withdraw resources and exclude others' access, use, management and exclusion rights.[91] That is, the mere recognition of rights in relation to land – including the recognition of carbon rights – risks being a pyrrhic victory for communities living in and around forests, if these rights lack the attributes of control and management and therefore fail to grant their holder the power to control and manage forested land.

Therefore, in processes of forest tenure reform, a key point of contestation has been not just *whether* local communities are granted rights, but also *what* rights they are granted. A particularly contentious struggle has been over the 'transfer of real decision-making powers, particularly management and exclusion rights, from the state to communities'.[92] From a perspective attentive to the rights of communities, critical questions thus arise about the degree to which communities 'hold and shape' decision-making rights over forest lands and resources and the extent to which the state 'undermines or recognises' community decision-making rights over forested

---

[85] Barry et al., 'Forest tenure reform': An orphan with only uncles', p. 37.

[86] Ibid., p. 22.

[87] Ibid., p. 37.

[88] Fisher and Lyster, 'Land and resource tenure: The rights of indigenous people and forest dwellers', p. 193.

[89] Barry et al., 'Forest tenure reform: An orphan with only uncles', p. 22.

[90] Ibid.

[91] Lyster, 'REDD+, transparency, participation and resource rights' p. 122.

[92] Barry et al., 'Forest tenure reform: An orphan with only uncles' p. 23.

land.[93] Advocates for forest peoples assert that tenure reform programmes need to recognise the right of communities to 'own, control and peacefully enjoy their lands, territories and other resources, and be secure in their means of subsistence'.[94] These demands extend beyond more limited calls for tenure rights, because they involve not just a claim to property rights, implicit in the term 'own', but also the innovation of broader rights including those of 'control', 'use' and 'enjoyment'.[95]

Given the real challenges for forest-dwelling communities in having tenure rights recognised, Robert Fisher and Rosemary Lyster have proposed that the concept of 'resource tenure' – rather than 'land tenure' – provides 'an appropriate avenue for identifying forest tenure in publicly owned forests'.[96] Such 'resource' tenure rights do not accord with land ownership or confer ownership of the underlying land, but are more akin to statutory tenures (such as mining leases, forestry concessions or fishing licences).[97] Nonetheless, Lyster and Fisher suggest that claims to 'resource tenure' could be a means to secure the rights of forest communities and allow them to claim property rights over the carbon rights in those forests.[98] However, the potential cost of such an approach, as Lee Godden warns, is that such carbon rights might be reduced to only usufructuary interests, with less priority and enforceability than other proprietary rights.[99] The analysis in the remainder of this chapter however shows that although this approach is problematic it resonates and aligns with broader trends in relation to natural resource governance, common property and community resource management that grant forest peoples limited rights to benefit from forest resources but do not grant them control or management rights over forested land . Although such trends are not necessarily determinative of future REDD+ trajectories, they do provide a sense of the policy context in which REDD+ implementation occurs, as well as the power of certain actors and ideas in this space, and thus are indicative of likely REDD+ developments. The next section therefore situates debates on carbon rights within broader trends relating to the governance of natural resources and CPRs, in order to better understand some of the likely trajectories with regard to carbon rights in REDD+ and how they operate to redistribute power and authority away from 'local' and towards 'global' actors.

C COMMON PROPERTY REGIMES AND NATURAL RESOURCES

This section contextualises debates on carbon rights in REDD+ within the broader literature on natural resource governance, common property and community

---

[93] Ibid., p. 23.
[94] Colchester, *Beyond Tenure: Rights-Based Approaches to Peoples and Forests*, p. 4.
[95] Ibid.
[96] Fisher and Lyster, 'Land and resource tenure', p. 197.
[97] Godden, 'Benefit-sharing in REDD+: Linking rights and equitable outcomes', p. 197.
[98] Fisher and Lyster, 'Land and resource tenure', p. 198.
[99] Godden, 'Benefit-sharing in REDD+: Linking rights and equitable outcomes', p. 197.

resource management in order to interrogate how even if local communities are acknowledged to have carbon rights, the nature of these rights and the social powers these rights convey are constrained. The analysis shows that even when the carbon rights of communities are recognised such rights generally only convey 'lower-order rights' of use and access, whereas the 'higher-order' control and authoritative rights are often granted to international actors. Situating the debates on carbon rights with reference to this literature helps illuminate how the broader property relations in which carbon rights are situated operate to globalise authority over forested lands. Discussions on carbon rights have focused on recognition of the land or resource tenure rights of forest communities by national or sub-national governments in order to protect such communities from potential risks, including that REDD+ implementation might alienate them from their land and resources, and to ensure that they can benefit from REDD+ implementation. However, such analyses often adopt a national or sub-national frame that often fails to properly account for the multiplicity of actors, including international and transnational actors, involved in REDD+. Given that tenure represents 'a set of agreements between social actors with respect to a resource',[100] it is critical to situate these discussions of carbon rights within a global frame and interrogate how the introduction of new social actors and a new set of arrangements transforms the distribution of social power between respective rights holders. The international interest in the measurement and verification of 'emission reductions' through forest carbon programmes, and potentially their propertisation, not only compels the need for clarification of carbon rights (as discussed above) but also transforms the degree of the social power that carbon rights grant the holder. Chapter 3 demonstrated how REDD+ programmes are underpinned by transnational carbon contracting. Contract is, as Anthony Scott writes, 'the main device by which one private (or sometimes public) party transfers some of his [sic] rights and powers of property, along with some or all of its characteristics, to another'.[101] If forested land is subject to a carbon contract, the contractual conditions prescribe obligations to manage that land in accordance with the contractual terms as well to a right to benefit from the REDD+ project. Thus, the rise of transnational carbon contracting, and the associated potential novel property rights in emission reductions from carbon sequestration programmes, allocates to international actors new rights that empower them to define and determine what sort of rights can be exercised by carbon rights holders and land rights holders. The discussion below provides the context for understanding how 'higher-order' rights that empower holders to exercise control and authoritative rights over natural resources are

---

[100] Barry et al., 'Forest tenure reform: An orphan with only uncles', p. 20.
[101] Scott, *The Evolution of Resource Property Rights*, p. 14.

C. Common Property Regimes and Natural Resources 271

increasingly being held and exercised by international actors, even as local communities might still possess 'lower' use rights to access the direct and indirect benefits from the resource.[102]

Further, contextualising the debates on carbon rights in REDD+ within this broader literature on natural resource governance, common property and community resource management also adds nuance to discussions about the need to recognise communal rights as well as legal pluralism in REDD+ implementation. Scholars attentive to questions of Indigenous rights have highlighted that it is not appropriate to apply liberal notions of individual property rights to Indigenous peoples and forest communities.[103] Similarly, scholars have highlighted how REDD+ will need to 'accommodate multiple and varied tenure systems' and have posed questions about how 'diverse tenure systems can be adequately incorporated within a multi-level governance framework such as REDD+'.[104] A number of scholars have stressed the desirability of 'legal pluralist' approaches to carbon rights to acknowledge local or customary legal systems.[105] Such acknowledgement of legal pluralism and customary tenure is both pertinent and necessary. However, the analysis in this chapter situates these calls within the context of broader developments in the natural resource governance space in order to show how communal rights and legal pluralism have been accommodated and deployed in developmental strategies as a 'compromise position', in ways that arguably discipline and constrain customary regimes through their incorporation into broader legal frameworks and global market relations. While it is positive to see a move away from development approaches that seek to replace diverse ontologies of property with the individualised private rights characteristic of Western modernity, there is nonetheless a real danger that the conditional accommodation of customary and communal rights could constrain rather than advance local empowerment and self-determination. Whilst commons have often been imagined as outside and against private property regimes, the purpose of such a strategic recognition of customary property regimes is to enable the commons to be incorporated into global capitalist strategies of accumulation. These models thereby promote *conditional* localised self-governance, but in doing so operate to ensure that local self-governance is only *exercised in specific ways* that facilitate 'global' interests.

---

[102] See T. Sikor, J. He, and G. Lestrelin, 'Property rights regimes and natural resources: A conceptual analysis revisited' (2017) 93 *World Development* 337–49.

[103] Fisher and Lyster, 'Land and resource tenure', p. 195; see also Godden and Tehan, 'REDD+: Climate justice and indigenous and local community rights in an era of climate disruption'; K. Birrell, L. Godden, and M. Tehan, 'Climate change and REDD+: Property as a prism for conceiving Indigenous peoples' engagement' (2012) 3(2) *Journal of Human Rights and the Environment* 196–216.

[104] E. Doherty and H. Schroeder, 'Forest tenure and multi-level governance in avoiding deforestation under REDD' (2011) 11(4) *Global Environmental Politics* 66–87 at 67.

[105] Takacs, *Forest Carbon: Law and Property Rights*, p. 6.

1 *Common Property Resources As a Development Strategy*

Partly in response to resistance to land privatisation programmes in the Global South, since the early 1990s there has been a 'cautious and qualified acceptance of the commons' and its strategic deployment in development planning, including at the World Bank.[106] Inspired by Hardin's 'tragedy of the commons' parable,[107] earlier land formalisation programmes linked to structural adjustment policies had aggressively sought to privatise common land on the assumption that individual land ownership was a necessary condition for capitalist markets.[108] However, when these policies faced an antagonist response and protests from social movements, there was within development planning circles a gradual 'acceptance of the agrarian or forest commons at least as a stop-gap, transitional institution'.[109] Drawing on new commons scholarship, especially the work of Elinor Ostrom,[110] development institutions endorsed the regulation of resources through CPRs – under certain conditions – as a 'rational' mode of management,[111] thereby transforming the commons from 'a relic to a live option in the World Bank's strategic "development" literature'.[112] Although the institutional adoption of this new discourse of the commons was seen by some as challenge to the 'legitimacy of elite discursive practices of capitalist development and expansion'[113] that were focused on individual, privatised rights, critical scholars have suggested instead that the way the commons were taken up within development thinking has, in fact, served broader agendas that aspired to the 'restructuring [of] Third World capacities and social–natural relations to accommodate transnational capital expansion'.[114] This strategic adoption of commons discourse by development institutions thus operated to foreground an understanding of the commons that was compatible with the smooth functioning of global markets, in contrast to an understanding of the commons as entailing modes of social relations that are radically antagonistic to capitalist globalisation and demand deep social transformation.[115]

---

[106] G. Caffentzis, 'A tale of two conferences: Globalization, the crisis of neoliberalism and question of the commons', www.globaljusticecenter.org/papers/caffentzis.htm.

[107] G. Hardin, 'The tragedy of the commons' (1968) 162(3859) *Science* 1243–8.

[108] G. Caffentzis, 'The future of "The Commons": Neoliberalism's "Plan B" or the original disaccumulation of capital?' (2010) 69 *New Formations* 23–41 at 26–28.

[109] Ibid., 29.

[110] O. Elinor, *Governing the Commons: The Evolution of Institutions for Collective Action* (Cambridge University Press, 1990).

[111] Caffentzis, 'The future of "The Commons"', 30.

[112] Ibid., 33.

[113] M. Goldman, '"Customs in common": The epistemic world of the commons scholars' (1997) 26(1) *Theory and Society* 1–37 at 24.

[114] Ibid., 26.

[115] G. Caffentzis and S. Federici, 'Commons against and beyond capitalism' (2014) 49 *Community Development Journal* 92–105 at 195.

C. Common Property Regimes and Natural Resources 273

The engagement of the World Bank with the commons can be traced to a 1989 World Bank discussion paper by Daniel Bromley and Michael Cernea, *The Management of Common Property Natural Resources*, which argued that the nature of common property regimes and resources has been fundamentally misunderstood by both academic scholars and World Bank project managers.[116] The authors distinguished 'common property regimes' from 'open access regimes' in order to position the former not as a 'free-for-all' but rather as a 'structured ownership arrangement', with set management rules, institutional arrangements and sanctions ensuring compliance between various co-owners.[117] Bromley and Cernea argued against Hardin's position that resource degradation can be attributed to a 'tragedy of the commons',[118] and suggested instead that the culprit was the 'dissolution of local-level institutional arrangements whose very purpose was to give rise to resource use patterns that were sustainable'.[119] Because they also rejected the possibility that governments can 'effectively' manage natural resources, Bromley and Cernea called for engagement with local resource users and warned that 'natural resource projects in the developing countries that do not actively incorporate the local users will ultimately fail'.[120] They therefore recommended that the 1990s sustainable development agenda focus on building rural managerial capacity in order to promote 'sustainable productive use of natural resources'.[121]

In 1990, Elinor Ostrom published her influential book *Governing the Commons: The Evolution of Institutions for Collective Action*. Widely seen as a 'landmark in the history of theories of commons governance',[122] the work demonstrated empirically the potential for collective action in natural resource governance.[123] Previously, in 1985, Ostrom had played a key role in the launch of the Common Property Resource Network, which in 1989 became the International Association for the Study of Common Property and is now called the International Association for the Study of the Commons.[124] In its focus on how people can work together to overcome collective action problems and the challenge of 'getting the institutions right',[125] scholarship on CPRs shared key concerns of new institutional economics, which focused on the role that institutions, formal rules, conventions and informal

---

[116] D. W. Bromley and M. M. Cernea, *The Management of Common Property Natural Resources* (The World Bank, 1989); see also Goldman, "Customs in common", 8.

[117] Bromley and Cernea, *The Management of Common Property Natural Resources*, p. iii.

[118] G. Hardin, 'The tragedy of the commons', p. iii.

[119] Bromley and Cernea, *The Management of Common Property Natural Resources*, p. iii.

[120] Ibid., pp. iii–iv.

[121] Ibid.

[122] F. Locher, 'Historicizing Elinor Ostrom: Urban politics, international development and expertise in the US context (1970–1990)' (2018) 19(2) *Theoretical Inquiries in Law* 533–58 at 534.

[123] Elinor, *Governing the Commons*; for a discussion of how this was taken up by lawyers see C. M. Rose, 'Ostrom and the lawyers: The impact of Governing the Commons on the American legal academy' (2011) 5(1) *International Journal of the Commons* 28–49.

[124] Locher, 'Historicizing Elinor Ostrom', 544.

[125] Elinor, *Governing the Commons*, p. 14.

codes play in regulating human behaviour, reducing uncertainty and thus minimising transaction costs.[126] Ostrom's way of conceptualising the commons 'provided a foundation for a whole wave of experimentation in community-based management founded on common-property resources'.[127] World Bank support for the production of expert knowledge on the commons gradually increased after its 1992 World Development Report *Development and the Environment* acknowledged the role that community-based arrangements can play in supporting sustainable development.[128] In 1995, a World Bank discussion paper bemoaned the neglect of common property resources by researchers, policy makers and development planners, and suggested that the 'productive potential' of CPRs was 'a major missing dimension of rural development strategies in developing countries'; the authors highlighted the convergence between CPR-centred policies/programmes and broader agendas in relation to participatory development, environmental sustainability and poverty alleviation.[129] The same year, the Common Property Resources Management Network (CPRNet) was established to connect World Bank staff with external practitioners and experts.[130] The establishment of this research group was based on a recognition that

> [i]n comparison with privately owned and managed, as well as state-controlled resources, CPRs play a crucial role in: (i) Reducing rural poverty and inequality; (ii) Maintaining local-level biodiversity and micro-level environmental stability; (iii) Enhancing agricultural productivity and diversity; and, (iv) Promoting collective sharing and group action.[131]

CPRNet's aims included 'enhancing awareness' about CPRs and 'resources that are managed collectively' as 'institutional modalities' within the World Bank.[132] It also sought to increase understanding of the 'dynamic interplay of various types of property rights' regimes on the local level' and the importance of CPRs for the 'correct targeting of World Bank Group investment operations'.[133] In 1998, an International Workshop on Community-Based Natural Resource Management

---

[126] Rose, 'Expanding the choices for the global commons', 49; on new institutional economics see D. C. North, *Institutions, Institutional Change, and Economic Performance* (Cambridge University Press, 1990).

[127] L. Mehta, M. Leach, and I. Scoones, 'Editorial: Environmental Governance in an Uncertain World' (2001) 32(4) *IDS Bulletin* 1–9 at 2.

[128] *World Development Report 1992; Development and the Environment* (The World Bank, 1992).

[129] N. S. Jodha, *Common Property Resources: A Missing Dimension of Development Strategies* (The World Bank, 1992).

[130] Caffentzis, 'The future of "The Commons"', 40.

[131] *The World Bank Group's Common Property Resource Management Network: Guide to CPRNet*, www.supras.biz/pdf/supras_008_wb_cprnetguide.pdf.

[132] Ibid.

[133] Ibid.

C. Common Property Regimes and Natural Resources

was held in Washington DC,[134] hosted by CPRNet and key strategic partner, the International Association for the Study of the Commons, founded and directed by Elinor Ostrom. Subsequently, a voluminous body of literature has been produced on CPRs, and the Vincent and Elinor Ostrom Workshop in Political Theory and Policy Analysis provided a central node for the development of theoretical frameworks for and ethnographic investigations of CPRs.[135]

By the late 1990s and early 2000s, the importance of commons as a form of property distinct from both private and public property, as well as the need to 'explain phenomena that do not fit into a dichotomous world of "the market" and "the state"',[136] was increasingly recognised in scholarship and by development institutions. Thinking beyond the state/market binary involved development of more complex analytical frameworks involving a diversity of institutional forms to understand social phenomena. A key question addressed by such scholarship was how the commons could be incorporated into market arrangements. One of the institutional design principles for CPRs that Ostrom proposed was clearly defined boundaries specifying who is authorised to use a resource.[137] Despite the internal institutional diversity of CPRs, such clearly defined boundaries mean that commons can appear to outsiders as 'a type of property institution ... that puts an entire stock of a resource under unitary and exclusive management'.[138] As Carol Rose identifies, depending on one's perspective such commons regimes can then take on a dual character, whereby '[a]lthough members ... may treat the resource as a "commons" amongst themselves, with respect to the rest of the world that resource is property'.[139] That is, 'they may look like a commons on the inside, but they are property on the outside'.[140] Once commons were delineated in this way, it became possible to experiment with different ways in which commons could be incorporated into broader institutional arrangements, such as structures that involve the combination of hybrid, regulatory property rights – such as carbon credits – alongside CPRs.[141]

---

[134] Ibid.; see also The International Workshop on Community-Based Natural Resource Governance (CBNRG), Washington DC, 10–14 May 1998, 'Workshop Report', info.worldbank.org/etools/docs/library/97605/conatrem/conatrem/documents/May98Workshop_Report. pdf.

[135] See P. D. Aligica, *Institutional Diversity and Political Economy: The Ostroms and Beyond* (Oxford University Press, 2014); P. D. Aligica and P. J. Boettke, *Challenging Institutional Analysis and Development: The Bloomington School* (Routledge, 2009); M. D. McGinnis (ed.), *Polycentric Governance and Development: Readings from the Workshop in Political Theory and Policy Analysis* (University of Michigan Press, 1999).

[136] E. Ostrom, 'Beyond markets and states: Polycentric governance of complex economic systems' (2010) 100(3) *American Economic Review* 641–72 at 641.

[137] Elinor, *Governing the Commons*, pp. 90–1.

[138] Rose, 'Expanding the choices for the global commons', 48.

[139] Ibid.

[140] Ibid.

[141] Ibid., 71.

Such experimentation with hybrid institutional structures simultaneously responded to the perceived need to scale up CPRs in order to address global commons challenges, such as climate change. Scale presents complex challenges for resource management: although empirical research has shown that 'close-knit groups' can come together to develop norms to manage common property resources, there remains considerable scepticism about whether CPR institutions can be effective for managing larger-scale or global commons used by diverse and heterogeneous groups,[142] especially when this requires the 'cooperation of appropriate international institutions and national, regional, and local institutions'.[143] The work of Ostrom and her collaborators suggested an institutional approach that accounted for both scale and pluralism: her scholarship identified both that global problems call for 'multilevel institutions that build on and complement local and regional institutions' and that 'institutional diversity may be as important as biological diversity'.[144] Concurrently, there was a push for greater recognition of legal pluralism and the 'co-existence of many different "legal" frameworks, laws and rules by which people might access natural resources' within development practice.[145] Law and development scholars argued that non-state legal forms and the 'normative and institutional complexity to which legal pluralism refers' needed to be taken more seriously, especially in the context of natural resource governance.[146]

In order to develop conceptual frameworks that account for legal pluralism and multilevel governance in relation to natural resources, scholars first focused on rethinking property rights by going 'beyond unitary conceptions of property' to understand property as a bundle of several types of rights in relation to resources.[147]

The following subsections all identify different facets of concurrent processes that facilitate the strategic incorporation of local commons within global markets and multi-layered governance systems in ways that enable the globalisation of authority over forested land alongside the localisation of responsibility. The next subsection examines how thinking on natural resource governance has been informed by a

---

[142] Ibid., 49.

[143] E. Ostrom, J. Burger, C. B. Field, R. B. Norgaard, and D. Policansky, 'Revisiting the commons: Local lessons, global challenges' (1999) 284(5412) *Science* 278–82 at 278.

[144] Ostrom et al., 'Revisiting the commons', 282 and 287; see also T. Dietz, E. Ostrom, and P. C. Stern, 'The struggle to govern the commons' (2003) 302(5652) *Science* 1907–12; E. Ostrom, *Understanding Institutional Diversity* (Princeton University Press, 2005); D. Armitage, 'Governance and the commons in a multi-level world' (2008) 2(1) *International Journal of the Commons* 7–32.

[145] Mehta et al., 'Editorial: Environmental Governance in an Uncertain World', 5.

[146] F. von Benda-Beckmann, 'Legal pluralism and social justice in economic and political development' (2001) 32(1) *IDS Bulletin* 46–56 at 53.

[147] R. S. Meinzen-Dick and R. Pradhan, 'Implications of legal pluralism for natural resource management' (2001) 32(4) *IDS Bulletin* 10–17 at 10; conceptually such a disaggregation of property has a longer history, see for example M. J. Horwitz, 'The historical foundations of modern contract law' (1974) 87 *Harvard Law Review* 917–56; A. Honoré, 'Ownership' in A. Guest (ed.), *Oxford Essays in Jurisprudence* (Oxford University Press, 1961) pp. 107–47.

C. Common Property Regimes and Natural Resources

conceptual schema that distinguishes between diverse 'bundles of rights' in relation to a particular resource, and how this has given rise to a realisation that different rights in this 'bundle' – such as authoritative rights, control rights and use rights – can be allocated to different actors. The subsequent subsection discusses polycentric and multilevel governance of natural resources. It pays particular attention to how models of multilevel governance have been proposed that would enable the incorporation of local-level common property and resource management regimes *within* markets operating at the international level. The final subsection examines how legal pluralism and the strategic recognition of diverse tenure forms have been deployed in ways that nonetheless allow for incorporation of such diverse legal and tenure system within global capitalist markets. The analysis show that within these sorts of hybrid arrangements, the commons are arguably conceptualised in a way analogous to Ronald Coase's theorisation of 'the nature of the firm':[148] an institutional arrangement that allows for certain coordination functions to be performed at a lower cost than would be incurred through market transactions, which is therefore conceptualised as a necessary element for the overall efficient operation of economic system.[149] It is in this sense that George Caffentzis critically described such an understanding of the commons that enables them to be strategically incorporated within global markets as 'commons *qua* firm'.[150] This thereby enables commons conceptualised as an institutional arrangement to be incorporated into the functioning of global markets in ways that neutralise the radical critique that the commons, as a political principle, presents of property and capitalist relations.

2 Property Rights Regimes and Natural Resources

This section examines how the disaggregation of different rights to natural resources has operated as another legal means by which authority over common-pool resources is transferred to global actors. During the 1990s, to better understand the range of outcomes different governance arrangements for common-pool resources produce, scholars developed analytical frameworks that conceptually disaggregated the various rights in the 'bundle of rights' that make up CPRs and how they are allocated to different actors. In 1992, Edella Schlager and Elinor Ostrom developed a 'conceptual schema for arranging property-rights regimes that distinguished among diverse bundles of rights that could be held by users of a resource system'.[151] This schema has 'profoundly influenced' the practice of natural resource governance and research in natural resource, common property and community

---

[148] R. H. Coase, 'The nature of the firm' (1937) 4(16) *Economica* 386–405.
[149] Caffentzis, 'The future of "The Commons"', 30–1.
[150] Ibid., 32.
[151] E. Schlager and E. Ostrom, 'Property-rights regimes and natural resources: A conceptual analysis' (1992) 68(3) *Land Economics* 249–62 at 249.

resource management.[152] Schlager and Ostrom's conceptual schema distinguishes between different rights (access withdrawal, management, exclusion and alienation) and situates them within a nested framework of 'operational-level' and 'constitutional-choice level' rules. 'Operational-level' rights include rights of 'access' (to enter a defined area) and 'withdrawal' (to obtain the products of a resource). 'Collective-choice level' rights include rights of management ('the right to regulate internal use patterns and transform the resource by making improvements'), exclusion ('the right to determine who will have an access right and how that right will be transferred') and alienation (the right to sell or lease management and/or exclusion rights).[153] In subsequent work, Agrawal and Ostrom make further distinctions between three aspects of 'management rights', namely, the right to: (i) decide how resources should be protected and used; (ii) decide how compliance should be monitored and enforced and (iii) adjudicate disputes.[154] The critical distinction between 'higher-level' ('constitutional-choice') rights and 'lower-level' ('operational') rights is that the holder of higher-level rights has the authority to define lower-level rights. Schlager and Ostrom describe this as 'the difference between exercising a right and participating in the definition of future rights to be exercised'.[155] For example, management rights may 'authoris[e] its holders to determine withdrawal rights' and 'determine how, when, and where harvesting from a resource may occur', while exclusion rights 'authorise its holders to devise operational-level rights of access' and 'define the qualifications that individuals must meet in order to access a resource'.[156] This conceptual framework therefore makes it possible to analytically identify what types of rights are accorded to a wide variety of social actors in the context of resource governance and to unpack the power relations between different actors in relation to a resource.

This schema, which has been increasingly influential in research on forest tenure, including in training manuals,[157] was adapted by the RRI for its work on documenting and promoting forest tenure reform,[158] and it has been taken up in and influenced REDD+ advocacy.[159] More recently, Thomas Sikor, Jun He and Guillaume Lestrelin have further adapted this framework in order to better account for the growing number of social actors involved in natural resource governance,

---

[152] Sikor et al., 'Property rights regimes and natural resources', 337.

[153] Schlager and Ostrom, 'Property-rights regimes and natural resources', 251.

[154] Discussed in Larson, *Tenure Rights and Access to Forests*, p. 13.

[155] Schlager and Ostrom, 'Property-rights regimes and natural resources', 251.

[156] Ibid.

[157] See, for example, Larson, *Tenure Rights and Access to Forests*; *What Rights? A Comparative Analysis of Developing Countries' National Legislation on Community and Indigenous Peoples' Forest Tenure Rights* (Rights and Resources Initiative, 2012); C. Stevens, R. Winterbottom, J. Springer, and K. Reytar, *Securing Rights, Combatting Climate Change* (World Resources Institute, 2014).

[158] *What Rights?*, p. 12.

[159] Stevens et al., *Securing Rights, Combatting Climate Change*, p. 14.

C. Common Property Regimes and Natural Resources

including the private, non-governmental and public local, national and international organisations. Their updated version of this conceptual schema facilitates analysis of contemporary changes in natural resource governance, including how payment for ecosystem services schemes, including REDD+, has transformed decision-making and property rights arrangements.[160] Sikor, He and Lestrelin propose a typology with three levels of rights: authoritative rights, control rights and use rights. The lower-level use rights determine social actors' ability to benefit from resources, encompassing both the 'right to obtain direct benefits derived from a resource (catch fish, harvest water, cut timber etc.)' and the 'right to obtain indirect benefits associated with resources, such as cash payments, the use of public goods, in-kind support'.[161] The middle-level rights, that is, the 'control rights', operate to 'determine the scope of direct and indirect use rights'. Control rights include management rights ('the right to regulate internal use and transform the resource'), exclusion rights ('right to determine who has rights to direct and indirect benefits'), monitoring rights (the right to monitor both direct and indirect benefits as well as the state of the resources) and transaction rights (rights to undertake activities to obtain the product of a resource or to realise benefits).[162] Finally, these authors add a higher-order level of 'authoritative rights', ones which 'empower their holder to authorize control rights'.[163] In this category they include 'definition rights', which relate to the power to define a resource in ways that delimit the 'discretionary space available for the exercise of control rights', as well as 'allocation rights', that is, the 'right to assign control rights to particular actors'.[164]

Sikor et al.'s conceptual framework helps make visible how ongoing developments in the practice of natural resource governance such as the growing influence of international norms – including those of the UNFCCC, certification schemes and codes of good practice – impact on the exercise of authoritative rights.[165] The application of their framework to empirical studies illuminates how contemporary changes in natural resource governance regimes generally do not lead to the outright dispossession of local communities, who often continue to possess use rights to natural resources. However, such changes have had the concurrent effect of denying the higher-order control and authoritative rights to local communities, and instead granting the exercise of such rights exclusively by state agencies or international actors.[166] What emerges, therefore, is a governance framework where 'international organizations and norms increasingly influence natural resource management on the ground while local communities' exclusion is compensated

---

[160] Sikor et al., 'Property rights regimes and natural resources', 338.
[161] Ibid., 339.
[162] Ibid.
[163] Ibid., 340.
[164] Ibid.
[165] Ibid., 346.
[166] Ibid., 338.

by indirect benefits'.[167] The framework developed by Sikor et al. is particularly valuable for enabling a more critical understanding of the 'unprecedented' payments potentially made to local communities through PES and REDD+ schemes. It shows that such payments are not only incentives to encourage compliance with management prescription and to address opportunity costs, but also that such payments should be understood as a form of 'compensated exclusions', which is minimal redress for the fact that local communities are increasingly denied a role in exercising control and authoritative rights.[168] Moreover, when this schema for the disaggregation of the 'bundle of rights' in CPRs is mapped onto the various rights in the forest carbon economy, it provides a lens for evaluating the respective power of different rights holders in the carbon economy. Applying this schema to the forest carbon economy shows that holders of carbon rights are generally granted rights only to access direct and indirect benefits from forest resources, whilst those with the right to implement REDD+ projects hold control or management rights, while holders of rights in 'emission reductions' or 'carbon credits' possess more authoritative rights and thus the power to determine how control rights and use rights are defined.

This conceptual schema was primarily designed to serve analytical and descriptive rather than prescriptive purposes. However, forest governance reforms (discussed below) have actively contributed to incentivising and producing the transformations that the conceptual framework documents. The next section critically evaluates programmes promoting for decentralisation of natural resource governance, arguing that although such programmes were intended to benefit local communities, in practice, local communities were rarely assigned more than 'operational-level' rights.[169] Therefore, in effect such programmes have functioned not only to transfer authority 'upwards' but also to responsibilise 'local' actors.

3 Decentralisation and Natural Resource Governance

Since the mid-1980s, discussions on the governance of natural resources have promoted greater decentralisation to 'improve' forest governance,[170] mirroring a broader push for decentralisation of state activities and localisation as part of

---

[167] Ibid.

[168] Ibid., 346–7.

[169] A. Agrawal and E. Ostrom, 'Collective action, property rights, and decentralisation in resource use in India and Nepal' (2001) 29(4) *Politics and Society* 485–514 at 492.

[170] See M. Moeliono, E. Wollenberg, and G. Limberg (eds.), *The Decentralization of Forest Governance: Politics, Economics and the Fight for Control of Forests in Indonesian Borneo* (Earthscan, 2009); C. Barr, I. A. P. Resosudarmo, A. Dermawan, J. McCarthy, M. Moeliono, and B. Setiono (eds.), *Decentralization of Forest Administration in Indonesia: Implications for Forest Sustainability, Economic Development and Community Livelihoods* (Center for International Forestry Research, 2006); for a discussion of the failures of decentralization in relation to forests see L. Arnold, 'Deforestation in decentralised Indonesia: What's law got to do with it?' (2008) 4(2) *Law, Environment and Development Journal* 75–101.

C. Common Property Regimes and Natural Resources

development interventions.[171] Of these, forests have been 'the most important [resource] in natural resource decentralization policy debates and the most studied in the natural resource decentralization literature'.[172] Anne Larson and Fernanda Soto situate discourses on decentralisation at the 'intersection between discussions of good governance and democracy, development and poverty alleviation, on the one hand, and studies of common property resources, community-based natural resource management, local rights, and access to resources, on the other'.[173] The democratic impetus for decentralisation has been to transfer power 'to authorities representative of and accountable to local populations',[174] as a 'growing tendency to see people less as a problem and more as a solution with regard to land and natural resource degradation' and to present their participation in resource governance as both necessary and desirable.[175] However, decentralisation processes – including their take-up more broadly in development thinking[176] – have also been driven by a scepticism of the state. Decentralisation prescription and policies, as Luis Eslava has identified, are part of an 'international trend that perceives the state as an oversized, unsustainable and unevenly developed jurisdiction', and are directed to the reconfiguration of the state through localisation rather than its dissolution.[177] The greater decentralisation of governance has therefore been promoted for different reasons by both conservatives and progressives, and these diverse agendas have contributed to 'a certain lack of conceptual clarity' around the term 'decentralisation'.[178] As a result, the promotion of community-based natural resource management[179] is marked by tensions and complexities, and aspirations for community-based forest management are best understood as a complex 'assemblage' that draws discrete elements and heterogeneous interests together.[180]

In practice, forest decentralisation policies 'sometimes result less in devolving local control and more in maintaining or even increasing state control over local

---

[171] See A. M. Larson and F. Soto, 'Decentralization of natural resource governance regimes' (2008) 33 *Annual Review of Environment and Resources* 213–39; on decentralization in development discourses more generally see L. Eslava, *Local Space, Global Life: The Everyday Operation of International Law and Development* (Cambridge University Press, 2015).

[172] Larson and Soto, 'Decentralization of natural resource governance regimes', 214.

[173] Ibid.

[174] J. C. Ribot, *Waiting for Democracy: The Politics of Choice in Natural Resource Decentralisation* (World Resources Institute, 2004) p. 9.

[175] Larson and Soto, 'Decentralization of natural resource governance regimes', 214.

[176] See R. Flaman, *Decentralisation: A Sampling of Definitions* (UNDP Working Paper, 1999).

[177] L. Eslava, 'Decentralization of development and nation-building today: Reconstructing Colombia from the margins of Bogotá' (2009) 2(1) *The Law and Development Review* 282–366 at 283.

[178] Larson and Soto, 'Decentralization of natural resource governance regimes', 214.

[179] W. Dressler, B. Büscher, M. Schoon, D. A. N. Brockington, T. Hayes, C. A. Kull, J. McCarthy, and K. Shrestha, 'From hope to crisis and back again? A critical history of the global CBNRM narrative' (2010) 37(1) *Environmental Conservation* 5–15.

[180] T. M. Li, 'Practices of assemblage and community forest management' (2007) 36(2) *Economy and Society* 263–93.

forests and forest communities'.[181] Analysis by Ribot et al. identified specific strategies adopted by centralised governments to undermine the local government's ability to make decisions, including by limiting the types of power transferred to local institutions.[182] Thus, real democratic decentralisation, which requires a 'secure domain of autonomous decision making' at the local level, has rarely been achieved.[183] In general, while decentralisation has granted local actors use rights to resources, these local actors have generally been excluded from exercising control or authoritative rights.[184]

Decentralisation is therefore best understood not as a process of democratisation but as a different mode and modality of governance. In the development literature, decentralisation is presented not as in opposition to or an alternative to centralisation, but as a complementary mode of governing that should be utilised when it presents the 'most effective ways and means of achieving a desired objective'.[185] Wendy Brown identifies the devolution of authority as a key feature of neoliberal governance, driven by both a 'formal antipathy to centralized state power' and an 'emphasis on problem solving achieved by stakeholders'.[186] She clearly and carefully distinguishes the neoliberal devolution of power and responsibility from 'thoroughgoing decentralization and local empowerment', noting that the former frequently delegates responsibility on the principle of subsidiarity to 'small and weak units [that are] unable to cope ... technically, politically, or financially'.[187] In Brown's account, a key effect of devolution is not effectiveness but rather the 'seeding' of competition between administrative units 'aimed at "entrepreneurialising" them'.[188] She argues that the neoliberal devolution of authority is therefore strategically related to *responsibilisation* as a social policy, in which the 'entity at the end of the pipeline' is tasked with cultivating themselves as a 'wholly accountable actor'.[189] In contrast to 'responsibility', which speaks of the human capacity for autonomy, Brown argues that its linguistic conversion to being *responsibilised* denotes an 'administered condition' that 'departs from the domain of agency', where the subject is instead governed through an 'external moral injunction'. The 'process-based transitive verb' *responsibilise* she claims, represents a further transformation and signals a *'regime* in

---

[181] Barry et al., 'Forest tenure reform: An orphan with only uncles', p. 34.
[182] J. C. Ribot, A. Agrawal, and A. M. Larson, 'Recentralizing while decentralizing: How national governments reappropriate forest resources' (2006) 34(11) *World Development* 1864–86 at 1864–5.
[183] Ibid., 1881.
[184] Sikor et al., 'Property rights regimes and natural resources', 344.
[185] UNDP, 'Factors to consider in designing decentralized governance policies and programmes to achieve sustainable people-centered development' (Management Development and Governance Division, February 1998) cited in Flaman, *Decentralisation: A Sampling of Definitions*, p. 3.
[186] W. Brown, *Undoing the Demos: Neoliberalism's Stealth Revolution* (Zone Books, 2015) pp. 131–4.
[187] Ibid., p. 132.
[188] Ibid.
[189] Ibid., p. 133.

C. Common Property Regimes and Natural Resources 283

which the singular human capacity for responsibility is deployed to constitute and govern subjects and through which their conduct is organized and measured, remaking and reorientating them for a neoliberal order'.[190]

The neoliberal strategic relation between devolution and responsibilisation therefore creates a model of decentralised governance that does not promote greater local democratisation, but rather the greater responsibilisation of local actors. Neoliberal models of decentralisation promote *conditional* localised self-governance, but also seek to ensure that such self-governance is *exercised in specific ways* that are facilitative of 'global' interests. Decentralisation thus represents not a dismantling of global authority but a *reconfiguration of its forms of exercise and implementation*, in which the 'local' can be strategically deployed as the level through which internationalised visions of development come into being. In the context of resource governance this is reflected in the fact that, even when rights to access, use and benefits have devolved to the local level, the way such rights can be exercised has already been determined by higher-order rights holders.

4 Polycentric Governance and Nested, Multilevel Institutional Arrangements

By the early 2000s, the scholarship on CPRs was increasingly focused on the difficult challenges involved in the management of large-scale resources that cannot be managed at the village level or even the national level. Rather, the effective management of such resources requires approaches that are global in scale and promote the 'cooperation of appropriate international institutions and national, regional, and local institutions'.[191] Elinor Ostrom and associated scholars thus explored how CPRs and the 'logic of incentive-led and locally autonomous institutions' can be scaled up to the regional or international level.[192] In doing so, she drew on previous work by Vincent Ostrom and the Indiana Workshop in Political Theory and Policy Analysis on 'polycentric governance',[193] which, although it has had a much longer genesis, arguably only came to be 'fully appreciated' and taken up widely within the 'policy context of devolution and decentralization'.[194] Through her work the concept of 'polycentricity' has had considerable take-up within the climate change literature, in descriptive and explanatory ways and as a normative

---

[190] Ibid. (emphasis in original).
[191] Ostrom et al., 'Revisiting the commons', 278.
[192] T. Forsyth and C. Johnson, 'Elinor Ostrom's legacy: Governing the commons, and the rational choice controversy' (2014) 45(5) *Development and Change* 1093–1110 at 1104.
[193] M. D. McGinnis (ed.), *Polycentric Governance and Development: Readings from the Workshop in Political Theory and Policy Analysis* (University of Michigan Press, 1999); see especially V. Ostrom, 'Polycentricity' (1972) in that volume.
[194] M. D. McGinnis, 'Introduction' in M. D. McGinnis (ed.), *Polycentric Governance and Development: Readings from the Workshop in Political Theory and Policy Analysis* (University of Michigan Press, 1999) p. 2.

284 *Scale, Multilevel Governance & Disaggregation of Property Rights in REDD+*

source of prescriptions on how to better govern this complex challenge.[195] Additionally, Ostrom has specifically proposed that the concept of polycentric governance can inform the implementation and analysis of international efforts around REDD+ and that 'careful consideration of polycentricity and the development of multilevel, integrated and socio-ecological assessments therefore hold significant potential for addressing some of the major challenges outlined for REDD'.[196]

Polycentric systems are characterised by 'multiple governing authorities at different scales rather than a mon-centric unit', where '[e]ach unit within a polycentric system exercises considerable independence to make norms and rules within a specific domain'.[197] Such systems typically combine the characteristics of 'multi-level' (local, provincial, national, regional, global), 'multi-type' (both nested jurisdictions and specialised cross-jurisdictional political units) and 'multi-sectoral' (engaging public, private, community-based and other organisations).[198] Polycentric governance 'implies the diffusion of sovereignty over several levels of governance and numerous institutions', as well as 'crosscutting "issue-specific" jurisdictions' with explicit roles for private, community and other non-governmental bodies as well as public actors.[199] Multilevel governance thus involves a 'series of reconfigurations of the relationships and modes of interaction between central states, other levels of government and other actors' with the effect that the 'power of government can increasingly be shaped and shared between actors operating at multiple levels'.[200] It has also been described as involving 'nested' institutions that sit within each other (a 'Russian doll' image is suggested by some authors), so that 'each local set of rules and incentives fits within the rules and objectives set at larger scales'.[201] Polycentric governance therefore encompasses both multi-actor governance – that

---

[195] A. Jordan, D. Huitema, J. Schoenefeld, and J. Forster, 'Governing climate change polycentrically: Setting the scene' in A. Jordan, D. Huitema, H. van Asselt, and J. Forster (eds.), *Governing Climate Change: Polycentricity in Action?* (Cambridge University Press, 2018), pp. 3–26, 5–6 and the other chapters in this book; E. Ostrom, *A Polycentric Approach for Coping with Climate Change: Background Paper to the 2010 World Development Report* (The World Bank, 2009); E. Ostrom, 'Polycentric systems for coping with collective action and global environmental change' (2010) 20(4) *Global Environmental Change* 550–7.

[196] H. Nagendra and E. Ostrom, 'Polycentric governance of multifunctional forested landscapes' (2012) 6(2) *International Journal of the Commons* 104–133 at 124.

[197] Ostrom, 'Polycentric systems for coping with collective action and global environmental change', 552.

[198] M. D. McGinnis, 'An introduction to IAD and the language of the Ostrom workshop: A simple guide to a complex framework' (2011) 39(1) *Policy Studies Journal* 169–83 at 171..

[199] J. A. van Zeben, 'Polycentricity' in B. Hudson, J. Rosenbloom, and D. Cole (eds.), *Routledge Handbook of the Study of the Commons* (Routledge, 2019) pp. 38–49, 41.

[200] D. Rodriguez-Ward, A. M. Larson, and H. G. Ruesta, 'Top-down, bottom-up and sideways: The multilayered complexities of multi-level actors shaping forest governance and REDD+ arrangements in Madre de Dios, Peru' (2018) 62(1) *Environmental Management* 98–116 at 100.

[201] T. Forsyth, 'Multilevel, multiactor governance in REDD' in A. Angelsen (ed.), *Realising REDD+: National Strategy and Policy Options* (Center for International Forestry Research, 2009), pp. 113–22, 116.

C. Common Property Regimes and Natural Resources   285

is, 'collaboration among different stakeholders to achieve public policy objectives' – as well as multilevel governance, or the 'implementation of public policy across diverse spatial scales and by actors who have dissimilar influence and values'.[202]

The concept of polycentric governance, especially in the Ostroms' formulation, is explicitly normatively linked to the practice of 'self-governance' such that polycentricity is seen as a 'fundamental prerequisite of *self-governance*' or the 'ability of groups of individuals to work out problems for themselves'.[203] Scholars from the Ostroms' Indiana Workshop in Political Theory argue that 'those groups who are able to manage CPRs effectively should be allowed to do so, if at all possible', because they consider that localised management provides greater sustainability and greater capacity for adaptive management and resilience of systems.[204] Their framework consequently promotes self-governance at different 'arenas of choice' or 'levels of analysis' – operational, management and constitutional – directed towards shaping the rules and making decisions pertinent to that 'level'.[205] However, despite this focus, the 'nested framework' remains hierarchically organised and thereby imposes constraints and places limits on self-governance. First, there is an implicit hierarchy in favour of higher levels, given how local arrangements are understood to be 'nested' within the overarching political, economic and cultural order and the 'explicit connection between micro-level processes of resource management and macro-level structures of constitutional order'.[206] In addition, the workshop scholars have specified two circumstances in which governmental intervention from 'higher levels' in the collective management of resources is necessary: 'when user groups fail to manage their resources effectively', and 'if user groups violate basic standards of fairness, accountability, or other issues of concern to society as a whole'.[207] These conditionalities built into the concept of 'nested' self-governance make explicit the double manoeuvre inherent in polycentric governance: implementation or management responsibility is devolved according to the principle of subsidiarity to the lowest applicable level, *but, simultaneously*, localised self-governance and self-management is made subject to criteria of 'effectiveness' and other 'basic principles' determined at a higher constitutional level. This model of 'nesting' therefore promotes capacities for self-governance at each operational level, but also constrains the exercise of such self-governance by making it subject to requirements imposed by actors at the higher levels. In terms of legal technique, this is somewhat analogous to the disaggregation of the concept of sovereignty as a 'bundle of rights' so as to

---

[202] Ibid., 114.
[203] McGinnis, 'Introduction', p. 3.
[204] Ibid., p. 4.
[205] M. D. McGinnis, 'An introduction to IAD and the language of the Ostrom workshop: A simple guide to a complex framework', 171.
[206] McGinnis, 'Introduction', pp. 2–3.
[207] Ibid., p. 4.

286 *Scale, Multilevel Governance & Disaggregation of Property Rights in REDD+*

facilitate forms of indirect rule within the Empire.[208] This legal arrangement thereby promotes a governmental approach that supports local autonomy, but simultaneously seeks 'to act on actions', setting conditions and 'artificially arranging things so that people, following only their own self-interest, *will do as they ought*'.[209]

The concepts of multilevel, nested and polycentric governance discussed above have gained considerable traction, more broadly speaking, in the field of environmental governance, but they have gained particular prominence in discussions on REDD+. Indeed, some have suggested that REDD+ 'will require a kind of multilevel governance system that is perhaps unique in the history of environmental policy'.[210] REDD+ is frequently described as a 'multilevel, multisector process' that necessarily engages a range of diverse – and at times conflictual – actors.[211] Scholars have argued that multilevel, multi-actor governance for REDD+ is necessary to ensure that REDD+ implementation is effective, efficient and equitable and to promote co-benefits.[212] Because REDD+ activities and their governance take place at multiple levels or scales, scholars have stressed the need for the mechanism to 'function effectively at all levels, from global to local, in order to succeed'.[213] Moreover, as a 'multilevel endeavour', REDD+ must ensure that 'global demands, national and subnational structures, and local people's needs and aspirations are all linked' as part of its efforts.[214] A key challenge is the vertical and horizontal coordination between international and transnational processes, national processes of REDD+-readiness and the development of REDD+ national plans, as well as 'local' or project-based activities focused on preventing deforestation and forest degradation. Scholars have thus highlighted the need for mechanisms that can promote better integration, including the 'match of *institutions and incentives across the levels*', 'the flow of *information* required to implement REDD+' and enabling 'the negotiation of actors with different *interests* across levels'.[215]

Mapping a more critical understanding of polycentric governance onto REDD+ implementation makes visible how multilayered arrangements in REDD+ that

---

[208] See H. S. Maine, *International Law: A Series of Lectures Delivered before the University of Cambridge, 1887* (J. Murray, 1888); for a discussion of Maine and indirect rule see K. Mantena, *Alibis of Empire: Henry Maine and the Ends of Liberal Imperialism* (Princeton University Press, 2010).

[209] Li, 'Practices of assemblage and community forest management', 266.

[210] M. Skutsch and P. E. Van Laake, 'REDD as multi-level governance in-the-making' (2008) 19(6) *Energy & Environment* 831–44 at 843.

[211] Rodriguez-Ward et al., 'Top-down, bottom-up and sideways', 98.

[212] Forsyth, 'Multilevel, multiactor governance in REDD', 122.

[213] Doherty and Schroeder, 'Forest tenure and multi-level governance in avoiding deforestation under REDD', 67.

[214] K. Korhonen-Kurki, M. Brockhaus, A. E. Duchelle, S. Atmadja, and T. T. Pham, 'Multiple levels and multiple challenges for REDD+' in A. Angelsen, M. Brockhaus, W. Sundelin, and L. Verchot, (eds.), *Analysing REDD+: Challenges and Choices* (Center for International Forestry Research, 2012) pp. 91–110, 91.

[215] Ibid., p. 92 (emphasis in original).

C. Common Property Regimes and Natural Resources

distribute governance to different actors at different scales nonetheless do so in a way that distributes greater power to international rather than local actors. Although it is common for discussions of REDD+ as a 'nested' framework to highlight the benefits of such devolution and how it might 'maximise equity and effectiveness by ensuring the willing participation of different actors at different scales', the analysis in this section suggests that self-governance at the lower levels is constrained by overarching constitutional-level imperatives, which require that 'objectives of REDD+ ... [be] clearly established and accepted by all parties'.[216] Thus, although discussions about promoting coordination within multilevel governance often operate on a technical register, this analysis has shown that they are in fact highly political as they distribute power and mediate tensions among a variety of interests.[217] Further, the different uses of forest land that are authorised by such governance frameworks 'reflects the influence and different levels of power, policies and decisions made across multiple sectors and scales'.[218] Such multilevel governance arrangements operate to shift authority over resources to international actors whilst constraining self-governance at the local level, where actors are increasingly responsibilised. The next section turns to consider how legal pluralism has been incorporated into multilayered governance frameworks in ways that facilitate the strategic incorporation of different legal systems into an overarching system of legal obligations.

5 Legal Pluralism and Customary Tenure

Concurrently with discussions on multilayered governance, in the early 2000s there was also a growing awareness in law and development debates of the number of local contexts characterised by the presence of multiple and overlapping legal systems. In particular, scholars highlighted that such legal pluralism is especially evident in the context of natural resource governance. Legal pluralism acknowledges the 'existence of non-state rules, rights and obligations that find their legitimacy in local customary laws or religious laws'[219] and the resulting overlapping and potentially competing norms, actors and institutions.[220] As a result, practitioners

---

[216] Forsyth, 'Multilevel, multiactor governance in REDD', 115 and 116.

[217] A. M. Larson, J. P. Sarmiento Barletti, A. Ravikumar, and K. Korhonen-Kurki, 'Multi-level governance: Some coordination problems cannot be solved through coordination' in A. Angelsen (ed.), *Transforming REDD+: Lessons and New Directions* (Center for International Forestry Research, 2018) pp. 81–92, 83.

[218] Ibid.

[219] Benda-Beckmann, 'Legal pluralism and social justice in economic and political development', 47.

[220] On legal pluralism generally see S. E. Merry, 'Legal pluralism' (1988) 22 *Law & Society Review* 869; J. Griffiths, 'What is legal pluralism?' (1986) 18(24) *The Journal of Legal Pluralism and Unofficial law* 1–55; on legal pluralism in transnational law see P. Zumbansen, 'Transnational legal pluralism' (2010) 1(1) *Transnational Legal Theory* 141–89.

and theorists working in the field of land and natural resource governance reform increasingly came to recognise the need to take legal pluralism seriously in order to avoid a repeat of earlier failures.[221] This gave rise to debates not only about the types of rights that were allocated to different social actors but also about the normative orders in which these rights were embedded and authorised by. Scholars also posed questions about the relative significance of different legal orders for the livelihood security of different sectors of the population and for achieving envisioned economic and social development outcomes.[222] Legal pluralism, focused as it is on the coexistence of different normative orders and forms of governance, thus has a different emphasis from that of nested governance, which establishes governance arrangements that operate at different scales but under one set of rules.[223] However, together they describe a complex situation of interlegality, where multiple claims are made to natural resources based on different legal systems and where there are overlapping property rights, sanctioned by different legal systems often competing with one another.[224]

This subsection interrogates the way in which legal pluralism has been mobilised within nested natural resource governance arrangements, by whom and for what purposes. It suggests that the acknowledgement of interlegality in natural resource governance arrangements for REDD+ has not promoted genuine legal plurality. Rather, the conditional recognition of legal pluralism in nested, polycentric natural resource governance arrangements has operated both to contain difference and to make it function in the interests of global capitalist markets. When they developed their conceptual framework, setting out different operational, management and constitutional rights relating to natural resources, Schlager and Ostrom were neutral about the form these legal rights should take, whether de jure, de facto or established by government or customary law. They did however express a normative preference that rules are produced by 'self-organised, collective-choice arrangements' at the level close to the physical and economic conditions of a particular site.[225] Subsequent work by Ruth Meinzen-Dick and Rajendra Pradhan built on their framework but also drew on insights from the literature on legal pluralism, to highlight that property rights are not 'unitary and fixed' but rather 'diverse and changing', thereby rethinking the relationship between normative orders and property rights in common-pool resources.[226] Meinzen-Dick and Pradhan suggest that

---

[221] Benda-Beckmann, 'Legal pluralism and social justice in economic and political development'.
[222] Ibid., 53.
[223] See Forsyth, 'Multilevel, multiactor governance in REDD', 116–17.
[224] See T. Sikor and C. Lund, 'Access and property: A question of power and authority' in T. Sikor and C. Lund (eds.), *The Politics of Possession: Property, Authority, and Access to Natural Resources* (John Wiley & Sons, 2010) pp. 1–22.
[225] Schlager and Ostrom, 'Property-rights regimes and natural resources', 255.
[226] Meinzen-Dick and Pradhan, 'Implications of legal pluralism for natural resource management'; they expand on this argument in R. S. Meinzen-Dick and R. Pradhan, 'Legal pluralism and dynamic property rights' (2002) CAPRi Working Paper No. 22.

the disaggregation of the rights to regulate, control and make decisions with respect to natural resources could facilitate the co-existence of multiple different legal regimes, where the different regimes govern these different levels of rights.[227] They highlight a number of benefits that arise from incorporating legal pluralism in common resource governance regimes, especially that increased 'flexibility' can operate as an 'important coping strategy' that makes governance arrangements more resilient.[228] Further, they suggest that 'multiple flexible and dynamic legal orders are more responsive to these uncertainties and changes than a single, fixed legal system with static property rights',[229] and that therefore legal pluralism can enable more 'adaptive responses' in the face of ecological, social and political uncertainties.[230] Meinzen-Dick and Pradhan therefore critique law reform measures that prioritise statutory law as the means to provide tenure security or promote economic 'efficiency', and instead point to the need to recognise multiple and overlapping bases of claims and see resource rights as 'negotiated outcomes' often determined through 'messy, dynamic processes'.[231]

In order to understand how legal pluralism and customary tenure rights have been mobilised in REDD+ and to what ends, it is instructive to consider the way in which customary tenure rights have been taken up in development debates since the early 2000s. In 2003 the World Bank released a key report, *Land Policies for Growth and Poverty Reduction*,[232] its first major pronouncement on land policy and development since 1975.[233] While the underlying impetus of the report was still the position that well-defined and enforceable property rights can promote economic growth, there were a number of significant departures from previous World Bank thinking both in how tenure rights are conceptualised and the means by which they can be secured. In particular, there was an explicit acknowledgement that 'the almost exclusive focus on formal title' in earlier policy documents was inappropriate.[234] The report recognised the need for greater engagement with customary tenure systems and acknowledged that customary systems of land ownership 'evolved over long periods of time in response to location-specific conditions' and often therefore 'constitute a way of managing land relations that is more flexible and more adapted to location-specific conditions than would be possible under a more

---

[227] Meinzen-Dick and Pradhan, 'Legal pluralism and dynamic property rights', p. 2.

[228] Ibid., 14.

[229] Ibid., 6.

[230] Ibid., 8–9.

[231] Meinzen-Dick and Pradhan, 'Implications of legal pluralism for natural resource management', 10 and 16.

[232] K. W. Deininger, *Land Policies for Growth and Poverty Reduction* (The World Bank, 2003).

[233] For background see K. Deininger and H. Bisswanger, 'The evolution of the World Bank's land policy: Principles, experience and future challenges' (1999) 14(2) *The World Bank Research Observer* 247–76.

[234] Deininger, *Land Policies for Growth and Poverty Reduction*, p. xlv.

290 Scale, Multilevel Governance & Disaggregation of Property Rights in REDD+

centralized approach'.[235] Although the overall report still accorded a strong priority to individual property rights, it also reflected a growing awareness that, due to the 'complexity of the institutional structures involved, in most situations simply introducing private property rights will be neither feasible nor cost-effective'.[236] The report concluded:

> The role of the state is to promote systems that ensure security of tenure by individuals. Tenure security increases the productivity of land and the incomes of those who depend on it. While the individualization of land rights is the most efficient arrangement in many circumstances, in a number of cases, for example, for indigenous groups, herders, and marginal agriculturalists, definition of property rights at the level of the group, together with a process for adjusting the property rights system to changed circumstances where needed, can help to significantly reduce the danger of encroachment by outsiders while ensuring sufficient security to individuals. As long as groups can internally decide on individuals' resource access and other issues following basic conditions of representativeness and transparency, securing group rights can contribute to better and more sustainable land management as well as more equitable access to productive resources.[237]

This influential report spoke to 'an emerging consensus that a "middle way" has to be found that essentially combines customary ownership with long-term leases that unlock the commercial value of land'.[238] In contrast to comprehensive privatisation, what was envisioned by development institutions was an approach to land policy that does not abolish customary systems of tenure, but 'build[s] on them by adapting the formal land administration system so that it recognizes and supports customary institutions' and thereby facilitates 'linking customary tenure systems to the formal economic and legal systems'.[239] Such linkages between customary tenure and formal institutions involve 'recognising the rights and authority of customary groups in relation to land' but simultaneously 'allowing leases or other agreements for customary land to be used by individuals, organisations or corporations'.[240] While this formulation leaves many questions about implementation open,[241] what these hybrid formalisation models allow for, and even encourage, are 'local' mechanisms of dispute resolution for disputes internal to a collective, *even as* they facilitate the regulation of 'external' disputes between that collective and external investors by

---

[235] Ibid., pp. 52–3.
[236] Ibid., p. 68.
[237] Ibid., p. 76.
[238] *Australian Aid: Promoting Growth and Stability – A White Paper on the Australian Government's Overseas Aid Program* (Australian Government AusAID, 2006) p. 36.
[239] *Making Land Work: Reconciling Customary Land and Development in the Pacific* (Australian Government, AusAID, 2008) p. 15.
[240] Ibid.
[241] D. Fitzpatrick, '"Best practice" options for the legal recognition of customary tenure' (2005) 36(3) *Development and change* 449–75.

C. Common Property Regimes and Natural Resources

formal state law.[242] This is envisioned as a compromise in which 'customary rights and authority are recognised, insiders and outsiders are given the security they need for investment, and mechanisms are provided for managing and resolving intractable disputes'.[243] What results is a complex framework of legal pluralism that recognises and deploys customary law for 'internal' disputes within a collective, but where interactions between the collective and external investors are subject to formal, state law as the ultimate container of social relations.

In relation to forest rights, there is a growing and important literature querying the appropriateness of liberal notions of individual property rights for Indigenous peoples and other forest communities.[244] In the context of REDD+ there has therefore been concern that the clarification or formalisation of tenure rights might inappropriately impose Western conceptions of individual property on forest communities.[245] Property in its varied iterations is, as Kathleen Birrell, Lee Godden and Maureen Tehan describe, 'imbued with rich social and cultural meaning', and very different ontologies and epistemologies of property characterise Indigenous and Western property regimes.[246] These authors therefore stress that REDD+ must provide 'adequate recognition of culturally-embedded property frameworks' to avoid subsuming Indigenous social relations, which are 'mediated in specific ways by customary property forms'.[247] Similarly, David Takacs has promoted the desirability of 'legal pluralist' approaches that integrate formal systems of property rights in sequestered carbon with customary legal systems.[248] In a report for Conservation International he recommends that

> [l]awmakers and project developers should take a legal pluralism approach. Forest carbon as property exists in a distinctly Western legal paradigm, and formal, statutory or treaty laws that govern its ownership will be constrained by certain notions of what constitutes 'law' and what constitutes 'property.' Yet customary legal systems operate at a local level to regulate human–human and human–nature relations, and these should be integrated to ensure sustainable forest carbon projects.[249]

There remain many unresolved questions regarding the implementation of legal pluralist approaches, including around how 'complex, multifaceted statute and customary law systems that govern lands and forests' can best be 'captured' and translated into 'the model of security of tenure that is proposed for REDD+'.[250] One

---

[242] *Making Land Work: Reconciling Customary Land and Development in the Pacific.*
[243] Ibid., p. 15.
[244] Lyster, 'REDD+, transparency, participation and resource rights', 120.
[245] See Birrell et al., 'Climate change and REDD+', p. 206.
[246] Ibid., p. 197.
[247] Ibid.
[248] Takacs, *Forest Carbon: Law and Property Rights*, p. 6.
[249] Ibid.
[250] L. Godden, 'Malaysia and the UN-REDD programme: Exploring possibilities for tenure pluralism in forest governance' in *The Impact of Climate Change Mitigation on Indigenous*

model that was adopted in some REDD+ pilot projects involves recognising community-owned and managed land, but establishing collective obligations to commit to specific land use activities through a community forest agreement.[251] However, the focus of this analysis is less on the procedural aspects than on interrogating the politics and effects of such strategic recognition of customary laws. The above discussion has shown how customary legal systems are being strategically recognised in ways that facilitate their incorporation into global capitalist strategies of accumulation such that they can used as a means of expanding market discipline rather than representing an alternative to, or even critique of, such relations. These developments therefore reflect modalities of 'environmentality' where (as Arun Agrawal has shown) forms of community-based governance of forests, community becomes the 'arena in which intimate governance unfolds'.[252] In contrast to 'government at a distance', which requires constant oversight and collection of information by external experts, 'intimate governance' operates by 'dispersing rule' and is reliant on 'practice and sociality'.[253] As Agrawal demonstrates, intimate governance redirects existing modes of power and enforcement within village and customary systems. He writes, 'the ability of regulation to make itself felt in the realm of everyday practice depends upon the channelling of existing flows of power within village communities towards new ends related to the environment'.[254] There is limited research on how external obligations have transformed the community institutions made responsible for meeting them in the REDD+ context. However, in other contexts scholars have shown that these modalities of governance have potential to lead to 'a proliferation of disciplinary technologies' and 'collective self-policing', where the operation of customary norms and rural codes intended to support community life and interaction instead coerce the performance of such external obligations.[255] There are therefore a number of reasons to be concerned about the ways in which legal pluralism and customary legal systems are strategically recognised in REDD+, how this incorporation facilitates rather than undermines the discipline imposed through international carbon contracts and global capitalist markets, and therefore how they may operate as a vector to better enable the forms of international authority that REDD+ seeks to establish.

---

and Forest Communities: International, National and Local Law Perspectives on REDD+ (Cambridge University Press, 2017) pp. 203–38, 223.

[251] See A. Awono, O. A. Somorin, R. E. Atyi, and P. Levang, 'Tenure and participation in local REDD+ projects: Insights from southern Cameroon' (2014) 35 Environmental Science & Policy 76–86; on village agreements see also M. Mulyani and P. Jepson, 'Social learning through a REDD+ "village agreement": Insights from the KFCP in Indonesia' (2015) 56(1) Asia Pacific Viewpoint 79–95.

[252] A. Agrawal, 'Environmentality: Community, intimate government, and the making of environmental subjects in Kumaon, India' (2005) 46(2) Current Anthropology 161–90 at 179.

[253] Ibid., 178–9.

[254] Ibid., 179.

[255] S. Federici, 'From commoning to debt: Financialization, microcredit, and the changing architecture of capital accumulation' (2014) 113(2) The South Atlantic Quarterly 231–44 at 237.

D CONCLUSION

This chapter has analysed how authority over forested land is reorganised through the property relations and multilevel governance frameworks proposed for REDD+. It showed that while the recognition of forest peoples' carbon rights is critical to ensure that they benefit from REDD+ projects, the nature of these rights and the forms of relational social power they convey are heavily constrained, and in particular that such carbon rights generally do not grant the holders the power to control and manage forested land. This analysis therefore warns that recognition of community carbon rights might constitute a 'pyrrhic' or 'hollow' victory that, while bringing certain undeniable material benefits, does not grant communities the authority to self-determine future land use. It has shown how, instead, the multi-layered system of rights in the carbon economy is another legal technology through which authority to determine how forested land is used is transferred to international actors, further marginalising local actors, even as they might retain some operational-level rights to use forested land or receive direct or indirect benefits from it. This chapter contextualised discussions about the definition and allocation of carbon rights and forest tenure within broader debates around natural resource governance, CPRs and community-based resource management in order to develop a more complex understanding of the distribution of power and authority in such multilevel governance frameworks. By considering how property rights were disaggregated in CPRs and processes of decentralisation, this chapter sought to show how REDD+ is echoing broader developments that transfer authority 'upwards' to global actors whilst simultaneously responsibilising 'local' actors. This chapter highlighted the need to analyse not just the rights granted at the local level but also the broader governance frameworks and relations of power they are enmeshed in. This therefore requires a more critical attention to how the strategic recognition of communal rights or customary laws at the 'local' level, can operate in ways that are facilitative of, and not disruptive to, the disciplinary imperatives of transnational contracting and global capitalist markets.

6

REDD+ at the 'Local' Level

Between Rights and Responsibilisation

A INTRODUCTION

This chapter examines the fraught terrain of REDD+ implementation 'on the ground', with a specific focus on three strategies that have been central in efforts to promote social safeguards: benefit-sharing, tenure reform and rights to consultation and to free, prior and informed consent (FPIC). Although REDD+ is an international project, it is constituted and takes shape through national and subnational institutions: REDD+ is, as Anu Lounela writes, 'a globally produced but place-based project'.[1] In many ways it is action at the local level that is ultimately determinative of its success or failure, as ultimately activities 'on the ground' will determine whether 'additional' sequestration or carbon 'savings' claimed in credits have a material basis. However, in implementing REDD+ 'on the ground', REDD+ proponents face serious challenges, especially given that they 'are caught between complex local realities, powerful (sub)national stakeholders and a changing global REDD+ landscape',[2] and thus to date, 'implementation of REDD+ has fallen far short of what was hoped'.[3]

It is now widely accepted that REDD+ must minimise social risks ('do no harm') and promote social benefits ('do good') in order to be both equitable and effective.[4] Chapter 1 provided a detailed overview of the way in which debates about the social impacts of REDD+ and the need to both mitigate potential risks and promote benefits for people living in and around forested areas have led to a convergence of views acknowledging the need to implement safeguards. There has also been a

---

[1]   A. Lounela, 'Climate change disputes and justice in Central Kalimantan, Indonesia' (2015) 56(1) *Asia Pacific Viewpoint* 62–78.

[2]   E. O. Sills (ed.), *REDD+ on the Ground: A Case Book of Subnational Initiatives across the Globe* (Center for International Forestry Research, 2014) pp. xx and 3.

[3]   Ibid., p. 3.

[4]   Ibid., p. 430; see also the discussion in Chapter 1.

A. Introduction

welcome recognition of the 'rights dimension' of REDD+ and the need to create synergies between it and human rights instruments.[5] While not all people living in and around forested areas identify as Indigenous, a particular focus has been the rights of Indigenous peoples articulated in the United Nations Declaration on the Rights of Indigenous Peoples (UNDRIP). Although only a 'soft law' instrument, the UNDRIP is widely seen as a 'triumph' for Indigenous rights,[6] especially after it was 'selectively endorsed' by the settler-colonial states of the Anglosphere who initially opposed it.[7] However, in contrast to more optimistic accounts of the potential 'synergies' between REDD+ and rights regimes, this chapter presents a cautionary analysis, attentive to how the integration of rights into development agendas can also precipitate the 'creeping transformation of a promised sphere of "rights" into a domain which may aptly be called "regulatory"'.[8]

This chapter understands the 'social' as a 'problem space' constituted by both the demands for rights, recognition and participation made by people living in and around forested areas, Indigenous peoples and their allies on the one hand, and the conditions that ensure and enable the viability of REDD+, including the necessary forms of social ordering that supports it, on the other. It therefore analyses the 'social' as terrain for addressing and mediating these different – and potentially competing – demands of rights and recognition 'from below' and the imperatives arising 'from above' to ensure that specific obligations and responsibilities are enforceable, which are critical to the viability of REDD+ as a performance-based scheme. It shows that all three strategies – benefit sharing, tenure reform, and rights to consultation and to FPIC – are caught between the imperatives of rights realisation 'from below' and greater responsibilisation of local peoples and communities 'from above'. This chapter examines how these competing demands play out in the proposals for benefit sharing, tenure reform and FPIC, and suggests that these three strategies might not necessarily be emancipatory for forest peoples, but rather they may operate to facilitate the greater disciplinary inclusion of forest peoples in the 'green economy' and thereby further consolidate the actualisation of new forms of global authority through REDD+.

---

[5] See A. Savaresi, 'The human rights dimension of REDD' (2012) 21(2) *Review of European Community & International Environmental Law* 102–13; A. Savaresi, 'REDD+ and human rights: Addressing synergies between international regimes' (2013) 18(3) *Ecology and Society* 5–13.

[6] See C. Charters and R. Stavenhagen (eds.), *Making the Declaration Work: The United Nations Declaration on the Rights of Indigenous Peoples* (International Work Group for Indigenous Affairs, 2009); M. Davis, 'Indigenous struggles in standard-setting: The United Nations Declaration on the Rights of Indigenous Peoples' (2008) 9(2) *Melbourne Journal of International Law* 439–71.

[7] S. R. Lightfoot, 'Selective endorsement without intent to implement: Indigenous rights and the Anglosphere' (2012) 16(1) *The International Journal of Human Rights* 100–22.

[8] S. Pahuja, 'Rights as regulation: The integration of development and human rights' in B. Morgan (ed.), *The Intersection of Rights and Regulation* (Ashgate, 2007) pp. 167–91, 168.

B MANAGING SOCIAL RISKS

The UNFCCC decisions on REDD+ have consistently called for developing country Parties to ensure 'the full and effective participation of relevant stakeholders', including both Indigenous peoples and 'local communities'.[9] Although a clear set of safeguards were articulated as part of the Cancun Agreements,[10] and considerable work has been done around understanding and implementing these safeguards,[11] operationalising them – putting them into practice and verifying their implementation – remains a major challenge. A CIFOR review found that, as a matter of practice, '[a]ttention to social safeguards needs to be increased and accelerated'.[12] CIFOR further noted the very significant challenges involved in ensuring the 'full and effective participation of local stakeholders' and 'promoting social co-benefits in a way that is efficient and equitable given the heterogeneity of livelihood portfolios and varying patterns of forest use and dependence among local stakeholders'.[13] Scholarship has also highlighted how the interests of and power dynamics between different actors influence the operationalisation of safeguards. For example, McDermott et al. found that 'the involvement of investor and/or donor government actors in decision-making is correlated with an idea of REDD+ as primarily focused on carbon, while the involvement of NGO actors is correlated with the idea of REDD+ as serving non-carbon values'.[14]

Understanding the local impacts and outcomes of 'actually existing' REDD+ has been challenging, given that case studies have shown 'contradictory'[15] outcomes, and the majority of the ethnographic work studying implementation of REDD+ remains 'unsynthesised across diverse sites and countries'.[16] A recent review and synthesis by Sarah Milne et al. identified a number of 'fundamental constraints' arising from 'practical difficulties in meeting high expectations around REDD+, and how they have led to local expressions of discontent' as well as how REDD+ has

---

[9] See Decision 1/CP.16 'The Cancun Agreements: Outcome of the work of the Ad Hoc Working Group on Long-Term Cooperative Action under the Convention' FCCC/CP/2010/7/Add.1 (15 March 2011), para 72.

[10] See Chapter 1.

[11] D. Ray, J. Roberts, S. Korwin, L. Rivera, and U. Ribet, *A Guide to Understanding and Implementing the UNFCCC REDD+ Safeguards* (Client Earth, 2013).

[12] Sills, *REDD+ on the Ground*, p. 439.

[13] Ibid., p. 430.

[14] C. L. McDermott, L. Coad, A. Helfgott, and H. Schroeder, 'Operationalizing social safeguards in REDD+: Actors, interests and ideas' (2012) 21 *Environmental Science and Policy* 63–72 at 70.

[15] M. Brockhaus, K. Korhonen-Kurki, J. Sehring, M. Di Gregorio, S. Assembe-Mvondo, A. Babon, M. Bekele, M. F. Gebara, D. B. Khatri, and H. Kambire, 'REDD+, transformational change and the promise of performance-based payments: A qualitative comparative analysis' (2017) 17(6) *Climate Policy* 708–30 at 723.

[16] S. Milne, S. Mahanty, P. To, W. Dressler, P. Kanowski, and M. Thavat, 'Learning from "actually existing" REDD+: A synthesis of ethnographic findings' (2019) 17(1) *Conservation & Society* 84–95 at 85.

B. Managing Social Risks

dominantly been framed in technical rather than political terms.[17] Their review identified key issues relating to 'enrolment' in REDD+ namely that 'those who need to be "on board" for REDD+ to succeed remain only partially engaged, or indeed not targeted at all'.[18] Moreover, the 'failure of many site-based REDD+ projects to deliver local benefits has led to community frustration and scepticism', especially given that financial investments have primarily flowed to the development of REDD+ bureaucracies and national strategies rather than to local forest users.[19] Milne et al. also identified how compliance demands have led to a greater focus on technical issues such as indicators, methodologies and reporting, rather than a substantive engagement with the problems of collective consent.[20] This accords with Pamela McElwee's findings that substantive problems in REDD+ implementation have generally been managed through technical measures, including the adoption of 'more bureaucratic and apolitical calculative checklist approaches for supposed participation'. This process of 'checklist-ification' has therefore functioned to reduce complexity and avoid discussion involving political issues.[21] In concluding, Milne et al. highlight that REDD+ has a 'proven capacity to misfire and mismatch', and they predict 'a long road of complicated and contingent outcomes ahead',[22] warning that the 'possibility for REDD+ to exacerbate social tensions or generate perverse or unintended outcomes must not be discounted, even if social and environmental safeguards are implemented'.[23]

Many serious challenges remain for the implementation and operationalisation of safeguards and to address persistent gaps between policy and practice in REDD+ implementation.[24] However, it is critical one interrogate not only whether safeguards are achieving their stated purpose but also to enquire into what other impacts or 'productive effects' safeguard policies are having in practice. That is, it is critical to interrogate what further purposes such safeguards might be serving and what 'instrument effects' – effects beyond those intended or desired – they might have. In this regard, it is telling that discussions about the social concerns arising from

---

[17] Ibid., 85.

[18] Ibid., 92.

[19] Ibid., 92.

[20] Ibid., 93.

[21] P. McElwee, 'From conservation and development to climate change: Anthropological engagements with REDD+ in Vietnam' in J. Barnes and M. Dove (eds.), *Climate Cultures: Anthropological Perspectives on Climate Change* (Yale University Press, 2015) pp. 82–104, 97.

[22] Milne et al., 'Learning from "actually existing" REDD', 10.

[23] Ibid., 93.

[24] S. Howell, '"No RIGHTS–No REDD": Some implications of a turn towards co-benefits' (2014) 41(2) *Forum for Development Studies* 253–72; J. Kill, *REDD: A Gallery of Conflicts, Contradictions and Lies* (World Rainforest Movement, 2014). See also P. Kanyinke Sena, M. Cunningham and B. Xavier, *Indigenous People's Rights and Safeguards in Projects Related to Reducing Emissions from Deforestation and Forest Degradation: Note by the Secretariat*, UN ESCOR, Permanent Forum on Indigenous Issues, 12th sess, Agenda Item 5, UN Doc E/C.19/2013/7 (5 February 2013) para 26.

REDD+ projects are not just focused on how forest carbon projects that might potentially impact people who live in and around forested areas but also on how such people, and especially any conflict arising with or between them, might impact the viability of REDD+ projects. That is, in the REDD+ literature the 'social' is not presented as just something that needs to be protected from potential impacts caused by REDD+ projects but rather as a domain that needs to be actively managed in order to ensure the feasibility of REDD+. Discussions about the implementation of safeguards at the 'local' level often emphasise how their realisation can serve 'efficiency' and 'effectiveness' objectives, given that negative social impacts arising from REDD+ projects could pose both short- and long-term risks to the viability of projects. For example, *The Eliasch Review* stresses that ensuring procedural rights means that REDD+ is 'more *likely to succeed* and benefit the poor'.[25] Other authors closely link the need for REDD+ to be 'pro-poor' with the fact that the mechanism 'deriv(es) much of its legitimacy and potential effectiveness from its ability to improve the welfare of the forest-dependent poor and foster development in some of the poorest regions of the world'.[26] A further argument made in support of 'pro-poor' approaches is that they help consolidate the labour base upon which payment for environmental services (PES) schemes depend and promote the 'niche-market' returns that co-benefits offer. A legal manual prepared by Baker McKenzie on the CDM discussed community opposition to such projects as being a 'risk' that might result in costly delays. It suggests that such risks can be 'mitigated by ensuring community consents are a condition precedent, and that the community (via community representatives) [be] consulted in all stages of the process'.[27]

Seen from 'above', through a governmental lens, the 'social' conditions deemed necessary for the successful implementation of REDD+ are multiple and not always easily aligned. The various objectives that need to be considered and managed include: avoiding conflict and maintaining stability in forest spaces; ensuring contractual performance and effective conservation outcomes; producing cost-effective offsets; efficiently utilising local populations as workers on these PES schemes; maintaining the social legitimacy of the 'carbon commodity' through rights promotion; enabling pricing mechanisms to have 'incentivising' effects at the 'lowest' and most decentralised level; and avoiding social dislocation and dispossession. Therefore, many REDD+ proponents have recognised that in order for REDD+ projects to be *sustainable* or *lasting*, to have the *social legitimacy* upon which the offset commodity depends and to be able to provide *investor confidence, security and*

---

[25] J. Eliasch, *Climate Change: Financing Global Forests: The Eliasch Review* (Earthscan, 2008) p. 192 (my emphasis).
[26] D. Brown, F. Seymour, and L. Peskett, 'How do we achieve REDD co-benefits and avoid doing harm?' in A. Angelsen (ed.), *Moving Ahead with REDD: Issues, Options and Implications* (Center for International Forestry Research, 2008) pp. 107–18.
[27] *Legal Issues Guidebook to the Clean Development Mechanism* (UNEP, 2004) p. 90.

B. Managing Social Risks

certainty, the rights of local communities need to be recognised and respected.[28] 'Given the ever-present potential of dissent, opposition or disruption, the successful implementation of REDD+ requires careful strategic engagement and subtle governance techniques in order to attempt to balance multiple objectives, which are sometimes in tension with one another or contradictory.[29] In particular, REDD+ implementation needs to actively manage and mediate the demands of forest peoples and their allies for rights, recognition and participation whilst also ensuring the realisation of the social conditions that are necessary for REDD+ to 'work'.

The 'social' therefore should be understood as a domain of governance that seeks to manage, mediate and bring into alignment potentially competing imperatives including contractual and regulatory imperatives 'from above' with demands for rights and benefits 'from below'. However, this means the 'social' is inherently also a terrain of struggle, a place where what Partha Chatterjee describes as the 'politics of the governed' is enacted. He formulated this term to describe a how claims made by those who might formally be considered 'illegal' to habitation and livelihood – even if such claims might not be judiciable as 'rights' – nonetheless need to be managed and/or negotiated by governmental agencies or other authorities 'according to calculations of political expediency'.[30]

There are a number of reasons why the implementation of REDD+ projects necessarily needs to operate within such a terrain of compromise. The first lies in the remote, often difficult-to-access nature of forest spaces where REDD+ is implemented, which constitute 'a site of struggle, but [one that] is difficult to control by coercive means'.[31] Thus, for REDD+ projects to remain viable over longer periods of time – as is necessary in order to demonstrate permanence – there needs to be a certain level of enrolment of local forest dwellers in REDD+ objectives and initiatives. The second reason is that social legitimation, secured through the participation of local stakeholders, is essential for the success of incentive-based conservation schemes such as REDD+.[32] Accounts of conflict or violent evictions risk upsetting the 'social licence' upon which these schemes – and the feelings of virtuousness they promise buyers – in part depend.

More broadly, the 'social' is a frame taken up by transnational experts seeking to manage the conduct of both forest dwellers and project proponents, in a context

---

[28] P. Anderson, *Free, Prior, and Informed Consent in REDD+: Principles and Approaches for Policy and Project Development* (RECOFTC and GIZ, 2011) p. 17.

[29] See T. M. Li, 'Practices of assemblage and community forest management' (2007) 36(2) *Economy and Society* 263–93.

[30] P. Chatterjee, *The Politics of the Governed; Reflections on Popular Politics in Most of the World* (Columbia University Press, 2004) p. 40.

[31] Li, 'Practices of assemblage and community forest management', 266.

[32] T. Krause and T. D. Nielsen, 'The legitimacy of incentive-based conservation and a critical account of social safeguards' (2014) 41 *Environmental Science & Policy* 44–51.

300   REDD+ at the 'Local' Level: Between Rights and Responsibilisation

where 'neither side pulls in a single direction'.[33] The governance of the 'social' thus calls upon, and gives rise to, a complex legality that reflects – and seeks to mediate – coexisting rights claims and regulatory imperatives.[34] What emerges is therefore what César Rodríguez-Garavito has described as an 'intensely controversial legal field in which the dominance of neoliberal legality – based on freedom of contract and due process – is constantly contested by the legality that is based on indigenous self-determination'.[35] The approaches adopted in order to manage this fraught social–legal terrain 'result from the complex interactions among actors of these two regulatory strategies at both international and national levels'.[36]

The promise of such governance strategies is that they can help 'assemble' a productive alignment of 'local' and 'global' interests. Such envisioned 'win-win' outcomes are frequently promoted in REDD+ discourses. For example, a 2014 report by the World Resources Institute (WRI), titled *Securing Rights, Combatting Climate Change*, provides 'global-scale' evidence to 'demonstrate the tremendous potential for reducing emissions by strengthening communities' rights'[37]; it presents the strengthening of community land and resource rights as a 'vital opportunity' to address the urgent crisis of climate change. In a similar vein, CIFOR has argued that 'community-managed forests could be a more cost-efficient and effective solution to reducing deforestation and ensuring the sustainable use of forests while benefiting local livelihoods'.[38] There is also increased empirical evidence that community-managed forests produce better conservation outcomes than do state-protected areas.[39] The promotion of such synergies between 'local' rights realisation and 'global' climate protection objectives is certainly desirable, yet such alignment is often more fragile, precarious and contingent than these accounts acknowledge. Moreover, there is a risk where 'local' interests are deployed or promoted in order to serve 'global' objectives that the granting of local rights can become *conditional upon* or *realisable only to the extent of* their facilitating a 'global' agenda: that is, only those rights whose realisation furthers, rather than challenges, market-based conservation will be promoted. However, an additional and arguably more acute concern is that in order to achieve a synergy between competing local and global interests, the

---

[33] T. M. Li, 'Indigeneity, capitalism, and the management of dispossession (2010) 51(3) *Current Anthropology* 385–414, 386

[34] Rodríguez-Garavito, C., 'Ethnicity.gov: Global governance, indigenous peoples, and the right to prior consultation in social minefields' (2011) 18 *Indiana Journal of Global Legal Studies* 263–305.

[35] Ibid., 282.

[36] Ibid.

[37] C. Stevens, R. Winterbottom, J. Springer, and K. Reytar, *Securing Rights, Combatting Climate Change* (World Resources Institute, 2014).

[38] Center for International Forestry Research, 'Deforestation much higher in protected areas than forests run by local communities', 23 August 2011, www.cifor.org/press-releases/deforestation-much-higher-in-protected-areas-than-forests-run-by-local-communities/.

[39] L. Porter-Bolland, E. A. Ellis, M. R. Guariguata, I. Ruiz-Mallén, S. Negrete-Yankelevich, and V. Reyes-García, 'Community managed forests and forest protected areas: An assessment of their conservation effectiveness across the tropics' (2012) 268 *Forest Ecology and Management* 6–17.

C DISCIPLINARY INCLUSION IN THE GREEN ECONOMY

governance strategies and modes of legal regulation to manage the domain of the 'social' might actively intervene in and reshape forest spaces in order to enable a better alignment of 'local' and 'global' interests.

The previous section demonstrated how the management of social issues in REDD+ implementation involves the mediation between the competing demands of rights 'from below' and regulatory imperative of responsibilisation 'from above'. REDD+ is being implemented at a time when the expansionist tendencies of contemporary capitalism mean that Indigenous peoples potentially face wholesale displacement due to deforestation, plantations, extractive industry projects, dams and other forms of 'land grabs'.[40] Therefore, understandably, the focus of much advocacy has been on avoiding similar outcomes from REDD+ schemes. Thus, while there is considerable – and critically important – concern about mitigating the potential threats of displacement and dispossession, less consideration has been given in the scholarship to examining the 'productive effects' of safeguard policies and the ways in which they may operate to transform social relations and produce specific subjectivities at the 'local' level.

Through his examination of the practices of forest management, Arun Agrawal has shown that environmental policies have helped create new environmental subjectivities and new forms of regulation of communities.[41] His scholarship highlights how the technologies of environmental government do not simply regulate pre-existing subjects but are actively engaged in the production of new environmental subjectivities.[42] He deployed the term 'environmentality', building on the Foucauldian conceptual framework of governmentality, to propose an approach to environmental politics that analyses the ways in which rural localities are incorporated into a wider set of political relations and is attentive to how issues of power/ knowledge, institutions and the production of subjectivities are interconnected.[43] Agrawal's work has shown how shifts in the relationship between states and localities have produced 'governmentalised localities' involving both the emergence of new environmental regulatory spaces within these localities, or 'regulatory communities', and the constitution of new 'environmental subjects' or 'people who have come to

[40] T. M. Li, 'Indigeneity, capitalism, and the management of dispossession' (2010) 51(3) *Current Anthropology* 385–414; see also S. Sassen, *Expulsions: Brutality and Complexity in the Global Economy* (Harvard University Press, 2014); S. Sassen, 'A savage sorting of winners and losers: Contemporary versions of primitive accumulation' (2010) 7(1) *Globalisations* 23–50.
[41] A. Agrawal, *Environmentality: Technologies of Government and the Making of Subjects* (Duke University Press, 2005) p. 3; see also A. Agrawal, 'Environmentality: Community, intimate government, and the making of environmental subjects in Kumaon, India' (2005) 46(2) *Current anthropology* 161–90.
[42] Agrawal, *Environmentality*, p. 6.
[43] Ibid., p. 8.

302   REDD+ at the 'Local' Level: Between Rights and Responsibilisation

think and act in new ways in relation to the environmental domain being governed', namely forests.[44] His work therefore demonstrates how practices of environmental governance have profound effects insofar as they 'redefine political relations, reconfigure institutional arrangements, and transform environmental subjectivities'.[45]

Drawing on Agrawal's conceptual framework, this chapter interrogates how the logic underpinning the management of social impacts in 'best practice' approaches to REDD+ implementation might be better understood not as orientated primarily towards protecting against exclusion but rather as directed towards *transforming* relations between forest peoples, their land and the global market. The actualisation of new forms of global authority over forested land involves 'reordering forest spaces according to international law and administrative specifications'.[46] Viewed from a governmentality perspective, this also entails, as Lee Godden argues, the reframing of 'communities' as 'project participants'.[47] Strategies to manage the social impact of REDD+ can be read in part as seeking to transform communities from (in the words of the Rights and Resources Initiative) 'unrecognized counter-parties'[48] into legally recognised 'partners' covered by 'village agreements' or other contractual arrangements.[49] In a context where forest peoples face real risks of dispossession and exclusion the promotion of participation and inclusion is generally viewed as rights-promoting and emancipatory. However, viewed from another perspective, transforming forest dwellers from 'unrecognized counter-parties' into 'partners' can also be seen as a form of disciplinary inclusion within global environmental markets that simultaneously transforms predominantly smallholder agriculturists into responsibilised, entrepreneurial 'ecosystem service' providers in the 'green economy'.

This analysis builds on anthropologist Tania Murray Li's reading of REDD+ projects as '[i]nterventions to fix Indigenous peoples to the land, and limit them to specific land uses, [which are] currently being intensified'.[50] Li argues that REDD+ operates as a form of environmental protection that has the effect of 'fixing [people],

[44] Ibid., pp. 6–7.

[45] Ibid., p. 7.

[46] L. Godden, 'Benefit-sharing in REDD+: Linking rights and equitable outcomes' in *The Impact of Climate Change Mitigation on Indigenous and Forest Communities: International, National and Local Law Perspectives on REDD+* (Cambridge University Press, 2017) pp. 172–200, 182.

[47] Ibid., p. 182.

[48] A. Alforte, J. Angan, J. Dentith, K. Domondon, L. Munden, S. Murday, and L. Pradela, *Communities As Counterparties: Preliminary Review of Concessions and Conflict in Emerging and Frontier Market Concessions* (Rights and Resources Initiative, 2014).

[49] For a discussion of the process of finalising 'village agreements' see M. Mulyani and P. Jepson, 'Social learning through a REDD+ "village agreement": Insights from the KFCP in Indonesia' (2015) 56(1) *Asia Pacific Viewpoint* 79–95; see also S. Howell, '"No RIGHTS–No REDD"', 253–72.

[50] T. M. Li, 'Fixing non-market subjects: Governing land and population in the Global South' (2014) 18 *Foucault Studies* 34–48.

C. Disciplinary Inclusion in the Green Economy 303

once again, in their distinct identities and their arboreal niche'.[51] As such, she characterises REDD+ as a mode of governing through difference, whereby people are 'fixed in place on ancestral/customary land' and 'fixed in their alterity'[52] via a process she describes as the 'communal fix'[53] or 'tribal slot'.[54] These practices echo forms of colonial governmentality based on indirect rule in which 'rather than [being] eradicated or aggressively modernized, native social and political forms would now be patronized as they become inserted into the institutional dynamics of imperial power'.[55] However, rather than simply repeating these forms of colonial governance that operate through difference, in REDD+ schemes difference is actively mobilised in ways that facilitate the inclusion of forest communities in neoliberal environmental markets.

This conceptual framework therefore calls for more critical attention to the potential 'instrument effects'[56] – effects beyond those intended or desired – of the various measures used to manage the social impacts of REDD+ and the way in which these may work to consolidate the reorganisation of authority that REDD+ represents. Moreover, it provides theoretical tools to interrogate the forms of environmental subjectivity that are constituted through processes of benefit-sharing, tenure reform, and consultation towards FPIC. The analysis in Section F examines whether these three strategies – benefit-sharing, tenure reform and consultation towards FPIC – should be understood as not simply mitigating the potential negative harms or risk of dispossession that REDD+ presents but also as operating to produce specific environmental subjects that can be *fixed in place* as workers on and/or beneficiaries of PES schemes, while their forests and land – newly commoditised as 'natural capital' – enter into international financial flows. It therefore suggests that these strategies are not simply protective: they also operate to more deeply embed market rationalities by facilitating the responsibilisation of the contracting subject upon which REDD+ depends. Before interrogating the three main strategies adopted to manage the social impacts of REDD+ the next two sections consider how the international legal frameworks pertaining to Indigenous peoples are compatible with, and arguably enabling of, forms of governmentality that operate through the accommodation and recognition of difference and the production of environmental subjects.

---

[51] Ibid., 46.

[52] Li, 'Fixing non-market subjects', 38; see also Li, 'Indigeneity, capitalism, and the management of dispossession'.

[53] Li, 'Indigeneity, capitalism, and the management of dispossession', 386–88.

[54] Li, 'Articulating Indigenous identity in Indonesia'; Li, 'Fixing non-market subjects', 39.

[55] K. Mantena, *Alibis of Empire: Henry Maine and the Ends of Liberal Imperialism* (Princeton University Press, 2010) p. 2.

[56] M. Foucault, *Discipline and Punish: The Birth of the Prison* (Knopf Doubleday Publishing Group, 1977); cited in B. Rajagopal, *International Law from Below: Development, Social Movements and Third World Resistance* (Cambridge University Press, 2003) p. 76.

D INDIGENOUS HUMAN RIGHTS, RECOGNITION AND CULTURAL DIFFERENCE

Contemporary international legal frameworks on the rights of Indigenous peoples are based on a paradigm focused on the recognition and protection of cultural difference. For most of the twentieth century an 'integrationist approach' dominated, one that emphasised the need for the assimilation and integration of Indigenous peoples into society. Since the mid-1980s, however, this has been replaced by a new paradigm centred on Indigenous rights, or a 'consultative approach'.[57] This transformation was marked by an 'overall reformulation of the normative parameters of the integrationist paradigm, resulting in an increasing recognition of Indigenous peoples as distinct subjects of rights under international law'.[58] This significant shift has led to a greater recognition of the rights of Indigenous peoples as well as their inclusion within formal decision-making structures, which 'seemed to signal an epic moment of change in politics'.[59] Such recognition and inclusion has thus been widely celebrated as a 'breakthrough, a significant shift and milestone marking progress in, and of, politics'.[60] However, it is also necessary, as Marjo Lindroth and Heidi Sinevaara-Niskanen write, to pose critical questions about the extent to which these shifts represent a (re)arrangement rather than a dismantling of colonial power relations between settlers and Indigenous peoples.[61] Scholars have shown how the move towards frameworks of recognition do not necessarily represent a dismantling of colonial forms of rule, but rather the adoption of different mechanisms of control. Glen Coulthard writes that the politics of recognition reflects a change in the form and nature of colonial relations from an 'unconcealed structure of domination to a mode of colonial *governmentality* that works through the limited freedoms afforded by state recognition and accommodation'.[62] In his analysis of the Canadian context, he has shown how 'colonial relations of power are no longer reproduced primarily through overtly coercive means, but rather through the asymmetrical exchange of mediated forms of state recognition and accommodation'.[63]

In international legal spaces, this shift coincided with changes in the forms of claim-making by some – but not all Indigenous advocates – who gradually moved

---

[57] Rodríguez-Garavito, 'Ethnicity.gov', 268.

[58] L. Rodríguez-Piñero, *Indigenous Peoples, Postcolonialism, and International Law: The ILO Regime (1919–1989)* (Oxford University Press, 2005) p. 6.

[59] M. Lindroth and H. Sinevaara-Niskanen, *Global Politics and Its Violent Care for Indigeneity: Sequels to Colonialism* (Springer, 2017) p. 3.

[60] Ibid., p. 4.

[61] Ibid.

[62] G. S. Coulthard, *Red Skin, White Masks: Rejecting the Colonial Politics of Recognition* (University of Minnesota Press, 2014) pp. 14–15 (emphasis in original).

[63] Ibid., p. 6.

D. Indigenous Human Rights, Recognition and Cultural Difference 305

away from claims grounded in assertions of 'sovereignty' and instead called for recognition of their human rights, especially rights of 'cultural identity'.[64] Closely linked to this move from a 'sovereignty' frame towards a focus on 'cultural rights' has been a greater emphasis on the right to 'internal' self-determination rather than a broader claim of 'external self-determination'.[65] Historically, calls for Indigenous self-determination – the founding principle of Indigenous rights – were inherently connected to demands for decolonisation. However, the 'modern conception' of self-determination does not necessarily include the right to separate from a state but instead is centred on 'a range of alternatives including the right to participate in the governance of the State as well as the right to various forms of autonomy and self-governance'.[66] As a result, '[s]elf-determination was essentially shorn of its connections to political power and redefined as the indispensable vehicle of preservation and flourishing of the culture of the group'.[67]

This focus on cultural identity has impacts both for the basis on which rights are claimed – that is, claims are grounded on cultural difference rather than based on citizenship or on demands for reparative justice for the wrongs of colonialism[68] – as well

---

[64] Articles written by James Anaya in the early 1990s (subsequently Special Rapporteur on the Rights of Indigenous Peoples 2008–14) are commonly identified as crucial in promoting this change in advocacy approach: S. J. Anaya, 'Indigenous rights norms in contemporary international law' (1991) 8 *Arizona Journal of International and Comparative Law* 1–39; S. J. Anaya, 'The capacity of international law to advance ethnic of nationality rights claims' (1991) 13(3) *Human Rights Quarterly* 403–11; see also S. J. Anaya, 'Divergent discourses about international law, Indigenous peoples, and rights over land and natural resources: Towards a realist trend' (2005) 16(2) *Colorado Journal of International Environmental Law and Policy* 237–58; for a critical analysis of this shift see K. Engle, 'Indigenous rights claims in international law: Self-determination, culture, and development' in D. Armstrong (ed.), *Routledge Handbook of International Law* (Routledge, 2009), pp. 331–43; K. Engle, *The Elusive Promise of Indigenous Development: Rights, Culture, Strategy* (Duke University Press, 2010); K. Engle, 'On fragile architecture: The UN Declaration on the Rights of Indigenous Peoples in the context of human rights' (2011) 22(2) *European Journal of International Law* 141–63; I. Schulte-Tenckhoff and A. Hasan Khan, 'The permanent quest for a mandate: Assessing the UN Permanent Forum on Indigenous Issues' (2011) 20(3) *Griffith Law Review* 673–701; I. Schulte-Tenckhoff, 'Treaties, peoplehood, and self-determination: Understanding the language of Indigenous rights' in E. Pulitano (ed.), *Indigenous Rights in the Age of the Declaration* (Cambridge University Press, 2012) pp. 64–86; I. Watson and S. Venne, 'Talking up Indigenous peoples' original intent in a space dominated by state interventions' in E. Pulitano (ed.), *Indigenous Rights in the Age of the Declaration* (Cambridge University Press, 2012) pp. 87–109.

[65] See E.-I. A. Daes, 'Some considerations on the right of indigenous peoples to self-determination' (1993) 3 *Transnational Law & Contemporary Problems* 1–11.

[66] E.-I. A. Daes, *Prevention of Discrimination and Protection of Indigenous Peoples: Indigenous Peoples' Permanent Sovereignty Over Natural Resources: Final Report of the Special Rapporteur*, E/CN.4/2004/30 (2004), 17 cited in T. Ward, 'The right to free, prior, and informed consent: Indigenous peoples' participation rights within international law' (2011) 10(2) *Northwestern University Journal of International Human Rights* 54–84 at 55.

[67] S. Wiessner, 'The cultural rights of indigenous peoples: Achievements and continuing challenges' (2011) 22(1) *European Journal of International Law* 121–40 at 122.

[68] See T. M. Li, 'Masyarakat Adat, difference, and the limits of recognition in Indonesia's forest zone' (2001) 35(3) *Modern Asian Studies* 645–76.

as the nature of rights recognised and protected. Such a focus on cultural rights has been promoted by key advocates such as James Anaya as a more pragmatic and 'realistic' route to protecting Indigenous rights.[69] However, critical scholars have highlighted various limitations of human rights models and this focus on the protection of cultural identity. Isabelle Schulte-Tenckhoff identifies a 'growing tendency to collapse Indigenous peoples and minorities' and to limit collective rights to 'human rights exercised by individuals in community with other members of their group, as opposed to group rights claimed by non-state groups as such'.[70] She thus warns that 'recognition of cultural rights comes at the price of the right of self-determination understood as a group right'.[71] Karen Engle has shown that the 'dark side' of such 'strategic essentialism'[72] and the focus on the human rights of cultural identity rather than on a broader claim of self-determination is that even when articulated in group terms such rights 'function to *protect* the group, rather than transform the underlying power structures *against* which they are protecting the group' and therefore might be 'short-sighted and even counterproductive'.[73] Anthropologist Charles Hale demonstrates how the regime of 'cultural recognition' 'shapes, delimits, and *produces* cultural difference rather than suppresses it' and thereby represents a 'transformation of power relations as opposed to resistance towards emancipation'.[74] His work on 'neoliberal multiculturalism' suggests that the recognition of cultural rights, including collective rights, is in fact compatible with neoliberal ideology and indeed risks producing deeper entanglement with neoliberalism's grid of intelligibility. Similarly, Rodríguez-Garavito has shown how the juridification of collective claims of cultural identity, self-determination and control over territory has led to the 'projection of the neoliberal subject onto the plane of collective rights' through a process of governance that he labels 'ethnicity. gov'.[75] Finally, a focus on cultural difference, rather than the experience of colonisation as a key characteristic of indigeneity, risks producing frameworks that are more orientated towards the *protection* and *maintenance* of certain characteristics

---

[69] Anaya, 'Divergent discourses about international law'.

[70] Schulte-Tenckhoff, 'Treaties, peoplehood, and self-determination", p. 64.

[71] Ibid., p. 67.

[72] Engle describes as 'strategic essentialism' the 'acceptance and deployment of static and essentialized notions of culture' as an advocacy strategy. She questions – and encourages activists and advocates to also question whether the 'the right to culture – and, perhaps human rights, more generally – is up to the task of the major economic and political restructuring that many advocates (if covertly) seem to seek': Engle, *The Elusive Promise of Indigenous Development*, p. 10.

[73] Engle, 'Indigenous rights claims in international law', p. 343; Engle, *The Elusive Promise of Indigenous Development*, Chapters 6 and 7; see also K. Gover, 'The elusive promise of indigenous developments: Rights, culture, strategy by Karen Engle' (2011) 12 *Melbourne Journal of International Law* 419–31.

[74] C. R. Hale, 'Neoliberal multiculturalism: The remaking of cultural rights and racial dominance in Central America' (2005) 28(1) *Political and Legal Anthropology Review* 10–28 at 13 and 16.

[75] Rodríguez-Garavito, 'Ethnicity.gov', 276.

E. Identifying 'Stakeholders': The Constitution of Environmental Subjects 307

deemed 'worthy' of human rights protections, rather than dismantling persistent colonial relations and interrogating how colonial relations have shaped specific constructions of indigeneity. The next section turns to consider how international legal frameworks have required Indigenous peoples to perform specific subject-positions or attributes and present themselves in specific ways in order to claim rights or be accorded legal protections.

E IDENTIFYING 'STAKEHOLDERS': THE CONSTITUTION OF ENVIRONMENTAL SUBJECTS

Colonial legal frameworks of recognition operate to produce specific subject-positions, categories of identity and the terms of their recognition. Glen Coulthard has drawn on the work of Franz Fanon to argue that where colonial rule does not operate exclusively through force, the maintenance of hegemony requires the production of 'colonised subjects'; that is, 'the production of the specific modes of colonial thought, desire and behaviour that implicitly or explicitly commit the colonized to the types of practices and subject-positions that are required for their continued domination'.[76] As examined in more detail in the sub-sections below, legal frameworks for the recognition of cultural rights do not merely define and thereby represent a pre-existing rights-bearing subject; rather, following Judith Butler, there is a sense in which 'judicial systems of power *produce* the subjects they subsequently come to represent',[77] due to law's power to set the terms of recognition. Legal frameworks thereby compel the performance of specific subject-positions by rights claimants in order for them to be recognised as entitled to the rights protections they seek. As Kathleen Birrell has argued, 'The creation of the Indigenous subject as a recognisable identity before a determinate law and, more broadly, within a contemporary liberal rights framework, entails the production of an abstraction – "socially produced and negotiated" – the performance of which attracts legal entitlements'.[78] She argues that the 'colonial schema in which . . . the conception of indigeneity operates compels a particular performance from the Indigenous subject, in order to appear before the law at all'.[79]

The power of legal frameworks resides partly in their capacity to set the terms of recognition and identification. As Tania Murray Li writes, the very idea that Indigenous peoples should have 'special rights, or that resource access should be linked to cultural identity and "traditional" environmental knowledge, would mean nothing if the bearer of those rights and qualities could not be identified and

---

[76] Coulthard, *Red Skin, White Masks*, p. 16.

[77] J. Butler, *Gender Trouble: Feminism and the Subversion of Identity* (Routledge, 1990) p. 2; cited in K. Birrell, *Indigeneity: Before and Beyond the Law* (Routledge, 2016) p. 4.

[78] K. Birrell, '"An essential ghost": Indigeneity within the legal archive' (2010) 33(1) *Australian Feminist Law Journal* 81–99 at 84.

[79] Birrell, *Indigeneity: Before and Beyond the Law*, p. 4.

308 REDD+ at the 'Local' Level: Between Rights and Responsibilisation

rendered recognisable by legal and bureaucratic criteria'.[80] Lindroth and Sinevaara-Niskanen's examination of international legal frameworks relating to Indigenous rights shows that '[t]he power of international law, as seen in the conventions and declarations on indigeneity, lies in its having ultimate authority in setting the terms of recognition and in producing and defining the content of a category of identity'.[81] International law thus plays a constitutive role with regard to understandings of indigeneity, as Patrick Thornberry argues, 'through recognition processes and incentives for groups to access international norms through [their] configuration or re-configuration as indigenous'.[82] The discussion below examines how international law has approached the question of defining who is considered 'Indigenous' as well as who is considered a 'local community' and therefore entitled to certain rights and protections. It shows that a consequence of the flexible and pragmatic approach to definition that has been adopted by international legal frameworks is that it implicitly requires those claiming rights as 'Indigenous peoples' or even 'local communities' to perform specific attributes in order to be granted the rights they claim.

1 Indigenous Peoples

The question of what defines 'Indigenous peoples' has vexed international law.[83] Indigenous peoples have asserted the right to self-definition is inherent to the right to self-determination, yet international legal frameworks have held that recognition of who is entitled to self-determination requires further criteria. However, in practice, in order to be recognised as subjects of this right to self-determination, Indigenous peoples find themselves having to meet certain implicit, externally imposed criteria that have been attached to this identity under international law.[84] The question of who is considered 'Indigenous' by law is, as Thornberry writes, 'mired in politics, suffused with ethical considerations [and shaped by a] complex amalgam of power, logic and right'.[85] The problems associated with establishing a definition of 'Indigenous peoples' (and by extension, clarifying the distinction between 'Indigenous' and other 'minority groups')[86] were purportedly resolved by a

[80] Li, 'Masyarakat Adat, Difference, and the Limits of Recognition, 652–53.
[81] Lindroth and Sinevaara-Niskanen, *Global Politics and Its Violent Care for Indigeneity*, pp. 11–12.
[82] P. Thornberry, *Indigenous Peoples and Human Rights* (Manchester University Press, 2013) p. 60.
[83] See for a discussion: D. E. Sanders, 'Indigenous peoples: Issues of definition' (1999) 8(1) *International Journal of Cultural Property* 4–13.
[84] Thornberry, *Indigenous Peoples and Human Rights*, p. 60.
[85] Ibid.
[86] E.-I. A. Daes and A. Eide, *Working Paper on the Relationship and Distinction between the Rights of Persons Belonging to Minorities and Those of Indigenous Peoples*, Economic and Social Council, Commission on Human Rights, Sub-commission on the Promotion and Protection of Human Rights, E/CN.4/Sub.2/2000/10 (19 July 2000).

E. *Identifying 'Stakeholders': The Constitution of Environmental Subjects*   309

prevailing view 'that no formal universal definition of the term [was] necessary'.[87] Instead, various 'working' rather than 'fixed' or binding definitions have been developed, alongside the identification of some *basic characteristics* to aid the process of 'functional determinations' on a case-by-case basis. The most prominent of these, the Martinez Cobo definition, insists on 'self-definition' as the central principle, but it is also structured around the concept of 'historical continuity' with 'pre-invasion' or 'pre-colonial' societies.[88] The 1989 International Labour Organisation Indigenous and Tribal Peoples Convention (ILO 169), which applies to both 'tribal peoples' and those 'regarded as Indigenous', provided the first legal definition of 'Indigenous peoples'.[89] The 1994 Draft UN Declaration on the Rights of Indigenous Peoples included the recognition of self-defined Indigenous identity.[90] In 1997, at the fifteenth session of the Working Group on the Draft Declaration on the Rights of Indigenous Peoples, a conclusion was reached that a 'definition of Indigenous peoples at the global level was not possible at that time', nor was it deemed necessary for the purpose of a declaration.[91] The UNDRIP therefore does not include any explicit provisions defining the subject of the rights it enumerates, although self-identification is implied in the provision regarding

---

[87] *The Concept of Indigenous Peoples: Background Paper Prepared for the Secretariat of the Permanent Forum on Indigenous Issues* (2004) PFII/2004/WS.1/3.

[88] J. R. Martinez Cobo, *Study on the Problem of Discrimination against Indigenous Populations* UN Doc E/CN.4/Sub.2/1986/7 and Add. 1–4 (1986).

[89] International Labour Organization (ILO), *Convention (No 169) Concerning Indigenous and Tribal Peoples in Independent Countries*, opened for signature 27 June 1989, 1650 UNTS 383 (entered into force 5 September 1991)('ILO 169'). Article 1 states:
This Convention applies to:

1. (a) tribal peoples in independent countries whose social, cultural and economic conditions distinguish them from other sections of the national community, and whose status is regulated wholly or partially by their own customs or traditions or by special laws or regulations;
   (b) peoples in independent countries who are regarded as Indigenous on account of their descent from the populations which inhabited the country, or a geographical region to which the country belongs, at the time of conquest or colonization or the establishment of present state boundaries and who, irrespective of their legal status, retain some or all of their own social, economic, cultural and political institutions.
2. Self-identification as Indigenous or tribal shall be regarded as a fundamental criterion for determining the groups to which the provisions of this Convention apply.
3. The use of the term peoples in this Convention shall not be construed as having any implications as regards the rights which may attach to the term under international law.

Note also that there was controversy around the use of the term 'peoples' which was only adopted after the Article 1(3) proviso to prevent it having any implications for a right to self-determination in international law was adopted.

[90] Note in particular draft Article 8, *Draft Declaration on the Rights of Indigenous Peoples* (1994) UN Doc. E/CN.4/Sub.2/1994/2/Add.1.

[91] See *The Concept of Indigenous Peoples: Background Paper Prepared for the Secretariat of the Permanent Forum on Indigenous Issues* PFII/2004/WS.1/3 (2004).

community rules and membership.[92] A 2012 report by the International Law Association (ILA) lists several indicia that 'should be used in order to ascertain whether or not a given community may be considered as Indigenous peoples'. These are self-identification, historical continuity, special relationship with ancestral lands, distinctiveness, non-dominance in society and perpetuation (or a desire to maintain and reproduce their distinct way of life).[93]

Adopting a more 'flexible' approach to defining the subject of Indigenous rights rather than requiring a 'fixed' or binding definition has clear advantages; however, perversely, in practice this has meant the form and content of the rights claimed have determined the characteristic of their subject. This flexible approach was celebrated by Erica-Irene Daes, long-term Chairperson of the UN Working Group on Indigenous Populations, on the basis that it was 'not desirable or possible to arrive at a universal definition at the present time'.[94] Patrick Thornberry similarly suggests that a search for a 'universal formula' might be 'misguided', and that there are real benefits of the adaptive flexibility of the current approach.[95] He argues, moreover, that the 'characteristics' of the 'subject' of Indigenous peoples' rights can be 'gleaned from the major specific texts on Indigenous rights'.[96] This echoes the approach proposed in a working paper by Asbjørn Eide, who affirms that 'being practical and realistic necessitates an approach that is purposive, and links the characteristics of groups to their aspirations and to the rights they are entitled to and realistically can exercise'.[97] Adopting such an approach, Thornberry identifies that the characteristics of the legal subject of Indigenous rights that can be 'gleaned' from the ILO Convention 169 include 'a specific social and cultural identity, customs, traditions and institutions'; 'a distinctive relationship with lands and territories'; a 'subsistence economy and traditional activities'; and distinctive knowledges, technologies and languages.[98] He concludes that, 'instead of defining beneficiaries and then allocating rights, international law has often proceeded the other way around. Rights have been set out and continue to be developed in such a way that the contours of the communities appropriating them become clearer'.[99] As Adil

---

[92] See General Assembly Resolution 61/295, *United Nations Declaration on the Rights of Indigenous Peoples*, UN GAOR 61st sess, 107th plen mtg, Supp No 49, UN Doc A/61/67 (13 September 2007). Articles 9 and Article 33.

[93] International Law Association, *Sofia Conference: Rights of Indigenous Peoples, Final Report* (2012).

[94] E.-I. A. Daes, *Report of the Working Group on Indigenous Populations on Its Fifteenth Session*, Sub-Commission on the Prevention of Discrimination and Protection of Minorities, E/CN.4/Sub.2/1997/14 (13 August 1997).

[95] Thornberry, *Indigenous Peoples and Human Rights*, p. 57.

[96] Ibid.

[97] A. Eide in the *Working Paper on the Relationship and Distinction between the Rights of Persons Belonging to Minorities and Those of Indigenous Peoples* E/CN.4/Sub.2/2000/10 (19 July 2000) para 50.

[98] Thornberry, *Indigenous Peoples and Human Rights*, p. 57.

[99] Ibid., p. 52.

E. Identifying 'Stakeholders': The Constitution of Environmental Subjects   311

Hasan Khan has identified, such analysis demonstrates the constructive nature of law and rights – namely, that rights do not attach themselves to pre-constituted subjects, but rather rights enumeration is itself part of the process of constructing the subjects to which it refers.[100] In contrast to a formalist approach to defining the subject of legal rights, this pragmatist approach that aims to 'describe' the subject of rights through a series of 'descriptive elements', in a circular fashion, effectively defines the subject by reference to the rights to which they are entitled.[101] This 'flexible' approach thus generates a paradox: although self-identification as Indigenous remains a key indicium, peoples are most likely to be 'read' or 'recognised' as Indigenous by external actors if their claims for rights have a specific content.

Certain discursive assumptions have increasingly made the performance of a specific relationship with the environment and enactment of environmental stewardship key to whether people are read as Indigenous. Chris Tennant argues that, in contrast to an earlier 'assimilationist' era (1945–71), when the predominant representation of Indigenous peoples was of the 'ignoble primitive' (uncivilised and living miserable lives requiring 'practice of development ... to lift them out of their backwardness'),[102] in the contemporary era these 'characteristics' have come to be considered as distinctive and deserving of protection. Tennant claims that since 1971 the dominant representation of Indigenous peoples has been as 'noble' and as having that 'which the modern world most lacks, namely a close relationship to nature and the environment'.[103] He shows that in the contemporary view the relationship of Indigenous peoples to modernity is scripted in accordance with three key interpretations of them: (a) as victims of progress; (b) as supporting and legitimating a critique of process and (c) as representing an aspiration to transcend modernity and progress through a 'return to the primitive'.[104] However, this conception has not provoked broader structural critiques of modernity, arguably because, as Birrell describes this conception of indigeneity is itself an 'expression of modernity', given that modernity requires a contrasting 'Other' of indigeneity and tradition to define itself again.[105] Thus, a dominant representation of Indigenous peoples has therefore come to be of a 'cultural subject' whose primary characteristic is historically continuous 'cultural difference', a representation that positions Indigenous peoples as both 'keepers of our past [and] custodians of *our* future'.[106] The

---

[100] A. Hasan Khan, 'How is the subject of international Indigenous peoples' rights made? Or, when the openness of law becomes its other' (paper presented at the 'Sculpting the Human' Association for the Study of Law, Culture and Humanities Conference, 2013).

[101] Ibid.

[102] C. Tennant, 'Indigenous peoples, international institutions, and the international legal literature from 1945–1993' (1994) 16(1) *Human Rights Quarterly* 1–57 at 12.

[103] Ibid.

[104] Ibid.

[105] Birrell, *Indigeneity: Before and Beyond the Law*, pp. 11–12.

[106] See E.-I. Daes, *Indigenous peoples: Keepers of Our Past, Custodians of Our Future* (International Work Group for Indigenous Affairs, 2008).

312   REDD+ *at the 'Local' Level: Between Rights and Responsibilisation*

UNDRIP contains numerous Articles aimed at protecting this very 'cultural integrity',[107] 'cultural difference'[108] and set of ancient 'traditions'.[109] It presents Indigenous culture as a culture whose 'difference' contributes to a state's 'cultural diversity'[110] and whose 'traditional' status augments humanity's knowledge and resources.[111]

A close relationship with nature has come to be seen as a 'core element of indigenousness' as well as a legitimation of Indigenous peoples' environmental agency.[112] As the 'importance of Indigenous involvement in environmental governance'[113] was affirmed through a growing number of laws and policies, scholars have asserted a 'mutually supportive' relationship or 'presumptive connection'[114] between Indigenous rights and environmental rights,[115] and an interconnection between 'environmental justice' and the rights of Indigenous peoples.[116] The increasing intersection of environmental law and Indigenous rights has the effect of producing a 'subject-position' of the 'ecological native',[117] who is posited as a steward of the environment on account of their special ecological knowledge and nature-friendly lifestyle.[118] There is a growing body of legal literature directed at, as Bradford Morse articulates, 'identify[ing] how asserting the recognized unique rights of Indigenous peoples through international and domestic law forums can provide a foundation for environmental sustainability to be accepted as a paramount principle'.[119] The Preamble of ILO 169 calls attention to 'the distinctive contributions of Indigenous and tribal peoples to the cultural diversity and *social and ecological harmony of humankind*'.[120] The Convention further affirms that the 'rights of the peoples concerned to the natural resources pertaining to their lands shall be

---

[107] UNDRIP, Article 8.

[108] UNDRIP, Articles 14, 15, 16 and 34.

[109] UNDRIP, Article 11, 12, 13 and 31.

[110] For example UNDRIP, Article 16.2.

[111] For example UNDRIP, Article 31.

[112] M. Lindroth and H. Sinevaara-Niskanen, 'At the crossroads of autonomy and essentialism: Indigenous peoples in international environmental politics' (2013) 7(3) *International Political Sociology* 275–93 at 287.

[113] B. J. Richardson, 'The ties that bind: Indigenous peoples and environmental governance' (2008) 4 *CLPE Research Paper Series* at 3.

[114] C. Metcalf, 'Indigenous rights and the environment: Evolving international law' (2003) 35(1) *Ottawa Law Review* 101–40 at 107.

[115] K. Bosselmann, 'The right to self-determination and international environmental law: An integrative approach' (1997) 1 *New Zealand Journal of Environmental Law* 1–40.

[116] L. Westra, *Environmental Justice and the Rights of Indigenous Peoples: International and Domestic Legal Perspectives* (Earthscan, 2008).

[117] See for example A. Ulloa, *The Ecological Native: Indigenous Peoples' Movements and Eco-Governmentality in Columbia* (Routledge, 2013).

[118] See also A. R. Ramos, 'The hyperreal Indian' (1994) 14(2) *Critique of Anthropology* 153–71.

[119] B. Morse, 'Indigenous rights as a mechanism to promote sustainability' in L. Westra, K. Bosselmann, and R. Westra (eds.), *Reconciling Human Existence with Ecological Integrity* (Earthscan, 2008).

[120] ILO Convention 169, Preamble (emphasis added).

E. Identifying 'Stakeholders': The Constitution of Environmental Subjects   313

specially safeguarded', particularly the rights 'to participate in the use, management and conservation of these resources'.[121] Similarly, Article 25 of the UNDRIP protects

> the right to maintain and strengthen their [Indigenous peoples'] *distinctive spiritual relationship* with their traditional owned or otherwise occupied and used lands, territories, waters and coastal seas and other resources and to *uphold their responsibilities to future generations in this regard.*[122]

Similar articulations emerge from the field of international environmental law, with the 1987 Brundtland Commission positioning Indigenous communities as a 'link' with humanity's 'ancient origins', who, as 'repositories of traditional knowledge' and 'traditional skills in sustainably managing very complex ecological systems', need to be recognised and protected.[123] Principle 22 of the Rio Declaration celebrates the 'vital role' Indigenous people and local communities play in environmental management due to their 'knowledge and traditional practices' and 'their identity, culture and interests', which must be recognised and supported in order to 'enable their effective participation in sustainable development'.[124] Although conservation traditionally followed a 'people-free parks' approach, since the late 1990s communities have become 'the locus of conservationist thinking', after being 'found' to be relevant stakeholders by international and national development organisations, conservation groups and philanthropic organisations.[125] Twenty years later, the Rio+20 outcome document stressed the 'importance of the participation of Indigenous peoples in the achievement of sustainable development' and of the UNDRIP in the 'context of global, regional, national and subnational implementation of sustainable development strategies'.[126]

While there are many examples of important environmental–Indigenous alliances, it is equally problematic to assume either an 'essential *affinity*' or an 'irreconcilable *conflict*' between Indigenous interests and environmental objectives, especially with regards to conservation projects.[127] Although depicting Indigenous

---

[121] ILO 169, Article 15.1.

[122] UNDRIP, Article 25 (emphasis added).

[123] Brundtland Commission Report, *Our Common Future World Commission on Environment and Development* (Cambridge University Press, 1987) pp. 114–15.

[124] See also *Convention on Biological Diversity*, opened for signature 5 June 1992, 1760 UNTS 79 (entered into force 29 December 1993), Article 8(j).

[125] A. Agrawal and C. C. Gibson, 'Enchantment and disenchantment: The role of community in natural resource conservation' (1999) 27(4) *World Development* 629–49 at 631.

[126] General Assembly Resolution 66/288, *The Future We Want*, UN GAOR 66th sess, 123rd plen mtg, Agenda Item 19, Supp No 49, A/RES/66/288 (11 September 2012), para 49. Indigenous peoples are also mentioned at numerous other points in the document, including the participation (para 43), the 'green economy' (para 58(j)), partnerships (para 71), 'traditional' knowledges (para 197), mountains (para 211), education (para 229), women (para 238) and forests (para 193).

[127] For a discussion of these complexities in the Australian context see E. Vincent and T. Neale, *Unstable Relations: Indigenous People and Environmentalism in Contemporary Australia* (Apollo Books, 2016).

and environmental rights as 'mutually supportive' might give rise to strategic benefits in specific contexts, such a positioning can also dangerously instrumentalise Indigenous rights, authorising rights on the basis that they are an 'effective strategy' for the protection of the global environment.[128] Such an approach risks producing what Li calls a 'compromise agreement', whereby 'social groups that are unique or different should have their knowledge and rights respected *if* and *when* it is instrumental to conservation objectives' in which 'only specific kinds of knowledge are relevant' and 'rights are conditional upon performance'.[129] Moreover, invocations of 'the right to environmental self-determination of Indigenous peoples'[130] risk reducing understandings of indigeneity to that of the 'noble savage' – a construction that has been heavily criticised for its 'green imperialism'.[131] Additionally, such representations often posit an imagined ideal that 'few Indigenous groups can live up to'.[132] Engle argues an 'unintended consequence' of the 'concept of culture as territory' is that it can operate as a tool for distinguishing who is Indigenous and deserving of protection and who is not. She writes:

> That is, if real Indians care about the land, those who are seen not to care for it properly might be restricted in their uses of it, or denied rights to it altogether. Second, given that the object of protection is the land, its stewardship sometimes takes priority over the autonomy of Indigenous peoples.[133]

Engle asserts that an 'even more serious consequence to the pursuit of a political and legal strategy based on a special relationship to land' can be that '[w]hen they do not behave towards the land in the idealized manner that has come to be expected of them, these groups might cease to be considered real Indians'.[134] She shows how, in some cases, communities have been required to 'learn' sustainable ways of living on the land that have been 'attributed to Indigenous origins and practices' in order to claim their collective ownership of that land.[135]

In conclusion, the flexible approach to the definition of 'Indigenous peoples' in international law, while allowing important openness, is also what has enabled the construction of a certain form of Indigenous subjectivity by law. This is achieved by a broader discursive frame that increasingly requires those claiming the rights afforded to Indigenous peoples to perform a specific subject-position that entails an assumed element of environmental stewardship in order to be read as 'Indigenous'.

---

[128] Cf. Bosselmann, 'The right to self-determination and international environmental law', 1.
[129] Li, 'Masyarakat Adat, Difference, and the Limits of Recognition in Indonesia's Forest Zone', 657.
[130] Bosselmann, 'The right to self-determination and international environmental law', 1.
[131] L. Lohmann, *Green Orientalism* (The Corner House, 1993); Ramos, 'The hyperreal Indian', 153–71.
[132] Engle, 'Indigenous rights claims in international law', p. 343.
[133] Engle, *The Elusive Promise of Indigenous Development*, p. 168.
[134] Ibid., 170.
[135] Ibid., 173.

E. Identifying 'Stakeholders': The Constitution of Environmental Subjects   315

Birrell warns that any such 'requisite demonstration of the elements of a legally prescribed "traditional" indigeneity . . . requires the performance of an unachievable embodiment of indigeneity'.[136] In the same way that a 'required performance of "authenticity" on the part of the Indigenous person before the law'[137] is problematic, a 'required performance' of environmental stewardship risks constraining Indigenous aspirations of self-definition and self-determination. Thus it is important to critically interrogate how international legal frameworks pertaining to Indigenous rights produce the subjects they regulate and circumscribe the types of rights claims that are legible to the law. This is especially the case given how the implicit requirement that Indigenous peoples perform a specific subject-position in order to claim rights can operate to undercut the desires and aspirations of Indigenous peoples. The next section turns to examine how this dynamic also plays out in relation to 'local communities'.

2 'Local Communities'

The term 'local communities' has received much less examination in international law than 'Indigenous peoples', and no international legal instruments specifically address the rights of 'local communities'. The Convention on Biological Diversity (CBD) calls on states to recognise the critical role played by 'custodians of biodiversity', including 'indigenous and local communities'.[138] The term also appears in the Nagoya Protocol on Access and Benefit-Sharing.[139] Discussions in the CBD have subsequently clarified that the phrase 'local communities' actually refers to two separate groups: 'Indigenous peoples' and 'local communities'.[140] However, as Adriana Bessa shows, the definition of these terms, and their interrelationship, 'remains fraught with political tensions and conceptual lack of clarity' and there is still no 'clear and generally accepted legal definition' of the concept of 'local communities'.[141]

In 2006, the Secretariat of the Permanent Forum on Indigenous Issues for the Expert Workshop on the Disaggregation of Data prepared a background paper for

---

[136] Ibid.

[137] Birrell, 'An essential ghost', 81.

[138] *Convention on Biological Diversity*; for a discussion see A. Bessa, 'Traditional local communities: What lessons can be learnt at the international level from the experiences of Brazil and Scotland?' (2015) 24(3) *Review of European, Comparative & International Environmental Law* 330–40, 332.

[139] *Nagoya Protocol on Access to Genetic Resources and the Fair and Equitable Sharing of Benefits Arising from Their Utilization to the Convention on Biological Diversity*, opened for signature 2 February 2011, UN Doc UNEP/CBD/COP/DEC/X/1, annex I (entered into force 12 October 2014).

[140] See the decision XII/12 from COP12 (2014) where Parties to the Convention on Biological Diversity finally agreed to use the term 'Indigenous peoples and local communities' in future decisions; see also Bessa, 'Traditional local communities', 332.

[141] Bessa, 'Traditional local communities', 332 and 339.

the CBD on the question 'Who are local communities?'[142] The paper begins by affirming that there is 'no set definition of "local or traditional communities"'[143] and concludes that, in 'international law, it is clear that a "definition" is not a pre-requisite for protection and that groups such as minorities have been guaranteed rights under international law without establishing a definition'.[144] The paper describes how

> [m]any communities may be considered local and may also be described as traditional communities. Some local communities may include peoples of Indigenous descent. They are culturally diverse and occur on all inhabited continents. For example, small farming communities in France, who have occupied and farmed their lands for many generations acquiring useful environmental knowledge including specialist knowledge about a variety of activities including sustainable agriculture, cheese making and wine making or even animal husbandry, represent a local or traditional community. Long term established rice and fish farmers in Asia may represent another type of local community.[145]

Michelle Rouke similarly notes that the term 'local communities' does not 'have a predefined meaning and there is no common agreement as to [its] ordinary meaning'.[146] However, from her textual analysis of the relevant provisions of the CBD and Nagoya Protocol, she provides insights into how the term should be interpreted. She highlights the role played by the limiting modifier 'embodying traditional lifestyles' in Article 8(j) of the CBD, which, she suggests, 'seemingly excludes any peoples who are the descendants of and identify as [international local communities], but who can no longer be said to be "embodying traditional lifestyles"'.[147]

Drawing on broader developments in human rights and environmental law, Adriana Bessa suggests that the term 'traditional local communities' applies to rural groups including small-scale farmers, artisanal fishing communities, and island and mountain communities 'that do not fit the strict test of indigeneity but nevertheless have traditionally maintained a lifestyle and socio-economic practices as well as knowledge and value systems, which are intimately connected to land and nature'.[148] She surveys a number of legal texts – predominantly those addressing natural resources – that recognise the rights and interests of 'local communities' and the need to preserve their traditional knowledges. These legal instruments 'rely on

---

[142] Convention on Biological Diversity, *Who are local communities?* UNEP/CBD/WS-CB/LAC/1/INF/5 (16 November 2006).

[143] Ibid., 2.

[144] Ibid., 3–4.

[145] Ibid., 2.

[146] M. Rourke, 'Who are "Indigenous and local communities" and what is "traditional knowledge" for virus access and benefit-sharing? A textual analysis of the Convention on Biological Diversity and its Nagoya Protocol' (2018) 25(3) *Journal of Law and Medicine* 707–26 at 724.

[147] Ibid.

[148] Bessa, 'Traditional local communities', 332.

E. Identifying 'Stakeholders': The Constitution of Environmental Subjects 317

the interconnection between communities' culture and nature preservation',[149] and on 'the legal narrative in which the notion of "community" is embedded, namely, attachment to land and dependence on local natural resources for their livelihoods, and the linkage between traditional lifestyles and conservation and sustainable use of these natural resources'.[150]

Although 'local communities' have been distinguished from 'Indigenous peoples', the former arguably 'can only be understood as comprising elements of the definition of Indigenous peoples'.[151] This has in turn led to 'restrictive approaches for the qualification' and 'eligibility' to be recognised as a 'traditional community'.[152] In Brazil, for example, recognition requires evidence that the communities in question 'occupy and use lands and natural resources as a way of maintaining their cultural, social, religious, ancestral and economic systems'; hold 'knowledge, innovations and practices relevant for nature conservation'; and have a 'long and continuous attachment to the lands they occupy and the richness of the local environment in terms of natural wealth'.[153] These are the attributes and characteristics that the REDD+ literature also attributes to 'local communities'. A 2013 report on REDD+ safeguards by ClientEarth and UK Aid describes 'local communities' as 'a broad concept that often goes undefined and unrecognized, but could be given an equally flexible interpretation as "Indigenous peoples"'.[154] It also suggests that, in some cases, specifically in the African context, the broader term 'local community' may be considered more appropriate than 'Indigenous peoples'.[155] The report notes the definition of 'local communities' adopted in the Southern African Development Community Protocol on Forestry as '[a] coherent, social group of persons with interests or rights related to forest or forest resources, in a particular area, which the persons hold or exercise communally in terms of an agreement, custom or law'.[156] Therefore, in practice, the term 'local communities' has been imbued with understandings of environmental stewardship and connection. Thus, claiming the rights afforded to 'local communities' – similar to claims based on indigeneity – requires the performance of specific ecological attributes as well as demonstration of skills in, aptitude for and desire to sustain, protect and conserve the environment. Yet the situation of those considered 'local communities' remains particularly precarious, and protection of such rights remains weak, because there is no international legal instrument specifically addressing the rights of 'local communities', Although

[149] Ibid.
[150] Ibid., 337.
[151] Ibid.
[152] Ibid., 338.
[153] Ibid., 338.
[154] D. Ray et al., *A Guide to Understanding and Implementing the UNFCCC REDD+ Safeguards* (Client Earth, 2013) p. 40.
[155] Ibid., p. 41.
[156] Ibid.; see also Southern African Development Community, *Protocol on Forestry*, 3 October 2002 (entered into force 17 July 2009) Article 2.1.

318 REDD+ at the 'Local' Level: Between Rights and Responsibilisation

various legal instruments assert state obligations towards 'local communities', there are no corresponding mechanisms for 'local communities' to lodge complaints at the national or international level if their rights are breached.[157] Therefore, in practice, the 'legal status of local communities and [their] enjoyment of collective rights may vary according to national circumstances'.[158]

3 Identifying the 'Subjects' of Safeguards in REDD+

The flexible approach that adopted to defining both 'Indigenous peoples' and 'local communities' within international law means that the processes of identifying specific subjects as 'Indigenous' or 'local', and thereby determining who can claim the rights afforded to these groups, are particularly power-laden. As a matter of international law, different protections are available to 'Indigenous peoples' than are available to 'local communities' or 'forest-dependent communities'. And, states have different obligations to the former than they have to the latter. Therefore, discussions concerning safeguards are careful to distinguish between distinctive rights of Indigenous peoples (and the resulting positive and negative obligations on states) and the more general universal human rights standards that apply to all, including 'local communities'.[159] However, any application of safeguard standards is necessarily preceded by an assessment to determine whether and what safeguards are applicable in a specific situation. As such, the application of safeguard policies often requires a case-by-case determination by legal experts and technocrats of whether a project will impact on either Indigenous peoples or 'local communities'. Moreover, as part of such a determination, Indigenous peoples and local communities are often required to perform a specific subject-position in order to be legible to the external experts or technocrats as subjects that should be protected by the applicable safeguard. The discussion below reviews different safeguard policies applicable in the REDD+ context to consider how they approach this task of identification. It shows that these documents, and the flexible approach to definition of 'Indigenous peoples' and 'local communities' at international law that they refer to, grants external experts considerable power to determine whether people within a project area are recognised as Indigenous or otherwise deserving of protection. In particular, the analysis suggests that the way these safeguard documents position Indigenous peoples and local communities as having innate capacities as environmental stewards and as therefore critical to the success of REDD+ risks creating a dangerous double-bind, whereby it becomes increasingly difficult for people living in and around forest areas to be identified as 'Indigenous' (or even 'local' or 'traditional') while simultaneously

---

[157] Bessa, 'Traditional local communities', 334.
[158] Ray et al., *A Guide to Understanding and Implementing the UNFCCC REDD+ Safeguards*, p. 41.
[159] Ibid., p. 44.

E. Identifying 'Stakeholders': The Constitution of Environmental Subjects 319

expressing opposition to or reluctance to participate in REDD+ projects that are presented as addressing a global environmental 'common concern'.

The Forest Carbon Partnership Facility (FCPF)and UN-REDD harmonised *Guidelines on Stakeholder Engagement in REDD+ Readiness with a Focus on the Participation of Indigenous Peoples and Other Forest-Dependent Communities* stresses that any consultation process for REDD+ should 'include a broad range of relevant stakeholders at the national and local levels', that the 'diversity of stakeholders needs to be recognized' and that 'the voices of forest-dependent and vulnerable groups must be heard, whether they are indigenous or not'.[160] However, the *Guidelines on Stakeholder Engagement* focus on a 'particular category of stakeholders who are often legal and/or customary rights holders', namely 'indigenous peoples and other forest-dependent communities'.[161] These peoples are described by the Guidelines as 'contribut[ing] to forest protection and depend[ing] on forests for their social and economic livelihoods as well as for cultural and spiritual well-being' and as 'often more vulnerable than other stakeholders' in the context of REDD+ activities.[162] The *Guidelines on Stakeholder Engagement* posit that 'a clear commitment will have to be made to ensure their rights are fully protected throughout the REDD+ program cycle'; however they do not provide advice on how to identify if 'Indigenous peoples' or 'local communities' are present in an area.[163] While the term 'forest-dependent communities' could arguably cover anyone living in and around a forest areas, the assertion in the *Guidelines on Stakeholder Engagement* that 'indigenous peoples and other forest-dependent communities have a special role to play in REDD+ given their traditional knowledge of and relationship to the forest and their presence on the ground' implicitly imposes specific criteria about the types of ecological knowledge and engagements such 'forest-dependent communities' should display.[164]

In terms of the specific safeguards applied, the FCPF is required to comply with World Bank Operational Policies and the UN-REDD Programme is required to 'follow a human rights-based approach and adhere to the UNDRIP, UN Development Group Guidelines on Indigenous Peoples' Issues, and International Labour Organization (ILO) Convention No. 169' and adhere to FPIC.[165] The question of who would be covered by the World Bank's Environmental and Social Standard on Indigenous Peoples/Sub-Saharan African Historically Underserved Traditional Local Communities (ESS7) was 'one of the most controversial aspects'

---

[160] UN-REDD Programme and FCPF, *Guidelines on Stakeholder Engagement in REDD+ Readiness with a Focus on the Participation of Indigenous Peoples and Other Forest-Dependent Communities*, 2.
[161] Ibid., 1.
[162] Ibid., 1–2.
[163] Ibid., 2.
[164] Ibid.
[165] Ibid.

shaping its development.[166] ESS7 applies to both 'Indigenous peoples' – although it recognises that the appropriate terminology may vary depending on the national context[167] – and 'Sub-Saharan African Historically Underserved Traditional Local Communities' (SAHUTLCs). It adopts a 'flexible' approach that is broad enough to encompass 'distinct social and cultural groups' that might not be recognised as Indigenous by national governments, provided they meet, 'in varying degrees', a number of identification criteria including self-identification and recognition by others; collective attachment to habitats, ancestral territories and natural resources; distinct customary cultural, economic, social or political institutions; and a distinct language or dialect.[168] This is similar to previous World Bank policies regarding 'Indigenous peoples' – Operational Directive 4.20 (1991) and Operational Policy 4.10 (2005) – which also did not provide a definition of 'Indigenous peoples' but listed characteristics for the purpose of identification.[169] However, while self-identification is seen as 'fundamental' in ILO 169,[170] ESS7 makes status 'conditioned on others' recognition of this identity'.[171] Earlier World Bank operational policies stated that a determination of whether Indigenous peoples are present in or have a collective attachment to a project area or are otherwise impacted by a project a project requires a 'technical judgment' by the World Bank's officials 'on the ground' with the assistance of other 'experts', namely 'qualified social scientists'.[172] ESS7 instead adopts the passive voice and simply states that it 'applies whenever Indigenous Peoples ... are present in, or have collective attachment to a proposed project area, as determined during the environmental and social assessment', without identifying how or by whom such an assessment is to be made.[173] Given the 'ambiguity' of the relevant criteria, the World Bank has 'significant leeway' in how such determinations are made.[174] Thus, although ESS7 covers a wider scope of potentially affected peoples and includes broader provisions on consent than earlier policies, it remains the case that the identification of whether Indigenous peoples or

---

[166] M. V. C. Ormaza and F. C. Ebert, 'The World Bank, human rights, and organizational legitimacy strategies: The case of the 2016 Environmental and Social Framework' (2019) 32(3) *Leiden Journal of International Law* 483–500 at 487.

[167] The World Bank, *ESS7: Indigenous Peoples/Sub-Sahara African Historically Underserved Traditional Local Communities*, para 6 ('ESS7').

[168] Ibid., para 8.

[169] World Bank, *Operational Directive 4.20: Indigenous Peoples*, (September 1991); World Bank, *Operational Policy 4.10: Indigenous Peoples* (July 2005).

[170] ILO Convention No 169, Article 1.2.

[171] Ormaza and Ebert, 'The World Bank, human rights, and organizational legitimacy strategies', 489.

[172] World Bank, *Operational Policy 4.10: Indigenous Peoples* (July 2005), para 8.

[173] ESS7, para 7.

[174] Ormaza and Ebert, 'The World Bank, human rights, and organizational legitimacy strategies', 499.

E. Identifying 'Stakeholders': The Constitution of Environmental Subjects   321

SAHUTLCs are present in a project area, or affected by a project, resides exclusively with the Bank.[175]

The UN-REDD *Programme Guidelines on Free, Prior and Informed Consent* are careful to identify that international norms relating to FPIC apply to 'Indigenous peoples' and that, therefore, 'States are required to recognize and carry out their duties and obligations to give effect to the requirement of FPIC as applicable to Indigenous peoples'.[176] The *Guidelines on FPIC* also include a discussion on 'identifying Indigenous peoples'.[177] After listing various indicia, they describe such identification as a 'constructive and pragmatic process', which must be based on the 'fundamental criterion of self-identification and full participation of the peoples concerned'.[178] While they stress a participatory approach to identification, the *Guidelines on FPIC* focus on 'external' criteria such as recognition in national legislation and policy, as well as note an 'intimate' relationship, or 'profound spiritual relationship' with lands, territories and resources.[179] They also implicitly ascribe particular ecological characteristics to Indigenous peoples, describing Indigenous peoples and 'forest-dependent communities' as 'essential to the success of REDD+', particularly because they have 'for centuries played a historical and cultural role in the sustainable management of these forests'.[180]

However, the UN-REDD Programme *Guidelines on FPIC* also affirms the rights of forest-dependent communities to participation and therefore provides that, 'at a minimum, States are required to consult forest-dependent communities in good faith regarding matters that affect them *with a view to agreement*', although noting that 'a blanket application of FPIC is not required for all forest-dependent communities'.[181] Nonetheless, the UN-REDD Programme *Guidelines on FPIC* recommend that

> States should evaluate the circumstances and nature of the forest-dependent com-
> munity in question, on a case by case basis, through among others a rights-based
> analysis, and secure FPIC from communities that share common characteristics
> with Indigenous peoples and whose underlying substantive rights are significantly
> implicated.[182]

The UN-REDD Programme *Guidelines on FPIC* thus acknowledge that the context is one where there is a 'growing call to secure consent from forest-dependent communities' as well as from 'Indigenous peoples'.[183] Several other guides to

---

[175] Ibid., 498.
[176] UN-REDD Programme, *UN-REDD Programme Guidelines on Free, Prior and Informed Consent* (January 2013) 11 ('*Guidelines on FPIC*').
[177] Ibid., Annex I.
[178] Ibid., 38–9.
[179] Ibid., 40.
[180] Ibid., 8.
[181] Ibid., 11 (emphasis added).
[182] Ibid., 12.
[183] Ibid., 13.

322 *REDD+ at the 'Local' Level: Between Rights and Responsibilisation*

safeguards or FPIC in REDD+ similarly blur this distinction between 'Indigenous peoples' and 'local communities' and suggest that one should aspire towards comprehensive rights recognition for all forest dwellers. The report *Free, Prior and Informed Consent in REDD+: Principles and Approaches for Policy and Project Development* guidelines prepared for The Centre for People and Forests (RECOFTC) and the German Development Agency (GIZ) states that '[a] proposed REDD+ project should map all tenure claims and a process to respect the right to FPIC should be developed to engage all communities whose lands and forests overlap with the proposed REDD+ project'.[184] Yet it remains the case that the distinction between the rights of 'Indigenous peoples' and those of 'local communities' is more pronounced in relation to whether there is a right to FPIC. Overall, in all these guidelines and reports, the questions of identification remain saturated by relations of power, as well as assumption that 'Indigenous peoples' and 'local communities' necessarily have inherent ecological characteristics, knowledges and behaviours.

F STRATEGIES TO MANAGE THE 'SOCIAL': BETWEEN RIGHTS AND RESPONSIBILISATION

The final section of this chapter discusses three key strategies adopted to manage the social impacts of REDD+ – benefit sharing, tenure reform and FPIC – and considers how each of these are caught between claims for rights 'from below' and imperatives of responsibilisation 'from above'. The analysis shows how these processes of benefit sharing, tenure reform and consultation towards consent operate as sites of struggle, given that these mechanisms can be deployed both to support claims for greater rights and authority for people who live in and around forested areas and to consolidate the formalisation of neoliberal contractual and market obligations and responsibilities. The discussion interrogates how some of the more radical potential of these safeguard mechanisms has been neutralised, and how these mechanisms therefore may not operate as hoped or envisioned by forest peoples and their advocates, but are instead potentially contributing to the disciplining of specific environmental subjects, including their 'fixing in place', and the consolidation of global authority in the 'green economy'.

1 *Benefit Sharing*

The sharing of 'benefits' arising from REDD+ schemes has been promoted as a key means by which the social risks of REDD+ can be mitigated and its social benefits promoted. The Cancun Agreements highlighted the need for REDD+ to contribute to sustainable development through co-benefits,[185] and the Warsaw Framework for

---

[184] Anderson, *Free, Prior, and Informed Consent in REDD+*, p. 32.
[185] Decision 1/CP.16, part D, preamble recital 2.

F. Strategies to Manage the 'Social': Between Rights and Responsibilisation   323

REDD+ and the Paris Agreement recognised the 'importance of incentivising non-carbon benefits'.[186] Yet such efforts, like every other aspect of REDD+, present a 'challenging hurdle' – perhaps, as some commentators suggest, 'one of the most challenging hurdles'.[187] These challenges arise partly out of the need to resolve the different types of benefits that might potentially accrue to different actors from REDD+.[188]

The references to benefit sharing in the REDD+ regime, much like the 'proliferation of references to benefit sharing' more generally, have been 'accompanied by a remarkable lack of conceptual clarity'.[189] There remains a lack of 'definition, detail and specificity' about both how such benefits are defined and how they will flow to forest-dwelling communities.[190] At present, the current REDD+ framework lacks a clear definition of such benefits or a 'viable means of situating them within national regulatory frameworks in order to facilitate effective implementation'.[191] Benefits can be defined broadly to include governance benefits (including land tenure reforms), ecosystem services provision (such as watershed conservation and biodiversity protection), adaptation and increased resilience, economic and livelihood benefits, as well as social and cultural benefits.[192] Further, the legal recognition of community-based natural resource management and the incorporation of traditional knowledge into environmental impact assessment or natural resource management can be seen as non-monetary benefits that grant beneficiaries formal recognition as project partners.[193] However, as Kathleen Birrell and Lee Godden have warned, 'the subtle re-articulation of community rights to the forest as "benefits" to be "shared" risks the commodification of a previously moral imperative'.[194] These authors are concerned about how the language of 'benefit-sharing' 'increasingly appears to substitute for', and may 'ultimately frustrate', broader human rights

---

[186] Decision 9/CP.19, 'Work programme on result-based finance to progress the full implementation of the activities referred to in decision 1/CP.16, paragraph 70', FCCC/CP/2013/10/Add.1 (31 January 2014), para 22; *Paris Agreement*, opened for signature on 22 April 2016, UNTS XXVII.7.d (entered into force 4 November 2016), Article 5.2.

[187] J. Costenbader, *REDD+ benefit sharing: A comparative assessment of three national policy approaches* (Forest Carbon Partnership Facility and UN-REDD Programme, 2011).

[188] See C. Luttrell, L. Loft, M. F. Gebara, and D. Kweka, 'Who should benefit and why? Discourses on REDD' in A. Angelsen, M. Brockhaus, W. D. Sunderlin, and L. V. Verchot (eds.), Analysing REDD+: Challenges and choices (Center for International Forestry Research, 2012), pp. 129–52, 129.

[189] E. Morgera, 'The need for an international legal concept of fair and equitable benefit sharing' (2016) 27(2) *European Journal of International Law* 353–83 at 354.

[190] Godden, 'Benefit-sharing in REDD+: Linking rights and equitable outcomes', pp. 174–5.

[191] Ibid., p. 176.

[192] R. Banfo, 'Non-carbon benefits in REDD+ implementation: Insights from Africa' (presentation, 3rd Voluntary Meeting of National REDD+ Focal Points, 23 May 2016), redd.unfccc.int/files/2_ghana_ncbs_ppt._revised_.pdf.

[193] Morgera, 'The need for an international legal concept of fair and equitable benefit sharing', 370.

[194] K. Birrell and L. Godden, 'Benefits and sharing: Realizing rights in REDD+' (2018) 9(1) *Journal of Human Rights and the Environment* 6–31 at 9.

324   REDD+ *at the 'Local' Level: Between Rights and Responsibilisation*

aspirations.[195] Presenting measures to protect the rights of forest dwellers not as a moral imperative but rather as a 'co-benefit' arising from REDD+ projects risks making the local realisation of rights subject to, or conditional upon, broader global, national or corporate agendas.[196] Therefore, the discussion below will not focus on reforms that might come under a broad definition of 'co-benefits' such as the protection of rights, but specifically examines agendas to achieve specific social objectives such as alleviating poverty and improving local livelihoods.

There are two distinct ways in which REDD+ projects can potentially benefit local livelihoods: first, through the equitable distribution of monetary gains from international and national financial support for REDD+-readiness and result-based payments from REDD+; and, second, via the benefits arising from changes in forest management practices that lead to increased stocks of – and thus possibilities of deriving incomes or livelihoods from – non-timber forest products and non-carbon ecosystem services.[197] The focus in the literature on achieving co-benefits through REDD+ implementation has been on policies aimed at ensuring 'a fair distribution of incentives for forest protection and carbon payments',[198] including through 'agreements between different stakeholders about the distribution of monetary benefits from the sale of carbon credits'.[199] This entails complex considerations of how benefits should be allocated, how beneficiaries should be determined and how benefit distribution is managed,[200] including questions about the equitable sharing of monetary benefits vertically between international, national, regional and local actors as well as horizontally, in the distribution at the local level between and within communities.[201] Scholarship has suggested that, in order to be effective, benefit-sharing mechanisms should incorporate shareholder engagement, incentive design, delivery mechanisms, transparency provisions and dispute settlement.[202] Thus, the implementation of benefit-sharing arrangements engages complex questions about the institutional design of mechanisms to support transparent, accountable and effective distribution of funds.[203]

The implementation of mechanisms for the distribution of co-benefits raises not only technical questions, but also complex questions of equity and what constitutes a 'fair' distribution. As Elisa Morgera has highlighted, the promotion of equity has

---

[195] Ibid.

[196] Ibid.

[197] Luttrell et al., 'Who should benefit and why?', 130–1.

[198] C. Streck, 'In the market: Forest carbon rights: Shedding light on a muddy concept' (2015) 4 *Carbon & Climate Law Review* 342–47 at 343.

[199] H. Lindhjem, I. A. K. Bråten, A. Gleinsvik, and I. Aronsen, *Experiences with benefit sharing: Issues and options for REDD-plus* (Pöyry Management Consulting (Norway), 2010), p. 2.

[200] S. Chapman, M. Wilder, and I. Millar, 'Defining the legal elements of benefit sharing in the context of REDD' (2014) 4 *Carbon & Climate Law Review* 270–81 at 270.

[201] Lindhjem et al., 'Experiences with benefit sharing', 3.

[202] Ibid., 8.

[203] Ibid., 7.

F. Strategies to Manage the 'Social': Between Rights and Responsibilisation 325

been a key rationale for the emergence of benefit sharing as a concept in international law.[204] Nonetheless, even as references to 'fair and equitable' benefit sharing within international law have increased over time, Morgera notes that 'empirical evidence indicates that in practice benefit sharing rarely achieves its stated objectives and may actually end up working against its purpose'.[205] She therefore emphasises the need to be attentive to the 'critical weight that power asymmetries have in all the relations to which benefit sharing applies'.[206] Despite the clear challenges in operationalising benefit sharing, Morgera suggests that the concept of 'benefit sharing' is important in providing a 'frame' that 'holds the promise to facilitate agreement upon specific forms of cooperation since different parties are being motivated by their perceptions of the benefits that would derive from it'.[207] Moreover, this is a 'frame' that is, as Birrell and Godden have highlighted, 'constituted by both global and local community imperatives'.[208] Understanding benefit sharing as a 'frame' highlights how the promise of benefits is able hold together the different imperatives and objectives of a number of diverse actors and thus facilitate alignment between the demand for rights 'from below' and the imperatives of responsibilisation 'from above'. Quite different rationales are provided for benefit sharing, including to 'create effective incentives by rewarding individuals, communities, organizations and businesses for actions that change land-uses and thereby reduce emissions' as well as to build 'legitimacy and support for the REDD+ mechanism' by ensuring that those affected by REDD+ are treated 'fairly and equitably'.[209] The frame of benefit sharing does important work in forging connections between heterogeneous elements and thereby 'reposing political questions as matters of technique'.[210] Rendering questions pertaining to benefit sharing as technical also deflects attention from the fact that the operationalisation of benefit sharing in many cases requires further interventions in livelihoods, land tenure and governance arrangements. Therefore, benefit sharing should not be understood simply as a tool to mitigate the potentially harmful impacts of REDD+ projects, but as a means by which REDD+ coalesces with and is incorporated into a broader project of establishing mechanisms for PES, which fundamentally transforms both livelihoods and human–nature relations. In this way, as Lee Godden has identified, '"benefits" have come to function as a new nexus of green governance'.[211]

---

[204] Morgera, 'The need for an international legal concept of fair and equitable benefit sharing', 380.

[205] Ibid., 356.

[206] Ibid., 356.

[207] Ibid., 356.

[208] Birrell and Godden, 'Benefits and sharing', 20.

[209] Lindhjem et al., 'Experiences with benefit sharing', 2.

[210] Li, 'Practices of assemblage and community forest management' (2007) 36(2) *Economy and Society* 263–93 at 264–5.

[211] Godden, 'Benefit-sharing in REDD', p. 191.

326   REDD+ at the 'Local' Level: Between Rights and Responsibilisation

The language and frame of benefit sharing aligns with institutional agendas to realise 'environmental assets' and increase 'environmental income' in order to promote poverty reduction. This programme of action, which complements the valuation of ecosystem services in the 'green economy', has been outlined in a series of reports prepared by the World Resources Initiative (WRI) in collaboration with UNEP, UNDP and the World Bank focused on the institutional and governance structures that can turn 'natural assets into wealth'. One of these reports, *The Wealth of the Poor: Managing Ecosystems to Fight Poverty* (2005), sought to draw attention to the 'full potential of ecosystems as a wealth-creating asset for the poor' by highlighting how 'environmental income', or income derived from ecosystems, 'can act as a fundamental stepping stone in the economic empowerment of the rural poor'.[212] It warns, however, that the rural poor are currently unable to 'reap the benefits of their good stewardship' of nature due to 'governance failures', including a 'lack of legal ownership and access to ecosystems, political marginalization, and exclusion from the decisions that affect how these ecosystems are managed'.[213] The report promotes instead a vision in which 'natural endowments' can operate as 'capital' for the poor:

> Ecosystem goods and services – the natural products and processes that ecosystems generate – are often the only significant assets the poor have access to. These natural endowments, if managed efficiently, can provide a capital base – a foundation for greater economic viability, and a stepping stone beyond mere subsistence. Yet the potential of these assets is often overlooked.[214]

Another report in this series, *Roots of Resilience: Growing the Wealth of the Poor* (2008), describes nature as an 'essential yet elusive asset for the world's poor' and proposes how such resources can be better realised, leveraged and scaled-up.[215] The report suggests that the 'increase in "environmental income" that results from ecosystem-based enterprises can stabilize the household economies of the poor, translating into better nutrition and health, greater access to education, more opportunities for saving and investment, and reduced vulnerability to financial shocks'.[216] Such an increase in 'environmental income' can be, the report argues, achieved through 'good resource stewardship, devolution of resource authority, and competent business models'.[217]

---

[212] *World Resources 2005: The Wealth of the Poor: Managing Ecosystems to Fight Poverty* (United Nations Development Programme, United Nations Environment Programme, The World Bank and World Resources Institute, 2005) p. 3.

[213] Ibid.

[214] Ibid., p. 16.

[215] *World Resources 2008: Roots of Resilience – Growing the Wealth of the Poor* (World Resources Institute (WRI) in collaboration with UNDP, UNEP and the World Bank, 2008) p. 3.

[216] Ibid.

[217] Ibid., p. 4.

F. Strategies to Manage the 'Social': Between Rights and Responsibilisation 327

What is striking in these WRI reports is how much they replicate the narrative structure of Hernando De Soto's famous 'bell-jar' metaphor:[218] the rural poor are presented as *already* extremely wealthy but suffering due to languishing assets that simply need to be transformed from 'nature' into 'natural capital' in order to be realised, and to release new income streams from nature. This narrative relies on invoking a view of nature as '[a source] of new economic values that are poised for potential capitalization and marketization'.[219] It suggests that the economic value of nature simply needs to be 'found', whereas critical geographers have shown that considerable work is involved in *fabricating* 'nature' as 'natural capital', including through the 'counting and calculative practices [that] conjure the metaphor of "natural capital" into manifest existence in the world'.[220] Further, the WRI narrative assumes that the rural poor have already adopted the rationality of *homo economicus* and are necessarily seeking to capitalise on natural assets.[221] In contrast, as Kathleen McAfee writes, in practice '[f]armers and forest dwellers often do not behave like the economically rational, benefit-maximizing individual at the core of neoclassical economic theory' and 'rarely base their decisions solely on expected pecuniary gains'.[222] This is not to assume that the rural poor necessarily 'reject new products and labor regimes in favor of locally oriented production on small family farms',[223] or cannot adapt to take advantage of new market opportunities, but simply to highlight that how the WRI narrative asserts a market-orientated subjectivity as pre-existing, when in fact these projects are actually actively engaged in 'constructing *homo economicus*' and 'creat[ing] the particular form of subjectivity necessary for the market economy to function'.[224] In this way, strategies to promote benefit sharing in REDD+ are linked to a much broader project of transforming rural actors into entrepreneurial subjects in the 'green economy' who are strategically leveraging 'natural capital' in order to realise 'environmental income'.

---

[218] H. de Soto, *The Mystery of Capital: Why Capitalism Triumphs in the West and Fails Everywhere Else* (Black Swan, 2000); for a critical analysis see S. Pahuja, *Decolonising International Law: Development, Economic Growth and the Politics of Universality* (Cambridge University Press, 2011) p. 218.

[219] S. Sullivan, 'Bonding nature(s)? Funds, financiers and values at the impact investing edge in environmental conservation' in S. Bracking, A. Fredriksen, S. Sullivan, and P. Woodhouse (eds.), *Valuing Development, Environment and Conservation* (Routledge, 2018) pp. 113–33, 102 (emphasis in original).

[220] S. Sullivan, 'On "natural capital", "fairy tales" and ideology' (2017) 48(2) *Development and Change* 397–423 at 398.

[221] See D. Williams, 'Constructing the economic space: The World Bank and the making of *homo oeconomicus*' (1999) 28(1) *Millennium: Journal of International Studies* 79–99; J. Read, 'A genealogy of homo-economicus: Neoliberalism and the production of subjectivity' (2009) 6 *Foucault Studies* 25–36.

[222] K. McAfee, 'Nature in the market-world: Ecosystem services and inequality' (2012) 55(1) *Development* 25–33 at 28–29.

[223] T. M. Li, 'Centering labor in the land grab debate' (2011) 38(2) *The Journal of Peasant Studies* 281–98 at 295.

[224] Williams, 'Constructing the economic space'.

328 REDD+ at the 'Local' Level: Between Rights and Responsibilisation

Scholarship on PES has shown that their benefits tend to flow to more powerful actors and larger landowners, and often risk excluding small landowners and the rural poor, even in contexts where policy interventions have specifically targeted more marginalised landowners.[225] As such there have been acute concerns that 'creating a market-based system of conservation will favour the wealthy and well connected, and ultimately exacerbate land and wealth inequality'.[226] The assumptions often arising in the PES literature that communities are 'single homogenous entities' and that contracts are a 'voluntary' reflection of 'community choice' have been problematised by empirical scholarship, which has showed that such assumptions actually work to 'disguise and depoliticize inter-community dynamics' and by doing so allow 'conservationists to avoid project complexities on the ground by outsourcing decisions about *how* conservation is achieved, and *who* benefits in the process'.[227] Although the rhetoric surrounding these projects focuses on ensuring the 3Es – equity, efficiency and effectiveness – in practice, 'case studies of PES projects reveal a pattern of problems that occur repeatedly across different settings'.[228] Kathleen McAfee argues that '[m]arket-based criteria for PES efficiency commonly conflict with social goals such as poverty alleviation'.[229] She claims these tensions are 'inherent *a priori* in the market paradigm' and have real practical manifestations, with the result that '[t]hose who design, implement, and participate directly in PES schemes are often forced to give up either equity or efficiency objectives in favour of the other'.[230] McAfee highlights an 'inverse relationship between scale and transactions costs': it being more costly to engage a large number of smallholders than a small number of large landholders, and, similarly, that it is 'often more expensive to involve less literate people, women, those who lack formal property titles, or Indigenous and other groups who hold land in common'.[231] While the language of opportunity costs provides an idiom for understanding what choices prevail in PES schemes, it is a framework that is seductive particularly for how it obscures power relations: 'Opportunity-cost criteria disguise the power relations that determine whose opportunities are more or less costly and *whose* land-use choices shall prevail and avoid consideration of *how* some people's opportunity costs became higher and *why* others' remain low'.[232] She thus argues:

> This [situation] points to a contradiction at the heart of the market paradigm linking conservation and development. The more strictly the fate of ecosystem-service-

---

[225] D. M. Lansing, 'Unequal access to payments for ecosystem services: The case of Costa Rica' (2014) 45(6) *Development and Change* 1310–31.

[226] Ibid., 1311.

[227] S. Milne and B. Adams, 'Market masquerades: Uncovering the politics of community-level payments for environmental services in Cambodia' (2012) 43(1) *Development and Change* 133–58 at 154 (emphasis in original).

[228] McAfee, 'Nature in the market-world', 27.

[229] Ibid., 28.

[230] Ibid., 28 (emphasis in original).

[231] Ibid., 30.

[232] Ibid. (emphasis in original).

F. Strategies to Manage the 'Social': Between Rights and Responsibilisation 329

producing land is determined by the logic of market efficiency, the more likely it becomes that environmental-services trading will reinforce existing inequalities in localities targeted for PES-based conservation or REDD/REDD+. Conversely, ecosystem-services projects designed primarily to support the poor will rarely meet market-efficiency standards.[233]

As such, there is a real risk that processes of benefit sharing will not promote an equitable distribution of income from REDD+, but rather may help to consolidate a paradigm where the marketisation of conservation is seen as a development strategy, so that the logic of market efficiency further shapes human–nature relationships and subjectivities and has the effect of reinforcing existing inequalities. In this way, benefit-sharing processes allow for some rights claims to be realised, but simultaneously operate to discipline and responsibilise rural communities as market actors in the 'green economy'. Moreover, these concerns about how benefit-sharing schemes might exacerbate existing inequalities are particularly acute given how questions of benefit sharing and tenure recognition overlap. The implementation of benefit sharing, as Kirsty Gover highlights, is 'premised upon a system which can identify designated individuals or communities that may hold the rights that ground the flow of benefits'.[234] In this sense, benefit sharing assumes 'recognition of the complex web of resource and use rights, and attendant governance within a community' and is therefore intertwined with tenure recognition.[235] Susan Chomba et al. found that the implementation of the REDD+ project they examined reinforced past injustices given that 'the historical context predetermined very unequal land ownership, and because of preferential allocation of benefit flows to landowners and project implementers at the expense of the wider community'.[236] These problems of unequal benefit flows could be aggravated by the tendency of REDD+ implementation to further consolidate control over land and resource access.[237] The next section therefore turns to examine in more detail the processes of tenure reform as a strategy to mitigate the social impacts of REDD+ and promote social benefits.

2 Tenure Reform

It is widely recognised that tenure reform is a necessary precondition for 'supposed benefits of REDD+ ... to accrue to Indigenous and other forest peoples'.[238] This section provides an overview of debates on tenure reform in REDD+, critically

---

[233] Ibid.

[234] Gover, 'REDD+, tenure and Indigenous property claims', p. 177.

[235] Ibid.

[236] S. Chomba, J. Kariuki, J. F. Lund, and F. Sinclair, 'Roots of inequity: How the implementation of REDD+ reinforces past injustices' (2016) 50 *Land Use Policy* 202–13 at 211.

[237] Ibid., 212.

[238] R. Fisher and R. Lyster, 'Land and resource tenure: The rights of Indigenous people and forest dwellers' in R. Lyster, C. MacKenzie, and C. McDermott (eds.), *Law, Tropical Forests and Carbon: The Case of REDD+* (Cambridge University Press, 2013) pp. 187–206, 193.

330 REDD+ at the 'Local' Level: Between Rights and Responsibilisation

evaluating how discourses on tenure reform mediate concurrent demands of rights 'from below' and responsibilisation 'from above'. It focuses particularly on how tenure reform is discussed and what purposes it is understood to serve, before turning to consider the specificities of forest tenure reform. The discussion uncovers the ambiguity in the term 'tenure reform': traditionally it referred to a redistributive practice of granting land to landless workers,[239] but in recent decades it has come to refer to neoliberal models of 'negotiated' or 'market-assisted' land reform directed towards clarifying obligations and transforming land into a marketised commodity.[240]

Tenure reform is not specifically included as part of the UNFCCC safeguards, although the Cancun Agreements request that developing country Parties address land tenure issues when developing and implementing national strategies and action plans.[241] Even though an influential 2009 report, *Tenure in REDD: Start-Point or Afterthought?*, by the International Institute for Environment and Development (IIED), highlighted the need to pay attention to tenure questions in REDD+ implementation,[242] and REDD+-readiness plans frequently identify clear and secure tenure as a prerequisite for REDD+ implementation, only a minority of such readiness plans include specific steps to clarify or reform tenure rights.[243] Tenure reforms are 'not yet a substantive part of REDD+ planning', an omission that, as Kirsty Gover identifies, raises 'serious questions about how tenure reform will impact on the interests of indigenous and local communities'.[244] Reviews have warmed that REDD+ may 'exacerbate land-related tensions in tropical forests' because 'REDD+ is often implemented in contexts where land tenure is neither clearly defined nor enforced' and that 'even if REDD+ discourse places great emphasis on tenure clarity and security, little has been done in this regard'.[245] Research by the RRI has found that although most countries with REDD+ strategies and all leading international REDD+ initiatives have committed to recognising tenure rights, there has actually been a significant decrease in the recognition of

---

[239] M. R. El-Ghonemy, 'Land reform development challenges of 1963–2003 continue into twenty-first century' FAO, www.fao.org/docrep/006/j0415t/j0415t05.htm.

[240] D. Barry, A. M. Larson, and C. J. P. Colfer, 'Forest tenure reform: An orphan with only uncles' in A. M. Larson, D. Barry, G. R. Dahal, and C. J. P. Colfer (eds.), *Forests for People: Community Rights and Forest Tenure Reform* (Earthscan, 2010) pp. 19–40, 23.

[241] Decision 1/CP.16, para 72.

[242] L. Cotula and J. Mayers, *Tenure in REDD – Start-Point or Afterthought?* (International Institute for Environment and Development, 2009).

[243] L. G. Williams, *Putting the Pieces Together for Good Governance of REDD+: An Analysis of 32 REDD+ Country Readiness Proposals* (World Resources Institute, 2013) p. 14.

[244] Gover, 'REDD+, tenure and Indigenous property claims', p. 134.

[245] J. P. S. Barletti and A. M. Larson, *Rights Abuse Allegations in the Context of REDD+ Readiness and Implementation: A Preliminary Review and Proposal for Moving Forward* (Center for International Forestry Research, 2017) p. 5.

F. Strategies to Manage the 'Social': Between Rights and Responsibilisation   331

rights on the ground between 2002–08 and 2008–13.[246] In 2013, experts advised that tenure issues in REDD+ are 'becoming increasingly urgent' and that greater clarity over tenure and recognition of customary rights was needed.[247] Subsequent evaluations found that addressing tenure and implementing benefit sharing remained 'unresolved challenges for REDD+ implementation'.[248] Exacerbating the problem, the UN-REDD Programme did not publish advice on tenure until 2012,[249] although a key aspect of its 2016–20 strategic framework is to produce more knowledge outputs on tenure in REDD+.[250] The UN-REDD Programme sees tenure reform as entailing 'important enabling conditions for REDD+' but does not impose specific reform expectations on host countries; rather, it supports 'a country-driven approach to tenure' that allows each country to 'determine the appropriate approach to deal with tenure issues based on its unique situation'.[251] The UN-REDD Programme provides technical advice and training on tenure questions and support activities to enable tenure clarification, and emphasises the importance of customary rights, gender mainstreaming and an 'integrated approach' that recognises the interconnectedness of forest tenure with broader land tenure and resource tenure issues.[252]

There are reasons for concern about the kind of tenure reform REDD+ will promote and how such reforms will take place. There are real risks that 'REDD+ policy could encourage the consolidation of tenure arrangements that do not sufficiently account for the interests of Indigenous and tribal peoples',[253] especially given that the focus on 'secure and clear' tenure 'suggests a bias in favour of current possessors and users of land'.[254] The discussions on tenure reform in REDD+ are underpinned by the duel – and competing – imperatives of securing rights of people living in and around forest areas 'from below' and imperatives of responsibilisation and ensuring investor confidence 'from above'. It is now common for the 'creation

---

[246] *Status of Forest Carbon Rights and Implications for Communities, the Carbon Trade and REDD+ Investments* (Rights and Resources Initiative, 2014) pp. 1–2.

[247] UN-REDD Programme, *Background Paper for the Expert Meeting: Options for Addressing Tenure under REDD+* (25–27 February 2013).

[248] A. Frechette, M. de Bresser, and R. Hofstede, *External Evaluation of the United Nations Collaborative Programme on Reducing Emissions from Deforestation and Forest Degradation in Developing Countries (the UN-REDD Programme): Volume I – Final Report* (July 2014) iii.

[249] B. Dickson, M. Bertzky, T. Christophersen, C. Epple, V. Kapos, L. Miles, U. Narloch, and K. Trumper, *REDD+ Beyond Carbon: Supporting Decisions on Safeguards and Multiple Benefits* (UN-REDD Programme, Policy Brief: Issue No 2, 2012).

[250] UN-REDD Programme, *Forest Tenure and Rights of Indigenous Peoples: Promoting Forest & Land Tenure Governance and the Rights of Indigenous Peoples & Forest Communities along REDD+ Implementation* (1 June 2017, modified 4 July 2018).

[251] UN-REDD Programme, 'Tenure Security', www.unredd.net/knowledge/redd-plus-technical-issues/tenure-security.html (accessed 22 March 2019).

[252] UN-REDD Programme, 'Tenure Security', www.unredd.net/knowledge/redd-plus-technical-issues/tenure-security.html (accessed 22 March 2019).

[253] Gover, 'REDD+, tenure and Indigenous property claims', p. 131.

[254] Ibid., p. 130.

of equitable legal structures governing the ownership of carbon rights and the ownership of the land in which the trees reside (and the ownership of the trees themselves)' to be described as 'crucial' to both efficiency and effectiveness in discussions on REDD+.[255] In this regard, the *Stern Review* stresses that 'defining property rights to forestland ... and determining the rights and responsibilities of landowners, communities and loggers, is key to effective forest management'.[256] Similarly, *The Eliasch Review* emphasises that 'only when property rights are secure, on paper and in practice do longer-term investments in sustainable management become worthwhile'.[257] The 2009 IIED report *Tenure in REDD: Start-Point or Afterthought?* foregrounded the centrality of tenure in order to ensure both the equity and efficiency of REDD+.[258] The CIFOR publication *Realising REDD+: National Strategy and Policy Options* states:

> [T]enure must be clarified, not only to create incentives for those managing the forests to properly assign benefits, but also to protect people whose rights could be usurped if REDD+ leads to a rush of command-and-control measures to protect forests, or if REDD+ leads to a resources race when the value of forests increases.[259]

Law firms Convington & Burling LLP and Baker McKenzie write that 'uncertainty surrounding land title is the single most significant impediment to effective preconditions for a REDD+ scheme',[260] and others have stressed how tenure formalisation is a necessary precondition for ensuring 'security of contracts' and 'accurate predictions of returns' in the carbon economy.[261] A 2013 report by USAID states that '[i]n order for investment to flow, property rights must be clear and secure'.[262] It highlights that security of property rights is a key safeguard for investors, given that it provides them with the confidence that their investments will result in an economic return. In the absence of such assurances, it warns, long-term investment is unlikely to flow into countries, potentially leading to the majority of REDD+ activities being located in a select few countries that have effective institutional enabling

---

[255] S. West, '"Command without control": Are market mechanisms capable of delivering ecological integrity to REDD?' (2010) 6(3) *Law, Environment and Development Journal* 298–319 at 310.

[256] N. H. Stern, *The Economics of Climate Change: The Stern Review* (Cambridge University Press, 2007) p. 27.

[257] J. Eliasch, *Climate Change: Financing Global Forests: The Eliasch Review* (Earthscan, 2008) p. 35.

[258] Cotula and Mayers, *Tenure in REDD – Start-Point or Afterthought?*

[259] W. D. Sunderlin, A. M. Larson, and P. Cronkleton, 'Forest tenure rights and REDD+: From inertia to policy solutions' in A. Angelsen (ed.), *Realising REDD+: National Strategy and Policy Options* (Center for International Forestry Research, 2009) p. 141.

[260] *Background Analysis of REDD Regulatory Frameworks* (Covington & Burling LLP and Baker & McKenzie, 2009) p. 40.

[261] C. Luttrell, K. Schreckenberg, and L. Peskett, *The Implications of Carbon Financing for Pro-Poor Community Forestry* (Overseas Development Institute, 2007).

[262] M. Sommerville, *Land Tenure and REDD+: Risks to Property Rights and Opportunities for Economic Growth* (USAID, 2013) p. 6.

F. Strategies to Manage the 'Social': Between Rights and Responsibilisation   333

environments.[263] Thus, within REDD+ implementation discourses, the imperatives for tenure rights relate to protecting rights but also 'establishing responsibilities' of people living in forest areas – who are described by some as 'populations with limited management capacity'[264] – and ensuring that institutional structures are in place to enforce such responsibilities.

Tenure reform therefore needs to be understood as a process that is not only focused on protecting rights, but also on 'fixing people in place' and creating responsibilised subjects. Critical commentators have argued that neoliberal land formalisation projects are not only aimed at the codification of existing social relations but also directed to the production of marketised social relations and the creation of *homo economicus*.[265] Hernando de Soto, in his influential book *The Mystery of Capital, Why Capitalism Triumphs in the West and Fails Everywhere Else*, stresses that the power of property comes from the way it 'transforms people with property interests into accountable individuals', thereby 'creating individuals from masses'.[266] For de Soto, formalisation is a disciplinary process and he celebrates how property's power manifests itself through the 'accountability it creates, from the constraints it imposes, the rules it spawns and the sanctions it can apply'.[267]

The analysis so far has emphasised how the prevailing discourse on tenure mediates the concurrent demands of rights 'from below' and responsibilisation 'from above'. The discussion now turns to consider two further ways in which the more radical rights-promoting possibilities inherent in calls for tenure reform have been neutralised and how instead the imperative towards responsibilisation is foregrounded in how tenure reform is implemented in REDD+. The discussion first considers the nature of the tenure rights granted over forested land and then the temporal sequencing of tenurial reform.

The discussion in Chapter 5 highlighted the need to be attentive to the nature and content of the rights granted over forested land through tenure reform programmes.[268] It described how processes of forest tenure reform were generally distinct from other forms of agrarian tenure reform. As a result, even when (collective) rights are granted to forested communities such rights often remain heavily constrained, as the state generally retains alienation rights as well as the ability to determine how forested land should be used. As such, even when rights to forested land are granted through tenure reform processes, such rights are generally 'hollow' and lack the attributes of management and control. Moreover, in the context of REDD+ projects, the rights to control how forested land will be used has often already been granted to international actors through processes of carbon contracting. Therefore, any tenure

[263] Ibid.
[264] Ibid., p. 5.
[265] Williams, 'Constructing the economic space'.
[266] de Soto, *The Mystery of Capital*, p. 53.
[267] Ibid., pp. 54–5.
[268] For further discussion see Chapter 5.

334 REDD+ at the 'Local' Level: Between Rights and Responsibilisation

rights granted to forest peoples are likely to be subject to internationally imposed obligations to use the land in specific ways to promote carbon sequestration.

The presence of such international contractual constraints is reinforced in 'best practice' international guidelines on tenure reform, which reiterate the need for any tenure reform process to be consistent with existing international obligations. The UN-REDD Programme has adopted the Voluntary Guidelines on the Responsible Governance of Tenure of Land, Fisheries, and Forests in the Context of National Food Security (VGGT) developed by the FAO[269] as part of its 'framework for tenure technical assistance'.[270] Although the VGGT are more focused on questions of rights than other more market-orientated guidelines and do provide considerable scope for legal pluralism, they nonetheless 'allocate responsibilities and authority between different actors' in ways that may constrain the more radical potential of tenure reform.[271] As stated therein, the VGGT are to be 'interpreted and applied consistent with existing obligations under national and international law',[272] and that States should ensure that 'all actions regarding the legal recognition and allocation of tenure rights and duties are consistent with their existing obligations under national and international law', including voluntary commitments.[273] More specifically, in situations where the state owns or controls land, fisheries and forests, the VGGT specify that it should 'determine the use and control of these resources in light of broader social, economic and environmental objectives' as well as ensure that actions are consistent with existing national and international legal obligations and voluntary commitments.[274] It is therefore apparent that in applying the VGGT in the REDD+ context, any recognition of tenure rights in forested land will be subject to international carbon sequestration commitments, including any contractual obligations pertaining to forested land.

Another way in which the more radical possibilities enabled by calls for tenure reform have been neutralised is through a lack of clarity about the temporal sequencing of tenure reform and resulting ambiguity about whether tenure reform should be understood as a positive *outcome of* a REDD+ project or a *precondition for* a REDD+ project. This is despite the fact that a key demand from Indigenous peoples and other forest peoples has been 'rights before REDD+' or 'no rights, no REDD+': namely that recognition of rights must come prior to the commencement

---

[269] *Voluntary Guidelines on the Responsible Governance of Tenure of Land, Fisheries, and Forests in the Context of National Food Security* (Committee on World Food Security and the Food and Agricultural Organization of the United Nations, 2012) ('VGGT'). See P. Seufert, 'The FAO voluntary guidelines on the responsible governance of tenure of land, fisheries and forests' (2013) 10(1) *Globalizations* 181–6 for an overview.

[270] UN-REDD Programme, *Forest Tenure and Rights of Indigenous Peoples*, 6.

[271] N. Tzouvala, 'A false promise? Regulating land-grabbing and the post-colonial state' (2019) 32(2) *Leiden Journal of International Law* 235–53 at 239.

[272] VGGT, para 2.2.

[273] Ibid., para 7.2.

[274] Ibid., para 8.1

F. Strategies to Manage the 'Social': Between Rights and Responsibilisation 335

of any REDD+ implementation processes.[275] In the REDD+ implementation literature, the descriptions of tenure clarification and formalisation are trapped within a circular logic where tenure reform processes are presented as both a necessary precondition for REDD+ implementation but REDD+ implementation is also presented as incentivising such reforms.[276] This circularity has allowed a certain ambiguity to persist regarding when tenure reform should take place. The UN-REDD Programme provides only very vague guidance in relation to the timing of tenure reform, describing how 'early-stage support' might include 'an analysis of the tenure situation as it relates to REDD+, the identification of policy gaps and the elaboration of work plans to develop enabling tenure conditions for REDD', but that '[e]fforts to address tenure issues in the context of REDD+ can be integrated with ongoing land tenure reform efforts'.[277] The FCPF Readiness Assessment Framework requires that as part of preparing their Readiness Preparation Proposal (R-PP) countries must conduct a national multi-stakeholder self-assessment that includes an assessment of land-use trends, including land tenure and titling, as well as governance and livelihood issues to inform the development of national strategy and national implementation frameworks.[278] However, although action plans for making short-, medium- and long-term progress on addressing land use, land tenure and titling, natural resource rights, livelihoods and governance issues need to be prepared as part of REDD+-readiness, such plans may be enacted alongside REDD+ implementation.[279] In their policy brief, USAID is more blunt in its assessment that tenure reform should not stall REDD+ implementation. The USAID brief recommends that 'investment in pilot projects or readiness should be contingent on the development and implementation of sound land policies and progress in achieving broader tenure security for affected populations';[280] but USAID also acknowledges that '[i]n most countries, it [would] not be practical to stall REDD+ investments until tenure concerns are fully addressed'.[281] Adopting a slightly different approach, the Kalimantan Forest Carbon Partnership (KFCP), a 'demonstration project' that was part of Australia's $200 million International Forest Carbon Initiative, which sought to rehabilitate 120,000 hectares of land

---

[275] See S. Long, E. Roberts, and J. Dehm, 'Climate justice inside and outside the UNFCCC: The example of REDD' (2010) 66 *Journal of Australian Political Economy* 221.

[276] A. Savaresi and E. Morgera, 'Ownership of land, forest and carbon' in John Costenbader (ed.), *Legal Frameworks for REDD: Design and Implementation at the National Level* (IUCN, 2009) pp. 15–34, 18.

[277] UN-REDD Programme, *UN-REDD Supporting Work on Tenure and REDD+* (November 2014), www.unredd.net/documents/global-programme-191/governance-452/tenure-and-redd-2647/13823-unredd-supporting-work-on-tenure-and-redd-13823.html.

[278] Forest Carbon Partnership Facility, *A Guide to the FCPF Readiness Assessment Framework*, June 2013, www.forestcarbonpartnership.org/sites/fcp/files/2013/July2013/FCPC%20framework %20text%207-25-13%20ENG%20web.pdf.

[279] Ibid., 11.

[280] Sommerville, *Land Tenure and REDD*, p. 12.

[281] Ibid.

336 REDD+ at the 'Local' Level: Between Rights and Responsibilisation

degraded by the disastrous Soeharto-era Ex-Mega Rice Project in Central Kalimantan, argued that tenure rights would be enabled through or by the project. The KFCP Design Document explicitly rejected clarification and recognition of land tenure as a precondition for the KFCP and argued instead that the project itself would *facilitate* tenure reforms:

> Clear land tenure laws cannot be made a precondition of project development, because no projects would then ever be developed or they would all be developed in the same handful of places. Rather, the projects themselves can be made the instrument of change, where community management rights are first given to local people in a step-wise process to full land tenure.[282]

However, if tenure rights are granted through formalisation only *after* contractual decisions have been made about how that land can be used, the rights granted are 'hollow' and lack the salient attributes of property, since title is already divested of the right to control land and decide future land-use activities. Such tenure reform through REDD+ projects cannot be seen to deliver the rights asserted by forest peoples to 'own, control, use and peacefully enjoy their lands, territories and other resources, and be secure in their means of subsistence'.[283] Instead, the way tenure formalisation processes are operating in REDD+ suggests that the granting of title rights is primarily orientated to responsibilising their holders as accountable subjects of the 'green economy'.

3 Free, Prior and Informed Consent

The right of communities to give FPIC has been a further mechanism promoted as critical to mitigating the potential social risks of REDD+ projects and ensuring that such projects promote social benefits. This section considers the debates around FPIC in international law and in the context of REDD+, especially differing interpretations of the purpose of FPIC and whether it entails a right to 'veto' projects as well as how it is operationalised in practice. The discussion reveals that although there is growing support for FPIC in the context of REDD+ implementation, there are a number of reasons to be concerned about how it operates in practice. As César Rodríguez-Garavito has shown, FPIC processes mark a point of convergence between two different legalities, whereby 'neoliberal legality based on freedom of contract and due process' is contested by a 'legality that is based on Indigenous self-determination'.[284] As such, even more than the strategies of benefit

---

[282] *Kalimantan Forests and Climate Partnership (KFCP): Design Document* (Australia Indonesia Partnership, 2009) p. 19, fn 11; see also R. Pearse and J. Dehm, *In the REDD: Australia's Carbon Offset Project in Central Kalimantan* (Friends of the Earth International, 2011) p. 16.

[283] M. Colchester, *Beyond Tenure: Rights-Based Approaches to Peoples and Forests. Some Lessons from the Forest Peoples Programme* (Forest Peoples Programme, 2007) p. 4.

[284] Rodríguez-Garavito, 'Ethnicity.gov', 282.

F. Strategies to Manage the 'Social': Between Rights and Responsibilisation 337

sharing and tenure reform discussed above, FPIC processes sit in a fraught space between demands for rights, autonomy and self-determination 'from below' and the imperatives of contractual obligations and responsibilisation 'from above'. This section demonstrates that there are reasons to be concerned that in the REDD+ context what is being foregrounded through the operationalisation of FPIC are neoliberal imperatives of contractual certainty rather than a commitment to Indigenous self-determination, which therefore risks promoting greater responsibilisation 'from above' rather than giving effect to claims for rights 'from below'.

The right to consultation towards FPIC is now recognised as a key right of Indigenous peoples in international law that has been affirmed by a number of UN treaty supervisory bodies and regional human rights courts.[285] ILO 169 states that signatory governments shall provide means for participation and consultation of Indigenous peoples affected by projects through their representative institutions, in good faith and with 'the objective of achieving agreement or consent to the proposed measures'.[286] FPIC has been affirmed in the UNDRIP and appears as an overarching principle in Article 19 of UNDRIP. Article 19 of UNDRIP, which requires that states 'consult and cooperate in good faith' with Indigenous peoples 'in order to obtain their free, prior and informed consent', is mentioned in several other provisions,[287] and this process must occur 'prior to the approval of any project affecting their lands or territories and other resources, particularly in connection with the development, utilization or exploitation of mineral, water or other resources'.[288] There are three major rationales for this right: to seek to restore to Indigenous peoples control over their land and resources; to enable Indigenous peoples' collective cultural integrity, pride and self-esteem; and to redress the power imbalance between Indigenous peoples and states.[289] FPIC is not an individual right but one inherently grounded in the right to self-determination,[290] and therefore 'recognizes collective rights and protects collective identities'.[291] According to international law, in order to be 'free, prior and informed' these processes must not be subject to 'coercion, intimidation or manipulation'; consent must be sought 'sufficiently in advance of any authorization or commencement of activities'; and sufficient information about the nature of the project, its reasons or purpose, duration, location and preliminary assessment of likely impacts must be provided.[292]

---

[285] For an overview see Ward, 'The right to free, prior, and informed consent'.

[286] ILO Convention 169, Article 6.

[287] UNDRIP, Article 10, 11, 19, 28, 29 and 32.

[288] UNDRIP, Article 32.

[289] *Free, Prior and Informed Consent: A Human Rights-Based Approach: Study on the Expert Mechanism on the Rights of Indigenous Peoples*, A/HRC/39/62 (10 August 2018), para 11.

[290] Ibid., para 6.

[291] Ibid., para 12.

[292] *Report of the International Workshop on Methodologies Regarding Free, Prior and Informed Consent and Indigenous Peoples* (New York, 17–19 January 2005), UN Permanent Forum on

338   REDD+ at the 'Local' Level: Between Rights and Responsibilisation

There is a growing consensus that FPIC is 'highly relevant' to REDD+, given that 'REDD+ will involve changes in forest management and use that can affect the rights and livelihoods of Indigenous peoples and local communities'.[293] Therefore, FPIC is promoted as a means both for 'communities to safeguard their rights and interests' and to better 'shape REDD+ initiatives to support communities in ways that will contribute to successful outcomes'.[294] Although the Cancun safeguards do not explicitly mention FPIC, they take note of the UNDRIP and state that 'respect for the knowledge and rights of indigenous peoples and members of local communities by taking into account relevant international obligations, national circumstances and laws' and the 'full and effective participation' of Indigenous peoples should be 'promoted and supported' when undertaking REDD+ activities.[295] The UN-REDD Programme and FCPF-harmonised *Guidelines on Stakeholder Engagement* provide differentiated obligations in relation to FPIC. These guidelines state that the UN-REDD Programme is expected to adhere to standards outlined in key relevant international instruments as well as to 'uphold the principle of free, prior and informed consent (FPIC) as stated in the UN Declaration on the Rights of Indigenous Peoples'.[296] UN-REDD prepared its own *UN-REDD Programme Guidelines on Free, Prior and Informed Consent* (January 2013) along with an associated legal companion.[297] For the FCPF, the ESS7 requires that the borrower country obtain the FPIC of affected Indigenous communities in certain circumstances, including where a project will 'have adverse impacts on land and natural resources subject to traditional ownership or under customary use or occupation'.[298] This is generally seen as a 'strong improvement' on earlier drafts of the ESF as well as the World Bank's previous Operational Policy 4.10 (OP 4.10) relating to Indigenous peoples, which only required free, prior and informed *consultation*, although it did provide that consent 'may exist even where some individuals or groups object to such project activities'.[299] Additionally a number of guidelines have been prepared by various organisations for FPIC in REDD+, including *Free, Prior and Informed Consent in REDD+: Principles and Approaches for Policy and Project*

Indigenous Issues, Fourth Session, E/C.19/2005/3 (17 February 2006), para 46; see also *Free, Prior and Informed Consent*, para 20–3.

[293] J. Springer and V. Retana, *Free, Prior and Informed Consent and REDD+: Guidelines and Resources* (WWF-US's People and Conservation Programme and WWF's global Forest and Climate Programme, 2014) p. 1.

[294] Ibid., p. 1.

[295] Decision 1/CP.16, Appendix I, para 2(c).

[296] *Guidelines on Stakeholder Engagement in REDD+ Readiness*, 2.

[297] UN-REDD Programme, *Legal Companion to the UN-REDD Programme Guidelines on Free, Prior and Informed Consent (FPIC): International Law and Jurisprudence Affirming the Requirement of FPIC* (January 2013).

[298] ESS7, para 24(a).

[299] ESS7, para 26. For a discussion of ESS7 see O. W. MacLaren and J.-A. Pariseau, 'The new World Bank safeguard standard for indigenous peoples: Where do we start' (2017) 45(1) *Syracuse Journal of International Law & Commerce* 35–57.

F. *Strategies to Manage the 'Social': Between Rights and Responsibilisation* 339

Development (2011), authored by Patrick Anderson and published by the Center for People and Forests (RECOFTC),[300] and WWF's working paper on *Free, Prior and Informed Consent and REDD+: Guidelines and Resources* (2014).[301] Despite these policy documents, several studies from the field have documented clear problems in the implementation of FPIC processes in REDD+, including the failure to meet standards outlined in policy documents, the use of inappropriate and inaccessible language in consultation processes, and a 'general pattern of uncertainty, unpreparedness and lack of planning'.[302] Additionally, the many still unanswered questions about REDD+'s financing and about the long-term trajectories of carbon markets make it almost impossible to provide sufficiently precise information on which a community might base an informed decision about a proposal.[303] The discussion below describes the challenges related to ensuring FPIC in the context of REDD+. It considers first the ongoing legal debates about its scope and operation, before turning to consider the tensions specific to the REDD+ context.

Even as consultation processes are increasingly recognised by all actors as 'not optional', scholars have highlighted how the nature of the duty to consult is subject to 'divergent interpretations and discursive methodologies'.[304] There continues to be a legal debate about the purpose and scope of FPIC rights, and especially whether they include an absolute right to give or refuse consent and thereby to 'veto' projects.[305] The text of the UNDRIP requires that States 'consult and cooperate in good faith' with affected communities 'in order to obtain their free, prior and informed consent'. As Karen Engle notes, this marks a clear departure from the 1993 draft of the declaration in which consent was a *requirement*, while in the UNDRIP consent is articulated as a *goal*. She highlights that the obligation articulated in UNDRIP is to 'consult and cooperate in good faith with the indigenous peoples concerned through their own representative institutions *in order to obtain* their free and informed consent prior to the approval of any projects affecting their lands, territories and other resources'.[306] The former UN Special Rapporteur on the situation of human rights and fundamental freedoms of Indigenous peoples, James Anaya, has provided a purposive interpretation of the obligation.[307] He articulates

---

[300] Anderson, *Free, Prior, and Informed Consent in REDD.*

[301] Springer and Retana, *Free, Prior and Informed Consent and REDD+: Guidelines and Resources.*

[302] S. Howell, "No RIGHTS–No REDD'", 253–72 at 265–66.

[303] Ibid., 255–6.

[304] S. J. Anaya and S. Puig, 'Mitigating state sovereignty: The duty to consult with Indigenous peoples' (2017) 67(4) *University of Toronto Law Journal* 435–64 at 447.

[305] Ibid., 449–50.

[306] UNDRIP, Article 19 and 32.2, discussed in Engle, 'On fragile architecture', 141–63 at 157, fn 56 (emphasis in Engle).

[307] J. Anaya, *Report of the Special Rapporteur on the Situation of Human Rights and Fundamental Freedoms of Indigenous Peoples, James Anaya,* General Assembly, A/HRC/12/34 (15 July 2009).

that the obligation 'applies whenever a State decision may affect indigenous peoples in ways not felt by others in society'.[308] The specific characteristics of the required consultation procedure may vary depending on context and in particular should be 'shaped by the nature of the right or interest at stake for the indigenous peoples concerned and the anticipated impact of the proposed measure'.[309] Anaya stresses that all consultations must be undertaken in 'good faith' and with the 'objective of achieving agreement or consent'; however, he contends that Article 19 'should not be regarded as according indigenous peoples a general "veto power" over decisions that may affect them'.[310] Instead, the purpose of the provision in his interpretation is to establish consent as 'the objective of consultations with indigenous peoples'.[311] Moreover, Anaya finds that the importance of this objective of achieving consent 'varies according to the circumstances and the indigenous interests involved', such that where a measure will have a 'significant, direct impact' on indigenous peoples' lives or territories it gives rise to a 'strong presumption' that the measure should not go ahead without consent.[312] Nonetheless, even though he stresses that where indigenous peoples' particular interests are affected the objective of any consultation should be to obtain their consent, this requirement 'does not provide indigenous peoples with a "veto power", but rather establishes the need to frame consultation procedures in order to make every effort to build consensus on the part of all concerned'.[313] Anaya is concerned that focusing the debate around whether or not Indigenous peoples 'hold a veto power' that could be 'wield[ed] to halt development projects' is 'not in line with the spirit or character of the principles of consultation and consent'.[314] Instead, he argues that the purpose should be to 'build dialogue', to 'work in good faith towards consensus and try in earnest to arrive at a mutually satisfactory agreement'.[315] In concluding, he suggests that Indigenous peoples should 'avoid inflexible positions when the proposed measures are based on legitimate public interests'.[316] In subsequent 2012 and 2013 reports focused on the extractive industries, Anaya further clarified the scope of the obligation.[317]

In its 2012 report, the International Law Association found that 'it is not possible to conclude that Article 19 may be interpreted as establishing a general right of veto in favour of the Indigenous communities concerned to block the adoption or

---

[308] Ibid., para 43.
[309] Ibid., para 46.
[310] Ibid.
[311] Ibid.
[312] Ibid., para 47.
[313] Ibid., para 48.
[314] Ibid.
[315] Ibid., para 49.
[316] Ibid., para 66.
[317] J. Anaya, *Report of the Special Rapporteur on the Rights of Indigenous Peoples, James Anaya*, Human Rights Council, 21st session, A/HRC/21/47 (6 July 2012); James Anaya, *Report of the Special Rapporteur on the Rights of Indigenous Peoples, James Anaya: Extractive Industries and Indigenous Peoples*, Human Rights Council, 24th session, A/HRC/24/41 (1 July 2013).

F. Strategies to Manage the 'Social': Between Rights and Responsibilisation   341

implementation of the governmental measures which may affect them per se'.[318] The ILA's analysis draws attention to cases where 'international institutions have recognized the existence of a full right of veto in favour of Indigenous peoples', including the Inter-American Court of Human Rights judgment in the *Saramaka* case[319] and in statements from other human rights treaties bodies. Noting that international practice concerning FPIC is heterogeneous, the ILA therefore concluded that the 'UNDRIP does not imply the existence of a right to veto – *in general terms* – with respect to *every kind of measure* that may affect indigenous peoples'.[320] However, it affirmed that the practice of international institutions appeared to be 'orientated towards recognizing the existence of a duty to actually obtain the consent of the indigenous communities concerned before carrying out activities of exploitation of their traditional lands'.[321] The ILA suggests that considering the provisions in light of their objective and purpose would imply that 'although States are not obliged to obtain the consent of indigenous peoples before engaging in *whatever kind* of activities which may affect them – this obligation exists any time that the lack of such a consent would translate into a violation of the rights of indigenous peoples that States are bound to guarantee and respect'.[322] Consent is thus positioned as a necessary precondition to the economic exploitation of the lands on which Indigenous peoples live, where such explanation would violate rights to autonomy, cultural integrity and cultural autonomy.[323]

In more recent academic writing, James Anaya and Sergio Puig identify and argue against a number of divergent positions adopted in relation to this duty to consult, critiquing both positions that focus on 'veto' powers as well as instrumentalist or minimalist positions. They revisit the purpose of the duty to consult as an 'accountability mechanism that focuses on reaching agreement in just terms and not merely on obtaining consent (on whatever terms)' in order to advance an interpretation of it as 'more than a mere right to be informed and heard but less than the right of veto'.[324] Anaya and Puig are therefore highly critical of the 'narrow' or 'minimalist' view of the duty to consult favoured by some business enterprises, where consultation is translated into 'check-the-box' exercises that seek input but where 'ultimate state decision-making power remain[s] substantially unchanged'.[325] They are similarly concerned about state authorities adopting an 'instrumentalist approach' to FPIC that interprets the duty to consult in only formal and procedural terms, in a

---

[318] International Law Association, *Sofia Conference: Rights of Indigenous Peoples*, 4.
[319] *Case of the Saramaka People v. Suriname*, Series C No. 172, Judgment of 28 November 2007.
[320] ILA, *Final Report* (2012), 6 (emphasis in original).
[321] Ibid., 6.
[322] ILA, *Final Report* (2012), 7 (emphasis in original).
[323] Ibid., 7.
[324] Anaya and Puig, 'Mitigating state sovereignty: The duty to consult with Indigenous peoples', 437, 438.
[325] Ibid., 450–2.

342   *REDD+ at the 'Local' Level: Between Rights and Responsibilisation*

way that 'obscures concern for any substantive rights that may be implicated'.[326] Anaya and Puig instead favour an approach grounded in human rights that sees consultation as serving a 'protective role' to 'mitigate' negative consequences for Indigenous peoples, but where it also provides a 'balancing function' in mediating the collective rights of Indigenous peoples with the rights of other rights-holders in a state-centric world.[327] This conception of the purpose and function of the duty to consult allows Anaya and Puig to justify certain limitations on the right to be consulted, provided that such limitations are 'pursuant to a valid public purpose or objective'.[328] They stress that any such limitations are only justifiable if they are 'necessary and proportionate' to such a public purpose, and that mere commercial purposes, private gains or revenue-seeking objectives do not constitute a 'valid public purpose'.[329] It remains an open question as to how 'public purpose' would be interpreted in the context of REDD+, where projects are authorised on the basis that increasing carbon sequestration is a key means of addressing climate change and a matter of global 'common concern'.

Although discussions on FPIC in REDD+ have generally endorsed a right to withhold consent, they have nonetheless subtly constrained Indigenous peoples' ability to refuse projects. The UN-REDD Programme *Guidelines on FPIC* draw on international human rights norms to affirm that 'consent must be freely given, obtained prior to implementation of activities and be founded upon an understanding of the full range of issues implicated by the activity or decision in question'.[330] These guidelines also stress that FPIC includes the right to *withhold* consent, stating explicitly that 'potentially impacted peoples have the right to participate in and consent to or withhold consent from a proposed action', and that the right to withhold consent is 'at the core of FPIC'.[331] The Center for People and Forests guide on FPIC is slightly more ambiguous, stating that a key motivation for ensuring FPIC is 'to give rights holders the power to veto REDD+ activities or policies on the basis of "unreasonable claims"'.[332] Elsewhere it describes the right to withhold consent as 'fundamental to FPIC', before clarifying that this is a community right and not a right of individual veto and also that 'giving and withholding of consent is time-specific – both can be re-visited and revised'.[333] This focus on 'living consent' as a recurring process involving continual monitoring, maintenance and reaffirmation

---

[326] Ibid., 448.

[327] Ibid., 452–4.

[328] Ibid., 461. This argument is also developed in J. Anaya, *Report of the Special Rapporteur on the Rights of Indigenous Peoples, James Anaya*, Human Rights Council, 24th session, A/HRC/24/41 (1 July 2013).

[329] Anaya and Puig, 'Mitigating state sovereignty', 461–2.

[330] UN-REDD Programme, *UN-REDD Programme Guidelines on Free, Prior and Informed Consent* (January 2013) 7.

[331] Ibid., 18, 20.

[332] Anderson, *Free, Prior, and Informed Consent in REDD*, p. 17.

[333] Ibid, p. 28.

F. Strategies to Manage the 'Social': Between Rights and Responsibilisation   343

entails many positive aspects, but the corollary position – that 'decisions to withhold consent are not necessarily forever binding and can also be revisited by rights holders as situations change'[334] – also entails risks for rights holders insofar as it suggests that a 'lack of consent is not so much a "no" as an invitation to come back with another offer'.[335] As Nathan Yaffe notes, such an approach where a 'no' is simply seen as part of 'getting to yes' demonstrates a 'disregard for Indigenous peoples as collectivities engaged in the act of defining the future they choose to pursue'.[336]

In addition to these debates about whether or not FPIC includes a 'veto' right, there are broader questions about the shifts that have occurred in the normative framework underpinning FPIC as well as how FPIC operates in practice. Yaffe argues that even as consent-seeking processes have become more common in development projects, there has been a 'normative drift' in the process whereby the 'normative foundation' of FPIC as grounded in rights of self-determination has 'been undermined'.[337] He is concerned that FPIC is increasingly embraced by corporations as a 'matter of risk management', even when they are not legally required to engage in consultation or obtain consent.[338] Yaffe suggests that through these processes, especially within the corporate context, FPIC has become 'unmoored from its normative underpinnings' as part of a broader agenda of Indigenous self-determination and in practice has come to 'resemble a procedural, box-checking requirement'.[339] His concern is not primarily with whether or not FPIC constitutes a veto right or lessor rights but rather that 'current practices could presage a future in which putative consent is obtained with respect to nearly all projects (whether or not as a matter of legal obligation), wherein FPIC functions primarily as a legitimising tool that insulates from critique the process of dispossessing Indigenous peoples and undermining their autonomy'.[340]

These concerns are pertinent in the REDD+ context because, although various guidelines on FPIC predominantly reference the principles of international human rights law and the rights of Indigenous peoples,[341] FPIC is also consistently discussed

---

[334] Ibid, p. 18.

[335] N. Yaffe, 'Indigenous consent: A self-determination perspective' 19(2) *Melbourne Journal of International Law* 703–49 at 725.

[336] Ibid.

[337] Ibid., 705.

[338] Ibid., 707.

[339] Ibid., 706.

[340] Ibid.

[341] See the *Report of the International Workshop on Methodologies Regarding Free, Prior and Informed Consent and Indigenous Peoples* (New York, 17–19 January 2005), UN Permanent Forum on Indigenous Issues, Fourth Session, E/C.19/2005/3 (17 February 2006) and *Final Study on Indigenous Peoples and the Right to Participate in Decision-Making: Report of the Expert Mechanism on the Right of Indigenous Peoples*, Human Rights Council, Expert Mechanism on the Rights of Indigenous Peoples, 4th session, A/HRC/EMRIP/2011/2 (26 May 2011).

and framed as a critical risk management strategy,[342] presented as key to managing risks not only to communities but also to the REDD+ project itself. Such a positioning of efforts to obtain 'community consent' as a risk management strategy, echoes the approach adopted in some corporate social responsibility accounts.[343] Such accounts focus on the risks of ignoring social and environmental issues, including financial risk, construction risk, operational risk, reputational risk, credit/corporate risk, host government risk and host country political risk, and highlight that these risks increase if there is 'social unrest and conflict caused by disagreement or disaffection' among affected communities.[344] Within this risk management frame, the ability to demonstrate community support is presented as an 'opportunity' that benefits companies because it makes it 'easier to gain regulatory approval for future projects, efficiently bring their products to market, attract skilled employees, or market their products to the growing pool of customers who consider production conditions and corporate sustainability practices in their purchasing decisions'.[345] Similar depictions of lack of consent as a risk *for project implementers* and investors is present even in 'best practice' manuals or guidelines on FPIC in REDD+. For example, *Free, Prior and Informed Consent in REDD+: Principles and Approaches for Policy and Project Development*, published by the Centre for People and Forests, presents deontological and utilitarian arguments for FPIC processes, emphasising that forest-dependent communities are 'essential to the success of REDD+' and that FPIC processes can assist in successfully implementing pre-determined REDD+ objectives.[346] The UN-REDD Programme *Operational Guidelines on Engagement of Indigenous Peoples and Other Forest Dependent Communities* similarly note that 'inadequate mechanisms for effective participation of local communities in land use decisions could seriously compromise the delivery of both local and global benefits and the long-term sustainability of REDD+ invest-ments'.[347] The UN-REDD Programme *Guidelines on FPIC*, in addition to asserting the 'strong normative case' for FPIC, foreground why obtaining FPIC makes 'good business sense', providing a list of reasons from the WRI's report on the business case for community consent.[348] This approach, which promotes obtaining FPIC as a risk management strategy, regardless of whether it is legally required, risks undermining

---

[342] See Anderson, *Free, Prior, and Informed Consent in REDD*.

[343] S. Herz, A. L. Vina, and J. Sohn, *Development without Conflict: The Business Case for Community Consent* (World Resources Initiative, 2007); I. Sosa, *License to Operate: Indigenous Relations and Free, Prior, Informed Consent in the Mining Industry* (Sustainalytics, 2011).

[344] *The Right to Decide: The Importance of Respecting Free, Prior and Informed Consent* (Amazon Watch, 2011).

[345] Herz et al., *Development without Conflict*, p. 6.

[346] Anderson, *Free, Prior, and Informed Consent in REDD*, p. 47.

[347] UN-REDD Programme, *UN-REDD Programme Operational Guidance: Engagement of Indigenous Peoples and Other Forest Dependent Communities* (2009) p. 3.

[348] UN-REDD Programme, *UN-REDD Programme Guidelines on Free, Prior and Informed Consent*, 16.

F. Strategies to Manage the 'Social': Between Rights and Responsibilisation   345

the broader normative commitment to self-determination that underpins FPIC, by understanding consent in more limited procedural terms.[349]

Finally, some of the empirical evidence from REDD+ project implementation suggests that the discursive space surrounding FPIC in REDD+ is structured in ways that limit the ability of forest peoples to veto carbon sequestration projects, as those individuals or groups who exhibit opposition to REDD+ may be characterised as either 'uninformed' or 'inauthentic'. In her discussion of REDD+, Tania Murray Li writes:

> It is not clear that forest villagers, whose participation is essential for a consensus version of REDD+, actually have the option to make the 'wrong' choice – to cut forests, to reject REDD+ programs and REDD+ funds in favour of different goals or different productive arrangements.[350]

Li's suggestion that a community's refusal to consent is read as a 'wrong' decision and that people making such decisions are perceived as uninformed, inauthentic or biased by project implementers is substantiated by other field accounts. In her discussion of a REDD+ pilot project in Sulawesi, Signe Howell documents how the Indonesian Ministry of Forestry attributed a community vote against the UN-REDD pilot project to 'inappropriate interference' by local NGOs.[351] In her study of the KFCP in Central Kalimantan, Anu Lounela has described how Ngaju Dayak villagers organising against the project, who had connections with advocacy NGOs such as Wahana Lingkungan Hidup Indonesia (Indonesian Forum for the Environment or WALHI) 'were considered egotistic by the village elite, of whom many gained economic benefits from the REDD+ project'.[352] These examples show how opposition to REDD+ has been characterised. On one reading, these issues – the characterisation of opposition to REDD+ as 'uninformed' or 'irrational', or attributing it to undue influence by ideological outsiders or (paradoxically) undue self-interest – can be attributed to deficiencies in local consultation and consent processes that were marred by paternalistic attitudes, stereotypes and vested interests, and thus, these problems could be remedied by a more rights-compliant approach to FPIC. However, a more critical reading suggests that such outcomes are not the result of a failure to properly comply with international legal norms pertaining to the duty to consult, but rather that such outcomes are, in part, a product of how international law has implicitly required Indigenous peoples to perform a specific subject-position in order to claim rights. That is, the ways in which Indigenous peoples are called upon to perform a particular 'subject-position' as ecological stewards can limit their ability to resist or oppose projects construed as addressing

---

[349] Yaffe, 'Indigenous consent', 707.
[350] Li, 'Fixing non-market subjects', 26.
[351] Howell, "No RIGHTS–No REDD", 263.
[352] A. Lounela, 'Climate change disputes and justice in Central Kalimantan, Indonesia' (2015) 56(1) *Asia Pacific Viewpoint* 62–78 at 74.

346 REDD+ at the 'Local' Level: Between Rights and Responsibilisation

a global ecological 'common concern'. This more critical reading suggests that the way international legal discourse has constructed the subject of Indigenous rights makes it very difficult for forest peoples claiming such rights to be legible as 'Indigenous', 'informed' and 'not consenting' simultaneously, especially in the context of environmental and conservation projects.

Finally, it is necessary to ask uncomfortable questions about the 'instrument effects' of FPIC processes and the productive effects they might have. It is arguable that in a context where indigeneity has been discursively constructed as linked to environmental stewardship – and REDD+ projects have been framed as addressing matters of global 'common concern' – processes of FPIC may actually operate to *incorporate* Indigenous peoples *into* REDD+ projects rather than allow Indigenous communities to articulate their own different future vision for forested territories. Even though the discursive construction of indigeneity in international law may mean that it is difficult for Indigenous peoples to be seen as simultaneously 'Indigenous', 'informed' and 'not consenting' to REDD+ projects, consultation and consent processes can still play a protective role in mitigating some of the negative consequences for Indigenous peoples from REDD+ projects and help to ensure that REDD+ projects do not breach substantive rights such as those to culture and cultural identity. Moreover, the obligations of project proponents to consult in order to obtain FPIC can provide critically important procedural rights, especially in situations where REDD+ projects might affect underlying substantive rights, for example, by displacing people or restricting access to cultural sites or activities. By doing so, processes of consultation and consent can operate to promote a model of REDD+ implementation that is more attentive to the partici-pation of Indigenous peoples and other local communities and the incorporation of their knowledges and skills into project design. Given that many conservation projects on the ground continue to exclude forest peoples participation – not to mention the destructive impacts of extractive, logging and plantation industries in surrounding areas – there is significant value in strategically asserting cultural rights to promote greater inclusion of Indigenous peoples in forest carbon offset projects and the more equitable distribution of resulting benefits.[353]

However, even as FPIC processes may help make REDD+ projects more equit-able, the extent to which they can assist Indigenous peoples and local communities to actually *resist* or *oppose* REDD+ schemes is more questionable, especially if such projects seek to foster participation and enable Indigenous 'cultural rights' of ecological management. As such, the effects of processes of consultation and consent may be to promote forms of disciplinary inclusion within REDD+ that simultaneously foreclose the abilities of peoples to freely determine their own future trajectories in accordance with their own aspirations and needs.

---

[353] I have participated in advocacy that has stressed FPIC as a precondition for REDD+ projects: see Pearse and Dehm, *In the REDD: Australia's Carbon Offset Project in Central Kalimantan.*

F. Strategies to Manage the 'Social': Between Rights and Responsibilisation 347

Additionally, the process of consenting and specifically the *articulation* of consent arguably has productive effects.[354] Speech act theory draws attention to how specific utterances do more than simply convey meaning: they also have communicative effect or illocutionary force, and in so doing bring something into being. They are thus *performative*, in that such utterances do things in the world.[355] Judith Butler has developed a theory of performativity that focuses not just on speech acts but also on other embodied acts, to show how gender – and by extension other subject-positions – is the product of repeated enactments, given that such actions always occur within an established field of social meanings.[356] As such, theories of performativity highlight both the constraints imposed by the process of being acted on and the conditions and possibilities enabled by acting. Even though theories of performativity rarely explicitly consider legal contracts, Angela Mitropoulos has shown how contracts represent 'the very sense of the performative' in that they are 'part of the making of what they say'.[357] Contractual instruments do not only allocate pre-existing rights to pre-existing subjects, they also bring into being and are constitutive of the 'self' and the concept of 'property' they presuppose.[358] Thus, the articulation of consent has performative effects, because this utterance helps constitute its speaker as a capable of self-management and fulfilling obligations, even in the face of an uncertain future.

Read critically, the guidelines on FPIC in REDD+ betray a tension: although the focus is on requiring a project proponent demonstrate they have obtained consent from the relevant community, the guidelines also implicitly require the community from whom consent is sought to demonstrate they have the requisite capacity to give consent. The tension manifests itself through the duel way in which the requirement that consent be 'informed' can be understood. Depending on how the emphasis is placed, this requirement that consent be informed can be presented both as an obligation imposed on project proponents to provide communities with proper information but *also* as a attribute that communities need to demonstrate to external observers. This ambiguity allows the requirement that a community be informed about a project by its proponents to morph into an implicit requirement that the community *demonstrate the capacity* 'to consider the project or program' and 'to develop a clear understanding [of] REDD+ implementations',[359] that is assessed in accordance with externally imposed criteria by the validating body. If a

---

[354] See also S. Young, *Indigenous Peoples, Consent and Rights: Troubling Subjects* (Routledge, 2019).

[355] J. L. Austin, *How to Do Things with Words* (Oxford University Press, 1975).

[356] See Butler, *Gender Trouble: Feminism and the Subversion of Identity*.

[357] A. Mitropoulos, *Contract and Contagion: From Biopolitics to Oikonomia* (Minor Compositions, 2012) p. 20.

[358] See D. G. Carlson, 'How to Do Things with Hegel' (1999) 78 *Texas Law Review* 1377–97; Mitropoulos, *Contract and Contagion* pp. 19–49.

[359] Anderson, *Free, Prior, and Informed Consent in REDD*, p. 26.

348   REDD+ *at the 'Local' Level: Between Rights and Responsibilisation*

community that does not consent to REDD+ is deemed to lack the 'capacity' to understand a project, then the proponents' obligation to 'inform' could be distorted to justify ongoing 'socialisation' of the local community to 'educate' them about the potential benefits of a project they have vetoed.

Moreover, such an implicit requirement (that a community demonstrate to external actors their capacity to properly understand or consider a REDD+ project) can justify external actors assessing – according to their own criteria – the community's decision-making processes and even the epistemological frameworks through which community members understand the world. If such 'capacity' is not deemed to be present, this could justify interventions, for example, the Center for People and Forests guide to FPIC notes that [a]dequate resources will also be needed by rights-holders to build up their capacity to consider the project or program', including 'appropriate training and skills development',[360] which 'should continue throughout the life of the project'.[361] The Center for People and Forests guide to FPIC shows how the question of 'capacity' to give concept also implicitly requires a community to demonstrate that they have particular models of internal governance and decision-making processes, modes of communicating, financial literacy, skill in particular ways of knowing and engaging with the world,[362] as well as a particular relationship with the monetary economy, including the 'capacity to manage funds in a transparent and accountable manner',[363] accounting proficiency and prudent financial planning.[364] While a collective's right to 'use their own decision-making institutions rather than an imposed system'[365] is explicitly affirmed, this right to internal self-governance is also tempered by external expectations of what constitutes proper 'good governance' or 'representation', especially where 'traditional institutions may be seen to be in conflict with international notions and expectations of "representation" and the need to include women, youth and marginalized people in decision-making'.[366] The articulation of consent is thereby also the enactment of what it is intended to demonstrate: a collective subjectivity that is free, self-managing and self-possessed and therefore sufficiently responsible to enter into contractual relations. In this sense, the articulation of consent, in a situation where those consenting could not do otherwise, is a performance that demonstrates a collective responsibilisation as an accountable, contractual subject, in the present and into the future.

---

[360] Ibid.
[361] Ibid., p. 45.
[362] Ibid.
[363] Ibid.
[364] Ibid., p. 46.
[365] Ibid., p. 35.
[366] Ibid.

G CONCLUSION

This chapter has interrogated the space of the 'social' as a complicated domain of governance that seeks to manage the competing demands of different actors at both the 'local' and 'global' level in order to assemble divergent interests and hold them together in a fragile alignment. It has highlighted that the contemporary logic of 'expulsion',[367] which hangs as a spectre over REDD+, is not the only logic at play in REDD+ implementation. Instead, it has suggested that the governance the social in REDD+ is orientated towards 'fixing people in place' and transforming forest peoples into responsibilised environmental service providers in the 'green economy'. This chapter has therefore provided a reading of the key strategies used to manage social concerns – benefit sharing, tenure reform and the right of consultation towards free, prior and informed consent – as mediating the potential tensions between calls for rights 'from below' and demands for responsibilisation 'from above'. A close reading of how these different strategies are discussed in REDD+ discourses and operationalised in practice suggests reasons for concern that the latter (regulatory and governance imperatives rather than the realisation of rights claims) are gaining the most traction in REDD+ implementation. The analysis suggests that while such strategies might assist communities in realising their interests *within* REDD+ projects and may help promote better REDD+ project implementation, they offer only limited possibilities for communities to resist or *oppose* REDD+. For many forest peoples there is nonetheless real value in pursuing such approaches: promoting more inclusive, participatory and rights-based models of REDD+ imple-mentation can make a real material difference to peoples who may have long histories of economic, social and political marginalisation. However, the clear limitations of these calls for benefit-sharing, tenure reform and a right of consult-ation towards FPIC highlights how 'neoliberalism incorporates techniques that domesticate and contain dissent within (certain) parameters', and how practices of dissent and resistance may 'be subject to entanglement within the very processes they seek to contest'.[368] This chapter has shown that these mechanisms should be understood not only as potentially inadequate ameliorative measures but also as having productive effects. The analysis has suggested that these mechanisms may, in fact, operate to create the forms of legibility, subjectivities and social relations that could further consolidate the reorganisation of authority that REDD+ represents. The analysis has particularly highlighted how these safeguard mechanisms work to transform forest peoples into responsibilised subjects of the green economy, and the ways in which international legal frameworks and discourses to protect the rights of Indigenous peoples and 'local communities' are implicated in these processes.

---

[367] See S. Sassen, *Expulsions: Brutality and Complexity in the Global Economy* (Harvard University Press, 2014).

[368] L. M. Coleman, 'The making of docile dissent: Neoliberalism and resistance in Columbia and beyond' (2013) 7(2) *International Political Sociology* 170–87 at 170.

Moreover, realising rights in REDD+ does not address the broader distributional questions raised by carbon markets and how they unequally allocate privileges, obligations and responsibilities. In particular, the schema of rights recognition that is operative in REDD+ is made dangerously conditional on people living in and around forest areas taking action in the name of a global 'common concern', even as the need to structurally transform the political economy that drives deforestation and excessive GHG emissions is obfuscated. In the same way that the offset relation seeks to legitimate environmentally destructive practices in one place by promoting environmental protection elsewhere, the offset relation also seeks to justify and redeem unsustainable lifestyles and consumption and production patterns in one part of the globe through a postulated ideal of 'traditional' forest communities, who are presented as the 'Other' to modernity and as possessing an inherent capacity and desire for ecological management.

However, what is lost in this focus on rights in REDD+ are both the distributional questions about what obligations are imposed on whom to address climate change and the need to push for broader systemic – cultural and ecological – change that rejects the substitutions of the offset economy. In the context of global climate mitigation, the focus on the 'inherent' capacity of Indigenous ecological subjects to act as 'leaders in the struggle to protect and rehabilitate the environment of our shared planet'[369] can operate perversely to undermine the differentiated responsibility of those who have done the most to cause the problem of climate change. Instead of addressing questions of historical and ongoing responsibility for GHG emissions, these mechanisms for managing social concerns are directed towards responsibilising forest peoples to be a certain type of ecological subject, who, can be trusted to protect forests.

Thus, the analysis in this chapter has suggested that these safeguard mechanisms play a critical role in establishing new forms of global authority over forested areas, by reorganising social relations and transforming people who live in and around forested areas into responsibilised 'project participants' and payment for ecosystem services providers in the green economy, thereby facilitating their potential disciplinary inclusion within global carbon markets in ways that risk displacing the social responsibilities of global elites to reduce their own oversized carbon footprints.

---

[369] B. Morse, 'Indigenous rights as a mechanism to promote sustainability' in L. Westra, K. Bosselmann, and R. Westra (eds.), *Reconciling Human Existence with Ecological Integrity* (Earthscan, 2008).

7

Conclusion

Possibilities for Climate Justice and Planetary Co-habitation

The unfolding ecological crisis will inevitably shape our future personal and collective lives. Yet the contours of possible futures are not yet fixed and, indeed, remain urgently contested, even as the disjointed present already foreshadows fragmented elements of climate barbarism, eco-socialism and green capitalism. Inherent in decisions over different legal responses to the climate crisis are fundamental questions about how we organise the forms of sociality – the forms of community and belonging – that give shape to our worlds: what values guide our actions and what it is we value. This book has traced the emergent relations of law, power and authority in one dominant – but not inevitable – future trajectory: the paradigm of the 'green economy' and associated agendas to make nature legible in economic terms and governable through market mechanisms. Its analysis of REDD+ is situated against the background of these broader developments, as REDD+ has widely been described as enabling of, and a key element of, the 'green economy'. In doing so, this book has sought to provide a critique of the sort of world that REDD+ looks forward to and expects.

REDD+ brings forests within international financial flows by commodifying the sequestered carbon emissions saved from avoided deforestation or other forms of forest degradation in the Global South and potentially allowing 'saved' emissions to be used as an 'offset' towards the GHG reduction targets of the Global North. It thus promotes the incorporation and realisation of nature within capitalist modes of valuation, so that nature – reinscribed as 'natural capital' and 'ecosystem services' – can become a new site of accumulation. A key aim of REDD+ implementation is to make nature, and the 'services' and 'functions' it provides, subject to a rationality of aggregate maximum productivity at the global, national and local level. In these processes, new claims to international authority have been authorised and articulated, although these remain in many ways provisional and aspirational. However, such claims to global authority have been partially materialised through institutional and organisational practices, and they have been partially actualised and given shape through the legal forms of property and contract.

This transformational project particularly affects the lives of those living in and around forested areas, and there has been considerable concern to manage the social impacts of REDD+ projects, with the implementation of safeguards seen as a key bastion against dispossession and coercion. However, the main safeguards proposed – benefit sharing, tenure reform and consultation towards FPIC – operate not only in protective ways but also to enact specific modes of governing forest communities by 'fixing them in place' as responsibilised subjects within the 'green economy'. This book showed how power in REDD+ is exercised through 'conducting the conduct' of national-level and local-level actors and by structuring a field of incentives so these actors 'behave as they ought'.[1] The logic of the offset, whereby pockets of sustainable or regenerative activities in the Global South legitimate additional polluting activities in the Global North, reappears in the logic of cultural difference, where the postulated alterity of forest peoples, and their presumed inherent capacity and desire for ecological management, operates to redeem the paradigmatic subject of modernity, who is ensnared in unsustainable relations of production and consumption. Obscured by this logic are both the distributional questions about what obligations are imposed on whom to address climate change and the need to push for broader systemic – cultural and ecological – change that rejects the substitutions of the offset economy. Rather than rejecting the extractivist mindset, REDD+ remains embedded a paradigm that sees nature as a resource to be exploited. Instead of reorganising production *within limits*, the carbon offsetting model imposes flexible limits that can be transcended, while concurrently seeking to intensify nature's capacity to 'repair' and promoting the maximisation of nature's sequestration capacities.

Statements made by community members impacted by the Australian-sponsored REDD+ demonstration in Indonesia, the Kalimantan Forest Carbon Project, perhaps articulate the inequality of the relations established by such offset schemes most poignantly. They write of the grassroots work to rehabilitate the project site through revegetation and ongoing resistance to palm oil and mining expansion in the area, noting that '[w]e have become ... part of the solution to climate change'.[2] Yet simultaneously they speak of how their initiatives 'have not been regarded as an important contribution in the global solution to climate change'.[3] There is, they claim, no global interest in learning from '[t]he initiatives of people throughout the world [that] constitute a model for managing the environment in a way that could save our families and all the inhabitants of the earth'.[4] Alongside the marginalisation

---

[1] T. M. Li, 'Fixing non-market subjects: Governing land and population in the Global South' (2014) 18 *Foucault Studies* 34–48.

[2] Petak Danum Kalimantan Tengah, *Our Land Is Not a Carbon Toilet for Dirty Industries of Developed Countries*, 2012, copy on file with author.

[3] Ibid.

[4] Ibid.

Conclusion: Possibilities for Climate Justice and Planetary Co-habitation   353

of these environmental knowledges they speak of the injustice that arises '[w]hen developed countries don't want to stop their own carbon emissions, [and] those who are most innocent have to shoulder the entire burden'.[5] Their comments highlight the messy entanglements that underpin a global political economy of unequal ecological exchange. Layered on top of these unequal exchanges is the ongoing slow attritional violence of already occurring climatic change and its impacts on local food production that exists alongside fears of further livelihood disruption from climate mitigation projects.

Forests are, both materially and metaphorically, a productive site for the examination of questions of authority and the process of authorisation, because they have physically and symbolically been sites of contested authority. The word 'forest', Robert Progue Harrison argues, originates from a judicial term, the etymology of which most likely derives from the Latin *foris*, meaning 'outside' or *forestare*, meaning 'to keep out, to place off limits, to exclude'.[6] In early English law, the term thus designated not a place or ecosystem but a jurisdiction, which by an exercise of royal prerogative was placed off limits from the common law.[7] The demand for 'deforestation' articulated in the thirteenth-century Charter of the Forest – the 'missing sister' of the Magna Carta – was a call for such areas to no longer be subject to the King's authority and instead to be returned to the commons.[8] The administrative category of 'forests' was globalised around the world through practices of colonisation. In Southeast Asia, for example, the idea of state territorial sovereignty over land designated as 'forests' only emerged in the nineteenth century, often through processes of colonial administration. Thus, as Nancy Peluso and Peter Vandergeest show, the 'assumption of state authority over forests is based on a relatively recent convergence of historical circumstances', and in many ways forests remain spaces where the claimed authority of the state has only actualised in limited ways.[9] Therefore, as anthropologist James Scott describes, forested spaces were often sites of escape or resistance, of self-governance, at the peripheries of and outside the territorial control of early state forms.[10] Even today, forests continue to be described as 'hinterlands'.

On a more symbolic register, trees are, as Margaret Davis has explored, imbued with metaphorical, imaginary and ontological characteristics, such that they are in

---

[5] Ibid.

[6] R. P. Harrison, *Forests: The Shadow of Civilisation* (The University of Chicago Press, 1992) p. 69.

[7] S. Dorsett and S. McVeigh, *Jurisdiction* (Routledge, 2012) p. 46.

[8] P. Linebaugh, *The Magna Carta Manifesto: Liberties and the Commons for All* (University of California Press, 2008).

[9] N. L. Peluso and P. Vandergeest, 'Genealogies of the political forest and customary rights in Indonesia, Malaysia, and Thailand' (2001) 60(3) *The Journal of Asian Studies* 761 at 762.

[10] J. Scott, *The Art of Not Being Governed: An Anarchist History of Upland Southeast Asia* (Yale University Press, 2009).

354 *Conclusion: Possibilities for Climate Justice and Planetary Co-habitation*

fact 'symbolically overloaded'.[11] Peter Goodrich points to how the tree has operated as a symbol for proper genealogy, consanguinity and 'things inherited through the lineal and carefully grounded degrees of familial and juridical belonging', and has thus been used as a metaphor in the common and civil law traditions for the authorised and pre-given place of the law.[12] In contrast to the singular tree, the forest has been construed as the 'other' or the 'periphery' of the city, and of civilisation.[13] Thus the imaginary of the forest has provided 'an outlying realm of opacity which has allowed civilisation to estrange itself, enchant itself, terrify itself, ironize itself'.[14] This mythology of forests as 'frontier' spaces persists in the present: representing space that marks a boundary between civilisation and the wilderness, between law and order and lawlessness. Frontier spaces are, as Angela Mitropoulos writes, spaces characterised by an 'unmissable terrain of conflict', where what is at stake is the reinscription or reimposition of the legal form of value and the establishment of contractual convention, and questions of origin and lineage are nowhere more disputed and uneasy.[15]

For law, forests are thus physically and metaphorically liminal frontier spaces. They are sites constructed as in need of the imposition of law, to create order and delineate rights and entitlements. But they are also spaces where the boundaries of law and property risk being undone, as sites that threaten to dissolve the bonds and institutions of the civic law. Therefore, it is not surprising that many narratives of forests foreground rival articulations of law and justice through 'tale[s] of forest rights, invocations of the commons, and an on-going centuries-old resistance to enclosure in all its legal, rhetorical and political forms'.[16] In this sense, the forest is also, as Cristy Clark and John Page highlight, an 'ontological *idea*, a legal memory of forest "liberties and customs"'.[17] They suggest two distinct metaphors: firstly of the *legal forest*, as 'an abstract positivist construct, a domineering paradigm where rights are technical, the "lawscape" detached, and private rights prevail', but also a competing notion of the *lawful forest*, which 'aspires for the many, not the few, a relational context where public or common rights resist private enclosure through occupation or performance'.[18] In this way, forests can be envisioned, literally and imaginatively, not as the periphery of law, but as the site of *another* law, which has the potential to interrupt, reformulate and remake international law.

---

[11] M. Davies, 'The consciousness of trees' (2015) 27(2) *Law & Literature* 217–35 at 218–19.
[12] P. Goodrich, 'Visive powers: Colours, trees and genres of jurisdiction' (2008) 2(2) *Law and Humanities* 213–31.
[13] See Harrison, *Forests: The Shadow of Civilisation*.
[14] Ibid., p. xi.
[15] A. Mitropoulos, *Contract and Contagion: From Biopolitics to Oikonomia* (Minor Compositions, 2012) p. 99.
[16] C. Clark and J. Page, 'Of protest, the commons, and customary public rights: An ancient tale of the lawful forest' (2019) 42(1) *University of New South Wales Law Journal* 26–59 at 27.
[17] Ibid. (emphasis in the original).
[18] Ibid.

Conclusion: Possibilities for Climate Justice and Planetary Co-habitation 355

The climate crisis is a socio-ecological biocrisis; it represents the point of tension between the limits of the atmosphere to absorb greenhouse gases and our ravenous capitalistic culture fixated on its desire for 'growth' powered by fossil fuels. The contradictions at the heart of debates on climate change are between capital and life, and between growth and limits.[19] Addressing these tensions will require interrogating the norms of development and growth that structure international law. It will also involve questioning the ways in which law is already complicit in the production of unsustainability rather than simply a benign tool for its amelioration. Additionally, this task calls for greater scepticism about the expansion of biopolitical regimes in the name of 'protecting' life, and a deep interrogation of the 'ways of life' that are protected and normalised through them, and a thoughtful exploration of alternative 'ways of living on this planet'.[20] Addressing the climate crisis also requires that we challenge the way commonality is assumed or posited 'from above' in a world deeply stratified by economic, gendered and racialised inequalities and hierarchies, and instead pay attention to the ways in which forms of commonality are built 'from below'. In concluding, addressing the climate crisis may also demand that we think beyond the false polarity of resource exploitation and stewardship – modalities of anthropogenic governance that presume *mastery over* nature – and instead learn about other relational ways of *living with* nature. Perhaps posing these questions – about how we live in and with nature, how we live in relation with one another and how we make worlds and our place in them – will present simple openings to a more engaged politics of environmental justice.

[19] Turbulence, 'Life in limbo?' (2009) 5 *Turbulence: Ideas for Movement* 3–7 at 6.
[20] F. Guattari, *The Three Ecologies* (Continuum International Publishing Group, 2008) p. 20.

Bibliography

TREATIES

Convention on Biological Diversity, opened for signature 5 June 1992, 1760 UNTS 79 (entered into force 29 December 1993)

Doha Amendment to the Kyoto Protocol, adopted on 8 December 2012, UNTS XXVII.7.c (entered into force 31 December 2020)

International Labour Organization (ILO), *Convention (No 169) Concerning Indigenous and Tribal Peoples in Independent Countries*, opened for signature 27 June 1989, 1650 UNTS 383 (entered into force 5 September 1991)

International Tropical Timber Agreement, 1983, opened for signature 18 November 1983, 1393 UNTS 119 (entered into force 1 April 1985)

International Tropical Timber Agreement, 1994, opened for signature 1 April 1994, 1955 UNTS 81 (entered into force 1 January 1997)

International Tropical Timber Agreement, 2006, opened for signature 3 April 2006, 2797 UNTS 75 (entered into force 7 December 2011)

Kyoto Protocol to the United Nations Framework Convention on Climate Change, opened for signature 16 March 1998, 2303 UNTS 148 (entered into force on 16 February 2005)

Nagoya Protocol on Access to Genetic Resources and the Fair and Equitable Sharing of Benefits Arising from Their Utilization to the Convention on Biological Diversity, opened for signature 2 February 2011, UN Doc UNEP/CBD/COP/DEC/X/1, annex I (entered into force 12 October 2014)

Paris Agreement, opened for signature on 22 April 2016, UNTS XXVII.7.d (entered into force 4 November 2016)

Southern African Development Community, *Protocol on Forestry*, 3 October 2002 (entered into force 17 July 2009)

United Nations Framework Convention on Climate Change, opened for signature 4 June 1992, 771 UNTS 107 (entered into force 21 March 1994)

UNFCCC DECISIONS

Decision 1/CP.1, 'The Berlin Mandate: Review of the adequacy of Article 4, paragraph 2(a) and (b), of the Convention, including proposals related to a protocol and decisions on follow up' FCCC/CP/1995/7/Add.1 (6 June 1995)

358   *Bibliography*

Decision 5/CP.6, 'The Bonn Agreement on the implementation of the Buenos Aires Plan of Action' FCCC/CP/2001/5 (29 October 2001)

Decision 15/CP.7, 'Principles, nature and scope of the mechanisms pursuant to Articles 6, 12 and 17 of the Kyoto Protocol', FCCC/CP/2001/13/Add.2 (21 January 2002)

Decision 16/CP.7, 'Guidelines for the implementation of Article 6 of the Kyoto Protocol', FCCC/CP/2001/13/Add.2 (21 January 2002)

Decision 17/CP.7, 'Modalities and procedures for a clean development mechanism, as defined in Article 12 of the Kyoto Protocol', FCCC/CP/2001/13/Add.2 (21 January 2002)

Decision 18/CP.7, 'Modalities, rules and guidelines for emissions trading under Article 17 of the Kyoto Protocol', FCCC/CP/2001/13/Add.2 (21 January 2002)

Decision 19/CP.9, 'Modalities and procedures for afforestation and reforestation project activities under the clean development mechanism in the first commitment period of the Kyoto Protocol' FCCC/CP/2003/6/Add.2 (30 March 2004)

Decision 1/CP.13 'Bali Action Plan' FCCC/CP/2007/6/Add.1 (14 March 2008)

Decision 2/CP.13, 'Reducing emissions from deforestation in developing countries: Approaches to stimulate action', FCCC/CP/2007/6/Add.1 (14 March 2008)

Decision 2/CP.15 'Copenhagen Accord' FCCC/CP/2009/11/Add.1 (30 March 2010)

Decision 4/CP.15 'Methodological guidance for activities relating to reducing emissions from deforestation and forest degradation and the role of conservation, sustainable management of forests and enhancement of forest carbon stocks in developing countries' FCCC/CP/2009/11/Add.1 (30 March 2010)

Decision 1/CP.16 'The Cancun Agreements: Outcome of the work of the Ad Hoc Working Group on Long-term Cooperative Action under the Convention' FCCC/CP/2010/7/Add.1 (15 March 2011)

Decision 2/CP.17 'Outcome of the work of the Ad Hoc Working Group on Long-Term Cooperative Action under the Convention' FCCC/CP/2011/9/Add.1 (15 March 2012)

Decision 12/CP.17 'Guidance on systems for providing information on how safeguards are addressed and respected and modalities relating to forest reference emission levels and forest reference levels as referred to in Decision 1/CP.16' FCCC/CP/2011/9/Add.2 (15 March 2012)

Decision 1/CP.18, 'Agreed outcome pursuant to the Bali Action Plan', FCCC/CP/2012/8/Add.1 (28 February 2013)

Decision 9/CP.19, 'Work programme on result-based finance to progress the full implementation of the activities referred to in Decision 1/CP.16, paragraph 70', FCCC/CP/2013/10/Add.1 (31 January 2014)

Decision 10/CP.19, 'Coordination of support for the implementation of activities in relation to mitigation actions in the forest sector by developing countries, including institutional arrangements', FCCC/CP/2013/10/Add.1 (31 January 2014)

Decision 11/CP.19, 'Modalities for national forest monitoring systems', FCCC/CP/2013/10/Add.1 (31 January 2014)

Decision 12/CP.19, 'The timing and frequency of presentation of the summary of information on how all the safeguards referred to in Decision 1/CP.16, appendix I, are being addressed and respected', FCCC/CP/2013/10/Add.1 (31 January 2014)

Decision 13/CP.19, 'Guidelines and procedures for the technical assessment of submissions from Parties on proposed forest reference emissions levels and/or forest reference levels', FCCC/CP/2013/10/Add.1 (31 January 2014)

Decision 14/CP.19, 'Modalities for measuring, reporting and verifying', FCCC/CP/2013/10/Add.1 (31 January 2014)

Decision 15/CP.19, 'Addressing the drivers of deforestation and forest degradation', FCCC/CP/2013/10/Add.1 (31 January 2014)

Bibliography

Decision 16/CP.21, 'Alternative policy approaches, such as joint mitigation and adaptation approaches for the integral and sustainable management of forests', FCCC/CP/2015/10/Add.3 (29 January 2016)

Decision 17/CP.21, 'Further guidance on ensuring transparency, consistency, comprehensiveness and effectiveness when informing on how all the safeguards referred to in Decision 1/CP.16, appendix I, are being address and respected', FCCC/SBSTA/2015/L.5/Add.3 (29 January 2016)

Decision 18/CP.21, 'Methodological issues related to non-carbon benefits resulting from the implementation of the activities referred to in Decision 1/CP.16, paragraph 70', FCCC/2015/10/Add.3 (29 January 2016)

Draft Decision -/CP.15 Policy 'Approaches and positive incentives on issues relating to reducing emissions from deforestation and forest degradation in developing countries; and the role of conservation, sustainable management of forests and enhancement of forest carbon sinks in developing countries' FCCC/AWGLCA/2009/L.7/Add.6 (15 December 2009)

Decision 1/CMP.1 'Consideration of commitments for subsequent periods for Parties included in Annex I to the Convention under Article 3, paragraph 9, of the Kyoto Protocol' FCCC/KP/CMP/2005/8/Add.1 (30 March 2006)

Decision 2/CMP.1 'Principles, nature and scope of the mechanisms pursuant to Article 6, 12 and 17 of the Kyoto Protocol' FCCC/KP/CMP/2005/8/Add.1 (30 March 2006)

Decision 16/CMP.1 'Land use, land-use change and forestry' FCCC/KP/CMP/2005/8/Add.3 (30 March 2006)

Decision 1/CMP.8, 'Amendment to the Kyoto Protocol pursuant to its Article 3, paragraph 9 (the Doha Amendment)', FCCC/KP/CMP/2012/13/Add.1 (28 February 2013)

Decision 8/CMA.1 'Matters relating to Article 6 of the Paris Agreement and paragraphs 36–40 of Decision 1/CP.21', FCCC/PA/CMA/2018/3/Add.1 (19 March 2019)

Green Climate Fund, 'Decision B.08/08', *Decisions of the Board – Eighth Meeting of the Board 14–17 October 2014*, GCF/B.08/45 (3 December 2014)

Green Climate Fund, 'Decision B.14/03', *Decisions of the Board – Fourteenth Meeting of the Board 12–14 October 2016*, GCF/B.14/17 (2 November 2016)

OTHER REPORTS AND RESOLUTIONS BY OR FOR INTERNATIONAL BODIES

Alston, P., *Climate Change and Poverty – Report of the Special Rapporteur on Extreme Poverty and Human Rights*, A/HRC/41/39 (25 June 2019)

Anaya, J., *Report of the Special Rapporteur on the Rights of Indigenous Peoples, James Anaya*, Human Rights Council, 21st session, A/HRC/21/47 (6 July 2012)

Anaya, J., *Report of the Special Rapporteur on the Rights of Indigenous Peoples, James Anaya: Extractive industries and Indigenous peoples*, Human Rights Council, 24th session, A/HRC/24/41 (1 July 2013)

Anaya, J., *Report of the Special Rapporteur on the Situation of Human Rights and Fundamental Freedoms of Indigenous Peoples, James Anaya*, General Assembly, A/HRC/12/34 (15 July 2009)

Beyani, C., *Protection of and Assistance to Internally Displaced Persons*, A/66/285 (9 August 2011)

Case of the Saramaka People v. Suriname, Inter-American Court of Human Rights, Series C No. 172, Judgment of 28 November 2007

Bibliography

Committee on Economic, Social and Cultural Rights, *Statement on Climate Change and the Covenant* (2018)

The Concept of Indigenous Peoples: Background Paper Prepared for the Secretariat of the Permanent Forum on Indigenous Issues (2004) PFII/2004/WS.1/3

Convention on Biological Diversity, *Who Are Local Communities?* UNEP/CBD/WS-CB/LAC/1/INF/5 (16 November 2006)

Crépeau, F., *Report of the Special Rapporteur on the Human Rights of Migrants*, A/67/299 (13 August 2012)

Daes, E.-I. A., *Prevention of Discrimination and Protection of Indigenous Peoples: Indigenous Peoples' Permanent Sovereignty over Natural Resources: Final Report of the Special Rapporteur*, E/CN.4/2004/30 (2004)

Daes, E.-I. A., *Report of the Working Group on Indigenous Populations on Its Fifteenth Session*, Sub-Commission on the Prevention of Discrimination and Protection of Minorities, E/CN.4/Sub.2/1997/14 (13 August 1997)

Daes, E.-I. A. and A. Eide, *Working Paper on the Relationship and Distinction between the Rights of Persons Belonging to Minorities and Those of Indigenous Peoples*, Economic and Social Council, Commission on Human Rights, Sub-commission on the Promotion and Protection of Human Rights, E/CN.4/Sub.2/2000/10 (19 July 2000)

Declaration of the United Nations Conference on the Human Environment (Report of the United Nations Conference on the Human Environment, Stockholm, 5–16 June 1972) A/CONF.48/14/Rev.1

Draft Declaration on the Rights of Indigenous Peoples (1994) UN Doc. E/CN.4/Sub.2/1994/2/Add.1

Economic and Social Council Resolution 2000/35, *Report on the Fourth Session of the Intergovernmental Forum on Forests*, 46th plen mtg, E/RES/2000/35 (18 October 2000)

Elver, H., *Interim Report of the Special Rapporteur on the Right to Food*, A/70/287 (5 August 2015)

The Extent to Which Climate Change Policies and Projects Adhere to the Standards Set Forth in the United Nations Declaration on the Rights of Indigenous Peoples: Concept Note Submitted by the Permanent Forum Special Rapporteurs, United Nations Permanent Forum on Indigenous Issues, Eighth Session, E/C.19/2009/5 (25 March 2009)

Final Study on Indigenous Peoples and the Right to Participate in Decision-Making: Report of the Expert Mechanism on the Right of Indigenous Peoples, Human Rights Council, Expert Mechanism on the Rights of Indigenous Peoples, 4th session, A/HRC/EMRIP/2011/2 (26 May 2011)

Forest Carbon Partnership Facility, *Carbon Fund: Methodological Framework* (Revised final, 22 June 2016)

Forest Carbon Partnership Facility, *R-PP Template Version 6, for Country Use* (April 20, 2012)

Forest Carbon Partnership Fund Participants Committee, Resolution PC/18/2014/2 'Adoption of FCPF General Conditions Applicable to Emissions Reductions Payment Agreement', 18th Meeting (PC18), Arusha, Tanzania 31 October–4 November 2014

Free, Prior and Informed Consent: A Human Rights-Based Approach – Study on the Expert Mechanism on the Rights of Indigenous Peoples, General Assembly, A/HRC/39/62 (10 August 2018)

General Assembly, *Provisional Record of the Thirty-Fifth Meeting*, 43rd session, A/43/PV.35 (25 October 1988)

General Assembly Resolution 41/128, *Declaration on the Right to Development*, 97th plen mtg, A/RES/41/128 (4 December 1986)

Bibliography

General Assembly Resolution 43/53, *Protection of Global Climate for Present and Future Generations of Mankind*, 70th plen mtg, A/RES/43/53 (6 December 1988)

General Assembly Resolution 44/228, *United Nations Conference on Environment and Development*, 85th plen mtg, A/RES/44/228 (22 December 1989)

General Assembly Resolution 61/295, *United Nations Declaration on the Rights of Indigenous Peoples*, UN GAOR 61st sess, 107th plen mtg, Supp No 49, UN Doc A/61/67 (13 September 2007)

General Assembly Resolution 62/98, *Non-Legally Binding Instrument on All Types of Forests*, UN GAOR 62nd sess, 74th plen mtg, Agenda Item 54, A/RES/62/98 (31 January 2008)

General Assembly Resolution 66/288, *The Future We Want*, UN GAOR 66th sess, 123rd plen mtg, Agenda Item 19, Supp No 49, A/RES/66/288 (11 September 2012)

General Assembly Resolution 70/1, *Transforming Our World: The 2030 Agenda for Sustainable Development*, UNGAOR 70th sess, 4th plen mtg, UN Doc A/RES/70/1 (21 October 2015)

General Assembly Resolution 1803, *Permanent Sovereignty over Natural Resources*, UNGAOR 17th sess, 1194th plen mtg, Agenda Item 39, UN Doc. A/5217 (14 December 1962)

General Assembly Resolution 3202(S-VI), *Programme of Action on the Establishment of a New International Economic Order*, A/RES/S-6/3203 (1 May 1974)

General Assembly Resolution 3281(XXIX), *Charter of Economic Rights and Duties of States*, Twenty-Ninth Session, Agenda Item 48, A/RES/29/3281 (12 December 1974)

General Assembly Resolution S-18/3, *Declaration on International Economic Co-operation, in particular the Revitalization of Economic Growth and Development of the Developing Countries*, 11th plenary meeting, A/RES/S-18/3 (1 May 1990)

Green Climate Fund, *Green Climate Fund support for the early phases of REDD+*, GCF/B.17/16 (2 July 2017)

Green Climate Fund, *Initial Social Model and Performance Measurement Framework for REDD+ Result-based Payments*, GCF/B.08/08/Rev.01 (17 October 2014)

Green Climate Fund, *Support for REDD-plus*, GCF/B.14/03 (10 October 2016)

Human Rights Committee, *General Comment No. 36 - Article 6: Right to Life*, CCPR/C/GC/36 (3 September 2019)

Id Balkassm, H. and P. Hasteh, *Study on the Extent to Which Climate Change Policies and Project Adhere to the Standards Set Forth in the United Nations Declaration on the Rights of Indigenous Peoples: Note by the Secretariat*, United Nations Permanent Forum on Indigenous Issues, Ninth Session, E/C.19/2010/7 (2 February 2010)

International Bank for Reconstruction and Development, *Charter Establishing the Forest Carbon Partnership Facility* (23 November 2015)

International Bank for Reconstruction and Development, *General Conditions Applicable to Emission Reductions Payment Agreements for the Forest Carbon Partnership Facility Emission Reductions Programs* (1 November 2014)

International Law Association, *Sofia Conference: Rights of Indigenous Peoples, Final Report* (2012)

International Union for the Conservation of Nature, *The Durban Action Plan* Revised Version, March 2004, cmsdata.iucn.org/downloads/durbanactionen.pdf

Kälin, W., *Report of the Representative of the Secretary-General on the Human Rights of Internally Displaced Persons*, A/65/282 (11 August 2010)

Knox, J., *Report of the Special Rapporteur on the Issue of Human Rights Obligations Relating to the Enjoyment of a Safe, Clean, Healthy and Sustainable Environment*, A/HRC/31/52 (1 February 2016)

Martínez Cobo, J. R., *Study on the Problem of Discrimination against Indigenous Populations*, UN Doc E/CN.4/Sub.2/1986/7 and Add. 1–4 (1986)

Bibliography

Ministerial Declaration and Message from the United Nations Forum on Forests to the World Summit on Sustainable Development, A/CONF.199/PC/8 (19 March 2002)

Murase, S., *Second Report on the Protection of the Atmosphere by Special Rapporteur*, International Law Commission, 67th session, A/CN.4/681 (2 March 2015)

Non-Legally Binding Authoritative Statement of Principles for a Global Consensus on the Management, Conservation and Sustainable Development of All Types of Forests, Report of the United Nations Conference on Environment and Development, Rio de Janeiro, A/CONF.151/26 (Vol. III) (14 August 1992)

Permanent Forum on Indigenous Issues: Report on the Seventh Session (21 April–2 May 2008), Economic and Social Council, E/2008/43, E/C.19/2008/13 (14 May 2008)

Report of the Expert Group Meeting on Identification of Principles of International Law for Sustainable Development, United Nations Commission on Sustainable Development, Geneva, 26–28 September 1995

Report of the International Workshop on Methodologies Regarding Free, Prior and Informed Consent and Indigenous Peoples (New York, 17–19 January 2005), UN Permanent Forum on Indigenous Issues, Fourth Session, E/C.19/2005/3 (17 February 2006)

Report of the Tenth Session, United Nations Forum on Forests (4 February 2011 and 8 and 9 April 2013) E/2013/42, E/CN.18/2013/18

Rio Declaration on Environment and Development, UN Doc. A/CONF.151/26 (vol. I); 31 ILM 874 (1992)

Rolnik, R., *Report of the Special Rapporteur on Adequate Housing As a Component of the Right to an Adequate Standard of Living, and on the Right to Non-Discrimination in This Context*, A/64/255 (6 August 2009)

Sena, P. K., M. Cunningham, and B. Xavier, *Indigenous People's Rights and Safeguards in Projects Related to Reducing Emissions from Deforestation and Forest Degradation: Note by the Secretariat*, UN ESCOR, Permanent Forum on Indigenous Issues, 12th sess, Agenda Item 5, UN Doc E/C.19/2013/7 (5 February 2013)

Tauli-Corpuz, V., *Report of the Special Rapporteur of the Human Rights Council on the Rights of Indigenous Peoples, Victoria Tauli-Corpuz*, General Assembly, A/71/229 (29 July 2016)

Tauli-Corpuz, V., *Report of the Special Rapporteur on the Rights of Indigenous Peoples*, A/HRC/36/46 (1 November 2017)

Tauli-Corpuz, V. and L.-A. Baer, *Results of the Copenhagen Meeting of the Conference of the Parties to the United Nations Framework Convention on Climate Change; Implications for Indigenous Peoples' Local Adaptation and Mitigation Measures*, Permanent Forum on Indigenous Issues, 9th session, E/C.19/2010/18 (2 March 2010)

Tauli-Corpuz, V. and A. Lynge, *Impact of Climate Change Mitigation Measures on Indigenous Peoples and Their Territories and Lands*, United Nations Permanent Forum on Indigenous Issues, Seventh Session, E/C.19/2008/10 (20 March 2008)

Trail Smelter Arbitration (USA v Canada, 1938/1941), UN.RIAA, Vol. III

UNFCCC, *Financing Options for the Full Implementation of Results-Based Actions Relating to the Activities Referred to in Decision 1/CP.16, paragraph 70, Including Related Modalities and Procedures: Technical Paper*, FCCC/TP/2012/3 (26 July 2012)

UNFCCC, *Issues Relating to Reducing Emissions from Deforestation in Developing Countries and Recommendations on Any Further Process. Submissions from Parties*, FCCC/SBSTA/2006/MISC.5 (11 April 2006) and Add.2 (10 May 2006)

UNFCCC, *Joint Submission by Costa Rica and Papua New Guinea: Reducing Emissions from Deforestation in Developing Countries: Approaches to Stimulate Action: Submission from Parties*, FCCC/CP/2005/MISC.1 (11 November 2005)

Bibliography

UNFCCC, *Reducing Emissions from Deforestation in Developing Countries: Approaches to Stimulate Action: Draft Conclusions Proposed by the President*, FCCC/CP/2005/L.2 (6 December 2005)

UNFCCC, *Reducing Emissions from Deforestation in Developing Countries: Approaches to Stimulate Action: Submissions from Parties*, FCCC/CP/2005/MISC.1 (11 November 2005)

UNFCCC, *Report of the Subsidiary Body for Scientific and Technological Advice on Its Twenty-Ninth Session, Held in Poznań from 1 to 10 December 2008*, FCCC/SBSTA/2008/13 (17 February 2009)

UNFCCC, *Report on the Second Workshop on Reducing Emissions from Deforestation in Developing Countries: Note by the Secretariat*, FCCC/SBSTA/2007/3 (17 April 2007)

UNFCCC, *Report on the Workshop on Methodological Issues Relating to Reducing Emissions from Deforestation and Forest Degradation in Developing Countries: A Note from the Secretariat*, FCCC/SBSTA/2008/11 (8 September 2008)

UNFCCC, *Report on a Workshop on Reducing Emissions from Deforestation in Developing Countries: Note by the Secretariat*, FCCC/SBSTA/2006/10 (11 October 2006)

UNFCCC, *Views on the Range of Topics and Other Relevant Information Relating to Reducing Emissions from Deforestation in Developing Countries. Submissions from Parties*, FCCC/SBSTA/2007/MISC.2 (2 March 2007) and Add.1 (3 April 2007)

UNFCCC, *Issues Relating to Indigenous Peoples and Local Communities for the Development and Application of Methodologies: Submissions from Parties*, FCCC/SBSTA/2009/MISC.1 (10 March 2009), Add.1 (17 April 2009) and Add.2 (27 June 2009)

UNFCCC, *Joint Submission under the Cancun Agreements: Reducing Emissions from Deforestation and Forest Degradation in Developing Countries, Submission by Australia and Indonesia to SBSTA*, FCCC/SBSTA/2011/MISC.7/Add.3 (9 December 2011)

UNFCCC, *Report on the Expert Meeting on Methodological Issues Relating to Reference Emission Levels and Reference Levels: Note by the Secretariat*, FCCC/SBSTA/2009/2 (14 May 2009)

UNFCCC, *Submission by the Plurinational State of Bolivia to the Ad Hoc Working Group on Long Term Co-operative Action*, FCCC/AWGLCA/2010/MISC.2 (30 April 2010)

UNFCCC, *Submission by the Plurinational State of Bolivia, Joint Mitigation and Adaptation Mechanism: 'Sustainable Forest Life'* (December 2011)

UNFCCC, *Submission of Views by the Democratic Republic of Congo on Behalf of the Coalition for Rainforest Nations on Article 6, paragraph 2 of the Paris Agreement. Views on Guidance on Cooperative Approaches* (2017)

UNFCCC, *Submission of Views by the Republic of Rwanda on Behalf of the Member States of the Central African Forestry Commission (COMIFAC) on APA Agenda Item 3* (2017)

UNFCCC, *Synthesis Report on Information on Various Approaches in Enhancing the Cost-Effectiveness of, and Promoting, Mitigation Actions: Note by the Secretariat*, FCCC/AWGLCA/2011/4 (30 March 2011)

UNFCCC, *Synthesis Report on the Aggregate Effects of the Intended Nationally Determined Contributions: Note by the Secretariat*, FCCC/CP/2015/7 (30 October 2015)

UNFCCC, *Views on a Workplan for the Ad Hoc Working Group on the Durban Platform for Enhanced Action: Submissions from Parties*, FCCC/ADP/2012/MISC.3 (30 April 2012)

UN-REDD Programme, *Background Paper for the Expert Meeting: Options for Addressing Tenure under REDD+* (25–27 February 2013)

UN-REDD Programme, *Framework Document* (2008)

UN-REDD Programme, *Harmonization of Readiness Components: Note by the Secretariat* (October 2009), UN-REDD/PB3/7

364 Bibliography

UN-REDD Programme, *Legal Companion to the UN-REDD Programme Guidelines on Free, Prior and Informed Consent (FPIC): International Law and Jurisprudence Affirming the Requirement of FPIC* (2013)

UN-REDD Programme, *UN-REDD Programme Guidelines on Free, Prior and Informed Consent* (2013)

UN-REDD Programme, *UN-REDD Programme Operational Guidance: Engagement of Indigenous Peoples & Other Forest Dependent Communities* (2009)

UN-REDD Programme and Forest Carbon Partnership Facility, *Guidelines on Stakeholder Engagement in REDD+ Readiness with a Focus on the Participation of Indigenous peoples and Other Forest-Dependent Communities* (20 April 2012)

UN-REDD Programme, *Forest Tenure and Rights of Indigenous Peoples: Promoting Forest & Land Tenure Governance and the Rights of Indigenous Peoples & Forest Communities along REDD+ Implementation* (1 June 2017, modified 4 July 2018)

UN-REDD Programme, *UN-REDD Programme Strategic Framework 2016–2020*

UN-REDD Programme, *The UN-REDD Programme Strategy 2011–2015* (2011)

Voluntary Guidelines on the Responsible Governance of Tenure of Land, Fisheries, and Forests in the Context of National Food Security (Committee on World Food Security and the Food and Agricultural Organization of the United Nations, 2012)

Working Paper on the Relationship and Distinction between the Rights of Persons Belonging to Minorities and Those of Indigenous Peoples, E/CN.4/Sub.2/2000/10 (19 July 2000)

The World Bank, *Environmental and Social Framework* (2017) pubdocs.worldbank.org/en/ 837721522762050108/Environmental-and-Social-Framework.pdf

The World Bank, *Environmental and Social Standard 7: Indigenous Peoples/Sub-Sahara African Historically Underserved Traditional Local Communities* (2017)

The World Bank, *Operational Directive 4.20: Indigenous Peoples* (September 1991)

The World Bank, *Operational Policy 4.10: Indigenous Peoples* (July 2005)

BOOKS, CHAPTERS IN BOOKS, JOURNAL ARTICLES, REPORTS AND NEWS ITEMS

A REDD+ Jurisdictional Approach to Achieve Green Development in Indonesia (Bandan Pengelola REDD+, 2014)

Abrahamsen, R., 'The power of partnerships in global governance' (2004) 25(8) *Third World Quarterly* 1453–67

Ackerman, F., B. Biewald, D. White, T. Woolf, and W. Moomaw, 'Grandfathering and coal plant emissions: The cost of cleaning up the Clean Air Act' (1999) 27(15) *Energy Policy* 929–40

Adams, B. and G. Luchsinger, *Climate Justice for a Changing Planet: A Primer for Policy Makers and NGOs* (UN Non-Governmental Liaison Service, 2009)

Adelman, S., 'Tropical forests and climate change: A critique of green governmentality' (2015) 11(2) *International Journal of Law in Context* 195–212

Affolder, N., 'A market for treaties' (2010) 11(1) *Chicago Journal of International Law* 159–96

Affolder, N., 'Transnational carbon contracting: Why law's invisibility matters' in C. Cutler and T. Dietz (eds.), *The Politics of Private Transnational Governance by Contract* (Routledge, 2017), pp. 215–236

Affolder, N., 'Transnational conservation contracts' (2012) 25(2) *Leiden Journal of International Law* 443–60

Bibliography

Affolder, N. A., 'The private life of environmental treaties' (2009) 103(3) *American Journal of International Law* 510–25

'After Paris, UN's new "light touch" role on markets to help spawn carbon clubs', *CarbonPulse*, 15 December 2015 carbon-pulse.com/13415/

Agarwal, A. and S. Narain, *Global Warming in an Unequal World: A Case for Environmental Colonialism* (Global Network for Human Rights and the Environment, 1990)

Agrawal, A., 'Environmentality: Community, intimate government, and the making of environmental subjects in Kumaon, India' (2005) 46(2) *Current Anthropology* 161–90

Agrawal, A., *Environmentality: Technologies of Government and the Making of Subjects* (Duke University Press, 2005)

Agrawal, A. and C. C. Gibson, 'Enchantment and disenchantment: The role of community in natural resource conservation' (1999) 27(4) *World Development* 629–49

Agrawal, A. and E. Ostrom, 'Collective action, property rights, and decentralisation in resource use in India and Nepal' (2001) 29(4) *Politics and Society* 485–514

Alam, S., S. Atapattu, C. G. Gonzalez, and J. Razzaque (eds.), *International Environmental Law and the Global South* (Cambridge University Press, 2015)

Alforte, A., J. Angan, J. Dentith, K. Domondon, L. Munden, S. Murday, and L. Pradela, *Communities As Counterparties: Preliminary Review of Concessions and Conflict in Emerging and Frontier Market Concessions* (Rights and Resources Initiative, 2014)

Aligica, P. D., *Institutional Diversity and Political Economy: The Ostroms and Beyond* (Oxford University Press, 2014)

Aligica, P. D. and P. J. Boettke, *Challenging Institutional Analysis and Development: The Bloomington School* (Routledge, 2009)

Aligica, P. D. and P. Boettke, 'The social philosophy of Ostrom's institutionalism' (2010) 10–19 Working Paper, Mercatus Centre, George Mason University

Aligica, P. D. and V. Tarko, 'Polycentricity: From Polanyi to Ostrom, and beyond' (2012) 25 *Governance: An International Journal of Policy, Administration, and Institutions* 237–62

Allen, C. and S. Clouth, *A Guidebook to the Green Economy – Issue 1: Green Economy, Green Growth and Low-Carbon Development – History, Definitions and a Guide to Recent Publications* (UN–DESA, 2012)

Alley, P., 'As the dust settles, some cause for optimism' *Global Witness blog*, 2009, www.globalwitness.org/archive/dust-settles-some-cause-optimism

Althor, G., J. E. Watson, and R. A. Fuller, 'Global mismatch between greenhouse gas emissions and the burden of climate change' (2016) 6 *Scientific Reports* 20281

Anaya, S. J., 'The capacity of international law to advance ethnic of nationality rights claims' (1991) 13(3) *Human Rights Quarterly* 403–11

Anaya, S. J., 'Divergent discourses about international law, indigenous peoples, and rights over land and natural resources: Towards a realist trend' (2005) 16(2) *Colorado Journal of International Environmental Law and Policy* 237–58

Anaya, S. J., 'Indigenous rights norms in contemporary international law' (1991) 8 *Arizona Journal of International and Comparative Law* 1–39

Anaya, S. J. and S. Puig, 'Mitigating state sovereignty: The duty to consult with indigenous peoples' (2017) 67(4) *University of Toronto Law Journal* 435–64

Anderson, K., 'Global governance: The problematic legitimacy relationship between global civil society and the United Nations' (2008) Working Paper No 2008-71, Washington College of Law

Anderson, P., *Free, Prior, and Informed Consent in REDD+: Principles and Approaches for Policy and Project Development* (RECOFTC (The Centre for People and Forests) and GIZ, 2011)

Anderson, T. and K. Stone, *Caught in the Net: How 'Net-Zero Emissions' Will Delay Real Climate Action and Drive Land Grabs* (ActionAid International, 2015)

Andersson, J. and E. Westholm, 'Closing the future: Environmental research and the management of conflicting future value orders' (2019) 44(2) *Science, Technology and Human Values* 237–62

Andonova, L. B., M. M. Betsill, and H. Bulkeley, 'Transnational climate governance' (2009) 9(2) *Global Environmental Politics* 52–73

Angelis, M. D., *The Beginning of History: Value Struggles and Global Capital* (Pluto Press, 2007)

Angelsen, A., 'The 3 REDD'1's' (2010) 16 *Journal of Forest Economics* 253–56

Angelsen, A., 'How do we set the reference levels for REDD payments?' in A. Angelsen (ed.), *Moving Ahead with REDD: Issues, Options and Implications* (Center for International Forestry Research, 2008), pp. 53–63

Angelsen, A., 'REDD+ as result-based aid: General lessons and bilateral of Norway' (2017) 21(2) *Review of Development Economics* 237–64

Angelsen, A., 'REDD+: What Should Come Next?' in S. Barrett, C. Carraro and J. de Melo (eds.), *Towards a Workable and Effective Climate Regime* (CEPR Press, 2016), pp. 405–21

Angelsen, A. (ed.), *Moving Ahead with REDD: Issues, Options and Implications* (Center for International Forestry Research, 2008)

Angelsen, A. (ed.), *Realising REDD+: National Strategy and Policy Options* (Center for International Forestry Research, 2009)

Angelsen, A. (ed.), *Transforming REDD+: Lessons and New Directions* (Center for International Forestry Research, 2018)

Angelsen, A. and S. Atmadja, 'What is this book about?' in A. Angelsen (ed.), *Moving Ahead with REDD: Issues, Options and Implications* (Center for International Forestry Research, 2008), pp. 1–9

Angelsen, A., D. Boucher, S. Brown, V. Merckx, C. Streck, and D. Zarin, *Guidelines for REDD+ Reference Levels: Principles and Recommendations. Prepared for the Government of Norway* (Meridian Institute, 2011)

Angelsen, A., M. Brockhaus, A. E. Duchelle, A. M. Larson, C. Martius, W. D. Sunderlin, L. V. Verchot, G. Wong, and S. Wunder, 'Learning from REDD+: A response to Fletcher et al.' (2017) 31(3) *Conservation Biology* 718–20

Angelsen, A., M. Brockhaus, W. D. Sunderlin, and L. V. Verchot (eds.), *Analysing REDD+: Challenges and Choices* (Center for International Forestry Research, 2012)

Anghie, A., 'Civilisation and commerce: The concept of governance in historical perspective' (2000) 45 *Villanova Law Review* 887–912

Anghie, A., '"The heart of my home": Colonialism, environmental damage, and the Nauru case' (1993) 34(1) *Harvard International Law Journal* 445–506

Anghie, A., *Imperialism, Sovereignty and the Making of International Law* (Cambridge University Press, 2007)

Anghie, A. and B. S. Chimni, 'Third World approaches to international law and individual responsibility in internal conflicts' (2003) 2(1) *Chinese Journal of International Law* 77–103

Argyrou, V., *The Logic of Environmentalism: Anthropology, Ecology and Postcoloniality* (Berghahn Books, 2005)

Armitage, D., 'Governance and the commons in a multi-level world' (2008) 2(1) *International Journal of the Commons* 7–32

Arnold, L., 'Deforestation in decentralised Indonesia: What's law got to do with it?' (2008) 4(2) *Law, Environment and Development Journal* 75–101

Bibliography

At a Crossroads: Consequential Trends in Recognition of Community-Based Forest Tenure from 2002–2017 (Rights and Resources Initiative, 2018)

Atapattu, S., *Human Rights Approaches to Climate Change: Challenges and Opportunities* (Routledge, 2015)

Atapattu, S. and C. G. Gonzalez, 'The North–South divide in international environmental law: Framing the issues' in S. Alam, S. Atapattu, C. G. Gonzalez, and J. Razzaque (eds.), *International Environmental Law and the Global South* (Cambridge University Press, 2015), pp. 1–20

Austin, J. L., *How to Do Things with Words* (Oxford University Press, 1975)

Australian Aid: Promoting Growth and Stability – A White Paper on the Australian Government's Overseas Aid Program (Australian Government AusAID, 2006)

Awono, A., O. A. Somorin, R. E. Atyi, and P. Levang, 'Tenure and participation in local REDD+ projects: Insights from southern Cameroon' (2014) 35 *Environmental Science & Policy* 76–86

Background Analysis of REDD Regulatory Frameworks (Baker & McKenzie, 2009)

Backram, H., 'Climate fraud and carbon colonialism: The new trade in greenhouse gases' (2004) 15(4) *Capitalism, Nature, Socialism* 5–20

Bäckstand, K. and E. Lövbrand, 'Planting trees to mitigate climate change: Contested discourses of ecological modernisation, Green governmentality and civic environmentalism' (2006) 6(1) *Global Environmental Politics* 50–75

Baer, P., G. Fieldman, T. Athanasiou, and S. Kartha, 'Greenhouse development rights: Towards an equitable framework for global climate policy' (2008) 21(4) *Cambridge Review of International Affairs* 649–69

Bailey, I., A. Gouldson, and P. Newell, 'Ecological modernisation and the governance of carbon: A critical analysis' (2011) 43(3) *Antipode* 682–703

Banerjee, S. B., 'Who sustains whose development? Sustainable development and the reinvention of nature' (2003) 24(1) *Organisation Studies* 143–80

Barletti, J. P. S. and A. M. Larson, *Rights Abuse Allegations in the Context of REDD+ Readiness and Implementation: A Preliminary Review and Proposal for Moving Forward* (Center for International Forestry Research, 2017)

Baroudy, E., 'Why we should be more optimistic about forests and climate change' The World Bank (blog), https://blogs.worldbank.org/climatechange/why-we-should-be-more-optimistic-about-forests-and-climate-change, 18 December 2017

Barr, C., I. A. P. Resosudarmo, A. Dermawan, J. McCarthy, M. Moeliono, and B. Setiono (eds.), *Decentralization of Forest Administration in Indonesia: Implications for Forest Sustainability, Economic Development and Community Livelihoods* (Center for International Forestry Research, 2006)

Barry, D., A. M. Larson, and C. J. P. Colfer, 'Forest tenure reform: An orphan with only uncles' in A. M. Larson, D. Barry, G. R. Dahal, and C. J. P. Colfer (eds.), *Forests for People: Community Rights and Forest Tenure Reform* (Earthscan, 2010), pp. 19–40

Baskin, J., 'The impossible necessity of climate justice?' (2009) 10(2) *Melbourne Journal of International Law* 424–38

Bates, G., *Environmental Law in Australia*, Ninth edition (LexisNexis, 2016)

Baxi, U., *Law and Poverty: Critical Essays* (NM Tripathi, 1988)

Bayon, R., A. Hawn, and K. Hamilton, *Voluntary Carbon Markets: An International Business Guide to What They Are and How They Work* (Earthscan, 2007)

Bedjaoui, M., *Towards a New International Economic Order* (United Nations Educational, Scientific and Cultural Organization, 1979)

Benda-Beckmann, F. von, 'Legal pluralism and social justice in economic and political development' (2001) 32(1) *IDS Bulletin* 46–56

Bernstein, S., *The Compromise of Liberal Environmentalism* (Columbia University Press, 2001)

Bernstein, S., M. Betsill, M. Hoffmann, and M. Paterson, 'A tale of two Copenhagens: Carbon markets and climate governance' (2010) 39(1) *Millennium: Journal of International Studies* 161–73

Bessa, A., 'Traditional local communities: What lessons can be learnt at the international level from the experiences of Brazil and Scotland?' (2015) 24(3) *Review of European, Comparative & International Environmental Law* 330–40

Betzold, C. and A. Flesken, 'Indigenous peoples in international environmental negotiations: evidence from biodiversity and climate change' in T. Kaime (ed.), *International Climate Change Law and Policy: Cultural Legitimacy in Adaptation and Mitigation* (Routledge, 2014), pp. 63–83

Beyerlin, U. and T. Marauhn, *International Environmental Law* (Hart/Beck, Nomos, 2011)

Beymer-Farris, B. A. and T. J. Bassett, 'The REDD menace: Resurgent protectionism in Tanzania's mangrove forests' (2012) 22(2) *Global Environmental Change* 332–41

Bhandary, R. R., 'Trying to eat an elephant (again): Opportunities and challenges in international cooperative approaches of the Paris Agreement' (2018) 12(3) *Carbon & Climate Law Review* 240–7

Bhatnagar, B. and A. C. Williams, 'Introduction' in B. Bhatnagar and A. C. Williams (eds.), *Participatory Development and the World Bank: Potential Directions for Change* (World Bank, 1992)

Biehl, J. and T. Eskerod, *Vita: Life in a Zone of Social Abandonment* (University of California Press, 2013)

Biermann, F., '"Common concern of humankind": The emergence of a new concept of international environmental law' (1996) 34(4) *Archiv des Völkerrechts* 426–81

Biniaz, S., 'Comma but differentiated responsibilities: Punctuation and 30 other ways negotiators have resolved issues in the international climate change regime' (2016) 6 *Michigan Journal of Environmental & Administrative Law* 37–63

Biniaz, S., 'Common but differentiated responsibility: Remarks by Susan Biniaz' (2002) 96 *Proceedings of the Annual Meeting (American Society of International Law)* 359–63

The BioCarbon Fund Experience: Insights from Afforestation/Reforestation Clean Development Mechanism Projects (The World Bank, 2012)

Birrell, K., '"An essential ghost": Indigeneity within the legal archive' (2010) 33(1) *Australian Feminist Law Journal* 81–99

Birrell, K., *Indigeneity: Before and Beyond the Law* (Routledge, 2016)

Birrell, K. and L. Godden, 'Benefits and sharing: realizing rights in REDD+' (2018) 9(1) *Journal of Human Rights and the Environment* 6–31

Birrell, K., L. Godden, and M. Tehan, 'Climate change and REDD+: Property as a prism for conceiving indigenous peoples' engagement' (2012) 3(2) *Journal of Human Rights and the Environment* 196–216

Bodansky, D., *Durban Platform: Issues and Options for a 2015 Agreement* (Centre for Climate and Energy Solutions, 2012)

Bodansky, D., *The Durban Platform Negotiations: Goals and Options* (Harvard Project on Climate Agreements, 2012)

Bodansky, D., 'A tale of two architectures: The once and future UN climate change regime' (2011) 43 *Arizona State Law Journal* 697–712

Bodansky, D., 'The Paris climate change agreement: A new hope?' (2016) 110(2) *American Journal of International Law* 288–319

Bibliography

369

Bodansky, D., J. Brunnée, and L. Rajamani, *International Climate Change Law* (Oxford University Press, 2017)

Bodin, B., E. Vaananen, and H. van Asselt, 'Putting REDD+ environmental safeguards into practice: Recommendations for effective and country-specific implementation' (2015) 2 *Carbon & Climate Law Review* 168–82

Boehnert, J., 'The green economy: Reconceptualising the natural commons as natural capital' (2015) 10(4) *Environmental Communication* 395–417

Böhm, S., 'How emissions trading at Paris climate talks has set us up for failure', *The Conversation*, 15 December 2015 theconversation.com/how-emissions-trading-at-paris-cli mate-talks-has-set-us-up-for-failure-52319

Böhm, S. and S. Dabhi (eds.), *Upsetting the Offset: The Political Economy of Carbon Markets* (MayFly Books, 2009)

Bond, P., *Politics of Climate Justice: Paralysis Above, Movement Below* (University of KwaZulu-Natal Press, 2012)

Borras, S. M., *Competing Views and Strategies on Agrarian Reform: International Perspective* (Ateneo de Manila University Press, 2008)

Borras, S. and J. Franco, 'From threat to opportunity? Problems with the idea of a "code of conduct" for land-grabbing' (2010) 13 *Yale Human Rights and Development Law Journal* 507–23

Borras, S. M., Jr., P. McMichael, and I. Scoones, 'The politics of biofuels, land and agrarian change: Editors' introduction' (2010) 37(4) *The Journal of Peasant Studies* 575–92

Bortscheller, M. J., 'Equitable but ineffective: How the principle of common but differentiated responsibilities hobbles the global fight against climate change' (2009) 10 *Sustainable Development Law & Policy* 49–69

Bosselmann, K., 'The right to self-determination and international environmental law: An integrative approach' (1997) 1 *New Zealand Journal of Environmental Law* 1–40

Bowman, M. and S. Minas, 'Resilience through interlinkage: The green climate fund and climate finance governance' (2019) 19(3) *Climate Policy* 342–53

Boyd, E., M. Boykoff, and P. Newell, 'The "new" carbon economy: What's new?' (2011) 43(3) *Antipode* 601–11

Boyd, E., N. Hultman, J. T. Roberts, E. Corbera, J. Cole, A. Bozmoski, J. Ebeling, R. Tippman, P. Mann, K. Brown, and D. M. Liverman, 'Reforming the CDM for sustainable development: Lessons learned and policy futures' (2009) 12 *Environmental Science and Policy* 820–31

Boyd, W., 'Climate change, fragmentation, and the challenges of global environmental law: Elements of a post-Copenhagen assemblage' (2010) 32 *University of Pennsylvania Journal of International Law* 457–550

Boyd, W., 'Ways of seeing in environmental law: How deforestation became an object of climate governance' (2010) 37 *Ecology Law Quarterly* 843–916

Boyd, W., C. Stickler, A. E. Duchelle, F. Seymour, D. Nepstad, N. H. A. Bahar, and D. Rodriguez-Ward, *Ending Tropical Deforestation: A Stocktake of Progress and Challenges. Jurisdictional Approaches to REDD+ and Low Emissions Development: Progress and Prospects* (World Resources Institute and Laboratory for Energy and Environmental Policy Innovation, 2018)

Braithwaite, J. P., 'Standard form contracts as transnational law: Evidence from the derivatives markets' (2012) 75(5) *The Modern Law Review* 779–805

Brand, U., N. Bullard, E. Lander, and T. Mueller (eds.), *Contours of Climate Justice: Ideas for Shaping New Climate and Energy Policies* (Dag Hammarskjöld Foundation, 2009)

Brand, U. and N. Sekler (eds.), *Postneoliberalism – A Beginning Debate* (The Dag Hammarskjöld Foundation, 2009)

Brand, U. and N. Sekler (eds.), 'Postneoliberalism: Catch-all word or valuable analytical and political concept? – Aims of a beginning debate' in U. Brand and N. Sekler (eds.), *Postneoliberalism – A Beginning Debate* (The Dag Hammarskjöld Foundation, 2009), pp. 5–15

Breidenich, C., D. Magrow, A. Rowley, and J. W. Rubin, 'The Kyoto Protocol to the United Nations Framework Convention on Climate Change' (1998) 92(2) *American Journal of International Law* 315–31

Briefing note: Unpacking the Warsaw Framework for REDD+: The requirements for implementing REDD+ under the United Nations Framework Convention on Climate Change (Climate Law and Policy, 2014)

Brockhaus, M., K. Korhonen-Kurki, J. Sehring, M. Di Gregorio, S. Assembe-Mvondo, A. Babon, M. Bekele, M. F. Gebara, D. B. Khatri, and H. Kambire, 'REDD+, transformational change and the promise of performance-based payments: A qualitative comparative analysis' (2017) 17(6) *Climate Policy* 708–30

Brockington, D., 'A radically conservative vision? The challenge of UNEP's towards a green economy' (2012) 43(1) *Development and Change* 409–22

Broder, J. M., 'U.S. climate envoy's good cop, bad cop roles' *New York Times*, 10 December 2009, www.nytimes.com/2009/12/11/science/earth/11stern.html

Bromley, D. W. and M. M. Cernea, *The Management of Common Property Natural Resources* (The World Bank, 1989)

Brown, D., K. Schreckenberg, G. Shepherd, and A. Wells, *Forestry As an Entry Point for Governance Reform* (Overseas Development Instituted Forestry Briefing, 2002)

Brown, D., F. Seymour, and L. Peskett, 'How do we achieve REDD co-benefits and avoid doing harm?' in A. Angelsen (ed.), *Moving Ahead with REDD: Issues, Options and Implications* (Center for International Forestry Research, 2008), pp. 107–18

Brown, M. L., *Redeeming REDD+: Policies, Incentives, and Social Feasibility for Avoided Deforestation* (Routledge and Earthscan, 2013)

Brown, W., '"The most we can hope for…": Human rights and the politics of fatalism' (2004) 103(2/3) *The South Atlantic Quarterly* 451–63

Brown, W., *Undoing the Demos: Neoliberalism's Stealth Revolution* (Zone Books, 2015)

Brundtland Commission Report, *Our Common Future World Commission on Environment and Development* (Cambridge University Press, 1987)

Brunnée, J., 'Common areas, common heritage, and common concern' in D. Bodansky, J. Brunnée, and E. Hey (eds.), *The Oxford Handbook of International Environmental Law* (Oxford University Press, 2008)

Brunnée, J., '"Common interest" echoes from an empty shell?: Some thoughts on common interest and international environmental law' (1989) 49 *Zeitschrift für ausländisches öffentliches Recht und Völkerrecht* 791–808

Brunnée, J., 'A conceptual framework for an international forests convention: Customary law and emerging principles' in Canadian Council of International Law (ed.), *Global Forests and International Environmental Law* (Kluwer Law, 1996), pp. 41–77

Brunnée, J., 'International environmental law: Rising to the challenge of common concern?' (2006) 100 *Proceedings of the Annual Meeting (American Society of International Law)* 307–10

Brunnée, J. and C. Streck, 'The UNFCCC as a negotiation forum: Towards common but more differentiated responsibilities' (2013) 13(5) *Climate Policy* 589–607

Bruno L., 'Why has critique run out of steam? From matters of fact to matters of concern' (2004) 30 *Critical Inquiry* 225–48

Bibliography

Bryant, G., 'Climate change: Back to the market or...?' *Progress in Political Economy*, 24 November 2014 ppesydney.net/climate-change-back-to-the-market-or

Buchanan, R. and S. Pahuja, 'Legal imperialism: Empire's invisible hand?' in P. A. Passavant and J. Dean (eds.), *Empire's New Clothes: Reading Hardt and Negri* (Routledge, 2004), pp. 73–93

Bulkeley, H., L. B. Andonova, M. M. Betsill, D. Compagnon, T. Hale, M. J. Hoffman, P. Newell, M. Peterson, C. Roger, and S. D. Vandveer, *Transnational Climate Change Governance* (Cambridge University Press, 2014)

Bullard, N. and T. Müller, 'Beyond the "green economy": System change, not climate change?' (2012) 55(1) *Development* 54–62

Bullock, S., M. Childs, and T. Picken, *A Dangerous Distraction: Why Offsetting Is Failing the Climate and People: The Evidence* (Friends of the Earth England, Wales and Northern Ireland, 2009)

Bumpus, A. G. and D. M. Liverman, 'Accumulation by decarbonization and the governance of carbon offsets' (2008) 84(2) *Economic Geography* 127–55

Bumpus, A. G. and D. M. Liverman, 'Carbon colonialism? Offsets, greenhouse gas reductions, and sustainable development' in R. Peet, P. Robbins, and M. J. Watts (eds.) *Global Political Ecology* (Routledge, 2011), pp. 203–24

Burke, A., S. Fishel, A. Mitchell, S. Dalby, and D. J. Levine, 'Planet politics: A manifesto from the end of IR' (2016) 44(3) *Millennium: Journal of International Studies* 499–523

Burkett, M., 'Small island states and the Paris Agreement' *Wilson Center*, 21 December 2015, www.wilsoncenter.org/article/small-island-states-and-the-paris-agreement

Burki, S. J. and G. E. Perry, *Beyond the Washington Consensus: Institutions Matter* (The World Bank, 1998)

Büscher, B., 'Nature on the move I: The value and circulation of liquid nature and the emergence of fictitious conservation' (2013) 6(1–2) *New Proposals: Journal of Marxism and Interdisciplinary Inquiry* 20–36

Butler, J., *Gender Trouble: Feminism and the Subversion of Identity* (Routledge, 1990)

Butler, J. and A. Athanasiou, *Dispossession: The Performative in the Political* (Polity, 2013)

Butt, S., R. Lyster, and T. Stephens, *Climate Change and Forest Governance: Lessons from Indonesia* (Routledge, 2015)

Caffentzis, G., 'The future of "the commons": Neoliberalism's "Plan B" or the original disaccumulation of capital?' (2010) 69 *New Formations* 23–41

Caffentzis, G., 'A tale of two conferences: Globalization, the crisis of neoliberalism and question of the commons' (2004), www.globaljusticecenter.org/papers/caffentzis.htm

Caffentzis, G. and S. Federici, 'Commons against and beyond capitalism' (2014) 49 *Community Development Journal* 92–105

Callon, M., 'Civilizing markets: Carbon trading between in vitro and in vivo experiments' (2009) 34(3–4) *Accounting, Organizations and Society* 535–48

Cameron, J., 'Forests' (1991) 1 *Yearbook of International Environmental Law* 201

Cames, M., R. O. Harthan, J. Füssler, M. Lazarus, C. M. Lee, P. Erickson, and R. Spalding-Fecher, *How Additional Is the Clean Development Mechanism? Analysis of the Application of Current Tools and Proposed Alternatives* (DG CLIMA, 2016)

Campbell, D., M. Klaes, and C. Bignell, 'After Copenhagen: The impossibility of carbon trading' (2010) 22 London School of Economics Law, Society and Economy Working Papers

Caney, S., 'Cosmopolitan justice, responsibility, and global climate change' (2005) 18 *Leiden Journal of International Law* 747–75

Carbon Credit Fraud: The White Collar Crime of the Future (Deloitte, 2009)

'Carbon finance: The role of the World Bank in carbon trading markets', *Bretton Woods Project*, 26 September 2018, www.brettonwoodsproject.org/2018/09/carbon-finance-role-world-bank-carbon-trading-markets/

Carbon Markets 101: The Ultimate Guide to Carbon Offsetting Mechanisms (Carbon Market Watch, 2019)

Carbon Pricing Watch 2016: An Advanced Brief from the State and Trends of Carbon Pricing 2016 Report, to be released in 2016 (The World Bank Group and ECOFYS, 2015)

Carlson, D. G., 'How to do things with Hegel' (1999) 78 *Texas Law Review* 1377–97

Carr, C. and F. Rosembuj, 'World Bank experiences in contracting for emission reductions' (2007) 2 *Environmental Liability* 114–19

Carroll, T., 'Introduction: Neo-liberal development policy in Asia and beyond the post-Washington consensus' (2012) 42(3) *Journal of Contemporary Asia* 350–8

Carry-Over of AAUs from the CP1 to CP2 – Future Implications for the Climate Regime (Point Carbon, 2012)

Castree, N. and G. Henderson, 'The capitalist mode of conservation, neoliberalism and the ecology of value' (2014) 7(1) *New Proposals: Journal of Marxism and Interdisciplinary Inquiry* 16–37

Caught REDD Handed: How Indonesia's Logging Moratorium Was Criminally Compromised on Day One and Norway Will Profit (Environmental Investigation Agency (EIA) and Telapak, 2011)

Chakrabarty, D., 'Planetary crises and the difficulty of being modern' (2018) 46(3) *Millennium: Journal of International Studies* 259–82

Chandler, D., *Empire in Denial: The Politics of State-Building* (Pluto Press, 2006)

Chapman, S., M. Wilder, and I. Millar, 'Defining the legal elements of benefit sharing in the context of REDD' (2014) 4 *Carbon & Climate Law Review* 270–81

Charters, C. and R. Stavenhagen (eds.), *Making the Declaration Work: The United Nations Declaration on the Rights of Indigenous Peoples* (International Work Group for Indigenous Affairs, 2009)

Chatterjee, P., *The Politics of the Governed; Reflections on Popular Politics in Most of the World* (Columbia University Press, 2004)

Chatterton, P., D. Featherstone, and P. Routledge, 'Articulating climate justice in Copenhagen: Antagonism, the commons, and solidarity' (2013) 45(3) *Antipode* 602–20

Childs, M., 'Privatising the atmosphere: A solution or dangerous con?' (2012) 12(1/2) *Ephemera: Theory and Politics in Organisation* 12–18

Chimni, B., 'Third world approaches to international law: A manifesto' (2006) 8 *International Community Law Review* 3–27

Chomba, S., J. Kariuki, J. F. Lund, and F. Sinclair, 'Roots of inequity: How the implementation of REDD+ reinforces past injustices' (2016) 50 *Land Use Policy* 202–13

Ciplet, D. and J. T. Roberts, 'Climate change and the transition to neoliberal environmental governance' (2017) 46 *Global Environmental Change* 148–56

Ciplet, D., J. T. Roberts, and M. R. Khan, *Power in a Warming World: The New Global Politics of Climate Change and the Remaking of Environmental Inequality* (MIT Press, 2015)

Clark, C. and J. Page, 'Of protest, the commons, and customary public rights: An ancient tale of the lawful forest' (2019) 42(1) *University of New South Wales Law Journal* 26–59

Clifton, S.-J., *A Dangerous Obsession: The Evidence against Carbon Trading and for Real Solutions to Avoid a Climate Crunch* (Friends of the Earth England, Wales and Northern Ireland, 2009)

Climate Change, Carbon Markets and the CDM: A Call to Action. Report of the High-Level Panel on the CDM Policy Dialogue (2012)

Bibliography

Climate Debt: A Primer (Third World Network, 2009)

Coase, R. H., 'The nature of the firm' (1937) 4(16) *Economica* 386–405

Coase, R. H., 'The problem of social cost' (1960) 3 *The Journal of Law and Economics* 1–44

Coen, D. R., *Climate in Motion: Science, Empire, and the Problem of Scale* (University of Chicago Press, 2018)

Cohen, M. R., 'The basis of contract' (1933) 46(4) *Harvard Law Review* 553–92

Cohen, M. R., 'Property and sovereignty' (1927) 13 *Cornell Law Quarterly* 8–30

Colchester, M., *Beyond Tenure: Rights-Based Approaches to Peoples and Forests. Some Lessons from the Forest Peoples Programme* (Forest Peoples Programme, 2007)

Colchester, M., T. Apte, M. Laforge, A. Mandondo, and N. Pathak, *Learning Lessons from International Community Forestry Networks: Synthesis Report* (Center for International Forestry Research, 2003)

Coleman, L. M., 'The making of docile dissent: Neoliberalism and resistance in Columbia and beyond' (2013) 7(2) *International Political Sociology* 170–87

Conant, J., 'Do trees grow on money?' (2011) *Earth Island Journal*, www.earthisland.org/journal/index.php/magazine/entry/do_trees_grow_on_money

Consolidation Report: Reducing Emissions from Deforestation and Forest Degradation in Indonesia (Ministry of Forestry of the Republic of Indonesia, 2008)

Cooke, B. and U. Kothari (eds.), *Participation: The New Tyranny?* (Zed Books, 2001)

Cooper, M., *Family Values: Between Neoliberalism and the New Social Conservatism* (MIT Press, 2017)

Cooper, M. E., *Life As Surplus: Biotechnology and Capitalism in the Neoliberal Era* (University of Washington Press, 2008)

Corbera, E., 'Problematizing REDD+ as an experiment in payments for ecosystem services' (2012) 4(6) *Current Opinion in Environmental Sustainability* 612–19

Corbera, E., M. Estrada, and K. Brown, 'Reducing greenhouse gas emissions from deforestation and forest degradation in developing countries: Revisiting the assumptions' (2010) 100 *Climatic Change* 355–88

Corbera, E., M. Estrada, P. May, G. Navarro, and P. Pacheco, 'Rights to land, forests and carbon in REDD+: Insights from Mexico, Brazil and Costa Rica' (2011) 2(1) *Forests* 301–42

Cordonier Segger, M.-C., M. Gehring, and A. Wardell, 'REDD+ instruments, international investment rules and sustainable landscapes' in C. Voigt (ed.), *Research Handbook on REDD-Plus and International Law* (Edward Elgar Publishing, 2016)

Cornwall, A., 'Unpacking "participation": Models, meanings and practices' (2008) 43(3) *Community Development Journal* 269–83

Corriveau-Bourque, A., F. Almeida, and A. Frechette, *Uncertainty and Opportunity: The Status of Forest Carbon Rights and Governance Frameworks in Over Half of the World's Tropical Forests* (Rights and Resources Initiative, 2018)

Cosbey, A., J.-E. Parry, J. Browne, Y. D. Babu, P. Bhandari, J. Drexhage, and D. Murphy, *Realizing the Development Dividend: Making the CDM Work for Developing Countries* (International Institute for Sustainable Development, 2005)

Costenbader, J., *Legal Frameworks for REDD – Design and Implementation at the National Level* (International Union for Conservation of Nature, 2009)

Costenbader, J., *REDD+ benefit sharing: A comparative assessment of three national policy approaches* (Forest Carbon Partnership Facility and UN-REDD Programme, 2011)

Cotula, L. and J. Mayers, *Tenure in REDD – Start-Point or Afterthought?* (International Institute for Environment and Development, 2009)

Coulthard, G. S., *Red Skin, White Masks: Rejecting the Colonial Politics of Recognition* (University of Minnesota Press, 2014)

Cover, R. M., 'Foreword: Nomos and narrative' (1983) 97 *Harvard Law Review* 4–68

Cowling, P., *REDD+ Market: Sending Out an SOS* (Conservation International, 2013)

Craven, M., 'Colonisation and domination' in B. Fassbender and A. Peters (eds.), *The Oxford Handbook of the History of International Law* (Oxford University Press, 2012), p. 888

Cronon, W., 'The trouble with wilderness; or, getting back to the wrong nature' in W. Cronon (ed.), *Uncommon Ground: Rethinking the Human Place in Nature* (W. W. Norton & Company, 1995), pp. 69–90

Crutzen, P. J., 'Geology of mankind' (2002) 415 *Nature* 23

Cullet, P., *Differential Treatment in International Environmental Law* (Ashgate, 2003)

Cullet, P., 'Differential treatment in environmental law: Addressing critiques and conceptualizing the next steps' (2016) 5(2) *Transnational Environmental Law* 305–28

Cullet, P., 'Differential treatment in international law: Towards a new paradigm of inter-state relations' (1999) 10(3) *European Journal of International Law* 549–82

Cullet, P., 'Principle 7–common but differentiated responsibilities' in J. Viñuales (ed.), *The Rio Declaration on Environment and Development: A Commentary* (Oxford University Press, 2015), pp. 229–44

Cutler, C. and T. Dietz, 'The politics of private transnational governance by contract: Introduction and analytical framework' in C. Cutler and T. Dietz (eds.), *The Politics of Private Transnational Governance by Contract* (Routledge, 2017), pp. 1–36

D'Alisa, G., F. Demaria, and G. Kallis, *Degrowth: A Vocabulary for a New Era* (Routledge, 2014)

Daes, E.-I. A., 'Some considerations on the right of indigenous peoples to self-determination' (1993) 3 *Transnational Law & Contemporary Problems* 1–11

Daes, E.-I. A., *Indigenous Peoples: Keepers of Our Past, Custodians of our Future* (International Work Group for Indigenous Affairs, 2008)

Dales, J. H., *Pollution, Property and Prices: An Essay in Policy-Making and Economics* (University of Toronto Press, 1968)

Davenport, D. S., 'An alternative explanation for the failure of the UNCED forest negotiations' (2005) 5(1) *Global Environmental Politics* 105–30

Davies, M., *Property: Meanings, Histories, Theories* (Routledge, 2007)

Davies, M., *Asking the Law Question*, Fourth edition (Thomson Reuters, 2017)

Davies, M., 'The consciousness of trees' (2015) 27(2) *Law & Literature* 217–35

Daviet, F. and G. Larsen, *Safeguarding Forests and People: A Framework for Designing a National System to Implement REDD+ Safeguards* (World Resources Initiative, 2012)

Davis, C., L. Williams, S. Lupberger, and F. Daviet, *Assessing Forest Governance: The Governance of Forests Initiative Indicator Framework* (World Resources Institute, 2013)

Davis, K. E., B. Kingsbury, and S. E. Merry, 'Indicators as a technology of global governance' (2010) 46(1) *Law & Society Review* 71–104

Davis, M., 'Indigenous struggles in standard-setting: The United Nations declaration on the rights of indigenous peoples' (2008) 9(2) *Melbourne Journal of International Law* 439–71

Dawson, A., 'Climate justice: The emerging movement against green capitalism' (2010) 109(2) *South Atlantic Quarterly* 313–38

de Águeda Corneloup, I. and A. P. Mol, 'Small island developing states and international climate change negotiations: The power of moral "leadership"' (2014) 14(1) *International Environmental Agreements: Politics, Law and Economics* 281–97

de la Cadena, M. and M. Blaser, *A World of Many Worlds* (Duke University Press, 2018)

Bibliography

de Campos Mello, V., *North–South Conflicts and Power Distribution in UNCED Negotiations: The Case of Forestry* (International Institute for Applied Systems Analysis, 1993)

De Lucia, V. 'Competing narratives and complex genealogies: The ecosystem approach in international environmental law' (2015) 27(1) *Journal of Environmental Law* 91–117

de Soto, H. *The Mystery of Capital: Why Capitalism Triumphs in the West and Fails Everywhere Else* (Black Swan, 2000)

Dehm, J., 'Carbon colonialism or climate justice?: Interrogating the international climate regime from a TWAIL perspective' (2016) 33 *Windsor Yearbook of Access to Justice* 129–161

Dehm, J., '"REDD faces all around": Implementing reducing emissions from deforestation and forest degradation in Indonesia' (2012) 10 *Local–Global* 98–125

Dehm, J., 'International law, temporalities and narratives of the climate crisis' (2016) 4(1) *London Review of International Law* 167–93

Dehm, J., 'The misery of international law: Confrontations with injustice in the global economy' (2018) 19 *Melbourne Journal of International Law* 763–72

Dehm, J., 'One tonne of carbon dioxide equivalent ($1tCO_2e$)' in J. Hohmann and D. Joyce (eds.), *International Law's Objects* (Oxford University Press, 2018), pp. 305–18

Dehm, J., 'Post Paris reflections: Fossil fuels, human rights and the need to excavate new ideas for climate justice' (2017) 8(2) *Journal of Human Rights and the Environment* 280–300

Dehm, J., 'Reflections on Paris: Thoughts towards a critical approach to climate law' (2018) *Revue québécoise de droit international* 61–91

Dehm, J., 'Tricks of perception and perspective: The disappearance of law and politics in carbon markets; Reading Alexandre Kossoy and Phillippe Ambrosi, "State and trends of the carbon market 2010"' (2011) 7(2) *Macquarie Journal of International and Comparative Environmental Law* 1–18

Dehm, J., 'Rupture and continuity: North/south struggles over debt and economic cooperation at the end of the cold war' in M. Craven, S. Pahuja, and G. Simpson (eds.), *International Law and the Cold War* (Cambridge University Press, 2020), pp. 287–314

Dehm, J. and A. Hasan Khan, 'North–South transboundary movement of hazardous wastes: The Basel ban and environmental justice' in P. Cullet and S. Koonan (eds.), *Research Handbook on Law, Environment and the Global South* (Edward Elgar Publishing, 2019), pp. 109–37

Dehm, S., 'Framing international migration' (2015) 3(1) *London Review of International Law* 133–68

Deininger, K., *Land Policies for Growth and Poverty Reduction* (The World Bank, 2003)

Deininger, K. and H. Bisswanger, 'The evolution of the World Bank's land policy: Principles, experience and future challenges' (1999) 14(2) *The World Bank Research Observer* 247–76

Deleuil, T., 'The common but differentiated responsibilities principle: Changes in continuity after the Durban Conference of the Parties' (2012) 21(3) *Review of European Community & International Environmental Law* 271–81

Demaria, F. and A. Kothari, 'The post-development dictionary agenda: Paths to the pluriverse' (2017) 38(12) *Third World Quarterly* 2588–99

Denier, L., S. Korwin, M. Leggett, and C. MacFarquhar, *The Little Book of Legal Frameworks for REDD+* (Global Canopy Programme, 2014)

Dickson, B., M. Bertzky, T. Christophersen, C. Epple, V. Kapos, L. Miles, U. Narloch, and K. Trumper, *REDD+ Beyond Carbon: Supporting Decisions on Safeguards and Multiple Benefits* (UN-REDD Programme, Policy Brief: Issue No 2, 2012)

Dietrich, C. R., *Oil Revolution* (Cambridge University Press, 2017)

Dietz, T., E. Ostrom, and P. C. Stern, 'The struggle to govern the commons' (2003) 302(5652) *Science* 1907–12

Bibliography

DiLeva, C., 'Common but differentiated responsbility: Remarks by Charles E. DiLeva' (2002) 96 *Proceedings of the Annual Meeting (American Society of International Law)* 363–6

Doherty, E. and H. Schroeder, 'Forest tenure and multi-level governance in avoiding deforestation under REDD' (2011) 11(4) *Global Environmental Politics* 66–87

Dooley, K., *An Overview of Selected REDD Proposals* (FERN and Forest Peoples Programme, 2008)

Dooley, K., T. Griffiths, H. Leake, and S. Ozinga, *Cutting Corners: World Bank's Forest and Carbon Fund Fails Forests and People* (FERN and Forest Peoples' Programme, 2008)

Dooley, K., T. Griffiths, F. Martone, and S. Ozinga, *Smoke and Mirrors: A Critical Assessment of the Forest Carbon Partnership Facility* (FERN and Forest Peoples' Programme, 2011)

Dooley, K. and A. Gupta, 'Governing by expertise: The contested politics of (accounting for) land-based mitigation in a new climate agreement' (2017) 17(4) *International Environmental Agreements: Politics, Law and Economics* 483–500

Dooley, K. and N. Reisch, 'Bonn II: REDD discussions at the June 2009 UNFCCC Climate Meeting', *EU Forest Watch* July 2009, www.redd-monitor.org/wp-content/uploads/2009/07/document_4448_4450.pdf

Dorsett, S. and S. McVeigh, *Jurisdiction* (Routledge, 2012)

Dowie, M., *Conservation Refugees: The Hundred-Year Conflict between Global Conservation and Native Peoples* (MIT Press, 2009)

Doyle, A., 'Space agencies, Google seek ways to save forests', *Reuters AlertNet*, 20 October 2009, www.alertnet.org/thenews/newsdesk/LK385966.htm

Dressler, W., B. Büscher, M. Schoon, D. A. N. Brockington, T. Hayes, C. A. Kull, J. McCarthy, and K. Shrestha, 'From hope to crisis and back again? A critical history of the global CBNRM narrative' (2010) 37(1) *Environmental Conservation* 5–15

Driesen, D. M., 'Free lunch or cheap fix: The emissions trading idea and the climate change convention' (1998) 26 *Boston College Environmental Affairs Law Review* 1–87

Dubash, N. K. and L. Rajamani, Beyond Copenhagen: Next steps (2010) 10(6) *Climate Policy* 593–9

Duchelle, A. E., M. Cromberg, M. F. Gebara, R. Guerra, T. Melo, A. Larson, P. Cronkleton, J. Börner, E. Sills, and S. Wunder, 'Linking forest tenure reform, environmental compliance, and incentives: Lessons from REDD+ initiatives in the Brazilian Amazon' (2014) 55 *World Development* 53–67

Duffield, M., *Development, Security and Unending War: Governing the World of Peoples* (Polity, 2007)

Durrant, N., 'Legal issues in biosequestration: Carbon sinks, carbon rights and carbon trading' (2008) 31(3) *UNSW Law Journal* 906–18

Dutschke, M. and A. Angelsen, 'How do we ensure permanence and assign liability?' in A. Angelsen (ed.), *Moving Ahead with REDD: Issues, Options and Implications* (Center for International Forestry Research, 2008), pp. 77–85

Dutschke, M. and A. Michaelowa, 'Development assistance and the CDM – How to interpret "financial additionality"' (2006) 11(2) *Environment and Development Economics* 235–46

Duyck, S., 'Delivering on the Paris promises? Review of the Paris Agreement's implementing guidelines from a human rights perspective' (2019) 9(3) *Climate Law* 202–23

The Ecologist, *Whose Common Future? Reclaiming the Commons* (Earthscan, 1993)

The Economics of Ecosystems and Biodiversity: Mainstreaming the Economics of Nature: A Synthesis of the Approach, Conclusions and Recommendations of the TEEB (TEEB, 2010)

Ecosystems and Human Well-Being: Current State and Trends, Vol 1 (The Millennium Ecosystem Assessment Board, 2005)

Bibliography

El-Ghoney, M.R., 'Land reform development challenges of 1963–2003 continue into twenty-first Century' FAO, www.fao.org/docrep/oo6/jo415t/jo415to5.htm

Eliasch, J., *Climate Change: Financing Global Forests: The Eliasch Review* (Earthscan, 2008)

Emerging Compliance Markets for REDD+: An Assessment of Supply and Demand (United States Agency for International Development, 2013)

Emissions Gap Report 2019 (United Nations Environment Programme, 2019)

Engaging the Private Sector in Results-Based Landscape Programs: Early Lessons from the World Bank's Forests and Landscapes Climate Finance Funds (Forest Carbon Partnership Facility and BioCarbon Fund Initiative for Sustainable Forest Landscapes, 2017)

Engle, K., *The Elusive Promise of Indigenous Development: Rights, Culture, Strategy* (Duke University Press, 2010)

Engle, K., 'Indigenous rights claims in international law: Self-determination, culture, and development' in D. Armstrong (ed.), *Routledge Handbook of International Law* (Routledge, 2009), pp. 331–43

Engle, K., 'On fragile architecture: The UN declaration on the rights of indigenous peoples in the context of human rights' (2011) 22(2) *European Journal of International Law* 141–63

Eni-Ibukun, T. A., *International Environmental Law and Distributive Justice* (Routledge, 2014)

Escobar, A., 'Beyond the third world: Imperial globality, global coloniality and antiglobalisation social movements' (2004) 25(1) *Third World Quarterly* 207–30

Eslava, L., 'Decentralization of development and nation-building today: Reconstructing Colombia from the margins of Bogotá' (2009) 2(1) *The Law and Development Review* 282–366

Eslava, L., 'Istanbul vignettes: Observing the everyday operation of international law' (2014) 2(1) *London Review of International Law* 3–47

Eslava, L., *Local Space, Global Life: The Everyday Operation of International Law and Development* (Cambridge University Press, 2015)

Eslava, L., 'TWAIL coordinates' *Critical Legal Thinking*, 2 April 2019 criticallegalthinking .com/2019/04/02/twail-coordinates

Esrin, D. and H. Kennedy, *Achieving Justice and Human Rights in an Era of Climate Disruption* (International Bar Association, 2014)

'EU carbon price volatility in January a sign of things to come', *S&P Global Platts Insight*, 10 January 2019 blogs.platts.com/2019/01/10/eu-carbon-price-volatility-sign-of-things-to-come/

Evans, S. and J. Gabbatiss, 'COP25: Key outcomes agreed at the UN climate talks in Madrid' *Carbon Brief*, 15 December 2019, www.carbonbrief.org/cop25-key-outcomes-agreed-at-the-un-climate-talks-in-madrid

Evans, S. and J. Timperley, 'COP24: Key outcomes agreed at the UN climate talks in Katowice' *Carbon Brief*, 16 December 2018, www.carbonbrief.org/cop24-key-outcomes-agreed-at-the-un-climate-talks-in-katowice

Extreme carbon inequality (Oxfam Media Briefing, 2015)

Fair Shares: A Civil Society Equity Review of INDCS. Report (CSO Equity Review Coalition, 2015)

Fairhead, J., M. Leach, and I. Scoones, 'Green grabbing: A new appropriation of nature?' (2012) 39(2) *The Journal of Peasant Studies* 237–61

The FCPF Carbon Fund: Piloting REDD+ Programs at Scale (Forest Carbon Partnership Fund, June 2013), www.forestcarbonpartnership.org/sites/fcp/files/2013/june2013/CF% 20Origination-web_o.pdf

Fearnside, P., 'Environmentalists split over Kyoto and Amazon deforestation' (2001) 28(4) *Environmental Conservation* 295–9

Bibliography

Federici, S., 'From commoning to debt: Financialization, microcredit, and the changing architecture of capital accumulation' (2014) 113(2) *The South Atlantic Quarterly* 231–44

Felli, R., 'On climate rent' (2014) 22(2–3) *Historical Materialism* 251–80

Ferguson, J., *The Anti-Politics Machine: 'Development,' Depolitization, and Bureaucratic Power in Lesotho* (Cambridge University Press, 1990)

Ferguson, P., *Post-Growth Politics: A Critical Theoretical and Policy Framework for Decarbonisation* (Springer International Publishing, 2018)

Fisher, R. and R. Lyster, 'Land and resource tenure: The rights of indigenous people and forest dwellers' in R. Lyster, C. MacKenzie, and C. McDermott (eds.), *Law, Tropical Forests and Carbon: The Case of REDD+* (Cambridge University Press, 2013), pp. 187–206

Fishman, A., E. Oliveira, and L. Gamble, *Tackling Deforestation through a Jurisdictional Approach: Lessons from the Field* (World Wide Fund for Nature, 2017)

Fitzpatrick, D., '"Best practice" options for the legal recognition of customary tenure' (2005) 36(3) *Development and Change* 449–75

Flaman, R., *Decentralisation: A Sampling of Definitions* (United Nations Development Programme Working Paper, 1999)

Fletcher, R., 'Against wilderness' (2009) 5(1) *Green Theory & Praxis: The Journal of Ecopedagogy* 169–79

Fletcher, R., 'Environmentality unbound: Multiple governmentalities in environmental politics' (2017) 85 *Geoforum* 311–15

Fletcher, R., 'How I learned to stop worrying and love the market: Virtualism, disavowal, and public secrecy in neoliberal environmental conservation' (2013) 31(5) *Environment and Planning D: Society and Space* 796–812

Fletcher, R., W. Dressler, B. Büscher, and Z. R. Anderson, 'Debating REDD+ and its implications: Reply to Angelsen et al.' (2017) 31(3) *Conservation Biology* 721–3

Fletcher, R., W. Dressler, B. Büscher, and Z. R. Anderson, 'Questioning REDD+ and the future of market-based conservation' (2016) 30(3) *Conservation Biology* 673–75

Fogel, C., 'The local, the global, and the Kyoto protocol' in M. L. Martello and S. Jasanoff (eds.), *Earthly Politics: Local and Global in Environmental Governance* (MIT Press, 2004)

The Forest Carbon Partnership Facility (Independent Evaluation Group, 2012)

The Forest Carbon Partnership Facility: 2018 Annual Report (Forest Carbon Partnership Facility, 2018)

Forest Carbon Partnership Facility: 2019 Annual Report (Forest Carbon Partnership Facility, 2019)

The Forest Sector (The World Bank, 1991)

Forests Sourcebook: Practical Guidance for Sustaining Forests in Development Cooperation (The World Bank, 2008)

Forsyth, T., 'Multilevel, multiactor governance in REDD' in A. Angelsen (ed.), *Realising REDD+: National Strategy and Policy Options* (Center for International Forestry Research, 2009), pp. 113–22

Forsyth, T. and C. Johnson, 'Elinor Ostrom's legacy: Governing the commons, and the rational choice controversy' (2014) 45(5) *Development and Change* 1093–1110

Foucault, M., *The Birth of Biopolitics: Lectures at the Collège de France 1978–1979* (Palgrave Macmillan, 2008)

Foucault, M., *Discipline and Punish: The Birth of the Prison* (Knopf Doubleday Publishing Group, 1977)

Foucault, M., *Power/Knowledge: Selected Interviews and Other Writings, 1972–1977* (Pantheon, 1980)

Bibliography

Foucault, M., *Security, Territory, Population: Lectures at the Collège de France 1977–1978* (Palgrave Macmillan, 2007)

Foucault, M., 'The subject and power' (1982) 8(4) *Critical Inquiry* 777–95

Foucault, M., *The Will to Knowledge: The History of Sexuality: Volume I* (Penguin, 1998)

'Founding statement', *Third World Approaches to International Law Review (TWAILR)* August 2019 twailr.com/about/founding-statement

Framework for Assessing and Monitoring Forest Governance (Program on Forests (PROFOR) and FAO, 2011)

Frechette, A., M. de Bresser, and R. Hofstede, *External Evaluation of the United Nations Collaborative Programme on Reducing Emissions from Deforestation and Forest Degradation in Developing Countries (the UN-REDD Programme): Volume 1 – Final Report* (2014)

Freestone, D., 'The establishment, role and evolution of the global environment facility: Operationalising common but differentiated responsibility?' in T. Malick Ndiaye and R. Wolfrum (eds.), *Law of the Sea, Environmental Law and Settlement of Disputes: Liber Amicorum Judge Thomas A. Mensah* (Brill Nijhoff, 2007), pp. 1077–107

Freestone, D., 'Interview with David Freestone' (2017) 3 *Carbon & Climate Law Review* 196–7

Freestone, D., *The World Bank and Sustainable Development: Legal Essays* (Martinus Nijhoff Publishers, 2013)

Freestone, D. and C. Streck (eds.), *Legal Aspects of Carbon Trading: Kyoto, Copenhagen, and Beyond* (Oxford University Press, 2009)

Freestone, D. and C. Streck (eds.), *Legal Aspects of Implementing the Kyoto Protocol Mechanisms: Making Kyoto Work* (Oxford University Press, 2005)

Fry, I., 'Reducing emissions from deforestation and forest degradation: Opportunities and pitfalls in developing a new legal regime' (2008) 17(2) *Review of European Community and International Environmental Law* 166–82

Gallagher, J. and R. Robinson, 'The imperialism of free trade' (1953) 6(1) *The Economic History Review: New Series* 1–15

Gathii, J. T., 'Good governance as a counter-insurgency agenda to oppositional and transformative social projects in international law' (1995) 5 *Buffalo Human Rights Law Review* 107–74

Gathii, J. T., 'The limits of the new international rule of law on good governance' in E. K. Obiora and O. C. Quashigah (eds.), *Legitimate Governance in Sub-Saharan Africa* (Kluwer Publishers, 1999), pp. 207–31

Gathii, J. T., 'Neoliberalism, colonialism and international governance: Decentering the international law of governmental legitimacy' (2000) 98 *Michigan Law Review* 1996–2055

Gathii, J. T., 'TWAIL: A brief history of its origins, its decentralised network, and a tentative bibliography' (2011) 3(1) *Trade, Law and Development* 26–64

Gautam, M., U. Lele, Ir. Erwinsyah, W. Hyde, H. Kartodiharjo, A. Khan, and S. Rana, *Indonesia: The Challenges of World Bank Involvement in Forests* (World Bank Operations Evaluation Department, 2000)

Getting to the Root: Underlying Causes of Deforestation and Forest Degradation, and Drivers of Forest Restoration (Global Forest Coalition, 2010)

Gibbon, P., 'The World Bank and the new politics of aid' (1993) 5(1) *The European Journal of Development Research* 35–62

Gideon, J., '"Consultation" or co-option? A case study from the Chilean health sector' (2005) 5(3) *Progress in Development Studies* 169–81

Gilman, N., 'The new international economic order: A reintroduction' (2015) 6(1) *Humanity: An International Journal of Human Rights, Humanitarianism, and Development* 1–16

Bibliography

Ginsburg, C. and S. Keene, *At a Crossroads: Consequential Trends in Recognition of Community-Based Forest Tenure From 2002–2017* (Rights and Resources Initiative, 2018)

Global Forest Resources Assessment 2015: How Are the World's Forests Changing?, Second edition (Food and Agricultural Organisation of the United Nations, 2016)

Global Warming of 1.5° C (Intergovernmental Panel on Climate Change, 2018)

Godden, L., 'Benefit sharing in REDD+: Linking rights and equitable outcomes' in M.F Tehan, L. Godden, M. A. Young, and K. Gover, *The Impact of Climate Change Mitigation on Indigenous and Forest Communities: International, National and Local Law Perspectives on REDD+* (Cambridge University Press, 2017), pp. 172–200

Godden, L., 'Malaysia and the UN-REDD programme: Exploring possibilities for tenure pluralism in forest governance' in M.F Tehan, L. Godden, M. A. Young, and K. Gover, *The Impact of Climate Change Mitigation on Indigenous and Forest Communities: International, National and Local Law Perspectives on REDD+* (Cambridge University Press, 2017), pp. 203–38

Godden, L., 'Preserving natural heritage: Nature as other' (1998) 22(3) *Melbourne University Law Review* 719–42

Godden, L. and M. Tehan, 'REDD+: Climate justice and indigenous and local community rights in an era of climate disruption' (2016) 34(1) *Journal of Energy & Natural Resources Law* 95–108

Goldman, M., '"Customs in common": The epistemic world of the commons scholars' (1997) 26(1) *Theory and Society* 1–37

Goldman, M., *Imperial Nature: The World Bank and Struggles for Social Justice in an Age of Globalization* (Yale University Press, 2006)

Gonzalez, C. G., 'Environmental justice, human rights, and the global south' (2015) 13 *Santa Clara Journal of International Law* 151–95

Goodrich, P., *The Laws of Love: A Brief Historical and Practical Manual* (Springer, 2006)

Goodrich, P., 'Visive powers: Colours, trees and genres of jurisdiction' (2008) 2(2) *Law and Humanities* 213–31

'Google tool to help watch over world's forests', *AFP* 10 December 2009

Gordon, R., 'Climate change and the poorest nations: Further reflections on global inequality' (2007) 78 *University of Colorado Review* 1559–624

Gordon, R. W., 'Macneil, Macaulay, and the discovery of power and solidarity in contract law' (1985) *Wisconsin Law Review* 565–79

Gore, T., *Extreme Carbon Inequality: Why the Paris Climate Deal Must Put the Poorest, Lowest Emitting and Most Vulnerable People First* (Oxfam International, 2015)

Gover, K., 'The elusive promise of indigenous developments: Rights, culture, strategy by Karen Engle' (2011) 12 *Melbourne Journal of International Law* 419–31

Gover, K., 'REDD+, tenure and indigenous property claims' in M. F. Tehan, L. Godden, M. A. Young, and K. Gover (eds.), *The Impact of Climate Change Mitigation on Indigenous and Forest Communities: International, National and Local Law Perspectives on REDD+* (Cambridge University Press, 2017), pp. 130–71

Graham, P., *Cooperative Approaches for Supporting REDD+: Linking Articles 5 and 6 of the Paris Agreement* (Climate Advisors, 2017)

Gray, I. P., *Climate finance, tropical forests and the state: Governing international climate risk in the Democratic Republic of Congo* (Master's thesis, Massachusetts Institute of Technology, 2012)

Gray, K., 'Property in thin air' (1991) 50(2) *The Cambridge Law Journal* 252–307

Grear, A., 'Deconstructing anthropos: A critical legal reflection on 'anthropocentric'law and anthropocene "humanity"' (2015) 26(3) *Law and Critique* 225–49

Bibliography

Grear, A., 'Towards "climate justice"? A critical reflection on legal subjectivity and climate injustice: Warning signals, patterned hierarchies, directions for future law and policy' (2014) 5 *Journal of Human Rights and the Environment* 103–33

Green, F. and R. Denniss, 'Cutting with both arms of the scissors: The economic and political case for restrictive supply-side climate policies' (2018) 150(1) *Climatic Change* 73–87

Greiber, T., M. Janki, M. Orellana, A. Savaresi, and D. Shelton, *Conservation with Justice: A Rights-Based Approach* (Center for International Forestry Research and International Union for Conservation of Nature, 2009)

Grewal, D. S., A. Kapczynski, and J. Purdy, 'Law and political economy: Toward a manifesto' *Law and Political Economy Blog* November 2017 lpeblog.org/2017/11/06/law-and-political-economy-toward-a-manifesto

Griffiths, J., 'What is legal pluralism?' (1986) 18(24) *The Journal of Legal Pluralism and Unofficial Law* 1–55

Griffiths, T., *Seeing 'RED'?: 'Avoided Deforestation' and the Rights of Indigenous Peoples and Local Communities* (Forest Peoples Programme, 2007)

Griffiths, T., *Seeing 'REDD'?: Forests, Climate Change Mitigation and the Rights of Indigenous Peoples and Local Communities*, Update for Poznań (UNFCCC COP14) (Forest Peoples Programme, 2008)

Griffiths, T., *Seeing 'REDD'?: Forest, Climate Change Mitigation and the Rights of Indigenous Peoples and Local Communities*, Updated Version (Forest Peoples Programme, 2009)

Griscom, B. W., J. Adams, P. W. Ellis, R. A. Houghton, G. Lomax, D. A. Miteva, W. H. Schlesinger, D. Shoch, J. V. Siikamäki, and P. Smith, 'Natural climate solutions' (2017) 114(44) *Proceedings of the National Academy of Sciences* 11645–50

Grotius, H., *Mare Liberum: Free Sea or a Dissertation on the Right Which the Dutch Have to Carry on Indian Trade* (Brill, 1609)

Grove, R., *Green Imperialism: Colonial Expansion, Tropical Island Edens and the Origins of Environmentalism, 1600–1860* (Cambridge University Press, 1996)

Guattari, F., *The Three Ecologies* (Continuum International Publishing Group, 2008)

Guha, R., *Environmentalism: A Global History* (Oxford University Press, 1999)

Gupta, J., *The Climate Change Convention and Developing Countries: From Conflict to Consensus?* (Kluwer Academic Publishers, 1997)

Gupta, J., *The History of Global Climate Governance* (Cambridge University Press, 2014)

Gupta, J., 'International law and climate change: The challenges facing developing countries' (2006) 16(1) *Yearbook of International Environmental Law* 119–53

Hale, C. R., 'Neoliberal multiculturalism: The remaking of cultural rights and racial dominance in Central America' (2005) 28(1) *Political and Legal Anthropology Review* 10–28

Hale, R. L., 'Coercion and distribution in a supposedly non-coercive state' (1923) 38(3) *Political Science Quarterly* 470–94

Hale, R. L., 'Rate making and the revision of the property concept' (1922) 22(3) *Columbia Law Review* 209–16

Hall, R., *REDD Myths: A Critical Review of Proposed Mechanisms to Reduce Emissions from Deforestation and Degradation in Developing Countries* (Friends of the Earth International, 2008)

Hall, R., *The Great REDD Gamble. Time to Ditch Risky REDD for Community-Based Approaches That Are Effective, Ethical and Equitable* (Friends of the Earth International, 2014)

Hall, R., *REDD: The Realities in Black and White* (Friends of the Earth International, 2010)

Hamilton, C., 'The Anthropocene as rupture' (2016) 3(2) *The Anthropocene Review* 93–106

Hamlin, T. B., 'Debt-for-nature swaps: A new strategy for protecting environmental interests in developing nations' (1989) 16 *Ecology Law Quarterly* 1065–88

Hamrick, K. and M. Gallant, *Fertile Ground: State of Forest Carbon Finance 2017* (Forest Trends Ecosystem Marketplace, 2017)

Hamrick, K. and M. Gallant, *Voluntary Carbon Market Insights: 2018 Outlook and First-Quarter Trends* (Ecosystem Marketplace, 2018)

Haraway, D. J., *Staying with the Trouble: Making Kin in the Chthulucene* (Duke University Press, 2016)

Hardin, G., 'The tragedy of the commons' (1968) 162(3859) *Science* 1243–8

Harris, P. G., 'Common but differentiated responsibility: The Kyoto Protocol and United States policy' (1999) 7 *NYU Environmental Law Journal* 27–48

Harrison, R. P., *Forests: The Shadow of Civilisation* (The University of Chicago Press, 1992)

Hartmann, E. and P. F. Kjaer, 'The status of authority in the globalizing economy: Beyond the public/private distinction' (2018) 25(1) *Indiana Journal of Global Legal Studies* 3–11

Harvey, D., *The New Imperialism* (Oxford University Press, 2005)

Hasan Khan, A., 'How is the subject of international Indigenous Peoples' rights made? Or, when the openness of law becomes its Other', Paper presented at *Sculpting the Human: Law, Culture and Biopolitics*, Conference Programme (Association for the Study of Law, Culture and the Humanities, 2013)

Hawkins, S., *Contracting for Forest Carbon: Elements of a Model Forest Carbon Purchase Agreement* (Duke Law, Forest Trends and the Katoomba Group, 2010)

Haywood, C., 'The European Union's emissions trading scheme: International emissions trading lessons for the Copenhagen Protocol and implications for Australia?' (2009) 26 *Environmental and Planning Law Journal* 310–29

Head, J. W., 'Environmental conditionality in the operations of international development finance institutions' (1991) 1 *The Kansas Journal of Law & Public Policy* 15–26

Heede, R., 'Tracing anthropogenic carbon dioxide and methane emissions to fossil fuel and cement producers, 1854–2010' (2014) 122(1–2) *Climatic Change* 229–41

Hepburn, C., 'Carbon trading: A review of the Kyoto mechanisms' (2007) 32(1) *Annual Review of Environment and Resources* 375–93

Hepburn, S., 'Carbon rights as new property: The benefits of statutory verification' (2009) 31 *Sydney Law Review* 239–71

Herold, M., A. Angelsen, L. V. Verchot, A. Wijaya, and J. H. Ainembabazi, 'A stepwise framework for developing REDD+ reference levels' in A. Angelsen, M. Brockhaus, W. D. Sunderlin, and L. V. Verchot (eds.), *Analysing REDD+: Challenges and Choices* (Center for International Forestry Research, 2012), pp. 279–300

Herz, S., A. L. Vina, and J. Sohn, *Development without Conflict: The Business Case for Community Consent* (World Resources Initiative, 2007)

Hickel, J., *The Divide: A Brief Guide to Global Inequality and Its Solutions* (Random House, 2017)

Hickel, J. and G. Kallis, 'Is green growth possible?' (2020) 25(4) *New Political Economy* 469–86

'"Historic" Paris Agreement paves way for World Bank to help countries deliver on climate commitments', *World Bank*, 12 December 2015, www.worldbank.org/en/news/feature/2015/12/12/paris-agreement-paves-way-for-world-bank-group-helping-countries-deliver-on-climate-commitments

Honest Engagement: Transparency and Civil Society Participation in REDD (Global Witness, 2008)

Bibliography 383

Honoré, A., 'Ownership' in A. Guest (ed.), *Oxford Essays in Jurisprudence* (Oxford University Press, 1961), pp. 107–47

Horwitz, M. J., 'The historical foundations of modern contract law' (1974) 87 *Harvard Law Review* 917–56

Houghton, R., 'Looking at the World Bank's safeguard reform through the lens of deliberative democracy' (2019) 32(3) *Leiden Journal of International Law* 465–82

Houghton, R. A., 'The future role of tropical forests in affecting the carbon dioxide concentration of the atmosphere' (1990) 19(4) *Ambio* 204–9

Howell, S., '"No RIGHTS–No REDD": Some implications of a turn towards co-benefits' (2014) 41(2) *Forum for Development Studies* 253–72

Huggins, A. and M. S. Karim, 'Shifting traction: Differential treatment and substantive and procedural regard in the international climate change regime' (2016) 5 *Transnational Environmental Law* 427–48

Human Development Report 2007/2008: Flighting Climate Change – Human Solidarity in a Divided World (United Nations Development Programme, 2007)

Human Rights Implications of Climate Change Mitigation Actions (CIDSE, Nature Code and Carbon Market Watch, 2015)

Humphreys, D., *Forest Politics: The Evolution of International Cooperation* (Earthscan, 1996)

Humphreys, D., *Logjam: Deforestation and the Crisis of Global Governance* (Earthscan, 2006)

Humphreys, S., 'Climate justice: The claim of the past' (2014) 5 *Journal of Human Rights and the Environment* 134–148

Humphreys, S., 'Conceiving justice: Articulating common causes in distinct regimes' in S. Humphreys (ed.), *Climate Change and Human Rights* (Cambridge University Press, 2010) pp. 299–319

Humphreys, S. (ed.), *Human Rights and Climate Change* (Cambridge University Press, 2009)

Humphreys, S., *Theatre of the Rule of Law: Transnational Legal Intervention in Theory and Practice* (Cambridge University Press, 2010)

Humphreys, S. and Y. Otomo, 'Theorizing international environmental law' in A. Orford, F. Hoffmann, and M. Clark (eds.), *The Oxford Handbook of the Theory of International Law* (Oxford University Press, 2016), pp. 797–819

Igoe, J., 'Nature on the move II: Contemplation becomes speculation' (2013) 6(1–2) *New Proposals: Journal of Marxism and Interdisciplinary Inquiry* 37–49

Implement in Haste, Repent at Leisure: A Call for Rethinking the World Bank's Carbon Fund, Based on an Analysis of the Democratic Republic of Congo Emissions Reduction – Project Idea Note (ER-PIN) (FERN and Forest Peoples' Programme, 2014)

Ince, O. U., 'Primitive accumulation, new enclosures, and global land grabs: A theoretical intervention' (2013) 79(1) *Rural Sociology* 104–31

'Inclusion of REDD+ in Paris Climate Agreement heralded as a major step forward on deforestation', *Mongabay* 14 December 2015 news.mongabay.com/2015/12/inclusion-of-redd-in-paris-climate-agreement-heralded-as-major-step-forward-on-deforestation/

Inclusive Green Growth: The Pathway to Sustainable Development (World Bank, 2012)

Intergovernmental Panel on Climate Change, *Global Warming of 1.5° C* (Special Report of the Intergovernmental Panel on Climate Change, 2018)

Intergovernmental Panel on Climate Change, *Special Report on Climate Change, Desertification, Land Degradation, Sustainable Land Management, Food Security, and Greenhouse Gas Fluxes in Terrestrial Ecosystems: Summary for Policymakers (Approved Draft)* (2019)

Isenberg, J. and C. Potvin, 'Financing REDD in developing countries: A supply and demand analysis' (2010) 10(2) *Climate Policy* 216–31

Jackson, T., *Prosperity without Growth: Economics for a Finite Planet* (Earthscan, 2009)

Jacobs, S., 'Tradition in a free society: The fideism of Michael Polanyi and the rationalism of Karl Popper' (2010) 36(2) *Tradition & Discovery: The Polanyi Society Periodical* 8–25

Jasanoff, S., 'Future imperfect: Science, technology, and the imaginations of modernity' in S. Jasanoff and S.-H. Kim (eds.), *Dreamscapes of Modernity: Sociotechnical Imaginaries and the Fabrication of Power* (University of Chicago Press, 2015), pp. 1–33

Jasanoff, S., 'A new climate for society' (2010) 27(2–3) *Theory, Culture and Society* 233–53

Jasanoff, S., *States of Knowledge: The Co-production of Science and the Social Order* (Routledge, 2004)

Jasanoff, S. and H. R. Simmet, 'No funeral bells: Public reason in a 'post-truth' age' (2017) 47(5) *Social Studies of Science* 751–70

Jodha, N. S., *Common Property Resources: A Missing Dimension of Development Strategies* (The World Bank, 1992)

Jodoin, S., *Forest Preservation in a Changing Climate: REDD+ and Indigenous and Community Rights in Indonesia and Tanzania* (Cambridge University Press, 2017)

Jodoin, S. and S. Mason-Case, 'What difference does CBDR make? A socio-legal analysis of the role of differentiation in the transnational legal process for REDD+' (2016) 5(2) *Transnational Environmental Law* 255–84

Johns, F., *Non-Legality in International Law: Unruly Law* (Cambridge University Press, 2013)

Johnson, B., 'The forestry crisis: What must be done' (1984) 13(1) *Ambio* 48–9

Johnson, H., P. O'Connor, W. D. Duncan, and S. A. Christensen, 'Statutory entitlements as property: Implications of property analysis methods for emissions trading' (2018) 43 *Monash University Law Review* 421–62

Jokubauskaite, G., 'The World Bank Environmental and Social Framework in a wider realm of public international law' (2019) 32(3) *Leiden Journal of International Law* 457–63

Jones, T. and S. Edwards, *The Climate Debt Crisis: Why Paying Our Dues If Essential for Tackling Climate Change* (Jubilee Debt Campaign and World Development Movement, 2009)

Jordan, A., D. Huitema, J. Schoenefeld, and J. Forster, 'Governing climate change polycentrically: Setting the scene' in A. Jordan, D. Huitema, H. van Asselt, and J. Forster (eds.), *Governing Climate Change: Polycentricity in Action?* (Cambridge University Press, 2018), pp. 3–26

Joyner, C. C., 'Common but differentiated responsibility' (2002) 96 *Proceedings of the Annual Meeting (American Society of International Law)* 358–9

Kalimantan Forests and Climate Partnership (KFCP): Design Document (Australia Indonesia Partnership, 2009)

Kallis, G., *Limits: Why Malthus Was Wrong and Why Environmentalists Should Care* (Stanford University Press, 2019)

Kanbur, R. and H. Shue, *Climate Justice: Integrating Economics and Philosophy* (Oxford University Press, 2018)

Kanowski, P. J., C. L. McDermott, and B. W. Cashore, 'Implementing REDD+: Lessons from analysis of forest governance' (2011) 14(2) *Environmental Science & Policy* 111–17

Karousakis, K., B. Guay, and C. Philibert, *Differentiating Countries in Terms of Mitigation Commitments Actions and Support* (Organisation for Economic Co-operation and Development, 2008)

Karsenty, A., 'The architecture of proposed REDD schemes after Bali: Facing critical choices' (2008) 10(3) *International Forestry Review* 443–57

Bibliography

Karsenty, A., A. Vogel, and F. Castell, '"Carbon rights", REDD+ and payments for environmental services' (2014) 35 *Environmental Science & Policy* 20–9

Katowice Climate Change Conference – December 2018 – Summary & Analysis (IISD Reporting Service, 2018)

'Katowice COP24 outcome incompatible with Paris Agreement,' *Center for International Environmental Law,* 15 December 2018, www.ciel.org/news/katowice-cop24-outcome-incompatible-with-paris-agreement

Kaul, I., I. Grunberg, and M. A. Stern (eds.), *Global Public Goods: International Cooperation in the 21st Century* (Oxford University Press, 1999)

Kelly, D. J., 'The case for social safeguards in a post-2012 agreement on REDD' (2010) 6(1) *Law, Environment and Development Journal* 61–81

Kennedy, D., 'The international human rights movement: Part of the problem?' (2002) 15 *Harvard Human Rights Journal* 101–25

Kennedy, D., 'The international human rights regime: Still part of the problem?' in R. Dickinson, E. Katselli, C. Murray, and O. W. Pedersen (eds.), *Examining Critical Perspectives on Human Rights* (Cambridge University Press, 2012), pp. 19–34

Kennedy, D., 'The "Rule of Law", political choices, and development common sense' in D. M. Trubek, and A. Santos (eds.), *The New Law and Economic Development: A Critical Appraisal* (Cambridge University Press, 2006), pp. 95–173

Kennedy, D., *A World of Struggle: How Power, Law, and Expertise Shape Global Political Economy* (Princeton University Press, 2016)

Kennett, S., A. J. Kwasniak, and A. R. Lucas, 'Property rights and the legal framework for carbon sequestration on agricultural land' (2005) 37 *Ottawa Law Review* 171–213

Kill, J., *REDD: A Gallery of Conflicts, Contradictions and Lies* (World Rainforest Movement, 2014)

Kishor, N. and K. Rosenbaum, *Assessing and Monitoring Forest Governance: A User's Guide to a Diagnostic Tool* (Program on Forests, PROFOR, 2012)

Kiss, A. C. and D. Shelton, *Guide to International Environmental Law* (Martinus Nijhoff Publishers, 2007)

Kissinger, G., M. Herold, and V. De Sy, *Drivers of Deforestation and Forest Degradation: A Synthesis Report for REDD+ Policy Makers* (Lexeme Consulting, 2012)

Klein, N., *This Changes Everything: Capitalism vs. the Climate* (Simon & Schuster, 2014)

Klijn, A.-M., J. Gupta, and A. Nijboer, 'Privatizing environmental resources: The need for supervision of clean development mechanism contracts?' (2009) 18(2) *Review of European Community & International Environmental Law* 172–84

Klingebiel, S. and H. Janus, 'Results-based aid: Potential and limits of an innovative modality in development cooperation' (2014) 5(2) *International Development Policy|Revue internationale de politique de développement*

Klinsky, S. and H. Dowlatabadi, 'Conceptualisations of justice in climate policy' (2009) 9 *Climate Policy* 88–108

Knicley, J. E., 'Debt, nature, and indigenous rights: Twenty five years of debt-for-nature evolution' (2012) 36 *Harvard Environmental Law Review* 79–122

Knox, A., D. Vhugen, S. Aguilar, L. Peskett, and J. Miner, *Forest Carbon Rights Guidebook: A Tool for Framing Legal Rights to Carbon Benefits Generated through REDD+ Programming* (United States Agency for International Development, 2012)

Knox-Hayes, J., 'Constructing carbon market spacetime: Climate change and the onset of neo-modernity' (2010) 100(4) *Annals of the Association of American Geographers* 953–62

Knox-Hayes, J., 'The spatial and temporal dynamics of value in financialization: Analysis of the infrastructure of carbon markets' (2013) 50 *Geoforum* 117–28

Bibliography

Korhonen-Kurki, K., M. Brockhaus, A. E. Duchelle, S. Atmadja, and T. T. Pham, 'Multiple levels and multiple challenges for REDD+' in A. Angelsen, M. Brockhaus, W. Sundelin, and L. Verchot (eds.), *Analysing REDD+: Challenges and Choices* (Center for International Forestry Research, 2012), pp. 91–110

Koskenniemi, M., 'Empire and international law: The real Spanish contribution' (2011) 61 *University of Toronto Law Journal* 1–36

Koskenniemi, M., 'Expanding histories of international law' (2016) 56(1) *American Journal of Legal History* 104–12

Koskenniemi, M., *From Apology to Utopia: The Structure of International Legal Argument* (Cambridge University Press, 2005)

Koskenniemi, M., International pollution in the system of international law (1984) 17 *Oikeustiede Jurisprudentia* 91–181

Koskenniemi, M., *The Politics of International Law* (Hart Publishing, 2011)

Kossoy, A. and P. Ambrosi, *State and Trends of the Carbon Market 2010* (World Bank, 2010)

Krajnc, A., 'Survival emissions: A perspective from the south on global climate change negotiations' (2003) 3(4) *Global Environmental Politics* 98–108

Krasmann, S., 'Targeted killing and its law: On a mutually constitutive relationship' (2012) 25(3) *Leiden Journal of International Law* 665–82

Krause, T. and T. D. Nielsen, 'The legitimacy of incentive-based conservation and a critical account of social safeguards' (2014) 41 *Environmental Science & Policy* 44–51

Krever, T., 'The legal turn in late development theory: The rule of law and the world bank's development model' (2011) 52 *Harvard International Law Journal* 287–319

La Viña, A. G. M. and A. de Leon, 'Conserving and enhancing sinks and reservoirs of greenhouse gases, including forests (Article 5)' in D. Klein, M. P. Carazo, M. Doelle, J. Bulmer, and A. Higham (eds.), *The Paris Agreement on Climate Change: Analysis and Commentary* (Oxford University Press, 2017), pp. 166–77

Lang, A., *World Trade Law after Neoliberalism: Reimagining the Global Economic Order* (Oxford University Press, 2011)

Lang, C., 'FoEI: Forests are more than carbon', *REDD-Monitor*, 29 October 2008

Lang, C., 'Global forest coalition attacks REDD', *REDD-Monitor*, 6 October 2008

Lang, C., 'How Kevin Conrad dismissed NGO requests not to weaken safeguards in the REDD text in Cancun', *REDD-Monitor*, 5 January 2011

Lang, C., 'Independent evaluation group review of the FCPF: "World Bank needs a high-level strategic discussion on its overall approach to REDD"', *REDD-Monitor*, 22 November 2012

Lang, C., 'Indigenous peoples censored at Poznań', *REDD-Monitor*, 15 December 2008

Lang, C., 'More reactions to COP20 and Lima's "roadmap to global burning"', *REDD-Monitor*, 2 January 2015

Lang, C., 'NGOs call for suspension of World Bank's REDD programme: "The approach to forest protection simply has not worked"', *REDD-Monitor*, 17 December 2017

Lang, C., 'REDD safeguards: What are they?', *REDD-Monitor*, 20 March 2015

Lang, C., 'REDD+ Myth: Sustainable forest management' (2014) 207 *World Rainforest Movement Bulletin*

Lang, C., 'Rights struck from draft text on REDD', *REDD-Monitor*, 9 December 2008

Lang, C., 'UN permanent forum on indigenous issues intervenes on REDD in Poznań', *REDD-Monitor*, 2 December 2008

Lansing, D. M., 'Carbon's calculatory spaces: The emergence of carbon offsets in Costa Rica' (2010) 28(4) *Environment and Planning D: Society and Space* 710–25

Lansing, D. M., 'Unequal access to payments for ecosystem services: The case of Costa Rica' (2014) 45(6) *Development and Change* 1310–31

Bibliography

Larson, A. M., 'Forest tenure reform in the age of climate change: Lessons for REDD+' (2011) 21 *Global Environmental Change* 540–549

Larson, A. M., *Tenure Rights and Access to Forests: A Training Manual for Research – Part I. A Guide to Key Issues* (Center for International Forestry Research, 2012)

Larson, A. M., D. Barry, and G. R. Dahal, 'Tenure change in the global south' in A. M. Larson, D. Barry, G. R. Dahal, and C. Colfer (eds.), *Forests for People: Community Rights and Forest Tenure Reform* (Earthscan, 2010), pp. 19–34

Larson, A. M., M. Brockhaus, W. D. Sunderlin, A. Duchelle, A. Babon, T. Dokken, T. T. Pham, I. A. P. Resosudarmo, G. Selaya, and A. A.-B. Huynh, 'Land tenure and REDD+: The good, the bad and the ugly' (2013) 23(3) *Global Environmental Change* 678–89

Larson, A. M. and E. Petkova, 'An introduction to forest governance, people and REDD+ in Latin America: Obstacles and opportunities' (2011) 2(1) *Forests* 86–111

Larson, A. M., J. P. Sarmiento Barletti, A. Ravikumar, and K. Korhonen-Kurki, 'Multi-level governance: Some coordination problems cannot be solved through coordination' in A. Angelsen, (ed.) *Transforming REDD+: Lessons and New Directions* (Center for International Forestry Research, 2018), pp. 81–92

Larson, A. M. and F. Soto, 'Decentralization of natural resource governance regimes' (2008) 33 *Annual Review of Environment and Resources* 213–39

Latour, B., 'Why has critique run out of steam? From matters of fact to matters of concern' (2004) 30(2) *Critical Inquiry* 225–48

Latour, B., 'Fourth Lecture: The Anthropocene and the destruction of (the image of) the globe' in *Facing Gaia: Eight Lectures on the New Climatic Regime* (John Wiley & Sons, 2017)

Laurance, W. F., 'Reflections on the tropical deforestation crisis' (1999) 91(2–3) *Biological Conservation* 109–17

Lawlor, K. and D. Huberman, 'Reduced emissions from deforestation and forest degradation (REDD) and human rights' in J. Campese, T. Sunderland, T. Greiber, and G. Oviedo (eds.), *Rights-Based Approaches: Exploring Issues and Opportunities for Conservation* (Center for International Forestry Research and International Union for Conservation of Nature, 2009), pp. 269–85

Lazarus, M., P. Erickson, and K. Tempest, *Supply-Side Climate Policy: The Road Less Taken* (SEI Working Paper No. 2015–13, 2015)

Lazarus, M., and H. van Asselt, 'Fossil fuel supply and climate policy: Exploring the road less taken' (2018) 150 *Climatic Change* 1–13

Legal Issues Guidebook to the Clean Development Mechanism (UNEP Riso Centre on Energy, Climate and Sustainable Development, 2004)

Lele, U., N. Kumar, S. A. Husain, A. Zazueta, and L. Kelly, *The World Bank Forest Strategy: Striking the Right Balance* (World Bank Operations Evaluations Department, 2000)

Lesniewska, F., 'UNFCCC REDD+ COP decisions: The cumulative effect on forest related law processes' (2013) 15 *International Community Law Review* 103–21

Li, T. M., 'Articulating indigenous identity in Indonesia: Resource politics and the tribal slot' (2000) 42 *Comparative Studies in Society and History* 149–79

Li, T. M., 'Centering labor in the land grab debate' (2011) 38(2) *The Journal of Peasant Studies* 281–98

Li, T. M., 'Fixing non-market subjects: Governing land and population in the global south' (2014) 18 *Foucault Studies* 34–48

Li, T. M., 'Indigeneity, capitalism, and the management of dispossession' (2010) 51 *Current Anthropology* 385–414

Li, T. M., 'Masyarakat Adat, difference, and the limits of recognition in Indonesia's forest zone' (2001) 35(3) *Modern Asian Studies* 645–76

Li, T. M., 'Practices of assemblage and community forest management' (2007) 36(2) *Economy and Society* 263–93

Li, T. M., *The Will to Improve: Governmentality, Development, and the Practice of Politics* (Duke University Press, 2007)

Lieb, E. J., 'Contracts and friendships' (2009) 59 *Emory Law Journal* 649–726

'Life in limbo?' (2009) 5 *Turbulence: Ideas for Movement* 3–7

Lightfoot, S. R., 'Selective endorsement without intent to implement: Indigenous rights and the Anglosphere' (2012) 16(1) *The International Journal of Human Rights* 100–22

Linacre, N., R. O'Sullivan, D. Ross and L. Durschinger, *REDD+ Supply and Demand 2015–2025: Forest Carbon, Markets and Communities Program* (United Stated Agency for International Development Forest Carbon, Markets and Communities Program, 2015)

Lindhjem, H., I. A. K. Bråten, A. Gleinsvik, and I. Aronsen, *Experiences with benefit sharing: Issues and options for REDD-plus* (Pöyry Management Consulting (Norway), 2010)

Lindroth, M. and H. Sinevaara-Niskanen, 'At the crossroads of autonomy and essentialism: Indigenous peoples in international environmental politics' (2013) 7(3) *International Political Sociology* 275–93

Lindroth, M. and H. Sinevaara-Niskanen, *Global Politics and Its Violent Care for Indigeneity: Sequels to Colonialism* (Springer, 2017)

Linebaugh, P., *The Magna Carta Manifesto: Liberties and the Commons for All* (University of California Press, 2008)

Liverman, D. M., 'Conventions of climate change: Constructions of danger and the dispossession of the atmosphere' (2009) 35(2) *Journal of Historical Geography* 279–96

Llewellyn, K. N., 'What price contract? – An essay in perspective' (1931) 40(5) *The Yale Law Journal* 704–51

Locher, F., 'Historicizing Elinor Ostrom: Urban politics, international development and expertise in the US context (1970–1990)' (2018) 19(2) *Theoretical Inquiries in Law* 533–58

Lodge, M. W., 'The common heritage of mankind' in D. Freestone (ed.), *The 1982 Law of the Sea Convention at 30: Successes, Challenges and New Agendas* (Martinus Nijhoff Publishers, 2013), pp. 59–68

Loft, L., A. Ravikumar, M. Gebara, T. Pham, I. Resosudarmo, S. Assembe, J. Tovar, E. Mwangi, and K. Andersson, 'Taking stock of carbon rights in REDD+ candidate countries: Concept meets reality' (2015) 6(4) *Forests* 1031–60

Lohmann, L., *Beyond Patzers and Clients: Strategic Reflections on Climate Change and the 'Green Economy'* (The Corner House, 2012)

Lohmann, L., 'Carbon trading, climate justice and the production of ignorance: Ten examples' (2008) 51 *Development* 359–65

Lohmann, L., *Carbon Trading: A Critical Conversation on Climate Change, Privatisation and Power* (Dag Hammarskjöld Foundation, 2006)

Lohmann, L., *Chronicle of a Disaster Foretold; REDD-with-Carbon-Trading* (The Corner House, 2008)

Lohmann, L., 'The endless algebra of climate markets' (2011) 22(4) *Capitalism, Nature, Socialism* 93–116

Lohmann, L., *Green Orientalism* (The Corner House, 1993)

Lohmann, L., 'Neoliberalism and the calculable world: The rise of carbon trading' in K. Birch and V. Mykhnenko (eds.), *The Rise and Fall of Neoliberalism: The Collapse of an Economic Order?* (Zed Books, 2010), pp. 77–93

Lohmann, L, 'Performative Equations and Neoliberal Commodification: The Case of Climate' in B. Buscher, W. Dressler, and R. Fletcher (eds.), *Nature^{TM} Inc.: Environmental Conservation in the Neoliberal Age* (The University of Arizona Press, 2014), pp. 158–80

Bibliography

Lohmann, L., 'Regulation as corruption in the carbon offset markets' in S. Böhm and S. Dabhi (eds.), *Upsetting the Offset* (MayFly Books, 2009), pp. 175–91

Lohmann, L., 'Uncertainty markets and carbon markets: Variations on Polanyian Themes' (2010) 15(2) *New Political Economy* 225–54

Long, A., 'Taking adaptation value seriously: Designing REDD to protect biodiversity' (2009) 3 *Carbon & Climate Law Review* 314–23

Long, S., E. Roberts, and J. Dehm, 'Climate justice inside and outside the UNFCCC: The example of REDD' (2010) 66 *Journal of Australian Political Economy* 222–46

Lounela, A., 'Climate change disputes and justice in Central Kalimantan, Indonesia' (2015) 56(1) *Asia Pacific Viewpoint* 62–78

Lövbrand, E. and J. Stripple, 'Making climate change governable: Accounting for carbon as sinks, credits and personal budgets' (2011) 5(2) *Critical Policy Studies* 187–200

Lovell, H. and N. S. Ghaleigh, 'Climate change and the professions: The unexpected places and spaces of carbon markets' (2013) 38(3) *Transactions of the Institute of British Geographers* 512–16

Lovell, H. and D. MacKenzie, 'Accounting for carbon: The role of accounting professional organisations in governing climate change' (2011) 43(3) *Antipode* 704–30

Lovera, S., 'REDD realities' in U. Brand, E. Lander, N. Bullard, and T. Mueller (eds.), *Contours of Climate Justice: Ideas for Shaping New Climate and Energy Policies* (Dag Hammarskjöld Foundation, 2009), pp. 45–53

Low, K. F. K. and J. Lin, 'Carbon credits as EU like it: Property, immunity, tragiCO$_2$medy?' (2015)' 27(3) *Journal of Environmental Law* 377–404

Luke, T. W., 'Environmentality' in J. S. Dryzek, R. B. Norgaard, and D. Schlosberg (eds.), *The Oxford Handbook of Climate Change and Society* (Oxford University Press, 2011), pp. 96–109

Luke, T. W., 'Environmentality as green governmentality' in E. Darier (ed.), *Discourses of the Environment* (Blackwell Publishers, 1999), pp. 121–51

Luke, T. W., 'On environmentality: Geo-power and eco-knowledge in the discourses of contemporary environmentalism' (1995) 31 *Cultural Critique* 57–81

Luttrell, C., L. Loft, M. F. Gebara, and D. Kweka, 'Who should benefit and why? Discourses on REDD' in A. Angelsen, M. Brockhaus, W. D. Sunderlin, and L. V. Verchot (eds.), *Analysing REDD+: Challenges and choices* (Center for International Forestry Research, 2012), pp. 129–52

Luttrell, C., K. Schreckenberg, and L. Peskett, *The Implications of Carbon Financing for Pro-Poor Community Forestry* (Overseas Development Institute, 2007)

Lyster, R., 'The new frontier of climate law: Reducing emissions from deforestation and degradation' (2009) 26 *Environmental and Planning Law Journal* 417–56

Lyster, R., 'REDD+, transparency, participation and resource rights: The role of law' (2011) 14 *Environmental Science and Policy* 118–26

Lyster, R., C. MacKenzie, and C. McDermott (eds.), *Law, Tropical Forests and Carbon: The Case of REDD+* (Cambridge University Press, 2013)

Macinante, J. D., 'Operationalizing cooperative approaches under the Paris Agreement by valuing mitigation outcomes' (2018) 12(3) *Carbon & Climate Law Review* 258–71

MacKenzie, D., 'Making things the same: Gases, emission rights and the politics of carbon markets' (2009) 34(3) *Accounting, Organizations and Society* 440–55

MacKenzie, D. A., F. Muniesa, and L. Siu, *Do Economists Make Markets?: On the Performativity of Economics* (Princeton University Press, 2007)

MacLaren, O. W. and J.-A. Pariseau, 'The new World Bank safeguard Standard for indigenous peoples: Where do we start' (2017) 45(1) *Syracuse Journal of International Law & Commerce* 35–57

Maguire, R., 'Deforestation, REDD and international law' in S. Alam, M. J. H. Bhuiyan, T. M. R. Chowdhury, and Re. J. Techera (eds.), *Routledge Handbook of International Environmental Law* (Routledge, 2013), pp. 697–716

Maguire, R., *Global Forest Governance: Legal Concepts and Policy Trends* (Edward Elgar Publishing, 2013)

Maguire, R., 'The role of common but differentiated responsibility in the 2020 climate regime' (2013) 4 *Carbon & Climate Law Review* 260–9

Mahanty, S., W. Dressler, S. Milne, and C. Filer, 'Unravelling property relations around forest carbon' (2013) 34(2) *Singapore Journal of Tropical Geography* 188–205

Maine, H. S., *International Law: A Series of Lectures Delivered before the University of Cambridge, 1887* (J. Murray, 1888)

Making Land Work: Reconciling Customary Land and Development in the Pacific (Australian Government AusAID, 2008)

Maljean-Dubois, S., 'The Paris Agreement: A new step in the gradual evolution of differential treatment in the climate regime?' (2016) 25(2) *Review of European, Comparative & International Environmental Law* 151–60

Manji, A., *The Politics of Land Reform in Africa: From Communal Tenure to Free Markets* (Zed Books, 2006)

Mantena, K., *Alibis of Empire: Henry Maine and the Ends of Liberal Imperialism* (Princeton University Press, 2010)

Marcu, A., *Carbon Market Provisions in the Paris Agreement (Article 6)* (Centre for European Policy Studies, 2016)

Marcu, A., *Issues for Discussion to Operationalise Article 6 of the Paris Agreement* (International Centre for Trade and Sustainable Development, 2017)

Marks, G. and L. Hooghe, 'Contrasting visions of multi-level governance' in I. Bache and M. V. Flinders (eds.), *Multi-level Governance* (Oxford University Press, 2004), pp. 15–31

Marks, S., 'Human rights and the bottom billion' (2009) 1 *European Human Rights Law Review* 37–49

Marks, S., 'Human rights and root causes' (2011) 74(1) *The Modern Law Review* 57–78

Marx, K., *Capital: A Critique of Political Economy*, Vol. 1 (Lawrence and Wishart, 1887)

Marx, K., *Grundrisse: Foundations of the Critique of Political Economy* (Penguin Books, 1939)

Mason, C. F. and A. J. Plantinga, 'The additionality problem with offsets: Optimal contracts for carbon sequestration in forests' (2013) 66(1) *Journal of Environmental Economics and Management* 1–14

Mason-Case, S., 'Inaugurating a new kind of "commons"' (draft manuscript on file with the author)

Mason-Case, S., 'On being companions and strangers: Lawyers and the production of international climate law' (2019) 32(4) *Leiden Journal of International Law* 625–51

Matsui, Y., 'Some aspects of the principle of "common but differentiated responsibilities"' (2002) 2(2) *International Environmental Agreements* 151–70

Mayer, B., *The International Law on Climate Change* (Cambridge University Press, 2018)

McAfee, K., 'Nature in the market-world: Ecosystem services and inequality' (2012) 55(1) *Development* 25–33

McBee, J. D., 'Distributive justice in the Paris Climate Agreement: Response to Peters et al.' (2017) 9(1) *Contemporary Readings in Law and Social Justice* 120–31

McDermott, C. L., L. Coad, A. Helfgott, and H. Schroeder, 'Operationalizing social safeguards in REDD+: Actors, interests and ideas' (2012) 21 *Environmental Science and Policy* 63–72

McDermott, C. L., K. Levin, and B. Cashore, 'Building the forest-climate bandwagon: REDD+ and the logic of problem amelioration' (2011) 11(3) *Global Environmental Politics* 85–103

McElwee, P., 'From conservation and development to climate change: Anthropological engagements with REDD+ in Vietnam' in J. Barnes and M. Dove (eds.), *Climate Cultures: Anthropological Perspectives on Climate Change* (Yale University Press, 2015), pp. 82–104

McGee, J. and J. Steffek, 'The Copenhagen turn in global climate governance and the contentious history of differentiation in international law' (2016) 28(1) *Journal of Environmental Law* 37–63

McGinnis, M. D., 'Introduction' in M. D. McGinnis (ed.), *Polycentric Governance and Development: Readings from the Workshop in Political Theory and Policy Analysis* (University of Michigan Press, 1999)

McGinnis, M. D., 'An introduction to IAD and the language of the Ostrom workshop: A simple guide to a complex framework' (2011) 39(1) *Policy Studies Journal* 169–83

McGinnis, M. D. (ed.), *Polycentric Governance and Development: Readings from the Workshop in Political Theory and Policy Analysis* (University of Michigan Press, 1999)

McLaren, D. P., D. P. Tyfield, R. Willis, B. Szerszynski, and N. O. Markusson, 'Beyond "Net-Zero": A case for separate targets for emissions reduction and negative emissions' (2019) 1 *Frontiers in Climate* 4

McVeigh, S. and S. Pahuja, 'Rival jurisdictions: The promise and loss of sovereignty' in C. Barbour and G. Pavlich (eds.), *After Sovereignty: On the Question of Political Beginnings* (Routledge, 2009), pp. 97–114

McVeigh, T., 'Borneo's majestic rainforest is being lilled by the timber Mafia', *The Guardian* 24 October 2010

Meadows, D. H., D. L. Meadows, J. Randers, and W. W. Behrens III, *The Limits to Growth* (Universe Books, 1972)

Meckling, J. O. and G. Y. Chung, 'Sectoral approaches for a post-2012 climate regime: A taxonomy' (2009) 9 *Climate Policy* 652–68

Mehta, L., M. Leach, and I. Scoones, 'Environmental governance in an uncertain world' (2001) 32(4) *IDS Bulletin* 1–9

Meinzen-Dick, R. S. and R. Pradhan, 'Implications of legal pluralism for natural resource management' (2001) 32(4) *IDS Bulletin* 10–17

Meinzen-Dick, R. S. and R. Pradhan, 'Legal pluralism and dynamic property rights' (2002) CAPRi Working Paper No. 22

Merry, S. E., 'Legal pluralism' (1988) 22(5) *Law & Society Review* 869–96

Merry, S. E., 'Measuring the world: Indicators, human rights, and global governance' (2011) 53(3) *Current Anthropology* 83–95

Metcalf, C., 'Indigenous rights and the environment: Evolving international law' (2003) 35(1) *Ottawa Law Review* 101–40

Mickelson, K., 'Beyond a politics of the possible? South–north relations and climate justice' (2009) 10(2) *Melbourne Journal of International Law* 411–23

Mickelson, K., 'Leading towards a level playing field, repaying ecological debt, or making environmental space: Three stories about international environmental cooperation' (2005) 43 *Osgoode Hall Law Journal* 137–70

Mickelson, K., 'Seeing the forest, the trees and the people: Coming to terms with developing country perspectives on the proposed global forests convention' in Canadian Council of International Law (ed.), *Global Forests and International Environmental Law* (Kluwer Law, 1996), pp. 239–64

Mickelson, K., 'South, north, international environmental law, international environmental lawyers' (2000) 11 *Yearbook of International Environmental Law* 52–81

Mickelson, K., 'The Stockholm conference and the creation of the South–north divide in international environmental law and policy' in S. Alam, S. Atapattu, C. G. Gonzalez, and J. Razzaque (eds.), *International Environmental Law and the Global South* (Cambridge University Press, 2015), pp. 109–29

Mickelson, K., 'Taking stock of TWAIL histories' (2008) 10(4) *International Community Law Review* 355–62

Milanovic, B., *Global Inequality: A New Approach for the Age of Globalization* (Harvard University Press, 2016)

Miles, K., *The Origins of International Investment Law: Empire, Environment and the Safeguarding of Capital* (Cambridge University Press, 2013)

Miller, C. A., 'Climate science and the making of a global political order' in S. Jasanoff (ed.), *States of Knowledge: The Co-production of Science and the Social Order* (Routledge, 2004)

Miller, C. A., 'Democratization, international knowledge institutions, and global governance' (2007) 20(2) *Governance: An International Journal of Policy, Administration, and Institutions* 325–57

Miller, D., *Global Justice and Climate Change: How Should Responsibilities Be Distributed?* (Tanner Lectures on Human Values, 2008)

Milne, S. and B. Adams, 'Market masquerades: Uncovering the politics of community-level payments for environmental services in Cambodia' (2012) 43(1) *Development and Change* 133–58

Milne, S., S. Mahanty, P. To, W. Dressler, P. Kanowski, and M. Thavat, 'Learning from "actually existing" REDD+: A synthesis of ethnographic findings' (2019) 17(1) *Conservation & Society* 84–95

Minang, P. A., M. Van Noordwijk, L. A. Duguma, D. Alemagi, T. H. Do, F. Bernard, P. Agung, V. Robiglio, D. Catacutan, and S. Suyanto, 'REDD+ readiness progress across countries: Time for reconsideration' (2014) 14(6) *Climate Policy* 685–708

Mirowski, P. and D. Plehwe (eds.), *The Road from Mont Pèlerin. The Making of the Neoliberal Thought Collective* (Harvard University Press, 2009)

Mitchell, T., *Rule of Experts: Egypt, Techno-Politics, Modernity* (University of California Press, 2002)

Mitchell, T., 'The work of economics: How a discipline makes its world' (2005) 46(2) *European Journal of Sociology* 297–320

Mitropoulos, A., *Contract and Contagion: From Biopolitics to Oikonomia* (Minor Compositions, 2012)

Mitropoulos, A., 'Oikopolitics, and storms' (2009) 3(1) *The Global South* 66–82

Moeliono, M., E. Wollenberg, and G. Limberg (eds.), *The Decentralization of Forest Governance: Politics, Economics and the Fight for Control of Forests in Indonesian Borneo* (Earthscan, 2009)

Moore, J. W., 'Anthropocene or capitalocene?' *Verso*, 1 December 2015 https://www .versobooks.com/blogs/2360-jason-w-moore-anthropocene-or-capitalocene

Moore, J. W. (ed.), *Anthropocene or Capitalocene?: Nature, History, and the Crisis of Capitalism* (PM Press, 2016)

Morgera, E., 'The need for an international legal concept of fair and equitable benefit sharing' (2016) 27(2) *European Journal of International Law* 353–83

Morse, B., 'Indigenous rights as a mechanism to promote sustainability' in L. Westra, K. Bosselmann, and R. Westa (eds.), *Reconciling Human Existence with Ecological Integrity* (Earthscan, 2008)

Bibliography

The Most Inconvenient Truth of All: Climate Change and Indigenous People (Survival International, 2009)

Mousie, J., 'Global environmental justice and postcolonial critique' (2012) 9(2) *Environmental Philosophy* 21–46

Moyn, S., *Not Enough: Human Rights in an Unequal World* (Harvard University Press, 2018)

Moyn, S., 'A powerless companion: Human rights in the age of neoliberalism' (2014) 77(4) *Law and Contemporary Problems* 147–69

Mulyani, M. and P. Jepson, 'Social learning through a REDD+ "village agreement": Insights from the KFCP in Indonesia' (2015) 56(1) *Asia Pacific Viewpoint* 79–95

Mutolib, A. and H. Ismono, 'Forest ownership conflict between a local community and the state: A case study in Dharmasraya, Indonesia' (2017) *Journal of Tropical Forest Science* 163–71

Mutua, M., 'What is TWAIL?' (2000) *Proceedings of the Annual Meeting (American Society of International Law)* 31–8

Myers, N., 'Tropical deforestation and climatic change: The conceptual background – Guest Editorial' in N. Myers (ed.), *Tropical Forests and Climate* (Springer, 1992), pp. 1–2

Myers, N. (ed.), *Tropical Forests and Climate* (Springer, 1992)

Nagendra, H. and E. Ostrom, 'Polycentric governance of multifunctional forested landscapes' (2012) 6(2) *International Journal of the Commons* 104–33

Natarajan, U., 'Human rights – Help or hindrance to combatting climate change?' *OpenDemocracy*, 9 January 2015, www.opendemocracy.net/en/openglobalrights-openpage-blog/human-rights-help-or-hindrance-to-combatting-climate-change/It

Natarajan, U., 'Third world approaches to international law (TWAIL) and the environment' in A. Philippopoulos-Mihalopoulos and V. Brookes (eds.), *Research Methods in Environmental Law: A Handbook* (Edward Elgar Publishing, 2017), pp. 207–36

Natarajan, U. and J. Dehm, 'Where is the environment? Locating nature in international law' *Third World Approaches to International Law Review (TWAILR)*, 30 August 2019 twailr .com/where-is-the-environment-locating-nature-in-international-law/

Natarajan, U. and J. Dehm (eds.), *Locating Nature: Making and Unmaking International Law* (Cambridge University Press, forthcoming)

Natarajan, U. and K. Khody, 'Locating nature: Making and unmaking international law' (2014) 27 *Leiden Journal of International Law* 573–93

Nature-Based Solutions to Address Climate Change (International Union for the Conservation of Nature, 2016)

Neto, E. R., 'REDD+ as a tool of global forest governance' (2015) 50(1) *The International Spectator: Italian Journal of International Affairs* 60–73

Newell, P. and M. Paterson, *Climate Capitalism: Global Warming and the Transformation of the Global Economy* (Cambridge University Press, 2010)

No to CO_2lonialism! Indigenous Peoples' Guide: False Solutions to Climate Change (Indigenous Environment Network, 2009)

Nordhaus, W., *A Question of Balance: Weighing the Options on Global Warming Policies* (Yale University Press, 2008)

Nordhaus, W. D., 'To slow or not to slow: The economics of the greenhouse effect' (1991) 101(407) *The Economic Journal* 920–37

Nordhaus, W. D., *The Climate Casino: Risk, Uncertainty, and Economics for a Warming World* (Yale University Press, 2013)

Norman, M. and S. Nakhooda, *The State of REDD+ Finance* (Centre for Global Development Climate and Forest Paper Series, Working Paper 378, September 2014)

North, D. C., *Institutions, Institutional Change, and Economic Performance* (Cambridge University Press, 1990)

O'Sullivan, R., 'CERSPA: A new template agreement for the sale and purchase of Certified Emission Reductions (CERs)' (2007) 2 *Environmental Liability* 120–4

Okereke, C., *Global Justice and Neoliberal Environmental Governance: Ethics, Sustainable Development and International Co-operation* (Routledge, 2007)

Okereke, C., H. Bulkeley, and H. Schroeder, 'Conceptualising climate governance beyond the international regime' (2009) 9(1) *Global Environmental Politics* 58–78

Öniş, Z. and F. Şenses, 'Rethinking the emerging post-Washington consensus' (2005) 36(2) *Development and Change* 263–90

Orford, A., 'In praise of description' (2012) 25(3) *Leiden Journal of International Law* 609–25

Orford, A., 'On international legal method' (2013) 1(1) *London Review of International Law* 166–97

Ormaza, M. V. C. and F. C. Ebert, 'The World Bank, human rights, and organizational legitimacy strategies: The case of the 2016 Environmental and Social Framework' (2019) 32(3) *Leiden Journal of International Law* 483–500

Ostrom, E., *Governing the Commons: The Evolution of Institutions for Collective Action* (Cambridge University Press, 1990)

Ostrom, E., 'Beyond markets and states: Polycentric governance of complex economic systems' (2010) 100(3) *American Economic Review* 641–72

Ostrom, E., *A Polycentric Approach for Coping with Climate Change: Background Paper to the 2010 World Development Report* (The World Bank, 2009)

Ostrom, E., 'Polycentric systems for coping with collective action and global environmental change' (2010) 20(4) *Global Environmental Change* 550–7

Ostrom, E., *Understanding Institutional Diversity* (Princeton University Press, 2005)

Ostrom, E., J. Burger, C. B. Field, R. B. Norgaard, and D. Policansky, 'Revisiting the commons: Local lessons, global challenges' (1999) 284(5412) *Science* 278–82

Ostrom, V., 'Polycentricity (Part 1)' in M. D. McGinnis (ed.), *Polycentricity and Local Public Economics: Readings from the Workshop in Political Theory and Policy Analysis* (University of Michigan Press, 1999), pp. 52–74

Ostrom, V., C. M. Tiebout, and R. Warren, 'The organisation of government in metropolitan areas: A theoretical inquiry' (1961) 55(4) *The American Political Science Review* 831–42

Our Forests, Our Future: Summary Report of the World Commission on Forests and Sustainable Development (World Commission on Forests and Sustainable Development, 1999)

Pahuja, S., 'Conserving the world's resources?' in J. Crawford and M. Koskenniemi (eds.), *The Cambridge Companion to International Law* (Cambridge University Press, 2012), pp. 398–420

Pahuja, S., *Decolonising International Law: Development, Economic Growth and the Politics of Universality* (Cambridge University Press, 2011)

Pahuja, S., 'Global poverty and the politics of good intentions' in R. Buchanan and P. Zumbansen (eds.), *Law in Transition: Human Rights, Development and Restorative Justice* (Hart Publishing, 2016), pp. 31–48

Pahuja, S., 'Laws of encounter: A jurisdictional account of international law' (2013) 1(1) *London Review of International Law* 63–98

Pahuja, S., 'Rights as regulation: The integration of development and human rights' in B. Morgan (ed.), *The Intersection of Rights and Regulation* (Ashgate, 2007), pp. 167–91

Palmer, C., 'Property rights and liability for deforestation under REDD+: Implications for "permanence" in policy design' (2011) 70(4) *Ecological Economics* 571–6

Palmer, C., M. Ohndorf, and I. A. MacKenzie, *Life's a Breach! Ensuring 'Permanence' in Forest Carbon Sinks under Incomplete Contract Enforcement* (CER-ETH (Center of Economic Research at ETH Zurich), 2009)

Bibliography

Pandering to the Loggers: Why WWF's Global Forest and Trade Network Isn't Working (Global Witness, 2011)

Parker, C., A. Mitchell, M. Trivedi, and N. Mardas, *The Little REDD+ Book: An Updated Guide to Governmental Proposals for Reducing Emissions from Deforestation and Degradation* (Global Canopy Program, 2009)

Parks, B. C. and J. T. Roberts, 'Climate change, social theory and justice' (2010) 27(2–3) *Theory, Culture and Society* 134–66

Parry, M., 'A property law perspective on the current Australian carbon sequestration laws, and the Green Paper model' (2010) 36 *Monash University Law Review* 321–60

Pasternak, S., *Grounded Authority: The Algonquins of Barriere Lake against the State* (University of Minnesota Press, 2017)

Paterson, M., 'Resistance makes carbon markets' in S. Böhm and S. Dabhi (eds.), *Upsetting the Offset: The Political Economy of Carbon Markets* (MayFly Books, 2009), pp. 244–55

Paterson, M., M. Hoffmann, M. Betsill, and S. Bernstein, 'Professions and policy dynamics in the transnational carbon emissions trading network' in L. Seabrooke and L. F. Henriksen (eds.), *Professional Networks in Transnational Governance* (Cambridge University Press, 2017), pp. 182–202

Paterson, M. and J. Stripple, 'Virtuous carbon' (2012) 21(4) *Environmental Politics* 563–82

Pattberg, P. and J. Stripple, 'Beyond the public and private divide: Remapping transnational climate governance in the 21st century' (2008) 8 *International Environmental Agreements* 367–88

Pearce, D., 'An intellectual history of environmental economics' (2002) 27 *Annual Review of Energy and Environment* 57–81

Pearce, D., A. Markandya, and E. B. Barbier, *Blueprint for a Green Economy* (Earthscan, 1989)

Pearce, F., *The Land Grabbers: The New Fight Over Who Owns the Earth* (Random House, 2012)

Pearse, R. and S. Böhm, 'Ten reasons why carbon markets will not bring about radical emissions reduction' (2014) 5 *Carbon Management* 325–37

Pearse, R. and J. Dehm, *In the REDD: Australia's Carbon Offset Project in Central Kalimantan* (Friends of the Earth International, 2011)

Peel, J., 'Re-evaluating the principle of common but differentiated responsibilities in transnational climate change law' (2016) 5(2) *Transnational Environmental Law* 245–54

Peel, J., *Science and Risk Regulation in International Law* (Cambridge University Press, 2010)

Peel, J., L. Godden, and R. J. Keenan, 'Climate change law in an era of multi-level governance' (2012) 1(2) *Transnational Environmental Law* 245–80

Peel, J. and H. M. Osofsky, 'A rights turn in climate change litigation?' (2018) 7(1) *Transnational Environmental Law* 37–67

Peluso, N. L., 'Coersing conservation? The politics of state resource control' (1993) *Global Environmental Change* 199–217

Peluso, N. L., *Rich Forests, Poor People: Resource Control and Resistance in Java* (University of California Press, 1992)

Peluso, N. L. and C. Lund, 'New frontiers of land control: Introduction' (2011) 38(4) *The Journal of Peasant Studies* 667–81

Peluso, N. L. and P. Vandergeest, 'Genealogies of the political forest and customary rights in Indonesia, Malaysia, and Thailand' (2001) 60(3) *The Journal of Asian Studies* 761

Pereira, R. and O. Gough, 'Permanent sovereignty over natural resources in the 21st century: Natural resource governance and the right to self-determination of indigenous peoples under international law' (2013) 14(2) *Melbourne Journal of International Law* 451–95

Bibliography

Perry-Kessaris, A., 'The re-co-construction of legitimacy of/through the doing business indicators' (2017) 13(4) *International Journal of Law in Context* 498–511

Peskett, L. and G. Brodnig, 'Carbon rights in REDD: Exploring the implications for poor and vulnerable people' (The World Bank, 2011)

Peskett, L. and Z. Harkin, *Risk and Responsibility in Reduced Emissions from Deforestation and Degradation* (Forest Policy and Environment Programme and Overseas Development Institute, 2007)

Peskett, L., D. Huberman, E. B. Jones, G. Edwards, and J. Brown, *Making REDD Work for the Poor* (Poverty and Environmental Partnership, 2008)

Peters, G. P., R. M. Andrew, S. Solomon, and P. Friedlingstein, 'Measuring a fair and ambitious climate agreement using cumulative emissions' (2015) 10 *Environmental Research Letters* 105004

Phelps, J., E. L. Webb, and A. Agrawal, 'Does REDD+ threaten to recentralize forest governance?' (2010) 328(5976) *Science* 312–13

Philibert, C., 'How could emissions trading benefit developing countries' (2000) 28 *Energy Policy* 947–56

Philibert, C., 'Lessons from the Kyoto Protocol: Implications for the future' (2004) 5(1) *International Review for Environmental Strategies* 311–22

Philibert, C. and J. Pershing, 'Considering the options: Climate targets for all countries' (2001) 1(2) *Climate Policy* 211–27

Pigou, A. C., *The Economics of Welfare* (Macmillan and Co., Ltd., 1932)

Piketty, T., *Capital in the Twenty-First Century* (Harvard University Press, 2014)

Piketty, T. and L. Chancel, *Carbon and inequality: From Kyoto to Paris: Trends in the Global Inequality of Carbon Emissions (1998–2013) and Prospects for an Equitable Adaptation Fund* (Paris School of Economics, 2015)

Platjouw, F. M., 'Reducing greenhouse gas emissions at home or abroad? The implications of Kyoto's supplementarity requirement for the present and future climate change regime' (2009) 18(3) *Review of European Community & International Environmental Law* 244–56

Polanyi, K., *The Great Transformation: The Political and Economic Origins of Our Time* (Beacon Press, 2001)

Polanyi, M., *The Logic of Liberty: Reflections and Rejoinders* (University of Chicago Press, 1981)

Polanyi, M., 'Profits and private enterprise' in R. T. Allen (ed.), *Society, Economics and Philosophy: Selected Papers Michael Polanyi* (Transaction Publishers, 1948)

Porter, G. and J. W. Brown, *Global Environmental Politics* (Westview Press, 1991)

Porter-Bolland, L., E. A. Ellis, M. R. Guariguata, I. Ruiz-Mallén, S. Negrete-Yankelevich, and V. Reyes-García, 'Community managed forests and forest protected areas: An assessment of their conservation effectiveness across the tropics' (2012) 268 *Forest Ecology and Management* 6–17

Posner, E. A. and D. Weisbach, *Climate Change Justice* (Princeton University Press, 2010)

Posner, E. A. and D. Weisbach, 'International Paretianism: A defense' (2012) 13 *Chinese Journal of International Law* 347–58

Potapov, P., A. Yaroshenko, S. Turubanova, M. Dubinin, L. Laestadius, C. Thies, D. Aksenov, A. Egorov, Y. Yesipova, and I. Glushkov, 'Mapping the world's intact forest landscapes by remote sensing' (2008) 13(2) *Ecology and Society* 51

The power of markets to increase ambition: New evidence supports efforts to realize the promise of Paris (Environmental Defense Fund, 2018)

The Production Gap Report (Stockholm Environment Institute, International Institute for Sustainable Development; Overseas Development Institute; Climate Analytics; Center for International Climate research and UN Environment Programme, 2019)

Bibliography

Prost, M. and A. T. Camprubí, 'Against fairness? International environmental law, disciplinary bias, and Pareto justice' (2012) 25(2) *Leiden Journal of International Law* 379–96

Protecting Carbon to Destroy Forests: Land, Enclosure and REDD+ (Carbon Trade Watch, 2013)

Prouty, A. E., 'The clean development mechanism and its implications for climate justice' (2009) 34 *Columbia Journal of Environmental Law* 513–40

Rajagopal, B., *International Law from Below: Development, Social Movements and Third World Resistance* (Cambridge University Press, 2003)

Rajamani, L., 'The Cancun Climate Agreements: Reading the text, subtext and tea leaves' (2011) 60(2) *International & Comparative Law Quarterly* 499–519

Rajamani, L., 'Ambition and differentiation in the 2015 Paris Agreement: Interpretative possibilities and underlying politics' (2016) 65(2) *International & Comparative Law Quarterly* 493–514

Rajamani, L., 'The changing fortunes of differential treatment in the evolution of international environmental law' (2012) 88(3) *International Affairs* 605–23

Rajamani, L., 'The devilish details: Key legal issues in the 2015 climate negotiations' (2015) 78(5) *The Modern Law Review* 826–53

Rajamani, L., *Differential Treatment in International Environmental Law* (Oxford University Press, 2006)

Rajamani, L., 'The Durban Platform for enhanced action and the future of the climate regime' (2012) 61(2) *International and Comparative Law Quarterly* 501–18

Rajamani, L., 'From Berlin to Bali and beyond: Killing Kyoto softly?' (2008) 57(4) *International & Comparative Law Quarterly* 909–39

Rajamani, L., 'The Making and unmaking of the Copenhagen Accord' (2010) 59(3) *International & Comparative Law Quarterly* 824–43

Rajamani, L., 'The principle of common but differentiated responsibility and the balance of commitments under the climate regime' (2000) 9(2) *Review of European Community & International Environmental Law* 120–31

Rajamani, L., 'Re-negotiating Kyoto: A review of the Sixth Conference of Parties to the Framework Convention on Climate Change Air and Atmosphere' (2001) 12 *Colorado Journal of International Environmental Law and Policy* 201–38

Rajamani, L. and E. Guérin, 'Central concepts in the Paris Agreement and how they evolved' in D. Klein, M. P. Carazo, M. Doelle, J. Bulmer, and A. Higham (eds.), *The Paris Agreement on Climate Change: Analysis and Commentary* (Oxford University Press, 2017), pp. 74–90

Ramos, A. R., 'The hyperreal Indian' (1994) 14(2) *Critique of Anthropology* 153–71

Randeria, S., 'Cunning states and unaccountable international institutions: Legal plurality, social movements and rights of local communities to common property resources' (2003) 44(1) *European Journal of Sociology* 27–60

Ratliff, D. P., 'The PCA optional rules for arbitration of disputes relating to natural resources and/or the environment' (2001) 14(4) *Leiden Journal of International Law* 887–96

Ravindranath, N. H. and J. A. Sathaye, *Climate Change and Developing Countries* (Kluwer Academic Publishers, 2002)

Ray, D., J. Roberts, S. Korwin, L. Rivera, and U. Ribet, *A Guide to Understanding and Implementing the UNFCCC REDD+ Safeguards* (Client Earth, 2013)

Read, J., 'A genealogy of homo-economicus: Neoliberalism and the production of subjectivity' (2009) 6 *Foucault Studies* 25–36

Read, J., *The Micro-Politics of Capital: Marx and the Prehistory of the Present* (SUNY Press, 2003)

Readfearn, G., and A. Morton, 'Australia is the only country using carryover climate credits, officials admit' *The Guardian*, 22 October 2019, www.theguardian.com/environment/2019/oct/22/australia-is-the-only-country-using-carryover-climate-credits-officials-admit

Recio, M. E., 'The Warsaw Framework and the future of REDD+' (2014) 24 *Yearbook of International Environmental Law* 37–69

Recommendations Related to the Role of Carbon Markets in the Paris Agreement (Carbon Market Watch, 2015)

REDD: Reaping Profits from Evictions, Land Grabs, Deforestation and Destruction of Biodiversity (Indigenous Environment Network, 2009)

Redford, K. H., C. Padoch, and T. Sunderland, 'Fads, funding, and forgetting in three decades of conservation' (2013) 27(3) *Conservation Biology* 437–8

'Report of the Third Conference of the Parties to the United Nations Framework Convention on Climate Change: 1–11 December 1997' (1997) 12(76) *Earth Negotiations Bulletin*

Rey, D. and S. Swan, *A Country-Led Safeguards Approach: Guidelines for National REDD+ Programmes* (SNV – The Netherlands Development Organisation, REDD+ Programme, 2014)

Reyes, O., 'Carbon markets after Durban' (2012) 12(1/2) *Ephemera: Theory and Politics in Organisation* 19–32

Reyes, O., *More Is Less: A Case against Sectoral Carbon Markets* (Carbon Trade Watch, 2011)

Ribot, J. C., *Waiting for Democracy: The Politics of Choice in Natural Resource Decentralisation* (World Resources Institute, 2004)

Ribot, J. C., A. Agrawal, and A. M. Larson, 'Recentralizing while decentralizing: How national governments reappropriate forest resources' (2006) 34(11) *World Development* 1864–86

Richardson, B. J., 'The ties that bind: Indigenous peoples and environmental governance' (2008) 4 *CLPE Research Paper Series*

The right to decide: The importance of respecting free, prior and informed consent (Amazon Watch, 2011)

Roberts, J. T. and B. C. Parks, 'Ecologically unequal exchange, ecological debt, and climate justice: The history and implications of three related ideas for a new social movement' (2009) 50 *International Journal of Comparative Sociology* 385–409

Robinson, A. and S. Tormey, 'Resisting "global justice": Disrupting the colonial "emancipatory" logic of the west' (2009) 30(8) *Third World Quarterly* 1395–409

Rockström, J., W. L. Steffen, K. Noone, Å. Persson, F. S. Chapin III, E. Lambin, T. M. Lenton, M. Scheffer, C. Folke, and H. J. Schellnhuber, 'Planetary boundaries: Exploring the safe operating space for humanity' (2009) 14(2) *Ecology and Society* 32

Rodríguez-Garavito, C., 'Ethnicity.gov: Global governance, indigenous peoples, and the right to prior consultation in social minefields' (2011) 18 *Indiana Journal of Global Legal Studies* 263–305

Rodríguez-Piñero, L., *Indigenous Peoples, Postcolonialism, and International Law: The ILO Regime (1919–1989)* (Oxford University Press, 2005)

Rodriguez-Ward, D., A. M. Larson, and H. G. Ruesta, 'Top-down, bottom-up and sideways: the multilayered complexities of multi-level actors shaping forest governance and REDD+ arrangements in Madre de Dios, Peru' (2018) 62(1) *Environmental Management* 98–116

Roots of Resilience — Growing the Wealth of the Poor (World Resources Institute (WRI) in collaboration with UNDP, UNEP and the World Bank, 2008)

Rose, C. M., 'Expanding the choices for the global commons: Comparing newfangled tradable allowance schemes to old-fashioned common property regimes' (1999) 10 *Duke Environmental Law & Policy Forum* 45–72

Rose, C. M., 'Ostrom and the lawyers: The impact of governing the commons on the American legal academy' (2011) 5(1) *International Journal of the Commons* 28–49

Rose, C. M., 'The several futures of property: Of cyberspace and folk tales, emission trades and ecosystems' (1998) 83 *Minnesota Law Review* 129–82

Rosenbaum, K. L., D. Schoene, and A. Mekouar, *Climate Change and the Forest Sector: Possible National and Subnational Legislation* (Food and Agriculture Organization of the United Nations, 2004)

Rosenberg, J., *The Empire of Civil Society: A Critique of the Realist Theory in International Relations* (Verso, 1994)

Rourke, M., 'Who are "indigenous and local communities" and what is "traditional knowledge" for virus access and benefit-sharing? A textual analysis of the convention on biological diversity and its Nagoya Protocol' (2018) 25(3) *Journal of Law and Medicine* 707–26

Rush, P., 'An altered jurisdiction: Corporeal traces of law' (1997) 6 *Griffith Law Review* 144–68

Russell, B. T., *Interrogating the Post-Political: The Case of Radical Climate and Climate Justice Movements* (PhD thesis, University of Leeds, 2012)

Russell, B. and A. Pusey, 'Movements and moments for climate justice: From Copenhagen to Cancun via Cochabamba' (2011) 11 *ACME: An International E-Journal for Critical Geographies* 15–32

Rutherford, S., 'Green governmentality: Insights and opportunities in the study of nature's rule' (2007) 31(2) *Progress in Human Geography* 291–307

Sachs, W. (ed.), *Global Ecology: A New Arena of Political Conflict* (Zed Books Ltd, 1993)

Sachs, W., 'One world' in W. Sachs (ed.), *The Development Dictionary: A Guide to Knowledge As Power* (Zed Books, 2010), pp. 111–26

Sachs, W., 'Sustainable development and the crisis of nature: On the political anatomy of an oxymoron' in M. Hajer and F. Fischer (eds.), *Living with Nature: Environmental Politics as Cultural Discourse* (Oxford University Press, 1999), pp. 23–41

Salomon, M. E., 'Why should it matter that others have more? – Poverty, inequality and the potential of international human rights law' (2011) 37(5) *Review of International Studies* 2137–55

Salzman, R. W., 'Distributing emission rights in the global order: The case for equal per capita allocation' (2010) 13 *Yale Human Rights and Development Journal* 281–306

Sanders, D. E., 'Indigenous peoples: Issues of definition' (1999) 8(1) *International Journal of Cultural Property* 4–13

Sand, P. H., 'International environmental law after Rio' (1993) 4(3) *European Journal of International Law* 377–89

Santilli, M., P. Moutinho, S. Schwartzman, D. Nepstad, L. Curran, and C. Nobre, 'Tropical deforestation and the Kyoto Protocol' (2005) 71(3) *Climatic Change* 267–76

Sasaki, N. and F. E. Putz, 'Critical need for a new definition of "forest" and "forest degradation" in a global climate change agreement' (2009) 20 *Conservation Letters* 1–20

Sassen, S., *Expulsions: Brutality and Complexity in the Global Economy* (Harvard University Press, 2014)

Sassen, S., 'A savage sorting of winners and losers: Contemporary versions of primitive accumulation' (2010) 7(1) *Globalisations* 23–50

Sassen, S., *Territory, Authority, Rights: From Medieval to Global Assemblages* (Princeton University Press, 2006)

Savaresi, A., 'A glimpse into the future of the climate regime: Lessons from the REDD+ architecture' (2016) 25(2) *Review of European, Comparative & International Environmental Law* 186–96

Savaresi, A., 'The human rights dimension of REDD' (2012) 21(2) *Review of European Community & International Environmental Law* 102–13

Savaresi, A., 'REDD+ and human rights: addressing synergies between international regimes' (2013) 18(3) *Ecology and Society* 5–13

Savaresi, A. and E. Morgera, 'Ownership of land, forest and carbon' in J. Costenbader (ed.), *Legal Frameworks for REDD: Design and Implementation at the National Level* (International Union for Conservation of Nature, 2009), pp. 15–34

Schlager, E. and E. Ostrom, 'Property-rights regimes and natural resources: A conceptual analysis' (1992) 68(3) *Land Economics* 249–62

Schlamadinger, B., L. Ciccarese, M. Dutschke, P. M. Fearnside, S. Brown, and D. Murdiyarso, 'Should we include avoidance of deforestation in the international response to climate change' in D. Murdiyarso and H. Herawati (eds.), *Carbon Forestry: Who Will Benefit?: Proceedings of Workshop on Carbon Sequestration and Sustainable Livelihoods held in Bogor on 16–17 February 2005* (Center for International Forestry Research, 2005), pp. 26–41

Schneider, L., 'Assessing the additionality of CDM projects: Practical experiences and lessons learned' (2009) 9(3) *Climate Policy* 242–54

Schneider, L. R., 'Perverse incentives under the CDM: an evaluation of HFC-23 destruction projects' (2011) 11(2) *Climate Policy* 851–64

Schneider, L. and A. Kollmuss, 'Perverse effects of carbon markets on HFC-23 and SF6 abatement projects in Russia' (2015) 5 *Nature Climate Change* 1061–63

Scholes, R. J. and I. R. Noble, 'Storing carbon on land' (2001) 294(5544) *Science* 1012–13

Schrijver, N., *The Evolution of Sustainable Development in International Law: Inception, Meaning and Status* (Martinus Nijhoff Publishers, 2008)

Schrijver, N., *Sovereignty over Natural Resources: Balancing Rights and Duties* (Cambridge University Press, 1997)

Schroth, F., *The politics of governance experiments: Constructing the Clean Development Mechanism* (Unpublished PhD thesis, Technischen Universität Berlin, 2016)

Schulte-Tenckhoff, I., 'Treaties, peoplehood, and self-determination: understanding the language of indigenous rights' in E. Pulitano (ed.), *Indigenous Rights in the Age of the Declaration* (Cambridge University Press, 2012), pp. 64–86

Schulte-Tenckhoff, I. and A. Hasan Khan, 'The permanent quest for a mandate: Assessing the UN permanent forum on indigenous issues' (2011) 20(3) *Griffith Law Review* 673–701

Scoones, I., R. Hall, S. M. Borras Jr, B. White, and W. Wolford, 'The politics of evidence: Methodologies for understanding the global land rush' (2013) 40(3) *The Journal of Peasant Studies* 469–83

Scott, A., *The Evolution of Resource Property Rights* (Oxford University Press, 2008)

Scott, D., 'Preface: Evil beyond repair' (2018) 22(1) *Small Axe: A Caribbean Journal of Criticism* vii–x

Scott, J., *The Art of Not Being Governed: An Anarchist History of Upland Southeast Asia* (Yale University Press, 2009)

Scott, J. C., *Seeing Like a State: How Certain Schemes to Improve the Human Condition Have Failed* (Yale University Press, 1998)

Scott, S. V., 'Is the crisis of climate change a crisis for international law: Is international law too democratic, too capitalist and too fearful to cope with the crisis of climate change?' (2007) 14 *Australian International Law Journal* 31–43

Segger, M.-C. C., A. Khalfan, M. Gehring, and M. Toering, 'Prospects for principles of international sustainable development law after the WSSD: Common but differentiated responsibilities, precaution and participation' (2003) 12(1) *Review of European Community & International Environmental Law* 54–68

Bibliography

Serageldin, I. and A. Steer (eds.), *Valuing the Environment: Proceedings of the First Annual International Conference on Environmentally Sustainable Development, Held at the World Bank, Washington DC September 30–1 October 1, 1993* (The World Bank, 1993)

Seufert, P., 'The FAO voluntary guidelines on the responsible governance of tenure of land, fisheries and forests' (2013) 10(1) *Globalizations* 181–6

Seymour, F., 'Forests, climate change and human rights: Managing risks and trade-offs' in S. Humphreys (ed.), *Climate Change and Human Rights* (Cambridge University Press, 2010), pp. 207–37

Seymour, F., N. Birdsall, and W. Savedoff, *The Indonesia–Norway REDD+ Agreement: A Glass Half-Full* (Center for Global Development, 2015)

Shelton, D., 'Common concern of humanity' (2009) 39 *Environmental Policy and Law* 83–6

Shiva, V., 'Resources' in W. Sachs (ed.), *The Development Dictionary: A Guide to Knowledge As Power* (Zed Books, 2010), pp. 228–42

Shue, H., *Climate Justice: Vulnerability and Protection* (Oxford University Press, 2014)

Shue, H., 'Global environment and international inequality' (1999) 75(3) *International Affairs* 531–45

Shue, H., 'Historical responsibility: Accountability for the results of actions taken' (SBSTA Technical Briefing, 2009)

Shue, H., 'Subsistence emissions and luxury emissions' (1993) 15(1) *Law & Policy* 39–60

Siegele, L., D. Roe, A. Giuliani, and N. Winer, 'Conservation and human rights – Who says what? A review of international law and policy' in J. Campese, T. Sunderland, T. Greiber, and G. Oviedo (eds.), *Rights-Based Approaches: Exploring Issues and Opportunities for Conservation* (Center for International Forestry Research and International Union for Conservation of Nature, 2009)

Sikor, T., J. He, and G. Lestrelin, 'Property rights regimes and natural resources: A conceptual analysis revisited' (2017) 93 *World Development* 337–49

Sikor, T. and C. Lund, 'Access and property: A question of power and authority' in T. Sikor and C. Lund (eds.), *The Politics of Possession* (Wiley-Blackwell, 2010), pp. 1–22

Sills, E. O. (ed.), *REDD+ on the Ground: A Case Book of Subnational Initiatives across the Globe* (Center for International Forestry Research, 2014)

Simms, A., A. Meyer, and N. Robbins, *Who Owes Who – Climate Change, Debt, Equity and Survival* (Christian Aid, 1999)

Sindico, F., 'Paris, climate change, and sustainable development' (2016) 6(1–2) *Climate Law* 130–41

Skutsch, M. and P. E. Van Laake, 'REDD as multi-level governance in-the-making' (2008) 19(6) *Energy & Environment* 831–44

Sluga, G., 'Capitalists and climate' *Humanity Journal Blog*, 6 November 2017, humanityjournal.org/blog/capitalists-and-climate

Smith, K., 'Offsets under Kyoto: A dirty deal for the south' in upsetting the offset' in S. Böhm and S. Dabhi (eds.), *Upsetting the Offset* (MayFly Books, 2009), pp. 2–4

Smith, M., *Against Ecological Sovereignty: Ethics, Biopolitics, and Saving the Natural World* (University of Minnesota Press, 2011)

Smith, N., 'Nature as accumulation strategy' (2007) 43 *Socialist Register* 19–41

Smith, N. 'There's no such thing as a natural disaster', *Understanding Katrina: Persepctives from the Social Sciences*, 11 June 2006 understandingkatrina.ssrc.org/Smith/

Smith, P., 'Chapter 11: Agriculture, forestry and other land use (AFOLU)' in O. Edenhofer (ed.), *Climate Change 2014: Mitigation of Climate Change* (Cambridge University Press, 2015)

Bibliography

Some views of indigenous peoples and forest-related organisations on the World Bank's "Forest carbon Partnership facility" and proposals for a "Global Forest Partnership" (Briefing by the Forest Peoples' Programme, 2008)

Sommerville, M., *Land Tenure and REDD+: Risks to Property Rights and Opportunities for Economic Growth* (USAID, 2013)

Sornarajah, M., *Resistance and Change in the International Law on Foreign Investment* (Cambridge University Press, 2015)

Sosa, I., *License to Operate: Indigenous Relations and Free, Prior, Informed Consent in the Mining Industry* (Sustainalytics, 2011)

Springer, J. and V. Retana, *Free, Prior and Informed Consent and REDD+: Guidelines and Resources* (WWF-US's People and Conservation Programme and WWF's Global Forest and Climate Programme, 2014)

State of the World's Forests: Enhancing the Socioeconomic Benefits from Forests (Food and Agricultural Organisation of the United Nations, 2014), www.fao.org/3/a-i3710e.pdf

Status of Forest Carbon Rights and Implications for Communities, the Carbon Trade and REDD+ Investments (Rights and Resources Initiative, 2014)

Steffen, W., K. Richardson, J. Rockström, S. E. Cornell, I. Fetzer, E. M. Bennett, R. Biggs, S. R. Carpenter, W. De Vries, and C. A. De Wit, 'Planetary boundaries: Guiding human development on a changing planet' (2015) 347(6223) *Science* 1259855

Stern, N. H., *The Economics of Climate Change: The Stern Review* (Cambridge University Press, 2007)

Stevens, C., R. Winterbottom, J. Springer, and K. Reytar, *Securing Rights, Combatting Climate Change* (World Resources Institute, 2014)

Stiglitz, J. E., *More Instruments and Broader Goals: Moving toward the Post-Washington Consensus* (Citeseer, 1998)

Stocker, T.F. et al. (eds.), *Climate Change 2013: The Physical Science Basis: Contribution of Working Group I to the Fifth Assessment Report of the Intergovernmental Panel on Climate Change* (Cambrdige University Press, 2013)

Stone, C. D., 'Common but differentiated responsibilities in international law' (2004) 98(2) *American Journal of International Law* 276–301

Stowell, D., *Climate Trading: The Development of Greenhouse Markets* (Palgrave Macmillan, 2005)

Streck, C., 'In the market: Forest carbon rights: Shedding light on a muddy concept' (2015) 4 *Carbon & Climate Law Review* 342–47

Streck, C., A. Howard, and R. Rajão, *Options for Enhancing REDD+ Collaboration in the Context of Article 6 of the Paris Agreement* (Meridian Institute, 2017)

Streck, C. and J. Lin, 'Making markets work: A review of CDM performance and the need for reform' (2008) 19(2) *European Journal of International Law* 409–42

Sukhdev, P., R. Prabhu, P. Kumar, A. Bassi, W. Patwa-Shah, T. Enters, G. Labbate, and J. Greenwalt, *REDD+ and the green economy: Opportunities for a mutually supportive relationship* (UN-REDD Programme, 2012)

Sullivan, G., 'Transnational legal assemblages and global security law: Topologies and temporalities of the list' (2014) 5(1) *Transnational Legal Theory* 81–127

Sullivan, S., 'Banking nature? The spectacular financialisation of environmental conservation' (2013) 45(1) *Antipode* 198–217

Sullivan, S., 'Bonding nature(s)? Funds, financiers and values at the impact investing edge in environmental conservation' in S. Bracking, A. Fredriksen, S. Sullivan, and P. Woodhouse (eds.), *Valuing Development, Environment and Conservation* (Routledge, 2018), pp. 113–33

Bibliography

Sullivan, S., 'The environmentality of "Earth Incorporated": On contemporary primitive accumulation and the financialisation of environmental conservation' (2010) Paper presented at the conference An Environmental History of Neoliberalism, Lund University 6–8 May 2010

Sullivan, S., 'Green capitalism, and the cultural poverty of constructing nature as service-provider' (2009) 3 *Radical Anthropology* 18–27

Sullivan, S., 'Nature on the move III: (Re)countenancing an animate nature' (2013) 6(1–2) *New Proposals: Journal of Marxism and Interdisciplinary Inquiry* 50–71

Sullivan, S., 'On "natural capital", "fairy tales" and ideology' (2017) 48(2) *Development and Change* 397–423

Sunderlin, W. D., A. M. Larson, and P. Cronkleton, 'Forest tenure rights and REDD+: From inertia to policy solutions' in A. Angelsen (ed.), *Realising REDD+: National Strategy and Policy Options* (Center for International Forestry Research, 2009), pp. 139–44

Sunderlin, W. D., A. M. Larson, and J. P. Sarmiento Barletti, 'Land and carbon tenure: Some but insufficient progress' in A. Angelsen, C. Martius, V. De Sy, A. E. Duchelle, A. M. Larson, and P. T. Thuy (eds.), *Transforming REDD+: Lessons and New Directions* (Center for International Forestry Research, 2018), pp. 93–103

Sustainable Management of Forests and REDD+: Negotiations Need Clear Terminology: Information Note (Food and Agricultural Organization, 2009)

Swyngedouw, E., 'Apocalypse forever?: Post-political populism and the spectre of climate change' (2010) 27(2–3) *Theory, Culture and Society* 213–32

Szabo, M., 'After Paris, UN's new "light touch" role on markets to help spawn carbon clubs' *Carbon Pulse*, 15 December 2015 carbon-pulse.com/13415/

Szabo, M., 'Paris Agreement rings in new era of international carbon trading' *Carbon Pulse*, 12 December 2015 carbon-pulse.com/13339/

Tacconi, L., F. Downs, and P. Larmour, 'Anti-corruption policies in the forest sector and REDD+' in A. Angelson (ed.), *Realising REDD+: National Strategy and Policy Options* (Center for International Forestry Research, 2009), pp. 163–74

Takacs, D., *Forest Carbon: Law and Property Rights* (Conservation International, 2009)

Takacs, D., 'Forest carbon (REDD+), repairing international trust, and reciprocal contractual sovereignty' (2012) 37 *Vermont Law Review* 653–736

Tangley, L., 'Saving tropical forests' (1986) 36 *BioScience* 4–8

Tanner, T. and J. Allouche, 'Towards a new political economy of climate change and development' (2011) 42(3) *IDS Bulletin* 1–14

Tehan, M. F., L. C. Godden, M. A. Young, and K. A. Gover, *The Impact of Climate Change Mitigation on Indigenous and Forest Communities: International, National and Local Law Perspectives on REDD+* (Cambridge University Press, 2017)

Tennant, C., 'Indigenous peoples, international institutions, and the international legal literature from 1945–1993' (1994) 16(1) *Human Rights Quarterly* 1–57

Third World Network, 'Bangkok Climate News Updates' (April 2011), www.twnside.org.sg/title2/climate/news/bangkok03/bkk3_news_up04.pdf

Third World Network, 'Indigenous peoples outraged at removal of rights in REDD outcome, Poznań News Update' 12 December 2008

Thomas, S., P. Dargusch, S. Harrison, and J. Herbohn, 'Why are there so few afforestation and reforestation Clean Development Mechanism projects?' (2010) 27 *Land Use Policy* 880–7

Thompson, M. C., M. Baruah, and E. R. Carr, 'Seeing REDD+ as a project of environmental governance' (2011) 14 *Environmental Science and Policy* 100–10

Thornberry, P., *Indigenous Peoples and Human Rights* (Manchester University Press, 2013)

Tienhaara, K., 'The potential perils of forest carbon contracts for developing countries: Cases from Africa' (2012) 39(2) *The Journal of Peasant Studies* 551–72

Torres, G., 'Who owns the sky' (2001) 19 *Pace Environmental Law Review* 227–86

Towards a Green Economy: Pathways to Sustainable Development and Poverty Eradication (United Nations Environment Programme, 2011)

Trick or Treat? REDD, Development and Sustainable Forest Management (Global Witness, 2009)

Trubek, D. M. and A. Santos (eds.), *The New Law and Development: A Critical Appraisal* (Cambridge University Press, 2006)

Tzouvala, N., 'A false promise? Regulating land-grabbing and the post-colonial state' (2019) 32(2) *Leiden Journal of International Law* 235–53

Ulloa, A., *The Ecological Native: Indigenous Peoples' Movements and Eco-Governmentality in Columbia* (Routledge, 2013)

Unruh, G. C., 'Understanding carbon lock-in' (2000) 28 *Energy Policy* 817–30

van Asselt, H., *The Politics of Fossil Fuel Subsidies and Their Reform* (Cambridge University Press, 2018)

van Asselt, H. and K. Kulovesi, 'Seizing the opportunity: Tackling fossil fuel subsidies under the UNFCCC' (2017) 17(3) *International Environmental Agreements: Politics, Law and Economics* 357–70

van Asselt, H., K. Kulovesi, and M. Mehling, 'Editorial – Negotiating the Paris rulebook: Introduction to the special issue' (2018) 12(3) *Carbon & Climate Law Review* 173–83

van Kooten, G. C., 'Forest carbon offsets and carbon emissions trading: Problems of contracting' (2017) 75 *Forest Policy and Economics* 83–8

van Zeben, J. A., 'Polycentricity' in B. Hudson, J. Rosenbloom, and D. Cole (eds.), *Routledge Handbook of the Study of the Commons* (Routledge, 2019), pp. 38–49

Venning, P., '"REDD" at the convergence of the environment and development debates – International incentives for national action on avoided deforestation' (2010) 6(1) *Law, Environment and Development Journal* 82–101

Vested Interests—Industrial Logging and Carbon in Tropical Forests (Global Witness, 2009)

Vidas, D., J. Zalasiewicz, and M. Williams, 'What is the Anthropocene—and why is it relevant for international law?' (2014) 25 *Yearbook of International Environmental Law* 3–23

Vincent, E. and T. Neale, *Unstable Relations: Indigenous People and Environmentalism in Contemporary Australia* (Apollo Books, 2016)

Voigt, C., 'Introduction: The kaleidoscopic world of REDD+' in C. Voigt (ed.), *Research Handbook on REDD-Plus and International Law* (Edward Elgar Publishing, 2016)

Voigt, C., *Research Handbook on REDD-Plus and International Law* (Edward Elgar Publishing, 2016)

Voigt, C. and F. Ferreira, 'Differentiation in the Paris Agreement' (2016) 6(1–2) *Climate Law* 58–74

Voß, J.-P. and F. Schroth, 'The politics of innovation and learning in polycentric governance' in A. Jordan, D. Huitema, H. van Asselt, and J. Forster (eds.), *Governing Climate Change: Polycentricity in Action?* (Cambridge University Press, 2018), pp. 99–116

Wainwright, J. and G. Mann, 'Climate leviathan' (2013) 45(1) *Antipode* 1–22

Wainwright, J. and G. Mann, *Climate Leviathan: A Political Theory of Our Planetary Future* (Verso Books, 2018)

Wallace-Wells, D., *The Uninhabitable Earth: Life after Warming* (Tim Duggan Books, 2019)

Ward, T., 'The right to free, prior, and informed consent: indigenous peoples' participation rights within international law' (2011) 10(2) *Northwestern University Journal of International Human Rights* 54–84

Bibliography

405

Warlenius, R., G. Pierce, V. Ramasar, E. Quistorp, J. Martínez-Alier, L. Rijnhout, and I. Yanez, 'Ecological debt: History, meaning and relevance for environmental justice' (2015) 18 *EJOLT Report*

Watson, C., E. Brickell, W. McFarland, and J. McNeely, *Integrating REDD+ into a Green Economy Transition* (Overseas Development Institute, 2013)

Watson, I. and S. Venne, 'Talking up indigenous peoples' original intent in a space dominated by state interventions' in E. Pulitano (ed.), *Indigenous Rights in the Age of the Declaration* (Cambridge University Press, 2012), pp. 87–109

Watson, R. T., I. R. Noble, B. Bolin, N. H. Ravindranath, D. J. Verardo, and D. J. Dokken, *Land Use, Land-Use Change and Forestry: A Special Report of the Intergovernmental Panel on Climate Change* (Cambridge University Press, 2000)

Watt, H. M., 'Private international law's shadow contribution to the question of informal transnational authority' (2018) 25(1) *Indiana Journal of Global Legal Studies* 37–60

The Wealth of the Poor: Managing Ecosystems to Fight Poverty (United Nations Development Programme, United Nations Environment Programme, The World Bank and World Resources Institute, 2005)

Webb, R. and J. Wentz, *Human Rights and Article 6 of the Paris Agreement: Ensuring Adequate Protection of Human Rights in the SDM and ITMO Frameworks* (Sabin Center for Climate Change Law Columbia Law School, 2018)

Weisslitz, M., 'Rethinking the equitable principle of common but differentiated responsibility: Differential versus absolute norms of compliance and contribution in the global climate change context' (2002) 13 *Colorado Journal of Environmental Law and Policy* 473–509

Wemaere, M., C. Streck, and T. Chagas, 'Legal ownership and nature of Kyoto units and EU allowances' in D. Freestone and C. Streck (eds.), *Legal Aspects of Carbon Trading: Kyoto, Copenhagen, and Beyond* (Oxford University Press, 2009), pp. 35–58

West, S., '"Command without control": Are market mechanisms capable of delivering ecological integrity to REDD?' (2010) 6(3) *Law, Environment and Development Journal* 298–319

Westra, L., *Environmental Justice and the Rights of Indigenous Peoples: International and Domestic Legal Perspectives* (Earthscan, 2008)

What Is an Emission Reduction Purchase Agreement (ERPA)? (Overseas Development Institute)

What Rights? A Comparative Analysis of Developing Countries' National Legislation on Community and Indigenous Peoples' Forest Tenure Rights (Rights and Resources Initiative, 2012)

Whitington, J., 'The prey of uncertainty: Climate change as opportunity' (2012) 12(1/2) *Ephemera: Theory and Politics in Organisation* 113–37

Whyte, J., 'The invisible hand of Friedrich Hayek: Submission and spontaneous order' (2019) 47(2) *Political Theory* 156–84

Wiersema, A., 'Climate change, forests and international law: REDD's descent into irrelevance' (2014) 47(1) *Vanderbilt Journal of Transnational Law* 1–66

Wiersum, K. F., '200 years of sustainability in forestry: Lessons from history' (1995) 19 *Environmental Management* 321–9

Wiessner, S., 'The cultural rights of indigenous peoples: Achievements and continuing challenges' (2011) 22(1) *European Journal of International Law* 121–40

Wilder, M. and L. Fitz-Gerald, 'Carbon contracting' in D. Freestone and C. Streck (eds.), *Legal Aspects of Implementing the Kyoto Protocol Mechanisms: Making Kyoto Work* (Oxford: Oxford University Press, 2005), pp. 295–309

Williams, D., 'Constructing the economic space: The World Bank and the making of *homo oeconomicus*' (1999) 28(1) *Millennium: Journal of International Studies* 79–99

Williams, L. G., *Putting the Pieces Together for Good Governance of REDD+: An Analysis of 32 REDD+ Country Readiness Proposals* (World Resources Institute, 2013)

Winkler, H., 'Mitigation (Article 4)' in D. Klein, M. P. Carazo, M. Doelle, J. Bulmer, and A. Higham (eds.), *The Paris Agreement on Climate Change: Analysis and Commentary* (Oxford University Press, 2017), pp. 141–165

Winkler, H., N. Höhne, G. Cunliffe, T. Kuramochi, A. April, and M. J. de Villafranca Casas, 'Countries start to explain how their climate contributions are fair: More rigour needed' (2018) 18(1) *International Environmental Agreements: Politics, Law and Economics* 99–115

Winkler, H. and L. Rajamani, 'CBDR&RC in a regime applicable to all' (2014) 14(1) *Climate Policy* 102–21

Winterbottom, R., *Taking Stock: The Tropical Forestry Action Plan after Five Years* (World Resources Institute, 1990)

Woodwell, G. M., 'Forests in a warming world: A time for new policies' *Tropical Forests and Climate* (Springer, 1992), pp. 245–51

The World Bank Participation Sourcebook (The World Bank, 1996)

World Development Report 1992: Development and the Environment (The World Bank, 1992)

World Development Report 1997: The State in a Changing World (The World Bank, 1997)

World Development Report 2002: Building Institutions for Markets (The World Bank, 2001)

World Development Report 2010: Development and Climate Change (The World Bank, 2010)

World People's Conference on Climate Change and the Rights of Mother Earth, *People's Agreement of Cochabamba* (2010) pwccc.wordpress.com/2010/04/24/peoples-agreement/

Wright, B. E., M. D. McGinnis, and E. Ostrom, 'Reflections on Vincent Ostrom, public administration, and polycentricity' (2011) 71(1) *Public Administration Review* 15–25

Wu, C. Q., 'A unified forum? The new arbitration rules for environmental disputes under the permanent court of arbitration' (2002) 3(1) *Chicago Journal of International Law* 263–70

Yaffe, N., 'Indigenous consent: A self-determination perspective' (2018) 19(2) *Melbourne Journal of International Law* 703–49

Yamin, F., 'Equity, entitlements and property rights under the Kyoto Protocol: The shape of "things" to come' (1999) 8(3) *Review of European, Comparative & International Environmental Law* 265–74

Yandle, B., 'Grasping for the heavens: 3-D property rights and the global commons' (1999) 10(1) *Duke Environmental Law and Policy Forum* 14–44

Yang, M., 'COP 24 round-up part 1: The Paris rulebook' *Inside Energy & Environment*, 18 December 2018, www.insideenergyandenvironment.com/2018/12/cop-24-round-up-part-one-the-paris-rulebook/

Young, M. A., 'Interacting regimes and experimentation' in *The Impact of Change Mitigation on Indigenous and Forest Communities: International, National and Local Law Perspectives on REDD+* (Cambridge University Press, 2017), pp. 329–45

Young, M. A., 'Introduction: The productive friction between regimes' in M. A. Young (ed.), *Regime Interaction in International Law: Facing Fragmentation* (Cambridge University Press, 2012), pp. 1–19

Young, M. A., 'REDD+ and interacting legal regimes' in C. Voigt (ed.), *Research Handbook on REDD-Plus and International Law* (Edward Elgar Publishing, 2016)

Young, M. A., 'REDD+ as an international legal regime' in *The Impact of Climate Change Mitigation on Indigenous and Forest Communities: International, National and Local Law Perspectives on REDD+* (Cambridge University Press, 2017), pp. 13–47

Young, S. M., *Indigenous Peoples, Consent and Rights* (Routledge, 2018)

Younging, G., *Elements of Indigenous Style: A Guide for Writing By an About Indigenous Peoples* (Brush Education, 2018)

Zahar, A., J. Peel, and L. Godden, *Australian Climate Law in Global Context* (Cambridge University Press, 2013)

Zhu, X. et al., 'Pathways for implementing REDD+: Experiences from carbon markets and communities' (UNEP Riso Centre, 2010), www.acp-cd4cdm.org/media/237951/pathwaysimplementinggreddplus.pdf

Zumbansen, P., 'The law of society: Governance through contract' (2007) 14(2) *Indiana Journal of Global Legal Studies* 191–233

Zumbansen, P., 'Transnational legal pluralism' (2010) 1(2) *Transnational Legal Theory* 141–89

Zwick, S., 'Katowice climate deal leaves carbon markets intact but incomplete', *Ecosystem Marketplace*, 15 December 2018, www.ecosystemmarketplace.com/articles/carbon-markets-look-set-to-emerge-from-katowice-intact-but-incomplete/

Zwick, S., 'The road from Paris: Green lights, speed bumps, and the future of carbon markets', *Ecosystem Marketplace*, 1 February 2016, www.ecosystemmarketplace.com/articles/green-lights-and-speed-bumps-on-road-to-markets-under-paris-agreement

WEB RESOURCES AND MISCELLANEOUS

Banfo, R., 'Non-carbon benefits in REDD+ implementation: Insights from Africa' (presentation, 3rd Voluntary Meeting of National REDD+ Focal Points, 23 May 2016) redd.unfccc.int/files/2_ghana_ncbs_ppt.__revised_.pdf

Call to Action to Reject REDD+ and Extractive Industries: To Confront Capitalism and Defend Life and Territories (December 2014) wrm.org.uy/wp-content/uploads/2014/11/Call-COP-Lima_NoREDD.pdf

Climate Justice Now! Statement, www.carbontradewatch.org/take-action-archive/climate-justice-now-statement-4.html

'Closing remarks – Forest Day 5, 2011' blog.cifor.org/5782/countries-draft-%E2%80%9Cglobal-business-plan%E2%80%9D-for-planet-at-climate-summit-figueres-says/

Constitution of the Republic of Indonesia 1945 (Indonesia)

Forest Carbon Partnership Facility, 'Carbon fund: Introduction to managing risk delivery' (PowerPoint slides of talk at FCPF Carbon Fund, 3rd Meeting, 2012)

Forest Carbon Partnership Facility, *A Guide to the FCPF Readiness Assessment Framework*, June 2013, www.forestcarbonpartnership.org/sites/fcp/files/2013/July2013/FCPC%20framework%20text%207-25-13%20ENG%20web.pdf

GCF in Brief: REDD+ (Global Climate Fund), www.greenclimate.fund/documents/20182/194568/GCF_in_Brief__REDD_.pdf/16e4f020-da42-42a2-ad52-d18314822710

GEO, 'Comprehensive new global monitoring system to track deforestation and forest carbon' (Media Release, 19 October 2009), www.earthobservations.org/documents/pressreleases/pr_09_10_forest_carbon_monitoring.pdf

Indigenous Environment Network, 'UN promoting potentially genocidal policy at World Climate Summit' (Media Release, 8 December 2015), www.ienearth.org/un-promoting-potentially-genocidal-policy-at-world-climate-summit/

International Emissions Trading Association, *Emission Reduction Purchase Agreement, Version 3.0* (2006), www.ieta.org/resources/Resources/Trading%20Documents/cdmerpav.3.ofinal.doc

Bibliography

International Emission Trading Association, *Key Design Options for Article 6: IETA Priorities* (April 2018), www.ieta.org/resources/International_WG/2018/Key%20design%20priorities%20for%20Article%206.pdf

The International Workshop on Community-based Natural Resource Governance (CBNRG), Washington DC, 10–14 May 1998, 'Workshop Report' info.worldbank.org/etools/docs/library/97605/conatrem/conatrem/documents/May98Workshop_Report.pdf

Letter from Bank Information Center, Environmental Investigation Agency and Rainforest Foundation Norway to Members of the FCPF Participants Committee, 29 October 2014 https://d5i6is0eze552.cloudfront.net/documents/Politiske-utspill/2014/FCPF-EIA-BIC-RFN-Letter-to-PC-on-ERPA-GC-CT-ID-17490.docx?mtime=20150630145459

'Mozambique and Democratic Republic of Congo sign landmark deals with World Bank to cut emissions and reduce deforestation' (Press Release, 19 February 2019), www.worldbank.org/en/news/press-release/2019/02/12/mozambique-and-democratic-republic-of-congo-sign-landmark-deals-with-world-bank-to-cut-carbon-emissions-and-reduce-deforestation

Petak Danum Kalimantan Tengah, *Our Land Is Not a Carbon Toilet for Dirty Industries of Developed Countries*, 2012, copy on file with author

'PROTEST: Indigenous peoples "2nd MAY REVOLT" at the UNPFII', *Carbon Trade Watch*, 12 May 2008, www.carbontradewatch.org/multimedia/protest-indigenous-peoples-2nd-may-revolt-at-the-u.html

Radical New Agenda Needed to Achieve Climate Justice': Poznań Statement from the Climate Justice Now! Alliance www.carbontradewatch.org/archive/poznan-statement-from-the-climate-justice-now-alliance-2.html

REDD: Indigenous Peoples Not Allowed to Speak at UNFCCC (2008), www.youtube.com/watch?v=brsqUgbBHu0

Scrap the ETS (2012) scrap-the-euets.makenoise.org/KV/

Shift2Neutral Pty Limited v Fairfax Media Publications Pty Limited [2014] NSWSC 86 (18 February 2014)

Shift2Neutral Pty Ltd v Fairfax Media Publications Pty Ltd [2015] NSWCA 274 (10 September 2015)

Social PreCOP, *Margarita Declaration on Climate Change* (2014) https://redd-monitor.org/2014/08/08/the-margarita-declaration-on-climate-change-we-reject-the-implementation-of-false-solutions-to-climate-change-such-as-carbon-markets-and-other-forms-of-privatization-and-commodification-of-life/

Stern, Todd, 'The new climate negotiations: Ambition, differentiation and flexibility', speech by Todd Stern, Special Envoy for Climate Change at World Futures Energy Summit, Abu Dhabi, 15 January 2013 2009-2017.state.gov/e/oes/rls/remarks/2013/202824.htm

System Change Not Climate Change – A People's Declaration from Klimaforum09 (2009) klimaforum.org/

Tauli-Corpuz, V., 'Statement on the announcement of the World Bank forest carbon partnership facility' 11 December 2007, www.un.org/esa/socdev/unpfii/documents/statement_vtc_toWB11dec.2007.doc

United Nations Permanent Forum on Indigenous Issues, 'Permanent forums hails General Assembly adoption of indigenous rights declaration, pledges to make it a living document' as Seventh Session Concludes: On special theme, says Indigenous Way of Life Threatened by Climate Change, Calls for Indigenous Participation in all Aspects of International Debate on Issue' (Media Release, 2 May 2008), www.un.org/News/Press/docs/2008/hr4953.doc.htm

UN-REDD Programme, *Frequently Asked Questions and Answers - The UN-REDD Programme and REDD+*, November 2010, www.unep.org/forests/Portals/142/docs/UN-REDD%20FAQs%20%5B11.10%5D.pdf

Bibliography

UN-REDD Programme, 'Info brief 5: Summaries of information: How to demonstrate REDD+ safeguards are being addressed and respected' (2016) unredd.net/documents/global-pro gramme-191/safeguards-multiple-benefits-297/15299-info-brief-summaries-of-information-1-en.html

UN-REDD Programme, *UN-REDD Supporting Work on Tenure and REDD+* (November 2014), www.unredd.net/documents/global-programme-191/governance-452/tenure-and-redd-2647/13823-unredd-supporting-work-on-tenure-and-redd-13823.html

VCS Submission: Operationalizing Article 6 of the Paris Agreement (29 September 2017), www.ieta.org/resources/International_WG/Article6/Portal/VCS%20Submission%20on%20Operationalizing%20Article%206,%2029%20SEP%202017.pdf

The World Bank, 'Forest carbon partnership facility launched at Bali climate meeting' (Media Release, 11 December 2007)

The World Bank, 'Forest carbon facility takes aim at deforestation' (Media Release, 11 December 2007), www.worldbank.org/archive/website01290/WEB/0-1493.HTM

The World Bank, *Forest Carbon Partnership Facility*, www.forestcarbonpartnership.org/fcp/node/12 accessed 18 February 2010

The World Bank, *Forest Carbon Partnership Facility: Information Memorandum* (13 June 2008)

The World Bank, *The World Bank Carbon Funds and Facilities*, www.worldbank.org/en/topic/climatechange/brief/world-bank-carbon-funds-facilities

The World Bank Group's Common Property Resource Management Network: Guide to CPRNet, www.supras.biz/pdf/supras_008_wb_cprnetguide.pdf

Index

accounting, 67–8, 72, 76, 93, 95, 186, 193, 206, 212, 217, 244, 348
  capacity, 249
  framework, 67, 69, 74, 141
  rules, 10, 23, 68, 141, 160, 191
Activities Implemented Jointly, 233
Ad Hoc Working Group on Further Commitments for Annex I Parties under the Kyoto Protocol (AWG-KP), 202
Ad Hoc Working Group on Long-term Cooperative Action (AWG-LCA), 63, 202
Ad Hoc Working Group on the Durban Platform of Enhanced Action, 203
adaptation. See climate adaptation
additionality, 20, 23, 61, 75, 142, 180, 200, 234–5
afforestation, 13, 103, 158–60, 201, See also afforestation and reforestation (A/R) projects
afforestation and reforestation (A/R) projects, 61–2, 186
aggregate global targets, 11, 132, 201
agrarian tenure. See tenure, agrarian
Agrawal, Arun, 278, 292, 301–2
agriculture, forestry and other land use (AFOLU), 13, 210
Anaya, James, 305–6, 339–42
Angelsen, Arild, 90, 181
Anthropocene, 1–2, 133
anti-corruption, 62, 155, 248–9
assemblage, 7, 17–18, 107, 131, 167, 193, 281, 349, See also REDD+, as an assemblage
assigned amount units (AAUs), 141, 197, 200
atmosphere, 24, 133, 149, 156–9, 260, 355
  common heritage and, 126
  emissions in, 50, 134–6, 192, 198, 224
  governance of, 27
  privatisation of, 196

  responsibility for, 31
  rights to, 197, 223
Australia, 90, 116, 118, 235, 264, 335, 353
authority, 3–5, 27–8, 30, 46–50, 129–31, 133, 167–70, 176, 257, 351, 353
  actualisation of, 4, 8, 168, 175, 302
  authorisation, 28, 47, 123, 128, 217, 351, 353
  devolution of, 282
  global, 4, 7, 28, 30, 122, 128, 130, 144, 166–7, 169, 217, 292, 351
  over forested land, 4, 6, 18, 29, 48–9, 122, 129–30, 144–53, 167, 175, 256, 270, 293, 353
  polycentric governance and, 46
  property and, 4, 49, 56, 169, 175–7, 192, 209, 278
  reorganisation of, 27–8, 48, 269, 303, 349
  rival forms, 30, 47

Bali Action Plan (2007), 60, 63, 97–8, 201–2, 223–4, 238
baselines, 20, 61, 70–1, 75, 242–3, See also reference levels, See also forest emission reference level and/or forest reference level (FERL/FRL)
  'business-as-usual', 180, 232
Bedjaoui, Mohammed, 149
benefit-sharing, 28, 77, 82, 106, 110, 112, 116, 121, 126, 188–9, 262, 294–5, 322–9
Berlin Mandate, 221
biblical injunction, 96
BioCarbon Fund Initiative for Sustainable Forest Landscapes, 87, 186
biodiversity, 17, 48, 72, 93, 98, 105, 160, 274
  custodians of, 315
  protection, 12, 16, 82, 98, 150, 154, 156, 267, 323
Bolivia, 29, 65, 67, 74
Brazil, 14, 35, 88, 149, 151, 233, 261–2, 317

Index

BRICS countries, 35, 229
Bromley, Daniel, 273
Butler, Judith, 307, 347

Caffentzis, George, 277
Call to Action to Reject REDD+ and Extractive Industries to Confront Capitalism and Defend Life and Territories, 25
Callon, Michel, 78
Canada, 116, 235
Cancun Agreements (2011), 60, 64–5, 69, 71–2, 80, 97–8, 117, 202–3, 225, 322, 330
capacity-building, 163, 186, 204, 212–13, 217, 238, 243–7
    Forest Carbon Partnership Facility and, 84
    in Bali Action Plan, 77
    in Cancun Agreements, 65
    REDD+-readiness and, 244
    UN-REDD+ Programme and, 86
capital, 42, 355
    -isation, 185
    -ist accumulation, 42, 292
    -ist development, 38, 166, 272
    -ist economy, 7, 143
    -ist expansion, 41, 272
    -ist globalisation, 272
    -ist imperatives, 40
    -ist markets, 41, 54, 259, 272, 288, 292–3
    -ist models of valuation, 351
    -ist relationship with limits, 41
    -ist social relations, 247, 277
capitalism, 1, 6, 25, 38, 103, 247, 301, See also growth, economic
    green, 3, 351
carbon contracts, 169–71, 174, 177–8, See also Emission Reduction Purchase Agreements (ERPAs)
    challenges in drafting, 178–84
    establishing norms through, 184–91
    forest, 177, 180, 182
    standard form, World Bank's role in developing, 178, 184
carbon credits, 9, 61, 65, 76, 201, 252, See also certified emission reductions (CERs), See also assigned amount units (AAUs), See also internationally transferred mitigation outcomes (ITMOs), See also carbon rights
    as a commodity, 195
    as property, 170, 192
carbon cycle, 23, 157
carbon dioxide, 4, 159, 203
    concentrations of, 157
    equivalent, 59, 68–9, 140–1, 196, 200
    removal of, 156

carbon footprint, 37, 134, 350, 353
carbon markets, 4, 194, 230
    as a 'governance experiment', 78
    critiques of, 23–4, 26
    inclusion of forests in, 59, 65, 67–8, 91, 94
    REDD+ and, 9–11
    World Bank driving development of, 184–5, 206
Carbon Offset and Reduction Scheme for International Aviation (CORSIA), 11
carbon offsets, 4, 94–7, 113–14, 174, 183, 232–7, 240, 350–2
    concept of, 12
    criticism of, 11–12, 23–4
    impacts of, 34
carbon rights, 182, 190–2, 256–66, 269–70
    clarification of, 261–2
    definition of, 259–60, 262–4
    unequal allocation of, 196, 198, 271
carbon sequestration, 8, 11–12, 22, 91, 141, 166, 186, 259–61
    as a global concern, 156–64
    permanence of, 75, 170, 180
carbon sinks, 8, 63–4, 98, 124, 261
    forests as global, 144, 156, 158, 161
carbon stocks, 8, 15, 64, 71, 160
    forest, 63, 71, 86, 97–8, 105
Center for International Forestry Research (CIFOR), 110–11, 243, 296, 300, 332
Center for People and Forests, 339, 342, 348
Central African Forest Initiative, 88
Cernea, Michael, 273
certified emission reductions (CERs), 61, 68, 199–200, 233, 235
    temporary certified emission reductions (tCERs), 160, 201
China, 35–6, 224, 227, 229, 233
Clean Development Mechanism (CDM), 33, 36, 60–2, 113, 140, 160, 186, 199–201, 207, 232–8, 249, 298
climate activists. See climate justice, activists
climate adaptation, 12, 15, 31–4, 74, 88–9, 105, 134, 202
climate change, 1–2, 123
    and human rights, 32–4
    anthropocentric causes, 13
    as a 'global' problem, 132–3
    as a common concern, 122–3, 125, 143, 166, 168
    as a problem of emissions, 135–6
    causes of, 33
    effects of, 31
    framing of, 131
    impacts of, 35
    REDD+ as 'false solution' to, 4–5, 35
    representations of, 122, 131, 166

Index

responses to, 2–3, 139
responsibility for, 34
'Southern' perspective on, 29
structural causes of, 38, 124
supranational jurisdiction and, 130
temporal framing of, 134
climate governance. *See* governance, climate
climate justice, 3–4, 29–39
  activists, 5
  compensative, 214
  conceptualisation of, 30, 38–9
  corrective, 31
  distributive, 36
  movements, 39
  procedural, 30–1
  statements for, 24
  structural, 31
Climate Justice Now! coalition, 24
climate mitigation, 13
  actions, commensurability of, 140
  and human rights, 32–3
  as future-orientated obligation, 134
  Bali Action Plan and, 202
  commitments, 4, 8, 204–5, 228
  cost-effectiveness of, 194
  costs of, 138
  distribution of burdens, 34
  effects of, 68
  frameworks, 34
  joint approaches to, 67, 74
  Kyoto Protocol and, 222
  leadership on, 230
  Paris Agreement and, 8, 206
  potential, 13, 85
  responses/strategies, 31, 62, 136, 156
  responsibility for, 33
Coalition for Rainforest Nations, 29, 209–10
Coase, Ronald, 138, 277
co-benefits, 16, 60, 73, 106, 110, 160, 286, 296, 298, 323–5
Cohen, Morris, 176–7
Collaborative Partnership on Forests, 105
colonialism, 6–7, 27, 37–8, 52, 100, 104, 134, 146–7, 149, 216, 255, 264, 303–4, 307, 353, *See also* imperialism
  colonial forestry, 104, 145
  international environmental law and, 54
  international law and, 52, 54
commodification, 5, 26–7, 40, 66, 113, 194, 323
common but differentiated responsibilities and respective capabilities (CBDR-RC), 35, 57, 173, 199, 213–31, 234, 237, 240, 243, 255, 350
common concern, 54–6, 122–30, 132, 143–4, 149, 153–4, 156–7, 163–8, 319, 342, 346, 350

conceptual foundations of, 125
difference from common heritage, 126–7
differences and similarities with common interest, 127–8
common heritage, 125–6, 148–9, 151, 153
common interest, 125, 127–8, 153
common property regimes (CPRs), 57, 256, 258, 269–77, 280, 293
  distinguished from 'open access regimes', 273
Common Property Resources Management Network (CPRNet), 274–5
commons, 40, 123, 126, 145, 258–9, 262, 272, 275, *See also* common property regimes (CPRs)
  global, 145, 151, 158, 276
  tragedy of the, 272–3
community-based forest management, 281, 292
community-based resource management, 57, 256, 258, 269, 271, 275, 278, 281, 293, 323
compensated reductions, 62, 213, 238, 240–3
Conferences of the Parties, 59, 67, 70–3
  COP3 (Kyoto, 1997), 233
  COP6 (The Hague, 2000), 235
  COP7 (Marrakech, 2001), 200, 234
  COP9 (Milan, 2003), 62, 160, 186, 240
  COP11 (Montreal, 2005), 62
  COP13 (Bali, 2007), 24, 63, 77, 81, 107–8, 186, 201, *See also* Bali Action Plan (2007)
  COP14 (Poznań, 2008), 24, 97, 116–17
  COP15 (Copenhagen, 2009), 64, 97, 117, 202, 224
  COP16 (Cancun, 2010), 64, 88
  COP17 (Durban, 2011), 72, 203, 225
  COP18 (Doha, 2012), 197, 203
  COP19 (Warsaw, 2013), 72, 187, 204, 226
  COP20 (Lima, 2014), 204, 227
  COP21 (Paris, 2015), 73, 203
  COP24 (Katowice, 2018), 60, 208, 209
  decisions on REDD+, 76, 162, 165
conservation, 15–16, 21, 63–4, 72, 91, 94, 96–102, 111, 125, 150, 152, 155, 160, 252, 300, 313–14, 328–9
  colonial origins of, 59, 104
  contracts, 168, 170–2, 177–8, 180
  rights-based approaches to, 101
Convention on Biological Diversity (CBD), 124–5, 153, 315, *See also* Nagoya Protocol on Access and Benefit-Sharing
Copenhagen Accord, 64, 137, 202, 224
Costa Rica, 29, 62, 241, 263
Cullet, Phillipe, 173, 229, 234
customary law, 266
customary tenure. *See* tenure, customary

Dales, J. H., 138–9
De Soto, Hernando, 327, 333

414

Index

decentralisation, 30, 46, 267, 280–3, 293
Declaration on International Economic Cooperation, 125
deforestation, 3, 8, 13, 18, 64, 73, 91–2, 97–8, 124, 149–50, 156–66, 201, 214, 241
  as a global common concern, 48, 122, 156, 162, 164, 166, 168
  avoided, 60, 62, 65, 68, 74, 113, 160, 180, 261, 351
  displacement of, 15, 75
  drivers of, 75, 123, 164–5, 248
  emissions from, 162, 181, 241–2
  rates of, 13, 149, 242
  representations of, 122
demonstration activities, 59, 66, 77–9, 90, 121
development, 23, 32, 38–9, 49, 51, 120, 138, 151–2, 216–17, 220–1, 232, 236, 273–4, 313
  green, 5
  right to, 35–6, 153, 199
  sustainable, 17, 40, 53, 65, 86, 88–9, 91–2, 105, 111, 136, 146, 152, 155, 185, 200, 206–8, 214, 219
development aid, 9–10, 67
distributive justice, 30–1, 34–7, 201, 214–15, 231–2, 243, 324
domination, 2, 7, 38, 95, 100, 149, 246, 304, 307
Durban Platform for Enhanced Action, 203, 225

ecological crisis, 1, 50, 351, 355, *See also* climate change
economic growth. *See* growth, economic
ecosystem services, 8, 40, 54, 72, 91, 93, 111, *See also* payment for ecosystem services
efficiency
  aggregate economic, 3, 138, 143, 208–9, 231, 243
  economic, 131, 137, 277, 289, 329
Eliasch Review, 10, 66, 80, 91, 94, 110, 160, 242, 298, 332
Eliasch, Johan, 91, 110
Emission Reduction Purchase Agreements (ERPAs), 84, 174, 178–9, 187–90, *See also* carbon contracts
emission reductions (ERs), 84, 178, 212, 260
emission rights, 34, 192, 199, 239
emissions trading schemes (ETSs), 80, 139–40, 191, 196, 239, 258
Engle, Karen, 306, 314, 339
Environmental and Social Standard on Indigenous Peoples/Sub-Saharan African Historically Underserved Traditional Local Communities (ESS7), 119–20, 319–21, 338
environmental economics, 59, 90, 137–8
environmental justice, 30, 38, 65, 312, 355, *See also* climate justice

environmental stewardship. *See* stewardship, environmental
environmentality, 30, 43, 292, 301, *See also* governmentality
equity, 3, 19, 31, 111, 153, 172–3, 199, 208, 211, 218, 225, 236, 239, 287, 324, 328
  common but differentiated responsibilities and respective capabilities (CBDR-RC) and, 220, 227
equivalence (claim of) between forest carbon and fossil carbon, 12, 95, 140–2
ESS7. *See* Environmental and Social Standard on Indigenous Peoples/Sub-Saharan African Historically Underserved Traditional Local Communities (ESS7)
European Union, 72, 88, 139, 235
experimental practices, 7, 56–7, 59, 76–9, 82, 90–1, 170, 212, 240, 258, 274–5, *See also* learning-by-doing
experimentalist governance. *See* governance, experimentalist
exploitation, 2, 37, 52, 90, 96, 104, 126, 144, 243, 337, 341, 355

Fanon, Franz, 307
FERN, 85, 110
Figueres, Christiana, 5
Fisher, Robert, 269
flexibility mechanisms, 60, 124, 230–1, 243
  in Kyoto Protocol, 61, 140, 208, 235
Forest Carbon Partnership Facility (FCPF), 10, 76, 81–7, 108, 118–19, 186, 190–1, 244–5, 262, 319
  Carbon Fund, 82–3, 178, 188
  Readiness Fund, 82–3
  Readiness Preparation Proposals (R-PPs), 83–5, 245–9, 335
forest emission reference level and/or forest reference level (FERL/FRL), 69–71, *See also* reference level, *See also* baselines
forest governance. *See* governance, forest
Forest Investment Programme (FIP), 81, 87
forest peoples, 2, 6, 28, 49, 85, 106, 109, 111, 116, 121, 183, 190–1, 264–5, 269, 298, 302, 329, 346, 352, *See also* Indigenous peoples, local communities
  authority over, 29
  carbon rights of, 293
  disciplinary inclusion of, 58, 295, 349
  livelihoods of, 60
  participation in REDD+, 319, 321
  responsibilisation of, 350
  rights of, 16, 21, 28, 60, 85, 153, 183, 267, 336
Forest Peoples Programme (FPP), 84–5

Index

Forest Principles, 102–3, 151–2
forest tenure. *See* tenure, forest
forest-dependent communities. *See* forest peoples
forest-dwelling communities. *See* forest peoples
forestry science, 103–4
forests, 10, 30, 48, 56, 59, 62, 68, 97, 145, 147, 150, 153, 160, *See also* afforestation, deforestation
 as carbon stocks, 15, 161
 as global commons, 158
 authority over. *See* authority, over forested land
 definition/meaning of, 20, 144–5
 global functions of, 153–6, 159
 inclusion in carbon markets, 7, 65, 67
 protection of, 13
 valued in economic terms, 8, 91–4
fossil fuels, 1, 11–12, 23, 135, 141, 143, 157–8, 355
Foucault, Michel, 27, 30, 42, 43, 301
free, prior and informed consent (FPIC), 28, 106, 108, 114, 117, 294–5, 321, 336–48, *See also UN-REDD Programme Guidelines on Free, Prior and Informed Consent (Guidelines on FPIC)*, Indigenous rights
 consultation and, 337–8
 debates around, 336
 problems with implementation, 339
 right of veto, 336, 339–43, 345
Friends of the Earth International (FoEI), 109

G7 Summit, 150
G77, 151, 233, 236
gender equality, 86, 110
Germany, 14, 87–8, 118
Global Environmental Facility, 99, 231
Global Forest Resources Assessment, 13
global inequality, 31, 213, 217, 229
global justice, 30, 36, *See also* climate justice
Global Witness, 103, 110
Godden, Lee, 156, 265–6, 269, 291, 302, 323, 325
Goldman, Michael, 184
Goldtooth, Tom, 113
good governance. *See* governance, good
Gover, Kirsty, 329–30
governance, 20, 22, 247–54, 292, 299–300, 335
 climate, 25, 44, 47, 138, 144, 162, 240, 242
 decentralised, 282–3
 environmental, 5–7, 101, 139, 258, 286, 301–2, 312
 experimentalist, 78
 forest, 72, 80, 84–6, 104, 111, 120, 147, 155, 167, 248, 250, 252–4, 280
 good, 15, 115, 164, 248–54, 281, 348
 multilevel, 42, 44, 256–7, 271, 276–7, 283–7
 nested, 42, 286, 288

 of natural resources, 12, 57, 256, 269, 271, 273, 276–83, 287–8
 of peoples who live in and around forested areas, 18, 106
 polycentric, 42, 44–6, 283–7
 reforms, 62
 self-. *See* self-governance
governmentality, 27, 302–3, *See also* environmentality
 colonial, 303–4
 green, 27, 30, 43
grandfathering, 197–9
green capitalism. *See* capitalism, green
Green Climate Fund (GCF), 76, 81, 88–9
green development. *See* development, green
green economy, 2, 5, 29–30, 39–42, 58, 92–3, 167, 175, 211, 214, 255, 257, 295, 302, 322, 326–7, 329, 336, 349, 351–2
 disciplinary inclusion in, 301–3
green governmentality. *See* governmentality, green
green grabbing, 6, 23, 27, 101, 107, *See also* land grabbing
green growth. *See* growth, green
green neoliberalism. *See* neoliberalism, green
greenhouse gas (GHG) emissions, 8, 50, 135, 162
 causes of, 143, 159
 responsibility for, 3, 159, 166, 221, 350
 stabilisation of, 134, 136
growth
 economic, 2, 38, 40, 51, 131, 136, 138, 216, 232, 237, 239, 251, 289, 355, *See also* capitalism
 green, 30, 40–1
Guidelines on Stakeholder Engagement in REDD+ Readiness with a Focus on the Participation of Indigenous Peoples and other Forest-Dependent Communities, 118, 319, 338

Hale, Robert, 176
Hardin, Garrett, 272–3, *See also* commons, tragedy of the
Hayek, Friedrich, 45
Hildyard, Nicolas, 216
human rights, 31–4, 119, 342–3, *See also* Office of the High Commissioner for Human Rights (OHCHR)
 and climate change, 32–4
 of Indigenous peoples. *See* Indigenous rights
 violations, 102
Humphreys, Stephen, 37, 96, 99–100, 250

imperialism, 6, 37, 52, 162, 176, 303, 314, *See also* colonialism
Indiana Workshop in Political Theory, 44, 283, 285

Index

Indigenous peoples, 5–6, 64, 72, 85, 107–11, 113–18, 190, 265, 301–2, 308–15, 317, *See also* self-determination
  as environmental stewards, 318, 346
  concept of wilderness and, 100
  definition of, 308–11, 320
  local communities, distinction between, 322
  rights of. *See* Indigenous rights
Indigenous rights, 15, 17, 72, 101–2, 111, 113, 115–16, 119, 257, 267, 271, 304–8, 343, *See also* free, prior and informed consent (FPIC)
  cultural rights, 305–7, 346, 350
Indonesia, 6, 14, 77, 90, 104, 146, 151, 251, 254, 345, 352
instrument-effects, 18, 28, 297, 303, 346
intended nationally determined contributions (INDCs). *See* nationally determined contributions (NDCs)
Intergovernmental Panel on Climate Change (IPCC), 133, 157–9
Intergovernmental Panel on Forests (1995-1997), 92, 156
International Association for the Study of the Commons, 273, 275
International Civil Aviation Organization (ICAO), 11
International Climate and Forest Initiative, 90
International Database on REDD+ Projects, 77
International Emissions Trading Association (IETA), 174, 184, 187, 205–7
international environmental law (IEL), 50–4
  and neo-colonialism, 7
  failures of, 7, 50–1
International Institute for Environment and Development (IIED), 93, 111, 260, 330, 332
International Labour Organization Indigenous and Tribal Peoples Convention (ILO 169), 119, 309, 312, 320, 337
international law, 1, 38, 51–2, 127, 176, 217, 304, 318, 325
  colonialism and. *See* colonialism
  complicit in climate crisis, 143, 166
  economic growth and, 136, 239
  environmental. *See* international environmental law
  private international law, 57, 169, 172
  relationship with nature, 2, 7
International Tropical Timber Agreements (ITTAs) (1983, 1994, 2006), 102–3, 150
International Union for the Conservation of Nature (IUCN), 111, 149
  World Parks Congress, 101
internationally transferred mitigation outcomes (ITMOs), 206, 210, *See also* carbon credits

Jodoin, Sébastien, 213–14, 240, 242
Joint Implementation, 140, 199–200
jurisdiction, 87, 284
  and authority, 123, 125
  balancing between international and domestic jurisdiction, 128
  competing, 44, 145
  global, 123, 127, 130
  national, 123, 127–8
  plurality of, 30, 49
  supranational, 130
justice. *See* distributive justice, *See* climate justice
Jutta Brunnée, 127–9, 136–53, 221

Kalimantan Forest Carbon Partnership (KFCP), 77, 90, 335–6, 345
Koskenniemi, Martti, 131, 175–6
Kyoto Protocol, 137, 139, 186–7, 192, 196–7, 199–201, 203, 221–3, 234–6, 239
  Doha Amendment to the Kyoto Protocol, 197, 203

land grabbing, 7, 108, *See also* green grabbing
land management, 13, 290
land rights, 109, 270, 290, *See also* tenure
land use, 87, 91, 157, 159, 292–3
  authority over, in Global South, 122
  carbon contracts and, 180
  opportunity costs and, 328
  REDD+ projects limiting, 109, 302
  RPPs and, 248, 335
  tenure rights and, 336
leakage, 15, 20, 61, 75, 160, 173, 180–1
learning-by-doing, 59, 77–9, 82, *See also* experimental
legal pluralism, 46, 147, 271, 276, 283–92, 334
legal realism, 169
Li, Tania Murray, 43, 302–3, 307, 314, 345
liberal environmentalism, 51, 136
Lima Call for Climate Action, 204, 227
local communities, 22, 24, 64, 72, 82, 85, 104, 108–10, 116–17, 147, 179, 183, 256–7, 265–6, 279, 296, 313, 330, 338, 344, 346
  definition of, 315–18
  Indigenous peoples, distinction between, 322
  rights of, 101, 257, 266–8, 271, 280, 299, 308
Lohmann, Larry, 194
Lomé IV Convention, 103
Lyster, Rosemary, 269

Margarita Declaration on Climate Change, 25
marketisation, 25, 40, 66, 329

Index

Marrakech Accords, 61, 141–2, 160, 186, 196, 200, 234, 236
Mason-Case, Sarah, 213–14, 240, 242
McAfee, Kathleen, 327–9
measuring, monitoring, reporting and verification (MMRV), 124, 163
monitoring, reporting and verification (MRV), 67, 71
Mickelson, Karin, 52–3, 146, 150–1
Millennium Ecosystem Assessment, 93
Miller, Clark, 133
Mitchell, Timothy, 78, 162
mitigation. *See* climate mitigation
Morgera, Elisa, 324
multilevel governance. *See* governance, multilevel

Nagoya Protocol on Access and Benefit-Sharing (Nagoya Protocol), 315–16
nationally appropriate mitigation actions (NAMAs), 238
nationally determined contributions (NDCs), 201, 204–9
intended nationally determined contributions (INDCs), 204, 226, 228
natural capital, 5, 40–1, 92, 94, 327, 351
natural resource governance. *See* governance, of natural resources
neoliberalism, 27, 34, 36, 43, 51, 90, 244, 251–2, 282, 306, 322, 349
green, 27, 184
neoliberal devolution of power, 282–3
neoliberal land reform, 330, 333
neoliberal legality, 300, 336
nested governance. *See* governance, nested
net-zero emissions, 11
New International Economic Order (NIEO), 52, 146
non-carbon benefits. *See* co-benefits
non-governmental organisations (NGOs), 4, 63, 65, 81, 85, 98, 106–12, 150, 189–90, 252, 296, 345
Non-Legally Binding Authoritative Statement of Principles for a Global Consensus on the Management, Conservation and Sustainable Development of All Types of Forests. *See* Forest Principles
Non-legally Binding Instrument on all Types of Forests, 103, 156
Norway, 14, 87–8, 90, 118, 235, 254

Office of the High Commissioner for Human Rights (OHCHR), 32
offsets. *See* carbon offsets

Organisation for Economic Co-operation and Development (OECD), 40
Ostrom, Elinor, 44, 272–8, 283–5, 288
Ostrom, Vincent, 44, 275, 283, 285
Otomo, Yoriko, 96, 99–100
Overseas Development Initiative (ODI), 109–10

Pahuja, Sundhya, 217, 251
Papua New Guinea, 29, 62, 241
Paretianism, 214, 239, 243
Paris Agreement, 8–9, 11, 14, 33, 60, 67, 81, 88, 174, 192, 201, 204–10, 212, 214, 227, 240, 323
differentiation and, 227–30
objectives, 137, 143
REDD+ and, 209–10
rule book. *See* Paris Rule Book
Paris Rule Book, 33, 60, 208, 209
payment for ecosystem services (PES), 24, 59, 95, 280, 298, 303, 328, 351
people who live in and around forested lands. *See* forest peoples
People's Agreement from the World People's Conference on Climate Change in Cochabamba (2010), 24
performativity, 12, 307–8, 314–15, 347–8
performance of subject-position, 307–8, 311, 314, 317–18, 345
performative nature of economics, 26, 78
permanence, 20, 61, 75, 170, 180, 299
permanent sovereignty over natural resources (PSNR), 146–7, 163, 261
Polanyi, Karl, 194
Polanyi, Michael, 44–5
political economy, 22, 43, 55, 123–4, 130, 143, 165, 196, 201, 214, 240, 250, 255, 353
polycentric governance. *See* governance, polycentric
polycentricity. *See* governance, polycentric
poverty, 164, 255
alleviation, 16, 60, 274, 281, 324, 328
eradication, 65, 105, 222, 232
reduction, 15, 17, 84, 88, 274, 289, 326
power, 30, 42–6, 130–1, 145, 169–70, 176, 245–6, 292, 351
over nature, 95–6
property and, 170
relations, 2, 8, 27, 50, 52, 79, 170, 257, 306, 328
power/knowledge, 27, 43, 184, 301
private law, 7, 57, 170–2, *See also* international law, private international law
impact on public authority/power and jurisdiction, 170, 174, 181

property rights, 16, 41, 111, 138–9, 168, 171, 176, 197, 251, 257, 266, 268, 275, 288, 291, *See also* authority, property and, carbon rights, common property regimes (CPRs)
access rights, 267
carbon credits as, 168, 170–1, 191–2
clarification of, 247
concept of property, 257
control rights, 277, 279–80
customary, 145, 267, 291, 319
disaggregation of, 57, 277, 289, 293
in trees and land, 261
management rights, 278–9
over forests, 153
recognition of, 176
REDD+ credits as quasi-property rights, 192
resource rights, 256, 259, 262, 265
use rights, 271, 277, 279–80, 282, 329
Prototype Carbon Fund (PCF), 185–6, 188, 231

quantified emission limitation and reduction commitments (QELRCs), 140, 196, 222, 235

Rajamani, Lavanya, 220, 223–4, 228, 234
REDD+. *See also* Warsaw Framework for REDD+ (2013), Reducing Emissions from Deforestation (RED)
aims of, 3, 15
alternative policy approaches, 74–6
as a 'false solution' to climate change, 4–5
as a carbon offset mechanism, 8, 11, 94–7
as a market-based mechanism, 4, 9, 168
as a proliferating project, 16
as a regime, 16–17
as a social project, 60, 106
as an assemblage, 7, 99
as a carbon offset mechanism, 4
as a concept/idea, 90–1
carbon markets and, 8–11, 94–7
criticisms of REDD+, 6
demonstration activities. *See* demonstration activities
development of framework for, 60–7
funding for, 9–10
jurisdictional approach, 181–2
Paris Agreement and, 209–10
potential benefits of, 109–11
result-based actions, 9, 67–9, 172
result-based payments, 10, 324
rights in, 115, 295
rights-based approaches, 87, 110, 117, 319, 349
safeguards. *See* safeguards

scholarship on, 19–28
social risks/impacts of, 28, 107–9, 116, 296–301, 322, 336
REDD+-readiness, 10, 14, 56, 59, 62, 66, 76, 80–1, 83–5, 87, 90, 118, 121, 215, 217, 244–55, 262, 286, 324, 330, 335
redistributive multilateralism, 35, 54, 218, 224, 230, 255
Reducing Emissions from Deforestation (RED), 63
reference levels, 61, 75, 80, 242, *See also* forest emission reference level and/or forest reference level (FERL/FRL), baselines
'business-as-usual', 180
remote sensing technologies, 71, 157, 161–2
responsibilisation, 184, 282–3, 287, 293–5, 301–3, 322, 325, 329–31, 333, 336–7, 348–50, 352
rights, 106, 111, 116, 300, *See also* property rights, *See also* Indigenous rights, human rights, land rights
rights-based approaches, 87, 101, 110, 117
Rights and Resources Initiative (RRI), 147, 262–3, 265, 278, 302, 330
Rio Earth Summit. *See* United Nations Conference on Environment and Development (1992)
romanticism, 99–101
Rose, Carol, 258, 275
rule of law, 249–51, 253
Russian Federation, 235

safeguards, 28, 71–4, 87, 106, 116–21, 317, 352, *See also* benefit-sharing, free, prior and informed consent (FPIC), tenure, reform, Environmental and Social Standard on Indigenous Peoples/Sub-Saharan African Historically Underserved Traditional Local Communities (ESS7), REDD+, social risks/impacts of
elaboration of, 116–21
environmental, 297
implementation of, 298
in Cancun Agreements, 72, 296, 338
non-carbon benefits and, 71–4
the subjects of, in REDD+, 318
Sassen, Saskia, 107
Schlager, Edella, 277–8, 288
Scott, James, 104, 353
Seeing 'RED'? Forests, Climate Change Mitigation and the Rights of Indigenous, 107
self-determination, 114, 146, 271, 293, 300, 305–6, 308, 314–15, 336–7, 343, 345
self-governance, 102, 175, 254, 271, 283, 285, 287, *See also* self-determination

Sena, Paul Kanyinke, 114
sequestration. *See* carbon sequestration
sinks. *See* carbon sinks
sovereignty, 3, 47, 62, 65, 72–3, 96, 126, 130, 132,
    145–7, 151–6, 169, 176, 199, 241, 254, 304
  as a 'bundle of rights', 285
  as managerial, 253
  common concern and, 128, 154
  ecological, 99
  over forests, 148, 153, 155–6, 164, 353
  polycentric governance and, 284
  Third World, 130, 146, 254
spontaneous order, 45–6
Stern Review, 91, 94, 137–8, 140, 160, 332
Stern, Nicholas. *See Stern Review*
stewardship, 95–6, 314, 326
  environmental, 311–12, 314–15, 317–18, 345, 355
subjectivity, 28, 42–3, 301–2, 329
  collective, 348
  environmental, 301, 303
  Indigenous, 314
  market-orientated, 327
  of *homo economicus*, 327, 333
subject-position, 30, 282, 307–8, 314, 318, 347,
    See also subjectivity
  as 'environmental stewards', 311, 314, 345,
    See also stewardship, environmental
  as 'ecological native', 312
Subsidiary Body for Scientific and Technological
    Advice (SBSTA), 63
Sullivan, Sian, 93–4
supplementarity, 235–6
Survival International, 109
sustainable development. *See* development,
  sustainable
sustainable forest management (SFM), 59, 74, 91,
    97–9, 102–6, 140
  controversy around, 98–9
  definition of, 98
System Change not Climate Change – A People's
    Declaration from Klimaforum09, 24

Takacs, David, 163, 259, 291
Tauli-Corpuz, Victoria, 101, 108, 112, 116
Tehan, Maureen, 265–6, 291
temperature increases, 8, 137, 203, 205
tenure, 49, 111, 164, 271
  agrarian, 267
  customary, 265, 289–90
  definition of, 266
  forest, 266–9, 278
  recognition, 265
  reform, 16, 28, 60, 106, 108, 111, 120, 262, 265–9,
    291, 294–5, 329–36

resource tenure, 269–70, 331
rights, 21, 257, 266–70, 289, 291
security, 86, 181, 264, 289–90
Third World Approaches to International Law
    (TWAIL), 51–3, 130
transboundary harm, 125
transnational law, 7, 143
trees, symbolic meaning of, 353–4
Tropical Forestry Action Plan (TFAP), 150

UNFCCC Web Platform, 68
United Kingdom, 14, 87–8, 193
United Nations Commission on International
    Trade Law (UNCITRAL), 174
United Nations Conference on Environment
    and Development (UNCED) (1992), 102,
    124–5, 127, 150–1, 158, 219, 221
United Nations Conference on Sustainable
    Development (2012), 39–40
United Nations Conference on the Human
    Environment (1972), 53, 148
United Nations Convention to Combat
    Desertification, 98
United Nations Declaration on the Rights of
    Indigenous Peoples (UNDRIP), 85, 109,
    116–17, 119, 147, 295, 309–12, 313, 319, 337–9,
    341
United Nations Environment Programme
    (UNEP), 5, 40, 81, 86, 93, 110, 187,
    326
United Nations Food and Agricultural
    Organization (FAO), 13, 81, 98, 151, 253, 263,
    334
United Nations Forum on Forests (UNFF), 98,
    105, 156
United Nations Framework Convention on
    Climate Change (UNFCCC), 4–6, 35, 56,
    59–60, 62, 70–1, 75–7, 79, 81–2, 89–90, 108,
    116–18, 120–1, 124, 131–2, 134, 136, 168, 172, 174,
    184, 201–2, 213–14, 219–20, 223, 225, 231–3, 236,
    240, 261–2, 279, 296, 330
United Nations Permanent Forum on Indigenous
    Issues (UNPFII), 108, 112–16
United States, 14, 87, 227, 235
UN-REDD Programme, 14, 73, 76, 81, 86–7, 91,
    110, 119, 244, 248, 319, 331, 334–5, 338, 345
  on tenure reform, 331
UN-REDD Programme Guidelines on Free, Prior
    and Informed Consent, 119, 321–2, 338, 342,
    344

valuation of nature, 5, 8, 59, 91–2
value
  economic, 90, 327

Voluntary Guidelines on the Responsible Governance of Tenure of Land, Fisheries, and Forests in the Context of National Food Security (VGGT), 334

Warsaw Framework for REDD+ (2013), 60, 66–70, 74–5, 88, 191, 210, 243, 322
Washington Consensus, 246–7, 250
wilderness, 49, 100
World Bank, 40, 84, 93, 104, 251–3, 289, *See also* Forest Carbon Partnership Facility, *See also* World Development Report
  carbon funds, 57, 170, 178, 207, 231
  carbon markets and, 184–9, 205
  commons and, 273
  CPRs and, 272, 274
  economic valuation of nature and, 92
  forest strategy and, 154
  Indigenous peoples and, 108, 113, 319–20, 338
  safeguards and, 119
  UN-REDD Programme and, 86
World Commission on Forests and Sustainable Development, 92
World Development Report, 44, 274
World Resources Institute (WRI), 149–50, 161, 253, 300, 326–7
World Summit on Sustainable Development 2002, 221

Young, Margaret, 98, 118

CPSIA information can be obtained
at www.ICGtesting.com
Printed in the USA
LVHW011609030821
694401LV00006B/367